Topic	Formula	Equation Number
Inference from a single sample	$s_{\bar{X}} = \dfrac{s}{\sqrt{N}}$	8.11
	$z = \dfrac{\bar{X} - \mu}{s_{\bar{X}}}$	8.2
	68% confidence interval: $\bar{X} \pm 1\ s_{\bar{X}}$	8.3
	95% confidence interval: $\bar{X} \pm 1.96\ s_{\bar{X}}$	8.4
	99% confidence interval: $\bar{X} \pm 2.58\ s_{\bar{X}}$	8.5
Inference from a difference between two means	$\bar{D} = \bar{X} - \bar{Y}$	9.1
repeated measurements (paired observations)	$\sum (D - \bar{D})^2 = \sum D^2 - \dfrac{(\sum D)^2}{N}$	See Example 9.1 and Example 10.9
	$s_D \text{ (or est } \sigma_D) = \sqrt{\dfrac{\sum (D - \bar{D})^2}{N - 1}}$	9.2
	$\phantom{s_D \text{ (or est } \sigma_D)} = \sqrt{\dfrac{\sum D^2 - \dfrac{(\sum D)^2}{N}}{N - 1}}$	See Example 9.1
	$s_{\bar{D}} \text{ (or est } \sigma_{\bar{D}}) = \dfrac{s_D}{\sqrt{N}}$	9.3
Inference from proportions		
Single sample's p (dichotomous variable)	$\bar{X} = p$	Sec. 8.6
	$S = \sqrt{pq}$	8.13
	$\sigma_p = \sqrt{\dfrac{p_{\text{pop}} q_1}{N}}$ 	8.14
	$z = \dfrac{\lvert p_{\text{sample}}}{\sqrt{\dfrac{p_{\text{pop}} q_{\text{pop}}}{N}}}$	8.15
Difference between two independent proportions	Estimate of $\sigma_{p_X - p_Y} = \sqrt{\dfrac{pq}{N_X} + \dfrac{pq}{N_Y}}$	9.9
	(p is obtained from all $N_X + N_Y$ observations; $q = 1 - p$.)	
	$\text{C.R.} = \dfrac{(p_X - p_Y) - 0}{\text{Estimate of } \sigma_{p_X - p_Y}}$	
	$\phantom{\text{C.R.}} = \dfrac{p_X - p_Y}{\sqrt{\dfrac{pq}{N_X} + \dfrac{pq}{N_Y}}}$	9.10
	$s_{\bar{D}} = \sqrt{s_{\bar{X}}^2 + s_{\bar{Y}}^2 - 2r_{XY}\, s_{\bar{X}}\, s_{\bar{Y}}}$	9.6
	$\text{C.R.} = \dfrac{\bar{D} - 0}{s_{\bar{D}}} = \dfrac{\bar{X} - \bar{Y}}{s_{\bar{D}}}$	9.4
Independent observations	$s_{\bar{D}} = \sqrt{s_{\bar{X}}^2 + s_{\bar{Y}}^2}$	9.8
	$\phantom{s_{\bar{D}}} = \sqrt{\dfrac{s_X^2}{N_X} + \dfrac{s_Y^2}{N_Y}}$	See Examples 9.2, 9.3, 9.4
	$\text{C.R.} = \dfrac{\bar{X} - \bar{Y}}{s_{\bar{D}}}$	See Examples 9.2, 9.3, 9.4

Small samples ($N < 30$): For small samples, use the t distribution instead of the normal distribution

Interference from a single mean	$t = \dfrac{\bar{X} - \mu}{s_{\bar{X}}}$	See Sec. 10.1
	$ = \dfrac{\bar{X} - \mu}{\dfrac{s_{\bar{X}}}{\sqrt{N}}}$	See Sec. 10.1

ELEMENTS OF STATISTICS FOR PSYCHOLOGY AND EDUCATION

McGRAW-HILL SERIES IN PSYCHOLOGY

CONSULTING EDITORS: Norman Garmezy, Richard L. Solomon, Lyle V. Jones, Harold W. Stevenson

Adams Human Memory
Beach, Hebb, Morgan, and Nissen The Neuropsychology of Lashley
Berkowitz Aggression: A Social Psychological Analysis
Berlyne Conflict, Arousal, and Curiosity
Blum Psychoanalytic Theories of Personality
Brown The Motivation of Behavior
Brown and Ghiselli Scientific Method in Psychology
Butcher MMPI: Research Developments and Clinical Applications
Campbell, Dunnette, Lawler, and Weick Managerial Behavior, Performance, and Effectiveness
Cofer Verbal Learning and Verbal Behavior
Crafts, Schneirla, Robinson and Gilbert Recent Experiments in Psychology
Crites Vocational Psychology
D'Amato Experimental Psychology: Methodology, Psychophysics, and Learning
Deese and Hulse The Psychology of Learning
Dollard and Miller Personality and Psychotherapy
Edgington Statistical Inference: The Distribution-free Approach
Ellis Handbook of Mental Deficiency
Ferguson Statistical Analysis in Psychology and Education
Fodor, Bever, and Garrett The Psychology of Language: An Introduction to Psycholinguistics and Generative Grammar
Forgus Perception: The Basic Process in Cognitive Development
Franks Behavior Therapy: Appraisal and Status
Ghiselli Theory of Psychological Measurement
Ghiselli and Brown Personnel and Industrial Psychology
Gilmer Industrial and Organizational Psychology
Gray Psychology Applied to Human Affairs
Guilford The Nature of Human Intelligence
Guilford Psychometric Methods
Giulford and Fruchter Fundamental Statistics in Psychology and Education
Guilford and Hoepfner The Analysis of Intelligence
Guion Personnel Testing
Haire Psychology in Management
Hirsch Behavior-genetic Analysis
Hirsh The Measurement of Hearing
Horowitz Elements of Statistics for Psychology and Education
Hurlock Adolescent Development
Hurlock Child Development
Hurlock Developmental Psychology
Jackson and Messick Problems in Human Assessment
Krech, Crutchfield, and Ballachey Individual in Society
Lakin Interpersonal Encounter: Theory and Practice in Sensitivity Training
Lawler Pay and Organizational Effectiveness: A Psychological View
Lazarus, A. Behavior Therapy and Beyond

LEONARD M. HOROWITZ
Stanford University

ELEMENTS OF STATISTICS FOR PSYCHOLOGY AND EDUCATION

McGRAW-HILL BOOK COMPANY

New York   St. Louis   San Francisco   Düsseldorf   Johannesburg   Kuala Lumpur   London
Mexico   Montreal   New Delhi   Panama   Rio de Janeiro   Singapore   Sydney   Toronto

**TO SUE, JONATHAN, AND JEREMY
WITH LOVE**

This book was set in Times Roman. The editors were Robert P. Rainier and Susan Gamer; the designer was Janet Durey Bollow; and the production supervisor was Sam Ratkewitch. The drawings were done by David Strassman.
The printer and binder was Kingsport Press, Inc.

**ELEMENTS OF
STATISTICS
FOR
PSYCHOLOGY AND
EDUCATION**

1234567890   KPKP   79876543

Library of Congress Cataloging in Publication Data

Horowitz, Leonard M
    Elements of statistics for psychology and education.

    (McGraw-Hill series in psychology)
      1. Psychometrics. I. Title.
[DNLM: 1. Psychometrics. 2. Statistics.
BF39 H816e 1974]
BF39.H65   519.5′02′415   73-13816
ISBN 0-07-030390-8

CONTENTS

PREFACE

One of my bookshelves has a row of statistics books over ten feet long. Every time a new addition arrives in the mail, I think of an old television commercial that showed a tired-looking housewife sampling freeze-dried coffees. With each taste, the woman would remark with unconvincing apathy: "Another freeze-dried coffee? I like it." But once the *sponsor's* brand passed her lips, her apathy changed to enthusiastic excitement.

Statistics books, like freeze-dried coffees, are very numerous these days. Most are decent, respectable books, and one wonders whether the world needs any more. But human nature being what it is, each author feels that his brand has something special to offer. I have been teaching statistics courses for many years now and have developed certain pedagogical notions and superstitions. Encouraged by my success in the classroom, I finally decided to translate these notions into book form. If my notions are sound, this sponsor's brand will have something special to offer.

One of my notions is that statistics is actually easier to understand and more interesting if the exposition contains clearly stated theoretical details. I feel that the theory enriches the practice enormously. Some of my colleagues, I know, prefer to teach the subject as a set of cookbook procedures, carefully choosing "what the student needs to know." But I believe that this is false economy. When we omit too many details, the material becomes dull, the topics do not hang together meaningfully, and the strain on the student's memory becomes unrealistic. In my experience, the less imaginative and less confident student suffers most of all from a cookbook approach. Neither his imagination nor his confidence has a chance to grow.

To some extent, of course, cookbook procedures have their place in a statistics course. I have often found it helpful to describe a procedure first, illustrate it fully, and then explain the theoretical underpinnings. Throughout this book I have relied heavily on my intuitions to adjust a balance of theory and method. At all times, though, my primary goal has been to help the student process the information efficiently and achieve a well-organized gestalt.

I have also tried to make judicious use of redundancy. Redundancy is helpful only if it is packaged in psychologically sensible wrapping. In general, I like to state a new idea once without redundancy—succinctly, directly, and unambiguously. Superfluous words sometimes camouflage and confuse. But once the idea is presented, redundancy is very important. Through diverse examples, I have tried to repeat the idea in different contexts and vary it in instructive ways. Thus, I have tried to write simply and clearly, with lots of examples set off in separate boxes.

To further achieve simplicity and clarity, I have occasionally included some "old-fashioned" topics. For example, some current textbooks are omitting material on empirical frequency distributions. I agree with the trend not to belabor this simple topic, but in my experience, students need contact with empirical frequency distributions as a basis for the subsequent theory. Empirical distributions form the stuff of statistical theory and provide a firm background for *theoretical* distributions. Then, after the reader has explored the empirical foundations, the book considers theoretical distributions and the more interesting topics of probability, sampling distributions, and hypothesis testing.

Throughout the text I have tried to provide a representative cross-section of psychological research. Wherever possible, I have used realistic examples of experimental and correlational studies. In this way I have hoped to sharpen the student's interest and skill in social science research.

A number of people have contributed to this effort, and I would like to acknowledge my deep gratitude. First, I would like to thank the many students, teaching assistants, and friends who read earlier drafts, caught errors, and made useful suggestions. I would also like to thank those friends whose help and encouragement made this project possible: Linda Barrick, whose secretarial skill, intelligence, and care enormously eased the production process; Lana Boutacoff and Cecilia Bahlman for their skill and patience as typists in earlier stages of the project; Nancy Eisenberg, Leon Manelis, and Elizabeth Loftus for their critical comments and suggestions. The book also reflects the influence of my own teachers and role models; I am especially grateful to Professors A. Chapanis, W. R. Garner, A. R. Jonckheere, and Q. McNemar, whose influence and style will be evident throughout. Most of all, I am indebted to my wife, Suzanne L. Horowitz, whose love and encouragement make it all worthwhile.

I also want to express my appreciation to the following organizations and publishers for permission to reproduce material found in the appendixes and elsewhere in the text. I am indebted to the Literary Executor of the late Sir Ronald A. Fisher, F.R.S., to Dr. Frank Yates, F.R.S., and to Oliver & Boyd, Edinburgh, for permission to reprint Tables III, IV, V, and VI from their book *Statistical Tables for Biological, Agricultural and Medical Research*. I am also indebted to Dr. Jack W. Dunlap, Prof. E. S. Pearson and the Biometrika Trustees, RAND Corporation, the American Statistical Association, and the Wm. C. Brown Company.

Certain sections of the text have been adapted from material in the author's *Statistics and Measurements in Psychology*, 1973, Wm. C. Brown Co., with permission of the Wm. C. Brown Co.

LEONARD M. HOROWITZ

1

STATISTICS IN PSYCHOLOGY

Statistical methods are used to collect and analyze data. Imagine an investigator about to conduct a study: He needs some general method for planning the study, treating the data, and interpreting the results. Statistical methods help him satisfy these needs. This book is designed to describe those methods and explain the theory behind them.

The word *statistics* comes from the Latin word *status*, which once meant *political state*. In an early form *statistics* referred to data about a political state—census data, military data, fiscal data. Now, though, the word has become generalized. The modern meaning covers data in quite a broad sense: It designates almost any kind of data as well as methods for treating the data.

The methods are used in various disciplines—biology, agriculture, economics, psychology, business, education, engineering. Table 1.1 shows a few

TABLE 1.1　Problems that illustrate the need for statistics

---

1. A political scientist is trying to forecast an election. He has polled 72 people. Candidate A was favored by 54 percent, 46 percent favored Candidate B. What conclusion can he draw?

2. A chemist has devised two ways of preparing a solution; call them Method 1 and Method 2. He now wants to see if the pH level is the same by either method. He prepares four specimens by each method and measures their pH levels. For Method 1, the pH levels are: 5.83, 6.72, 5.80, 5.79; for Method 2, they are: 5.90, 5.84, 5.79, 5.88. Do the two methods differ?

3. A manufacturing company tries to produce high-quality light bulbs. To test their quality, an industrial engineer has selected 200 bulbs. Four bulbs of this set were defective. What can the engineer conclude about the quality of the bulbs as a whole?

4. The admissions department of a college wants to predict students' ultimate success. Several tests were administered to freshmen. How can predictions now be made?

5. A farmer has studied 5 plots of land which make up a tenth of the farm. He has noted the alfalfa yield of each. The yields are: 0.8, 1.3, 2.0, 1.7, and 2.1 tons of alfalfa per acre. How much alfalfa can he expect from the farm as a whole?

6. A baseball player has had a batting average of 0.280. When the new season opens, he gets 15 hits in 30 times at bat. Has his batting average really improved—or is his recent record a lucky streak?

---

typical problems that arise in different professions. In each case the investigator has collected some data and needs to draw a conclusion. Each problem requires a simple statistical method. Different disciplines, of course, adapt the methods to suit their own special needs, but basically the methods are all alike. This book emphasizes methods that the psychologist needs the most; the examples therefore concern the problems of psychology. Psychology is so diverse, though, that the procedures will span quite a wide range.

Let us open the discussion with a fundamental question: Why are statistical procedures needed? What are these methods all about, and what is their role in psychology?

1.1　SOME REASONS FOR STATISTICAL METHODS IN PSYCHOLOGY

Statistical methods contribute to psychology in various ways. For one thing, certain psychological concepts are really *defined* in statistical terms. A concept like the IQ, for example, can only make sense with statistics. Suppose two people have IQs of 110. These IQs are not necessarily identical. Perhaps the people were tested on different tests; 110 on one might not equal 110 on the other. With statistical methods, we can explore the difference and find other ways to compare the people.

Second, statistics aids in prediction. Certain specialties in psychology try to predict behavior—predicting who will succeed on a job, who will benefit from psychotherapy, who will become violent under stress. Special statistical methods have been devised to make the best possible predictions. The psychologist finds these methods indispensable.

Third, modern psychology is empirical; its conclusions come largely from research, and research makes abundant use of statistics. When we perform an experiment or conduct a survey, we need to evaluate the outcome statistically. We can therefore anticipate the statistical analyses when we plan the research. By thinking ahead, we often avoid awkward, untreatable situations. In that way our research plans are improved.

Finally, statistics and psychology share a common intellectual history. To appreciate the history of one is to understand the other better. Certain old philosophical questions that have been discussed for years have matured along two different lines; one evolved into psychology, the other into statistics. Perhaps a historical introduction can help capture the statistical flavor of psychological research: It will pose the problem and state the major goal.

The problem historically

Psychology started with questions about the mind. *Mind* was needed as a concept to help scholars discuss the most human phenomena—reasoning, thinking, believing, knowing, desiring. One early question concerned the process of *knowing*. It was posed this way: An adult's mind knows many facts and relationships—it knows its way around the world, the size and shape of objects, the consequences of different acts—a host of lawful regularities. But how does the mind acquire this knowledge of the world? In modern terms, how do human beings learn laws about the universe? The question was originally philosophical, and three positions were adopted as answers—those of the *rationalist*, the *naive empiricist*, and the *statistical empiricist*.

Deductive inference

According to the rationalist, every human mind at birth contains the power to reason; through reasoning it *deduces* most of the everyday laws. For the rationalist, a "syllogism" best illustrates how the mind works. Here is an example. Suppose a person knows, first, that no bald creatures need a hairbrush. Second, suppose all lizards are bald creatures. These two given facts are diagramed in Fig. 1.1.

Statement 1 concerns two kinds of creatures—"bald creatures" and "creatures who need a hairbrush." Let us call the bald creatures Set B (for "bald") and the creatures needing a hairbrush Set N (for "needers"). If a creature is in Set B, it is not in Set N (since bald creatures do not need a hairbrush). Therefore, the circles do not overlap in Fig. 1.1. The sets are said to be *mutually exclusive*: Ingredients of one are not in the other.

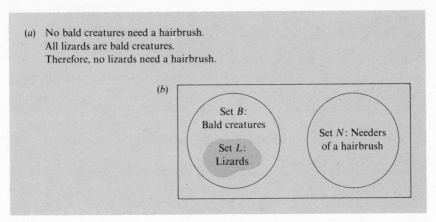

FIG. 1.1   An illustration of deductive inference through syllogistic reasoning. (*a*) Syllogism. (*b*) Diagram.

Statement 2 concerns lizards and bald creatures. Let us call the lizards Set L. By Statement 2, the lizards are all in Set B: Thus all of Set L lies inside Set B. Figure 1.1 therefore shows Circle L inside Circle B—Set L is a subclass of Set B.

According to the rationalist, the mind can now deduce a law—whatever is true for Set B as a whole must also hold true for Set L. One fact about Set B is already clear: Its members are not in Set N. Hence, the rule must hold for lizards too: Members of Set L are not in Set N. Thus, lizards, as bald creatures, do not need hairbrushes. And the mind has deduced a law.

This kind of inference is called *deductive inference*. A law is known about a general class first. Then that law is applied to a particular group within the general class. Deductive inference is described as an inference from the *general* case to the *particular* case.

Inductive inference

But how do we learn general laws in the first place? Deductive inference, after all, requires a general law first. One forerunner of psychology, the school of empiricism, offered this explanation: A newborn child knows nothing; his mind is a blank tablet without any knowledge. Through his senses the child acquires a welter of new experiences—individual experiences based on individual objects. Each experience leaves its mark or impression on the mind: an impression of whiteness, of smallness, of softness, of drunkenness. From these impressions, general laws are inferred. For the empiricist, the machinery of the mind produces general laws from a series of isolated experiences. The mind infers the general law from particular experiences.

Still, how can generalizations ever be trusted? Sense organs, after all, can only provide single, isolated experiences. But a *generalization* covers *all* hard objects, *all* schizophrenics. This kind of inference is called *inductive inference*; it is an inference about the general case from observations of particular cases. Somehow we need to show that the generalization is true.

Can we ever prove that an inductive inference is absolutely true? Early thinkers thought so, and their view has been called *naive empiricism*. The philosophical opinion changed in the eighteenth century, though, with the philosophy of David Hume. The later, more sophisticated, view was called *statistical empiricism*.

According to the statistical empiricist, there is only one way to *prove* an inductive inference: that is to examine every possible case. To prove a law about schizophrenics, you would have to observe all schizophrenics. If you could not study them all, you could not prove the law. Thus, it is generally impossible to *prove* a general law. Instead, the statistical empiricist argues, we can only state the generalization as a *hypothesis*. Hypotheses, of course, vary in their plausibilities; some are very plausible, others are less plausible. Statistical methods help us judge how plausible a hypothesis is. They tell how much confidence a hypothesis deserves.

This approach always accompanies the experimental method. An experimenter usually studies a small group of animals or humans. His small group is called a *sample*. From the sample he hopes to generalize to a larger group— to *all* animals or *all* humans. The larger, general class is called a *population*. Perhaps the experimenter wants to learn about the population of paranoids. He might therefore study 200 paranoids. Special rules are followed in selecting the sample and in drawing the inference. Statistical methods provide these rules.

1.2 TO ILLUSTRATE THE PROBLEM

Let us consider a concrete problem. According to a rumor of some years ago, a vitamin-enriched diet helps improve a retarded child's IQ. Suppose a psychologist wanted to examine this hypothesis. He could adopt several different strategies. For example, he might experiment with pairs of retarded *twins*.

Say he studied five pairs of retarded twins. One twin of each pair might receive a specially enriched diet; the other might receive the regular diet. Then after 6 months, each twin's IQ would be measured. Hypothetical data appear in Table 1.2. Group E had the enriched diet; Group R, the regular diet.

After the 6-month program, Group E's average IQ was 74; Group R's was 70. On the average, then, Group E earned a 4-point advantage. Can this difference be trusted? Can we generalize to the *population* of retarded children?

An exact answer to this question will emerge in later chapters. For now, though, let us consider the answer intuitively: We hesitate to generalize from this sample for several reasons. For one thing, the difference is small: 74 is not

TABLE 1.2 IQ scores after the 6-month program

Pair of twins	Group E (twin receiving enriched diet)	Group R (twin receiving regular diet)
Pair A	75	70
Pair B	71	66
Pair C	82	69
Pair D	69	75
Pair E	73	70
	Average = 74	Average = 70

very different from 70. If it had been a 10-point difference—or a 30-point difference—it would deserve more trust.

Second, the scores in this sample vary a lot. Some lie in the 60s, others in the 70s and 80s. If the IQ's in Group E were *all* about 74 and those in Group R were all about 70, we would be readier to generalize. But when they vary so much, accidental outcomes seem more likely.

Third, the sample does not contain very many observations. A difference based on 50 pairs of twins—or 200 pairs—would deserve more trust than one based on only five pairs.

The decision to generalize, then, depends on three factors—the size of the difference, the variability of the scores, and the number of observations. In this sample, the difference between 74 and 70 is small, the scores are quite variable, and only five pairs of twins were observed. We generally trust a difference more when it is large, when it is based on *many* observations, and when the observations are not too variable.

Methods for generalizing are called *inferential statistics*. To use the methods, the experimenter has to summarize his data first. Table 1.2, for example, needs three kinds of summarizing: First, how many scores are involved? The number of scores is denoted N; for each group in Table 1.2, $N = 5$. Second, what is each group's average score? The two averages are 74 and 70. Third, how much do the scores vary? For Group E, they range from 69 to 82; for Group R, from 66 to 75. These kinds of measures are called *descriptive statistics:* They prepare the investigator for inferential statistics.

Descriptive statistics are always computed first; then the investigator uses statistical inference to draw his conclusions. Chapters 2 and 3 will consider descriptive methods in more detail. Later chapters will discuss the methods of inference.

1.3 OBJECTIVITY IN RESEARCH

Before we examine the methods, let us consider the philosophy behind them. Research usually involves numbers: Some trait is measured, and the measure gets reported as a number. Ideally, the measure is objective—free of human whims and biases. Contemporary psychology generally requires an investigator to describe the conditions of his observations explicitly so that other investigators can replicate the work. Therefore, the investigator should be able to specify the variables, devise clear ways of measuring them, and explain his procedures explicitly. The more explicit an investigator can be about his procedures, the more easily his research can be repeated—and the more we can trust the discipline as a whole.

But still, people sometimes ask, is objectivity *always* desirable—and appropriate—in psychology? Psychologists at one extreme believe it is. They sometimes cite the words of Lord Kelvin, the British physicist: "When you can measure what you are speaking about and express it in numbers, you know something about it; when you cannot measure it, ... your knowledge is ... meagre and unsatisfactory." Lord Kelvin's position is probably too extreme for most people's taste today; for one thing, it ignores the contributions of the Darwins and the Freuds to the history of Western thought. But it does establish one clear anchor point on a continuum of opinions.

At the other extreme, some psychologists downplay the importance of measuring. *Measurable* phenomena, they argue, make up only a limited fraction of the world's phenomena. For them, human nature and human relationships are just not quantifiable. According to this view, psychology does not need samples, numbers, and statistical methods: When a psychologist quantifies, he overlooks some of the most interesting psychological truths. A few wise intuitions about human nature are worth more than a lot of irrelevant objective data. This view establishes the other extreme.

The issue keeps reappearing in the history of psychology. Not long ago it appeared as a debate over the clinical method versus the statistical method. The debate became tempered in time, and today most psychologists accept a compromise view. Let us review the debate and consider the compromise.

Statistical versus clinical approaches

Clinical psychologists are said to use the clinical method when they examine a patient in depth. They interview the person and test him at length. Then they try to construct a picture of the person—his motives and fantasies, hopes and frustrations, strengths and weaknesses, perceptions and thoughts. The psychologist usually finds himself generating hypotheses about the person. Then, as new information emerges, these hypotheses are reviewed, revised, and refined.

The statistical method, in contrast, is less global. Statistically minded psychologists pose questions that are usually simple and explicit. The questions often concern a large group of individuals: A hypothesis might be stated and an experiment would be performed. Or two traits might be measured and their relationship determined. A statistical psychologist often tries to *predict:*

He might administer a test to predict job success. He might perform an experiment to predict a drug's effect.

Now which approach is better—the clinical or the statistical? Clinicians have praised the clinical method this way: "Dynamic, subtle, sympathetic, rich, deep, sophisticated, true-to-life, understanding!" Their opponents, though, have answered: "Mystical, vague, hazy, unreliable, crude, primitive, prescientific, sloppy, uncontrolled, muddleheaded!" Statistically minded psychologists have praised their own statistical method instead: "Objective, reliable, verifiable, testable, rigorous, scientific, precise, careful, down-to-earth, hardheaded, sound!" But the clinicians have described the statistical method this way: "Mechanical, cut-and-dried, artificial, arbitrary, trivial, forced, superficial, rigid, academic, oversimplified, pseudoscientific!"[1]

Today most psychologists do see merit in both approaches. The statistical method, on the one hand, helps a psychologist make simple, straightforward predictions. After all, statistical methods were designed for just that purpose, and no other method can do better.

The clinical method, on the other hand, is more personal. Imagine a skilled and sensitive clinician seeing a patient in psychotherapy. He comes to know that person very well. By reeducating the patient, he can help the patient in subtle ways. The changes are not direct changes that appear in a definite proportion of all patients. Instead, they are small changes that occur day after day in this one patient.

A good clinician is sometimes said to be intuitive. We call an observation *intuitive* when we can *recognize* a phenomenon but cannot verbalize its properties. Simple intuitions occur every day: You see a friend after a long separation, and you recognize the friend at once. If you tried to describe the friend in words, though, your best description would be too vague; you might as well be describing a dozen other people. Apparently we use many cues when we recognize complex phenomena, and the cues cannot always be put into words. The clinical method depends on cues of this kind.

Even the best clinician, though, needs the statistical method as well. In some of his work he wants to generalize beyond one person. Perhaps he hopes to generalize about human nature or about methods of therapy. His ideas may be intuitive, but if he wants to *generalize*, he needs objective data and statistical methods. Otherwise, his conclusions are only hunches.

Some clinical variables are hard to objectify. Suppose a clinician wanted to study ways of reducing fear. Fear would have to be objectified and measured. Some ingenious methods have already been devised for measuring fear. Let us consider two of them.

---

[1] Adapted from Meehl, P. E. *Clinical vs. Statistical Prediction.* Minneapolis: University of Minnesota Press, 1954.

Measuring fear in lower animals

One method has been used with lower animals. The animal, usually a rat, is placed in an alleyway, and a special harness is attached to its head. A string is connected to the harness, and the string is released at a constant rate. The animal can only move as fast as the string is let out. This string passes through a hook-and-spring mechanism; whenever the animal tugs on the string, the experimenter can record the force of the tug. Suppose a frightening object were placed at the end of the alleyway. The animal would pull away, and the examiner could record the force of the animal's pull. This force is used as a measure of the animal's fear. Thus, the "fear" might range from 0 gm to, say, 200 gm.

This straightforward procedure objectifies fear: The investigator attaches a harness apparatus to the animal; then he introduces a frightening stimulus; and finally he records the force of pull. These operations are said to *define* fear objectively. The procedure as a whole is called an operational definition of fear. An *operational definition* defines a variable by the operations used to measure it.

Measuring fear in humans

Fear has also been operationalized for humans. Imagine an investigator studying snake phobias, irrational fears of snakes. In one study[2] the fear was operationalized this way: The subject was asked to perform tasks that brought him closer and closer to a live, but caged, snake. The experimenter noted how close the subject would come. Almost everyone will watch a snake from a doorway, but some people will not come any closer than that.

The experimenter standardized a procedure for testing subjects. Each subject was asked to approach, touch, and lift a harmless snake. A score was assigned to every level of difficulty. The different levels are shown in Table 1.3. The experimenter used this method to measure each subject's level of fear. The procedure of Table 1.3, then, operationalizes fear for snake phobics.

Thus, fear can be defined in more ways than one: The harness-method can define fear for rats. Table 1.3 can define fear for snake phobics.[3] And the two kinds of fear are not identical concepts. Facts based on one may not

---

[2] Adapted from Larsen, S. R. *Strategies for Reducing Phobic Behavior*. Ph.D. dissertation, Stanford University, 1965.

[3] Some questions may occur to you about the numbers in Table 1.3: "11" does suggest more fear than "10," you might argue, and "10" does suggest more fear than "9," but the psychological step from "9" to "10" might not equal the step from "10" to "11." That is, the step sizes might differ. Measurements of this kind can be contrasted with measurements of weight, say. When we measure weight, the "9-lb to 10-lb" step is the same as the "10-lb to 11-lb" step: A standard 1-lb weight can be added to 9 lb to produce 10 lb or to 10 lb to produce 11 lb. In Chap. 4, we shall further consider the philosophy of measurement.

TABLE 1.3 An operational definition of fear in snake phobics

Score (degree of fear)	Item
26	Refuses to approach room that houses snake and look through doorway.
25	Goes to threshold of room, looks into room, but does not enter.
24	Enters 0–1 ft into room.
23	Enters 1–2 ft into room.
22	Enters 2–3 ft into room.
21	Enters 3–4 ft into room.
20	Enters 4–5 ft into room.
19	Enters 5–6 ft into room.
18	Enters 6–7 ft into room.
17	Enters 7–8 ft into room.
16	Enters 8–9 ft into room.
15	Enters 9–10 ft into room.
14	Enters 10–11 ft into room.
13	Enters 11–12 ft into room.
12	Enters 12–13 ft into room.
11	Enters 13–14 ft into room.
10	Enters 14 ft or more into room. (Cage is located 14.6 ft into room.)
9	Places hand in cage, does not touch snake.
8	Dabs at snake 1–5 times. ("Dab" means that the subject touches the snake very briefly, no more than $\frac{1}{4}$ sec, and pulls away almost instantly.)
7	Dabs at snake 6 or more times.
6	Brushes snake lightly 1–5 times. ("Brush" means the subject moves his hand along the snake's body for about $\frac{1}{2}$ sec in response to experimenter's request that he touch snake for 10 sec.)
5	Brushes snake lightly 6 or more times.
4	Rests hand on snake for 1–5 consecutive sec.
3	Rests hand on snake for 6 or more consecutive sec.
2	Picks up part of snake but does not lift its whole body.
1	Picks up snake (clearing the floor of the cage) and holds it for 1–5 sec.
0	Picks up snake and holds it for 6 or more sec.

hold for the other. A concept, after all, is linked to the procedures that measure it. If the measuring procedures differ, the concepts differ. For that reason, an investigator should always describe his procedures with care.

1.4   LYING WITH STATISTICS

Every day we hear generalizations—that the cost of living rose 5 percent last year, that a certain toothpaste produces fewer cavities, that men have more heart disease than women. The generalizations sometimes seem plausible, and other times seem absurd. Through experience we learn to approach these statements skeptically. Mark Twain summarized his own skepticism this way: "There are three kinds of lies—lies, damned lies, and statistics."

Indeed, a liar can use statistics to advantage: He can violate basic assumptions and then use the methods to justify his claims. He can misapply the methods and mislead the reader. To evaluate a claim, we therefore need background information: How did the investigator obtain his data? Were his methods appropriate? Was his sample representative? Did his data meet the assumptions?

There are many ways to lie with statistics—some malicious and some less serious. By studying statistical methods, a person grows sensitive to these devices. As an illustration, let us consider two simple ways of lying.

Varying an operational definition

One way of lying is to let an operational definition shift during a discussion. The concept of unemployment, for example, is often used by political propagandists. But how should the concept be defined? How should we measure the number of people who are unemployed in this country? Should we count part-time workers? If so, should we include people who have *chosen* to work part-time?

The definition of unemployment varies in different discussions. One year the U.S. Bureau of the Census reported that 4 million Americans were unemployed. That same year a Soviet official, using *his* definition, reported that 14 million Americans were unemployed. And each statement in its own way was probably true.

Citing a result out of context

Another way of lying is to report a result out of context. Suppose an attitude were measured over a 10-year period—from 1960, say, to 1970. And suppose the attitude changed over that period. A hypothetical change is shown in Fig. 1.2a; the change seems quite dramatic.

Now suppose we examined the attitude change over a longer period—say, 1900 to 1980. Figure 1.2b reports that change. Notice that the 80-year period includes the briefer 10-year period. Now the smaller change seems rather

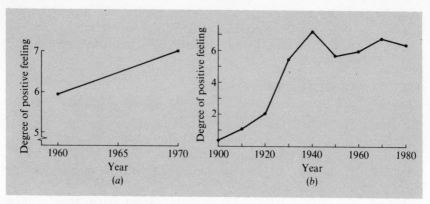

FIG. 1.2 Graphs of the change in some hypothetical attitude: (*a*) from 1960 to 1970; (*b*) from 1900 to 1980.

slight—only a ripple in a much larger wave. Out of context, though, it can look very large.

These devices illustrate two ways of manipulating the truth. Other subtler devices will emerge in later chapters. By recognizing them, an investigator sharpens his critical powers so he can better judge the claims he hears. This is another good reason for studying statistics.

2

DESCRIPTIVE STATISTICS: EMPIRICAL DISTRIBUTIONS OF DATA

Imagine a test that measures anxiety. Say it contains 150 statements like "I am a high-strung person" and "I always have enough energy when faced with difficulty." The subject reads each statement and circles T or F to tell whether the statement is true or false. For some statements T indicates anxiety, for others F indicates anxiety; the examiner then counts the number of these anxiety responses. This number is a score which operationally defines anxiety. It can range from 0 to 150.

Now suppose 100 subjects are tested; the testing yields 100 scores. (The symbol N tells the number of scores, so in this case, $N = 100$.) The 100 scores are shown in Table 2.1. Let us use these data to illustrate some descriptive procedures.

TABLE 2.1

Raw scores on a psychological test				*Same scores in numerical order*			
97	89	96	106	144	115	107	98
107	115	112	100	137	115	107	97
82	83	106	94	136	114	107	97
123	114	94	88	133	114	106	97
97	126	144	112	131	113	106	97
108	74	102	112	130	112	106	96
103	120	99	109	129	112	105	95
127	107	91	101	127	112	105	94
97	110	121	105	127	112	105	94
97	104	88	131	127	111	104	92
119	91	104	101	126	111	104	91
110	118	99	111	124	111	104	91
90	92	121	116	123	111	104	90
133	98	109	105	121	111	103	90
89	106	137	118	121	110	102	89
108	127	111	107	120	110	102	89
104	109	116	110	120	110	102	88
90	115	109	101	119	109	101	88
112	115	105	117	119	109	101	87
102	100	99	95	118	109	101	85
78	127	129	113	118	108	100	84
119	104	102	87	117	108	100	83
108	111	107	130	116	108	99	82
136	84	120	107	116	108	99	78
110	114	124	85	115	107	99	74

2.1   THE FREQUENCY DISTRIBUTION

The listing in Table 2.1 contains too much information, and our minds cannot grasp the essence of it. We therefore need to arrange the data into some more succinct form. When the scores are ordered from smallest to largest, we can easily see their range: 74 to 144. But even so, the listing is too large.

One problem in Table 2.1 is that every score forms a separate category—74, 78, 82, 83. This much precision is really not needed, and broader categories would show the trend more clearly Broader categories are shown in Table 2.2. There are 15 categories and every category is the same size—5 points wide.

Usually 12 to 20 categories are formed. To form the categories, the investigator first notes the range of scores: The scores range from 74 to 144—a 70-point range. This 70-point range needs to be divided into about 12 categories. $70/12 = 5^+$, so we make each category 5 points wide: One category contains the scores from 70 to 74; another contains the scores from 75 to 79; and so on. Altogether there are 15 categories. The size of each category is called *the interval size*; it is denoted i. In Table 2.2, $i = 5$.

TABLE 2.2 Same scores categorized

Category	Frequency
140–144	1
135–139	2
130–134	3
125–129	5
120–124	6
115–119	10
110–114	15
105–109	17
100–104	13
95–99	10
90–94	7
85–89	6
80–84	3
75–79	1
70–74	1
	$N = 100$

Usually each category is arranged so that its lower number is a multiple of i. In Table 2.2, where i equals 5, each lower number is a multiple of 5: 70, 75, 80. The categories are: 70–74, 75–79, 80–84, and so on. If i equaled 4, the categories would be 72–75, 76–79, 80–83, etc. If i equaled 6, the categories would be 72–77, 78–83, 84–89, and so on.

Once the categories are formed, the scores are tallied and counted. Table 2.2 shows the number of scores in each category. This number is called the category's *frequency*. And the table as a whole is called a *frequency distribution*.

(Table 2.2 describes actual data, so it is called an *empirical* frequency distribution. Other times, the distribution is purely hypothetical or theoretical; it might be the distribution that some theory has predicted. We then call it a *theoretical* frequency distribution. Theoretical distributions will be examined in later chapters.)

The frequency distribution tells at a glance how the scores are distributed. In Table 2.2, they cluster around 110. The most popular scores lie between 90 and 125. Scores rarely fall in the 70s or in the 130s.

Also notice that the frequency column sums to N: In Table 2.2, it sums to 100. Since every score gets counted in some one category, the total has to include all N scores.

Discrete versus continuous scores

Measurements are broadly divided into two types—discrete and continuous. Let us consider discrete measurements first. Suppose we measured the size of a man's family by counting his children. Certain numbers are possible— 1, 2, 3—but others are not; 1.47 is not possible. Or suppose we examined a set of pennies; we could measure the number of heads. Again, certain numbers are possible while others—like 8.04—are not. Measures like these—2 children, 5 heads—are called *discrete*: Certain particular values are possible, others are not. Furthermore, the measure is exact.

On the other hand, suppose a person's weight were measured—say, 162 lb. This value is not exact. The truth might be closer to 161.8 lb, and 161.784 lb even closer; 162 is really an approximation. But scales are not precise enough —and human eyes are not acute enough—to determine the exact value. Therefore, the ideal measure gets rounded off to 162: "162" really stands for a value between 161.5 and 162.5. Measures of this kind are said to be *continuous*: Such numbers are approximations; the true value could lie anywhere along the number continuum. Physical measurements like length and weight are usually continuous. If a tone's loudness were 63 decibels, the true loudness would lie between 62.5 and 63.5 decibels.

What about *psychological* measurements like test scores? Should we view the test score 43 as discrete or continuous? Many readers will consider test scores to be discrete; but by convention, they are usually considered continuous. Thus, an IQ of 112 is viewed as an approximation—a value between 111.5 and 112.5. In the category 105–109, 105 really means 104.5 to 105.5; and 109 really means 108.5 to 109.5. Therefore, the category really extends from 104.5 to 109.5. Its *real limits* are said to be 104.5 and 109.5. The category 75–79 has the real limits 74.5 and 79.5.

2.2   WAYS TO GRAPH A FREQUENCY DISTRIBUTION

A frequency distribution is often drawn as a graph. Three kinds of graph are commonly used—the histogram, the polygon, and the ogive. They help form the basis of statistical theory.

Histogram

A histogram depicting the data of Table 2.2 is shown in Fig. 2.1. The score categories appear along the X axis, and the frequencies along the Y axis. A bar extends over each category and rises to a certain height; that height tells the category's frequency. The bar for the category 90–94 has a height of 7. Notice that each bar extends to the category's real limits. The bar 90–94 extends from 89.5 to 94.5; the next bar, from 94.5 to 99.5. The histogram in Fig. 2.1 shows at a glance that the middle categories were more popular.

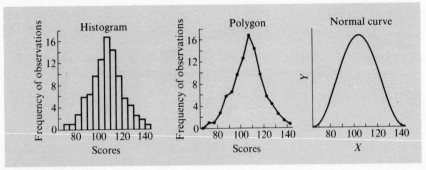

FIG. 2.1 A histogram and a polygon of the data in Table 2.2, and a normal curve.

A histogram has one important characteristic. The amount of *area* within a category is proportional to the category's frequency. Consider the category 90–94. If its bar is 1 unit wide and 7 units high, its area would equal 7 square units. Another category, 80–84, would contain 3 square units. And so on. If all these areas were measured, the total would equal 100 square units. Altogether, then, the histogram has 100 square units.

Now what *percent* of the total area lies in the category 90–94? This category's 7 square units are 7 percent of the total area. Seven percent is also the *percentage of people* with scores in that category. These two percentages are always identical—*the percentage of the histogram's area* in some region and *the percentage of people with scores* in that region. If 6 percent of a histogram falls beyond the score 120, then 6 percent of the people had scores beyond 120. If 35 percent of a histogram falls between 95 and 109, then 35 percent of the people had scores between 95 and 109.

EXAMPLE 2.1

For the histogram in Fig. 2.1, how many people had scores below 94.5?

Solution Consider the corresponding table, Table 2.2; the bottom five categories contain 18 people: $7 + 6 + 3 + 1 + 1 = 18$. These people comprise 18/100, or 18 percent, of the distribution. Thus, 18 percent of the examinees had scores below 94.5; and 18 percent of the histogram's area lies below 94.5.

EXAMPLE 2.2

What proportion of the histogram lies between 94.5 and 104.5?

Solution If you actually measured this area, it would make up 23 percent of the histogram. Twenty-three people had scores in that region, and they form 23 percent of the group.

EXAMPLE 2.3

Locate the lowest 11 percent of the distribution and the top 6 percent.

Solution Consult either the histogram or the frequency distribution. The lowest 11 percent lies below the 89.5. The top 6 percent lies above the score 129.5.

Polygon

A second kind of graph is the polygon. A polygon is shown in the middle of Fig. 2.1. The axes are the same as the histogram's. However, a dot appears at the middle of each category, and the height of the dot tells the frequency of scores. Only one person had a score between 75 and 79, so a dot appears at frequency " 1 " above the middle value, 77.

This middle value is called the category's *midpoint*. Check that 77 is the midpoint of category 75–79: The category extends from 74.5 to 79.5, at 5-point distance. Half of this distance lies between 74.5 and 77, and half lies between 77 and 79.5. To compute a midpoint, in general, first note the value of i; in Fig. 2.1, $i = 5$. Compute half of i, and add this amount to the lower real limit: $\frac{1}{2} (5) = 2.5$; and $74.5 + 2.5 = 77$.

A dot appears over each midpoint, and the dots are all connected. Notice the dot over the category 65–69: This category's frequency is 0; the 0 is plotted in order to close the figure at the left. Also notice the 0 plotted for the category 145–149; that point closes the figure at the right.

If the polygon were superimposed on the histogram, the two areas would be equal. A polygon rearranges the histogram's area to make the figure a little smoother, though the total area is unchanged. There are still as many square units of area as there are people, and the proportion of area in any region still reflects the proportion of examinees.

Notice the polygon's general shape: It is high in the middle where scores are more frequent. Toward the extremes the scores grow sparse. Also, the frequencies drop symmetrically on both sides. Psychological measurements are often distributed this way. A general, idealized version is shown at the bottom of Fig. 2.1. This theoretical form is called the normal curve; we shall discuss it further in Chap. 4.

Ogive

A third kind of graph is the ogive. An ogive is shown in Fig. 2.2. It tells how many people fell below each score. How many people, for example, fell below 99.5? Ten people were in category 95–99, and 18 people were below them—altogether, 28 people. This frequency is called the *cumulative* frequency. It tells how many scores were below some value.

An ogive reports cumulative frequencies. The X axis shows the different scores, and the Y axis shows the cumulative frequency. A dot appears over

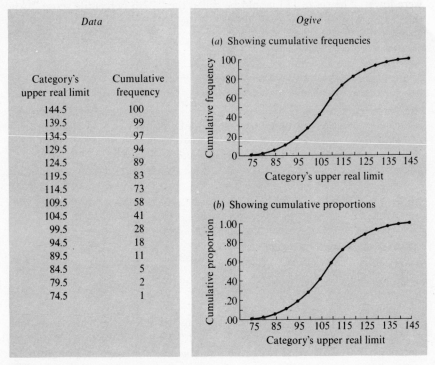

Data		Ogive

Category's upper real limit	Cumulative frequency
144.5	100
139.5	99
134.5	97
129.5	94
124.5	89
119.5	83
114.5	73
109.5	58
104.5	41
99.5	28
94.5	18
89.5	11
84.5	5
79.5	2
74.5	1

(a) Showing cumulative frequencies

(b) Showing cumulative proportions

FIG. 2.2 An ogive of the data in Table 2.2.

each category's upper real limit; it tells the cumulative frequency at that point. For category 95–99, the upper real limit is 99.5; the cumulative frequency is 28. Thus, a dot appears where X equals 99.5 and Y equals 28. For category 100–104, the cumulative frequency is 41; a dot appears where X equals 104.5 and Y equals 41. Then the various points get connected.

Notice the last category in Fig. 2.2: Its cumulative frequency equals N—in this case, 100. This cumulative frequency has to equal N since all N scores fall below the top of that category.

If each cumulative frequency were divided by N, it would tell the *proportion* of people below each score. The values are then called *cumulative proportions*. In Fig. 2.2b, cumulative proportions are plotted instead of cumulative frequencies. At the score 129.5, the Y value is .94. Thus .94 of the cases lie below 129.5.

2.3   PERCENTILES

A score has no meaning until we know its location in a distribution. The concept of a *percentile* tells that location. Suppose someone received the score 113 on a test, and suppose 27 percent of the examinees had scores that lower. The score 113 would be called the "27th percentile score." And the person with that score would fall "at the 27th percentile." We sometimes write: $P_{27} = 113$.

EXAMPLE 2.4

In the data of Table 2.2, what is P_{94}, the 94th percentile score?

Solution Ninety-four percent of the cases lie below 129.5, so $P_{94} = 129.5$. Notice that P_{94} is a *score*—the score that separates the lowest 94 percent of the distribution from the top 6 percent.

EXAMPLE 2.5

In the data of Table 2.2, what is P_{11}?

Solution Again, P_{11} is a *score*, the 11th percentile score. From Table 2.2, $P_{11} = 89.5$.

Sometimes a person's percentile standing tells more than his score does. A person at the 5th percentile has exceeded 5 percent of the other people, no matter what score he got. The score alone would not be as meaningful.

Special labels are used to designate particular percentile scores. The 25th percentile score is called the first quartile score. It is denoted Q_1. Therefore P_{25} is the same score as Q_1: Twenty-five percent of the examinees have scores that are lower. The 50th percentile score is called the second quartile score (Q_2), and the 75th percentile score is called the third quartile score (Q_3). Quartile scores divide the distribution into quarters. Thus, $Q_1 = P_{25}$; $Q_2 = P_{50}$; and $Q_3 = P_{75}$.

Sometimes *decile scores* are reported. Decile scores divide the distribution into tenths. The first decile score, for example, corresponds to the 10th percentile score. It is designated D_1. The second decile score, D_2, corresponds to P_{20}. And so on.

The 50th percentile score is called the *median*. Notice that the median is a *score*—the score that divides the distribution in half. Half the scores are below the median, the rest are above it. The median score is identical to the second quartile score (Q_2) and to the fifth decile score (D_5). Thus, the median $= P_{50} = D_5 = Q_2$.

How to compute the median

Whenever you compute the median of a distribution, your answer must be a score. The median of Table 2.2 has to lie between 70 and 144. Now what score in Table 2.2 cuts the distribution in half? Whatever it is, half of the scores lie below it and half lie above it.

"Half of the scores" refers to scores of 50 people. Therefore, we need to find the score that segregates the 50 lowest people. Start at the bottom category and gradually move upward, counting the number of people. At category 100–104 the cumulative frequency is 41 people—not yet the needed 50. Thus, category 100–104 is too low; the median must lie in the next category, 105–109.

Category 105–109 contains 17 people, but only 9 of them are needed to make the required 50. Let us assume that the 17 people are spread evenly throughout the category. Each person would occupy 1/17 of the category. And 9 people would occupy 9/17 of the category. That part of the category is shown in Fig. 2.3.

Now what *score* lies 9/17 of the way into category 105–109? The category extends from 104.5 to 109.5—a 5-point distance. And 9/17 of the distance equals 9/17 (5) = 2.6 points. And 2.6 points into the category brings us to 104.5 + 2.6 = 107.1. Thus, the median equals: 104.5 + 9/17 (5) = 107.1.

The median can usually be computed without a formula. If you do prefer a formula, though, we can write one this way: Let C denote the category that contains the 50th percentile score. Let f denote its frequency, and let $cf_{\text{lower limit}}$ denote the cumulative frequency below that category. In the formula, N is the number of scores, and i is the interval size. The formula is written:

$$\text{Median} = \begin{bmatrix} C\text{'s lower} \\ \text{real limit} \end{bmatrix} + \frac{.50\,N - cf_{\text{lower limit}}}{f}\,(i) \tag{2.1}$$

For the distribution of Table 2.2, C is the category 105–109, N is 100, and

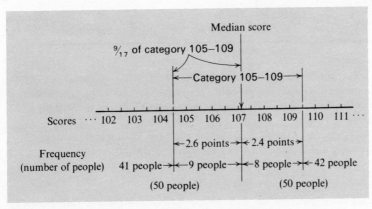

FIG. 2.3 The median score in a frequency distribution.

i equals 5. The cumulative frequency at 104.5 is 41, and the frequency of category C is 17. Therefore:

$$\text{Median} = 104.5 + \frac{.50(100) - 41}{17} \quad (5)$$

$$= 104.5 + \frac{9}{17}(5) = 107.1$$

EXAMPLE 2.6

Table 2.3 presents data on the Minnesota Psycho-Analogies Test,[1] an intelligence test that requires subjects to solve a series of analogies. The distribution contains 158 scores, and the interval size is 3. Compute P_{90}.

TABLE 2.3 Data on Minnesota psycho-analogies test

Score	Frequency (f)	Cumulative frequency (Cf)
27–74	4	158
69–71	15	154
66–68	21	139
63–65	21	118
60–62	24	97
57–59	16	73
54–56	23	57
51–53	15	34
48–50	7	19
45–47	3	12
42–44	4	9
39–41	1	5
36–38	3	4
33–35	1	1
	$N = 158$	

Solution P_{90}, the 90th percentile score, falls along the score continuum. It has to lie between 33 and 74—probably closer to 74. And 90 percent of the cases lie below that value. "90 percent of the cases" refers to $.90(158) = 142.2$ cases.

Now 139 cases lie below 68.5. Therefore P_{90} must lie in the next category, 69–71. To make 142.2 cases, 3.2 more cases are needed—3.2 of the 15 cases.

[1] These data are taken from: Levine, A. S. Minnesota Psycho-Analogies Test. *Journal of Applied Psychology*, 1930, *34*, pp. 300–305.

Therefore, P_{90} is 3.2/15 of the distance into category 69–71. The category is 3 points wide, 3.2/15 of it equals 0.6 points. Therefore, P_{90} equals:

$$68.5 + 3.2/15\,(3) = 68.5 + 0.6 = 69.1$$

A formula for P_{90} can be devised this way: We adapt the median's formula. Let C now denote the category that contains the 90th percentile score. And replace $.50N$ by $.90N$.

$$P_{90} = \begin{bmatrix} C\text{'s lower} \\ \text{real limit} \end{bmatrix} + \frac{.90N - cf_{\text{lower limit}}}{f} \quad (i) \qquad\qquad (2.2)$$

$$= 68.5 + \frac{.90(158) - 139}{15} \quad (3)$$

$$= 68.5 + \frac{3.2}{15}\,(3) = 69.1$$

Another Solution P_{90} can also be computed this way. P_{90} is the value that separates the top 10 percent of the cases from those below it. Let us therefore locate the highest 10 percent of the cases—.10 (158) = 15.8 cases.

Category 72–74 contains 4 cases. To make 15.8 cases, 11.8 more cases are needed; they have to come from the next lower category, 69–71. We enter this category at 71.5, preceeding downward. Now how far into the category should we go?

11.8 cases comprise 11.8/15 of the distance—11.8/15 of the 3-point distance. P_{90} therefore lies 11.8/15 (3) = 2.4 points below the upper real limit, 71.5. It equals $71.5 - 2.4 = 69.1$. Therefore $P_{90} = 69.1$.

In Example 2.6 notice that P_{90} is a *point*—69.1—that separates the lowest 90 percent of the distribution from the top 10 percent. The scores range from 33 to 74, and P_{90} is closer to 74. As a *point*, P_{90} does not necessarily equal any one person's score. Instead, it cleanly separates the distribution into two parts: 90 percent of the cases fall on one side, 10 percent on the other side: P_{90} is the common boundary between the two regions.

EXERCISES

2.1 What are the real limits of the following categories? (Assume that the data involve continuous measurements.)
  (*a*) 16–19
    Answer: 15.5–19.5
  (*b*) 78–90
    Answer: 77.5–90.5
  (*c*) 1.0–1.4
    Answer: 0.95–1.45

2.2 Compute i for the following categories. (Assume that the data involve continuous measurements.)
   (a) 16–19
        Answer: 4
   (b) 78–90
        Answer: 13
   (c) 1.0–1.4
        Answer: 0.5

2.3 Here is a distribution of 25 test scores. (i) Make a frequency distribution using an interval size of 2. (ii) From your frequency distribution, compute the 64th percentile score.

30	29	25	22	20
19	20	19	18	19
16	16	17	16	17
15	14	12	15	12
8	9	12	2	6

Answer: (ii) 18

2.4 Here is a frequency distribution of test scores. Find the median score and the 75th percentile.

Score	Number of Cases
95–99	4
90–94	9
85–89	17
80–84	7
75–79	3

Answer: Median = 87.4; $P_{75} = 91.2$

2.5 Imagine a certain frequency distribution. Let us define Difference A as the difference between the 10th and 20th percentile scores. Let us define Difference B as the difference between the 40th and 50th percentile scores. Why would Difference A usually be bigger than Difference B?

   Answer: Fewer people get scores at the extremes, so the histogram is usually shallower at the extremes. Therefore the people between P_{10} and P_{20} (10 percent of the examinees) are spread further apart, so the score P_{10} is further from the score P_{20} than P_{40} is from P_{50}.

3

DESCRIPTIVE MEASURES AND SYMBOLIC NOTATION

Here are two distributions of scores:

Distribution 1: 13, 15, 15, 15, 17

Distribution 2: 43, 45, 45, 45, 47

The scores in one range from 13 to 17; those in the other, from 43 to 47. The two distributions have different centers. One is centered at 15, the other at 45.

Now consider these two distributions. They have the same center, but the scores differ in their variability.

Distribution 3: 43, 45, 45, 45, 47

Distribution 4: 5, 25, 45, 65, 85

The scores of one are much more variable; they range from 5 to 85. Those of the other are closer together.

To describe a distribution of scores, then, we need two kinds of measures. One should describe the distribution's center, the other should describe its variability.

3.1   MEASURES OF CENTER (AVERAGES)

An *average* is a measure of a distribution's center. Psychologists mainly use three kinds of averages—the mode, the median, and the mean.

Mode

The mode is the most popular score in a distribution. It is the score that occurs most often. If the scores are in their original form, the mode is the one that occurs most often. For the scores 87, 93, 93, 95, the mode is 93.

To determine the mode of a *frequency distribution*, find the most popular *category*. That category's midpoint is the mode. In Table 3.1, the most popular category is 105–109. Therefore, the mode is 107.

Sometimes no one score is the most popular. Two different scores might be tied for the title. Then the distribution would have two modes. The distribution 87, 93, 93, 97, 97 has two modes, 93 and 97.

The mode is a crude kind of average. For one thing, it is not necessarily unique; a distribution might have two or three modes. Second, it is not necessarily central; it might be a high score or a low score. Third, it is not very stable: If the same subjects were tested again, the mode might be quite different.

Median

The median has already been defined as the 50th percentile score—the value that cuts the distribution in half. Figure 2.3 showed how to compute the median of a frequency distribution.

We can also compute a median from the original raw scores: First, arrange the scores from smallest to largest. If N is an *odd* number, the median is literally the middle score. It equals the $[(N + 1)/2]$th score of the distribution. Consider the scores: 5, 6, 7, 10, 14. The median is the third score, 7.

When N is an *even* number, examine the score on each side of the middle. The median is halfway between them. The median is therefore halfway between the score of the $(N/2)$th person and that of the $[(N/2) + 1]$th person. Consider these scores: 5, 6, 7, 10, 14, 21. The median is halfway between 7 and 10. It equals 8.5.

The median is more stable than the mode, and quite often, it is the most useful kind of average. It will reappear throughout later chapters.

Mean

The most widely used average, however, is the mean. The mean is the sum of all the scores divided by the number of scores. This measure uses all the data, it tends to be more stable, and it will reappear throughout later chapters. It is a very useful measure.

To compute the mean, sum all the scores and divide by N. For the scores 4, 3, 6, 7, the sum is 20 and N is 4; the mean is 5.0. Let us write the rule symbolically:

$$\text{Mean} = \frac{\Sigma X}{N}$$

In these symbols, ΣX is an instruction to sum all the scores; N is the number of scores. Symbols of this kind will be needed throughout our work. Let us therefore pause at this time to consider some basic notation.

3.2 SYMBOLIC NOTATION

Consider the listing of scores below. Four subjects were tested, and each subject has an identification number—1, 2, 3, 4. The letter X is used to denote a score; the subscript tells whose score it was. Subject 1's score is denoted X_1; X_1 equals 4. Subject 2's score is denoted X_2; it equals 3. Any individual's score is denoted X_i; there are N such scores.

Subject's Identification Number	X_i (Score)
Subject 1	$4 (= X_1)$
Subject 2	$3 (= X_2)$
Subject 3	$6 (= X_3)$
Subject 4	$7 (= X_4)$

(a) The capital Greek letter sigma (Σ) is an instruction to sum; ΣX_i means "sum all the scores." It is more precise to write $\sum_{i=1}^{N} X_i$—the sum of the X_i values from the first (where $i = 1$) to the last (where $i = N$). Thus:

$$\sum_{i=1}^{N} X_i = X_1 + X_2 + X_3 + \cdots + X_N$$

For the four scores above, $\sum_{i=1}^{N} X_i = \sum_{i=1}^{4} X_i = 20$.

The symbol $\overline{X}$ (read "X bar") denotes the mean. The rule for computing $\overline{X}$ is therefore written:

$$\overline{X} = \frac{\sum_{i=1}^{N} X_i}{N} \tag{3.1}$$

(Later we shall simplify this notation.) In the data above, $\overline{X} = 20/4 = 5.0$.

(b) A second notation is $\sum\limits_{i=1}^{N} X_i^2$. This instruction tells you to square each score (X_i^2) and then to sum the squared scores. For the scores above, $\sum\limits_{i=1}^{N} X_i^2 = 4^2 + 3^2 + 6^2 + 7^2 = 110$.

(c) A third notation is $\left(\sum\limits_{i=1}^{N} X_i\right)^2$. This notation tells you first to sum the scores $\left(\sum\limits_{i=1}^{N} X_i\right)$ and then to square the total. For the data above, $\left(\sum\limits_{i=1}^{N} X_i\right)^2 = (20)^2 = 400$. Notice the difference between $\sum\limits_{i=1}^{N} X_i^2$ and $\left(\sum\limits_{i=1}^{N} X_i\right)^2$. The first is a sum of squared scores, the second is the square of a sum. Usually for a set of data, $\left(\sum\limits_{i=1}^{N} X_i\right)^2$ is larger.

(d) Now suppose each subject received two scores. Let one be denoted X_i; let the other be denoted Y_i. Consider the data below:

Subject	X_i	Y_i	$(X_i + Y_i)$
Subject 1	$4 (= X_1)$	$1 (= Y_1)$	$5 (= X_1 + Y_1)$
Subject 2	$3 (= X_2)$	$2 (= Y_2)$	$5 (= X_2 + Y_2)$
Subject 3	$6 (= X_3)$	$6 (= Y_3)$	$12 (= X_3 + Y_3)$
Subject 4	$7 (= X_4)$	$3 (= Y_4)$	$10 (= X_4 + Y_4)$
	$\sum\limits_{i=1}^{N} X_i = 20$	$\sum\limits_{i=1}^{N} Y_i = 12$	

The next notation is the term: $\sum\limits_{i=1}^{N} (X_i + Y_i)$. This instruction tells you first to add each subject's pair of scores and then to sum the $(X_i + Y_i)$ values. The column "$X_i + Y_i$" gives each subject's total, and the sum of this column equals 32.

Notice that:

$$\sum_{i=1}^{N} (X_i + Y_i) = \sum_{i=1}^{N} X_i + \sum_{i=1}^{N} Y_i$$

If every entry in a set of scores is composed of two parts, Part 1 + Part 2, the total of the entries can be computed in two ways. You can sum the entries directly: $\sum\limits_{i=1}^{N} (X_i + Y_i)$. Or you can sum the Part 1 scores, then sum the Part 2 scores, and then add the two subtotals: $\sum\limits_{i=1}^{N} X_i + \sum\limits_{i=1}^{N} Y_i$.

This conclusion makes sense: If every subject had two sources of income—a main source, say, and a subsidiary source—you could compute the group's total income in two ways: (i) You could record every subject's total income and then sum these figures. Or (ii) you could compute two subtotals—the sum of the main incomes and the sum of the subsidiary incomes—and then add the two subtotals.

(*e*) Two other notations will give us further algebraic flexibility. The term $\sum_{i=1}^{N} (X_i + 2)$ is an instruction to increase each X_i by 2 points and then sum the increased scores. This total can be written:

$$\sum_{i=1}^{N} (X_i + 2) = [(X_1 + 2) + (X_2 + 2) + (X_3 + 2) + \cdots + (X_N + 2)].$$

Subject 1's increased score	Subject 2's increased score	Subject 3's increased score	Subject N's increased score

By rearranging the pieces, we can write the total this way:

$$[(X_1 + X_2 + X_3 + \cdots + X_N) + (2 + 2 + 2 + \cdots + 2)]$$

Therefore, $\sum_{i=1}^{N} (X_i + 2)$ is composed of two subtotals—the sum of the X_i's and the sum of the 2's. Notice that there are as many 2's as there are X_i's—namely, N of them.

$$\sum_{i=1}^{N} (X_i + 2) = \sum_{i=1}^{N} X_i + \sum_{i=1}^{N} 2$$

$$= \sum_{i=1}^{N} X_i + N \cdot 2$$

Thus, for the data above, the total becomes:

$$\sum_{i=1}^{N} (X_i + 2) = \sum_{i=1}^{N} X_i + N \cdot 2 = 20 + 4 \cdot 2 = 28$$

As a general rule, suppose every X_i is increased by a constant; the sum of the increased scores equals:

$$\sum_{i=1}^{N} (X_i + c) = \sum_{i=1}^{N} X_i + N \cdot c \qquad (3.2)$$

(*f*) Finally, suppose every score in a set gets *multiplied* by some constant. Say every score gets multiplied by 3, and the tripled scores are then summed.

The instruction would be written: $\sum\limits_{i=1}^{N} 3X_i$. Let us examine this sum.

$$\sum_{i=1}^{N} 3X_i = 3X_1 + 3X_2 + 3X_3 + \cdots + 3X_N$$

$$= 3[X_1 + X_2 + X_3 + \cdots + X_N]$$

$$= 3\sum_{i=1}^{N} X_i$$

In other words, the sum of the tripled scores equals: "3 times the sum of the scores." For the data above, the sum of the tripled scores equals $3\sum\limits_{i=1}^{N} X_i = 3 \cdot 20 = 60$. As a general rule:

$$\sum_{i=1}^{N} cX_i = c\sum_{i=1}^{N} X_i \tag{3.3}$$

Thus, the constant c can be moved to the left of the summation sign. In other words, cX_i values can be summed in two ways: (i) Each X_i can be multiplied by c and the resulting values then get summed. Or (ii) the X_i's can first be summed and this sum then gets multiplied by c. The two answers are identical.

Dropping the subscript *i*
This discussion has used X_i as a precise way of denoting a score. If there is no confusion, though, it is easier to ignore the subscript and denote the score as X. Then the sum of the scores would be written ΣX. The sum of the squared scores would be ΣX^2, and the square of the sum would be $(\Sigma X)^2$. If a constant were added to each score, we would write $\Sigma(X + c) = \Sigma X + N \cdot c$. If every score were multiplied by a constant, we would write $\Sigma cX = c\Sigma X$. The mean would be written: $\bar{X} = \Sigma X/N$.

This simpler notation is very convenient. Let us adopt it in general. When possible confusion arises, though, we can resume use of the more precise form.

3.3   PROPERTIES OF THE MEAN

Addition rule for $\bar{X}$
Suppose a set of scores has a certain mean. And suppose a constant amount is added to each score. Now let the mean be recomputed. What would the new mean be?

Intuitively, the new mean would equal the former mean plus the added constant. Consider the scores 0, 4, 7, 9. Their mean is 5. Every score is raised by 2 points, and the scores become 2, 6, 9, 11. The new mean equals 7. Thus, the mean increases from 5 to 7. If a constant is added to every score, the mean increases by the same amount. Let us call this general rule the *addition rule*.

The addition rule is easy to prove. Let each score be denoted X and now increase each X to "$X + c$." To compute the new mean, sum these increased scores and divide by N:

$$\text{New mean} = \frac{\Sigma(X + c)}{N} = \frac{\Sigma X + N \cdot c}{N} = \frac{\Sigma X}{N} + \frac{N \cdot c}{N}$$

$$= \bar{X} + c$$

What if we subtracted a constant from every score? Then the mean would be *reduced* by that amount. If every score were reduced by 3, the mean would drop from 5 to 2.

Suppose $\bar{X}$ itself were subtracted from every score. What would the new mean be? For any set of scores, $\bar{X}$ is a constant number; for the set 4, 0, 7, 9, $\bar{X}$ equals 5. Let us therefore subtract 5 points from every score. The scores become $-1, -5, 2, 4$ and the mean drops from 5 to 0. The new mean equals the former mean minus $\bar{X}$. Whenever $\bar{X}$ is subtracted from every score, the mean drops to 0.

When a score is reduced by $\bar{X}$ points, we express it as $X - \bar{X}$. This value is called a *deviation score*. A deviation score is also denoted x; it tells the score's distance from $\bar{X}$. Deviation scores always have a mean of 0.

Score X	Deviation score $x = X - \bar{X}$	Score X	Deviation score $x = X - \bar{X}$
4	-1	12	-9
0	-5	24	$+3$
7	$+2$	24	$+3$
9	$+4$	24	$+3$
Mean = 5	Mean = 0	Mean = 21	Mean = 0

Multiplication rule for $\bar{X}$

Suppose every score is *multiplied* by some constant, and suppose the mean is recomputed. What would the new mean equal? Consider the scores 0, 4, 7, 9 again, and multiply each one by 6. The scores become 0, 24, 42, 54, and their mean equals 30. The mean has increased sixfold from 5 to 30. The new mean equals the former mean *times* the constant. Let us call this result the *multiplication rule*.

The multiplication rule is also easy to prove. Each score X becomes cX. The cX values are then summed and divided by N. The new mean becomes:

$$\text{New mean} = \frac{\Sigma cX}{N} = c\frac{\Sigma X}{N} = c\overline{X}$$

The constant c might be a fraction—say, $\frac{1}{3}$. Then each score would be multiplied by $\frac{1}{3}$, and the new mean would become $\frac{1}{3}$ of its original value. We can therefore extend the rule to division: If every score is *divided* by a constant, the mean also gets divided by that constant.

EXAMPLE 3.1

A personality test is administered to 30 males and 20 females. The scores of the males are labeled X, those of the females are labeled Y. The mean for the males ($\overline{X}$) is 100; that for the females ($\overline{Y}$) is 90.

(a)   Suppose we add 5 points to each female's score. What would $\overline{Y}$ become?
Solution.   The new mean would equal $90 + 5 = 95$.

(b)   Suppose every X score is multiplied by $\frac{1}{2}$. What would $\overline{X}$ become?
Solution.   The new mean would equal $\frac{1}{2}(100) = 50$.

(c)   What is the mean of all 50 scores?

Solution   To compute the overall mean, first compute the total for the males (ΣX) and the total for the females (ΣY). Then add these totals together to obtain the overall total. Finally divide by 50.

$$\overline{X} = \frac{\Sigma X}{N_X} \qquad \overline{Y} = \frac{\Sigma Y}{N_Y}$$

$$100 = \frac{\Sigma X}{30} \qquad 90 = \frac{\Sigma Y}{20}$$

$$\Sigma X = 3{,}000 \qquad \Sigma Y = 1{,}800$$

The total of all 50 scores equals $\Sigma X + \Sigma Y = 3{,}000 + 1{,}800 = 4{,}800$. The mean of the 50 scores is therefore: $4{,}800/50 = 96$.

EXAMPLE 3.2

Prove algebraically that the sum of the deviation scores is 0.

Solution   The sum of the deviation scores is written $\Sigma(X - \overline{X})$.

In general: $\Sigma(X + Y) = \Sigma X + \Sigma Y$.

Therefore: $\Sigma(X - \overline{X}) = \Sigma X - \Sigma \overline{X}$.

Now what does $\Sigma \bar{X}$ mean? This notation $\left(\text{really } \sum_{i=1}^{N} \bar{X}\right)$ tells us to add $\bar{X} +$ $\bar{X} + \bar{X} + \cdots$ (N times), or simply $N \cdot \bar{X}$.

$$\Sigma(X - \bar{X}) = \Sigma X - N \cdot \bar{X}$$
$$= \Sigma X - N \cdot \frac{\Sigma X}{N}$$
$$= \Sigma X - \Sigma X$$
$$= 0$$

*3.4 COMPUTING THE MEAN OF A FREQUENCY DISTRIBUTION

Table 3.1 presents the frequency distribution we developed before. Let us now compute its mean. First we shall consider a direct, but tedious, method; then we shall develop a shorter method.

TABLE 3.1 Computing $\bar{X}$ from a frequency distribution

Column 1	Column 2	Column 3	Column 4	Column 5	Column 6
Category	Midpoint (the lowest midpoint is 72)	Each midpoint is reduced by 72	Each value is now divided by 5 (d value)	Frequency (f)	(f · d)
140–144	142	70	14	1	14
135–139	137	65	13	2	26
130–134	132	60	12	3	36
125–129	127	55	11	5	55
120–124	122	50	10	6	60
115–119	117	45	9	10	90
110–114	112	40	8	15	120
105–109	107	35	7	17	119
100–104	102	30	6	13	78
95–99	97	25	5	10	50
90–94	92	20	4	7	28
85–89	87	15	3	6	18
80–84	82	10	2	3	6
75–79	77	5	1	1	1
70–74	72	0	0	1	0
				100	701
				N	Σfd

* This section can be omitted in a shorter course.

The frequency distribution does not report exact scores. Therefore, we need to approximate each examinee's score. Consider category 140–144; we can use its midpoint 142 as its most representative score—142 approximates the score of the person in that category. Likewise, 117 approximates the score of the ten people in category 115–119. To compute the mean, then, we consider all 100 scores and sum them: one 142, two 137s, three 132s, five 127s, and so on. (The different scores are listed in Column 2.) The total—10,705—is then divided by 100 to yield the mean, 107.05.

Shorter method

Notice the midpoints in Column 2. The lowest one is 72, so we can subtract 72 from each value to achieve smaller numbers. The resulting values are shown in Column 3. These values are easier to handle; they range from 0 to 70.

But the numbers can be simplified further. Each entry is a multiple of the interval size 5, so we can divide each entry by 5. The resulting values are shown in Column 4: 0, 1, 2, 3, ... 14. These values are called "coded deviations," or "d values." The lowest one is 0; each successive one increases by 1 point.

Consider the mean of the d values. One hundred values need to be summed: one 14, two 13s, three 12s, five 11s, and so on. This sum is shown in Column 6; it equals 701. The mean of the d values is therefore: $701/100 = 7.01$. Its formula is written: $\overline{X}_{d\,values} = \Sigma(f \cdot d)/N$.

We can now use this mean—7.01—to reconstruct the original mean. (a) First consider the entries of Column 4—one 14, two 13s, three 12s, ... If each one is multiplied by i, we obtain the entries of Column 3—one 70, two 65s, three 60s, ... Therefore, Column 3's mean equals $(7.01)(i) = (7.01)(5) = 35.05$.

$$\overline{X}_{\text{Column 3}} = i \cdot \overline{X}_{d\,values} = i \cdot \frac{\Sigma(f \cdot d)}{N}$$

(b) Now consider the entries of Column 3—one 70, two 65s, three 60s, ... If each one is increased by 72 points, we obtain the entries of Column 2—one 142, two 137s, three 132s, ... Therefore, Column 2's mean equals 35.05 plus 72: 107.05. In general:

$$\overline{X}_{\text{Column 2}} = \text{Lowest midpoint} + \overline{X}_{\text{Column 3}}$$
$$= \text{Lowest midpoint} + i \cdot \frac{\Sigma(f \cdot d)}{N} \qquad (3.4)$$

To summarize, we compute the mean by the following steps. (i) First note the lowest midpoint and the interval size i. In Table 3.1, the lowest midpoint is 72, and i is 5. (ii) Assign d values to the different categories: 0, 1, 2, 3, ... (iii) Then compute the mean using these d values; for the data, $\bar{X}_{d\ values} = 7.01$. (iv) Multiply $\bar{X}_{d\ values}$ by i, and add the lowest midpoint: 5 (7.01) + 72. This step reconstructs the original mean 107.05.

Any arbitrary midpoint could be subtracted from the values in Column 2. Suppose 102 were subtracted instead of 72. Each result would then be divided by 5, and the d values would become:

$$-6, -5, -4, -3, -2, -1, 0, 1, 2, 3, 4, 5, 6, 7, 8$$

$\bar{X}_{d\ values}$ would equal 1.01, and the original mean would equal: $\bar{X} = 5\ (1.01) + 102 = 107.05$.

3.5   MEAN AS THE "CENTER OF GRAVITY"

The mean also has a physical meaning. Imagine a weightless board that looks like the base of a histogram. Different score values occur along its length. Now let a 1-unit weight signify each person's score. The scores 3, 3, 3, 5, 6 would be diagramed as in Fig. 3.1.

Now where is the "center of gravity"? Where should a fulcrum be placed to equalize the weights on each side? To anwer this question, compute the mean: $\bar{X} = 4.0$. The fulcrum should be placed at the value 4.0 if the board is to balance.

Figure 3.2 illustrates this fact. In Case a the fulcrum occurs at 4.0, and the

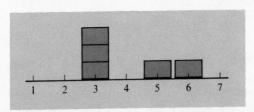

FIG. 3.1

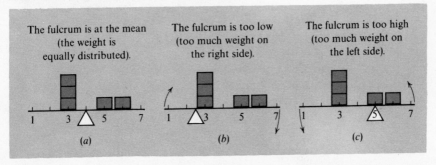

The fulcrum is at the mean (the weight is equally distributed).

The fulcrum is too low (too much weight on the right side).

The fulcrum is too high (too much weight on the left side).

(a)   (b)   (c)

FIG. 3.2

board is balanced: The push on the left offsets the push on the right. Two other cases are shown for comparison; in one the fulcrum is too high, in the other it is too low.

3.6 MEASURES OF VARIABILITY

Next we consider some measures of variability. Here are two sets of scores with identical means. Set A: 44, 45, 46; Set B: 25, 45, 65. The two sets only differ in their variabilities. In one the scores are close together; in the other, they differ widely. This variability can be described in different ways.

Range

One measure is the range—the difference between the highest score and the lowest score. In Set A, the range equals $46 - 44 = 2$; in Set B, it equals $65 - 25 = 40$. The range is informative, but it only involves two scores; therefore, it does not differentiate between, say, the set 25, 45, 45, 65 and the more variable set 25, 30, 60, 65.

Quartile deviation

Another measure is the *quartile deviation*. Like the range, it involves just two values—Q_1 (the 25th percentile score) and Q_3 (the 75th percentile score). The quartile deviation is half of their difference. It is denoted Q.

$$Q = \tfrac{1}{2}(Q_3 - Q_1) \tag{3.5}$$

The quartile deviation is often reported along with the median. Suppose a set of scores has a median of 43, and suppose Q equals 10. We might then picture Q_1 to be 10 points *below* the median and Q_3 to be 10 points *above* the median. (Q_1 would equal 33, Q_3 would equal 53, and Q would equal $\tfrac{1}{2}(53 - 33) = 10$.) A crude histogram would look like Fig. 3.3.

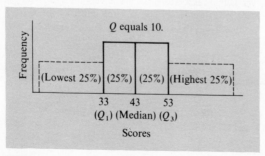

FIG. 3.3

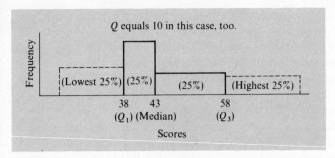

FIG. 3.4

If the scores were really distributed this way, the quartile deviation would be useful. But the scores might be distributed in some other way. For example, Q_1 might be 5 points below the median, and Q_3 15 points above the median. Q_1 would equal 38, Q_3 would equal 58, and Q would still be 10: $\frac{1}{2}$ (58 − 38) = 10. One-fourth of the distribution would now lie below 38; another fourth between 38 and 43; another fourth between 43 and 58; the top fourth above 58. The histogram would look like Fig. 3.4. Therefore, Q could be misleading: It tends to suggest the first histogram, which might not be valid.

Average deviation

Another measure is the average deviation. Consider the 10 scores in Table 3.2. They range from 0 to 16, and their mean is 8. Now consider each score's distance from $\overline{X}$. For each score we express this distance as $X - \overline{X}$. When X is 11, $X - \overline{X}$ equals 11 − 8 = 3; 11 is therefore 3 points above $\overline{X}$. When X is 2, $X - \overline{X}$ equals 2 − 8 = −6; 2 is therefore 6 points below $\overline{X}$. Distances

TABLE 3.2 Computation of average deviation

Person	Score	$X - \overline{X}$	$|X - \overline{X}|$
A	11	3	3
B	2	−6	6
C	0	−8	8
D	4	−4	4
E	5	−3	3
F	14	6	6
G	8	0	0
H	16	8	8
I	12	4	4
J	8	0	0
	$\overline{X} = 8.0$		$\Sigma|X - \overline{X}| = 42$

$$\text{A.D.} = \frac{\Sigma|X - \overline{X}|}{N} = \frac{42}{10} = 4.2$$

from $\overline{X}$ are called deviation scores; they appear in the third column of Table 3.2.

When the scores vary a lot, their deviation scores are generally large. When the scores are close together, their deviation scores are small. We can therefore describe the scores' variability by describing the typical deviation score. Unfortunately, though, we cannot simply average the deviation scores for their sum is always 0.

But we *can* average the *absolute* deviation scores. (An absolute value is the value without a sign.) The absolute value of -6 is 6; it is written $|-6|$. An absolute deviation score is written $|X - \overline{X}|$. It tells the score's distance from $\overline{X}$—regardless of direction. Such values are shown in the fourth column of Table 3.2.

The average deviation (A.D.) is the mean of these values.

$$\text{A.D.} = \frac{\Sigma|X - \overline{X}|}{N} \tag{3.6}$$

For the data of Table 3.2, A.D. equals $42/10 = 4.2$.

The average deviation appears more frequently in the older literature of psychology. Another measure—the standard deviation—is generally preferred today. It also is based on deviation scores.

Standard deviation

The standard deviation is the most common measure of variability; it is denoted S. To compute a standard deviation, change every score to a deviation score, $X - \overline{X}$. Then *square* each deviation score; the squaring eliminates negative values. Then compute the mean of the squared values: Sum them and divide by N. Finally, take the square root. The entire procedure is written:

$$S = \sqrt{\frac{\Sigma(X - \overline{X})^2}{N}} = \sqrt{\frac{\Sigma x^2}{N}} \tag{3.7}$$

Sometimes the standard deviation is called the "root-mean-squared-deviation." This label summarizes all the operations for computing S: We take the square *root* of the *mean* of the *squared deviation* scores. The computation is illustrated in Table 3.3.

TABLE 3.3 Computation of standard deviation

Person	Score	$X - \bar{X}$	$(X - \bar{X})^2$
A	11	3	9
B	2	−6	36
C	0	−8	64
D	4	−4	16
E	5	−3	9
F	14	6	36
G	8	0	0
H	16	8	64
I	12	4	14
J	8	0	0
	$\bar{X} = 8.0$		$\Sigma(X - \bar{X})^2 = 250$

$$\frac{\Sigma(X - \bar{X})^2}{N} = \frac{250}{10} = 25$$

$$S = \sqrt{\frac{\Sigma(X - \bar{X})^2}{N}} = \sqrt{25} = 5$$

Computational formula

S is *defined* as $\sqrt{[\Sigma(X - \bar{X})^2]/N}$. For some purposes, however, this formula is cumbersome. Suppose $\bar{X}$ were 8.521. The formula would demand a lot of awkward subtracting and squaring. Other more convenient formulas can be derived. Let us consider one of them. It contains two important terms—ΣX^2, the sum of the squared scores, and $(\Sigma X)^2$, the squared sum. For the data of Table 3.3, $\Sigma X^2 = 890$, $(\Sigma X) = 80$, and $(\Sigma X)^2 = 6{,}400$. The formula is:

$$S = \frac{1}{N}\sqrt{N\Sigma X^2 - (\Sigma X)^2} \qquad (3.8)$$

For Table 3.3,

$$S = \tfrac{1}{10}\sqrt{10(890) - (80)^2} = \tfrac{1}{10}\sqrt{2{,}500}$$
$$= 5.0$$

Let us now derive this formula. Begin with the definition of S: $S = \sqrt{[\Sigma(X - \bar{X})^2]/N}$. Square both sides to eliminate the radical sign.

$$S^2 = \frac{\Sigma(X - \bar{X})^2}{N}$$

Now expand $(X - \overline{X})^2$. In general, $(A + B)^2$ equals $A^2 + 2AB + B^2$. Therefore, $(X - \overline{X})^2$ equals $X^2 - 2X\overline{X} + \overline{X}^2$. Thus:

$$S^2 = \frac{\Sigma(X^2 - 2X\overline{X} + \overline{X}^2)}{N}$$

Next we sum each term within the parentheses:

$$S^2 = \frac{\Sigma X^2 - \Sigma 2X\overline{X} + \Sigma \overline{X}^2}{N}$$

$$= \frac{\Sigma X^2}{N} - \frac{\Sigma 2X\overline{X}}{N} + \frac{\Sigma \overline{X}^2}{N}$$

For any set of data, $2\overline{X}$ is a constant value. Thus, $\Sigma 2\overline{X}X$ is like ΣkX. The constant can be placed in front of the summation sign: $k\Sigma X$. So $\Sigma 2\overline{X}X = 2\overline{X}\Sigma X$. Furthermore, $\Sigma \overline{X}^2$ is the sum $\overline{X}^2 + \overline{X}^2 + \overline{X}^2 + \cdots$ (once for every subject); it equals $N \cdot \overline{X}^2$. Therefore:

$$S^2 = \frac{\Sigma X^2}{N} - 2\overline{X}\frac{\Sigma X}{N} + \frac{N \cdot \overline{X}^2}{N}$$

$$= \frac{\Sigma X^2}{N} - 2\overline{X} \cdot \overline{X} + \overline{X}^2 = \frac{\Sigma X^2}{N} - \overline{X}^2$$

(If we now replace the radical sign, the formula becomes:

$$S = \sqrt{\frac{\Sigma X^2}{N} - \overline{X}^2} \tag{3.9}$$

This formula is sometimes useful.)

To derive the other formula, replace $\overline{X}$ by $\Sigma X/N$.

$$S^2 = \frac{\Sigma X^2}{N} - \overline{X}^2$$

$$S^2 = \frac{\Sigma X^2}{N} - \left(\frac{\Sigma X}{N}\right)^2 = \frac{\Sigma X^2}{N} - \frac{(\Sigma X)^2}{N^2}$$

$$= \frac{N\Sigma X^2}{N^2} - \frac{(\Sigma X)^2}{N^2}$$

$$S^2 = \frac{N\Sigma X^2 - (\Sigma X)^2}{N^2}$$

Finally replace the radical sign, and the formula becomes:

$$S = \sqrt{\frac{N\Sigma X^2 - (\Sigma X)^2}{N^2}}$$

$$= \frac{1}{N}\sqrt{N\Sigma X^2 - (\Sigma X)^2}$$

Variance
If the standard deviation is squared, the formula becomes:

$$S^2 = [\Sigma(X - \bar{X})^2]/N$$

S^2 is called the scores' variance. It is really a special kind of mean—the mean of all the squared deviation scores:

Variance $= S^2 =$ mean of the $(X - \bar{X})^2$ values

$$= \frac{\Sigma(X - \bar{X})^2}{N}$$

Variance plays an important role in certain statistical procedures that we shall examine in later chapters.

3.7   PROPERTIES OF S

Addition rule for S
Suppose a constant were added to every score in a set of scores. The standard deviation would not be affected. Say we raised every score by one point: The mean would also increase one point, so each deviation score would stay unchanged. Therefore S itself would not change. We can state the rule this way: If a constant value is added to every score, the standard deviation is not affected. If a constant value is *subtracted* from every score, the standard deviation is not affected either.

Multiplication rule for S
Now try *multiplying* every score by some value—say, 3. This time S is affected—it gets tripled: When every score gets tripled, the mean gets tripled. And each deviation score, formerly $X - \bar{X}$, becomes $3X - 3\bar{X}$, or $3(X - \bar{X})$. S also gets tripled. If every score is multiplied by some constant factor, S gets multiplied by that factor too.

Let us prove this point algebraically. Let $S = \sqrt{[\Sigma(X - \bar{X})^2]/N}$. Now suppose every score is multiplied by k. The score becomes kX, and the mean becomes $k\bar{X}$. The standard deviation becomes:

TABLE 3.4 The weighting of a subtest depends on its standard deviation

		Examination 1	Examination 2	Examination 1 + Examination 2
Original data	Student A:	5 (High)	10	15
	Student B:	5 (High)	10	15
	Student C:	3	30 (High)	33 (High)
	Student D:	3	30 (High)	33 (High)
		$\bar{X} = 4$	$\bar{X} = 20$	
		$S = 1$	$S = 10$	
To equalize the means: Add 16 points to every score of Examination 1. (Its S is unchanged.)	Student A:	21	10	31
	Student B:	21	10	31
	Student C:	19	30	49
	Student D:	19	30	49
		$\bar{X} = 20$	$\bar{X} = 20$	
		$S = 1$	$S = 10$	
To equalize the standard deviations: Multiply every score of Examination 1 by 10. (Its S increases to 10.)	Student A:	50	10	60
	Student B:	50	10	60
	Student C:	30	30	60
	Student D:	30	30	60
		$\bar{X} = 40$	$\bar{X} = 20$	
		$S = 10$	$S = 10$	
		↑———equal———↑		

$$\sqrt{\frac{\Sigma(kX - k\overline{X})^2}{N}} = \sqrt{\frac{\Sigma k^2(X - \overline{X})^2}{N}} = \sqrt{\frac{k^2\Sigma(X - \overline{X})^2}{N}}$$

$$= k\sqrt{\frac{\Sigma(X - \overline{X})^2}{N}} = kS$$

The weighting of subtests

Suppose three tests are administered; each examinee receives three scores. The scores might be three examination scores—say, two midterms and a final. Now suppose each person's scores are added together to form a three-score total.

When test scores are added in this way, how much does each one count? Does the final examination contribute more to the total than either midterm? The answer, as you will see, depends on its standard deviation. The standard deviation of a test determines its weight in the total.

Consider the data of Table 3.4. Four subjects were tested, and each subject had two scores—a score on Examination 1 and a score on Examination 2. Each subject's scores have been summed in the last column.

First notice the original data: On the first examination Subjects A and B scored high, Subjects C and D scored low. On the second examination Subjects C and D scored high, Subjects A and B scored low. If the two examinations counted *equally*, a high score on one would offset a low score on the other; and the totals would all be alike. But notice the totals: They mainly reflect Examination 2. When a score is high on Examination 2, the total is high. Apparently, Examination 2 carries the greater weight.

Why is this? And how can the two sets be equalized? You might try equalizing the means: Add 16 points to each score of Examination 1. Then both means equal 20. But the problem is still not solved; Examination 2 still carries the greater weight.

The trouble is, the scores on the first examination *vary* so little; their S is too small. To equalize the standard deviations, multiply each score of Examination 1 by 10. Both standard deviations become 10, and the variabilities are equal. Now the two sets do offset one another: Subject A was high on one and low on the other; his total becomes 60. As a general rule, the subtest with the larger S carries the greater weight. When the standard deviations are equal, the weightings are equal.

*3.8 COMPUTING S FROM A FREQUENCY DISTRIBUTION

The frequency distribution of Chap. 2 is shown in Table 3.5. Let us now compute its standard deviation. First we compute S by a direct, but tedious, method. Then we shall develop a short-cut.

---

* This section can be omitted in a shorter course.

TABLE 3.5 Computing S from a frequency distribution

Column 1	Column 2	Column 3	Column 4	Column 5	Column 6	Column 7
Category	Midpoint (the lowest midpoint is 72)	Each midpoint is reduced by 72	Each value is now divided by 5 (d value)	frequency (f)	$f \cdot d$	$f \cdot d^2$
140–144	142	70	14	1	14	196
135–139	137	65	13	2	26	338
130–134	132	60	12	3	36	432
125–129	127	55	11	5	55	605
120–124	122	50	10	6	60	600
115–119	117	45	9	10	90	810
110–114	112	40	8	15	120	960
105–109	107	35	7	17	119	833
100–104	102	30	6	13	78	468
95–99	97	25	5	10	50	250
90–94	92	20	4	7	28	112
85–89	87	15	3	6	18	54
80–84	82	10	2	3	6	12
75–79	77	5	1	1	1	1
70–74	72	0	0	1	0	0
				100	701	5,671
				↑ N	↑ Σfd	↑ Σfd^2

First of all, try to apply the formula $\dfrac{1}{N}\sqrt{N\Sigma X^2 - (\Sigma X)^2}$. Each midpoint can be used as a score. To compute ΣX, sum the 100 scores: One 142, two 137s, three 132s, five 127s, and so on. This sum equals 10,705. Then compute ΣX^2 by adding $(142)^2$ once, $(137)^2$ twice, $(132)^2$ three times, $(127)^2$ five times, and so on. This sum equals 1,164,895. The formula becomes

$$\frac{1}{100}\sqrt{100(1,164,895) - (10,705)^2} = 13.75$$

Shorter method
To simplify the midpoints, subtract 72 from each one and divide by 5. The resulting d values are shown in Column 4. Let us use these d values to compute S: First sum the 100 d values, then sum the 100 *squared d* values. To sum the d values, add: one 14, two 13s, three 12s, five 11s, and so on. That total—Σfd in Table 3.5—equals 701. To sum the *squared d* values, add: $(14)^2$ once, $(13)^2$ twice, $(12)^2$ three times, $(11)^2$ five times, and so on. This sum—Σfd^2 in Table 3.5—equals 5,671.

Finally, compute S:
In general,

$$S = \frac{1}{N}\sqrt{N\Sigma X^2 - (\Sigma X)^2}$$

Therefore:

$$S_{d\,values} = \frac{1}{N}\sqrt{N\Sigma fd^2 - (\Sigma fd)^2}$$

$$= \frac{1}{100}\sqrt{100(5,671) - (701)^2} = 2.75$$

Let us now use this value to reconstruct the original standard deviation (*a*) First consider the data of Column 4. If every entry of Column 4 is multiplied by i, we obtain the entries of Column 3. According to the multiplication rule, Column 3's standard deviation equals $(i)(2.75) = (5)(2.75) = 13.75$. Thus, $S_{Column\,3} = i \cdot S_{d\,values}$.

(*b*) Now consider the data of Column 3. If every entry of Column 3 is increased by 72 points, we obtain the entries of Column 2. According to the addition rule, Column 2's standard deviation is the same as Column 3's. Thus, the standard deviation is still 13.75.

As a general rule, then, the standard deviation of the d values only needs to be multiplied by i.

$$S = i \cdot S_{d\,values}$$

$$= i \cdot \frac{1}{N}\sqrt{N\Sigma fd^2 - (\Sigma fd)^2}$$

$$= \frac{i}{N}\sqrt{N\Sigma fd^2 - (\Sigma fd)^2} \qquad (3.10)$$

EXERCISES

True or false?

3.1 If X is a variable and C is a constant, $\Sigma(X + C) = \Sigma X + C$.
   Answer: F

3.2 If $x = X - \bar{X}$, then $\Sigma ax = 0$.
   Answer: T

3.3 For two sets of scores, X and Y, $\Sigma XY = (\Sigma X)(\Sigma Y)$.
Answer: F

3.4 If every score in a distribution were doubled, the value of Q would be doubled.
Answer: T

3.5 If a is a constant and X is a variable, $\Sigma aX^2 = a\Sigma X^2$.
Answer: T

Problems

3.6 Two scores for each of five subjects are listed below. Call one the subject's X score and the other his Y score.

Subject	X	Y
A	3	2
B	2	1
C	0	5
D	9	0
E	5	3

(a) Compute: (i) ΣX, (ii) ΣX^2, (iii) $(\Sigma X)^2$, (iv) ΣY, (v) ΣY^2, (vi) $(\Sigma Y)^2$, (vii) $(\Sigma X)(\Sigma Y)$.
Answer: (i) $\Sigma X = 19$; (ii) $\Sigma X^2 = 119$; (iii) $(\Sigma X)^2 = 361$; (iv) $\Sigma Y = 11$; (v) $\Sigma Y^2 = 39$; (vi) $(\Sigma Y)^2 = 121$; (vii) $(\Sigma X)(\Sigma Y) = 209$

(b) Form a column labeled $(X + Y + 3)$, and enter a value for every subject. By summing this column, compute $\Sigma(X + Y + 3)$.
Answer: 45

(c) In the same way compute: (i) $\Sigma(X + 5)$, (ii) $\Sigma(3X + 2Y)$, (iii) $\Sigma[(X - 3)(Y + 1)]$.
Answer: (i) 44; (ii) 79; (iii) -6

(d) Consider the expression in (b), which can be expanded to:

$$\Sigma(X + Y + 3) = \Sigma X + \Sigma Y + N \cdot 3$$
$$= \Sigma X + \Sigma Y + 15$$

Enter your computed values of ΣX and ΣY into the right-hand side of this equation and show that your answer equals the answer of (b).

(e) Likewise expand the expressions in (i), (ii), and (iii) of (c). Recompute these values using the expanded expressions.

(f) If each X score and each Y score are multiplied by 3: (i) What will the sum of the squared X scores be? (ii) What will the square of the sum of the Y scores be?
Answer: (i) 1,071; (ii) 1,089

3.7 Here is a group of four scores: 3, 3, 5, 7.
  (a) Compute $(\Sigma X)^2$.
  Answer: 324
  (b) Compute ΣX^2.
  Answer: 92
  (c) Compute $\Sigma(X + 3)$.
  Answer: 30

3.8   In a certain set of data, a is a constant equal to 10. $\bar{Y} = 5$ and $\Sigma X = 4$. Compute the value of $\Sigma \bar{X}(a - Y)$.
Answer: 20

3.9 $\Sigma X = 10$, $\Sigma Y = 20$, $\Sigma(X + Y + 3) = 60$. Therefore, $N =$ _____.
Answer: 10

3.10   What is the median of the following groups of scores?
(a)   1, 3, 12, 13, 14
    Answer: 12
(b)   2, 10, 12, 19, 21, 40
    Answer: 15.5

3.11   In a certain distribution the average deviation is 10. If every score were multiplied by 3 and then increased by 4 points, the average deviation would become_____.
Answer: 30

3.12   Use the shortcut method to find the mean, variance, and standard deviation.

Category	f
60–64	2
55–59	1
50–54	3
45–49	1
40–44	2

Answer: $\bar{X} = 52$; $S^2 = 50$; $S = 7.1$

3.13   Here is a set of ten numbers: 19, 28, 12, 3, 31, 21, 25, 37, 15, 9.
(a)   Compute (i) the mean and (ii) the standard deviation.
    Answer: Mean = 20; standard deviation = 10
(b)   Add 5 points to each measurement. Compute (i) the new mean and (ii) the new standard deviation.
    Answer: New mean becomes 25; new standard deviation becomes 10.
(c)   If a constant amount is added to each score in a distribution of scores: (i) How is the mean affected? (ii) How is the standard deviation affected?
    Answer: (i) Mean increases by amount of constant. (ii) Standard deviation is unaffected.
(d)   If you subtracted 15 from each score, what would the new mean and standard deviation be?
    Answer: New mean would be 5. New standard deviation would be 10.
(e)   Double each of the original measurements. Compute (i) the new mean and (ii) the new standard deviation.
    Answer: New mean becomes 40. New standard deviation would be 20.
(f)   If each score in a distribution is multiplied by a constant amount: (i) How is the mean affected? (ii) How is the standard deviation affected?
    Answer: (i) Mean is multiplied by the constant. (ii) Standard deviation is multiplied by the constant.

(*g*) If you took $\frac{1}{5}$ of each score, what would the new mean and standard deviation be?
Answer: New mean would be 4. New standard deviation would be 2.

3.14 There are 15 scores in a certain set. $\Sigma X = 95$. Compute $\Sigma(X - 3)$.
Answer: 50

3.15 Find two scores for which $N\Sigma X^2 = (\Sigma X)^2$. [That is, $N\Sigma X^2 - (\Sigma X)^2$ is 0, so the standard deviation is 0.]
Answer: Any two scores that are identical, e.g., 1 and 1

3.16 A set of 10 scores has the following characteristics: The mean value of X is 1, and the mean value of X^2 is 2. Suppose you are given the following instructions: Reduce every X by 1; then multiply this result by 5; and finally, sum across all subjects. What would the final result equal?
Answer: 50

3.17 For 20 scores, $\Sigma X = 15$; $\Sigma Y = 20$; $\Sigma XY = 50$. Compute $\Sigma[(X - 1)(Y + 2)]$.
Answer: 20

3.18 The term *sum of squares*, which is often denoted *ss*, refers to the sum of the squared deviation scores, x^2. Prove algebraically that this term equals:

$$ss = \Sigma x^2 = \Sigma X^2 - \frac{(\Sigma X)^2}{N}$$

3.19 There are 7 members in a commune, and they are all employed. The mean weekly salary is $55, and the median is $50.
(*a*) What is the commune's entire weekly income?
Answer: $385
(*b*) One member of the commune is already the most highly paid. Suppose he now receives an increase of $6 a week. (i) What is the new mean? (ii) What is the new median?
Answer: (i) $55.86 (ii) $50

3.20 A class of 50 students contains 30 men and 20 women. The entire class's mean score on a quiz is 80. Suppose the mean for the men students is 70. What is the mean for the women students?
Answer: 95

3.21 Consider these two kinds of information that you might have about a distribution of scores: *Situation A:* You know that the 75th percentile score is 30 points above the median, and the 25th percentile score is 10 points below the median. *Situation B:* You know that the quartile deviation, Q, equals 20. What can you say from the information in Situation A that may not be true of Situation B?
Answer: From Situation A, we can infer something about the shape of the distribution; from Situation B, we cannot.

4

THE NORMAL CURVE, z SCORES, AND RELATED TOPICS

We have now graphed different frequency distributions and described the distribution's center and variability. A frequency distribution can assume many different shapes. Some shapes are symmetrical, others are not. Some concentrate scores in the center, others do not. Various histograms are shown in Fig. 4.1.

4.1 THE NORMAL CURVE

One type of distribution is the *normal distribution*. This bell-like shape is very common in psychological data. Test scores are often distributed in this way. So are other psychological measurements, like IQs, measures of visual acuity, and performance on learning tasks. A histogram illustrating a normal distribution appears in Fig. 4.1.

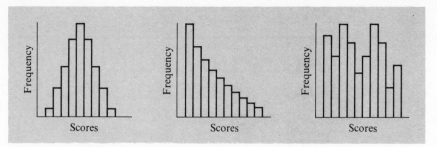

FIG. 4.1   Histograms of different shapes.

A normal distribution has three major characteristics. First, its scores are most numerous in the middle; scores near the mean are more common. Second, scores grow less and less common away from the middle. Third, the scores' frequencies decline symmetrically on both sides of the middle; a score 10 points above the mean is about as common as one 10 points below the mean.

Figure 4.2 shows histograms that illustrate normal distributions. Each histogram shows a distribution of IQs. The distributions differ in the size of the Ns; in one case N is very small, in another case N is extremely large.

Notice how smooth the histogram and polygon become as N grows larger. When there are enough cases, the distribution approaches a completely smooth, ideal form, which is called the *normal curve*. This ideal form is also called the *gaussian curve*, after Gauss, the German mathematician, who studied its characteristics in detail. The normal curve is a theoretical, idealized version of many polygons found in nature (Fig. 4.3). The X axis is analogous to the different possible scores, and the Y axis is analogous to the score's frequency. The curve's general shape resembles the shape of typical polygons. Like many simple curves, this one can be described by a mathematical equation that we shall examine later.

Sketching the normal curve

Suppose you wanted to sketch a normal curve that described some polygon— say a polygon for data with $\overline{X} = 48$ and $S = 3$. (This normal curve appears in Fig. 4.4 along with the polygon it describes.) To sketch the normal curve, first find the curve's highest point. The score under that point is the mean score. The mean always occurs in the *middle* of a normal distribution. If we drew a line down the middle, the line would cut the curve in half.

Consider the curve's highest point, its peak. As the curve leaves the peak it bends downward. A short distance from the peak, it stops bending downward and starts to bend upward. This transition point is called the curve's *inflection point*. The inflection points are shown in Fig. 4.4. Notice the score that is just under the inflection point: *That score is always one standard deviation*

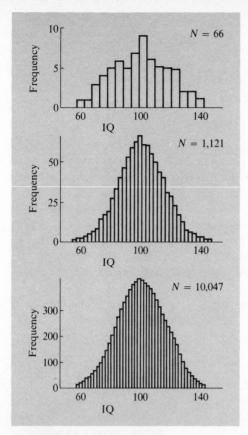

FIG. 4.2 Histograms showing the distribution of IQs for different sizes of N. (As the number of cases increases, the histogram becomes smoother.)

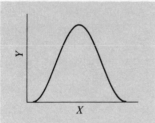

FIG. 4.3

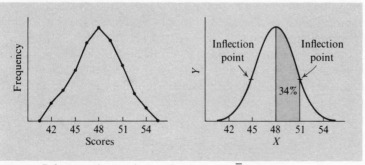

FIG. 4.4 Polygon and normal curve for data with $\overline{X} = 48$ and $S = 3$.

from the mean—it is S points from $\overline{X}$. In Fig. 4.4 it is 3 points from $\overline{X}$—on the left side 45, on the right side 51.

(This is the major reason for using the standard deviation as a measure of variability: It describes a certain distance in a normal curve—the distance between $\overline{X}$ and the score under the curve's inflection point.)

In Fig. 4.4 the region is crosshatched between the mean score and the score one standard deviation above the mean. In any normal curve, that region contains 34 percent of the curve's total area. In Fig. 4.4 it lies between the score 48 and the score 51. Another comparable region lies between the scores 45 and 48; that region, too, contains 34 percent of the curve's area.

Now let us use the normal curve to describe the polygon: If 34 percent of the *normal curve* falls between 48 and 51, then roughly 34 percent of the *polygon* must fall between 48 and 51. "Percentage of area" can be translated to "percentage of people," so roughly 34 percent *of the examinees* should have their scores between 48 and 51. Another 34 percent should fall between 45 and 48.

Consider a further example. Suppose a distribution of scores has a mean of 87 and a standard deviation of 12, and suppose the scores are normally distributed. The score one standard deviation below the mean equals 75, and the score one standard deviation above the mean equals 99. A normal curve describing this polygon would have 34 percent of its area between 75 and 87 and another 34 percent between 87 and 99. Therefore, 34 percent of the *polygon* should lie in each of these regions.

Here is another example. Table 2.1 contained 100 scores whose $\overline{X} = 97.1$ and whose $S = 13.5$. Consider those data again. Approximately 34 percent of the 100 scores should lie between 97.1 and 110.6. If you actually counted the scores in that range, you would find 33 such scores. Furthermore, 34 scores should lie between 83.6 and 97.1; actually there are 36 scores in that region.

In theory, then, we expect 34 percent of the scores to lie between $\overline{X}$ and the score one standard deviation from $\overline{X}$. Other distances from the mean have also been calibrated. Consider a score that is *half* a standard deviation from $\overline{X}$: If $\overline{X}$ were 45 and S were 10, the score would be 40 on one side and 50 on the other side. Tables are available to show how much of the normal curve's area lies between $\overline{X}$ and that score. One of these tables is reproduced as Table 4.1. Since the score is *half* a standard deviation from $\overline{X}$, consult ".50" in Column 1. The corresponding value in Column 2—19.15 percent—tells how much of the curve it bounds: About 19 percent of a normal distribution lies between $\overline{X}$ and whatever score is *half* a standard deviation from $\overline{X}$.

We can also use Table 4.1 to learn how much of the curve lies between $\overline{X}$ and the score .80 standard deviation from $\overline{X}$. The answer is 28.81 percent. Or between $\overline{X}$ and the score 1.30 standard deviations from $\overline{X}$. The answer is 40.32 percent.

Table 4.1 has two important features. First, distances are always calibrated

TABLE 4.1 Percent of total area under the normal curve
(A more detailed table appears as Table A.1 in the appendix.)

Score's distance from $\overline{X}$: number of standard deviations (z score)	Percent of area between score and $\overline{X}$
.00	0.00
.10	3.98
.20	7.93
.30	11.79
.40	15.54
.50	19.15
.60	22.57
.70	25.80
.80	28.81
.90	31.59
1.00	34.13
1.10	36.43
1.20	38.49
1.30	40.32
1.40	41.92
1.50	43.32
1.60	44.52
1.70	45.54
1.80	46.41
1.90	47.13
2.00	47.72
2.10	48.21
2.20	48.61
2.30	48.93
2.40	49.18
2.50	49.38
2.60	49.53
2.70	49.65
2.80	49.74
2.90	49.81
3.00	49.86
3.50	49.98
3.75	49.99

from the mean. The mean must be one point of reference whenever this table is used. Second, the distances of Column 1 are always expressed as " number of standard deviations." To use Column 1, you need to know *how many standard deviations* (.50, 1.00, 1.30) the score is from the mean.

A more detailed version of Table 4.1 appears in Table A.1 in the appendix.

EXAMPLE 4.1

Suppose a normal distribution has a mean of 110 and a standard deviation of 20.

(*a*) What score is 1.20 standard deviations above the mean?

Solution The score is 1.20 (20) = 24 points above the mean; it equals 110 + 24 = 134.

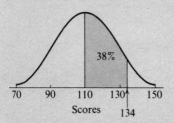

(*b*) What percentage of the normal curve lies between the mean score and the score 134?

Solution Since 134 is 1.20 standard deviations from $\bar{X}$, find 1.20 in Column 1 of Table 4.1 (or Table A.1 in the appendix). The corresponding entry of Column 2 is 38 percent. Therefore, 38 percent of the normal curve's area lies between 110 and 134.

(*c*) Suppose 200 people had been tested. Theoretically, how many earned scores between 110 and 134?

Solution Thirty-eight percent of 200 people = 76 people.

(*d*) What percentage of the normal curve lies below 134?

Solution The curve below 134 contains two parts, the part below $\bar{X}$ and the part from $\bar{X}$ to 134. Fifty percent of the curve lies below $\bar{X}$, and 38 percent lies between $\bar{X}$ and 134. Altogether 88 percent of the curve lies below 134.

(*e*) What percentage lies above 134?

Solution 100 percent − 88 percent = 12 percent

EXAMPLE 4.2

A normal distribution has a mean of 110 and a standard deviation of 20. What percentage of the distribution lies between the scores 100 and 130?

Solution Distances are always calibrated from the mean 110. Therefore, we must consider two separate regions—the part from 100 to $\bar{X}$, and the part from $\bar{X}$ to 130.

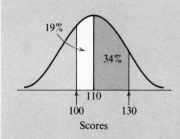

The score 100 is *half* a standard deviation below $\bar{X}$. From Table A.1, 19 percent of the curve lies between it and $\bar{X}$. The score 130 is 1.00 standard deviation above $\bar{X}$. From Table A.1, 34 percent of the curve lies between it and $\bar{X}$. Altogether 53 percent of the curve lies between 100 and 130.

EXAMPLE 4.3

A normal distribution has a mean of 110 and a standard deviation of 20. What percentage of the distribution lies between the scores 120 and 130?

Solution   Again, distances are calibrated from the mean 110. A table of the normal curve can be used to tell how much of the curve lies between $\bar{X}$ and 130: That region contains 34 percent of the area. But part of this area should not be included. The unwanted part contains 19 percent of the area. (120 is half a standard deviation from $\bar{X}$.) Therefore, the region from 120 to 130 equals the 34 percent region minus the 19 percent region: 15 percent of the curve's area lies between the scores 120 and 130.

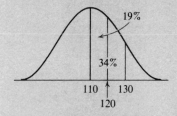

4.2   CONVERTING SCORES TO PERCENTILE RANKS

The percentile rank of a score tells what percentage of the distribution lies below that score. Suppose a score in a normal distribution is .30 standard deviation below $\bar{X}$. Twelve percent of the distribution would fall between that score and $\bar{X}$, so 38 percent would fall below that score (Fig. 4.5). The score is said to fall at the 38th percentile. If the score happens to be 112, then 112 falls at the 38th percentile. Any score in a normal distribution can be converted to a percentile rank with the aid of Table A.1.

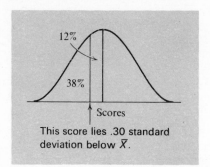

12%

38%

↑ Scores

This score lies .30 standard deviation below $\bar{X}$.

FIG. 4.5

EXAMPLE 4.4

Compute the percentile rank of a score (*a*) 1 standard deviation below $\bar{X}$, and (*b*) 1.5 standard deviations above $\bar{X}$.

Solution   (*a*) From Table A.1, 34 percent of the distribution lies between $\bar{X}$ and the score. Therefore, 16 percent of the distribution lies *below* the score. The score falls at the 16th percentile.

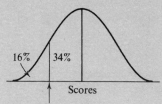

16%   34%

↑ Scores

The score that falls at
the 16th percentile

(*b*) From Table A.1, 43 percent of the distribution lies between $\bar{X}$ and the score. Therefore, 93 percent of the distribution lies *below* this score. The score falls at the 93d percentile.

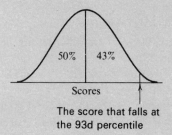

50%   43%

Scores   ↑

The score that falls at
the 93d percentile

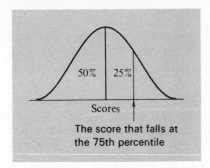

50%   25%

Scores

The score that falls at
the 75th percentile

FIG. 4.6

We can also use Table A.1 to convert a percentile rank back to the original score. Consider the 75th percentile of a normal distribution (Fig. 4.6). Whatever the original score was, it had two properties: First, it was above the mean. Second, 25 percent of the distribution fell between it and the mean. Locate the area ".25" in Table A.1; the nearest value is .2486. The corresponding entry in Column 1 is .67. Whatever the score was, it fell approximately .67 standard deviation above $\overline{X}$. [If $S = 20$, the score was 13.4 points above $\overline{X}$: $(0.67)(20 \text{ points}) = 13.4$ points. If $\overline{X} = 50$, the score was 63.4.]

EXAMPLE 4.5

(*a*)   What score falls at the 40th percentile in a normal distribution?

Solution   Ten percent of the distribution lies between this score and $\overline{X}$. Therefore, this score lies approximately .25 standard deviation below $\overline{X}$.

(*b*)   If $\overline{X} = 80$ and $S = 20$, what score falls at the 40th percentile?

Solution   The score is .25 standard deviation below $\overline{X}$. Since $(.25)(20 \text{ points}) = 5$ points, the score is: $80 - (.25)(20) = 80 - 5 = 75$.

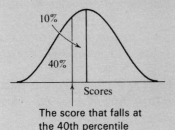

10%

40%

Scores

The score that falls at
the 40th percentile

*4.3 EQUATION OF THE NORMAL CURVE

Strictly speaking, we should not speak of *the* normal curve since there are many different normal curves. There is a different curve for each polygon that you might want to describe. One normal curve, for example, describes a polygon with $\overline{X} = 48$ and $S = 3$. That curve is highest over the X value 48, and 34 percent of its area lies between 48 and 51. Another normal curve describes a polygon with $\overline{X} = 97.1$ and $S = 13.5$. It is highest over $X = 97.1$, and 34 percent of its area lies between 97.1 and 110.6. These normal curves have certain properties in common, but strictly speaking, each curve is different.

The general equation for a normal curve can be written:

$$Y = \frac{1}{S\sqrt{2\pi}}\, e^{-(X-\overline{X})^2/2S^2}$$

In this equation, certain symbols refer to constant values: $\pi = 3.1416$ and $e = 2.7183$. To write the equation for any particular normal curve we would also need to specify the values of $\overline{X}$ and S in the equation. These values determine which particular polygon is being described.

For example, suppose we let $\overline{X} = 48$ and $S = 3$. The equation would then refer to one particular normal curve:

$$Y = \frac{1}{3\sqrt{2\pi}}\, e^{-(X-48)^2/2(3^2)}$$

$$= \frac{1}{7.53}\, e^{-(X-48)^2/18} = .1330\, e^{-(X-48)^2/18}$$

In this equation, Y is given as a function of X. For any value of X, the equation tells the corresponding value of Y. Let us choose some particular X and compute the corresponding value of Y. Say X equals 39, or 48, or 53. Table 4.2 gives the resulting Y values, and the graph is plotted in Fig. 4.7.

The normal curve's properties depend on the equation. Notice first that Y is greatest when X equals $\overline{X}$. In that case, $(X - \overline{X}) = 0$, so e is raised to the 0th power. Any quantity to the 0th power equals 1, so $Y = (1/3\sqrt{2\pi})(1) = .1330$. Any other value of X would raise e to a negative power, and the resulting value of Y would be smaller.

Second, notice that the curve is symmetrical. Consider a value of X that is 4 points above $\overline{X}$ and one that is 4 points below $\overline{X}$. The equation contains $(X - \overline{X})^2$. Because of the squaring, the resulting Y is the same for either X. Thus, the normal curve has exactly the same height when X is 15 points below $\overline{X}$ as it does when X is 15 points above $\overline{X}$. The two halves of the normal curve

---

* This section can be omitted in a shorter course.

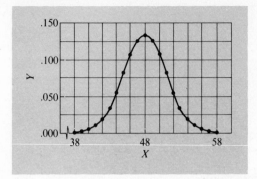

FIG. 4.7 Graph of the normal curve with $\overline{X} = 48$ and $S = 3$, sketched from the points shown in Table 4.2.

TABLE 4.2 Different values of X and Y in the equation for the normal curve with $\overline{X} = 48$ and $S = 3$

Equation: $Y = \dfrac{1}{3\sqrt{2\pi}} e^{-(X-\overline{X})^2/2S^2} = .1330e^{-(X-48)^2/18}$

X	$(X-48)^2$	$\dfrac{(X-48)^2}{18}$	$e^{-(X-48)^2/18}$	$Y = .1330e^{-(X-48)^2/18}$
58	100	5.56	.00	.000
57	81	4.50	.01	.001
56	64	3.56	.03	.004
55	49	2.72	.07	.009
54	36	2.00	.14	.019
53	25	1.39	.25	.033
52	16	0.89	.41	.055
51	9	0.50	.61	.081
50	4	0.22	.80	.106
49	1	0.06	.94	.125
48	0	0.00	1.00	.133
47	1	0.06	.94	.125
46	4	0.22	.80	.106
45	9	0.50	.61	.081
44	16	0.89	.41	.055
43	25	1.39	.25	.033
42	36	2.00	.14	.019
41	49	2.72	.07	.009
40	64	3.56	.03	.004
39	81	4.50	.01	.001
38	100	5.56	.00	.000

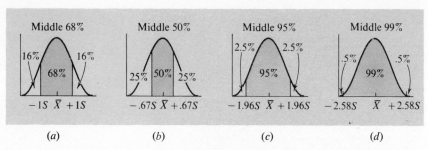

FIG. 4.8   Boundaries for the middle 50, 68, 95, and 99 percent of the normal distribution.

look alike. A line down the middle would split the curve's area in half. If a histogram can be described by a normal curve, half of its area lies on each side of the center, so the score in the middle is both the mean and the median.

Finally, notice that Y is theoretically never 0. For *any* value of X, the Y is greater than 0. Theoretically, *any* value of X, however large or small, is possible. We say that the normal curve is asymptotic to the X axis. Both tails of the curve come closer and closer to 0 without ever quite reaching 0.

The normal curve's equation is derived from the principles of probability. These principles will be developed in Chaps. 5 and 6. In practice, the psychologist rarely needs the equation itself. But he frequently needs to sketch the curve and use the table.

4.4   SETTING SYMMETRICAL BOUNDARIES

Imagine two scores on opposite sides of the mean but equally distant from the mean. Perhaps one score is one standard deviation above the mean and the other is one standard deviation below the mean. The region between them would contain 68 percent of the distribution. As shown in Fig. 4.8a, these two scores bound the middle 68 percent of the distribution.

An extremity of a curve is sometimes called its *tail*; therefore, in Fig. 4.8a, each tail contains 16 percent of the distribution. To bound the middle 50 percent of the distribution, we need scores that are each 0.67 standard deviation from the mean. As shown in Fig. 4.8b, each tail then contains 25 percent of the distribution.

Figure 4.8c shows how to bound the middle 95 percent: Locate scores that are each 1.96 standard deviations from $\overline{X}$, leaving 2½ percent in each tail. Finally, Fig. 4.8d shows how to bound the middle 99 percent: Locate scores that are 2.58 standard deviations from $\overline{X}$, leaving 0.5 percent in each tail.

EXAMPLE 4.6

In a certain normal distribution $\overline{X} = 83$ and $S = 12$. (a) What scores bound the middle 95 percent of the cases? (b) The middle 50 percent of the cases?

Solution (a) The boundaries lie 1.96 standard deviations on each side of the center. Since 1.96 $(S) = 1.96$ (12 points) = 23.5 points, the boundaries would extend 23.5 points on each side of $\bar{X}$—from 59.5 to 106.5.

The middle 95 percent of the cases lies between $\bar{X} \pm 1.96(S) = 83 \pm 23.5$ points.

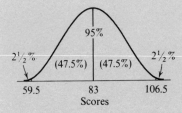

(b) The boundaries lie 0.67 standard deviation on each side of the center. Since 0.67 $(S) = 0.67$ (12 points) = 8 points, the boundaries would extend 8 points on each side of $\bar{X}$—from 75 to 91. The middle 50 percent of the cases lies between $\bar{X} \pm 0.67$ $(S) = 83 \pm 8$ points.

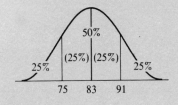

4.5 STANDARD SCORES (z SCORES)

In statistical work we often have to translate a score into some alternate form. Consider the score 55 in a normal distribution with $\bar{X} = 45$ and $S = 10$. To use Table A.1, we have to translate the score 55 into "the score which is 1 standard deviation from the mean." It is convenient to abbreviate this phrase by writing $z = 1$. A *z score* tells how many standard deviations a score is from the mean. The score 55 is thus translated into a z score of 1.

If a score is denoted X, the corresponding z score is written:

$$z = \frac{X - \bar{X}}{S} \tag{4.1}$$

Thus, in the example $z = (55 - 45)/10 = 1$. The numerator tells how many *points* X is from $\bar{X}$; divided by S, it tells how many standard deviations.

Imagine the score 129 in a distribution with $\overline{X} = 120$ and $S = 6$. Then $z = 1.5$; the score is 1.5 standard deviations from $\overline{X}$. If the distribution is normal, the score falls at the 93d percentile.

If the score is smaller than $\overline{X}$, the z score is negative. If $X = 117$, $\overline{X} = 120$, and $S = 6$, then $z = -.50$. Therefore, the score 117, falling half a standard deviation *below* the mean, falls at the 31st percentile.

EXAMPLE 4.7

A large group has been tested on two tests—Test V, which measures verbal ability, and Test Q, which measures quantitative ability. Here are one person's results: (1) On Test V he scored 105. The distribution of scores was normal, $\overline{X}$ was 95, and S was 4. (2) On Test Q he fell at the 88th percentile. Which performance was better, the verbal or the quantitative?

Solution   On Test V:

$$z = \frac{X - \overline{X}}{S} = \frac{105 - 95}{4} = 2.5$$

Therefore, the score on Test V fell at the 99th percentile. The score on Test Q, on the other hand, fell at the 88th percentile. Therefore, the subject's performance was relatively better on Test V.

Scores on intelligence tests are usually called IQs. But an IQ can always be viewed as an arbitrary score. Like any set of scores, IQs have their particular mean and standard deviation. Today there are many different intelligence tests. The tests' means are usually made to equal 100, but their standard deviations differ widely.

Suppose two people were tested for intelligence, one on Test 1 and the other on Test 2. Person 1's IQ was 110 (measured by Test 1) and Person 2's IQ was 115 (measured by Test 2). Now suppose Test 1 yielded a standard deviation of 10, while Test 2 yielded a standard deviation of 20. Here are the summarized data:

Person 1	Person 2
(on Test 1)	(on Test 2)
IQ = 110	IQ = 115
$\overline{X} = 100$	$\overline{X} = 100$
$S = 10$	$S = 20$

To compare the two people, change their IQs to z scores. Person 1's z equals 1.00; Person 2's equals 0.75. If both sets of scores were normally distributed, we could make the following statement: Person 1 fell at the 84th percentile, while Person 2 fell at the 77th percentile. Person 1 scored higher within *his* group than Person 2 did within his group.

4.6   THE MEAN AND STANDARD DEVIATION OF z SCORES

Suppose the scores of a set are *all* transformed to z scores. The z scores then have one important property: *Their mean is always 0 and their standard deviation is always 1.* Consider the scores of Table 4.3; their $\bar{X} = 8$ and their $S = 5$. The last column reports each score as a z score. Notice the mean and standard deviation of the z scores. The mean became 0 because each original X was reduced 8 points. The standard deviation became 1.0 because each $(X - \bar{X})$ was divided by 5. Let us prove these two points more formally.

TABLE 4.3   Converting scores to z scores

Subject	X	z score
A	4	−0.8
B	2	−1.2
C	11	0.6
D	0	−1.6
E	5	−0.6
F	14	1.2
G	8	0.0
H	16	1.6
I	8	0.0
J	12	0.8
	$\bar{X} = 8.0$	Mean of z scores $= 0.0$
	$S = 5.0$	Standard deviation of z scores $= 1.0$

First let us prove that the mean z score is 0. This mean equals the sum of the z scores divided by N:

$$\bar{z} = \frac{\sum z}{N}$$

$$= \frac{1}{N}\sum z$$

Each z score can be written as $\dfrac{(X - \bar{X})}{S}$ so

$$\bar{z} = \frac{1}{N}\sum \frac{(X - \bar{X})}{S}$$

And S is a constant number, so it can be placed before the summation sign:

$$\bar{z} = \frac{1}{N}\frac{1}{S}\sum (X - \bar{X})$$

The deviation scores always sum to 0, so:

$$\bar{z} = \frac{1}{N}\frac{1}{S}(0) = 0$$

Thus the mean equals 0.

Next, let us prove that the standard deviation of any set of z scores equals 1. The general formula for the squared standard deviation is:

$$S^2 = \frac{\sum (X - \bar{X})^2}{N}$$

For z scores, this formula becomes:

$$S_z^2 = \frac{\sum (z - \bar{z})^2}{N} = \frac{\sum (z - 0)^2}{N} = \frac{\sum z^2}{N}$$

$$= \frac{1}{N}\sum z^2$$

Each z score can be written $(X - \bar{X})/S$ so:

$$S_z^2 = \frac{1}{N}\sum \frac{(X - \bar{X})^2}{S^2}$$

S^2 is a constant number, so it can be placed before the summation sign:

$$S_z^2 = \frac{1}{N}\frac{1}{S^2}\sum (X - \bar{X})^2$$

Rearranging the terms:

$$S_z^2 = \frac{1}{S^2}\frac{\sum (X - \bar{X})^2}{N} = \frac{1}{S^2}\cdot S^2$$

$$= 1$$

Therefore:

$$S_z = \sqrt{1} = 1$$

Thus, the standard deviation always equals 1.

4.7 TRANSFORMING SCORES

A set of scores can be transformed to yield *any* mean and *any* standard deviation. One simple method is this: First transform the scores to z scores and then transform the z scores. For example, Table 4.4 shows how to transform the scores of Table 4.3 so as to make $\bar{X} = 100$ and $S = 15$. The procedure is given in three steps: First, all scores are converted to z scores; the $\bar{X}$ becomes

TABLE 4.4 Transforming scores to make $\bar{X} = 100$ and $S = 15$

Subject	X	Step 1: Change to z scores	Step 2: Multiply by 15	Step 3: Add 100
A	4	−0.8	−12.0	88
B	2	−1.2	−18.0	82
C	11	0.6	9.0	109
D	0	−1.6	−24.0	76
E	5	−0.6	−.90	91
F	14	1.2	18.0	118
G	8	0.0	0.0	100
H	16	1.6	24.0	124
I	8	0.0	0.0	100
J	12	0.8	12.0	112
	$\bar{X} = 8$			$\bar{X} = 100$
	$S = 5$			$S = 15$

0 and the S becomes 1. Then each z score is multiplied by 15, the desired standard deviation. This step makes the standard deviation 15 while the mean remains 0. Finally, 100, the desired mean, is added to every score. This step makes $\bar{X} = 100$ and $S = 15$.

Actually, an IQ score is usually a transformed score. First the test designer constructs a test without worrying about the mean and standard deviation. He administers this test to a large group, the *normative group*, which is representative of future examinees. The scores they obtain are called *raw scores*, and their $\bar{X}$ and S are computed. Then these scores are transformed to scores having a mean of 100 and an S of, say, 15. The transformed scores *are* the IQs. In Sec. 4.9 we shall discuss the procedure further.

4.8 DEVIATIONS FROM NORMALITY

Most topics in this book depend very heavily on the normal curve. Not all distributions of scores are normal, however. Sometimes the distribution is far from bell-shaped; perhaps it has an excess of scores on one side. Figure 4.9 shows some non-normal distributions.

Skewness
Suppose subjects are asked to react to a stoplight as quickly as possible, and suppose their reaction times are measured. The distribution might take the form of Fig. 4.10. A subject's reaction time has to be greater than 0, of course, but there is no upper limit on the score. The distribution can trail off into exceedingly long reaction times. A distribution with a long tail of this kind is said to be *skewed*. In a distribution of reaction times, the long tail is on the

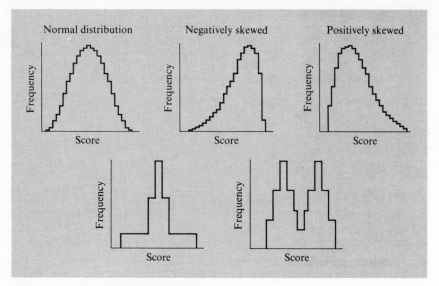

FIG. 4.9 Normal and non-normal distributions.

right. The distribution is said to be "skewed to the right" or "positively skewed."

In contrast, Fig. 4.11 is a distribution of scores on a very easy test. This distribution is said to be "skewed to the left" or "negatively skewed." Most people achieved high scores but no one could do better than a perfect score; on the other hand, the scores could trail downward to very low scores.

In a *normal* distribution, the mean, the median, and the mode coincide. They all refer to the same score at the center of the distribution. In a *skewed* distribution, however, the mean, the median, and the mode are not the same. Consider this distribution of scores: 5, 7, 7, 8, 8, 10, 10, 10, 10, 10. The distribution is negatively skewed. The mode is 10, the median is 9, and the mean is 8.5. The mode is the most popular score, so it occurs where the distribution has its peak. On the other hand, the mean is pulled downward toward the tail.

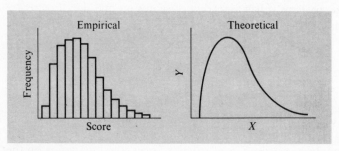

FIG. 4.10

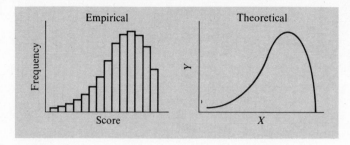

FIG. 4.11

Statisticians have observed that the mean, the median, and the mode in a skewed distribution become separated in alphabetical order. Figure 4.12 illustrates this separation. The mean moves toward the long tail, the mode stays under the curve's highest point, and the median falls between the two (but closer to the mean). Thus, the mean and the median turn out to be closer together, as they would be in a dictionary. Statisticians have found empirically that the difference between the mean and the median is usually about half the difference between the median and the mode.

If the mode of a distribution is 88 and the median is 96, then the distribution is clearly skewed—positively skewed. Furthermore, the difference between the two measures is 8 points, so the difference between the mean and the median would be about 4 points. The mean would therefore be about 100.

Measures exist for telling how skewed a distribution is. In this book we shall never need such a measure, but one simple measure is the difference between the mean and the median, divided by the standard deviation. The more the mean and the median differ, the more skewed the distribution; but the difference is only meaningful relative to the distribution's variability.

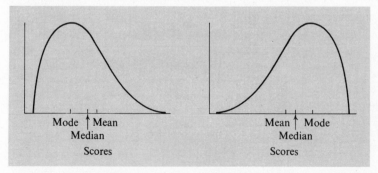

FIG. 4.12 Mean, median, and mode in a skewed distribution. (Notice that the mean is pulled toward the tail.)

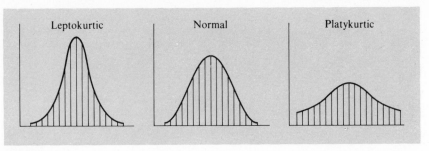

FIG. 4.13

Kurtosis

A *skewed* distribution is not symmetrical. But even if a distribution *is* symmetrical, it is not necessarily normal. The distribution may be thin and narrow in the center with very long tails. In that case, the distribution is said to be *leptokurtic*; too much of its area falls in the tails. Other times the curve is *platykurtic*: An excess of scores falls near the middle, making the distribution squat with very short tails. Figure 4.13 shows some examples of leptokurtic and platykurtic distributions.

In Chap. 9 we shall consider a special distribution called the *t* distribution. That distribution is symmetrical but leptokurtic. Therefore, Table A.1 in the appendix will not be accurate for describing it.

EXAMPLE 4.8

A certain test has $\bar{X} = 100$ and $S = 10$, and an individual earns the mean score, 100. Under what circumstance does he fall at the 50th percentile? Under what circumstance does he fall at some other percentile?

Solution If the distribution is symmetrical, the mean score equals the median, so the individual falls at the 50th percentile.

If the distribution is skewed, though, the two halves are not symmetrical. In that case the mean score differs from the median score. When the distribution is *positively* skewed, the mean is higher than the median. Half of the distribution lies below the median, so *more than half* lies below the mean. The score 100, therefore, would exceed the 50th percentile.

When the distribution is *negatively* skewed, on the other hand, the mean falls below the median. Half of the distribution falls below the median, so *less than half* falls below the mean. The score, therefore, would fall below the 50th percentile.

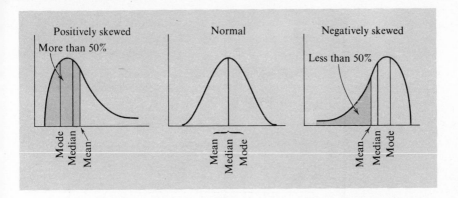

In a normal distribution a person who is one standard deviation above the mean falls at the 84th percentile. If the distribution is not normal, however, we cannot make such inferences. *A table of the normal curve is only valid when the distribution of scores is normal.*

*4.9   NORMALIZING A SKEWED DISTRIBUTION

To use certain statistical procedures, an investigator needs to start with a normal distribution of scores. If the distribution is skewed, those procedures are not valid. However, a skewed distribution can be transformed into a normal one. The procedure is sometimes useful and worth examining.

Table 4.5 presents a skewed distribution of scores. The distribution's skewness is very apparent from the distribution's asymmetry. In Column 3 the table also reports each score as a z score; especially notice the extremes. The highest score yields $z = 1.29$ while the lowest score yields $z = -4.98$. The highest score is not even 2 standard deviations from $\overline{X}$, while the lowest is nearly 5 standard deviations below $\overline{X}$. The distribution seems to have a long tail at the low end.

Before we normalize this distribution, let us briefly consider the meaning of a score like 61. Suppose an investigator administered a test of 100 questions which he designed to measure verbal aptitude, and suppose he assigned one point for each correct answer. The score 61 means that the subject answered 61 questions correctly. Now how does 61, as a measure of verbal aptitude, compare with 62? We don't know. Perhaps a subject finds it easy to get a score of 60 or 61 but extremely hard to answer one more question for a score of 62. Psychologically, the difference between 61 and 62 may be larger than the difference between 60 and 61: 62 might reflect a lot more aptitude than 61, and 61 might reflect just a little more than 60.

Measurements of this kind are called *ordinal* measurements. The numbers

* This section can be omitted in a shorter course.

TABLE 4.5   Normalizing a skewed distribution

(Column 1) Score (X)	(Column 2) Frequency (f)	(Column 3) z score	(Column 4) Upper limit cumulative frequency	(Column 5) Midpoint cumulative frequency (f below + ½ of this category)	(Column 6) Midpoint cumulative proportion z	(Column 7) normalized z	(Column 8) 5.1z + 64.4 (normalized z, rounded off)
71	6	1.29	162	159	.981	2.08	75
70	8	1.10	156	152	.938	1.54	72
69	14	.90	148	141	.870	1.13	70
68	15	.71	134	126.5	.781	.78	68
67	23	.51	119	107.5	.664	.42	67
66	16	.31	96	88	.543	.11	65
65	14	.12	80	73	.451	−.12	64
64	12	−.08	66	60	.370	−.33	63
63	12	−.27	54	48	.296	−.54	62
62	9	−.47	42	37.5	.231	−.73	61
61	8	−.67	33	29	.179	−.91	60
60	7	−.86	25	21.5	.133	−1.11	59
59	5	−1.06	18	15.5	.096	−1.31	58

58	3	−1.25	13	11.5	.071	−1.47	57
57	2	−1.45	10	9	.056	−1.59	56
56	1	−1.65	8	7.5	.046	−1.69	56
55	1	−1.84	7	6.5	.040	−1.75	55
54	0	−2.04	6	6	.037	−1.79	55
53	1	−2.24	6	5.5	.034	−1.83	55
52	0	−2.43	5	5	.031	−1.87	55
51	0	−2.63	5	5	.031	−1.87	55
50	0	−2.82	5	5	.031	−1.87	55
49	1	−3.02	5	4.5	.028	−1.91	55
48	0	−3.22	4	4	.025	−1.96	54
47	1	−3.41	4	3.5	.022	−2.02	54
46	0	−3.61	3	3	.019	−2.08	54
45	1	−3.80	3	2.5	.015	−2.17	53
44	0	−4.00	2	2	.012	−2.25	53
43	0	−4.20	2	2	.012	−2.25	53
42	0	−4.39	2	2	.012	−2.25	53
41	1	−4.59	2	1.5	.009	−2.37	52
40	0	−4.78	1	1	.006	−2.52	52
39	1	−4.98	1	0.5	.003	−2.70	51

$N = 162$
$\bar{X} = 64.4$
$S = 5.1$

$\bar{X} = 64.4$
$S = 5.1$

are *ordered* correctly—a higher number reflects more aptitude—but the numbers have no further meaning than that. The 1-point difference between 62 and 61 may be quite different from the 1-point difference between 61 and 60. If the scores 11, 212, and 219 are ordinal measurements, an investigator could call them 1, 2, and 3. Or, if he preferred, 11, 12, and 13. Or even 10, 30, and 100. As long as the new values maintained the original order, they would be just as good.

In contrast, consider physical measurements like weight. Suppose three objects have the weights 60, 61, and 62 gm. In that case, the numbers have a stricter meaning. As before, higher numbers reflect more weight; but in addition, the difference between 60 and 61 *does* equal the difference between 61 and 62. The 1-point difference has a definite and consistent meaning: A 1-gm weight added to the lower weight always produces the higher weight. The 1-point difference is no longer flexible.

Measurements of weight differ in another way, too, from ordinal measurements. The *ratio* of two weights is meaningful. The weight of 48 gm is, in a meaningful sense, three times the weight of 16 gm: If three objects each weigh 16 gm, their combined weight equals that of the 48 gm. In weight measurements the 0 point truly denotes no weight at all, so the difference $48 - 0$ (the weight of the heavier object) is truly three times the difference $16 - 0$ (the weight of the lighter object).

Such measurements are called *ratio measurements*. A ratio measurement has three major properties: First, the *order* of the numbers conveys meaning; the higher the number, the more of the trait. Second, a difference between two values has a consistent meaning; all 1-point differences or all 7-point differences are equal. Third, ratios between two values are meaningful; 16 in. is really twice as long as 8 in.

Another kind of measurement, the *interval measurement*, has two of these three properties. Interval measurements therefore seem to fall in between ordinal and ratio measurements. In this case, the order of the number conveys meaning, and a difference between two numbers has a consistent meaning. But ratios are not meaningful. The common temperature scales are interval measurements. Consider 3 objects at 60°F, 61°F, and 62°F. First, the higher number denotes more heat. And second, the interval $61 - 60$ equals the interval $62 - 61$; the same amount of heat, when added to the lower, raises its temperature to that of the higher. However, an object of 48°F is not twice as hot as one of 24°F. At 0°F, an object still has some heat, so $48 - 0$ and $24 - 0$ do not designate amounts beyond no heat at all. Thus, in a physical sense, the ratio has no meaning.

In Table 4.5, the measurements are *ordinal* measurements. We can assign different numbers to each subject as long as subjects remain ordered in the same way. And by choosing the new numbers wisely, we can eliminate the skewness.

First, look ahead at the finished product (Column 8). You will notice that the highest six people are assigned the score 75, and the eight people below them, the score 72. While the original scores 71 and 70 were separated by one point, the "normalized" scores are separated by three points (75 vs. 72). The other end of the distribution is not expanded; the original scores 39 and 40 change to the scores 51 and 52.

To normalize the distribution, first determine the proportion of the distribution that falls at or below each original X score. Consider the score 61. What proportion of the cases fall at or below 61? There are 25 cases in the categories below 61. The category 61 itself contains eight cases, but that category extends from 60.5 to 61.5. Let us therefore assume that four scores fall below 61.0 and four fall above 61.0. (That is, let us assume that the eight scores are spread evenly throughout this category.) Then, a total of $25 + (\frac{1}{2})(8) = 25 + 4 = 29$ scores fall at or below the score 61.0. The value 29 appears in Column 5, and Column 6 expresses it as a proportion of the total N: $29/162 = .179$. Thus, Column 6 tells what *proportion* of the distribution falls at or below each original X score.

Similarly, .870 of the distribution falls below the score 69.0. If the distribution *were* normal, what z score would correspond to the score 69.0? In a normal distribution, what z score has .870 of the distribution below it? According to Table A.1, when $z = 1.13$, .870 of the distribution falls below the score (Fig. 4.14). Let us therefore replace the original score 69 (its z was $+0.90$) with the new value $z = +1.13$.

How about the raw score 63? Here .296 of the distribution falls below 63. What would its z score be if the distribution were normal? If the distribution were normal, the z score at this point would be $z = -0.54$ (Fig. 4.15). Therefore, we replace the original score 63 (its z was -0.27) with the new value $z = -0.54$. These new z values are called normalized z scores.

Like any set of z scores, the normalized z's have a mean of 0 and a standard deviation of 1. To obtain any desired $\overline{X}$ and S, multiply each normalized z by the desired S and add the desired $\overline{X}$. For example, suppose you wanted the distribution to have the same $\overline{X}$ and S as the original scores; then multiply each normalized z by 5.1 and add 64.4. The resulting values appear in the last

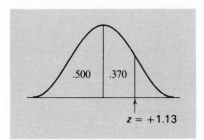

.500   .370

$z = +1.13$

FIG. 4.14

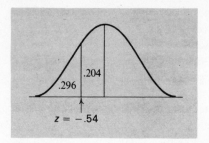

FIG. 4.15

column of Table 4.5. (For convenience, they are usually rounded off to whole numbers.) The frequency distributions in Table 4.6 show the effect of the normalizing. The scores are now normally distributed, so inferences from a table of the normal curve are now valid.

If you wanted $\overline{X}$ to equal 50 and S to equal 10, you would multiply each normalized z by 10 and add 50. When the scores are transformed in this way— (normalized, $\overline{X} = 50$, and $S = 10$)—the resulting scores are called T scores.

The famous intelligence tests are typically normalized in this way. First, the test designer constructs a test that yields any arbitrary set of scores. The distribution of raw scores is then normalized, and the scores are adjusted to make $\overline{X}$ equal 100 and S equal 10 or 15. A manual, which accompanies the test, contains tables that convert each raw score to a normalized score. The normalized scores are then called IQs.

If you were measuring someone's IQ, you would administer the test and compute his raw score. Then you would consult the published table to translate the raw score to the IQ. The distribution of IQs has been normalized, so you can convert the IQ to a z score, and with a table of the normal curve,

TABLE 4.6   Frequency distributions of the values in Table 4.5

Original distribution (skewed)		Normalized distribution (normal)	
Category	Frequency	Category	Frequency
69–71	28	75–77	6
66–68	54	72–74	8
63–65	38	69–71	14
60–62	24	66–68	38
57–59	10	63–65	42
54–56	2	60–62	29
51–53	1	57–59	15
48–50	1	54–56	7
45–47	2	51–53	3
42–44	0		
39–41	2		$N = 162$
	$N = 162$		

infer the individual's percentile rank. Perhaps it would be simpler to report percentiles in the first place, but the notion of the IQ has become very much ingrained in our culture and presents no serious problem of interpretation.

4.10   MEASURE OF CORRELATION

Now let us consider one last descriptive statistic, a measure of correlation. The most common measure is the Pearson *correlation coefficient,* which can be defined in terms of z scores. In this section we consider the concept of correlation, define the correlation coefficient, and illustrate a way to compute it. Later, in Chap. 12, we shall examine the measure more fully.

Concept of correlation

The concept of correlation is widely used in psychology. We hear claims that certain traits go together: Intelligence correlates with performance in school; learning time correlates with the subject's motivation; a word's frequency in English correlates with a speaker's ease of perceiving the word; a subject's personality correlates with his physique.

A correlation may be positive, negative, or zero. Height and weight are *positively* correlated. Tall people tend to be heavier, short people tend to be lighter. Of course, this relationship is not perfect since some short people weigh more than some tall people. The correlation is *negative* when the relationship is inverse: Individuals who are high on one trait tend to be low on the other. Word frequency, for example, correlates negatively with word length; frequent words are usually shorter.

The correlation is said to be a *zero correlation* when the traits are not related. An individual who is high on one trait might be high, medium, or low on the other trait. All combinations seem to occur. When the two traits are uncorrelated, they are said to be *distributed independently.*

First consider a simple, non-numerical example. Suppose four people are tested. Each person is asked to flip two pennies, Penny 1 and Penny 2. Then each person is assigned two scores, a score on Penny 1 and a score on Penny 2. The score can be H (for heads) or T (for tails). Here is one possible result:

	Penny 1	*Penny 2*
Subject 1's result	H	H
Subject 2's result	H	T
Subject 3's result	T	H
Subject 4's result	T	T

Situation I. A Zero Correlation

Situation I illustrates a zero correlation: Subject 1 got an H both times, Subject 4 got a T both times, and Subjects 2 and 3 got one H and one T. All kinds of combinations occurred. There was no systematic relationship between the two events. Therefore, the Penny 1 score and the Penny 2 score are uncorrelated; they are independent of each other.

To illustrate a *positive* correlation, suppose an invisible rod connects the two pennies. Then the score on Penny 1 *would* be related to the score on Penny 2. This relationship is shown in Situation II: An H on one accompanies an H on the other, and a T on one accompanies a T on the other. Finally,

Situation II. A Positive Correlation			Situation III. A Negative Correlation		
	Penny 1	*Penny 2*		*Penny 1*	*Penny 2*
Subject 1's result	H	H	Subject 1's result	H	T
Subject 2's result	H	H	Subject 2's result	H	T
Subject 3's result	T	T	Subject 3's result	T	H
Subject 4's result	T	T	Subject 4's result	T	H

Situation III illustrates a *negative* correlation: In Situation III, an H on one penny accompanies a T on the other.

Pearson's correlation coefficient

Frequently the scores are numerical and we need to describe the degree of correlation. The most common measure is Pearson's correlation coefficient, which is symbolized r. It originated with Sir Francis Galton, an English psychologist, and was extended by his student, Karl Pearson.

Consider the pairs of scores in Table 4.7. One score of each pair is denoted X, the other is denoted Y. (The r itself is denoted r_{XY}.) The mean of the X scores is 30, and the standard deviation is 5. The mean of the Y scores is 50, and the standard deviation is 10.

Table 4.7 shows one way to compute r_{XY}. First we convert each set of scores to z scores. (That makes the scores of one set comparable to those of the other set.) Thus, each X becomes a z_X, and each Y becomes a z_Y. For Subject A, $z_X = (26-30)/5 = -.80$; Subject A's score is therefore .8 standard deviation below the mean. The corresponding z_Y score is -1.8. Subject A's Y score therefore falls 1.8 standard deviations below the mean of the Y scores.

Then we multiply each z_X by the subject's z_Y and record the products in the last column. Then, to obtain r, we compute the mean of these $z_X \cdot z_Y$ products: We sum them and divide by N. The complete formula is written:

$$r_{XY} = \frac{\sum z_X z_Y}{N}$$

TABLE 4.7　Computing r through z scores

Person	Trait X	Trait Y	z_X	z_Y	$z_X \cdot z_Y$
A	26	32	−0.8	−1.8	+1.44
B	24	40	−1.2	−1.0	+1.20
C	22	44	−1.6	−0.6	+0.96
D	33	44	+0.6	−0.6	−0.36
E	27	48	−0.6	−0.2	+0.12
F	36	52	+1.2	+0.2	+0.24
G	30	56	0.0	+0.6	0.00
H	38	56	+1.6	+0.6	+0.96
I	30	60	0.0	+1.0	0.00
J	34	68	+0.8	+1.8	+1.44

$$\bar{X} = 30 \qquad \bar{Y} = 50 \qquad \qquad \qquad \sum z_X z_Y = +6.00$$
$$S_X = 5 \qquad S_Y = 10$$
$$r_{XY} = \frac{\sum z_X z_Y}{N} = \frac{+6.00}{10}$$
$$= +0.60$$

In Table 4.7, the mean of the $z_X \cdot z_Y$ column is positive. In general, negative z_X's accompany negative z_Y's, and positive z_X's accompany positive z_Y's. Most of the $z_X \cdot z_Y$ products are positive, so the mean is positive.

When r is negative, the mean $z_X \cdot z_Y$ is negative: Negative z_X's would generally accompany positive z_Y's. Most of the products would be negative, so their mean would be negative.

The *sign* of r therefore describes the relationship as negative or positive. +.30 means a positive relationship; −0.60 means a negative relationship.

When r equals 0, the scores are not related. In that case, some negative z_X's accompany negative z_Y's, and other negative z_X's accompany positive z_Y's. Thus, some products are negative, while others are positive. If the negative products completely offset the positive ones, $\sum z_X \cdot z_Y = 0$, and r is 0.

If r differs from 0, the number tells how strong the relationship is. The further it is from 0, the stronger the relationship. The relationship is strongest when r equals +1.00 or −1.00. Thus, the possible values of r range from −1.00 through 0.00 to +1.00. In Table 4.7, $r = +0.60$—a moderately high, positive correlation.

To understand r, it is helpful to examine the data on a graph. Figure 4.16 presents the data of Table 4.7 graphically. Each subject's pair of scores appears as a dot on the graph. Notice that the points mainly fall in two quadrants— the lower left-hand quadrant and the upper right-hand quadrant. People with high X scores usually earned high Y scores; those with low X scores usually earned low Y scores.

Figure 4.17 shows other sets of data, too. When $r = +1.00$, the points

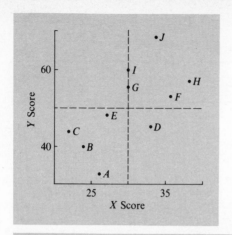

FIG. 4.16 Graph of data in Table 4.1.

(a) $r = +1$

Subject	X	Y	z_X	z_Y
A	7	10	−.8	−.8
B	5	8	−1.2	−1.2
C	14	17	.6	.6
D	3	6	−1.6	−1.6
E	8	11	−.6	−.6
F	17	20	1.2	1.2
G	11	14	.0	.0
H	19	22	1.6	1.6
I	11	14	.0	.0
J	15	18	.8	.8

$\overline{X} = 11 \qquad \overline{Y} = 14$
$S_X = 5 \qquad S_Y = 5$

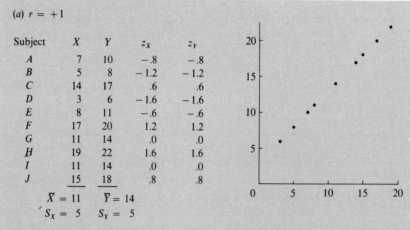

(b) $r = 0$

Subject	X	Y	z_X	z_Y
A	7	8	−.8	−1.2
B	5	10	−1.2	−.8
C	14	18	.6	.8
D	3	17	−1.6	.6
E	8	22	−.6	1.6
F	17	14	1.2	.0
G	11	20	.0	1.2
H	19	14	1.6	.0
I	11	6	.0	−1.6
J	15	11	.8	−.6

$\overline{X} = 11 \qquad \overline{Y} = 14$
$S_X = 5 \qquad S_Y = 5$

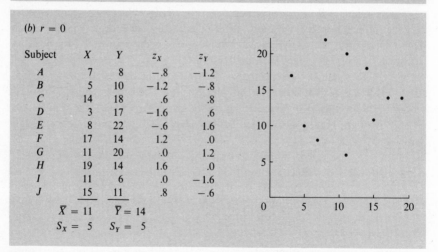

FIG. 4.17 Data illustrating two cases: (a) $r = +1$ and (b) $r = 0$.

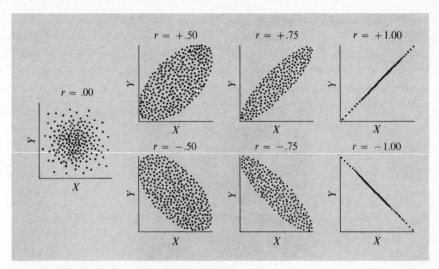

FIG. 4.18 Graphs of data with different values of r.

fall along a perfectly straight line, and the relationship is perfect. The subject with the lowest X score has the lowest Y score; the one with the next highest X score has the next highest Y score, and so on. Each subject's z_X matches his z_Y, so a person's relative standing on X matches his relative standing on Y.

On the other hand, suppose $r = 0.00$. The z_X bears no relation to the z_Y. A positive z_X sometimes accompanies a negative z_Y and sometimes accompanies a positive z_Y. All combinations occur. Figure 4.17 illustrates a zero correlation. When $r = 0.00$, the points fall haphazardly on the graph.

When r differs from 0, the points seem to fall within an ellipse. Some examples are shown in Fig. 4.18. The ellipse grows thinner as r increases. Eventually, when r equals -1.00 or $+1.00$, the ellipse becomes a straight line.

Computational formula for r

Usually it is not convenient to convert each X score to a z_X score and each Y score to a z_Y score. Instead, other formulas are preferred. To make the formula more convenient, z_X can be replaced by $(X - \overline{X})/S_X$ and z_Y by $(Y - \overline{Y})/S_Y$. The derivation is shown in the appendix at the end of the chapter. From this derivation we obtain the following formula:

$$r = \frac{N \sum XY - (\sum X)(\sum Y)}{\sqrt{N \sum X^2 - (\sum X)^2} \sqrt{N \sum Y^2 - (\sum Y)^2}}$$

This formula is more convenient. To use it, you need the following information: the sum of the raw scores, $\sum X$ and $\sum Y$; the sum of the squared scores, $\sum X^2$ and $\sum Y^2$; and $\sum XY$. To compute $\sum XY$, multiply each subject's pair of scores and sum the products.

For the data of Table 4.7:

$$\sum X = 300 \qquad \sum Y = 500 \qquad \sum XY = 15,300$$
$$\sum X^2 = 9,250 \qquad \sum Y^2 = 26,000 \qquad N = 10$$

Therefore:

$$r = \frac{10(15,300) - (300)(500)}{\sqrt{10(9,250) - (300)^2}\ \sqrt{10(26,000) - (500)^2}} = +0.60$$

EXAMPLE 4.9

A classic study of intelligence was performed in the 1930s. The investigators[1] found 19 pairs of identical twins who had been separated early in life and raised in separate environments. Each twin's IQ was measured on the Stanford-Binet

Pair	Difference in educational advantages (X)	Difference in IQ (Y)
A	37	24
B	32	12
C	28	19
D	22	17
E	19	7
F	15	12
G	15	10
H	14	15
I	12	−2
J	12	−1
K	11	4
L	11	1
M	10	5
N	9	1
O	9	−1
P	9	−9
Q	8	2
R	7	8
S	7	6

[1] Newman, H. H., F. N. Freeman, and K. J. Holzinger. *Twins: A Study of Heredity and Environment.* Chicago: University of Chicago Press, 1937.

intelligence test; the quality of his education was rated on a scale ranging from 0 to 50. Then, for each pair, the authors recorded the difference in IQ and the difference in educational advantages. The resulting data are shown below. (A negative difference in IQ means that the twin with the better education had the lower IQ.)

Is the IQ difference related to the educational difference? Compute r.

Solution First we summarize the data:

$$\sum X = 287 \qquad \sum Y = 130$$
$$\sum X^2 = 5{,}703 \qquad \sum Y^2 = 2{,}122$$
$$\sum XY = 2{,}953$$
$$N = 19$$

Then:

$$r = \frac{N \sum XY - (\sum X)(\sum Y)}{\sqrt{N \sum X^2 - (\sum X)^2} \; \sqrt{N \sum Y^2 - (\sum Y)^2}}$$

$$= \frac{19(2{,}953) - (287)(130)}{\sqrt{19(5{,}703) - (287)^2} \; \sqrt{19(2{,}122) - (130)^2}}$$

$$= \frac{56{,}107 - 37{,}310}{\sqrt{108{,}357 - 82{,}369} \; \sqrt{40{,}318 - 16{,}900}}$$

$$= +0.76$$

Thus, the IQ difference is strongly related to the educational difference.

Correlation means prediction

If someone is above average in height, we expect him to be above average in weight. If his IQ is low, we expect him to do poorly in school. Correlation means prediction: We can always use one variable to help predict the other. The main purpose of a psychological test is to make predictions about other variables.

For example, suppose the staff of a college admissions office were trying to predict ultimate grade-point averages. They might administer a one-hour test to every student just before the freshman year. Four years later, they might compute each student's grade-point average. The value of r would also be computed. Suppose the admissions office tested thousands of students and obtained the data of Fig. 4.19. Thousands of datum points make a very thorough and accurate picture; future students would also fit into this picture.

Test scores can be gotten in one easy hour of mass testing. But grade-point averages cost four years of individual time, effort, and money. If grade-point averages could be *predicted* from test scores, some errors of admission and consequent heartache could be spared. The data of Fig. 4.19 can help achieve this goal.

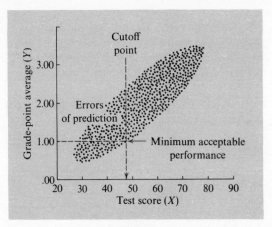

FIG. 4.19 Hypothetical data relating test scores to grade-point averages.

First, the admissions office must set the minimum acceptable grade-point average. Say this value is 1.00. They would like to screen out those people whose grade-point averages will ultimately fall below 1.00. Who are those people? In Fig. 4.19 they all have test scores below 47. Therefore, in the future, the admissions office might require a score above 47 for admission. The college could thus eliminate potential failures.

This procedure does create one serious error. There are always some individuals whose test scores are low, but whose actual college performance is good. They might be people who become unusually anxious during a mass testing. Or they might be people who have not yet mastered the art of taking multiple-choice tests. It would be a mistake to reject those people from the college. Thus, as its next step, the admissions office would seek ways of identifying those people, perhaps through biographical data or personality tests. In Chap. 12 we shall examine these problems more fully.

APPENDIX   *Derivation of the computational formula for r.*
First, *r* is defined by the *z*-score formula:

$$r = \frac{\sum z_X \cdot z_Y}{N}$$

Each *z* score is then replaced by its raw-score equivalent:

$$z_X = \frac{X - \bar{X}}{S_X} \quad \text{and} \quad z_Y = \frac{Y - \bar{Y}}{S_Y}$$

The formula for r becomes:

$$r = \frac{\sum z_X z_Y}{N}$$

$$= \frac{\sum \left[\dfrac{(X-\bar{X})}{S_X} \dfrac{(Y-\bar{Y})}{S_Y} \right]}{N} = \frac{1}{N} \sum \left[\frac{(X-\bar{X})}{S_X} \frac{(Y-\bar{Y})}{S_Y} \right]$$

Since S_X and S_Y are constant numbers, they can be placed in front of the summation sign:

$$r = \frac{1}{N} \frac{1}{S_X} \frac{1}{S_Y} \sum [(X-\bar{X})(Y-\bar{Y})]$$

Then $(X-\bar{X})$ is multiplied by $(Y-\bar{Y})$.

$$r = \frac{1}{NS_X S_Y} \sum [XY - X\bar{Y} - Y\bar{X} + \bar{X}\bar{Y}]$$

Then each term is summed:

$$r = \frac{1}{NS_X S_Y} [\sum XY - \bar{Y}\sum X - \bar{X}\sum Y + N\bar{X}\bar{Y}]$$

$$= \frac{1}{NS_X S_Y} \left[\sum XY - \frac{\sum Y}{N}\sum X - \frac{\sum X}{N}\sum Y + N\frac{\sum X}{N}\frac{\sum Y}{N} \right]$$

$$= \frac{1}{NS_X S_Y} \left[\sum XY - \frac{(\sum X)(\sum Y)}{N} \right]$$

$$= \frac{1}{NS_X S_Y} \left[\frac{N\sum XY - (\sum X)(\sum Y)}{N} \right]$$

Recall the formulas for S_X and S_Y:

$$S_X = \frac{1}{N}\sqrt{N\sum X^2 - (\sum X)^2} \quad \text{and} \quad S_Y = \frac{1}{N}\sqrt{N\sum Y^2 - (\sum Y)^2}$$

Therefore

$$r = \frac{N\sum XY - (\sum X)(\sum Y)}{N^2 \left[\dfrac{1}{N}\sqrt{N\sum X^2 - (\sum X)^2} \right]\left[\dfrac{1}{N}\sqrt{N\sum Y^2 - (\sum Y)^2} \right]}$$

$$= \frac{N\sum XY - (\sum X)(\sum Y)}{\sqrt{N\sum X^2 - (\sum X)^2}\ \sqrt{N\sum Y^2 - (\sum Y)^2}}$$

Occasionally, another formula for r is also useful: $r = \dfrac{\sum xy}{NS_X S_Y}$.

(In this formula, x refers to the deviation score $X - \bar{X}$, and y refers to the deviation score $Y - \bar{Y}$.) This formula will be useful in the theory that we develop. To derive it, we begin with the z-score formula:

$$r = \frac{\sum z_X z_Y}{N}$$

The z scores are then expressed in terms of deviation scores:

$$z_X = \frac{X - \bar{X}}{S_X} = \frac{x}{S_X} \quad \text{and} \quad z_Y = \frac{Y - \bar{Y}}{S_Y} = \frac{y}{S_Y}$$

Then r becomes:

$$r = \frac{\sum z_X z_Y}{N}$$

$$= \frac{\sum \dfrac{x}{S_X}\dfrac{y}{S_Y}}{N} = \frac{1}{N}\sum \frac{x}{S_X}\frac{y}{S_Y}$$

$$= \frac{1}{N}\frac{1}{S_X}\frac{1}{S_Y}\sum xy$$

$$= \frac{\sum xy}{N S_X S_Y}$$

EXERCISES

4.1   What proportion of the normal curve's area lies between the mean and the following value of z:

(a)   .80   (d)   2.00   (g)   −1.50
(b)   .20   (e)   −1.00   (h)   .50
(c)   −.35   (f)   .45   (i)   −.05

Answer: (a) .29, (b) .08, (c) .14, (d) .48, (e) .34, (f) .17, (g) .43, (h) .19, (i) .02

4.2   What proportion of the normal curve's area lies to the right of the following z scores?

(a)   1.0   (d)   −2.00
(b)   1.67   (e)   1.90
(c) −1.67   (f)   −.55

Answer: (a) .16, (b) .05, (c) .95, (d) .98, (e) .03, (f) .71

4.3   What proportion of the normal curve's area does not lie between the following z scores?

(a)   −1.96 and 1.96   (d)   −0.05 and 0
(b)   −.15 and 1.50   (e)   −1.30 and −.30
(c)   .67 and 1.0   (f)   1.60 and 2.00

Answer: (a) .05, (b) .51, (c) .91, (d) .98, (e) .72, (f) .97

4.4   What proportion of the normal curve's area lies between these two values of z?

(a)   .05 and .50   (d)   1.0 and 2.0
(b)   −.30 and −.10   (e)   −1.96 and 1.96
(c)   −.40 and .40   (f)   0 and 1.00

Answer: (a) .17, (b) .08, (c) .31, (d) .14, (e) .95, (f) .34

4.5 The scores on a test were transformed to z scores. Grades were assigned this way:

z score	Grade
Above 1.60	A
.40 to 1.60	B
−1.00 to .40	C
−1.50 to −1.00	D
Below −1.50	F

(a) What proportion of the class got each grade?
Answer: A, .05; B, .29; C, .50; D, .09; F, .07

(b) What proportion of the class got a grade of C or better?
Answer: .84

(c) If a certain score fell at the 75th percentile, what would the letter grade be?
Answer: B

(d) If the score fell at the 33d percentile, what would the letter grade be?
Answer: C

4.6 A distribution of grades in a course has a mean of 70 and a standard deviation of 10. Letter grades are to be assigned this way: A, 15 percent; B, 35 percent; C, 35 percent; D, 15 percent.

(a) What grade divides the A's from the B's?
Answer: 80.4

(b) What grade divides the B's from the C's?
Answer: 70

4.7 What z score corresponds to the 44th percentile score of a normal distribution?
Answer: −0.15

4.8 What percentile score corresponds to $z = -0.7$ in a normal distribution?
Answer: 24th percentile score

4.9 In a normal distribution, what is the percentile score of:

(a) the mean?
Answer: 50th percentile score

(b) the median?
Answer: 50th percentile score

(c) Q_3?
Answer: 75th percentile scope

(d) the score halfway between $\bar{X}$ and $\bar{X} + 3S$?
Answer: 93d percentile score

4.10 In a normal distribution, what is the z-score distance (or difference):

(a) between P_{10} and P_{20}?
Answer: 0.44

(b) between P_{40} and P_{50}?
Answer: 0.25

4.11   The IQs on a certain intelligence test are distributed normally with a mean of 100 and a standard deviation of 15.

(a)   Determine the first quartile score, Q_1.
Answer: 90

(b)   What percentage of examinees would have IQs above 130?
Answer: 2.28 percent

(c)   What score values bound the middle 80 percent of the distribution?
Answer: $z = -1.28$ and $z = 1.28$; scores are 80.8 and 119.2

(d)   Determine the 99th percentile score.
Answer: 134.95

(e)   What percentage of examinees would have IQs below 70?
Answer: 2.28 percent

4.12   A certain test yields a normal distribution of scores with a mean of 100 and a standard deviation of 20.

(a)   Determine Q_3.
Answer: 113.4

(b)   Determine P_1.
Answer: 53.4

(c)   What percentage of the score distribution would fall between the scores of 70 and 130?
Answer: 86.64 percent

4.13   Imagine two normal distributions of weights among college students, one for males and one for females. For males, $\bar{X} = 152$ and $S = 15$; for females, $\bar{X} = 130$ and $S = 12$. What percentage of the males weigh less than the average (mean) female?
Answer: 7.08 percent

4.14   An intelligence test has two subtests; call them Subtest A and B. An individual falls at the 20th percentile on Subtest A, and his z score is -1.4 on Subtest B. Assume that both subtests give a normal distribution of scores. Which performance is better?
Answer: Subtest A is superior

4.15 Q is the quartile deviation. It equals $(Q_3 - Q_1)/2$. What percentage of a normal distribution falls between the score which is $2Q$ below the mean and the score which is $2Q$ above the mean?
Answer: 82 percent

4.16   A school has a special class for slow learners. The IQs of students in the school are normally distributed; $\bar{X} = 100$, $S = 15$. To qualify for the class a student must have an IQ lower than $z = -2.00$.

(a)   What is the highest IQ of students in the class?
Answer: 70

(b)   What percent of the students in the school qualify for the class?
Answer: 2.3 percent of the school

(c) The school also has a special class for students with IQs above $z = 1.5$. What is the lowest IQ of students in this class?
Answer: 122.5

(d) What percent of the students in the school qualify for this class?
Answer: 6.7 percent

4.17 A normal distribution has a mean of 82. A person earns a score of 76, and his z score is -1.00.

(a) His score falls at the _____th percentile.
Answer: 16th

(b) The value of S is _____.
Answer: 6

(c) Q_3 would approximately equal _____.
Answer: 86

4.18 (a) Here is a set of 10 z scores: $-1.7, -1.1, -0.8, -0.5, -0.1, 0.1, 0.5, 0.8, 1.1, 1.7$. Transform these z scores to compose a set of 10 scores whose $\bar{X} = 50$ and whose $S = 10$.
Answer: 33, 39, 42, 45, 49, 51, 55, 58, 61, 67

(b) Here is a set of z scores: $-1.6, -1.2, -0.8, -0.6, 0.0, 0.0, 0.6, 0.8, 1.2, 1.6$. Transform these z scores to compose a set whose $\bar{X} = 10$ and whose $S = 2$.
Answer: 6.8, 7.6, 8.4, 8.8, 10.0, 10.0, 11.2, 11.6, 12.4, 13.2

(c) Here is a set of z scores: $-2.0, -0.8, -0.6, 0.0, 0.0, 0.0, 0.0, 0.6, 0.8, 2.0$.
(i) Use these z scores, first, to compose a set of z_X scores for 10 subjects —one for each subject. Then use the z scores again to compose a set of z_Y scores for the same subjects. Arrange the pairs of z_X and z_Y scores so as to make $r_{XY} = 0$.
(ii) Now manipulate the z_X scores and the z_Y scores so as to yield a set of data with the following characteristics: $N = 10$, $r_{XY} = 0$, $\bar{X} = 100$, $S_X = 10$, $\bar{Y} = 0$, $S_Y = 2$.
Answer:

(i) Subject	z_X	z_Y	(ii) X	Y
1	-2.0	0.8	80	1.6
2	-0.8	-2.0	92	-4.0
3	-0.6	0.0	94	0.0
4	0.0	-0.8	100	-1.6
5	0.0	-0.6	100	-1.2
6	0.0	0.6	100	1.2
7	0.0	2.0	100	4.0
8	0.6	0.0	106	0.0
9	0.8	0.0	108	0.0
10	2.0	0.0	120	0.0

(Other arrangements are also possible.)

4.19   Here is a set of 10 z scores ($\bar{X} = 0$, $S = 1$): -1.7, -1.1, -0.8, -0.5, -0.1, $+0.1$, $+0.5$, $+0.8$, $+1.1$, $+1.7$. Convert this set of scores to a set for which:

   (a) $\bar{X} = 15$, $S = 1$
         Answer: 13.3, 13.9, 14.2, 14.5, 14.9, 15.1, 15.5, 15.8, 16.1, 16.7

   (b) $\bar{X} = 0$, $S = 2$
         Answer: -3.4, -2.2, -1.6, -1.0, -0.2, 0.2, 1.0, 1.6, 2.2, 3.4

   (c) $\bar{X} = 15$, $S = 2$
         Answer: 11.6, 12.8, 13.4, 14.0, 14.8, 15.2, 16.0, 16.6, 17.2, 18.4

4.20   Here is a set of data reporting X scores and Y scores for 10 subjects.

X	Y
16	0
20	52
22	84
22	18
24	74
26	40
28	96
28	48
30	116
34	132

$$\sum X = 250 \qquad \sum Y = 660$$
$$\sum X^2 = 6{,}500 \qquad \sum Y^2 = 59{,}560$$
$$\sum XY = 18{,}100$$

   (a)   Compute r, showing your calculations.
         Answer: $r = .80$

   (b)   Plot the data on a sheet of graph paper. Do not connect the points.

4.21   Start with the formula $S^2 = [\sum (X - \bar{X})^2]/N$.

   (a)   Rewrite this formula to make it appropriate for z scores. That is, replace X by z, and simplify the formula in any way you can.
         Answer: S^2 of z scores $= (\sum z^2)/N$

   (b)   Show that $\sum z^2 = N$.
         Answer: Since $S_z = 1$, $S_z{}^2 = 1$. Therefore, $(\sum z^2)/N = 1$, so $\sum z^2 = 1$.

4.22   Suppose, for every subject, $z_X = z_Y$. What is r_{XY}?
       Answer: $r_{XY} = 1$

4.23   Construct a distribution of scores for which $\bar{X} = 10$, $S = 0$, and $N = 5$.
       Answer: 10, 10, 10, 10, 10

5

PROBABILITY

So far we have examined different kinds of frequency distributions and different ways of describing them. The most common distributions can be described by the normal curve, and we have considered normal distributions in detail. Our major goal, though, is to *infer*, not to describe. Once we know 50 subjects' mean scores, we want to make an inference about *all* subjects in the population. Since these inferences will be expressed in probabilistic terms, we now turn to the concept of probability.

5.1 DEFINITION OF PROBABILITY

Suppose we draw a card from a deck, or toss a penny, or roll a die. No one knows what will happen at any given moment. But in the long run, the results are predictable. A single penny might land heads or tails, we don't know which; but if the penny is tossed many times, a certain regularity emerges: Half the time it lands heads, and half the time it lands tails. Probability is used in situations like this; the outcome at any moment is uncertain, but the results in the long run are predictable.

Probability can be defined in either of two ways. Neither definition is perfect, and they are used interchangeably.

1   Classical probability

Suppose an event has n possible outcomes which are equally likely, and suppose only one outcome occurs at a time. Now suppose that n_A of these outcomes have the characteristic A. Then the probability of A is defined as the ratio n_A/n. We write:

$$P(A) = \frac{n_A}{n} \tag{5.1}$$

What is the probability of drawing a king from a deck of cards? There are 52 equally likely alternatives so $n = 52$. And 4 of these outcomes are kings so $n_A = 4$. The probability is therefore:

$$P(\text{king}) = \frac{n_A}{n} = \frac{4}{52} = \frac{1}{13}$$

This definition is circular, though: It requires the outcomes to be equally likely. And "equally likely" really means "equally probable," so the definition implies a preestablished notion of probability.

2   Relative frequency (empirical) probability

An event's probability is sometimes defined as its relative frequency of occurring. Suppose a distribution contains 200 scores and 84 of them fall above 26. What is the probability that a score falls above 26? The probability is defined by the relative frequency:

$$P(X > 26) = \frac{84}{200} = .42$$

This definition also poses a problem. Each time the test is administered, the probability $P(X > 26)$ changes. In general, though, investigators like to think of an event as having some single, long-run probability.

As a matter of fact, there is no precise definition of probability. At times the classical definition is convenient; other times, the relative frequency definition is more appropriate. The context usually tells which definition is intended. In either case, the probability can range from 0 to 1. If $P = 0$, the event does not occur at all; if $P = 1$, the event is certain to occur.

EXAMPLE 5.1

A subject answers a 4-item multiple-choice test by guessing. Only one choice is correct. What is the probability that he guess correctly on the first item?

Solution One choice is correct, so $n_A = 1$; with 4 alternatives, $n = 4$. Therefore, $P(\text{correct}) = \frac{1}{4}$.

EXAMPLE 5.2

A certain hospital reports 510 female births in 1969 and 490 male births. What is the probability of a male birth?

Solution Altogether there were $510 + 490 = 1,000$ births. The relative frequency of male births was $490/1,000 = 0.49$. Therefore, $P(\text{male}) = 0.49$.

EXAMPLE 5.3

What is the probability in a normal distribution that a score lies within 1.96 standard deviations of the mean—between $(\bar{X} - 1.96S)$ and $(\bar{X} + 1.96S)$?

Solution Thirty-five percent of the distribution falls within this region, so the probability is .95. That is:

$$P([\bar{X} - 1.96S] < X < [\bar{X} + 1.96S]) = 0.95$$

5.2 THE MEAN AND EXPECTATION

We can use the relative frequency definition to reexamine the mean. Suppose a distribution contains 5 scores; $N = 5$. Let the scores be: 2, 3, 3, 3, 9. The mean equals $\sum X/N = 20/5 = 4.0$. There are only 3 different score-categories (2, 3, and 9), and we can denote each score category as C_i.

Here is the frequency distribution. Each category is listed along with its relative frequency (or probability).

C_i	Frequency $= f_i$	Relative frequency $= P(C_i)$
2	1	$\frac{1}{5} = .20$
3	3	$\frac{3}{5} = .60$
9	1	$\frac{1}{5} = .20$
	$N = 5$	1.00

The mean of this distribution, $\overline{X} = 4.0$, can also be defined this way:

$$\overline{X} = \sum [C_i \cdot P(C_i)] \qquad (5.2)$$

To compute the mean, multiply each score-category C_i by its probability; then sum these values:

$$\tfrac{1}{5}(2) + \tfrac{3}{5}(3) + \tfrac{1}{5}(9) = 4.0$$

Expressed this way, the mean is sometimes called a "weighted sum" of the scores. Each score is weighted by its probability.

Later in the chapter this formula will be very useful. To derive it, let us begin with the basic definition of $\overline{X}$: $\sum X/N$. The five scores are summed; 2 is counted once, 3 is counted three times, and 9 is counted once:

$$\sum X = 1(2) + 3(3) + 1(9) = 20$$
$$= f_1 C_1 + f_2 C_2 + f_3 C_3$$

Then the total is divided by N:

$$\overline{X} = \frac{\sum X}{N} = \frac{1(2) + 3(3) + 1(9)}{5} = \frac{20}{5}$$

$$= \frac{f_1 C_1 + f_2 C_2 + f_3 C_3}{N}$$

$$= \frac{f_1 C_1}{N} + \frac{f_2 C_2}{N} + \frac{f_3 C_3}{N}$$

But each f_i/N is the probability of that category, $P(C_i)$. So

$$\overline{X} = \frac{\sum X}{N} = P_1 C_1 + P_2 C_2 + P_3 C_3$$

$$= \sum [C_i \cdot P(C_i)]$$

Statisticians sometimes call this mean the *expectation*. It tells us what value to expect on the average. In general, the expectation of X is written:

$$E(X) = \sum [X_i \cdot P(X_i)] \tag{5.3}$$

Be sure to notice the difference between E, the expectation, and $\sum$, the summing operation.

The expectation of X^2 would be written: $E(X^2) = \sum [X_i^2 \cdot P(X_i^2)]$. If $E(X^2) = 15$, then on the average, X^2 equals 15. To compute $E(X^2)$ for a set of data, first consider the X values: Perhaps 2, 3, and 9 occur with probabilities .20, .60, and .20. The X^2 values are 4, 9, and 81, and they occur as often as the corresponding X values occur: In .20 of the cases $X^2 = 4$; in .60 of the cases $X^2 = 9$; in .20 of the cases $X^2 = 81$. Therefore:

$$E(X^2) = \sum [X_i^2 \cdot P(X_i^2)]$$
$$= .20(4) + .60(9) + .20(81)$$
$$= 22.4$$

5.3 SETS AND ELEMENTS

Next we need to consider the concept of a *set*. We defined a set in Chap. 1 as a collection of things. The books in a library form a set; examination scores form a set; the different outcomes of a pair of dice form a set.

Each ingredient of a set is called an *element*. One way to define a set is to list its elements. The set of whole numbers from 1 to 5 is written: $S = \{1,2,3,4,5\}$. A set can also be defined by a rule which tells the elements it contains. The set of bald creatures in San Francisco is written: $S = \{X : X$ is a bald creature in San Francisco$\}$. Any X that obeys the rule is in the set; it has to be a bald creature in San Francisco.

Suppose the elements of one set are all also elements of a larger set. The smaller set is then called a *subset* of the larger one. The set of all jacks is a subset of the set of all picture cards. The set of all picture cards is a subset of the set of all cards.

Let us call some set Set W (W for "whole"), and suppose Set A is a subset of Set W. Every element of A is included in W. We can describe this arrangement by a Venn diagram (Fig. 5.1). The rectangle in the diagram denotes the larger Set W. The inner circle denotes the smaller Set A. Set W, for example, might be the set of all animals, and Set A might be the set of all mammals.

Probabilities can be viewed in terms of sets and subsets. Suppose a box

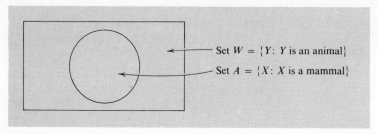

Set $W = \{Y : Y$ is an animal$\}$

Set $A = \{X : X$ is a mammal$\}$

FIG. 5.1

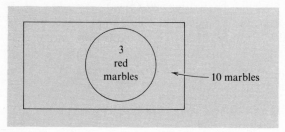

3
red
marbles

10 marbles

FIG. 5.2

contains 10 marbles, and 3 of them are red. Set W then contains 10 elements, and Set A (the subset) contains 3 of them (Fig. 5.2). If the marbles are all mixed, what is the probability of drawing a red one? This probability equals a ratio of two numbers, the number of elements in the subset divided by the number of elements in Set W:

$$P(\text{red}) = \frac{n_A}{n} = \frac{3}{10} = 0.3$$

5.4   DIFFERENT RELATIONSHIPS BETWEEN TWO SETS

Now consider two sets, A and B, both subsets of the larger Set W. Different relationships could exist between A and B, and these relationships are worth considering.

Case 1

In this case one set (say, A) is a subset of the other (B). For example, A might be the set of all lions and B, the set of all mammals. (And W might be the set of all animals.) We could describe the arrangement as shown in Fig. 5.3.

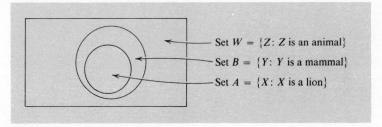

Set $W = \{Z: Z$ is an animal$\}$

Set $B = \{Y: Y$ is a mammal$\}$

Set $A = \{X: X$ is a lion$\}$

FIG. 5.3

Case 2

In this case A and B are mutually exclusive; they have no elements in common. No element of A is included in B, and no element of B is included in A. Suppose Set W refers to all people who have ever lived. Set A might be "people born before 1700," and Set B might be "people born after 1900." Nobody in one is included in the other. We could describe the situation as in Fig. 5.4. The circles do not overlap since they have no elements in common. The sets are said to be mutually exclusive.

Suppose a die is rolled and the 6 possible outcomes are considered. These outcomes might be called "Set S"; $S = \{1,2,3,4,5,6\}$. The subset $S_{odd} = \{1,3,5\}$ and the subset $S_{even} = \{2,4,6\}$ are mutually exclusive; no element in one appears in the other. But the subset $S_{under 5} = \{1,2,3,4\}$ and the subset $S_{over 3} = \{4,5,6\}$ are not mutually exclusive; they both contain the element 4.

Case 3

In this last case Sets A and B are said to *overlap* or *intersect*. One or more elements appear both in A and in B. For example, suppose 100 people (Set W) attend a meeting. Some are teachers (Set T) and some are Californians (Set C). (Some, of course, are neither teachers nor Californians.) Furthermore, some people at the meeting are in both sets; they are Californian teachers.

The composition of the group could be diagrammed as in Fig. 5.5. Elements that appear in both sets are shown where the circles overlap. To make the

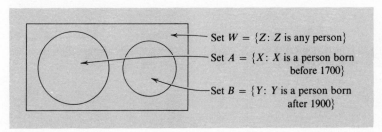

Set $W = \{Z: Z$ is any person$\}$

Set $A = \{X: X$ is a person born before 1700$\}$

Set $B = \{Y: Y$ is a person born after 1900$\}$

FIG. 5.4

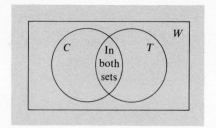

FIG. 5.5

example concrete, suppose the 100 people are divided this way: There are 10 Californians and 25 teachers, and the intersection contains 3 people (Fig. 5.6). The diagram shows several things. For one thing, it shows how the 10 Californians are divided—3 are teachers and 7 are not. It also shows how 25 teachers are divided—3 are Californians and 22 are not. Everybody else falls outside of T and outside of C—neither teachers nor Californians.

Sets derived from A and B

Set A and Set B are subsets of W. Other sets which are also subsets of W can be constructed from A and B. These new sets are called (i) the *union* of A and B, and (ii) the *intersection* of A and B.

Union of A and B

The union of two sets contains all the elements in Set A plus all the elements in Set B. It contains individuals that are *either* in A *or* in B. The union of dogs and cats contains creatures that qualify as either. The union of kings and red cards contains all the kings and all the red cards.

The union of two sets is denoted A ∪ B. The symbol ∪ stands for union. A union of two sets is usually a large category since members can qualify in two or more ways. Let us consider A ∪ B for each of our cases.

Case 1

If A is a subset of B, A ∪ B is simply Set B. The union of lions and animals contains creatures that are either lions or animals. Since all the lions are counted as animals, the union is the set of animals. When A is a subset of B, then A ∪ B = B.

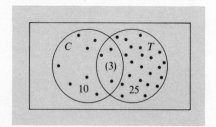

FIG. 5.6

Case 2

If A and B are mutually exclusive, A ∪ B contains all the elements of Set A plus all the elements of Set B. A ∪ B of our earlier example contains people born before 1700 plus people born after 1900. (It includes everybody except people born from 1700 to 1900.) When A and B are mutually exclusive, A ∪ B = A + B.

Case 3

If the two sets overlap, A ∪ B contains three groups of elements: (i) elements in A but not in B, (ii) elements in the intersection, and (iii) elements in B but not in A. A ∪ B of our earlier example contains (i) teachers who are not Californians, (ii) Californian teachers, and (iii) Californians who are not teachers.

Intersection of A and B

We also need some way to designate the intersection of two sets. The intersection is itself a set, and it is denoted A ∩ B. (The horseshoe is sometimes read as "and." An element in A ∩ B meets a double criterion: "both A *and* B.")

Set A ∩ B in the earlier example denotes the set of "Californian teachers." Notice that A ∩ B is a subset of A, and it also is a subset of B: Californian teachers are all Californians, and they are all teachers.

What is the intersection of sets in Case 1, where all of Set A is included in B? All of the A's are also in B, so the intersection contains all of Set A. In Case 1, therefore, A ∩ B = A: The intersection of lions and animals contains all of the lions.

What about Case 2, where A and B are mutually exclusive? In Case 2, no member of A is included in B, and of course, no member of B is included in A. The intersection, therefore, contains no members at all; A ∩ B has no elements.

Number rule

The symbol $n(A)$ tells the number of elements in A. $n(B)$ tells the number in B; $n(A \cap B)$, the number in the intersection; and $n(A \cup B)$, the number in the union. When A and B are mutually exclusive, $n(A \cap B)$ equals 0. On the other hand, if $n(A \cap B) = 5$, then 5 elements are "both A and B."

Consider the diagram again which described the composition of 100 people. Set C contains Californians, and Set T contains teachers. $n(C) = 10$; $n(T) = 25$; and with 3 people in the intersection, $n(C \cap T) = 3$ (Fig. 5.7).

How many elements of C are not in the intersection? Three Californians *are* in the intersection—$n(C \cap T) = 3$—so 7 Californians are not. Let us therefore record 7 in the nonoverlapping part of Set C. Similarly, 22 teachers are not in Set C, so 22 appears in the nonoverlapping part of Set T.

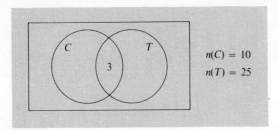

FIG. 5.7

Figure 5.8 completely analyzes the situation. It contains 7 Californians who are not teachers, 3 Californian teachers, and 22 teachers who are not Californians. You can easily compute $n(C \cup T)$ from this diagram: $n(C \cup T)$ equals $7 + 3 + 22 = 32$.

Notice that $n(C \cup T)$ is not simply $n(C)$ plus $n(T)$. "$n(C) + n(T)$" counts the elements in the intersection twice, once with $n(C)$ and once with $n(T)$. To compute $n(C \cup T)$, add $n(C) + n(T)$, *but subtract $n(C \cap T)$ from one of them*:

$$n(C \cup T) = n(C) + n(T) - n(C \cap T)$$
$$= (7 + 3) + (3 + 22) - 3$$
$$= \quad 10 \quad + \quad 25 \quad - 3$$
$$= 32$$

This rule can also be used to compute $n(C \cap T)$:

$$n(C \cap T) = n(C) + n(T) - n(C \cup T)$$
$$= \quad 10 \quad + \quad 25 \quad - \quad 32$$
$$= 3$$

Furthermore, the rule also applies to Case 1 and Case 2. In Case 1, Set A is included in Set B, so $n(A \cap B) = n(A)$. The number of elements in the union is:

$$n(A \cup B) = n(A) + n(B) - n(A \cap B)$$
$$= n(A) + n(B) - n(A)$$
$$= n(B) \qquad\qquad\qquad\qquad (5.4)$$

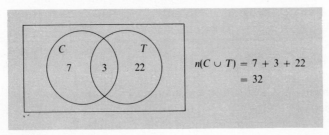

FIG. 5.8

In Case 1, therefore, the number of elements in the union equals $n(B)$. Let Set A contain 3 lions and Set B, 14 animals; $n(A \cup B) = 3 + 14 - 3 = 14$ elements.

The sets in Case 2 are mutually exclusive, so $n(A \cap B) = 0$. Therefore:

$$n(A \cup B) = n(A) + n(B) - n(A \cap B)$$
$$= n(A) + n(B)$$

When two sets are mutually exclusive, the number of elements in their union equals $n(A)$ plus $n(B)$. Let Set A contain 4 aces, and Set B, 12 picture cards; $n(A \cup B) = 4 + 12 = 16$ elements.

5.5 PROBABILITIES ABOUT THE UNION OF TWO SETS

A probability always involves a set and a subset. Consider the probability of a queen when you draw a card from a deck. The larger set (Set W) has 52 possible outcomes, and the subset (the queens) has 4 possible outcomes. $n(Q) = 4$ and $n(W) = 52$. The probability of a queen equals:

$$P(Q) = \frac{n(Q)}{n(W)} = \frac{4}{52} = \frac{1}{13}$$

The question becomes more interesting if it includes the word *or*: What is the probability of drawing a card that is either A *or* B? This time the question asks the probability that an element of W is in $A \cup B$. Suppose $A \cup B$ contains 15 elements; then 15 elements in W can be called "A or B." And if W contains 25 elements, the probability equals:

$$P(A \text{ or } B) = \frac{n(A \cup B)}{n(W)}$$
$$= \frac{15}{25} = .60$$

This probability is also written $P(A \cup B)$.

Let us use the expansion rule to expand $P(A \cup B)$.

$$P(A \cup B) = \frac{n(A \cup B)}{n(W)} = \frac{n(A) + n(B) - n(A \cap B)}{n(W)}$$
$$= \frac{n(A)}{n(W)} + \frac{n(B)}{n(W)} - \frac{n(A \cap B)}{n(W)}$$

$$P(A \cup B) = P(A) + P(B) - P(A \cap B) \qquad (5.5)$$

To compute the probability that an individual is either A or B, first add the two simpler probabilities $P(A) + P(B)$. Then subtract $P(A \cap B)$, the probability that an element of W lies in the intersection.

The following examples illustrate this rule for each of the cases.

EXAMPLE 5.4 (Case 1)

What is the probability that a card drawn from a deck is either a jack (J) or a picture card (P)?

Solution There are 52 possible outcomes, so $n(W) = 52$. Set J (the jacks) contains 4 possibilities, and Set P (the pictures) contains 12 possibilities. Set J, however, is *included in* Set P, so all the J's are P's.

The question asks about $J \cup P$. Now $n(J \cup P) = n(J) + n(P) - n(J \cap P) = 4 + 12 - 4 = 12$. Therefore, 12 cards are "jacks or picture cards." The probability, then, is:

$$P(J \cup P) = \frac{n(J \cup P)}{n(W)} = \frac{12}{52} = \frac{3}{13}.$$

Another way to compute this value is:

$$P(J \cup P) = P(J) + P(P) - P(J \cap P) = \frac{4}{52} + \frac{12}{52} - \frac{4}{52}$$

$$= \frac{12}{52} = \frac{3}{13}$$

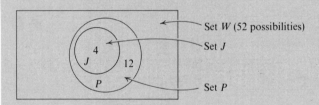

Set W (52 possibilities)
Set J
Set P

EXAMPLE 5.5 (Case 2)

What is the probability that a card drawn from a deck is a jack or a king?

Solution Out of 52 possible outcomes, there are 4 jacks (Set J) and 4 kings (Set K). The two sets do not overlap, so $P(J \cap K) = 0$. Therefore,

$$P(J \cup K) = P(J) + P(K) - P(J \cap K)$$

$$= P(J) + P(K)$$

$$= \frac{4}{52} + \frac{4}{52} = \frac{8}{52} = \frac{2}{13}$$

EXAMPLE 5.6 (Case 2)

What is the probability that a card drawn from a deck is an ace or a picture card?

Solution   Since aces (Set A) and picture cards (Set P) are mutually exclusive, $P(A \cap P) = 0$. Therefore:

$$P(A \cup P) = P(A) + P(P) - P(A \cap P)$$

$$= \frac{4}{52} + \frac{12}{52} - 0$$

$$= \frac{16}{52} = \frac{4}{13}$$

EXAMPLE 5.7 (Case 2)

In a normal distribution of scores, what is the probability that an examinee has a z score greater than $+1.00$ or less than -1.00?

Solution   The characteristics "$z > 1.00$" and "$z < -1.00$" are mutually exclusive; a given person cannot be both. Therefore, $P(z > 1.00 \cap z < -1.00) = 0$. Hence, the probability of one *or* the other is:

$$P(z > 1.00 \cup z < -1.00) = P(z > 1.00) + P(z < -1.00)$$

$$= .16 + .16 = .32$$

When the outcomes are mutually exclusive, $P(A \cup B)$ is just the sum of the simple probabilities $P(A)$ and $P(B)$. This simple rule can be extended for any number of alternatives:

$$P(A \cup B \cup C \cup D) = P(A) + P(B) + P(C) + P(D)$$ (if the alter-   (5.6)
natives are
all mutually
exclusive)

Suppose the events A, B, C, and D are mutually exclusive, and suppose they have these probabilities: $P(A) = .14$; $P(B) = .03$; $P(C) = .21$; and $P(D) = .62$. Then the probability of "A or B or C" is:

$$P(A \cup B \cup C) = P(A) + P(B) + P(C) = .14 + .03 + .21 = .38$$

Case 3, on the other hand, is not so simple. The alternatives are not mutually exclusive, and the simple rule does not apply.

EXAMPLE 5.8 (Case 3)

What is the probability that a card drawn from a deck is either a jack or a spade?

Solution   Out of 52 possible outcomes, there are 4 jacks (Set J) and 13 spades (Set S). However, the intersection of these sets, $J \cap S$, contains 1 card, the jack of spades.

One way to solve the problem is to compute $n(J \cup S) = n(J) + n(S) - n(J \cap S)$. This value equals $4 + 13 - 1 = 16$. Thus, 16 cards are "either a jack or a spade." The probability is therefore:

$$P(J \cup S) = \frac{n(J \cup S)}{n(W)} = \frac{16}{52} = \frac{4}{13}$$

Another way to solve the problem is to work directly with probabilities:

$$P(J) = \frac{4}{52}; \quad P(S) = \frac{13}{52}; \quad \text{and} \quad P(J \cap S) = \frac{1}{52}.$$

Therefore:

$$P(J \cup S) = P(J) + P(S) - P(J \cap S)$$

$$= \frac{4}{52} + \frac{13}{52} - \frac{1}{52} = \frac{16}{52} = \frac{4}{13}$$

EXAMPLE 5.9 (Case 3)

One hundred voters in a community consist of 30 Republicans (Set R) and 50 female voters (Set F). Ten Republicans happen to be females, and 20 Republicans happen to be male. What is the probability that a given voter is either a female or a Republican?

Solution   For the community of 100 people,

$$P(R) = \frac{30}{100}; \quad P(F) = \frac{50}{100}; \quad \text{and} \quad P(R \cap F) = \frac{10}{100}.$$

Therefore the probability that a voter is "R or F" is:

$$P(R \cup F) = P(R) + P(F) - P(R \cap F)$$

$$= .30 + .50 - .10$$

$$= .70$$

Be sure you can visualize the situation as a Venn diagram:

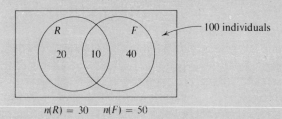

$n(R) = 30 \quad n(F) = 50$

As the diagram shows, 70 people qualify as "female or Republican." The other 30 people are male Democrats.

EXAMPLE 5.10 (Case 3)

A certain mental hospital contains 200 patients. Fifty of them are schizophrenic (S), and 40 are feebleminded (F). Therefore, $P(S) = .25$ and $P(F) = .20$. Ten schizophrenics happen to be feebleminded, so $P(S \cap F) = .05$.

(a) Compute the probability that a patient in the hospital is either schizophrenic or feebleminded. (b) Compute the probability that a patient is neither schizophrenic nor feebleminded.

Solution

$$(a) \quad P(S \cup F) = P(S) + P(F) - P(S \cap F)$$
$$= .25 + .20 - .05$$
$$= .40$$

In the entire hospital $.40(200) = 80$ people are either schizophrenic or feebleminded. The composition of the patient community is shown in the Venn diagram below:

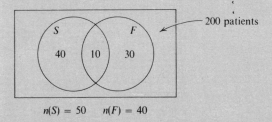

$n(S) = 50 \quad n(F) = 40$

(b) Since 80 patients are "S or F," the other patients fall outside the union. These 120 people are not S, and they are not F. Therefore, the probability that a patient is neither schizophrenic nor feebleminded equals $120/200 = .60$.

5.6 CONDITIONAL PROBABILITY

Consider Example 5.10 again. Fifty patients were in Set S, and 40 were in Set F. The intersection S ∩ F contained 10 patients and these 10 patients, of course, were in *both* sets.

Now consider the patients in Set S alone: What is the probability—within *their* group—of a feebleminded person? We already know the value of $P(F)$ for all 200 members of Set W: $P(F) = n(F)/n(W) = 40/200 = .20$. But this time the question is restricted to Set S: What is the probability of finding an F just among the 50 members of Set S? In Set S there are 10 feebleminded individuals. The probability of an F within Set S is therefore $10/50 = .20$. This probability is written $P(F|S)$, and it is called a *conditional probability*. It is computed:

$$P(F|S) = \frac{n(F \cap S)}{n(S)} = \frac{10}{50} = .20$$

$P(F|S)$ tells the probability of an F given this one condition: that you only observe members of Set S. Therefore, it is usually read: "The probability of F *given* S."

In this example, $P(F|S)$ happens to equal $P(F)$. Both values equal .20. Therefore, the feebleminded individuals are just as probable among schizophrenics as they are in the hospital community at large. In other cases, though, the two values differ. Consider Example 5.9 again: A community of 100 voters contains 30 Republicans (R) and 50 females (F). Ten voters are female Republicans (F ∩ R).

Now $P(R)$ equals .30 for the entire community. But what is the probability of a Republican among just the female voters? What is $P(R|F)$? To determine this conditional probability, we limit our attention to Set F (Fig. 5.9). The 50 females of Set F contain 10 Republicans:

$$P(R|F) = \frac{n(R \cap F)}{n(F)} = \frac{10}{50} = .20$$

In other words, a Republican is less probable among female voters; Republicans in the community tend more to be male. In general, when $P(A)$

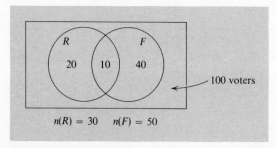

$n(R) = 30 \quad n(F) = 50$

FIG. 5.9

differs from $P(A|B)$, then A and B are correlated. This example illustrates a correlation between the voter's sex and his party affiliation in that community of 100 voters.

Consider the formula once again for computing $P(R|F)$.

$$P(R|F) = \frac{n(R \cap F)}{n(F)} = \frac{10}{50}$$

If we divide the numerator and the denominator both by $n(W)$, they both become simple probabilities:

$$P(R|F) = \frac{n(R \cap F)}{n(F)} = \frac{n(R \cap F)/n(W)}{n(F)/n(W)} = \frac{P(R \cap F)}{P(F)}$$

The conditional probability can therefore be viewed as a ratio of two simple probabilities. For the data given above, $P(R \cap F) = .10$ and $P(F) = .50$. Therefore:

$$P(R|F) = \frac{.10}{.50} = .20$$

How about the conditional probability, $P(F|R)$? This term tells the probability of a *female* within the set of Republicans:

$$P(F|R) = \frac{n(F \cap R)}{n(R)} = \frac{P(F \cap R)}{P(R)} = \frac{.10}{.30} = .33$$

For the entire community, $P(F) = .50$; half of the 100 voters are female. But for the group of Republicans, the probability drops to .33; relatively fewer females are in Set R.

Whenever A and B are subsets of W, two conditional probabilities can be considered—$P(B|A)$ and $P(A|B)$. $P(B|A)$ tells the probability of B within Set A; $P(A|B)$ tells the probability of A within Set B.

$$(1) \quad P(B|A) = \frac{P(A \cap B)}{P(A)}$$

$$(2) \quad P(A|B) = \frac{P(A \cap B)}{P(B)}$$

(5.7)

Each of these equations involves $P(A \cap B)$, the simple probability that an individual falls in the intersection. Let us solve each equation for $P(A \cap B)$.

$$\text{From (1),} \quad P(A \cap B) = P(A) \cdot P(B|A)$$
$$\text{From (2),} \quad P(A \cap B) = P(B) \cdot P(A|B)$$

(5.8)

Therefore, two ways exist for computing $P(A \cap B)$. One way is to multiply $P(A)$ times the conditional probability $P(B|A)$. The other way is to multiply $P(B)$ times the conditional probability $P(A|B)$.

These rules are applied to the problems below.

EXAMPLE 5.11

The probability of a certain disease among men is .10. Throughout many families, the disease occurs as often among fathers as it does among sons—in both cases, $P = .10$. We can write $P(F) = .10$ (for fathers) and $P(S) = .10$ (for sons).

Now suppose the conditional probability $P(S|F)$ is also known—the probability that the son is afflicted in families where the father is afflicted. In such families the probability is .90 for the sons, so $P(S|F) = .90$. Clearly the disease runs in families: Throughout *all* families, $P(S) = .10$. Given that the father is afflicted, though, the probability for the son is .90.

(a) What is the probability in all families that the father and the son both have the disease?

Solution

$$P(F \cap S) = P(F) \cdot P(S|F) = (.10)(.90) = .09$$

In 9 families out of 100, then, both father and son have the disease.

(b) What is the probability that either the father or the son has the disease?

Solution

$$P(F \cup S) = P(F) + P(S) - P(F \cap S)$$
$$= .10 + .10 - .09 = .11$$

EXAMPLE 5.12

In a certain community of men, the probability is .06 that the man's salary exceeds $25,000; let us denote this probability $P(\text{rich})$. Furthermore, the probability that the man has had a college education is denoted $P(\text{educated})$;

$P(\text{educated}) = .30$. Finally, the conditional probability $P(\text{educated}|\text{rich}) = .67$.
(*a*) Compute the probability that an individual has both traits.

Solution

$$P(\text{rich} \cap \text{educated}) = P(\text{rich}) \cdot P(\text{educated}|\text{rich})$$
$$= (.06) \cdot (.67) = .04$$

(*b*) Compute the conditional probability $P(\text{rich}|\text{educated})$.

Solution

$$P(\text{rich} \cap \text{educated}) = P(\text{educated}) \cdot P(\text{rich}|\text{educated})$$
$$.04 = (.30) \cdot P(\text{rich}|\text{educated})$$
$$P(\text{rich}|\text{educated}) = \frac{.04}{.03} = .13$$

Therefore, the educated men in the community have a higher chance of being rich. Their probability is .13, while that for the community as a whole is $P(\text{rich}) = .06$.

EXAMPLE 5.13

Two sets of scores are normally distributed. The scores show a perfect correlation, $r_{XY} = 1.00$, so a person's z score on one test equals his z score on the other. Compute the probability that a person falls at $z > 1.00$ on *both* tests.

Solution The probability that $z > 1.00$ on Test X is .16. Let us denote this probability $P(\text{high X}) = .16$. Similarly, $P(\text{high Y})$ equals .16. Since the tests are perfectly correlated, $P(\text{high Y}|\text{high X}) = 1.00$: $z_X = z_Y$, so everybody high on Test X also scores high on Test Y.

The probability of excellence on both tests, then, equals:

$$P(\text{high X} \cap \text{high Y}) = P(\text{high X}) \cdot P(\text{high Y}|\text{high X})$$
$$= (.16) \cdot (1.00) = .16$$

When the scores are perfectly correlated, the probability is .16 that $z > 1.00$ on both tests.

5.7   INDEPENDENT EVENTS

When $P(A|B)$ equals $P(A)$, A and B are said to be *independent* (or *uncorrelated*). And if $P(A|B)$ equals $P(A)$, then the other conditional probability, $P(B|A)$, equals its simple probability $P(B)$. Let us prove this point.

First, $P(A \cap B) = P(A) \cdot P(B|A);$
Furthermore, $P(A \cap B) = P(B) \cdot P(A|B);$
Therefore, $P(A) \cdot P(B|A) = P(B) \cdot P(A|B).$

Now $P(A) = P(A|B)$; therefore, we can replace $P(A|B)$ by $P(A)$:

$$P(A) \cdot P(B|A) = P(A) \cdot P(B)$$

Hence

$$P(B|A) = P(B)$$

Thus, if A and B are independent, each conditional probability equals the corresponding simple probability; $P(A) = P(A|B)$, and $P(B) = P(B|A)$: The probability of A within Set B is the same as $P(A)$. And the probability of B within Set A is the same as $P(B)$.

Furthermore, when A and B are independent, $P(A \cap B)$ can be simplified. In general, $P(A \cap B) = P(A) \cdot P(B|A)$. But when A and B are independent:

$$P(A \cap B) = P(A) \cdot P(B)$$

The probability of "A and B" therefore equals the product $P(A)$ times $P(B)$.

EXAMPLE 5.14

In a certain school the probability is .16 that a student's IQ exceeds 115; let us call this probability P(bright). And the probability is .10 that a student is musically talented; P(musical) = .10. If the two characteristics are independent, what is the probability that a student is both bright and musical?

Solution

$$P(\text{bright} \cap \text{musical}) = P(\text{bright}) \cdot P(\text{musical})$$
$$= (.16)(.10) = .016$$

Notice that the conditional probability P(bright|musical) equals the simple probability P(bright): To prove that point, compute the probability of a bright person within the set of musical people:

$$P(\text{bright}|\text{musical}) = \frac{P(\text{bright} \cap \text{musical})}{P(\text{musical})} = \frac{.016}{.10} = .16$$

EXAMPLE 5.15

Color blindness among males has a probability of .08. And myopia, let us say, has a probability of .25. If the two traits are independent, compute the probability that a man is afflicted with both disabilities.

Solution

$$P(CB \cap M) = P(CB) \cdot P(M) = (.08)(.25) = .02$$

Thus, 2 percent of all men are afflicted with both. Make sure that you understand this result intuitively: Color-blind men comprise .08 of all men. But a quarter of all people are myopic, so a quarter of the color-blind men are myopic too. A quarter of .08 equals .02, the fraction that is both myopic *and* color-blind.

5.8   PROBABILITY IN SEQUENTIAL EVENTS

The general rule $P(A \cap B) = P(A) \cdot P(B|A)$ is useful in many different situations. Sometimes $A \cap B$ denotes a sequence of two events—first A, then B. Here are some examples of sequential situations.

EXAMPLE 5.16 (NONINDEPENDENT EVENTS)

An urn contains 8 balls—5 white ones and 3 yellow ones. An experimenter draws two balls in succession, Ball 1 and then Ball 2. Say Ball 1 is yellow (Y) and Ball 2 is white (W). Let us write Y_1 to mean "yellow on Ball 1" and W_2 to mean "white on Ball 2." The symbol $Y_1 \cap W_2$ tells that Ball 1 is yellow and Ball 2 is white. (Other possible outcomes would be written: $Y_1 \cap Y_2$, $W_1 \cap Y_2$, and $W_1 \cap W_2$.) What is the probability of $W_1 \cap W_2$?

Solution   We can write:

$$P(W_1 \cap W_2) = P(W_1) \cdot P(W_2|W_1)$$

The conditional probability $P(W_2|W_1)$ tells the probability that Ball 2 is white, given that Ball 1 was white: Initially $P(W_1) = \frac{5}{8}$. But once W_1 occurs, only 7 balls remain in the urn—4 white ones and 3 yellow ones. Given W_1, then, the probability of W_2 drops to $\frac{4}{7}$; $P(W_2|W_1) = \frac{4}{7}$.

To compute the probability $P(W_1 \cap W_2)$, then:

$$P(W_1 \cap W_2) = P(W_1) \cdot P(W_2|W_1).$$

$$= \frac{5}{8} \cdot \frac{4}{7} = \frac{20}{56} = \frac{5}{16}$$

EXAMPLE 5.17 (NONINDEPENDENT EVENTS)

Two cards, Card 1 and Card 2, are drawn from a deck of 52 cards. What is the probability that Card 1 is a jack and Card 2 is a king?

Solution   Let us denote this probability $P(J_1 \cap K_2)$. Then:

$$P(J_1 \cap K_2) = P(J_1) \cdot P(K_2|J_1)$$

$$= \frac{4}{52} \cdot \frac{4}{51} = \frac{16}{2,652}$$

(Notice why $P(K_2|J_1)$ equals $\frac{4}{51}$: After a jack is drawn as Card 1, 4 kings remain in the deck of 51 cards.)

Similarly, you might compute $P(K_1 \cap J_2)$, the probability of drawing a king as Card 1 and a jack as Card 2. That probability would equal 16/2,652. Now, what is the probability that a two-card sequence contains a jack and a king, no matter which order they appear in? They might appear as $J_1 \cap K_2$ (the jack drawn first), or as $K_1 \cap J_2$ (the king drawn first). These two possibilities are mutually exclusive, so the probability of *either* one equals $16/2652 + 16/2652 = 32/2652$.

EXAMPLE 5.18 (INDEPENDENT EVENTS)

A die and then a coin are tossed. What is the probability that the coin falls "heads" and the die falls "3"?

Solution

$$P(H \cap 3) = P(H) \cdot P(3) = \frac{1}{2} \cdot \frac{1}{6} = \frac{1}{12}$$

EXAMPLE 5.19 (INDEPENDENT EVENTS)

Two pennies are tossed. Compute the probability of a head on Coin 1 and a tail on Coin 2; that is, compute $P(H_1 \cap T_2)$.

Solution

$$P(H_1 \cap T_2) = P(H_1) \cdot P(T_2) = \frac{1}{2} \cdot \frac{1}{2} = \frac{1}{4}$$

Notice the four possible outcomes: $H_1 \cap H_2$, $H_1 \cap T_2$, $T_1 \cap H_2$, and $T_1 \cap T_2$. These different outcomes occur equally often, so the outcome $H_1 \cap T_2$ occurs one-fourth of the time.

When two coins are tossed, what is the probability of one head and one tail (in either order)? Two different outcomes meet this requirement: $H_1 \cap T_2$ (the head on Coin 1) or $T_1 \cap H_2$ (the head on Coin 2). The probability of each alternative is $\frac{1}{4}$, so the probability of *either* one equals $\frac{1}{4} + \frac{1}{4} = \frac{1}{2}$.

5.9 THE NATURE OF COMPOUND EVENTS

Next we shall examine situations that are more complex. Perhaps several coins are tossed at once, or 4 cards are drawn from a deck. These situations will help us extend the concept of probability further.

First we need some definitions. When a situation is composed of two or more events, each event is called a *simple event*. A toss of three coins contains three simple events. The situation as a whole is usually called a *compound event* or an *experiment*. If each simple event is denoted E_1, E_2, E_3, the entire 3-coin experiment is denoted E_1-E_2-E_3.

Suppose E_1-E_2-E_3 refers to the toss of three pennies. One experimental outcome would be H_1-T_2-T_3: a head on the first penny and a tail on the other two. How many different outcomes of E_1-E_2-E_3 are possible? Or consider this question. Suppose E_1-E_2-E_3 refers to the first three cards dealt from a deck; how many different 3-card deals are possible? Questions like these are all basically alike. They can be answered through one basic rule.

Basic rule
If a different things can happen as Event 1 and if b different things can happen as Event 2, then $a \times b$ different two-event outcomes are possible.

EXAMPLE 5.20

A customer in a restaurant chooses a dinner that contains a main course (M) and a beverage (B). He has three main courses to choose from and two beverages. How many different dinners are possible?

Solution The main courses are denoted M_1, M_2, and M_3, and the beverages, B_1 and B_2. Then $a \times b = 3 \times 2 = 6$. The six possible dinners are: M_1B_1, M_1B_2, M_2B_1, M_2B_2, M_3B_1, and M_3B_2. These six possibilities can be visualized as a matrix; each cell of the matrix reports a different two-course dinner.

The Beverage

		B_1	B_2
The Main Course	M_1	M_1B_1	M_1B_2
	M_2	M_2B_1	M_2B_2
	M_3	M_3B_1	M_3B_2

If the customer can also choose one of five desserts, the number of possible dinners becomes $a \times b \times c = 3 \times 2 \times 5 = 30$; Each M_iB_j combination gets paired with each dessert to yield $6 \times 5 = 30$ dinners.

Consider an experiment with three simple events: E_1-E_2-E_3. Suppose E_1 has three possible outcomes, E_2, nine possible outcomes, and E_3, seven possible outcomes. The entire experiment would have $3 \times 9 \times 7 = 189$ possible outcomes. This basic principle appears in a variety of problems, which are often classified into five types. The following section describes these five variations.

Variation 1   (*n* simple events, and each event has *r* possible outcomes)

Suppose three pennies are tossed—Penny 1, Penny 2, and Penny 3—and the experiment is denoted E_1-E_2-E_3. Each simple event has two outcomes, a head or a tail. Altogether there are $2 \times 2 \times 2 = 2^3 = 8$ experimental outcomes. The 8 outcomes are shown below in two ways. Particularly notice the diagram on the left, which is called a tree diagram. Each pathway through the tree describes a different experimental outcome.

E_1	E_2	E_3		E_1	E_2	E_3
(Penny 1)	(Penny 2)	(Penny 3)		(Penny 1)	(Penny 2)	(Penny 3)
			Outcome 1:	H	H	H
			Outcome 2:	H	H	T
			Outcome 3:	H	T	H
			Outcome 4:	H	T	T
			Outcome 5:	T	H	H
			Outcome 6:	T	H	T
			Outcome 7:	T	T	H
			Outcome 8:	T	T	T

In general, suppose an experiment contains *n* simple events. The experiment as a whole would be denoted E_1-E_2-E_3- $\cdots$ -E_n. If each simple event has *r* possible outcomes, the entire experiment contains r^n different possible outcomes.

EXAMPLE 5.21

A certain maze has four choice points. As a rat runs through the maze, it finds three options at each choice point: It can turn right, turn left, or proceed straight. How many different response patterns are possible?

Solution   The response at each choice point is a simple event, so the four choice points can be denoted E_1-E_2-E_3-E_4. With three alternatives at each choice point, there are $3^4 = 81$ possible response patterns.

EXAMPLE 5.22

A multiple-choice test contains 10 questions, and every question offers four response alternatives. Here is one answer-sheet pattern:

Item	1	A	Ⓑ	C	D
	2	Ⓐ	B	C	D
	3	A	B	Ⓒ	D
	4	A	B	Ⓒ	D
	5	A	Ⓑ	C	D
	6	A	B	C	Ⓓ
	7	A	B	C	Ⓓ
	8	A	B	Ⓒ	D
	9	A	B	C	Ⓓ
	10	A	B	Ⓒ	D

How many different answer-sheet patterns are possible?

Solution Each response is a simple event, and the entire experiment contains 10 simple events. With four alternatives for each event, r^n equals 4^{10} possible patterns.

EXAMPLE 5.23

A certain maze has four choice points and three options at each choice point, R, L, or S. (*a*) What is the probability that a rat turns right at the first three choice points and then turns left: $E_1\text{-}E_2\text{-}E_3\text{-}E_4 = R\ R\ R\ L$?

Solution This pathway is *one* of the $3^4 = 81$ possible pathways. Its probability therefore equals $\frac{1}{81}$.

(*b*) What is the probability that the rat turns right at the first and third choice points?

Solution Pathways that meet this criterion could be denoted $R\!\!-\!\!L\!\!-\!\!R\!\!-\!\!L$, with branches R, R above and S, S below.

A total of $1 \times 3 \times 1 \times 3 = 9$ pathways meet this criterion. This probability therefore equals $\frac{9}{81} = \frac{1}{9}$.

Variation 2 (Permutations of *n* objects)

Suppose an experimenter has four pictures to show to a subject. The pictures are all different, and the subject will make a judgment about them one by one. Let us call the pictures A, B, C, and D. First the experimenter shows one of the four pictures; then he selects one of the remaining three; then one of the remaining two; and so on. How many different orders are possible?

This experiment contains four simple events: E_1-E_2-E_3-E_4. Any picture can appear as E_1, so E_1 has four alternatives. E_2 has three alternatives; E_3, two alternatives; and E_4, one alternative. Altogether there are $4 \times 3 \times 2 \times 1 = 24$ possible experimental outcomes. The 24 different orders are shown below.

First E_1	Second E_2	Third E_3	Fourth E_4		First E_1	Second E_2	Third E_3	Fourth E_4
A	B	C——D	Order 1:	A	B	C	D
		D——C	Order 2:	A	B	D	C
	C	B——D	Order 3:	A	C	B	D
		D——B	Order 4:	A	C	D	B
	D	B——C	Order 5:	A	D	B	C
		C——B	Order 6:	A	D	C	B
B	A	C——D	Order 7:	B	A	C	D
		D——C	Order 8:	B	A	D	C
	C	A——D	Order 9:	B	C	A	D
		D——A	Order 10:	B	C	D	A
	D	A——C	Order 11:	B	D	A	C
		C——A	Order 12:	B	D	C	A
C	A	B——D	Order 13:	C	A	B	D
		D——B	Order 14:	C	A	D	B
	B	A——D	Order 15:	C	B	A	D
		D——A	Order 16:	C	B	D	A
	D	A——B	Order 17:	C	D	A	B
		B——A	Order 18:	C	D	B	A
D	A	B——C	Order 19:	D	A	B	C
		C——B	Order 20:	D	A	C	B
	B	A——C	Order 21:	D	B	A	C
		C——A	Order 22:	D	B	C	A
	C	A——B	Order 23:	D	C	A	B
		B——A	Order 24:	D	C	B	A

When n objects are presented in order, the experiment contains n simple events: E_1-E_2- $\cdots$ -E_n. E_1 has n possible outcomes, and each succeeding event has one less alternative. Altogether there are $n \times n - 1 \times n - 2 \times \cdots \times 2 \times 1$ experimental outcomes. This term is called "n factorial"; it is written $n!$. For example, $4! = 4 \times 3 \times 2 \times 1 = 24$.

EXAMPLE 5.24

An experimenter is preparing a list of 6 nonsense syllables. The first item is generally learned faster, so he plans to vary the order of items. How many different orders are possible?

Solution The experiment contains 6 simple events: E_1-E_2-E_3-E_4-E_5-E_6. Altogether $n! = 6! = 720$ orders are possible.

The different orders of objects are called *permutations* of the objects. The letter P refers to the possible permutations. $_nP_n$ refers to the permutations of n objects; the first n tells that n objects are available, and the second n tells that all n objects will eventually appear: n simple events. $_nP_n$ is usually read as follows: "the number of permutations of n objects when all n of them are to be used."

$$_nP_n = n!$$

(5.9)

Variation 3 (Permutations: n objects are available but s of them look alike)

Suppose four objects are permuted and you consider the $4! = 24$ possible orderings. This time, though, suppose three of them are identical; perhaps these three are gray while the fourth one is black. Let A, B, and C be the gray objects, and **D** be the black one. The order B A C **D** would look exactly like the order C B A **D**. In both cases the viewer would see three gray objects followed by a black one: X X X **X**. The order X X **X** X, though, would be different: two grays, a black, and then a gray. Now, how many different— that is, *distinguishably* different—arrangements of A, B, C, and D can be formed?

First consider the answer and some examples. Let $_nD_n$ denote the number of different permutations of the n objects. If s of them look alike, then:

$$_nD_n = \frac{n!}{s!}$$

For example, suppose three objects of the four look alike; then $_nD_n = 4!/3! = 4$. There are four distinguishably different permutations. These permutations would be: **X X X X, X X X X, X X X X,** and **X X X X.**

X X X X	X X X X	X X X X	X X X X
D A B C	A D B C	A B D C	A B C D
D A C B	A D C B	A C D B	A C B D
D B A C	B D A C	B A D C	B A C D
D B C A	B D C A	B C D A	B C A D
D C A B	C D A B	C A D B	C A B D
D C B A	C D B A	C B D A	C B A D

Here is the reason for the formula. Consider one arrangement of the objects—say, A C B D, which can be viewed as X X X X. Suppose we permute A, B, and C, but keep **D** in Position 4: B A C D, C B A D, and so on. All permutations would yield the X X X **X** pattern. Now, how many permutations can be formed of A, B, and C to yield X X X **D**? There are 3! permutations, and they all yield the X X X X pattern. For any single type of pattern like X X X X, there are $s! = 3!$ permutations which look alike. The 24 permutations of A, B, C, and D, then, can be subdivided into four groups of six permutations. In general:

$n! = $ (Number of *distinguishably* $\times$ ($s!$ permutations
                 different permutations)   which look alike)

$n! = $ $_nD_n$ $\times$ $s!$

Therefore:

$$_nD_n = \frac{n!}{s!}$$

EXAMPLE 5.25

Consider the letters in the word START. The letter T appears twice, so $s = 2$. If the letters were all different (as in, say, STARK), there would be $5! = 120$ possible orders of letters. But because of the two T's, some permutations look alike: $S T_1 A R T_2$ looks like $S T_2 A R T_1$. How many distinguishably different orders of the letters are possible?

Solution $n = 5$ and $s = 2$. Therefore $_nD_n = n!/s! = 5!/2! = 60$ distinguishably different arrangements.

EXAMPLE 5.26

Suppose the letters of the word S T A R T are arranged haphazardly. What is the probability that they spell the word S T A R T?

Solution Only one arrangement of the 60 possible arrangements spells the word S T A R T. The probability is therefore 1/60.

This rule can be extended to cases with s_1 objects of one kind, s_2 of another kind, and s_3 of a third kind. The number of distinguishably different permutations of the n objects becomes:

$$_nD_n = \frac{n!}{s_1! s_2! s_3!} \tag{5.10}$$

EXAMPLE 5.27

Consider six stimuli: three are red, two are green, and 1 is blue. How many distinguishably different permutations of the six objects are possible?

Solution

$$_nD_n = \frac{n!}{s_1! s_2!} = \frac{6!}{3! 2!} = \frac{6 \times 5 \times 4 \times 3 \times 2 \times 1}{(3 \times 2 \times 1)(2 \times 1)} = 60$$

EXAMPLE 5.28

Consider five slips of paper, and suppose an H appears on three slips and a T appears on two slips. How many distinguishably different orderings of the slips are possible?

Solution

$$_nD_n = \frac{n!}{s_1! s_2!} = \frac{5!}{3! 2!} = 10$$

EXAMPLE 5.29

Imagine a board that contains five slots. Suppose three balls roll randomly around the board—perhaps a red one, a green one, and a blue one. Each ball eventually falls into a different slot. How many different arrangements of balls in slots are possible?

Solution   Imagine two extra, invisible balls which occupy the two slots that remain vacant. Then $n = 5$; but the two invisible balls look alike so $s = 2$. The number of different arrangements of balls in slots, then, is $5!/2! = 60$. [If the three real balls looked alike too, then there would be three balls of one kind ($s_1 = 3$) and two (invisible) balls of another kind ($s_2 = 2$).] The number of distinguishably different arrangements would be $5!/3!2! = 10$ possible arrangements.

Variation 4   (Permutations: n different objects are available but only r are used)

An experimenter has six different stimuli to show a subject. If he showed all six, he could choose any of $6!$ different orders. Suppose he only wants to show three stimuli, though, to any one subject. How many different orders of objects might be shown? We speak here of the "permutations of three objects chosen from a set of six." The number of such permutations is denoted $_nP_r = {_6}P_3$. The subscript six refers to the set of six objects; P_3 tells that three of them are selected. The experiment therefore contains three simple events: E_1-E_2-E_3. First the experimenter chooses one of the six alternatives (E_1); then he chooses one of the remaining five alternatives (E_2); and finally he chooses one of the remaining four (E_3). The number of permutations is $6 \times 5 \times 4 = 120$.

In general,

$$_nP_r \text{ equals } "n \times n - 1 \times n - 2 \cdots" \text{ to } r \text{ factors}$$

EXAMPLE 5.30

Ten books are available for an exhibit, but the shelf can only hold three of them. How many different orders of books can appear on the shelf?

Solution   The experiment is denoted E_1-E_2-E_3. Ten choices exist for E_1, nine choices for E_2, and eight choices for E_3. $_{10}P_3 = 10 \times 9 \times 8 = 720$ possible arrangements.

EXAMPLE 5.31

How many different trigrams can be formed from the letters B, L, O, S, Y? A trigram is three letters long—e.g., BLO, LOB, BLS—and a given letter is only to appear once in a trigram.

Solution Let us denote a trigram by three blank spaces: ___ ___ ___ .
Each blank is a separate event: E_1 E_2 E_3. There are five alternatives for E_1,
four alternatives for E_2, and three alternatives for E_3. $_5P_3 = 5 \times 4 \times 3 = 60$.
Thus, 60 different trigrams can be formed.

EXAMPLE 5.32

The letters B, L, O, S, Y are arranged haphazardly to form trigrams like those
described above. What is the probability that the resulting trigram contains a
B in Position 1 and an S in Position 2?

Solution Altogether there are 60 possible trigrams. Those meeting the requirement could be denoted B ___ S ___ ___ . Position 3 can be filled by three
possible letters—L, O, or Y. Therefore $1 \times 1 \times 3 = 3$; three arrangements
meet the requirement, and the probability equals $\frac{3}{60} = \frac{1}{20}$.

We have written the formula for $_nP_r$ as "$n \times n-1 \times n-2 \times \cdots$" to r
factors. This formula resembles $n!$ except for one thing: the last $n-r$ factors
have been removed. Therefore, the formula for $_nP_r$ can be written this way:

$$_nP_r = \frac{n!}{(n-r)!} = n \times n-1 \times n-2 \cdots (\text{to } r \text{ factors}) \qquad (5.11)$$

Consider the value of $_{10}P_3$; it equals $10 \times 9 \times 8$. By writing $10!/(10-3)!$
the denominator cancels the numerator's last 7 factors, leaving $10 \times 9 \times 8$.
$_5P_2$ is written either 5×4 or $5!/3!$.

It is convenient to let $0!$ equal 1. Then $_nP_n$ fits the rule too:

$$_nP_n = \frac{n!}{(n-n)!} = \frac{n!}{0!} = n!$$

Variation 5 (Combinations)

Imagine five objects A, B, C, D, and E, and consider the permutations of 3:
$_5P_3 = 5 \times 4 \times 3 = 60$. The 60 permutations are shown below:

ABC	ABD	ABE	ACD	ACE	ADE	BCD	BCE	BDE	CDE
ACB	ADB	AEB	ADC	AEC	AED	BDC	BEC	BED	CED
BAC	BAD	BAE	CAD	CAE	DAE	CBD	CBE	DBE	DCE
BCA	BDA	BEA	CDA	CEA	DEA	CDB	CEB	DEB	DEC
CAB	DAB	EAB	DAC	EAC	EAD	DBC	EBC	EBD	ECD
CBA	DBA	EBA	DCA	ECA	EDA	DCB	ECB	EDB	EDC

Notice the first six permutations. They all involve the same three objects—A, B, and C—but in different orders. The second group contains permutations of the objects A, B, and D; the third, permutations of A, B, and E; and so on.

Each group is called a *combination* of the objects. A combination refers to a collection of objects regardless of their order: ABC, ACB, BAC, BCA, CAB, and CBA are all examples of a single combination.

Certain questions that an experimenter asks concern *combinations*, not permutations. For example, let us designate five people as A, B, C, D, and E, and consider the different three-man committees that might be formed. The committee A B C is the same committee as B A C. How many different committees can be formed?

The symbol $_nC_r$ denotes the number of possible r-object combinations. It equals:

$$_nC_r = \frac{n!}{(n-r)!\,r!} \tag{5.12}$$

If $n = 5$, the number of three-man committees equals:

$$_5C_3 = \frac{5!}{2!\,3!} = \frac{5 \times 4 \times 3 \times 2 \times 1}{(2 \times 1)(3 \times 2 \times 1)} = 10$$

To derive the formula for $_nC_r$, first consider the number of permutations of r objects: $_nP_r = n!/(n-r)!$. Any given collection of r objects can be permuted in $r!$ ways, and these $r!$ permutations all yield the same combination. Therefore, any one *combination* allows $r!$ *permutations*. One combination of three objects, for example, allows $3! = 6$ permutations. The $_nP_r$ permutations can therefore be subdivided this way:

(Total number of permutations) =

$$\begin{pmatrix}\text{Number of } r\text{-object} \\ \text{combinations}\end{pmatrix} \times \begin{pmatrix} r! \; \textit{permutations} \\ \text{of the objects in} \\ \text{a single} \\ \text{combination} \end{pmatrix}$$

$$_nP_r = \quad _nC_r \quad \times \quad r!$$

$$_nC_r = \quad _nP_r/r!$$

$$= \frac{n!}{(n-r)!} \Big/ r!$$

$$= \frac{n!}{(n-r)!\,r!}$$

EXAMPLE 5.33

How many three-member groups can be formed out of seven people? (Group ABC is the same group as Group BCA.)

Solution

$$_7C_3 = \frac{7!}{4!\,3!} = 35 \text{ different groups}$$

EXAMPLE 5.34

Consider five pennies, Penny 1 through Penny 5. Suppose three pennies are "heads" and two are "tails." (Penny 1, Penny 3, and Penny 4, for example, might be the heads, while the others are the tails.) How many different three-penny combinations can be formed?

Solution $_5C_3 = 5!/2!\,3! = 10$, so 10 different three-penny combinations are possible.

EXAMPLE 5.35

Five pennies can fall in $2^5 = 32$ possible patterns: H H H H H, H H H H T, and so on. What is the probability that one of these patterns contains 3 heads and 2 tails?

Solution First determine how many patterns show 3 heads and 2 tails: $_5C_3 = 10$. The probability is therefore $^{10}\!/_{32}$.

EXERCISES

True or False?

5.1 A population contains the scores 51, 52, 53, and 54. You do not know their frequencies, and you do not know how many scores there are. You only know the probability of each score's occurrence. For this population, you could compute:

(*a*) the mean
   Answer: T
(*b*) the standard deviation
   Answer: T
(*c*) the median
   Answer: T
(*d*) Q_1
   Answer: T

Problems

5.2 Here is a set of data.

X_i	P_i
1	.20
5	.10
12	.40
15	.30

(a) Compute the mean using the expectation formula: Mean $= E(X)$.
    Answer: 10

(b) "Variance" is really a special kind of mean—a mean of $(X - \bar{X})^2$ values. Think of each $(X - \bar{X})^2$ value occurring as often as the corresponding X value. For any given value, $P[(X - \bar{X})^2]$ is the same as the corresponding $P(X)$. Using this fact, compute the variance from the expectation formula: Variance $= E[(X - \bar{X})^2]$.
    Answer: 27.8

5.3 Here is a set of data.

X_i	P_i
4	.50
6	.10
7	.10
8	.10
9	.10
10	.10

(a) Compute $E(X)$, $E(X^2)$, and $E(X - \bar{X})^2$.
    Answer: 6.0; 41.0; 5.0

(b) The variance can be computed in two different ways. One way involves the squared deviation scores: Variance $= E[(X - \bar{X})^2]$. The other involves the following formula:

$$\text{Variance} = E(X^2) - [E(X)]^2.$$

(This formula comes from the alternate formula for computing S^2: $\Sigma X^2/N - \bar{X}^2$.) Compute the variance by each method and show that your answers agree.

5.4 There are only four different score values in a certain frequency distribution. Each score is reported below as a deviation from the mean. Its relative frequency is also reported.

$X - \bar{X}$	$P =$ relative frequency
$+2$	.3
$+1$	.4
-3	.2
-4	.1

(*a*) Check the statements below that one could compute from the information given above.

_____ N
_____ ΣX of the original distribution
_____ the mean of the original distribution
_____ the median of the original distribution
_____ the 30th percentile score of the original distribution
_____ the mode of the original distribution
Answer: none

(*b*) Compute S^2, the variance of the distribution.
Answer: 5

5.5 In a survey of 100 students, the investigator determined the number who were currently studying various languages. Here are the results: Spanish, 28; German, 30; French, 42; Spanish and German, 8; Spanish and French, 10; German and French, 5; all three languages, 3.

(*a*) Make a Venn diagram to show the various relationships. Use three overlapping circles.

(*b*) How many students were studying no language at all?
Answer: 20

(*c*) How many had French as their only language?
Answer: 30

(*d*) Within this group, what is the probability that a student study German? [Call this probability $P(G)$.]
Answer: .30

(*e*) Determine $P(G \cup F)$.
Answer: .67

(*f*) Determine $P(F \cap S)$.
Answer: .10

(*g*) Determine $P(F|G)$.
Answer: $5/30 = .17$

(*h*) Determine $P(G|F)$.
Answer: $5/42$

(*i*) Determine $P(G|F \cap S)$.
Answer: .30

5.6 Men and women were polled after they viewed a film. The results show how many people of each sex liked or disliked the film:

	Liked the film (L)	Disliked the film (D)	
Men (M)	40	60	100
Women (W)	210	190	400
	250	250	500

(a)   Compute $P(L)$.
Answer: .50

(b)   Compute $P(M)$.
Answer: .20

(c)   Compute $P(L|M)$.
Answer: .40

(d)   Two of these probabilities taken together tell whether " liking the film " is independent of sex. Which two? Are the two variables independent?
Answer: $P(L)$ and $P(L|M)$. No

(e)   Compute $P(M|L)$.
Answer: $^{40}/_{250} = .16$

5.7   Complete the following table so that " liking the film " is independent of sex.

	Liked the film (L)	Disliked the film (D)	
Men (M)	40	60	100
Women (W)			400
			500

Answer: Women: 160; 240

(a)   Compute $P(L)$ and $P(L|M)$.
Answer: $P(L) = .40$; $P(L|M) = .40$

(b)   Compute $P(M)$ and $P(M|L)$.
Answer: $P(M) = .20$; $P(M|L) = .20$

5.8 $P(A) = .40$ and $P(B) = .50$. If A and B are independent, $P(A \cup B) = $ _____.
Answer: .70

5.9   Suppose $P(A \cup B) = 1/2$, $P(A) = 1/4$, and $P(B) = 3/8$.

(a)   Compute $P(A \cap B)$.
Answer: $\frac{1}{8}$

(b)   Consider individuals who have characteristic A. What proportion of them will have characteristic B?
Answer: $\frac{1}{2}$

(c)   What is the probability that an individual has characteristic A and *not* characteristic B?
Answer: $\frac{1}{8}$

5.10   If $P(A|B) = .50$, the highest possible value of $P(A \cap B)$ is _____.
Answer: .50

5.11   In how many ways can 5 differently colored stimulus objects be arranged in a row?
Answer: 120

5.12   In how many ways can 10 people be seated on a bench if only 4 seats are available?
Answer: $10 \cdot 9 \cdot 8 \cdot 7 = 5,040$

5.13   How many arrangements are possible for seating 5 men and 4 women in a row so that the women occupy the even places?
Answer: for odds: 120; for evens: 24; 120 × 24 = 2,880

5.14   How many 4-digit numbers can be formed with the 10 digits $0, 1, 2, 3, \ldots 9$:
   (a)   if repetitions are allowed and 0 can occur as a first digit?
         Answer: 10 × 10 × 10 × 10 = 10,000
   (b)   if repetitions are not allowed and 0 can occur as a first digit?
         Answer: 10 × 9 × 8 × 7 = 5,040
   (c)   if the last digit must be 0 and repetitions are not allowed?
         Answer: 9 × 8 × 7 = 504

5.15   Five red stimulus objects, two white stimulus objects, and 3 blue stimulus objects are arranged in a row. If all objects of one color are indistinguishable from one another, how many different arrangements are possible?

Answer: $\dfrac{10!}{5!\,3!\,2!} = 2{,}520$

5.16   In how many ways can small groups of 5 people be selected out of 9 people?

Answer: $_9C_5 = \dfrac{9!}{5!\,4!} = 126$

5.17   Five items are available for a test. How many different 1-item tests can be formed? 2-item tests? 3-item tests? 4-item tests? 5-item tests?
Answer: 1-item tests: $5 = {_5C_1}$; 2-item tests: $10 = {_5C_2}$; 3-item tests: $10 = {_5C_3}$; 4-item tests: $5 = {_5C_4}$; 5-item tests: $1 = {_5C_5}$

5.18   From 7 consonants and 5 vowels, how many words (meaningful and meaningless) can be formed consisting of 4 different consonants and 3 different vowels if consonants and vowels must alternate?
Answer: (7 × 6 × 5 × 4)(5 × 4 × 3) = 50,400

5.19   Suppose a box contains 3 white balls and 2 black balls. Let E_1 stand for the event "The first ball drawn is black" and E_2 for the event "The second ball drawn is black." The balls are not replaced after being drawn.
   (a)   What is the probability of E_1?
         Answer: $P(E_1) = \tfrac{2}{5}$
   (b)   If the first ball drawn is in fact black, what is the probability of E_2?
         Answer: $P(E_2 \mid E_1) = \tfrac{1}{4}$
   (c)   If the first ball drawn is white, what is the probability of E_2?
         Answer: $P(E_2 \mid W_1) = \tfrac{2}{4}$
   (d)   What is the probability of the joint event E_1E_2?
         Answer: $P(E_1E_2) = P(E_1)P(E_2 \mid E_1) = (\tfrac{2}{5})(\tfrac{1}{4}) = \tfrac{1}{10}$

5.20   Suppose you roll two dice once, a red die and a white one. What is the probability of obtaining a 5 on the red die and a 6 on the white one?
Answer: $\tfrac{1}{6} \times \tfrac{1}{6} = \tfrac{1}{36}$

5.21   Suppose you roll two dice once. What is the probability that 11 spots occur?
Answer: $\frac{1}{36} + \frac{1}{36} = \frac{1}{18}$

5.22   (a)   In a normal distribution of scores, what is the probability that a person's
z score exceed $+1.65$?
Answer: .05
(b)   In a normal distribution of scores, what is the probability that a person
get a z score more deviant from the mean than 1.96 (in either direction)?
Answer: .05
(c)   What is the probability that a person's score on each of two tests is more
than 2.58 standard deviations away from the mean—if the two test
scores are independent and normally distributed?
Answer: .01 × .01 = .0001

5.23   In an ordinary, well-shuffled deck of cards:
(a)   what is the probability of drawing a heart?
Answer: .25
(b)   what is the probability of drawing either a heart or a spade?
Answer: .50
(c)   what is the probability of drawing either a heart or a red card?
Answer: .50
(d)   what is the probability of drawing a red card?
Answer: .50
(e)   what is the probability of drawing a card that is both 3 and a heart (i.e.,
the 3 of hearts)?
Answer: $\frac{1}{13} \times \frac{1}{4} = \frac{1}{52}$
(f)   what is the probability of drawing a card that is both red and a heart?
Answer: .25

5.24   (a)   Suppose the scores on two tests are uncorrelated (independent). What
is the probability that a subject is both in the lowest quarter of the distribution on one test (*either one*) and in the highest quarter on the other?
Answer: $\frac{1}{8}$
(b)   Suppose r between the two tests is $+1.00$. What then is the probability
that a subject is both in the lowest quarter on one of the tests and in the
highest quarter on the other?
Answer: 0
(c)   Suppose r between the two tests is -1.00. What then is the probability
that a subject is both in the lowest quarter on one of the tests (*either one*)
and in the highest quarter on the other?
Answer: $P(L_1 \cap H_2) + P(H_1 \cap L_2) = \frac{1}{4} + \frac{1}{4} = \frac{1}{2}$

5.25   Subjects in an experiment were asked to work on two problems, Problem A
and Problem B. Let $P(A)$ denote the probability that a subject solved Problem
A, and let $P(B)$ denote the probability that he solved Problem B. Suppose
$P(A) = .20$, $P(B) = .10$, and $P(A|B) = .60$. Determine $P(B|A)$.
Answer: .30

5.26 The probability that a man vote for a certain candidate is .28. The probability that his wife vote for that candidate is .32. The conditional probability that his wife vote for the candidate, given that he does, is .72. Compute the following probabilities:

(a) that both the man and his wife vote for the candidate.
Answer: .28 × .72 = .2016

(b) that either vote for the candidate.
Answer: .40

(c) the conditional probability that the man does, given that his wife does.
Answer: .63

5.27 A box contains five white kittens and four black kittens. An experimenter selects two kittens in a row. What is the probability that he pulls out a black kitten first and then a white kitten?
Answer: $5/18$

6

THE BINOMIAL
DISTRIBUTION

In this chapter we examine the binomial distribution, a theoretical frequency distribution. The binomial distribution allows us to compute complicated probabilities with ease. It is also related to the normal distribution in an interesting way.

6.1 INTRODUCTION TO THE BINOMIAL DISTRIBUTION

Suppose five subjects participate in an experiment. Each subject tosses a penny once, and the subject's outcome (a head or a tail) constitutes one simple event. Together the five simple events comprise the full experiment: E_1-E_2-E_3-E_4-E_5. This experiment has 32 possible outcomes. Let us analyze these outcomes into different types of patterns. How many of them contain three heads and two tails? As Example 5.34 showed, there are $_5C_3 = 10$ outcomes of that type.

Pattern: 3H and 2T	Subject 1	Subject 2	Subject 3	Subject 4	Subject 5
Outcome 1:	T	T	H	H	H
Outcome 2:	T	H	T	H	H
Outcome 3:	T	H	H	T	H
Outcome 4:	T	H	H	H	T
Outcome 5:	H	T	T	H	H
Outcome 6:	H	T	H	T	H
Outcome 7:	H	T	H	H	T
Outcome 8:	H	H	T	T	H
Outcome 9:	H	H	T	H	T
Outcome 10:	H	H	H	T	T

On the other hand, consider the outcomes with four heads and one tail. How many outcomes fit that pattern? $_5C_4 = 5$ and the 5 patterns are shown below.

Pattern: 4H and 1T	Subject 1	Subject 2	Subject 3	Subject 4	Subject 5
Outcome 1:	T	H	H	H	H
Outcome 2:	H	T	H	H	H
Outcome 3:	H	H	T	H	H
Outcome 4:	H	H	H	T	H
Outcome 5:	H	H	H	H	T

Now consider *all* the different types—"five heads and 0 tails," "four heads and one tail," and so on. These various types are shown in Table 6.1. The table also tells how many patterns fit each type. Notice that the numbers sum to 32.

Sometimes an outcome is described by a score. The score might tell, say, how many heads appear in the pattern. Scores of this kind also appear in Table 6.1; they range from 0 (0 heads and five tails) to 5 (five heads and 0 tails). The score "3," then, is a shorthand way of describing the pattern "three heads and two tails." As the table shows, 0 and 5 are relatively rare outcomes; 2 and 3 are fairly common. "3," for example, accounts for 10 of the 32 patterns.

TABLE 6.1   Experimental outcomes that occur when five subjects each toss one penny

Type of outcome (pattern)	Score (the number of heads)	Number of outcomes that produce this pattern
5H and 0T	5	$\dfrac{5!}{5!0!} = 1$
4H and 1T	4	$\dfrac{5!}{4!1!} = 5$
3H and 2T	3	$\dfrac{5!}{3!2!} = 10$
2H and 3T	2	$\dfrac{5!}{2!3!} = 10$
1H and 4T	1	$\dfrac{5!}{1!4!} = 5$
0H and 5T	0	$\dfrac{5!}{0!5!} = 1$
		32 possible outcomes

Binomial expansion

$(a + b)^5$ is an instruction to multiply five $(a + b)$ terms together. When this multiplication is performed, the answer is:

$$(a + b)^5 = a^5 + 5a^4b + 10a^3b^2 + 10a^2b^3 + 5ab^4 + b^5$$

$(a + b)^5$ is called a binomial; its expansion will help us reconstruct Table 6.1 very rapidly. Therefore, as our next step, let us review the steps in expanding the binomial.

When $(a + b)^n$ is expanded, there are $n + 1$ terms. The expansion of $(a + b)^5$ contains 6 terms. The first term contains $a^n b^0$ (that is, a^n), and the last term contains $a^0 b^n$ (that is, b^n). In each successive term, the power of a drops by 1, and the power of b increases by 1:

$$(a + b)^5 : a^5 \quad a^4b \quad a^3b^2 \quad a^2b^3 \quad ab^4 \quad b^5$$
$$(a + b)^n : a^n \quad a^{n-1}b \quad a^{n-2}b^2 \quad \cdots \quad a^r b^{n-r} \quad \cdots \quad ab^{n-1} \quad b^n$$

In general, each term has the form $a^r b^{n-r}$.

Next, each term is multiplied by some coefficient. This coefficient is always $_nC_r$. For example, the coefficient that appears in front of a^2b^3 is $_5C_2 = 5!/(2!3!)$.

Finally, the terms are added together.

$$(a + b)^5 = {}_5C_5\,a^5 + {}_5C_4\,a^4b + {}_5C_3\,a^3b^2 + {}_5C_2\,a^2b^3 + {}_5C_1ab^4 + {}_5C_0\,b^5$$

$$= \frac{5!}{5!}\,a^5 + \frac{5!}{4!\,1!}\,a^4b + \frac{5!}{3!\,2!}\,a^3b^2 + \frac{5!}{2!\,3!}\,a^2b^3 + \frac{5!}{1!\,4!}\,ab^4 + \frac{5!}{5!}\,b^5$$

$$= a^5 + 5a^4b + 10a^3b^2 + 10a^2b^3 + 5ab^4 + b^5$$

$$(a + b)^n = \frac{n!}{n!}\,a^n + \frac{n!}{(n-1)!\,1!}\,a^{n-1}b + \frac{n!}{(n-2)!\,2!}\,a^{n-2}b^2 + \cdots$$

$$+ \frac{n!}{r!\,(n-r)!}\,a^rb^{n-r} + \cdots + \frac{n!}{n!}\,b^n$$

Certain experiments can be described by a binomial expansion. The experiment must contain n simple events, and each event must have the same two possible outcomes, a or b. For example, suppose five pennies are tossed. $(H + T)$ describes the alternatives for each simple event, H or T. And $(H + T)^5$ tells that the experiment is composed of five simple events like it. $(H + T)^5$ is expanded this way:

$$(H + T)^5 = H^5 + 5H^4T + 10H^3T^2 + 10H^2T^3 + 5HT^4 + T^5$$

Each term of the expansion describes one type of result. $10H^3T^2$, for example, describes outcomes with three heads and two tails; there are 10 outcomes of that type. $5H^4T$ describes outcomes with four heads and one tail; there are five outcomes of that type. Thus, the expansion fully describes the results shown in Table 6.1. Altogether there are $2^n = 2^5 = 32$ outcomes, so the coefficients must sum to 32: $1 + 5 + 10 + 10 + 5 + 1 = 32$.

EXAMPLE 6.1

Consider a six-item test, and suppose each item is scored right (R) or wrong (W). As an experiment, someone guesses each answer. If he guessed perfectly, his pattern would contain six R's and 0 W's. If he missed one item, his pattern would contain five R's and one W. (a) How many different outcomes are possible altogether? (b) Describe the different types of results.

Solution   (a) The experiment involves six simple events. Each simple event has two alternatives—R or W—so altogether there are $2^6 = 64$ possible results.

(b) Each simple event is described as $(R + W)$; the experiment as a whole, $(R + W)^6$. We therefore expand the binomial $(R + W)^6$.

$$(R + W)^6 = \frac{6!}{6!\,0!}\,R^6 + \frac{6!}{5!\,1!}\,R^5W + \frac{6!}{4!\,2!}\,R^4W^2 + \frac{6!}{3!\,3!}\,R^3W^3$$

$$+ \frac{6!}{2!\,4!}\,R^2W^4 + \frac{6!}{1!\,5!}\,RW^5 + \frac{6!}{0!\,6!}\,W^6$$

$$= R^6 + 6R^5W + 15R^4W^2 + 20R^3W^3 + 15R^2W^4 + 6RW^5 + W^6$$

As a check, the coefficients must sum to 2^6: $1 + 6 + 15 + 20 + 15 + 6 + 1 = 64$.

Each term describes a different type of result: R^6, for example, describes a perfect paper, a score of 6. That score is only achieved in one way: R R R R R R. $6R^5W$ describes a test with five correct responses and one error; that score occurs in six different ways: W R R R R R, R W R R R R, and so on.

Let us define the experiment's "score" as the number of correct responses. The score can range from 0 (none right) to 6 (all right). The following table summarizes these different results.

Type of pattern	Score	Number of outcomes which produce this pattern
6R and 0W	6	1
5R and 1W	5	6
4R and 2W	4	15
3R and 3W	3	20
2R and 4W	2	15
1R and 5W	1	6
0R and 6W	0	1
		64 possible outcomes

6.2 BINOMIAL DISTRIBUTION AND PROBABILITIES

The binomial expansion also helps compute probabilities. This section will illustrate that procedure.

Suppose a multiple-choice test has six items, and each item offers four alternatives. The probability is $\frac{1}{4}$ that any one answer is correctly guessed. What is the probability that all six answers are correctly guessed? The items are independent, so this probability equals $(\frac{1}{4})^6 = \frac{1}{4096}$. (Put another way, there are 4 choices per item, hence $4^6 = 4096$ possible answer sheets. Only one is entirely correct—say, B C C A D A—so the probability equals $\frac{1}{4096}$.)

Now let us complicate the question. What is the probability that the subject correctly guesses five items and misses one item? What is the probability that he earns the score 5? Consider one way of earning a 5: (Item 1)R; (Item 2)W; (Item 3)R; (Item 4)R; (Item 5)R; (Item 6)R. The probability of this particular pattern is $(\frac{1}{4})(\frac{3}{4})(\frac{1}{4})(\frac{1}{4})(\frac{1}{4})(\frac{1}{4}) = (\frac{1}{4})^5(\frac{3}{4}) = \frac{3}{4096}$. But there are other ways of earning the same score: Perhaps Item 1 is missed (and the other items are correct). Or perhaps Item 3 is missed. There are $_6C_5 = 6!/5!\,1! = 6$ patterns that contain 5R's and 1W. The probability of each pattern is $(\frac{1}{4})^5(\frac{3}{4}) = \frac{3}{4096}$; so altogether, the probability of 5R's and 1W is $6(\frac{1}{4})^5(\frac{3}{4}) = \frac{18}{4096}$. This conclusion is shown in Table 6.2.

TABLE 6.2 The probability of different scores described by the binomial

Score (r)	An example of one pattern that gives this score — Item 1 2 3 4 5 6	Probability of this one pattern $(1/4)^r(3/4)^{n-r}$	Number of patterns that give this score $_nC_r$	Probability of this score
6	R R R R R R	$(1/4)^6 = 1/4096 = .0002$	$\dfrac{6!}{6!0!} = 1$	$1(.0002) = .000$
5	W R R R R R	$(1/4)^5(3/4) = 3/4096 = .0007$	$\dfrac{6!}{5!1!} = 6$	$6(.0007) = .004$
4	W W R R R R	$(1/4)^4(3/4)^2 = 9/4096 = .0022$	$\dfrac{6!}{4!2!} = 15$	$15(.0022) = .033$
3	W W W R R R	$(1/4)^3(3/4)^3 = 27/4096 = .0066$	$\dfrac{6!}{3!3!} = 20$	$20(.0066) = .132$
2	W W W W R R	$(1/4)^2(3/4)^4 = 81/4096 = .0199$	$\dfrac{6!}{2!4!} = 15$	$15(.0198) = .297$
1	W W W W W R	$(1/4)(3/4)^5 = 243/4096 = .0594$	$\dfrac{6!}{1!5!} = 6$	$6(.0594) = .356$
0	W W W W W W	$(3/4)^6 = 729/4096 = .1781$	$\dfrac{6!}{0!6!} = 1$	$1(.1781) = .178$

Algebraic Summary:

Score $= r$ — Pattern contains r cases of R and $n - r$ cases of W.	Probability of one pattern $= (1/4)^r(3/4)^{n-r}$	Number of patterns that yield the score $r = {}_nC_r$	Probability of the score $r = {}_nC_r(1/4)^r(3/4)^{n-r}$

Table 6.2 lists all the different scores and their probabilities. In Column 1 the scores range from 0 to n. Column 2 shows one pattern as an example of each score. The pattern contains r correct responses and $n - r$ errors—for the score 4, 4R's and 2W's. Column 3 then reports the probability of that example. The probability always equals $(\frac{1}{4})^r(\frac{3}{4})^{n-r}$. But other patterns also yield that score, and Column 4 tells how many. The score 4, for example, is produced in $_6C_4 = 15$ different ways.

Finally, Column 5 reports the probability of each score: Each value in Column 5 equals the probability of any one pattern (Column 3) times the number of possible patterns (Column 4). The resulting probabilities sum to 1.00.

The binomial expansion can perform this job with much less bookkeeping. First, expand the binomial; let R denote "right" and W denote "wrong."

$$(R + W)^6 = R^6 + 6R^5W + 15R^4W^2 + 20R^3W^3 + 15R^2W^4 + 6RW^5 + W^6$$

Now replace R by the *probability* of a correct response: $P(R) = \frac{1}{4}$. This probability is usually denoted p, so $p = \frac{1}{4}$. Also replace W by the *probability* of an error: $P(W) = \frac{3}{4}$. That value is usually denoted q, so $q = \frac{3}{4}$.

$$
\begin{aligned}
(p + q)^6 &= p^6 + 6p^5q + 15p^4q^2 + 20p^3q^3 + 15p^2q^4 + 6pq^5 + q^6 \\
&= (\tfrac{1}{4})^6 + 6(\tfrac{1}{4})^5(\tfrac{3}{4}) + 15(\tfrac{1}{4})^4(\tfrac{3}{4})^2 + 20(\tfrac{1}{4})^3(\tfrac{3}{4})^3 \\
&\quad + 15(\tfrac{1}{4})^2(\tfrac{3}{4})^4 + 6(\tfrac{1}{4})(\tfrac{3}{4})^5 + (\tfrac{3}{4})^6 \\
&= \frac{1}{4096} + \frac{18}{4096} + \frac{135}{4096} + \frac{540}{4096} + \frac{1215}{4096} + \frac{1458}{4096} + \frac{729}{4096}
\end{aligned}
$$

$(R + W)^6$, then, has been replaced by $(\frac{1}{4} + \frac{3}{4})^6$. (Notice that the terms all sum to 1.)

The expansion of $(p + q)^6$ can be interpreted this way. Each term describes some general outcome: p^2q^4, for example, refers to 2 right answers and 4 wrong ones. This probability, $(\frac{1}{4})^2(\frac{3}{4})^4$, tells the probability of any one pattern of 2R's and 4W's, like R W R W W W. The coefficient is $_6C_2$, so 15 patterns can be formed from 2R's and 4W's. With all 15 patterns, the probability of the score 2 is:

$$P(\text{Score} = 2) = {}_6C_2(\tfrac{1}{4})^2(\tfrac{3}{4})^4 = 15(^{81}/_{4096}) = 0.297$$

To summarize, the binomial $(A + B)^n$ describes certain kinds of experiments. The experiment must contain n simple events, and each event must have two possible outcomes. If the simple events are all independent, the binomial is used to compute the *probability* of each outcome: To compute a probability from $(A + B)^n$, replace A by p (the probability of A); and replace B by q (the probability of B). Then expand $(p + q)^n$. The resulting probabilities form a *binomial distribution*.

EXAMPLE 6.2

Five pennies are tossed, and each outcome is scored H or T. The probability of H is $\frac{1}{2}$, and the events are independent. Describe the different possible outcomes and their probabilities.

Solution

$$(H + T)^5 = H^5 + 5H^4T + 10H^3T^2 + 10H^2T^3 + 5HT^4 + T^5$$
$$(p + q)^5 = p^5 + 5p^4q + 10p^3q^2 + 10p^2q^3 + 5pq^4 + q^5$$
$$(\tfrac{1}{2} + \tfrac{1}{2})^5 = (\tfrac{1}{2})^5 + 5(\tfrac{1}{2})^4(\tfrac{1}{2}) + 10(\tfrac{1}{2})^3(\tfrac{1}{2})^2$$
$$+ 10(\tfrac{1}{2})^2(\tfrac{1}{2})^3 + 5(\tfrac{1}{2})(\tfrac{1}{2})^4 + (\tfrac{1}{2})^5$$

$$= \frac{1}{32} + \frac{5}{32} + \frac{10}{32} + \frac{10}{32} + \frac{5}{32} + \frac{1}{32}$$

$$= .03 + .16 + .31 + .31 + .16 + .03$$

The probability of one particular pattern—say, H T T H H—is $\frac{1}{32}$. But altogether, 10 patterns contain 3H's and 2T's. The probability of 3H's and 2T's, then, is .31. The binomial distribution is summarized below.

Score (Number of heads)	Nature of the outcome	Probability of this score	Number of times this score is expected In 64 expts.	In 100 expts.
5	5H and 0T	$\frac{1}{32} = .03$	2	3
4	4H and 1T	$\frac{5}{32} = .16$	10	16
3	3H and 2T	$\frac{10}{32} = .31$	20	31
2	2H and 3T	$\frac{10}{32} = .31$	20	31
1	1H and 4T	$\frac{5}{32} = .16$	10	16
0	0H and 5T	$\frac{1}{32} = .03$	2	3
		1.00	64 expts.	100 expts.

From Example 6.2, you can easily compute the probability of 4 or more heads: $P(4 \text{ or more heads}) = P(4 \text{ heads}) + P(5 \text{ heads}) = .16 + .03 = .19$. The probability of 2 or fewer heads equals $P(2 \text{ heads}) + P(1 \text{ head}) + P(0 \text{ heads}) = .31 + .16 + .03 = .50$.

EXAMPLE 6.3

An urn contains white balls and red balls. The probability of a red ball, $P(R)$, equals $\frac{1}{3}$. An experimenter draws a ball from the urn, notes its color, and replaces it. Then he repeats the procedure two more times. What is the probability that he draws at least one red ball?

Solution

$$(R + W)^3 = R^3 + 3R^2W + 3RW^2 + W^3$$
$$(p + q)^3 = p^3 + 3p^2q + 3pq^2 + q^3$$
$$(\tfrac{1}{3} + \tfrac{2}{3})^3 = (\tfrac{1}{3})^3 + 3(\tfrac{1}{3})^2(\tfrac{2}{3}) + 3(\tfrac{1}{3})(\tfrac{2}{3})^2 + (\tfrac{2}{3})^3$$

$$= \frac{1}{27} + \frac{6}{27} + \frac{12}{27} + \frac{8}{27}$$

$P(\text{at least 1 red ball}) = P(3 \text{ red}) + P(2 \text{ red}) + P(1 \text{ red})$
$$= \tfrac{1}{27} + \tfrac{6}{27} + \tfrac{12}{27}$$
$$= \tfrac{19}{27}$$

EXAMPLE 6.4

The probability of a certain gene in the American population is .30. An experimenter selects eight representative Americans and notes how many have the gene. (*a*) Describe the possible outcomes and their probabilities. (*b*) What is the probability that six people have the gene and two do not?

Solution   (*a*) Selecting eight people is like tossing eight pennies or drawing eight balls. Let G mean that the gene is present; let g mean that the gene is absent. This experiment contains eight simple events. Each event has two possible outcomes, G or g.

$$(G + g)^8 = G^8 + 8G^7g + 28G^6g^2 + 56G^5g^3 + 70G^4g^4 + 56G^3g^5$$
$$+ 28G^2g^6 + 8Gg^7 + g^8$$
$$(p + q)^8 = (.30 + .70)^8$$
$$= (.30)^8 + 8(.30)^7(.70) + 28(.30)^6(.70)^2 + 56(.30)^5(.70)^3$$
$$+ 70(.30)^4(.70)^4 + 56(.30)^3(.70)^5 + 28(.30)^2(.70)^6$$
$$+ 8(.30)(.70)^7 + (.70)^8$$

(*b*) The probability of 6G's and 2g's is:

$$P(6\text{G's and 2g's}) = \frac{8!}{6!\,2!}(.30)^6(.70)^2 = .010$$

The outcome, 6G's, is sometimes viewed as a score. An investigator might write $P(X = 6) = .010$.

6.3 SKEWNESS AND THE BINOMIAL DISTRIBUTION

Suppose a subject guesses the answers to a 4-item test. His score could range from 0 to 4, as the binomial expansion describes.

$$(R + W)^4 = R^4 + 4R^3W + 6R^2W^2 + 4RW^3 + W^4$$
$$(p + q)^4 = p^4 + 4p^3q + 6p^2q^2 + 4pq^3 + q^4$$

Once we knew the value of p, we could specify each score's probability.

Now consider three situations with different values of p. Situation A is a true-false test: Each item has two alternatives which are equally attractive, so $p = \frac{1}{2}$. Situation B is a four-alternative multiple-choice test, and $p = \frac{1}{4}$. Situation C is a ten-alternative multiple-choice test, and $p = \frac{1}{10}$. Consider $(p + q)^4$ in each case.

Situation A, $p = \frac{1}{2}$:

$$(p + q)^4 = (\tfrac{1}{2})^4 + 4(\tfrac{1}{2})^3(\tfrac{1}{2})$$

.0625 .2500

$$+ 6(\tfrac{1}{2})^2(\tfrac{1}{2})^2 + 4(\tfrac{1}{2})(\tfrac{1}{2})^3 + (\tfrac{1}{2})^4$$

.3750 .2500 .0625

Situation B, $p = \frac{1}{4}$:

$$(p + q)^4 = (\tfrac{1}{4})^4 + 4(\tfrac{1}{4})^3(\tfrac{3}{4})$$

.0039 .0469

$$+ 6(\tfrac{1}{4})^2(\tfrac{3}{4})^2 + 4(\tfrac{1}{4})(\tfrac{3}{4})^3 + (\tfrac{3}{4})^4$$

.2109 .4219 .3164

Situation C, $p = \frac{1}{10}$:

$$(p + q)^4 = (\tfrac{1}{10})^4 + 4(\tfrac{1}{10})^3(\tfrac{9}{10})$$

.0001 .0036

$$+ 6(\tfrac{1}{10})^2(\tfrac{9}{10})^2 + 4(\tfrac{1}{10})(\tfrac{9}{10})^3$$

.0486   .2916

$$+ (\tfrac{9}{10})^4$$

.6561

The different possible scores are shown in Table 6.3 with their probabilities.

TABLE 6.3   Three situations that illustrate the skewness of $(p + q)^4$ when p differs from $\frac{1}{2}$

Situation A: $p = \frac{1}{2}, q = \frac{1}{2}$

Score	Probability of this score	Expected frequency of this score (a) when 50 subjects are tested	(b) when 100 subjects are tested
4	.06	3.0	6.0
3	.25	12.5	25.0
2	.38	19.0	38.0
1	.25	12.5	25.0
0	.06	3.0	6.0
	1.00	50.0 subjects	100.0 subjects

Situation B: $p = \frac{1}{4}, q = \frac{3}{4}$

Score	Probability of this score	Expected frequency of this score (a) when 50 subjects are tested	(b) when 100 subjects are tested
4	.00⁺	0.0	0.0
3	.05	2.5	5.0
2	.21	10.5	21.0
1	.42	21.0	42.0
0	.32	16.0	32.0
	1.00	50.0 subjects	100.0 subjects

Situation C: $p = .10, q = .90$

Score	Probability of this score	Expected frequency of this score (a) when 50 subjects are tested	(b) when 100 subjects are tested
4	.00⁺	0.0	0.0
3	.00⁺	0.0	0.0
2	.05	2.5	5.0
1	.29	14.5	29.0
0	.66	33.0	66.0
	1.00	50.0 subjects	100.0 subjects

When $p = \frac{1}{2}$, the distribution is symmetrical: The probability of a perfect score, $P(X = 4)$, equals the probability of a 0 score, $P(X = 0)$. And the highest probability occurs in the middle where $X = 2$.

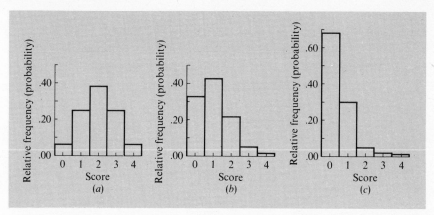

FIG. 6.1 Histograms showing the binomial distributions of Table 6.3. (*a*) Situation *A*: $p = \frac{1}{2}$, $q = \frac{1}{2}$. (*b*) Situation *B*: $p = \frac{1}{4}$, $q = \frac{3}{4}$. (*c*) Situation *C*: $p = .10$, $q = .90$.

If p is not $\frac{1}{2}$, the distribution is skewed. Consider Situation B, for example. The probability is very low that $X = 4$, but rather high that $X = 0$. Situation C is even more extreme. The probability is tiny that $X = 4$, but very high that $X = 0$.

These distributions appear as histograms in Fig. 6.1. Notice how skewed the distribution becomes as p moves away from $\frac{1}{2}$. The farther p is from $\frac{1}{2}$, the more skewed the distribution.

6.4 MEAN AND STANDARD DEVIATION OF THE BINOMIAL DISTRIBUTION

$(p + q)^4$ describes the probabilities for any one person's scores. But suppose the experiment were repeated many times. Say 100 subjects or 10,000 subjects took the test. They would generate a whole distribution of scores. What is the mean of the expected distribution?

Let us consider the scores of Situation A; that distribution appears in Fig. 6.1. The mean is denoted μ_{binomial}. (μ is the Greek letter *mu*.) For Situation A, μ_{binomial} equals 2. Therefore, on the average, examinees are expected to earn a score of 2 by guessing.

In any binomial distribution $(p + q)^n$, the mean is easy to compute; it equals np.

$$\mu_{\text{binomial}} = np \qquad (6.1)$$

In Situation A, $n = 4$ and $p = \frac{1}{2}$. Therefore $\mu_{\text{binomial}} = 4(\frac{1}{2}) = 2$. When the experiment is repeated many times, the average score would equal 2.

To confirm this value, suppose the experiment were repeated 10,000 times; say 10,000 people took the test. With everyone guessing, here is the expected distribution:

Score	Expected frequency
4	625
3	2500
2	3750
1	2500
0	625

10,000 people tested

The mean equals:

$$\overline{X} = \frac{\sum X}{N} = \frac{625(4) + 2500(3) + 3750(2) + 2500(1) + 625(0)}{10,000} = \frac{20,000}{10,000} = 2$$

The formula $\overline{X} = \sum[X_i \cdot P(X_i)]$ could also be used to compute the mean.

$$\overline{X} = \sum[X_i \cdot P(X_i)] = (4).0625 + (3).2500 + (2).3750 + (1).2500 + (0).0625$$
$$= 2$$

Therefore, we would expect the mean to equal 2. This expected mean is also called the *expectation* of X. It tells what score to expect on the average. With many subjects, $E(X) = \mu_{\text{binomial}} = np$. In Situation B, $E(X) = np = 4(\frac{1}{4}) = 1.00$: The average examinee should earn a score of 1.00. For Situation C, $E(X) = 0.40$.

The standard deviation of a binomial distribution is also easy to compute. This standard deviation is denoted σ_{binomial}. (σ is the Greek letter sigma.) It equals:

$$\sigma_{\text{binomial}} = \sqrt{npq} \tag{6.2}$$

For Situation A, the standard deviation is

$$\sqrt{npq} = \sqrt{4(\frac{1}{2})(\frac{1}{2})}$$
$$= \sqrt{1} = 1$$

To confirm this value, consider the distribution of 10,000 scores again, and compute the standard deviation. Use the general formula

$$S = \sqrt{\frac{\sum(X - \bar{X})^2}{N}}$$

$$S =$$
$$\sqrt{\frac{625(4-2)^2 + 2500(3-2)^2 + 3750(2-2)^2 + 2500(1-2)^2 + 625(0-2)^2}{10,000}}$$

$$= \sqrt{\frac{625(2)^2 + 2500(1)^2 + 3750(0)^2 + 2500(-1)^2 + 625(-2)^2}{10,000}}$$

$$= \sqrt{\frac{10,000}{10,000}} = 1$$

S^2 can also be viewed as a mean, a mean of squared deviation scores. Therefore, S^2 can be computed this way:

$$S^2 = \sum[(X_i - \bar{X})^2 \cdot P[X_i - \bar{X}]^2] \qquad (6.3)$$

With this formula:

$$S^2 = .0625(4-2)^2 + .2500(3-2)^2 + .3750(2-2)^2 + .2500(1-2)^2$$
$$+ .0625(0-2)^2$$

$$= 1$$
$$S = \sqrt{1} = 1$$

The two formulas,

$$\mu_{\text{binomial}} = np \qquad \text{and} \qquad \sigma_{\text{binomial}} = \sqrt{npq}$$

make the mean and standard deviation of a binomial distribution easy to compute. These two formulas are derived in the chapter appendix as Proofs 6.1 and 6.2.

The mean and standard deviation are given at the top of page 142 for each distribution in Table 6.3.

$(p + q)^n = (\frac{1}{2} + \frac{1}{2})^4$		$(p + q)^n = (\frac{1}{4} + \frac{3}{4})^4$		$(p + q)^n = (\frac{1}{10} + \frac{9}{10})^4$	
Score	probability	Score	probability	Score	probability
4	.0625	4	.0039	4	.0001
3	.2500	3	.0469	3	.0036
2	.3750	2	.2109	2	.0486
1	.2500	1	.4219	1	.2916
0	.0625	0	.3164	0	.6561

$\mu_{binomial} = np = 2$	$\mu_{binomial} = np = 1$	$\mu_{binomial} = np = 0.4$
$\sigma_{binomial} = \sqrt{npq}$	$\sigma_{binomial} = \sqrt{npq}$	$\sigma_{binomial} = \sqrt{npq}$
$= \sqrt{4(\frac{1}{2})(\frac{1}{2})}$	$= \sqrt{4(\frac{1}{4})(\frac{3}{4})}$	$= \sqrt{4(\frac{1}{10})(\frac{9}{10})}$
$= 1$	$= 0.87$	$= 0.60$

Thus, the experimenter readily knows what score to expect, on the average, and how much variability.

EXAMPLE 6.5

A multiple-choice test contains eight items, and each item offers three alternative choices. If the examinees all guess at the answers, what mean score is expected? What standard deviation?

Solution The test scores could range from 0 to 8. The different outcomes would be described by the binomial expansion $(p + q)^n = (\frac{1}{3} + \frac{2}{3})^8$. The expected mean is:

$$\mu_{binomial} = np = 8(\frac{1}{3}) = 2.67$$

The expected standard deviation is:

$$\sigma_{binomial} = \sqrt{npq} = \sqrt{8(\frac{1}{3})(\frac{2}{3})} = 1.33$$

Thus, we would expect the average subject to answer 2.67 items correctly by guessing. [Notice that it makes no difference *how many* people take the test; $E(X)$ is still 2.67.]

EXAMPLE 6.6

An experimenter has devised a new maze for testing laboratory rats, and the maze has eight choice points. The probability is $\frac{1}{3}$ that a rat respond correctly at each choice point. If many rats were tested, how many correct responses would you expect on the average? What standard deviation would you expect?

Solution

$$\mu_{\text{binomial}} = np = (8)(\tfrac{1}{3}) = 2.67$$

$$\sigma_{\text{binomial}} = \sqrt{npq} = 1.33$$

The average rat is expected to make 2.67 correct responses. Different rats' scores should have a standard deviation of 1.33.

EXAMPLE 6.7

According to a certain geneticist, every human being can be classified as either G or g. The probability is .30 that a person is G. Suppose the geneticist selects eight people for a study. He describes the eight-person group by a score which tells how many G individuals are in it. The probability of each score is given by: $(p + q)^8 = (.30 + .70)^8$.

Now suppose the geneticist examines many of these eight-person groups. What score would the average group exhibit? How much variability would occur in the scores of different groups?

Solution

$$\mu_{\text{binomial}} = np = 8(.30) = 2.4$$

$$\sigma_{\text{binomial}} = \sqrt{npq} = \sqrt{8(.30)(.70)} = 1.30$$

On the average, the different groups would show 2.4 G individuals. The standard deviation of different groups' scores would equal 1.30.

6.5 NORMAL CURVE APPROXIMATION TO THE BINOMIAL DISTRIBUTION

At times the binomial distribution resembles the normal curve. And when it does, the normal curve's properties can be used to describe the binomial distribution. This section illustrates that procedure.

Consider the binomial distribution $(p + q)^n$ when $p = \tfrac{1}{2}$. To be concrete, suppose a subject is guessing the answers to a true-false test. The expected scores are described by $(\tfrac{1}{2} + \tfrac{1}{2})^n$: For a 3-item test, $n = 3$; for a 10-item test, $n = 10$. Figure 6.2 describes the different distributions for these different-sized tests.

The binomial distribution looks more and more like a normal curve as n gets larger. In general, the binomial distributions in Fig. 6.2 can be described this way. First, each distribution resembles a normal curve, especially if n is large. Second, its mean equals np, and its standard deviation equals $\sqrt{npq}$. Therefore, in cases like these, we can sketch a binomial distribution by

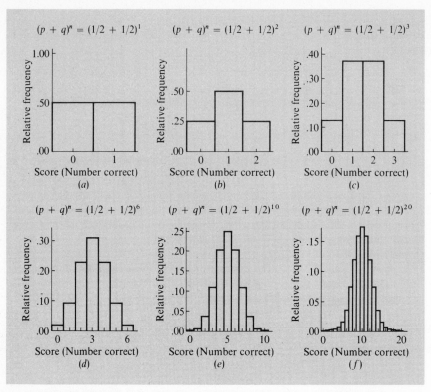

FIG. 6.2 Binomial distributions of $(p + q)^n$ when $p = \frac{1}{2}$ and $q = \frac{1}{2}$. (a) One-item test; (b) two-item test; (c) three-item test; (d) six-item test; (e) ten-item test; (f) twenty-item test.

drawing a normal curve; its mean is set equal to np; its standard deviation, to $\sqrt{npq}$. Then the normal curve is said to *approximate* the binomial distribution.

Here is a problem that illustrates the approximation: A subject was asked to judge brandies. He was given a pair of brandies, a cheap one and an expensive one, and he had to judge which was which. He was tested on 6 pairs, so his score could range from 0 to 6. What is the probability that he achieved the score 5? First let us answer this question by the exact method; then we will examine the normal curve approximation.

Exact method
First we expand the binomial.

$$(p + q)^6 = p^6 + 6p^5q + 15p^4q^2 + 20p^3q^3 + 15p^2q^4 + 6pq^5 + q^6$$
$(\frac{1}{2} + \frac{1}{2})^6$:   .02   .09   .23   .31   .23   .09   .02

The probability of "5" is .09.

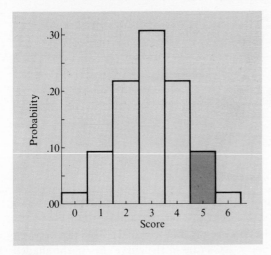

FIG. 6.3

The distribution might also be drawn as a histogram. Figure 6.3 tells the distribution of scores to expect in the long run. $\mu_{\text{binomial}} = np = 3$, so the histogram's mean equals 3. Its standard deviation equals $\sqrt{npq} = 1.23$. Especially notice the histogram's bar at 5; that bar occupies .09 of the graph's total area.

Normal curve approximation

Now let us approximate this histogram with a normal curve (Fig. 6.4). The normal curve's mean is set equal to 3 ($\mu_{\text{binomial}} = 3$), and its standard deviation, to 1.23 ($\sigma_{\text{binomial}} = 1.23$). In the *histogram* the bar at 5 extended from 4.5 to 5.5. Now, how much of the *normal curve* lies between $X = 4.5$ and $X = 5.5$?

To answer this question, compute the z score at 4.5 and the z score at 5.5.

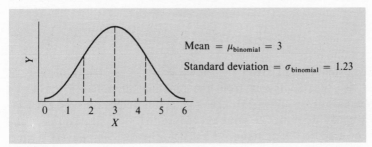

Mean $= \mu_{\text{binomial}} = 3$

Standard deviation $= \sigma_{\text{binomial}} = 1.23$

FIG. 6.4

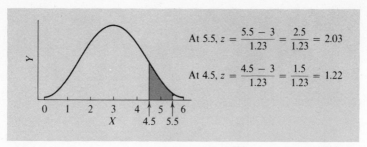

$$\text{At } 5.5, z = \frac{5.5 - 3}{1.23} = \frac{2.5}{1.23} = 2.03$$

$$\text{At } 4.5, z = \frac{4.5 - 3}{1.23} = \frac{1.5}{1.23} = 1.22$$

FIG. 6.5

Then from a table of the normal curve, determine the area between the two z scores (Fig. 6.5).

Of the normal curve, .4788 lies between $\overline{X}$ and $z = 2.03$; .3888 lies between $\overline{X}$ and $z = 1.22$. Therefore, .4788 − .3888 (.09 of the curve) lies in the shaded region. And since the normal curve approximates the histogram, .09 of the *histogram* must fall between 4.5 and 5.5. The probability of 5, then, is roughly .09. This approximate probability agrees perfectly with the exact value.

What is the probability that a subject earn a score of 5 or more by guessing? In the histogram, "5 or more" extends from 4.5 to the far right. How much of the *normal curve* extends beyond 4.5?

$$\text{At } 4.5, z = \frac{4.5 - 3}{1.23} = \frac{1.5}{1.23} = 1.22$$

.1112 of the normal curve's area falls beyond $z = 1.22$. Hence, 11 percent of the normal distribution falls beyond 4.5. The probability of "5 or more" is therefore .11. (Computed from the binomial distribution, the exact probability equals .09 + .02 = .11; again, the two answers agree well.)

Finally, let us approximate the probability of a score 2 or less. The histogram's area for the score "2 or less" extends from 2.5 to the far left. How much of the normal curve extends to the left of 2.5?

$$\text{At } 2.5, z = \frac{2.5 - 3}{1.23} = -0.41$$

.3409 of the normal curve's area falls below $z = -0.41$, so the probability of "2 or less" is .34. (Computed from the binomial distribution, the exact probability equals .02 + .09 + .23 = .34. Again, an excellent agreement.)

Some textbooks describe the same procedure this way. Say you need the probability of a score "5 or more." First, let $X = 5$; then convert X to a z score, but as you do, subtract ½ from $|X - \overline{X}|$. That is, compute:

$$z = \frac{|X - \overline{X}| - \frac{1}{2}}{S} = \frac{|X - \mu_{binomial}| - \frac{1}{2}}{\sigma_{binomial}} \qquad (6.4)$$

$$= \frac{|5 - 3| - \frac{1}{2}}{1.23} = 1.22$$

(This z has the same value as the one above.) The "$\frac{1}{2}$" in this formula is called the *correction for continuity*. It is a "correction" in that we need the histogram's area to the right of 4.5, not to the right of 5.

This formula can be used for any X. To find the probability of the score 2 or less, compute:

$$z = \frac{|X - \overline{X}| - \frac{1}{2}}{S} = \frac{|2 - 3| - \frac{1}{2}}{1.23} = \frac{0.5}{1.23} = 0.41$$

When $p = \frac{1}{2}$, the normal curve's approximation is excellent. When p differs from $\frac{1}{2}$, though, the binomial distribution becomes increasingly skewed and the normal curve's approximation becomes poor. If p is fairly close to $\frac{1}{2}$, the error is not serious, but as p gets more extreme, the error does grow serious. Statisticians use the following rule of thumb to decide whether the normal curve's approximation is safe: The product np and the product nq should both exceed 10. For example, suppose $p = \frac{1}{4}, q = \frac{3}{4}$, and $n = 16$. The approximation should not be used since np is only 4. The binomial distribution would be too skewed, and the normal curve's approximation would not be valid.

EXAMPLE 6.8

The probability of a certain trait is .40. Suppose an investigator examines a representative group of 30 people. (*a*) Describe the binomial distribution that summarizes the different outcomes. (*b*) Use the normal curve to approximate the probability that 16 or more people have the trait.

Solution (*a*) The possible outcomes can be described by the binomial expansion $(.40 + .60)^{30} = (.40)^{30} + 30(.40)^{29}(.60) + \cdots + (.60)^{30}$. Each term tells the probability of some different outcome. The distribution could be described by a histogram with the following mean and standard deviation:

$$\mu_{binomial} = np = 30(.40) = 12$$

$$\sigma_{binomial} = \sqrt{npq} = \sqrt{30(.40)(.60)} = 2.7$$

The average group would contain 12 people who exhibit the trait. This value would vary from experiment to experiment, with a standard deviation of 2.7.

(b) A normal curve approximates the histogram described above:

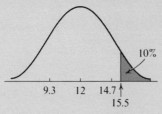

Experiment's outcome: Number of people
   out of 30 who exhibit the trait

Let us compute the probability of "16 or more" (really, 15.5 or more) in this distribution. Using the correction for continuity:

$$z = \frac{|X - \bar{X}| - \frac{1}{2}}{S} = \frac{|16 - 12| - \frac{1}{2}}{2.7} = \frac{3.5}{2.7} = 1.3$$

From a table of the normal curve, .10 of the curve's area falls beyond $z = 1.3$. Therefore, the probability is about .10 that 16 or more people exhibit the trait.

In Example 6.8, 30 people were examined, and the group's score or outcome could range from 0 to 30. Whenever a distribution describes the possible outcomes of an experiment, it is called a *sampling distribution*. A binomial distribution is therefore one kind of sampling distribution. In later chapters we shall examine other kinds.

6.6 THE "UNUSUALNESS" OF A SAMPLE OUTCOME

Suppose an experimenter tosses 64 pennies and notes the number of heads. The different possible outcomes can be described by the binomial distribution $(\frac{1}{2} + \frac{1}{2})^{64}$, or by the normal curve that approximates it (Fig. 6.6). The

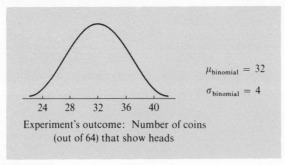

Experiment's outcome: Number of coins
   (out of 64) that show heads

FIG. 6.6

average experiment would show 32 heads, and the distribution's standard deviation would equal 4.

Now suppose 36 of the 64 coins showed heads. This result would not seem surprising or unusual; after all, 36 heads is very close to the expectation 32. On the other hand, suppose 51 coins showed heads. That result *would* seem surprising. Now what makes 36 seem reasonable while 51 seems surprising? Perhaps you reply that 36 is more *probable* than 51. True, but then again, 36 is not very probable either: The probability of 36 heads is only .0605. When many different outcomes are possible—0 through 64—no one outcome is very probable.

Then what makes 36 seem reasonable while 51 seems surprising? An outcome seems reasonable *if it is near the expectation*—in this case, near 32. An outcome far from the expectation seems unusual. As 36 is only one standard deviation from 32, it seems reasonable. On the other hand, 51 is 4.75 standard deviations from 32.

Let us adopt some arbitrary criterion to separate reasonable events from unusual ones. Experimenters often use the 5 percent criterion. According to this criterion, "unusual events" lie in the extreme 5 percent of the distribution. To use this criterion, we need to locate the extreme 5 percent of the distribution—the part farthest from $\overline{X}$.

What is the extreme 5 percent of a *normal* distribution? Usually this phrase denotes the area in the two extreme tails: the 2.5 percent above $z = 1.96$, and the 2.5 percent below $z = -1.96$; together they make up the extreme 5 percent. An event is called unusual, then, if its $|z|$ exceeds 1.96.

Statisticians use the letter α (alpha) to describe the criterion of unusualness. "$\alpha = .05$" says that the extreme 5 percent is considered unusual.

"$\alpha = .01$" says that the extreme 1 percent is considered unusual. The criterion $\alpha = .01$ is called the 1 percent criterion. In a normal distribution an event is unusual by this criterion if its z score exceeds 2.58.

Consider the toss of 64 pennies again. Is the outcome "48 heads" unusual by the criterion $\alpha = .05$? First locate 48 in the distribution:

$$z = \frac{|X - \overline{X}| - \frac{1}{2}}{S} = \frac{|48 - 32| - \frac{1}{2}}{4} = 3.875$$

"48 heads" is more than 1.96 standard deviations from $\overline{X}$. It does fall in the extreme 5 percent of the distribution, so it *is* unusual by the criterion $\alpha = .05$. It would also be called unusual by the criterion $\alpha = .01$.

6.7   HYPOTHESIS TESTING

Once we adopt a criterion of unusualness, we can separate "reasonable" situations from "unreasonable" ones. If a penny is tossed 64 times, "36 heads" is reasonable; all features of the situation jibe: p (the probability of a head) is $\frac{1}{2}$, the expectation is 32, and " 36 heads " fits comfortably into the sampling distribution.

The result "48 heads," though, is not reasonable; with $\alpha = .05$, the result is unusual. For if p equals $\frac{1}{2}$, then "48 heads" is disturbingly far from the expectation, and fact and theory do not seem to jibe. True, "48 heads" may be one of those rare events that does occasionally happen. But another explanation is possible: p may not equal $\frac{1}{2}$. Perhaps the coin is biased in some way; perhaps heads really are more frequent than tails. The result "48 heads" makes us question the assumption that $p = \frac{1}{2}$.

Sometimes the value of p is simply not known, and the investigator can only hypothesize its value. Then, to evaluate the hypothesis, he examines one group of subjects. For example, suppose a researcher is investigating brain damage in poor readers. He does not know how often brain damage occurs, but according to his theory, half of the population of poor readers is brain damaged. He then states his hypothesis.

Hypothesis: $p = \frac{1}{2}$

Is this hypothesis reasonable? First, the investigator studies one group of subjects—30 subjects who are representative of the population of poor readers. According to the hypothesis, 15 subjects or so should be brain damaged; $np = 30(\frac{1}{2}) = 15$. The group's "score" might not be exactly 15, but it should be reasonably close. If it *is* reasonably close, the investigator accepts the hypothesis. If it is not reasonably close (by his criterion of unusualness), he rejects the hypothesis.

The investigator therefore prepares to examine 30 subjects. If p equals $\frac{1}{2}$, the sampling distribution is:

$$(p + q)^n = (\tfrac{1}{2} + \tfrac{1}{2})^{30} = (\tfrac{1}{2})^{30} + 30(\tfrac{1}{2})^{29}(\tfrac{1}{2}) + \cdots$$

This sampling distribution is approximated by the normal curve of Fig. 6.7. The distribution's mean equals 15; its standard deviation equals 2.74.

Suppose the data show that 25 subjects are brain damaged. Does this result jibe with the hypothesis? Does it fit comfortably into the sampling distribution? Let us locate "25" in the sampling distribution.

$$z = \frac{|X - \overline{X}| - \frac{1}{2}}{S} = \frac{|25 - 15| - \frac{1}{2}}{2.74} = 3.74$$

The result "25" is disturbingly far from the center; it does not fit comfortably into the distribution. Therefore, the investigator cannot accept the hypothesis. He rejects the hypothesis, concluding that p is probably not $\frac{1}{2}$.

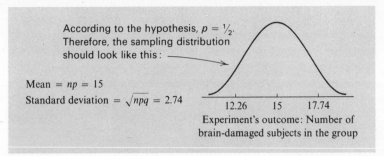

According to the hypothesis, $p = \frac{1}{2}$.
Therefore, the sampling distribution
should look like this: ——

Mean $= np = 15$
Standard deviation $= \sqrt{npq} = 2.74$

12.26   15   17.74
Experiment's outcome: Number of
brain-damaged subjects in the group

FIG. 6.7

This general procedure is called "hypothesis testing." An experimenter first states some hypothesis and considers the sampling distribution it implies. Then he performs the experiment once. He locates his result in the sampling distribution to see whether it jibes with the hypothesis. If it does, he accepts the hypothesis. If not, he rejects the hypothesis. Hypothesis testing will be examined more fully in Chap. 7.

APPENDIX: *Proofs*

Proof 6.1 *Proof that* $\mu_{\text{binomial}} = np$.
The binomial is expanded this way:

$$(p+q)^n = p^n + np^{n-1}q + \frac{n(n-1)}{2} p^{n-2}q^2 + \cdots + npq^{n-1} + q^n$$

| Probability of Score n | Probability of Score n − 1 | Probability of Score n − 2 | Probability of Score 1 | Probability of Score 0 |

To compute the mean, let us use this general equation:

Mean $= \sum [X_i P(X_i)]$

Each score (n, n − 1, n − 2, ... 1, 0) needs to be multiplied by its probability. The sum of the terms will then equal the mean. Therefore:

$$\mu_{\text{binomial}} = np^n + (n-1)np^{n-1}q + (n-2)\frac{n(n-1)}{2} p^{n-2}q^2 + \cdots + 1npq^{n-1} + 0q^n$$

| Score | Its probability |

The last term equals 0. Every other term contains the factor np; let us therefore factor np from each term.

$$\mu_{\text{binomial}} = np \left[p^{n-1} + (n-1)p^{n-2}q + \frac{(n-1)(n-2)}{2} p^{n-3}q^2 + \cdots + q^{n-1} \right]$$

$$= np(p+q)^{n-1}$$

Since $(p + q)$ equals 1, $(p + q)$ to any power equals 1. Therefore:

$$\mu_{\text{binomial}} = np$$

Proof 6.2   *Proof that* $\sigma_{\text{binomial}} = \sqrt{npq}$.
(*a*) First let us modify the formula for S^2, adapting it to the binomial distribution.

$$S^2 = \frac{\sum X^2}{N} - \bar{X}^2$$

$\dfrac{\sum X^2}{N}$ is the *mean* of the squared scores. Since a mean can be written as the sum of each value weighted by its probability, $\dfrac{\sum X^2}{N}$ can be written $\sum [X^2 \cdot P(X^2)]$. Thus, the general formula for S^2 becomes:

$$S^2 = \sum [X^2 \cdot P(X^2)] - \bar{X}^2$$

(*b*) Let us apply this formula to the binomial distribution.
1. $\bar{X}^2$ in the formula is easy to interpret. In the binomial distribution the mean equals np; therefore $\bar{X}^2$ equals $(np)^2$.
2. Now consider $\sum [X^2 \cdot P(X^2)]$. " The probability of each X^2 " refers to the probability of each squared $\mathbf{n, n-1, \ldots 0}$. These probabilities are given by the binomial expansion. The squared scores are $\mathbf{n^2, (n-1)^2, (n-2)^2, \ldots 1^2, 0^2}$. Each one needs to be multiplied by its probability. Therefore:

$$\sum [X^2 \cdot P(X^2)] = \mathbf{n}^2 p^n + (\mathbf{n-1})^2 np^{n-1}q + (\mathbf{n-2})^2 \frac{n(n-1)}{2} p^{n-2}q^2$$

$$+ \cdots + \mathbf{1}^2 npq^{n-1} + \mathbf{0}^2 q^n.$$

| Squared score | Its probability |

The last term equals 0; and np can be factored out of every other term.

$$\sum [X^2 \cdot P(X^2)] = np \left[np^{n-1} + (n-1)^2 p^{n-2}q + \frac{(n-2)^2(n-1)}{2} p^{n-3}q^2 + \cdots + 1^2 q^{n-1} \right]$$

To examine this result further, let us darken certain terms:

$$\sum [X^2 \cdot P(X^2)] = np \left[\mathbf{n}p^{n-1} + (\mathbf{n-1})(n-1)p^{n-2}q + (\mathbf{n-2}) \frac{(n-1)(n-2)}{2} p^{n-3}q^2 + \cdots + \mathbf{1}q^{n-1} \right]$$

The darkened terms are $\mathbf{n, n-1, n-2, \ldots, 1}$. They are like scores that range from n to 1.

Suppose each darkened term were 1 point lower: $n-1, n-2, n-3, ..., 0$. Then the expression in the brackets would be the mean of the binomial distribution $(p+q)^{n-1}$. It would equal $[(n-1)p]$. We can summarize by writing:

$$\sum [X^2 \cdot P(X^2)] = np \begin{bmatrix} \text{a term that would equal the mean of } (p+q)^{n-1} \text{ if the scores} \\ \text{ranged from } n-1 \text{ to } 0. \end{bmatrix}$$

But every score is 1 point too high. When every score in a distribution is raised 1 point the mean is raised 1 point. Instead of $[(n-1)p]$, the term in the brackets equals $[(n-1)p+1]$

$$\sum [X^2 \cdot P(X^2)] = np[(n-1)p+1]$$
$$= np[np-p+1] = n^2p^2 - np^2 + np$$

3. Finally, the variance of the binomial distribution can be determined.

$$S^2 = \sum [X^2 \cdot P(X^2)] - \bar{X}^2$$
$$\sigma^2_{\text{binomial}} = [n^2p^2 - np^2 + np] - (np)^2$$
$$= np - np^2 = np(1-p)$$
$$= npq$$

$$\sigma_{\text{binomial}} = \sqrt{npq}$$

EXERCISES

6.1 Consider the experiment of tossing four pennies: Penny 1, Penny 2, Penny 3, Penny 4.

(a) What is the probability of: a head on Penny 1, a tail on Penny 2, a head on Penny 3, and a tail on Penny 4?
Answer: $\frac{1}{16}$

(b) In how many ways can the results show two heads and two tails?
Answer: 6

(c) What is the probability of two heads and two tails?
Answer: $6(\frac{1}{2})^2(\frac{1}{2})^2 = \frac{3}{8}$

(d) If the experiment were performed 160 times, how many times would you expect two heads and two tails?
Answer: 60

6.2 In a typical ESP deck of cards, there are 25 cards, five symbols appearing five times each. A subject is about to be tested for ESP: A card is selected, held up, and the subject makes his guess. The card is returned to the deck, the deck is shuffled, another card is selected, and the subject makes another guess, for a total of 10 trials. The subject's score is defined as the number of times he guesses correctly.

(a) In the expression $(p+q)^n$, what are the values of p, q, and n?
Answer: $p = .20, q = .80, n = 10$

(b) What is the probability of a score of 8 or more?
Answer: $P(8 \text{ or more}) = 45(.2)^8(.8)^2 + 10(.2)^9(.8) + (.2)^{10} = .0000779$

(c) Which is more probable, the score 0 or the score 2?
Answer: $P(0) = .64(.8)^8$; $P(2) = 1.80(.8)^8$; $P(2)$ is therefore greater

6.3   Find the probability that in a four-children family there will be:
(a) exactly one boy; (b) exactly three boys; (c) at least one boy; (d) all girls.
Assume that the probability of a boy is $\frac{1}{2}$.
Answer: (a) $\frac{1}{4}$; (b) $\frac{1}{4}$; (c) $\frac{15}{16}$; (d) $\frac{1}{16}$

6.4   Out of 64 families with four children how many would you expect to have:
(a) exactly one boy; (b) exactly three boys; (c) at least one boy; (d) all girls?
Answer: (a) 16; (b) 16; (c) 60; (d) 4

6.5   The probability that a male (selected at random) is color-blind is .08. Suppose
a sample of four men is picked at random. What is the probability: (a) that
all four men are color-blind; (b) that two men are color-blind and two are
normal; (c) that at least one of the men is color-blind?
Answer: (a) $(.08)^4 = .00004096$; (b) $6(.08)^2(.92)^2 = .03250176$; (c) $1 - (.92)^4 = .28$

6.6   If you took 100 samples like the one in question 6.5 (that is, you did the
"experiment" 100 times), in how many of them would you expect to find at
least one color-blind man?
Answer: 28

6.7   Suppose a student takes an eight-item true-false test and answers each
question by guessing.
(a)   What is the probability that he obtain a score of 8 correct?
      Answer: $\frac{1}{256}$
(b)   What is the probability that he obtain a score of 6 or higher?
      Answer: $\frac{37}{256}$
(c)   If all students taking the test were guessing, what would you expect the
      mean score to be?
      Answer: 4
(d)   If all students taking the test were guessing, what would you expect the
      standard deviation to be?
      Answer: $\sqrt{2} = 1.414$

6.8   Expand $(p + q)^6$. If an animal is placed in a maze with six choice points
(where each choice point has two alternative turns, left or right), and the
animal has not yet learned its way around the maze:
(a)   What is the probability of his making four left turns and two right turns?
      Answer: $\frac{15}{64}$
(b)   What is the probability of his making two correct turns and four in-
      correct turns?
      Answer: $\frac{15}{64}$

6.9   Expand the binomial $(p + q)^5$. If $p = .30$ for the occurrence of event E, what
is the probability that the event occur three times out of five opportunities, if
successive occurrences of the event are independent of one another?
Answer: $10(.3)^3(.7)^2 = .1323$

6.10 Suppose the probability of selecting an extravert (as defined by some theorist)
is .40. Five individuals are selected independently to form a sample.

(a) What is the exact probability that three of the individuals selected are extraverts and two are not?

Answer: $\dfrac{5!}{3!2!}(.4)^3(.6)^2 = .2304$

(b) If many samples like the one above were taken, what would be the mean number of extraverts per sample?
Answer: $\mu_{binomial} = 2$

(c) Let us define a sample's score as the number of extraverts in it. If many samples were taken, what would be the standard deviation of this distribution of scores?
Answer: $\sigma_{binomial} = \sqrt{(5)(.4)(.6)} = 1.1$

(d) What is the exact probability that *three or more* of the individuals selected are extraverts?

Answer: $\dfrac{5!}{3!2!}(.4)^3(.6)^2 + \dfrac{5!}{4!1!}(.4)^4(.6) + (.4)^5 = .31744$

6.11 Find the probability of getting three, four, five, or six heads when a penny is tossed 10 times. (a) Use the binomial distribution. (b) Use the normal curve approximation.

Answer: $\dfrac{60}{512} + \dfrac{105}{512} + \dfrac{126}{512} + \dfrac{105}{512} = .7734$

6.12 Use the normal curve approximation: What is the probability on a 40-item True-False test that a person achieves a score of 24 or more by guessing?
Answer: .1335

6.13 Use the normal curve approximation: What is the probability of 25 sevens when a pair of dice is tossed 100 times?
Answer: .0090

6.14 Use the normal curve approximation: A machine produces bolts of which 10 percent are defective. Find the probability in a sample of 400 bolts that between 35 and 45 are defective.
Answer: .6424

6.15 Suppose $p = .10$ that a person selected at random will some day incur mental illness. If 10,000 10-person samples are examined, the mean number of persons per sample who will some day incur mental illness is _____.
Answer: 1

7

STATISTICAL THEORY AND HYPOTHESIS TESTING

A *set*, we said earlier, refers to a collection of things. A set can be identified in two different ways. Sometimes the investigator lists all of its members. The set of states on the West Coast is: {Alaska, Washington, Oregon, California}. Other times, the set is too large, and we describe it best by a verbal description. "The set of all brain-damaged boys in public schools" is one such case. No one could list all of its members; the set is too large, and furthermore, brain damage is not always evident.

Now frequently an investigator wants to generalize to *every* member of some set. Perhaps he wants to know about *all* 8-year-olds. Or perhaps he wants to know about all American 8-year-old schizophrenic boys. Either of these sets is prohibitively large. Statistical inference is needed in just such cases; the investigator wants to learn about *all* members of some set, but the set as a whole is too large for him to examine every member. He therefore restricts his study to relatively few members of the set. From those few, he generalizes to all.

First, the investigator has to select the members that he *will* study—a subset of the larger set. This subset may include just a few cases, or it may include several thousand cases. The subset is called a *sample*, and the larger set is called the *population*. Sometimes the terms *sample* and *population* refer to people or objects; other times they refer to measurements of those people or objects. Both meanings are used, and the context usually tells which one is meant.

A statistical inference, then, is a conclusion about a population that is inferred from a sample. Perhaps an investigator hopes to learn how the million voters of a city will vote in the next election. He cannot poll the entire population, so he might study a sample of 200 voters.

Any descriptive measure can be computed from the data of a sample— the mean $(\overline{X})$, the standard deviation (S), a correlation coefficient (r), the proportion of people with some trait (p). Now theoretically, the same measure could be computed from data of the entire population. In practice, of course, the population is usually too large for us to record every score. But *theoretically*, the mean of all the scores, the standard deviation, and the correlation coefficient exist.

Any descriptive measure on the scores of a *sample* is called a *sample statistic*. Sample statistics are denoted by Roman alphabet letters—$\overline{X}$, S, r, p. The corresponding theoretical measure on the scores of the *population* is called a *population parameter*. Population parameters are denoted in one of two ways—either by a Greek letter or by a Roman letter with the subscript "pop." The mean of a population is denoted μ; the standard deviation, σ. The relative frequency of some trait in a population[1] is denoted p_{pop}. A population's correlation coefficient is denoted either ρ (rho) or r_{pop}.

The goal of statistical inference, then, is this: The investigator hopes to infer something about a population parameter. He observes a sample of data and computes a sample statistic. From the sample statistic, he then draws an inference about the population parameter. By examining $\overline{X}$, he might draw an inference about μ. By examining p, he might draw an inference about p_{pop}.

7.1 BASIC ASSUMPTION: A REPRESENTATIVE SAMPLE

Statistical inference always begins with one basic requirement: The sample must be representative of the population. It should contain a good cross section. Any trait in the population should have about the same relative

---

[1] Usage varies in the notation for a population's p. When there is no possible confusion, it is sometimes denoted simply p. That was true in the examples of Chap. 6. From now on, however, let us be more precise and use p_{pop}. (The corresponding Greek letter π (pi) never caught on as a way of denoting this parameter.)

frequency in the sample. A sample of college students, for example, would not typify the general population: In general, its members would be younger than the general population, brighter, better informed, and so on. The sample of college students would be a *biased* sample of the general population. It might typify the population of college students, but not the general population.

Statistical theory always assumes that the sample is representative. One procedure for drawing a representative sample is called *random sampling*. Random sampling is the simplest method, but other methods also exist. These other methods will make more sense after we have examined the analysis of variance technique. For now, let us restrict ourselves to random samples.

To draw a random sample, the experimenter first specifies all the members of the population. Perhaps they are listed in some file or in some directory. Then he needs to devise a system for drawing the sample. The sample is random if it has two characteristics. First, everyone in the population should have an equal probability of being selected. Second, one person's selection should not affect another person's chances; the selections should be independent.

Table of random numbers

To make the sample random, an investigator often uses a table of random numbers. This table contains many pages filled with digits from 0 to 9. The table is composed in such a way that the digits are all equally probable. These digits are also independent—a 3, for example, occurs as often next to a 7 as it does next to a 9. The most extensive table of this kind was generated electronically by the Rand Corporation. Table B.1 in the appendix is part of that table.

Now suppose an experimenter were drawing a sample from a population of 10,000 individuals. Each person in the population might be assigned a number between 0000 and 9999. Then the experimenter would draw a four-digit number from the table. If the number were 8097, he would select Individual 8097 as his first subject.

96	20	74	41	56	74
58	17	52	66	95	33
05	12	80	97	19	00
13	49	90	63	19	06
64	42	18	08	14	28

Then he would repeat the procedure until he had drawn enough subjects for his sample.

The number in the table should be selected in an unsystematic way. Sometimes an investigator closes his eyes and lets his finger fall on a pair of two-digit numbers; these numbers then refer him to some particular column and some particular row of the book. The entry in that column and that row is then taken as his random number.

Sampling with and without replacement

A sample can be drawn with or without replacement. When an investigator samples with replacement, he draws an element for his sample—a person, an animal, a plant—and returns it to the population before he draws the next element. That way, the probability that an element is reselected is the same as the initial probability that it was selected. Suppose a population contains 1,000 men who are numbered 1, 2, 3, ... 1,000. The experimenter might begin drawing a sample, perhaps drawing Subject 593. Subject 593 would then be returned to the population before the next subject was drawn.

If Subject 593 were *removed* from the population, however, he could not be reselected; the probability of being reselected would be 0. In that case, we would speak of sampling *without* replacement. When two cards are dealt from a deck, the dealer samples without replacement. Perhaps he deals the king of spades (K_S) and then the jack of hearts (J_H). The probability of K_S is $\frac{1}{52}$. Once it is removed from the deck, the population contains 51 cards; and the probability of J_H becomes $\frac{1}{51}$. The probabilities change as each new card is selected.

A random sample can be drawn with or without replacement; the important point is that every possible sample has the same chance of being drawn. Usually experimenters sample without replacement. Once a subject is drawn, that subject is no longer a candidate for further selection. Thus, N subjects are deliberately chosen to be N different people.

Biased samples

Biases sometimes occur in a sample despite the investigator's best intentions. One widely publicized example was the poll taken in 1936 by a magazine that is now defunct. The pollsters studied a sample of 2,300,000 people from the population of American voters. They hoped to forecast the presidential election that year, generalizing from their sample to the population of all American voters. In their sample Alfred M. Landon was favored over Franklin D. Roosevelt, and they confidently predicted Landon's success. Their prediction, however, was wrong; Roosevelt received 60 percent of the votes cast.

Why the upset? Since that day the sample has been reexamined. It seems that questionnaires were mailed to individuals on various lists—lists of automobile owners, telephone subscribers, and so on. The low-income people in those days did not appear on such lists, so they were not represented in the sample. The sample was therefore not representative of all American voters, and the statistical inference was faulty.

Samples often fail to be representative. Suppose an investigator mails out questionnaires; he asks each recipient to complete the questionnaire and return the data. The returns, of course, might be a small subset of all the original questionnaires. And this subset need not typify the population at all. In fact, it might be very atypical: The respondents might be more cooperative than most people, more interested in social science research, more mature, or better educated.

The theory we shall develop—and this point must be emphasized—only holds if the sample is not biased. When a psychologist studies white rats, he must generalize to white rats—and only to the subset of white rats typified by his sample. If he generalizes to *all* rats, or to dogs, or to humans, he has crossed the boundaries of statistical theory. At that point, he depends on his intuitions and his own assumptions. His intuitions and assumptions might be valid, but they lie outside the realm of statistical theory. And if the sample is biased to begin with, the theory cannot be blamed for wrong conclusions.

Sometimes a sample cannot be drawn at random: For example, the population's members might not be cataloged anywhere, so the investigator could not select randomly. How then can the investigator be sure that his sample is representative of the population? Frankly, he cannot be. Sometimes it is helpful to draw a *large* sample. As we develop the theory, you will see that, in some respects, a large sample better typifies the population than a small sample; so to some extent there is safety in large numbers. But again, if the sample is biased, a large sample is every bit as misleading as a small one.

In certain derivations that we shall examine later, we assume that the population is *infinitely* large. At times this assumption is not valid: The population may contain the 1,200 children in a school, not an *infinite* number of children. Or it may contain the 831,256 voters in a city, not an infinite number of people. When the population contains a *finite* number of people, then strictly speaking, our derivations and formulas ought to be modified. In actual practice, though, this modification usually turns out to be minor, and it is therefore ignored. As long as the sample is considerably smaller than the population—say, it has no more than 5 percent of the population's members— then we treat the population as though it were *infinitely* large. This working approximation is very convenient, and in general, the error it causes is tiny.

7.2 BASIC CONCEPT: THE SAMPLING DISTRIBUTION

The concept of a sampling distribution is basic to the theory of statistics. We now turn to that concept.

Consider the population of all male human beings, and imagine a random sample of three males. Let us compute some descriptive statistic from the sample's data. We might compute the mean IQ—perhaps 108. Or the sum of the IQ's—324. Or the median height—perhaps 67 in. Or the number of people who are color-blind—perhaps one.

For simplicity, let us select one of these measures—say, the number of people who are color-blind. We can call this statistic " c " (for " color-blind "). And suppose *many* experimenters performed the experiment. Each experimenter would compute his own sample's c. For one sample, c might equal 1: one color-blind person. For another sample, c might equal 0; for another, c might equal 2 or 3. The lowest value of c is 0, the highest value is 3.

If we collated all the different sample c's, we would have an entire distribution of c's. This distribution is called a sampling distribution. It describes all the different sample outcomes and their relative frequencies. If we measured a sample's mean IQ, the sampling distribution would describe all the different means of different experiments. If we measured the median height, the sampling distribution would describe all the different medians. If we measured the sample's "$\sum X$," the sampling distribution would describe all the different $\sum X$'s.

Statisticians sometimes distinguish between an *empirical* sampling distribution and a *theoretical* sampling distribution. If an experimenter performed an experiment over and over—say he collected many different $\overline{X}$'s or many different c's—his distribution of $\overline{X}$'s or c's would be an *empirical* sampling distribution. But if he used a *theory* to describe the distribution (and never really collected data at all), the distribution would be a *theoretical* sampling distribution.

We can often use probability theory to describe a sampling distribution. For example, consider the c's of different samples: Suppose many three-person samples were examined. For each sample, c might equal 3, 2, 1, or 0. In the population of male humans the probability of color blindness is .08. (Since .08 is a population parameter, we could write: $p_{pop} = .08$.)

Theoretically, then, the different sample c's are described by the binomial distribution: $(p_{pop} + q_{pop})^3 = (.08 + .92)^3$.

$$(.08 + .92)^3 = (.08)^3 \quad + \quad 3(.08)^2(.92) + \quad 3(.08)(.92)^2 + (.92)^3$$
$$= .001 \quad + \quad .018 \quad + \quad .203 \quad + \quad .779$$

relative frequency of *3* color-blind men	relative frequency of *2* color-blind men	relative frequency of *1* color-blind man	relative frequency of *0* color-blind men

The theory, then, describes an enormous number of different samples. These expected outcomes could be listed in a table. That table would report the theoretical sampling distribution of c's.

Sample's Outcome (c)	Relative frequency
3 color-blind men	.001
2 color-blind men	.018
1 color-blind man	.203
0 color-blind men	.779

A sampling distribution always suggests differences. We *expect* some samples to be higher, others to be lower. One sample in a thousand should contain three color-blind men. Most samples, though, should contain 0 or one color-blind men. Because of chance factors, then, the sample outcomes vary. $\sigma = \sqrt{npq}$ describes this variability: $\sqrt{3(.08)(.92)} = .47$.

The standard deviation of a sampling distribution is called a *standard error*; .47, then, is the standard error of this sampling distribution. Later, we shall examine other kinds of standard errors.

EXAMPLE 7.1

Imagine five genetically mutant animals. These five animals form the entire population of such animals. Each animal's blood was analyzed for a certain biochemical, with these resulting scores: 5, 9, 9, 10, 12. The mean of the population (μ) equals 9.

Now suppose the investigator randomly samples two animals from the population, and suppose he computes the mean. Perhaps the two scores are 9 and 10, and $\bar{X}$ equals 9.5. Consider all the different samples the experimenter might draw. Describe the theoretical sampling distribution of the different sample means.

Solution   In Chap. 8 we shall examine a quick, efficient way to solve this problem. For now, let us list all the possible samples and their means.

Possible Sample	First Score Drawn	Second Score Drawn	Sample's Mean
1	5	5	5.0
2	5	9	7.0
3	5	9	7.0
4	5	10	7.5
5	5	12	8.5
6	9	5	7.0
7	9	9	9.0
8	9	9	9.0
9	9	10	9.5
10	9	12	10.5
11	9	5	7.0
12	9	9	9.0
13	9	9	9.0
14	9	10	9.5
15	9	12	10.5
16	10	5	7.5
17	10	9	9.5
18	10	9	9.5

19	10	10	10.0
20	10	12	11.0
21	12	5	8.5
22	12	9	10.5
23	12	9	10.5
24	12	10	11.0
25	12	12	12.0

If the samples are drawn at random, each score would have an equal chance of appearing. Therefore, each two-score combination would have the same probability. These combinations are shown in the table along with their means. Let us collate the means into a more compact distribution. The following table gives the theoretical sampling distribution of means.

Sample's Mean	Frequency
12.0	1
11.5	0
11.0	2
10.5	4
10.0	1
9.5	4
9.0	4
8.5	2.
8.0	0
7.5	2
7.0	4
6.5	0
6.0	0
5.5	0
5.0	1
	25

This sampling distribution tells the various possible outcomes and their relative frequencies. It tells what sample means to expect. Ninety-two percent of the means lie between 7.0 and 11.0. Their mean is 9.0, and their standard deviation is 1.61. Thus, the sampling distribution has a mean of 9.0 and a standard error of 1.61.

7.3 HYPOTHESIS TESTING

Usually an investigator does not know details about the population. He does not know exact scores, he does not know μ, σ, or p_{pop}. Instead, he can only form hypotheses about these parameters.

Suppose the investigator formed a hypothesis about p_{pop}. Say he hypothesized how often some trait occurs in the population—e.g., $p_{pop} = .55$. This hypothesis has two immediate implications. First, the *average* sample should show this trait in .55 of its cases. Second, the standard error should equal $\sigma = \sqrt{npq} = \sqrt{n(.55)(.45)}$. If the *hypothesis* is valid, *these two implications* should be valid.

A hypothesized p_{pop}, then, (together with n) implies a certain sampling distribution. The hypothesis " $p_{pop} = .55$ " suggests a particular sampling distribution. And any sample should fall comfortably into that sampling distribution. If the sample *does* fit comfortably, the hypothesis and the sample are consistent; they jibe. If the sample does *not* fit comfortably, the hypothesis and the sample are at odds.

Let us be more explicit. Hypothesis testing can be outlined in five steps. First, the investigator states a hypothesis about the population parameter. The hypothesis itself is denoted H_0. That hypothesis might concern p_{pop}, μ, σ, or any other parameter.

Step 1   State a convenient hypothesis, H_0.

How does the investigator generate a hypothesis? Sometimes he has a theory or an intuition. The theory might concern the mean IQ of adult schizophrenics—e.g., $\mu = 100$. It might concern the frequency of diabetics among anxious people—e.g., $p_{pop} = .30$. It might concern the correlation between spatial ability and verbal ability—e.g., $r_{pop} = 0$.

At other times the investigator states a hypothesis that he would like to *disprove*. He deliberately states a hypothesis that he does not believe and that he hopes to discredit. Perhaps he suspects that p_{pop} really differs from .50: He might hypothesize that $p_{pop} = .50$, examine this hypothesis, and show how absurd it is. In that way he can conclude that p_{pop} is *not* .50.

The investigator may eventually accept H_0, or he may eventually reject H_0. If he rejects H_0, he needs to replace it by some alternative. As Step 2, then, the investigator states an alternative to H_0. This alternative is usually denoted H_1. Say H_0 has claimed $p_{pop} = .50$; then H_1 might claim $p_{pop} \neq .50$.

Step 2   State the alternative hypothesis, H_1.

Third, the experimenter examines H_0. H_0 always suggests some sampling distribution. Suppose H_0 claimed that $p_{pop} = .50$. And suppose the experimenter is about to study a sample of 64 people. Consider the distribution of all the samples he might draw. The sampling distribution would be described by: $(p + q)^{64} = (.50)^{64} + 64(.50)^{63}(.50) + \cdots$. In the average sample, $np = 32$ people would exhibit the trait. The standard error would equal $\sqrt{npq} = 4$. H_0 has implied all this.

> *Step 3* Note the implications of H_0. Examine the sampling distribution: its mean, its standard error.

Next the investigator draws one random sample and examines the data. He locates the result in the sampling distribution of Step 3. Does the one sample's result fit comfortably in the distribution? (If so, the sample and the hypothesis jibe.) How far is the sample from the distribution's center?

In locating the result, the investigator usually computes a z score. This z score tells its distance from the distribution's center. If the z is *small*, the sample fits well; it jibes with H_0. If the z is *large*, the two are at odds: H_0 and the sample disagree.

> *Step 4* Examine the outcome of one random sample. Locate it in the hypothesized distribution.

Finally, the investigator makes a decision. If the result fits comfortably in the hypothesized sampling distribution, the investigator accepts H_0. More extreme results are quite probable. But if the result falls in the distribution's tail, H_0 and the sample are at odds. The investigator rejects H_0; and rejecting H_0 he accepts H_1.

> *Step 5* Make a decision: Accept H_0 or reject it.

Hypothesis testing is related to a famous form of logical reasoning. In classical logic, two kinds of inference are distinguished. One is called the *ponendo ponens* form of inference; the other is called the *tollendo tollens* form. Let us review these two terms first. Then we can relate them to hypothesis testing.

Consider the following type of proposition. "If A is true, then B is true." "If Jones is guilty, he was on the street at noon." "If the scores are normally distributed, 68 percent of them lie within *S* points of the mean." The first clause (A) is the antecedent clause; it states the condition. The second clause (B) is the consequent clause; it tells A's effect. The proposition does not claim that A is true, it does not claim that B is true. It only claims that A *implies* B: *If* A is true, then B is true.

Now suppose someone could prove that A *is* true. Then he would know at once that B is true. By affirming Part A, we can affirm Part B. *Ponere* in Latin means "to affirm"; and *ponnedo ponens* is translated "affirming (one part) by affirming (the other part)." If Jones is guilty, he was on the street at noon. Now let someone prove Jones is guilty. Once that is proved, Part B is true: He was on the street at noon.

Now consider the other form. We begin with the same proposition: "If A is true, then B is true." But suppose someone proves *B is false.* He would know at once that A is false. (For if A were *true*, B would be true.) If Jones is guilty, he was on the street at noon. But, according to eyewitnesses (say), B is false: Jones was *not* on the street at noon. Therefore, we infer that A is false: Jones is not guilty. *Tollere* in Latin means "to deny"; *tollendo tollens* is translated "denying (one part) by denying (the other part)." By denying Part B, we deny Part A.

Hypothesis testing resembles the *tollendo tollens* form: "If the population's parameter equals A, its sampling distribution should assume Form B." According to the one sample, though, Form B seems wrong; therefore, A also seems wrong. The parameter, we infer, does not equal A.

This procedure does not *prove* or *disprove* H_0. It is only a strategy to help the investigator make a decision. It helps him decide when to believe H_0, when to reject H_0. It definitely allows room for error, and soon we shall have to examine that error.

7.4 LEVELS OF SIGNIFICANCE

When does a sample jibe with H_0, and when does it not? Psychologists once felt that a *z* score of 3.0 was a good criterion: If a sample fell 3 or more standard deviations from the center of the hypothesized sampling distribution, it failed to jibe with H_0. Nowadays, however, we are less rigid, and each experimenter is free to set his own criterion.

One common criterion is the .05 level of significance. According to this criterion, we reject H_0 if the sample falls in the outer 5 percent of the hypoth-

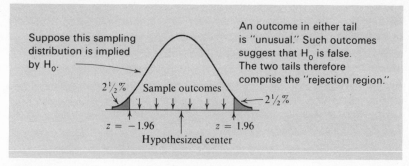

Suppose this sampling
distribution is implied
by H_0.

An outcome in either tail
is "unusual." Such outcomes
suggest that H_0 is false.
The two tails therefore
comprise the "rejection region."

$2\frac{1}{2}\%$ Sample outcomes

$2\frac{1}{2}\%$

$z = -1.96$ $z = 1.96$
Hypothesized center

FIG. 7.1 Hypothesized sampling distribution.

esized distribution. If the distribution is normal, the outer 5 percent is 1.96
standard deviations from the center. This criterion is illustrated in Fig. 7.1.

Suppose an investigator is about to test a hypothesis. He draws a sample.
If the hypothesis is valid, the sample should fit—it should fall somewhere
near the distribution's center. If the sample falls in one of the tails, the agreement is poor; H_0 is rejected. Let us therefore call the outer 5 percent of the
distribution the 5 percent rejection region. A sample in the rejection region
leads us to reject H_0.

Type I error

Occasionally, by chance, every experimenter *does* draw an unusual sample:
Perhaps H_0 is perfectly true, but by chance, the sample falls in the rejection
region. The experimenter then mistakenly rejects a perfectly valid hypothesis.
And needless to say, he draws the wrong conclusion.

Suppose an experimenter adopts the 5 percent criterion and suppose H_0 is
perfectly true. But through bad luck, suppose he draws a rare sample, one
in the 5 percent rejection region. Then he mistakenly rejects H_0. This kind
of error is called a *Type I error*. A Type I error is defined as the kind of error
that occurs when an experimenter mistakenly rejects H_0: The experimenter
is misled by a rare kind of sample.

How often do Type I errors occur? To answer this question, suppose H_0
is true. Now think of all the possible samples the experimenter might draw.
A random sample could fall anywhere in the distribution. How often would
it fall in the 5 percent rejection region? That probability is .05, so the probability of a Type I error is .05.

The symbol α (alpha) tells the probability of a Type I error. If the .05 level
is adopted, we write $\alpha = .05$: The probability of a Type I error is .05.

An experimenter does not have to adopt the .05 level. He might choose the
.01 level. Then events are considered unusual when they reach the outer
1 percent of the distribution. In a normal distribution these events exceed
$z = 2.58$. What is the probability of a Type I error? Again suppose H_0 is

true, and think of all the possible samples. One sample in a hundred would fall in the 1 percent rejection region, thereby misleading the experimenter. When the .01 level is adopted, then, the probability of a Type I error is .01. Thus, the .01 level makes a Type I error less likely. [On the other hand, another type of error grows *more* likely when $\alpha = .01$. This kind of error is the *Type II error*. It occurs when an investigator *accepts* an H_0, though H_1 (not H_0) is the correct hypothesis. We shall examine this kind of error later.]

The .05 level and the .01 level are the most common criteria. Occasionally, an experimenter adopts the .001 level of significance. In a normal distribution the .001 rejection region exceeds a z score of 3.29. This criterion is very strict: The experimenter only rejects H_0 when the sample is really deviant. And the probability of a Type I error is tiny—.001.

Sometimes a Type I error can be serious and expensive; other times it does no harm. Suppose an experimenter committed a Type I error, performed another experiment, and discovered the error. The error might be inconvenient but not very damaging. On the other hand, suppose a school board redesigned a city's schools because of a Type I error. Or suppose a government agency modified an elaborate medical program in some drastic way. The error would be very serious and expensive. If an experimenter lets $\alpha = .001$, this kind of error is lowered. Usually α equals .05 or .01, but not always. When a Type I error is serious, α might equal .001. When a Type I error is harmless, α might even equal .10.

A statistical test is like a gamble or bet. First, the players state the rules—the conditions, the risks involved, the possible losses, the odds. Then the die is cast, the roulette wheel is spun. From then on, no further changes are allowed. Likewise, an experimenter states the rules first: He notes H_0, establishes α, and plans his sample. Then the experiment is performed. Thus, α is really one of the ground rules; it has to be set from the start.

Example 7.2 resembles many earlier problems of hypothesis testing. From now on, though, we shall set α as part of Step 1.

EXAMPLE 7.2

An investigator conducted a political poll. He recognized three possible conclusions: (1) Most people favor the issue: $p_{pop} > .50$. (2) Most people oppose the issue: $p_{pop} < .50$. Or (3) p_{pop} equals .50—opinion is either divided, or people are undecided. (Conclusion 3 offers a specific value for p_{pop}, so we shall use that value to state H_0.)

A hundred people were polled. Sixty of them favored the issue and voted "yes." What conclusion can be drawn?

Solution

Step 1   State $H_0: p_{pop} = .50$. Also establish α. Suppose a Type I error is rather harmless; then α is set at .05.

Step 2   State $H_1: p_{pop} \neq .50$.

Step 3   Consider the sampling distribution implied by H_0. It is described by: $(p + q)^{100} = (.50 + .50)^{100}$. Its mean is $np = (100)(.50) = 50$ people voting "yes." Its standard deviation is $\sqrt{npq} = \sqrt{100(.50)(.50)} = 5$. A normal curve approximates the sampling distribution:

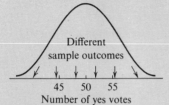

Different
sample outcomes

45   50   55
Number of yes votes

Step 4   Locate the result "60" in the hypothesized distribution:

$$z = \frac{|60 - 50| - \frac{1}{2}}{5} = \frac{9.5}{5} = 1.90$$

Step 5   Make a decision. The result "60" *does* fit comfortably in the distribution—not in the 5 percent rejection region. Therefore, H_0 is accepted: $p_{pop} = .50$.

Experimenters often express the conclusion this way: "H_0 is accepted, $p > .05$." This statement conveys two ideas—first, that α was set at .05; second, that over 5 percent of the hypothesized distribution is more extreme than "60."

EXAMPLE 7.3

A *population* of 13-year-old girls was tested on an intellectual task (a certain problem). Of the girls .60 responded correctly, so $p_{pop} = .60$. The investigator now wonders about the population of boys: Does $p_{pop} = .60$ for the population of boys? Or do boys differ from girls in this way?

Thirty-six boys were tested; 18 of them responded correctly.

Solution

Step 1   State $H_0: p_{pop} = .60$ for the group of boys. Suppose a Type I error is fairly risky; then α is set at .01.

Step 2   State $H_1: p_{pop} \neq .60$.

Step 3   Note the sampling distribution which H_0 implies. The exact distribution is $(p + q)^{36} = (.60 + .40)^{36}$. The distribution's mean is $np = (36)(.60) = 21.60$; its σ is $\sqrt{npq} = 2.94$. The distribution is approximated by a normal curve:

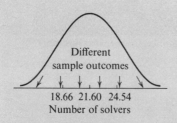

Different sample outcomes

18.66 21.60 24.54
Number of solvers

Step 4 Examine one sample's result; locate it in the distribution. Result "18" falls 1.1 standard deviations below the center:

$$z = \frac{|18 - 21.60| - \frac{1}{2}}{2.94} = \frac{3.10}{2.94} = 1.1$$

Step 5 Make a decision at $\alpha = .01$. Does the result lie comfortably within the hypothesized distribution? Or does it lie in the 1 percent rejection region? "18" does lie comfortably in the distribution, so H_0 is accepted. Experimenters sometimes express the conclusion this way: "H_0 is accepted, $p > .01$."

Option of suspending judgment

In problems of this kind, the experimenter finally reaches a decision—to accept H_0 or reject H_0. The procedure for making the final decision is sometimes called a *decision rule*. With α set at some level, the decision rule can be expressed this way:

Decision Rule 1: Reject H_0 if the sample falls in the rejection region. Otherwise, accept H_0.

In Example 7.2, the sample fell far from the rejection region, and the decision rule was easy to apply.

Some experimenters dislike this decision rule. They argue, suppose the result is marginal. Say $\alpha = .01$, so the rejection region falls beyond $z = 2.58$. And suppose a sample's z equals 2.53. According to Decision Rule 1, H_0 must be accepted. But why not admit the genuine ambiguity?

Decision Rule 1 only offers two choices—to *accept* H_0, to *reject* H_0. Some experimenters prefer more flexibility than that. They would prefer *three* options: to accept H_0, to reject H_0, or to *suspend judgment*. Some experimenters therefore adopt a decision rule like this one:

Decision Rule 2: Accept H_0 if z is less than 1.96. Reject H_0 if z exceeds 2.58. Otherwise, suspend judgment.

Then, when z falls in the ambiguous zone, the experimenter collects more data, perhaps even repeating the experiment.

Decision Rule 1 is the more conventional procedure, and we shall adopt it in later chapters. However, *any* strategy could be adopted if it were sensible and objective. Sometimes an experimenter simply reports his result and leaves the interpretation to the reader: For example, he might first compute the z value—say, $z = 2.53$. Then he might tell the probability of events this extreme: $p < .02$. (If α were set at .02, H_0 would be rejected.) The investigator, though, does not take a stand; he leaves that to the reader.

Statistical theory provides the general method. But different strategies can be used in applying that method.

7.5   ONE-TAILED VERSUS TWO-TAILED TESTS

Suppose an experimenter tests a hypothesis in the usual way: He sets α at .05, studies the hypothesized sampling distribution, and observes a single sample. If the sample falls in the 5 percent rejection region, he rejects H_0.

The 5 percent rejection region contains two tails of the curve—with 2.5 percent in each tail. The graph of Fig. 7.2 shows these two tails. If the sample falls in either tail, H_0 is rejected. Therefore, this kind of statistical test is called a *two-tailed test*.

In some problems, however, the 5 percent rejection region logically lies *in just one tail*. For example, the 5 percent rejection region might be the *highest* 5 percent of the distribution (Fig. 7.3). In that case, the statistical test is called a *one-tailed test*. Let us consider an example. Suppose an experimenter wants to learn whether subjects can discriminate between an expensive beer and a cheap beer. Call the two brands Brand E (expensive) and Brand C (cheap).

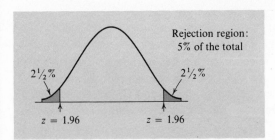

Rejection region:
5% of the total

$2\frac{1}{2}\%$ $2\frac{1}{2}\%$

$z = 1.96$ $z = 1.96$

FIG. 7.2

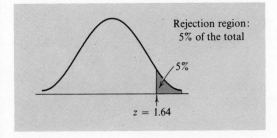

Rejection region:
5% of the total

5%

$z = 1.64$

FIG. 7.3

The experimenter plans to test 100 subjects, and each subject will judge which beer is E and which is C. Each subject's response will be correct or incorrect. By guessing, 50 subjects of 100 should be correct. According to H_0, then, p_{pop} equals .50.

In this problem H_0 is easy to state: $p_{pop} = .50$. But what is H_1, the alternative hypothesis? You might think of writing: $p_{pop} \neq .50$. But that alternative is not valid here; it implies that p_{pop} might equal any value other than .50—one above .50 or one below .50. Could p_{pop} be less than .50? Might subjects discriminate *more poorly* than chance? A conclusion of this type would not make sense: p_{pop} might be *above* .50 but not below .50. Therefore, the two reasonable alternatives are these:

$H_0 : p_{pop} = .50$

$H_1 : p_{pop} > .50$

What if 18 subjects of the 100 were correct? What would the experimenter conclude? Eighteen is somewhat less than the expected 50. But the experimenter would still consider 18 a chance deviation from 50 and accept H_0. He would conclude that p_{pop} equals .50. Any result at 50 or below would support H_0. Only results *above* 50 would contradict H_0 and support H_1. That is why the 5 percent rejection region is concentrated in one tail; events in the lower tail support H_0.

Some statisticians express the hypotheses this way:

$H_0 : p_{pop} \leq .50$

$H_1 : p_{pop} > .50$

These alternatives cover all the possible outcomes.

In this example, then, the rejection region lies in the upper 5 percent of the distribution—the part beyond $z = 1.64$. When a sample's z exceeds 1.64, the sample falls in the 5 percent rejection region, and H_0 gets rejected. The graphs in Fig. 7.4 show the rejection region for a one-tailed test at various levels of α.

Consider the kinds of questions that lead to a one-tailed test. Here are some examples. (1) Are girls better than boys in solving anagrams? (According to

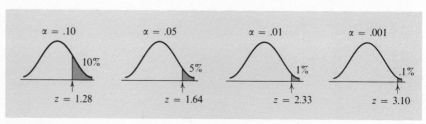

FIG. 7.4

H_0, the best performers are both—half boys and half girls. According to H_1, the best performers are mainly girls.) (2) Does a new drug produce more immunities than an older drug? (According to H_0, successful immunities come from both—half from the old drug, half from the new drug. According to H_1, more immunities come from the new drug.) (3) Do rats have a tendency to turn right? (According to H_0, rats turn right half the time. According to H_1, they more often turn right.) (4) Can subjects recognize an expensive beer over a cheap beer? (According to H_0, subjects are correct half the time. According to H_1, they are correct more often.)

For each example, H_0 and H_1 could be expressed this way: According to H_0, $p_{pop} = .50$. According to H_1, $p_{pop} > .50$. In each case, H_1's claim is the same—that p_{pop} deviates from .50 *in one direction*. p_{pop}, it claims, *exceeds* .50: Girls perform better, the new drug is better, more rats turn right, beer-drinkers judge correctly. Since H_1 is directional, a one-tailed test is needed.

A two-tailed test, on the other hand, allows for both directions. Here are some examples. (1) Do boys and girls differ in solving anagrams? Girls may be better, or girls may be worse. The claim " $p_{pop} \neq .50$ " allows for either extreme—perhaps $p_{pop} > .50$, perhaps $p_{pop} < .50$. (2) Do two drugs differ in producing immunities? The new drug may be better, the new drug may be worse. In cases like these, H_0 is still $p_{pop} = .50$. But H_1 is nondirectional: $p_{pop} \neq .50$. When H_1 is nondirectional, a two-tailed test is needed.

When a one-tailed test is used, the experimenter should make his plans beforehand. Some experimenters are so eager to reject H_0 that they misuse the one-tailed test. Say an experimenter has adopted the .05 level, and say a two-tailed test is appropriate. Then, perhaps the data show that $z = 1.73$. The experimenter, let us say, eager to reject H_0, now shifts to a one-tailed test. Since z exceeds 1.64, he rejects H_0. Such experimenters would reject H_0 at the .05 level whenever $|z|$ exceeded 1.64. But 10 percent of the distribution exceeds $|z| = 1.64$. The experimenter would therefore be setting α at .10, but calling it .05. And the probability of a Type I error would be .10, not .05. To avoid such temptations, the experimenter should verbalize his plan beforehand.

EXAMPLE 7.4

A manufacturer has developed a toy for infants. He believes that infants prefer the toy in red. To test his hunch, he tested 64 children. Each child was shown two forms of the toy, one in red and one in another color. The experimenter then noted which toy the infant approached first. The results showed that 42 children selected the red toy. Do children generally prefer the toy in red?

Solution

Step 1 $H_0: p_{pop} = .50$. Let us set α equal to .01.

Step 2 $H_1: p_{pop} > .50$ (a one-tailed test).

Step 3   Consider the sampling distribution for samples of 64 children. The distribution is described by $(p + q)^{64} = (.50 + .50)^{64}$. The mean of the distribution is $np = (64)(.50) = 32$. The standard deviation is $\sqrt{npq} = 4$. The sampling distribution could be approximated by a normal curve.

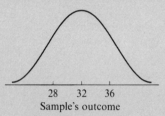

28   32   36
Sample's outcome

Step 4   Note the outcome of one sample: 42 children preferred the toy in red. Locate "42" in the sampling distribution.

$$z = \frac{|42 - 32| - \frac{1}{2}}{4} = 2.38$$

Step 5   For a one-tailed test with $\alpha = .01$, the rejection region falls beyond $z = 2.33$. The sample's result, $z = 2.38$, *does* lie in the rejection region, so H_0 gets rejected. At $\alpha = .01$, then, H_0 is rejected, $p < .01$. Therefore, we conclude, $p_{pop} > .50$. Children generally prefer the toy in red.

As we proceed, we shall develop other techniques for analyzing data, techniques beyond the method of hypothesis testing. Sometimes these other techniques provide information that is far more important for the investigator than accepting or rejecting a hypothesis. In contemporary psychological research, though, hypothesis testing is very widely used, and it will appear repeatedly in later chapters.

EXERCISES

7.1   Someone claims that he can detect a taste difference between two brands of a popular drink. This claim is put to the test by presenting two cups, one containing Brand A, the other Brand B. The person is asked to tell which of the cups contains Brand A. (Care is taken to control various factors other than taste that might influence his choice.) Then the person is tested again and again to make a total of 12 trials.

    (*a*)   Assume the person is just chance guessing. Use the binomial expansion to find: (i) the probability that he make exactly 12 correct choices; (ii) the probability that he make exactly 9 correct choices; (iii) the probability that he make 9 or more correct choices.

        Answer: (i) $(.5)^{12} = \dfrac{1}{4096} = .000244$

               (ii) $\dfrac{12!}{9!\,3!}(.5)^9(.5)^3 = \dfrac{220}{4096} = .0537$

$$(iii) \frac{12!}{9!3!}(.5)^9(.5)^3 + \frac{12!}{10!2!}(.5)^{10}(.5)^2 + \frac{12!}{11!1!}(.5)^{11}(.5) + (.5)^{12}$$

$$= \frac{299}{4096}$$

$$= .073$$

(b) Compute the three probabilities above using the normal curve approximation.

Answer: $\mu = 6$; $\sigma = \sqrt{(12)(\frac{1}{2})(\frac{1}{2})} = 1.73$

(i) $z_{11.5} = 3.18$	(ii) $z_{8.5} = 1.45$	(iii) $z_{8.5} = 1.45$
$p = .0007$	$z_{9.5} = 2.02$	$p = .0735$
	$p = .0518$	

(c) The person is correct on 8 trials out of the 12. Test the hypothesis that he was in fact chance guessing.

Answer: $z_{7.5} = .87$; $P(8 \text{ or more}) = .19$. *Accept* H_0 *that person is chance guessing.*

7.2 Should an experimenter use a one-tailed or a two-tailed test to examine the following questions?

(a) Do girls and boys differ in their quantitative ability?
Answer: 2

(b) Do rats perform better when they are rewarded with more reinforcers?
Answer: 1

(c) Do animals exhibit more anxiety if they are deprived of early sensory stimulation?
Answer: 1

(d) Do two species of monkeys differ in their reaction to stress?
Answer: 2

(e) Are tenth graders better than eighth graders in visual-motor coordination?
Answer: 1

(f) Are decorticate animals slower in becoming conditioned than normal animals?
Answer: 1

7.3 In an experiment 42 rats out of 60 turned right at the first choice point. (Think of each rat's performance as a simple ingredient event like the flip of a penny.) Would you conclude from this experiment that rats in general prefer to turn right at this choice point?

Answer: H_0: *p(turning right)* $= \frac{1}{2}$. $\mu = 30$, $\sigma = \sqrt{60(\frac{1}{2})(\frac{1}{2})} = 3.87$. $z_{41.5} = 2.96$. *Probability (42 or more)* $= .0015$. *Reject* H_0.

7.4 In a random sample of 25 persons, 7 were found to be left-handed, and 18 right-handed. Test the hypothesis that right- and left-handedness occur with equal frequencies in the population.

Answer: H_0: $p(right\text{-}handed) = \frac{1}{2}$. $\mu = 12.5$, $\sigma = 2.5$, $z = 2.0$. *Reject* H_0 *at 5 percent level; accept* H_0 *at 1 percent level*

7.5 A student is investigating the validity of the saying "Gentlemen prefer blondes." In a random sample of 36 gentlemen, 12 preferred blondes. Using the 5 percent level of significance (and the normal curve approximation to the binomial distribution), test the following hypothesis: In the population, the proportion of gentlemen who prefer blondes is .5.
Answer: H_0: $p(prefer\ blondes) = \frac{1}{2}$. $\mu = 18$; $\sigma = 3$; $z = -1.83$. *Accept* H_0 *at 5 percent level*

7.6 Suppose in some election that 50 percent of all the eligible voters favor the Democrats.
   (a) What is the probability that a sample of 25 individuals show 20 or more people favoring the Democrats?
   Answer: $\mu = 12.5$; $\sigma = 2.5$; $z = 2.8$; *probability* $= .0026$
   (b) What is the probability that a sample of 25 individuals show 80 percent or more of the individuals favoring the Democrats?
   Answer: $z = 2.8$; *probability* $= .0026$
   (c) What is the probability that a sample of 400 individuals show 80 percent or more favoring the Democrats?
   Answer: $\mu = 200$; $\sigma = 10$; $z = 11.95$; *probability* $= 0$

7.7 Suppose in a presidential election, the winner receives 60 percent of all the votes cast. Assume, therefore, that .60 is the probability that a voter vote for this candidate. If voters were polled just before the election, how often would a sample of 100 voters have shown a majority (51 voters or more) favoring this winning candidate? Use the normal curve approximation to answer this question.
Answer: $\mu = 60$; $\sigma = 4.9$; $z = -1.94$; *such samples would occur .97 of the time*

7.8 In a concept-identification task, the subject is asked to sort many cards into Category A or Category B and he is told after each sorting whether he was correct or not. How many times in a row must the subject sort the cards correctly before you can reject the hypothesis that he was guessing: (a) using the 5 percent level of significance; (b) using the 1 percent level of significance.
Answer: Probability of n consecutive correct guesses $= (\frac{1}{2})^n$

n	1	2	3	4	5	6	7
Probability of this result	$\frac{1}{2}$	$\frac{1}{4}$	$\frac{1}{8}$	$\frac{1}{16}$	$\frac{1}{32}$	$\frac{1}{64}$	$\frac{1}{128}$
	.5	.25	.125	.063	.031	.016	.0078
					5% level		1% level

7.9 Suppose you were testing a hypothesis that $p = .50$ and you were using the 1 percent level of significance with a two-tailed test. How large a sample would you need in order to conclude that a sample outcome of .53 was not merely a chance deviation from the hypothesized .50? (Do not bother using the correction for continuity.)

Answer: The sample should have more than 1,849 cases

8

THE SAMPLING DISTRIBUTION OF MEANS

8.1 THE DISTRIBUTION OF SAMPLE MEANS

Imagine an enormous population of people, and suppose their IQs have all been measured. Theoretically, IQ scores are continuous, so *any* value could exist. Now imagine the mean of all the scores. (The population may be too large for us to record every score, but theoretically at least, we can *imagine* the population's mean.) This mean is denoted μ (mu). We can also imagine the population's standard deviation (theoretically), and that value is denoted σ (sigma). Greek letters, then, designate the population parameters.

If an investigator wants to learn about μ or σ, he usually needs to draw a representative sample from the population; then he studies that sample. The sample's mean, $\overline{X}$, is easy to compute. But because of chance factors, the sample's mean usually differs from μ: Some samples contain an excess of high scores; for them, $\overline{X}$ is higher than μ. Other samples contain an excess of low scores; for them, $\overline{X}$ is lower than μ. Different samples have slightly different $\overline{X}$'s.

To illustrate how sample means vary, I artificially produced a population of scores. This population contained 10,000 normally distributed scores. Each score was written on a separate slip of paper. The scores ranged from 0 to 100; their mean was 50.0, and their standard deviation was 15.8. This one time, then, the population parameters were known:

Characteristics of the population: Scores normally distributed

$$\mu = 50.0$$
$$\sigma = 15.8$$

Now imagine yourself selecting a sample of 10 scores from that population. Suppose you sample with replacement; you reach into the container, randomly draw a score, note it, and return it to the population. Then you select another score. You repeat the procedure until you have noted 10 scores; then you compute the mean. The mean would equal some value in the neighborhood of 50, say 52.3. Now suppose another sample of 10 scores were drawn from the same population; this time perhaps the mean is 46.9. Then a third, a fourth, and so on. Ninety-six students from my class each selected one sample. Their means are shown in Table 8.1.

TABLE 8.1 Distribution of sample means
(for each sample $N = 10$)

Interval	Frequency	
62.0–63.9	1	
60.0–61.9	1	
58.0–59.9	3	
56.0–57.9	7	
54.0–55.9	9	Mean of sample means = 49.99
52.0–53.9	12	Standard deviation (S) of
50.0–51.9	15	sample means = 5.01
48.0–49.9	15	
46.0–47.9	13	
44.0–45.9	9	
42.0–43.9	6	
40.0–41.9	3	
38.0–39.9	1	
36.0–37.9	1	
	—	
	96 samples	

Notice how the means vary. One extreme sample had a mean of 37.8, another had a mean of 62.3; the others fell between these extremes. The distribution of means in Table 8.1 is approximately normal. When *scores* in a population are normally distributed, the *means of different samples* are normally distributed too. Also, notice the mean of all the sample means; that mean approximately equals μ. In Table 8.1 the mean of all the sample means is 49.99; 49.99 is very close to μ.

> Characteristics of *sample means:* Normally distributed
> Their mean approximates μ

Standard error of the mean

You could also compute the *standard deviation* of the 96 sample means in Table 8.1: That standard deviation equals 5.01. It describes the variability among the sample means. The standard deviation in this case is called the *standard error of the mean.* Whenever the standard error of the mean is small, the means do not vary much; they fit closely around μ. When the standard error of the mean is large, the means vary more. In Table 8.1 most of the means—about 68 percent of them—fall within 5.01 points of 49.99.

The standard error of the mean has important uses which we shall examine soon. Statisticians have developed a simple formula for computing the standard error of the mean theoretically. Later we shall examine the theory and derive the formula. With this formula, you never really need to compile a distribution of means like the one in Table 8.1. Instead, the formula tells how variable these sample means would be.

The formula has two ingredients. First, you need to know the variability of *scores in the population*—σ. (In the artificial population of 10,000 scores, $\sigma = 15.8$. If σ is not known, you need some estimate of it. Later we shall also consider ways to estimate it.) Second, you need to know the size of the samples. In Table 8.1 each mean was based on 10 scores, so $N = 10$. The standard error of the mean is a ratio of two values; the result is denoted $\sigma_{\bar{X}}$.

$$\sigma_{\bar{X}} = \frac{\sigma}{\sqrt{N}} \tag{8.1}$$

Theoretically, then, the standard error of the mean for samples of 10 scores is $15.8/\sqrt{10} = 5.00$: The means of many 10-score samples, then, should have a standard deviation of 5.00. This value agrees well with the empirical value in Table 8.1—5.01.

The formula reflects two characteristics of $\sigma_{\bar{X}}$. First, $\sigma_{\bar{X}}$ is larger when the *scores* are more variable: The more the *scores* vary, the more the *sample means* vary. If σ were larger than 15.8, $\sigma_{\bar{X}}$ would be larger than 5.00, and the means of Table 8.1 would vary more. Second, $\sigma_{\bar{X}}$ is smaller when the sample size is large. If N were 50 instead of 10, $\sigma_{\bar{X}}$ would be smaller. Means of large samples are not as variable.

Suppose each sample contained 50 scores. The standard error of the mean would be $15.8/\sqrt{50} = 2.24$. Hence, the standard deviation of the 50-score sample means would equal 2.24. To interpret this figure, imagine many 50-score samples. I had 96 students each draw a sample of 50 scores from the population. Their resulting means are shown in Table 8.2. Again the means

TABLE 8.2 Distribution of sample means (for each sample $N = 50$)

Interval	Frequency	
55.0–55.9	1	
54.0–54.9	3	
53.0–53.9	5	
52.0–52.9	9	
51.0–51.9	13	Mean of sample means = 49.95
50.0–50.9	17	Standard deviation (S) of
49.0–49.9	16	sample means = 2.23
48.0–48.9	14	
47.0–47.9	9	
46.0–46.9	6	
45.0–45.9	2	
44.0–44.9	1	
	—	
	96 samples	

were normally distributed. And their average, 49.95, was close to μ. Notice the variability of these means: The standard deviation is 2.23, which agrees well with the theoretical value, 2.24. Large samples bring the various means closer together—hence, closer to μ.

If N were 100, the means would vary even less; the standard error would become $\sigma/\sqrt{N} = 15.8/\sqrt{100} = 1.58$. If N were 1,000, it would become 0.50. Samples of 1,000 scores would show remarkably little variation: 68 percent of them would lie within 0.5 points of μ—between 49.5 and 50.5.

Figure 8.1 shows theoretical sampling distributions for different sample sizes. In each case, imagine a population of normally distributed scores; $\mu = 50$ and $\sigma = 15.8$. Then imagine samples drawn randomly from this population. Their means would be normally distributed, and the average of these means would equal μ.

Let us consider very small samples first: Suppose each sample contained just one score: $N = 1$. In that case $\sigma_{\bar{X}} = \sigma/\sqrt{N} = 15.8/\sqrt{1} = 15.8$. This

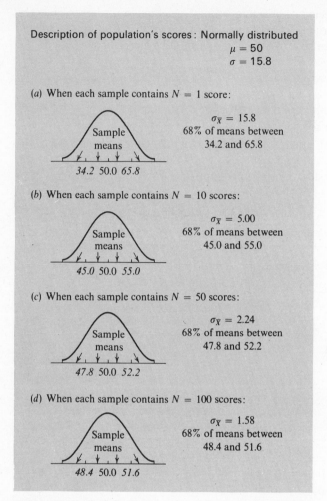

Description of population's scores: Normally distributed
$$\mu = 50$$
$$\sigma = 15.8$$

(a) When each sample contains $N = 1$ score:

Sample means

34.2 50.0 65.8

$\sigma_{\bar{X}} = 15.8$
68% of means between
34.2 and 65.8

(b) When each sample contains $N = 10$ scores:

Sample means

45.0 50.0 55.0

$\sigma_{\bar{X}} = 5.00$
68% of means between
45.0 and 55.0

(c) When each sample contains $N = 50$ scores:

Sample means

47.8 50.0 52.2

$\sigma_{\bar{X}} = 2.24$
68% of means between
47.8 and 52.2

(d) When each sample contains $N = 100$ scores:

Sample means

48.4 50.0 51.6

$\sigma_{\bar{X}} = 1.58$
68% of means between
48.4 and 51.6

FIG. 8.1 Theoretical distribution of sample means for different sample sizes.

distribution of sample means appears in the top curve of Fig. 8.1. These "means" are as variable as the original scores; their standard deviation is 15.8.

When $N = 100$, $\sigma_{\bar{X}} = \sigma/\sqrt{N} = 15.8/\sqrt{100} = 1.58$, so the sample means are very close together; their standard deviation is only 1.58. The bottom curve shows this distribution of sample means. Sixty-eight percent of the sample means lie within 1.58 points of μ.

The other two graphs describe the distribution of sample means when $N = 10$ and when $N = 50$. Notice the clear progression: As N gets larger, $\sigma_{\bar{X}}$ gets smaller; the sample means grow closer together.

Strictly speaking, the term *standard error of the mean* refers to the theoretical quantity $\sigma_{\bar{x}}$, not to the empirical value computed in Tables 8.1 and 8.2. The word "error" is used because sample means do not usually equal μ. A sample mean can be viewed as an *estimate* of μ. However, this estimate is rarely perfect; it usually contains some error. When sample means vary from one another, they also vary from μ. If they vary a lot, some means are far from μ; and means far from μ contain more error. The larger $\sigma_{\bar{x}}$, the larger the possible error.

EXAMPLE 8.1

Suppose the scores in a population are normally distributed with $\mu = 122.0$ and $\sigma = 9.0$. Someone draws a sample of 100 scores. He then repeats the procedure many times, recording the mean of each sample. (*a*) What value would you expect as the mean of all the sample means? (*b*) What value would you expect as the standard deviation of the sample means? (*c*) Sketch the distribution of sample means; how many samples per hundred would have means above 124.0?

Solution (*a*) The mean of all the sample means would approximately equal μ: 122.0.

(*b*) The standard deviation of the sample means would approximately equal

$$\sigma_{\bar{x}} = \frac{\sigma}{\sqrt{N}} = \frac{9}{\sqrt{100}} = 0.9$$

(*c*) Here is the theoretical distribution of sample means. It is a normal distribution with a mean of 122.0 and a standard deviation of 0.9.

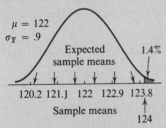

$\mu = 122$
$\sigma_{\bar{x}} = .9$

Expected sample means   1.4%

120.2 121.1 122 122.9 123.8
Sample means
124

The sample mean 124.0 lies 2.2 standard errors from the center:[1] $z = (124.0 - 122.0)/0.9 = 2.2$. According to a table of the normal curve, 1.4 percent of the curve's area exceeds $z = 2.2$. Therefore the sample mean would exceed 124.0 in roughly 1.4 samples per hundred.

---

[1] A correction for continuity is usually not applied to problems involving sample means. We assume that the scores are "continuous," so theoretically *any* value can occur. A sample's mean could equal 122.4, 122.43, 122.431, and so on. It is not restricted to discrete values like 121, 122, and 123. Therefore, the normal curve describes the scores accurately; the normal curve is not merely an *approximation* to the binomial distribution.

EXAMPLE 8.2

Intelligence tests can be made to yield some particular μ and some particular σ. Now suppose a certain intelligence test yields $\mu = 100$ and $\sigma = 16$. A representative sample of 64 people is about to be tested. (*a*) What is the probability that this sample's mean is 102 or more?

Solution   The distribution of sample means is shown below. The mean of these means equals 100; their standard error equals $16/\sqrt{64} = 2.0$.

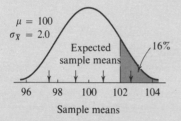

To locate 102 in this distribution, convert it to a z score: $z = (\overline{X} - \mu)/\sigma_{\overline{x}} = (102 - 100)/2 = 1.00$. Sixteen percent of the distribution exceeds 102, so $P\{\overline{X} > 102\} = .16$.

(*b*) What is the probability that a sample mean lies below 94?

Solution   The value 94 is 3 standard errors below 100: $z = (94 - 100)/2 = -3.00$. Less than 1 percent of the curve lies below 94, so $P\{\overline{X} < 94\}$ is less than .01.

The standard error of the mean has two major applications that are examined next. For one thing, $\sigma_{\overline{x}}$ is used to test hypotheses about μ. It is also used to help us determine what μ equals. In the rest of this chapter, we shall examine these two applications. After that we shall prove that $\sigma_{\overline{x}} = \sigma/\sqrt{N}$. Then we shall consider the best way to estimate σ if σ is not known.

8.2   APPLICATIONS OF $\sigma_{\overline{x}}$: HYPOTHESIS TESTING

Sample means vary; one $\overline{X}$ exceeds μ, another falls below μ. If the sample means are normally distributed, most of them fall within two standard errors of μ.

Suppose a certain population of normally distributed scores has $\sigma = 12$. For samples of 81 scores, the standard error of the mean is 1.3. Now suppose one sample is examined, and $\overline{X}$ for that sample is 79. Most sample means—and 79 is probably one of them—fall within 2.6 points of μ.

But μ itself is not known. We can only speculate—or hypothesize—about the value of μ. To be believable, of course, the hypothesis should jibe with the datum that $\overline{X} = 79$. *Reasonable* hypotheses have to agree with the empirical facts.

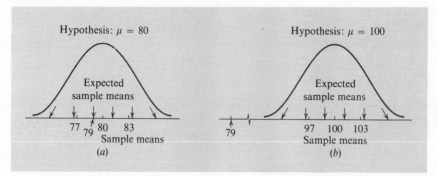

FIG. 8.2 Hypothesis testing. The normal curve shows the theoretical distribution of sample means that the hypothesis implies. (*a*) The hypothesized mean and the sample mean are consistent. (*b*) The hypothesized mean and the sample mean are not consistent.

Might μ equal 80, for example? The sample mean 79 is certainly consistent with the claim $\mu = 80$. As shown in Fig. 8.2*a*, 79 is less than one standard error from 80.

On the other hand, might μ equal 100? Suppose for a moment that μ *is* 100. Figure 8.2*b* tells what sample means to expect: The most likely means lie within 2 standard errors of 100. But 79 does not fit comfortably into that distribution at all; it is 16.2 standard errors from the center. Thus, the empirical fact ($\overline{X} = 79$) and the hypothesis ($\mu = 100$) are at odds. The data cannot be challenged, but the hypothesis might be wrong: μ is probably not 100.

Thus, we can use $\sigma_{\overline{X}}$ to test hypotheses about μ. Let us adopt the 1 percent level—$\alpha = .01$—and test the hypothesis that $\mu = 100$. The procedure requires 5 steps:

First, state a convenient hypothesis about μ. (This hypothesis is designated H_0.) In the example, H_0 is $\mu = 100$.

Second, note the alternative to the hypothesis. (The alternative is designated H_1.) Therefore, H_1 is $\mu \neq 100$.

Third, consider the sampling distribution implied by the hypothesis. If the population's scores are normally distributed, the sampling distribution would also be normal. What sample means would be expected? What are the most common sample means? What would the standard error be? Figure 8.3 shows the sampling distribution that the hypothesis implies.

Fourth, examine one sample's mean. Locate this $\overline{X}$ in the hypothesized sampling distribution. If the sample's mean is 79, locate 79 in the hypothesized distribution:

$$z = \frac{\overline{X} - \mu}{\sigma_{\overline{X}}}$$

$$= \frac{79 - 100}{1.3} = \frac{-21.0}{1.3} = -16.2$$

(8.2)

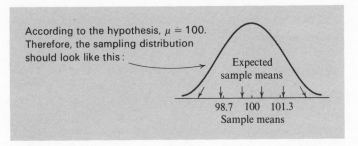

According to the hypothesis, $\mu = 100$. Therefore, the sampling distribution should look like this:

Expected sample means

98.7 100 101.3
Sample means

FIG. 8.3

In this hypothesized distribution, 79 lies more than 16 standard deviations below the center.

Finally, evaluate the hypothesis. Does $\overline{X}$ fall within the middle 99 percent of the distribution ($\alpha = .01$)? If so, the hypothesis is tenable; otherwise, it is not. In this example, $\overline{X}$ does *not* fit comfortably into the hypothesized distribution: If $\mu = 100$, then the one bit of data—$\overline{X} = 79$—is a rare event; a sample whose $\overline{X}$ is 79 is unusual—a less than one in a hundred kind of sample. If μ really equals 100, the probability is less than .01 that $\overline{X}$ be as extreme as 79. But according to the data, $\overline{X}$ *does* equal 79. Hence, the hypothesis is probably false. At $\alpha = .01$ the hypothesis "$\mu = 100$" is therefore rejected. Instead, the alternative hypothesis is accepted: $\mu \neq 100$.

EXAMPLE 8.3

An investigator composed some standard passages for studying the reading process. He timed thousands of college students reading this passage, and he estimated the μ and σ of the population. According to his estimates, $\mu = 13.5$ min, and $\sigma = 2.0$ min. The scores were normally distributed.

Next the investigator decided to examine a new style of print which was designed to improve reading speed. He had his passages printed in the new style, and he administered them to 16 students selected at random. The mean of the sample was 12.0 min.

If the new style does not differ from the old style, the 16-student sample is like a random sample from the general population. (For the general population $\mu = 13.5$.) Test the hypothesis at $\alpha = .05$ that $\mu = 13.5$ for this sample's population, too.

Solution

Step 1   State H_0: $\mu = 13.5$. According to this hypothesis, sample means center around 13.5. (Their standard error is $2.0/\sqrt{16} = 0.5$.)

Step 2   State H_1: $\mu \neq 13.5$.

Step 3 Examine the sampling distribution:

According to H_0, $\mu = 13.5$. If many 16-score samples were drawn from the population, their $\bar{X}$'s would vary. The sampling distribution would look like this:

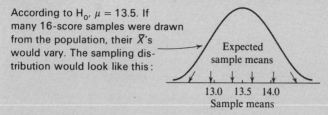

Expected sample means

13.0 13.5 14.0
Sample means

Step 4 Locate the one sample's outcome:

$$z = \frac{\bar{X} - \mu}{\sigma_{\bar{X}}} = \frac{12 - 13.5}{0.5} = -3.0$$

Step 5 Make a decision. The sample mean 12.0 does not fit comfortably into the hypothesized distribution. It falls more than 1.96 standard deviations from the center. Therefore, at $\alpha = .05$, H_0 is rejected. Instead, we conclude, $\mu \neq 13.5$. Apparently, the new-styled sample does not belong to a population with $\mu = 13.5$. (The sample's population seems to have a lower μ. Apparently, the new style of print *is* read faster.)

EXAMPLE 8.4

An investigator used a certain maze to study the learning process in rats. He collected extensive norms and from his norms he estimated the population parameters: $\mu = 120$ errors and $\sigma = 15$ errors. The scores were normally distributed. Recently a new strain of rats was developed. According to the advertisements, this new strain learns significantly faster. To test this claim, the investigator examined 36 rats of the new strain. The sample mean was 117 errors. Is this sample like a random sample from the general population? Use $\alpha = .05$, and test the hypothesis that $\mu = 120$ for the new strain, too.

Solution

Step 1 State H_0: $\mu = 120$. According to this hypothesis, sample means center around 120. (Their standard error is $15/\sqrt{36} = 2.5$.)

Step 2 State H_1: $\mu \neq 120$.

Step 3 Note the sampling distribution which the hypothesis implies

According to H_0, $\mu = 120$.
The sampling distribution should look like this:

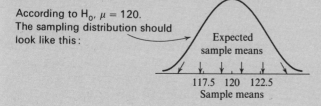

Expected sample means

117.5 120 122.5
Sample means

Step 4   Locate the one sample's outcome in the sampling distribution:

$$z = \frac{\bar{X} - \mu}{\sigma_{\bar{X}}} = \frac{117 - 120}{2.5} = -1.2$$

Thus, 117 *does* fit comfortably into the hypothesized distribution.

Step 5   Make a decision. The sample mean 117 is only 1.2 standard errors from the hypothesized μ. Therefore, at $\alpha = .05$, H_0 is accepted: $\mu = 120$. (The advertised strain does fit comfortably into the general population, so those rats do *not* seem to learn significantly faster.)

8.3   APPLICATIONS OF $\sigma_{\bar{X}}$: ESTABLISHING A CONFIDENCE INTERVAL

Sometimes an investigator needs to estimate some parameter of a population. Say he needs to estimate μ. There are two ways to make this estimate; one is called a *point estimate*. A point estimate is a single number that tells the investigator's best guess about μ. For example, the investigator might examine a random sample from the population, compute $\bar{X}$, and report $\bar{X}$ as his best guess about μ. $\bar{X}$ is then a point estimate of μ.

The other kind of estimate is called an *interval estimate*. Instead of estimating μ by a single number, the investigator computes a *range* of likely values. The range is chosen so that it probably does include μ. The range itself is called a *confidence interval*. Its boundaries are called *confidence limits* or *fiducial limits*.

Let us establish a confidence interval as a way of estimating μ. Suppose the scores in a certain population are normally distributed and $\sigma = 10$. An investigator draws a sample of 25 scores. The standard error of the mean, then, is $10/\sqrt{25} = 2.0$. The investigator also notes the mean of one sample: $\bar{X} = 22.4$.

The value of μ is not known, of course, but whatever it is, the sampling distribution looks as shown in Fig. 8.4. Since $\sigma_{\bar{X}} = 2.0$, 68 percent of the sample means fall within 2.0 points of μ (on either side). And 95 percent of the sample means fall within $(1.96)(\sigma_{\bar{X}}) = (1.96)(2.0) = 3.92$ points of μ. If μ were known—say $\mu = 24.7$—we could reconstruct the whole distribution: 68 percent of the sample means would fall between 22.7 and 26.7; 95 percent would fall between 20.8 and 28.6.

But μ is not known. Only one bit of data is known, the *sample's* mean: $\bar{X} = 22.4$. This $\bar{X}$ falls somewhere in the distribution. Perhaps it lies relatively close to μ, perhaps it lies 1 standard deviation above μ. Let us consider two extreme possibilities. Case 1: Suppose 22.4 actually lies 1.96 standard deviations above μ. What would μ equal? μ would certainly be less than 22.4: It

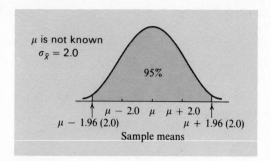

FIG. 8.4

would lie 1.96 standard errors below $\overline{X}$. Now " 1.96 standard errors below $\overline{X}$ " is 1.96 $\sigma_{\overline{X}} = 1.96(2.0) = 3.92$ points below $\overline{X}$. μ would equal 22.4–3.92, or 18.48. This relationship is shown in Fig. 8.5a.

On the other hand, consider another extreme, Case 2. Suppose $\overline{X} = 22.4$ actually lies *below* μ. Suppose $\overline{X}$ lies 1.96 standard errors *below* μ—that is, $(1.96)(2.0) = 3.92$ points below μ. Then μ would exceed 22.4, and it would equal 26.32. This relationship is shown in Fig. 8.5b.

Thus, we have considered two extreme possibilities. In Case 1, the sample mean 22.4 was quite a distance *above* μ; μ then equaled 18.48. In Case 2, the sample mean 22.4 was quite a distance *below* μ; μ then equaled 26.32. Chances are, $\overline{X}$ lies somewhere between these two extremes—somewhere between " 1.96 standard errors below μ " and " 1.96 standard errors above μ." Therefore, μ probably lies somewhere between 18.48 and 26.32. The probability is .95 that the sample mean 22.4 lies within 1.96 standard errors of μ. Hence, the probability is .95 that we have managed to identify μ correctly. The resulting interval, 18.48–26.32, is therefore called the 95 percent confidence interval.

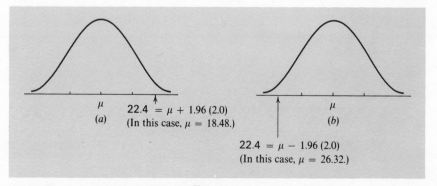

FIG. 8.5 Two extreme cases for locating $\overline{X} = 22.4$. (*a*) 22.4 is 1.96 standard errors above μ. (*b*) 22.4 is 1.96 standard errors below μ.

The procedure can be summarized this way:

> 95% confidence interval for μ: $\overline{X} \pm 1.96\sigma_{\overline{X}}$
> $22.4 \pm 1.96(2.0)$
> 22.4 ± 3.92
> 95% confidence interval for μ: 18.48–26.32

The phrase "95 percent confidence" reflects our confidence that $\overline{X}$ does fall between the two extremes; the probability that it does is .95. Therefore, the probability is .95 that the resulting interval manages to capture μ.

What if $\overline{X}$ were *more* than 1.96 standard errors from μ? Suppose $\overline{X}$ happened to be 2.5 standard errors above μ (Fig. 8.6). (In other words, suppose μ equaled 17.4.) Such extreme sample means are rare, but when they happen, the procedure fails: The 95 percent confidence interval (18.48–26.32) is not broad enough to include this μ.

To set broader limits, an investigator might establish the "99 percent confidence interval." He would reason this way: 99 percent of all sample means fall within 2.58 standard errors of μ. Therefore, let us consider the two extreme cases. First, suppose $\overline{X}$ lies 2.58 standard errors *below* μ; what is μ? Then suppose $\overline{X}$ lies 2.58 standard errors *above* μ; what is μ? The two answers set the extremes; they form the 99 percent confidence limits for μ.

$$99\% \text{ confidence interval: } \overline{X} \pm 2.58\sigma_{\overline{X}}$$
$$\overline{X} \pm 2.58(2.0)$$
$$\overline{X} \pm 5.16$$
$$99\% \text{ confidence interval: } 17.24\text{–}27.56.$$

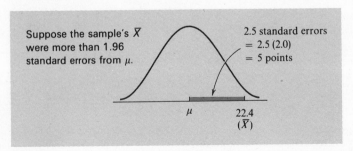

Suppose the sample's $\overline{X}$ were more than 1.96 standard errors from μ.

2.5 standard errors
= 2.5 (2.0)
= 5 points

μ 22.4
($\overline{X}$)

FIG. 8.6

Notice that the 99 percent confidence limits are further apart than the 95 percent confidence limits. The 99 percent limits do not pinpoint μ as well; but the probability is greater that the interval manages to capture μ.

The most common confidence limits can be summarized this way:

$$68\% \text{ confidence limits: } \bar{X} \pm 1\sigma_{\bar{X}} \tag{8.3}$$

$$95\% \text{ confidence limits: } \bar{X} \pm 1.96\sigma_{\bar{X}} \tag{8.4}$$

$$99\% \text{ confidence limits: } \bar{X} \pm 2.58\sigma_{\bar{X}} \tag{8.5}$$

EXAMPLE 8.5

An investigator plans to examine the effects of illumination on reading speed. In a pilot study, he tests 49 subjects. The scores are normally distributed, and from his data he takes σ to equal 21 sec. The sample's $\bar{X}$ is 240 sec.

Sample data: $\bar{X} = 240$ sec
$N = 49$ subjects
$\sigma = 21$ sec (best available estimate)

(a) What is the 99 percent confidence interval for μ?

Solution   First, we need to compute the standard error of the mean.

$$\sigma_{\bar{X}} = \frac{\sigma}{\sqrt{N}} = \frac{21}{\sqrt{49}} = 3.00$$

The 99 percent interval, then, equals:

99% confidence interval: $\bar{X} \pm 2.58\sigma_{\bar{X}} = 240 \pm 2.58(3.00)$
$\qquad\qquad\qquad\qquad\qquad\qquad = 240 \pm 7.74$
99% confidence interval: 232.26–247.74

Thus, the sample's mean, $\bar{X} = 240$, probably lies within 2.58 standard errors of μ. If it does, then μ lies between 232.26 sec and 247.74 sec.

(b) Next the investigator starts planning a major study. The same task is to be used, and he wants to allow enough time for every subject to complete the task. How much time should he allow?

Solution   To be prepared for the slowest subject, he might assume that $\mu = 247.74$. Scores in the population would then be distributed this way:

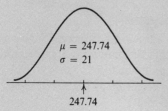

$\mu = 247.74$
$\sigma = 21$

247.74

The scores would range from approximately 193.56 (2.58 standard deviations below μ) to 301.92 (2.58 standard deviations above μ). Therefore, by allowing 6 min—360 sec—the experimenter would be prepared for the slowest subject.

8.4 PROOF THAT $\sigma_{\bar{X}} = \dfrac{\sigma}{\sqrt{N}}$

Next we need to derive the equation for the standard error. To perform this derivation, let us first lay some groundwork. We begin by considering the mean and variance of sums. Then we shall use the results to derive $\sigma_{\bar{X}}$.

Mean and variance of sums

Here are some data on four subjects. Each subject has two scores, an X score and a Y score. The X scores can be described this way: $\bar{X} = 10$, $S_X{}^2 = 0.5$. The Y scores can be described this way: $\bar{Y} = 4.0$, $S_Y{}^2 = 4.5$.

	X	Y	$X + Y$
Subject 1	9	4	13
Subject 2	10	7	17
Subject 3	11	4	15
Subject 4	10	1	11
Mean	10.0	4.0	
Variance (S^2)	0.5	4.5	

Furthermore, the correlation between X and Y happens to equal 0. To prove that r_{XY} is 0, notice these facts: Subject 2 and Subject 4 have X scores equal to $\bar{X}$; for them, $z_X = 0$, so their $z_X \cdot z_Y$ product would equal 0. The other two subjects, Subject 1 and Subject 3, have Y scores equal to $\bar{Y}$. For them, $z_Y = 0$, so their $z_X \cdot z_Y$ product would also equal 0. In every case then, $z_X \cdot z_Y = 0$, so $\sum z_X \cdot z_Y = 0$. Hence $r_{XY} = (\sum z_X z_Y)/N = 0$.

Every subject's scores have been summed to yield a total score $X + Y$. What is the mean of these $X + Y$ scores? What is their variance? You might compute their mean and variance directly from the data above. The resulting mean would equal 14.0, and the variance would equal 5.0.

These results suggest two things. First, the mean of the sums seems to equal the sum of the two separate means, $\bar{X}$ and $\bar{Y}$.

$$\text{Mean of } (X + Y) = \overline{X} + \overline{Y} \tag{8.6}$$

In the data, $14 = 10 + 4$. Second, the variance of the sums, 5, is related to the variance of the parts. In general, the relationship can be described this way:

$$S^2_{X+Y} = S_X{}^2 + S_Y{}^2 + 2r_{XY} S_X S_Y \tag{8.7}$$

When the correlation between X and Y is 0, though, the variance of the sums equals the variance of the X scores plus the variance of the Y scores:

$$S^2_{X+Y} = S_X{}^2 + S_Y{}^2$$

In the data, $r_{XY} = 0$, so $S^2_{X+Y} = 0.5 + 4.5$.

These formulas are easy to derive. To derive the formula for the mean, sum the $X + Y$ scores—there are N such scores. Then divide by N.

$$\text{Mean of ``}X + Y\text{''} = \frac{\sum (X + Y)}{N}$$

$$= \frac{\sum X + \sum Y}{N} = \frac{\sum X}{N} + \frac{\sum Y}{N}$$

$$= \overline{X} + \overline{Y}$$

To derive the formula for S^2_{X+Y}, express each $(X + Y)$ as a deviation from $\overline{X} + \overline{Y}$. The deviation scores are then squared, summed, and divided by N.

$$S^2_{X+Y} = \frac{\sum [(X + Y) - (\overline{X} + \overline{Y})]^2}{N}$$

Now rearrange the terms in the brackets:

$$S^2_{X+Y} = \frac{\sum [(X - \overline{X}) + (Y - \overline{Y})]^2}{N} = \frac{\sum [x + y]^2}{N}$$

Next perform the squaring and then sum.

$$S^2_{X+Y} = \frac{\sum [x^2 + 2xy + y^2]}{N} = \frac{\sum x^2}{N} + \frac{\sum y^2}{N} + \frac{2 \sum xy}{N}$$

$\sum x^2/N$ is the variance of the X scores, $S_X{}^2$; $(\sum y^2)/N$ is the variance of the Y scores, $S_Y{}^2$.

What about the term $(\sum xy)/N$? This term is related to the correlation coefficient, r_{XY}:

$$r_{XY} = \frac{\sum xy}{N S_X S_Y}$$

Therefore:

$$\frac{\sum xy}{N} = r_{XY} S_X S_Y$$

Thus, the equation for S^2_{X+Y} can be written:

$$S^2_{X+Y} = S_X{}^2 + S_Y{}^2 + 2r_{XY} S_X S_Y$$

If $r_{XY} = 0$, $S^2_{X+Y} = S_X{}^2 + S_Y{}^2$

Sometimes an investigator adds three or more scores together to yield a single composite score. Perhaps the scores are scores on three subtests. Let us call them W, X, and Y. The total might be denoted T; then any subject's T equals his $W + X + Y$. Now what is the variance of the T scores? If the parts are uncorrelated—$r_{WX} = 0$, $r_{WY} = 0$, and $r_{XY} = 0$—then the variance of the T scores is the sum of the three part variances.

$$S_T{}^2 = S_W{}^2 + S_X{}^2 + S_Y{}^2 \qquad (r_{WX} = 0; r_{WY} = 0; \text{ and } r_{XY} = 0.)$$

This relationship holds for any number of parts—as long as the parts are uncorrelated.

EXAMPLE 8.6

A test was administered to 100 individuals. The test contained two parts. For Part 1, $S = 3$; for Part 2, $S = 4$. Finally, each subject's total score was computed: Part 1 + Part 2. (a) If the correlation between the parts is 0, what is the standard deviation of the totals?

Solution

$$S^2{}_{Total} = S^2{}_{Part\ 1} + S^2{}_{Part\ 2} = 3^2 + 4^2 = 25$$

$$S_{Total} = \sqrt{25} = 5$$

(b) Suppose the value of r between the parts is .70. Compute S_{X+Y}.

Solution

$$S^2_{\text{Total}} = S^2_{X+Y} = S^2_X + S^2_Y + 2r_{XY}S_X S_Y$$

$$= 3^2 + 4^2 + 2(.70)(3)(4) = 41.8$$

$$S_{\text{Total}} = \sqrt{41.8} = 6.5$$

EXAMPLE 8.7

A certain aptitude test has 10 component parts, and these parts are summed to yield a total score (T). The test was designed so that no two parts are correlated. For each part, $S = 4$. Compute S_T, the standard deviation of the total test scores.

Solution   Visualize the data this way:

	Score on part 1	Score on part 2	$\cdots$	Score on part 10	Total score (T)
Subject 1	7	4	$\cdots$	7	79
Subject 2	4	9	$\cdots$	2	64
$\vdots$	$\vdots$	$\vdots$		$\vdots$	$\vdots$
Subject i	6	5		4	83
$\vdots$	$\vdots$	$\vdots$		$\vdots$	$\vdots$
Standard deviation	$S_1 = 4$	$S_2 = 4$	$\cdots$	$S_{10} = 4$	$S_T = ?$

S^2_T equals the sum of the separate S^2 terms. For each part $S^2 = 4^2 = 16$, so the variance of the total scores equals:

$$S^2_T = 4^2 + 4^2 + \cdots (10 \text{ terms}) = 10(4^2) = 160$$

$$S_T = \sqrt{160} = 12.6$$

In general, suppose m separate parts all have the same variance, S^2. Suppose these parts are then summed to yield a total score. If all the intercorrelations equal 0, the variance of the totals, S_T^2, equals mS^2.

Derivation of $\sigma_{\bar{x}}$

Next let us prove that $\sigma_{\bar{x}}$ equals $\sigma/\sqrt{N}$. Consider a population of scores with $\mu = 50$ and $\sigma = 10$, and suppose scores are drawn at random. Since they are drawn at random, every score in the population has an equal chance of being selected. And one score's selection is independent of another's.

Suppose the sample contains N scores; let us call it Sample 1. Then suppose another sample is drawn, Sample 2; it too contains N scores. Then a third, a fourth, and so on. Suppose this procedure is repeated many, many times—say, an infinite number of times—and imagine the resulting data:

	Score 1	Score 2	Score 3	Score 4	$\cdots$	Score N	Sample's mean $(\bar{X})$
Sample 1	43	50	27	44	$\cdots$	69	51
Sample 2	62	47	48	58	$\cdots$	50	54
$\vdots$							
Sample 1,000,000							
$\vdots$							

The last column depicts each sample's mean—an infinite number of sample means. And each mean, of course, is based on N scores. Let us consider the standard deviation of all these means. *That standard deviation, whatever it is, is the standard error of the mean.* We need to examine it theoretically.

To examine this standard deviation, let us modify the table. Consider a column labeled " sample's total," and imagine each sample's $\sum X$. Let us call the total T.

	Score 1	Score 2	Score 3	$\cdots$	Score N	$T = \Sigma X$
Sample 1	43	50	27		69	$\vdots$
Sample 2	62	47	48		50	$\vdots$
$\vdots$	$\vdots$	$\vdots$	$\vdots$		$\vdots$	$\vdots$
Sample 1,000,000						
$\vdots$	$\vdots$	$\vdots$	$\vdots$		$\vdots$	$\vdots$
Variance of the column	$\uparrow$ $100 = \sigma^2$	$\uparrow$ $100 = \sigma^2$	$\uparrow$ $100 = \sigma^2$		$\uparrow$ $100 = \sigma^2$	$\uparrow$ $N \cdot 100 = N \cdot \sigma^2$
Standard deviation of the column	$10 = \sigma$	$10 = \sigma$	$10 = \sigma$		$10 = \sigma$	

Consider the variance of these T's. Their variance happens to be related to σ^2, the variance of scores in the population. We can prove that the variance of the T's equals $N\sigma^2$. First, consider Column 1 in the table. This column lists the first *score* of each sample. The number of samples is infinitely large, so theoretically, Column 1 contains an infinite number of scores (all of the "first scores"). Now the variance of the scores in Column 1 happens to equal σ^2. Here is why: Whenever a set of scores is very large, its variance reliably approximates the *population's* variance. The larger the set, the more we can trust its variance to approximate σ^2. The variance of a set which is *infinitely* large theoretically equals σ^2. Column 1's listing is infinitely large, so its variance equals σ^2. (In the example, σ^2 equals 10^2, or 100.)

Likewise, Column 2 is infinitely large—a listing of the *second* score of each sample. The variance of this listing also equals σ^2. In the same way, each column contains an infinite listing of scores; therefore, each column's variance theoretically equals σ^2.

Theoretically, no column of scores is correlated with any other column. The scores have been drawn at random so they are independent—uncorrelated. The listing in Column 1 is not correlated with the listing in Column 2. The listing in any column, "Column i," is not correlated with the listing in any other column, "Column j."

Now let us consider the variance of the totals—the column of T's. The variance of the totals equals the sum of each column's variance. Theoretically:

The variance of the column of T's =

$$\sigma^2 \quad + \quad \sigma^2 \quad + \quad \sigma^2 \quad + \cdots (N \text{ times})$$

(Variance of Column 1) (Variance of Column 2) (Variance of Column 3)

Variance of the T's $= N\sigma^2$
$$\sigma_T^2 = N\sigma^2$$

Hence, the standard deviation of the T's equals:

$$\sigma_T = \sqrt{N\sigma^2} = \sigma\sqrt{N}$$

However, we are not really interested in the listing of T's. Instead we are interested in the listing of *means*. Each mean is a sample total (T) divided by N. The relationship between T and $\overline{X}$ is shown in the table at the top of page 198.

	T column, sample's total, $\sum X$ *or T*	*X̄ column, sample's mean,* $\sum X/N = T/N = \bar{X}$
Sample 1	839	839/N
Sample 2	724	724/N
Sample 3	968	968/N
⋮		
Sample 1,000,000	⋮	⋮
⋮		
Standard deviation	$\sigma_T = \sigma\sqrt{N}$	?

A sample's $\bar{X}$ equals its T divided by N. But in general, suppose each entry in a set of numbers is divided by some constant (like N); then the standard deviation also gets divided by that constant. Now that standard deviation of the T column equals $\sigma\sqrt{N}$. So the standard deviation of the $\bar{X}$ column equals the same value divided by N: $\sigma_T/N = \sigma\sqrt{N}/N$.

$$\sigma_{\bar{X}} = \frac{\sigma\sqrt{N}}{N} = \frac{\sigma}{\sqrt{N}}$$

This result tells the standard deviation of an infinite listing of means. Theoretically, then, it equals the standard error of the mean.

8.5 COMPUTING A BEST ESTIMATE OF σ

The formula for $\sigma_{\bar{X}}$ contains σ, the standard deviation of scores in the population. To use $\sigma_{\bar{X}}$, then, we either need the value of σ, or else we need to estimate it. In practice, of course, the exact value of σ is usually not known, so we need to estimate it.

How would you estimate σ? As one approach, you might draw a random sample of scores, then compute $S = \sqrt{[\sum (X - \bar{X})^2]/N}$, and then use S as your estimate of σ. But S is not a good estimate of σ. S systematically underestimates σ.

To clarify this point, consider the more general problem: When shall we say that a sample statistic is a *good* estimate of the population parameter? Why is a sample's $\bar{X}$ a good estimate of μ and why is a sample's S a poor estimate of σ?

First, consider the sample's mean. $\bar{X}$ is called a *good* or an *unbiased* estimate of μ. For suppose an experimenter estimated μ over and over: Suppose he drew sample after sample and recorded each sample's $\bar{X}$. The average of all his estimates would be perfect; the average $\bar{X}$ *would* equal μ. Admittedly, $\bar{X}$ would be larger than μ in some samples, smaller than μ in other samples.

But the average $\overline{X}$ would equal μ. We say that the expectation of $\overline{X}$ is μ, and we write: $E(\overline{X}) = \mu$. There is no systematic error. That is why a sample's mean is called an unbiased—hence, a good—estimate of μ.

This is not so, however, with a sample's S. When S is computed from a sample, it is said to be a *biased* estimate of σ. S, in the long run, tends to be smaller than σ. On the average—over many samples—a sample's S *under-estimates* σ. The expectation of S, $E(S)$, is less than σ. Therefore, we need to consider why this bias occurs. After that, we will derive a better estimate of σ, one that is not biased. This unbiased estimate of σ will be denoted s, and it will equal

$$\sqrt{\frac{\sum (X - \overline{X})^2}{N - 1}}$$

The reason S underestimates σ

Imagine yourself computing the variance of a population: You note every score in the population and record its deviation from μ. Then you square each deviation—$(X - \mu)^2$. Finally, you average the squared deviations—by summing them and dividing by N. Now a variance can always be viewed as a mean—a mean of all the squared deviations. So the population's variance, σ^2, can be viewed as a mean too—the mean of all the $(X - \mu)^2$ values in the population.

But suppose the population were extremely large. The investigator could not actually compute σ^2; he could only estimate σ^2 from a single sample. Suppose he randomly drew 10 scores from the population: 19, 21, 15, 13, 5, 9, 23, 9, 13, 23. How might he estimate σ^2?

If he knew μ, he could estimate σ^2 this way: He could convert each score to an $(X - \mu)^2$ and then compute the mean of the ten $(X - \mu)^2$ values. A *sample's* mean, after all, is a good estimate of the *population's* mean. From a sample of $(X - \mu)^2$ values, the investigator could estimate the mean of the whole population's $(X - \mu)^2$ values.

> "The mean of the sample's ten $(X - \mu)^2$ values"
> estimates
> "the mean of the whole population's $(X - \mu)^2$ values"
> (which equals σ^2).

Thus, the investigator could compute $[\sum (X - \mu)^2]/10$ as a good estimate of σ^2.

Usually, of course, μ is not known. But for the moment, suppose the investigator does know μ, and suppose $\mu = 14$. Assuming that $\mu = 14$, let us estimate σ^2. Each $(X - \mu)^2$ would become $(X - 14)^2$. And $[\sum (X - 14)^2]/10$ would equal 37. If $\mu = 14$, the best estimate of σ^2 would equal 37.

Of course, μ might not equal 14. Perhaps μ equals 15. In that case, each $(X - \mu)^2$ would become $(X - 15)^2$. And the best estimate of σ^2 would equal 36.

Table 8.3 considers different possible μ's. For each case σ^2 is estimated. If $\mu = 15$, the estimate is 36. If μ equals 14 or 16, the estimate is 37. (Notice that the estimate is smallest when $\mu = 15$.)

The ideal estimate of σ^2, then, is based on squared deviations from μ: These $(X - \mu)^2$ values provide an unbiased estimate of σ^2. To use this method, though, we need to know μ. And μ, of course, is usually not known.

Suppose an investigator, not knowing μ, wanted to estimate μ. His best estimate would be the sample's $\overline{X}$; for the 10-score sample, $\overline{X} = 15$. μ might really equal 13.4 or 14.1 or 17.9, but he would estimate it to be 15: $\overline{X} = 15$. Now suppose he used $\overline{X}$ to estimate σ^2. He would compute squared deviations around $\overline{X}$: $[\sum (X - \overline{X})^2]/N = [\sum (X - 15)^2]/10 = 36$. (This term, of course, is S^2.)

If μ *did* equal $\overline{X}$, the estimate 36 would be fine. But suppose μ differed from $\overline{X}$. Then the ideal estimate ought to be higher: If $\mu = 13$, the ideal estimate ought to be 40; if $\mu = 14$, the ideal estimate ought to be 37; if $\mu = 16$, the ideal estimate ought to be 37. If μ differed the slightest bit from $\overline{X}$, the ideal estimate ought to be higher. The term $S^2 = [\sum (X - \overline{X})^2]/N$ gives the smallest possible estimate. (This point is proved in the chapter appendix.) S^2 is only a valid estimate when $\overline{X}$ and μ coincide. Usually $\overline{X}$ and μ do differ a little, so usually S^2 underestimates σ^2.

Let us examine the problem algebraically. Here is a derivation that will relate S^2 to the ideal estimate of σ^2. The ideal estimate involves $(X - \mu)$ values. Each $(X - \mu)$ can be written in two parts:

$$(X - \mu) = (X - \overline{X}) + (\overline{X} - \mu)$$

$$\uparrow \phantom{(X - \overline{X}) +} \uparrow$$

$$\text{Part 1} \text{Part 2}$$

Part 1 tells the score's deviation from $\overline{X}$; Part 2 tells $\overline{X}$'s deviation from μ.

[The first score in the sample was 19, and the sample's $\overline{X}$ was 15. Now suppose μ equals 13. Then $X - \mu = 19 - 13 = 6$. This six-point deviation can be written in two parts: Part 1 equals $(X - \overline{X}) = (19 - 15) = 4$; Part 2 equals $(\overline{X} - \mu) = (15 - 13) = 2$.]

Next, consider the squared deviation scores:

$$(X - \mu) = (X - \overline{X}) + (\overline{X} - \mu) \text{analogous to } c = a + b$$
$$(X - \mu)^2 = [(X - \overline{X}) + (\overline{X} - \mu)]^2 c^2 = (a + b)^2$$
$$ = (X - \overline{X})^2 + (\overline{X} - \mu)^2 + 2(X - \overline{X})(\overline{X} - \mu) = a^2 + b^2 + 2ab$$

TABLE 8.3 The best estimate of σ^2 given different values of μ

	Case 1 If μ equals 12:		Case 2 If μ equals 13:		Case 3 If μ equals 14:	
	X	$(X-\mu)^2$	X	$(X-\mu)^2$	X	$(X-\mu)^2$
	19	49	19	36	19	25
	21	81	21	64	21	49
	15	9	15	4	15	1
	13	1	13	0	13	1
	5	49	5	64	5	81
	9	9	9	16	9	25
	23	121	23	100	23	81
	9	9	9	16	9	25
	13	1	13	0	13	1
	23	121	23	100	23	81
		450		400		370
Ideal estimate of σ^2 equals:	$\dfrac{\sum(X-\mu)^2}{N}=\dfrac{450}{10}$ $=45$		$\dfrac{\sum(X-\mu)^2}{N}=\dfrac{400}{10}$ $=40$		$\dfrac{\sum(X-\mu)^2}{N}=\dfrac{370}{10}$ $=37$	

	Case 4 If μ equals 15:		Case 5 If μ equals 16:		Case 6 If μ equals 17:	
	X	$(X-\mu)^2$	X	$(X-\mu)^2$	X	$(X-\mu)^2$
	19	16	19	9	19	4
	21	36	21	25	21	16
	15	0	15	1	15	4
	13	4	13	9	13	16
	5	100	5	121	5	144
	9	36	9	49	9	64
	23	64	23	49	23	36
	9	36	9	49	9	64
	13	4	13	9	13	16
	23	64	23	49	23	36
		360		370		400
Ideal estimate of σ^2 equals:	$\dfrac{\sum(X-\mu)^2}{N}=\dfrac{360}{10}$ $=36$		$\dfrac{\sum(X-\mu)^2}{N}=\dfrac{370}{10}$ $=37$		$\dfrac{\sum(X-\mu)2}{N}=\dfrac{400}{10}$ $=40$	

Now sum all of the sample's $(X-\mu)^2$ values: $\sum(X-\mu)^2$.

$$\sum(X-\mu)^2 = \underset{1}{\sum(X-\overline{X})^2} + \underset{2}{\sum(\overline{X}-\mu)^2} + \underset{3}{\sum 2(X-\overline{X})(\overline{X}-\mu)}.$$

Consider Term **2**, $\sum (\overline{X} - \mu)^2$. For any sample of data, $(\overline{X} - \mu)^2$ is a constant number; in the example, $(\overline{X} - \mu)^2 = (15 - 13)^2 = 2^2$. Therefore, $\sum (\overline{X} - \mu)^2$ is the sum of a constant number—so it equals $N(\overline{X} - \mu)^2$.

Also consider Term **3**, $\sum 2(X - \overline{X})(\overline{X} - \mu)$. Since "2" and "$(\overline{X} - \mu)$" are both constants, this term is written: $2(\overline{X} - \mu) \sum (X - \overline{X})$. But $\sum (X - \overline{X})$, the sum of all the deviation scores, always equals 0. Therefore, the entire term equals 0.

To summarize, then:

$$\sum (X - \mu)^2 = \sum (X - \overline{X})^2 + N(\overline{X} - \mu)^2$$

Finally, divide $\sum (X - \mu)^2$ by N. The result is an unbiased estimate of σ^2.

$$\frac{\sum (X - \mu)^2}{N} = \frac{\sum (X - \overline{X})^2}{N} + \frac{N(\overline{X} - \mu)^2}{N}$$

The unbiased estimate of $\sigma^2 = S^2 + (\overline{X} - \mu)^2$.

This equation explains why S^2 is a poor estimate of σ^2: S^2 is too small. S^2 plus "something more" gives a good estimate of σ^2. The "something more" equals $(\overline{X} - \mu)^2$.

Suppose $\overline{X} = 15$ and $\mu = 13$. Then $(\overline{X} - \mu)^2 = 2^2 = 4$, and S^2 would be 4 points too small. S^2 might equal 36, but the ideal estimate should equal $36 + 4 = 40$. If $\overline{X}$ and μ differed by 3 points, then $(\overline{X} - \mu)^2$ would equal 9; and S^2 would be 9 points too small.

Generally, then, S^2 gives too small an estimate of σ^2. To be exact, S^2 is $(\overline{X} - \mu)^2$ points too small. If we knew what $(\overline{X} - \mu)^2$ equaled, we could correct the estimate. But μ is usually not known, so $(\overline{X} - \mu)^2$ is not known either.

A solution to the problem

There *is* a way to estimate $(\overline{X} - \mu)^2$, though. This value plus S^2 gives the ideal estimate of σ^2.

Consider many different samples—say, k different samples. And theoretically, imagine each sample's value of $(\overline{X} - \mu)^2$. Then imagine the mean of all these $(\overline{X} - \mu)^2$ values: We sum all k of them and divide by k:

$$\text{Mean value of } (\overline{X} - \mu)^2 = \frac{\sum (\overline{X} - \mu)^2}{k}$$

But this term happens to be the variance of the sample $\overline{X}$'s: Their theoretical center is μ, so $(\overline{X} - \mu)^2$ is a squared deviation from the center. For an infinite number of samples, this term would equal $\sigma_{\overline{X}}^2$—the squared form of $\sigma_{\overline{X}}$. Theoretically, then, the *average* value of $(\overline{X} - \mu)^2$ is the same as $\sigma_{\overline{X}}^2$. For the average sample, $(\overline{X} - \mu)^2$ should equal $\sigma_{\overline{X}}^2$.

Now let us return to the derivation. For any one sample:

The unbiased estimate of $\sigma^2 = S^2 + (\overline{X} - \mu)^2$

Now consider each term in this equation when it is averaged over many samples. That is, consider each term's expectation.

$$E(\text{the unbiased estimate of } \sigma^2) = E(S^2) + E(\overline{X} - \mu)^2$$

$$\sigma^2 = (\text{the average sample's } S^2) + \sigma_{\bar{x}}^2$$

$$\sigma^2 = (\text{the average sample's } S^2) + \frac{\sigma^2}{N}$$

Next rearrange the terms:

$$\sigma^2 - \frac{\sigma^2}{N} = (\text{the average sample's } S^2)$$

$$\frac{N\sigma^2 - \sigma^2}{N} = (\text{the average sample's } S^2)$$

$$\frac{N-1}{N}\sigma^2 = (\text{the average sample's } S^2)$$

For the average sample, then, S^2 is only a fraction of σ^2; it equals $N - 1/N$ of the population's variance, σ^2.

Suppose a sample contained 10 scores, hence, $N = 10$; for the average 10-score sample, S^2 would equal $\frac{9}{10}$ of σ^2. Or suppose $N = 100$; for the average 100-score sample, S^2 would equal $\frac{99}{100}$ of σ^2. When the sample is small, the bias is more serious.

Finally, let us solve the equation for σ^2:

$$\frac{N-1}{N}\sigma^2 = (\text{the average sample's } S^2)$$

$$\sigma^2 = \frac{N}{N-1}(\text{the average sample's } S^2)$$

For the average sample, then:

$$\sigma^2 = \frac{N}{N-1}S^2$$

$$\sigma^2 = \frac{N}{N-1}\frac{\sum (X - \overline{X})^2}{N}$$

$$\sigma^2 = \frac{\sum (X - \overline{X})^2}{N-1}$$

Averaged over many samples, $[\sum (X - \overline{X})^2]/(N - 1)$ does equal σ^2. Therefore, this formula provides a better estimate of σ^2. It *is* an unbiased estimate of σ^2 since $[\sum (X - \overline{X})^2]/(N - 1)$, on the average, *does* equal σ^2: Its expectation equals σ^2.

Use this formula whenever you want to estimate σ^2 from the data of one sample. We denote this unbiased estimate "s^2". It is also denoted "est σ^2".

$$s^2 = \text{est } \sigma^2 = \frac{\sum (X - \bar{X})^2}{N - 1} \tag{8.8}$$

$$s = \text{est } \sigma = \sqrt{\frac{\sum (X - \bar{X})^2}{N - 1}} \tag{8.9}$$

EXAMPLE 8.8

A set of data contains 26 scores. $\sum X = 52$ and $\sum X^2 = 204$. Estimate σ^2 and σ.

Solution First compute $\sum (X - \bar{X})^2$:

$$\sum (X - \bar{X})^2 = \left[\sum X^2 - \frac{(\sum X)^2}{N} \right] \tag{8.10}$$

$$= 204 - \frac{(52)^2}{26} = 100$$

This term, the "sum of squares," is then divided by $N - 1$:

$$s^2 = \text{est } \sigma^2 = \frac{\text{sum of squares}}{N - 1} = \frac{\sum (X - \bar{X})^2}{N - 1}$$

$$= \frac{100}{26 - 1} = \frac{100}{25} = 4$$

$$s = \text{est } \sigma = \sqrt{4} = 2$$

From this one sample, then, the best estimate of σ is 2.

EXAMPLE 8.9

An investigator has computed $S = \sqrt{[\sum (X - \bar{X})^2]/N} = 6.00$ from a sample of 10 scores. Estimate σ.

Solution

$$S^2 = \frac{\sum (X - \bar{X})^2}{N} = 36$$

There are two ways to compute s^2. One is to compute $\sum (X - \bar{X})^2$ and then divide by $N - 1$:

$$\sum (X - \bar{X})^2 = NS^2 = 10(36) = 360$$

$$s^2 = \frac{\sum (X - \bar{X})^2}{N - 1} = \frac{360}{10 - 1} = 40$$

$$s = \sqrt{40} = 6.32$$

The estimate of σ, then, is 6.32—a little larger than $S = 6.00$.

s can also be computed this way:

$$s^2 = \frac{N}{N - 1} S^2 = \frac{10}{9} (36) = 40$$

$$s = \sqrt{40} = 6.32$$

In these two examples, s differs appreciably from S. Clearly s, not S, should be used as an estimate of σ. When N is large, though, s and S do not differ very much. Statisticians sometimes use this rule of thumb: When N is 30 or smaller, it is essential to use s, not S, as an estimate of σ. For larger samples, though, the two values are so close that either one can be used to estimate σ.

EXAMPLE 8.10

In a certain set of data, $N = 100$ and $S = 9.00$. Estimate the standard error of the mean as precisely as possible.

Solution

$$s^2 = \frac{N}{N - 1} S^2 = \frac{100}{27} (81) = 81.82$$

$$s = \sqrt{81.82} = 9.05$$

To estimate the standard error of the mean, we now replace σ by s.

$$\sigma_{\bar{X}} = \frac{\sigma}{\sqrt{N}}$$

$$s_{\bar{X}} = \text{Estimate of } \sigma_{\bar{X}} = \frac{s}{\sqrt{N}} \tag{8.11}$$

$$= \frac{9.05}{\sqrt{100}} = 0.905$$

This estimate of $\sigma_{\bar{X}}$ can be denoted $s_{\bar{X}}$: $s_{\bar{X}} = s/\sqrt{N}$. $s_{\bar{X}}$, then, is the best estimate of $\sigma_{\bar{X}}$.

In this example, $N = 100$. With samples this large, investigators sometimes use S as an estimate of σ. The investigator might write:

$$\sigma_{\bar{X}} = \frac{\sigma}{\sqrt{N}}$$

$$\text{Estimate of } \sigma_{\bar{X}} = \frac{S}{\sqrt{N}} \tag{8.12}$$

This estimate of $\sigma_{\bar{X}}$ would be denoted $S_{\bar{X}}$. $S_{\bar{X}}$, of course, is not as precise an estimate as $s_{\bar{X}}$. For Example 8.10 $S_{\bar{X}}$ would equal $9.00/\sqrt{100} = .900$. Just as S underestimates σ, so $S_{\bar{X}}$ underestimates $\sigma_{\bar{X}}$. When N is large, though, $S_{\bar{X}}$ is not far off.

Some textbooks indiscriminately call all of these formulas "the standard error of the mean." $\sigma_{\bar{X}}$, of course, is the exact value. To use it, the investigator needs to know the population parameter σ. The other formulas are *estimates*. $s_{\bar{X}}$ is the better estimate since it makes use of s.

We can summarize the various formulas by the following table.

Value used for σ	*Formula for computing (or estimating)* $\sigma_{\bar{X}}$	
σ (Population parameter is known)	$\sigma_{\bar{X}} = \dfrac{\sigma}{\sqrt{N}}$ (Exact)	(8.1)
$s = \sqrt{\dfrac{\sum (X - \bar{X})^2}{N - 1}}$ (*Best* estimate of σ)	$s_{\bar{X}} = \dfrac{s}{\sqrt{N}}$ (*Best* estimate of $\sigma_{\bar{X}}$)	(8.11)
$S = \sqrt{\dfrac{\sum (X - \bar{X})^2}{N}}$ (*Biased* estimate of σ)	$S_{\bar{X}} = \dfrac{S}{\sqrt{N}}$ (*Biased* estimate of $\sigma_{\bar{X}}$)	(8.12)

In most problems it is as easy to compute s from the data as S. In those cases, use s, not S, as your estimate of σ.

*8.6 $\sigma_{\bar{X}}$ FOR A DICHOTOMOUS VARIABLE

Suppose a set of scores contained 0s and 1s. For example, suppose children were observed in a nursery school, and the observer watched for aggressive behavior. Perhaps "1" means that aggressive behavior did occur, while "0" means that aggressive behavior did not occur. When scores can assume just two different values—like 0 and 1—the variable is called *dichotomous*.

---

* This section can be omitted in a shorter course.

Consider a sample of 10 such scores:

	X	
		Summary statistics:
Subject 1	1	
Subject 2	0	$n_1 = 6$
Subject 3	0	
Subject 4	1	
Subject 5	1	$n_0 = 4$
Subject 6	0	
Subject 7	1	
Subject 8	1	$N = n_0 + n_1 = 10$
Subject 9	0	
Subject 10	1	
		$\bar{X} = \frac{6}{10} = .60$
		$S = \sqrt{.24} = .49$

Various statistics could be computed from these data: $\sum X = 6; \bar{X} = \sum X/N = \frac{6}{10} = 0.6; S = \sqrt{.24} = .49$. In data like these, the mean and standard deviation are particularly easy to compute. The mean is simply the sum of the 1s divided by N. For the data above, let n_0 equal the number of 0s, and n_1, the number of 1s. Since $\sum X$ is the same as n_1, the mean equals n_1/N. This mean, n_1/N, also tells the *proportion* of 1s. Let us denote the proportion of 1s by p. Then $\bar{X} = n_1/N = p$.

The standard deviation is also easy to compute. Since p is the proportion of 1s, let q be the proportion of 0s. The formula for S then becomes $\sqrt{pq}$. To derive this formula, first consider $\sum (X - \bar{X})^2$ for the data above. The mean of the data is p, so $\sum (X - \bar{X})^2$ is the same as $\sum (X - p)^2$. Every time a "1" occurs, $(X - \bar{X})^2$ equals $(1 - p)^2$. And every time a "0" occurs, $(X - \bar{X})^2$ equals $(0 - p)^2$. Next, let us record every score's squared deviation from $\bar{X}$: There are n_1 cases of $(1 - p)^2$ and n_0 cases of $(0 - p)^2$. The sum of squares, then, is

$$\sum (X - \bar{X})^2 = \sum (X - p)^2 = n_1(1 - p)^2 + n_0(0 - p)^2$$

Therefore:

$$S^2 = \frac{\sum (X - \bar{X})^2}{N} = \frac{n_1}{N}(1 - p)^2 + \frac{n_0}{N}(0 - p)^2$$

But n_1/N is the proportion of 1s, p. And n_0/N is the proportion of 0s, q. Therefore:

$$S^2 = \frac{\sum (X - \bar{X})^2}{N} = p(1 - p)^2 + q(0 - p)^2$$

$$= pq^2 + p^2q$$

$$= pq(q + p)$$

Now $p + q = 1$, so:

$$S^2 = \frac{\sum (X - \bar{X})^2}{N} = pq$$

$$S = \sqrt{\frac{\sum (X - \bar{X})^2}{N}}$$

$$S = \sqrt{pq} \tag{8.13}$$

EXAMPLE 8.11

A group of 50 subjects was tested. The scores were entirely 0s and 3s: 45 subjects scored 0, while 5 subjects scored 3. Compute the distribution's standard deviation.

Solution If the scores were 0s and 1s, the standard deviation would equal

$$\sqrt{pq} = \sqrt{\frac{45}{50} \cdot \frac{5}{50}} = \sqrt{(.90)(.10)} = \sqrt{.09} = .30$$

But the distribution contained 0s and 3s, not 0s and 1s. Compare the distribution of 0s and 3s with a distribution of 0s and 1s.

Distribution of 0s and 1s (distribution L)		Distribution of 0s and 3s (distribution R)	
Score	*Frequency*	*Score*	*Frequency*
1	5	3	5
0	45	0	45
$S = \sqrt{pq} = .30$		$S = ?$	

Let us call these distributions L (for "left") and R (for "right"). We can relate the two distributions this way. If we triple every score in Distribution L, we produce Distribution R. In general, when every score in a distribution is multiplied by a constant, the standard deviation increases by that constant. The standard deviation of Distribution R, then, is 3 times .30. Distribution R's standard deviation equals $3\sqrt{pq} = 3(.30) = .90$.

Standard error of the mean

With a dichotomous variable, the mean score tells what "proportion of people scored 1." $\overline{X}$ and p are identical. Therefore, we can think of p as the sample's mean and imagine many samples drawn from the population. Different samples would yield different means—different p's. Now what is $\sigma_{\overline{x}}$ for these different sample means?

First, consider the population's scores—all 0s and 1s. The proportion of 1s in the population can be denoted p_{pop}, and the proportion of 0s, q_{pop}. Then $p_{pop} + q_{pop} = 1$. The population's mean is therefore p_{pop}; its standard deviation is $\sqrt{p_{pop}q_{pop}}$.

A population of dichotomous scores: Scores are 0s and 1s.

$$\mu = p_{pop}$$

$$\sigma = \sqrt{p_{pop}q_{pop}}$$

Now imagine one sample of N scores. Its mean (or p) is noted. Then another sample is drawn, and its mean is also noted. Then another sample. And so on for many samples. How much variability would these means—or p's—exhibit?

In general, the variability among means is described by $\sigma_{\overline{x}} = \sigma/\sqrt{N}$. σ tells the standard deviation of scores in the population. For the dichotomous population, $\sigma = \sqrt{p_{pop}q_{pop}}$. Therefore:

$$\sigma_{\overline{X}} = \frac{\sigma}{\sqrt{N}} = \frac{\sqrt{p_{pop}q_{pop}}}{\sqrt{N}} = \sqrt{\frac{p_{pop}q_{pop}}{N}} \qquad \text{(dichotomous population of 0s and 1s)}$$

This term, then, tells how variable the sample $\overline{X}$'s—or sample p's—are. Since each sample p is a proportion, this form of the $\sigma_{\overline{x}}$ is called the *standard error of the proportion*. It describes the variability among sample proportions. The standard error of the proportion is usually denoted σ_p. Do not be confused by the symbols; σ_p is just a special kind of $\sigma_{\overline{X}}$.

$$\sigma_p = \sqrt{\frac{p_{pop}q_{pop}}{N}} \qquad (8.14)$$

EXAMPLE 8.12

An item on a test is scored right (1) or wrong (0). The probability is .10 that a subject responds correctly. Therefore, in the average sample, .10 of the subjects would respond correctly. (The mean of all the 0s and 1s would equal 0.10.)

Suppose we consider samples of 25 subjects. For different samples, the proportion of 1s would vary. How much variability would occur among the different sample p's?

Solution

$$\sigma_p = \sqrt{\frac{p_{pop} q_{pop}}{N}} = \sqrt{\frac{(.10)(.90)}{25}} = \sqrt{\frac{.09}{25}} = .06$$

Theoretically, the various sample p's would have a standard deviation of .06.

Relationship to the binomial distribution

The formula for σ_p can be derived from the binomial distribution. Let us perform that derivation. It will help you integrate several different topics.

First, consider a binomial distribution—say, $(p + q)^5$ with $p = .20$ and $q = .80$. (Perhaps the investigator plans to study a trait whose probability is .20. And perhaps his sample will contain 5 individuals.) A sample's outcome could range from 5 (*everyone* exhibits the trait) to 0 (*no one* exhibits the trait). The sampling distribution is shown below:

Sample's outcome: The number of people who exhibit the trait (a frequency)	Probability of this outcome (computed from the binomial distribution)
5	.00032
4	.00640
3	.05120
2	.20480
1	.40960
0	.32768

This distribution shows all the possible outcomes. Each outcome is a frequency—the number of people who exhibit the trait. Since the outcomes are frequencies, let us call this distribution "Distribution F" (for "frequency"). The mean of Distribution F is $Np = 1.0$; thus, the *average* sample would contain 1.0 person who exhibits the trait. [2] The standard deviation of Distribution F is $\sqrt{Npq} = \sqrt{.80} = .90$. The figure .90 describes the variability among the various outcomes—among the 0s, 1s, 2s, ..., 5s.

[2] We previously expressed the mean as np. Here, however, it appears as Np, so the two formulas need to be reconciled.

Generally, problems on the binomial distribution use n to denote the number of simple events in the experiment. N, on the other hand, denotes the number of people in a sample. In the present case, though, the two terms are the same: The number of simple events— the total number of 1s and 0s—equals the number of subjects in the sample. n therefore equals N.

Now consider some particular sample—say, a sample whose outcome is 2: 2 people exhibit the trait. We could describe the same outcome this way: "$\frac{2}{5}$ of the sample's subjects exhibit the trait." Here the outcome is expressed as a proportion. Instead of "3," we report "$\frac{3}{5}$" or "0.6." Instead of "4," we report that "$\frac{4}{5}$," or "0.8," of the sample's members exhibit the trait. Suppose every outcome were reported as a proportion. Distribution F would require one change: Every outcome would have to appear as a proportion. Each frequency (0, 1, 2, ...) would be divided by 5—or in general, by N. The proportions would range from $\frac{5}{5} = 1.00$ to $\frac{0}{5} = 0.00$. The resulting distribution might be called "Distribution P" (for "proportion"). Whereas Distribution F reports the outcomes as *frequencies*—5, 4, 3, 2, 1, 0—Distribution P reports them as *proportions*—$\frac{5}{5}$, $\frac{4}{5}$, $\frac{3}{5}$, $\frac{2}{5}$, $\frac{1}{5}$, $\frac{0}{5}$.

Sample's outcome: The proportion of people who exhibit the trait	Probability of this outcome (computed from the binomial distribution)
$\frac{5}{5} = 1.00$	.00032
$\frac{4}{5} = 0.80$	.00640
$\frac{3}{5} = 0.60$	.05120
$\frac{2}{5} = 0.40$	.20480
$\frac{1}{5} = 0.20$	.40960
$\frac{0}{5} = 0.00$	.32768

The mean and standard deviation of Distribution F were easy to compute. The mean was $Np = 1.0$; the standard deviation was $\sqrt{Npq} = .90$. But what is the mean of Distribution P? What is the standard deviation? Distribution P is really Distribution F with one change: Every "score" has been divided by a constant value—by N (in this case, 5). When every score is divided by some constant, the $\overline{X}$ and the S also get divided by that constant. Therefore, the mean of Distribution P equals the mean of Distribution F *divided by N*. And the S of Distribution P equals the S of Distribution F *divided by N*.

The mean of Distribution P therefore equals $\dfrac{Np}{N} = p$. Its standard deviation equals $\dfrac{\sqrt{Npq}}{N} = \sqrt{\dfrac{pq}{N}}$. This value describes the variability among the sample proportions. And it therefore equals σ_p.

Thus, a binomial distribution can be depicted in two forms. In one form, the sample outcomes appear as *frequencies*. The mean then equals Np—the number of individuals in the average sample who exhibit the trait. The standard deviation equals $\sqrt{Npq}$.

In the other form, the outcomes appear as proportions—the *proportion* of subjects who exhibit the trait. This proportion might be $0/N$, $1/N$, $2/N$, and so on. The average sample would show p (e.g., .40) of all its members exhibit-

ing the trait. And the variability among sample p's would be $\sqrt{\dfrac{pq}{N}}$.

σ_p, then, tells the standard deviation of a sampling distribution of proportions. To interpret σ_p, always imagine a distribution of sample outcomes.
Each outcome tells what proportion of the sample's members displayed the
trait. This sampling distribution, then, is a *sampling distribution of proportions*.
And its standard deviation, σ_p, is the *standard error of the proportion*.

Now let us use σ_p to test hypotheses about p_{pop}. These problems can also
be solved by the earlier method of Sec. 6.7.

EXAMPLE 8.13

An investigator has a theory about reading disabilities. According to his
theory, half of all poor readers have some degree of brain damage. That is,
the probability of brain damage is .50 in the disabled population, according to
the theory.

The investigator examines a representative sample of 30 subjects with
reading disabilities. He tests them and finds that 25 are brain-damaged.
Expressed as a proportion, $^{25}\!/_{30} = .83$ of the sample's members are brain-
damaged. This proportion is denoted p_{sample}. Thus, $p_{\text{sample}} = .83$.

Test the hypothesis that p_{pop} is .50. Adopt the 5 percent level of significance.

Solution

Step 1   State H_0: $p_{\text{pop}} = .50$. According to this hypothesis, .50 of the average
sample's members would show brain damage.

Step 2   Note H_1, the alternative hypothesis: $p_{\text{pop}} \neq .50$. Ultimately one
of the two hypotheses will be accepted.

Step 3   Consider the sampling distribution. Suppose p_{pop} does equal .50.
Different samples would show different sample p's—different proportions of
subjects with brain damage. For one, p_{sample} might equal .57: 17 brain-damaged
children out of 30. For another, p_{sample} might equal .47: 14 brain-damaged
children out of 30. The variability among sample p's is described by

$$\sigma_p = \sqrt{\frac{p_{\text{pop}} q_{\text{pop}}}{N}} = \sqrt{\frac{(.50)(.50)}{30}} = .091$$

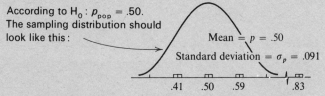

According to H_0: $p_{\text{pop}} = .50$.
The sampling distribution should
look like this:

Mean $= p = .50$

Standard deviation $= \sigma_p = .091$

.41   .50   .59   .83

Experiment's outcome: The proportion
of brain-damaged subjects in a sample

The different sample p's would be $\%_0$, $\frac{1}{30}$, $\frac{2}{30}$, ..., $\frac{30}{30}$. The exact distribution is given by the binomial $(.50 + .50)^{30}$. Let us use the normal curve to approximate this binomial distribution.

Step 4 Consider the result of one sample: In the one sample, .83 of the members were brain-damaged. Does .83 fit comfortably into the hypothesized distribution?

We need to locate "$p_{\text{sample}} = .83$" in this sampling distribution. You might think of computing the z score:

$$z = \frac{p_{\text{sample}} - p_{\text{pop}}}{\sigma_p} = \frac{.83 - .50}{.091}$$

But we can improve upon this z score. The normal curve only *approximates* the binomial distribution; we really need to consider the binomial distribution, not the normal distribution. What proportion of the *binomial* distribution falls at the outcome "$\frac{25}{30} = .83$" or beyond it?

This problem, of course, is the same one we analyzed in Sec. 6.7. In that section (page 150) the z score was computed with a correction for continuity:

$$z = \frac{|25 - 15| - .5}{2.74}$$

25 out of 30 were brain-damaged
$Np = (30)(.50) = 15$
$\sqrt{Npq} = \sqrt{(30)(.50)(.50)} = 2.74$

Now "$z = \dfrac{p_{\text{sample}} - p_{\text{pop}}}{\sigma_p}$" has most of the same terms, *but they have been divided by N*: Instead of 25, we have entered $\frac{25}{30}$ as p_{sample}; instead of 15, we have entered $\frac{15}{30}$ as p_{pop}; instead of 2.74, we have entered $2.74/30 = .091$ as σ_p. Since every term has been divided by N, the correction for continuity needs to be divided by N. The correction for continuity becomes $.5/N = .5/30$. And the z becomes:

$$z = \frac{|p_{\text{sample}} - p_{\text{pop}}| - 0.5/N}{\sigma_p} \tag{8.15}$$

$$= \frac{|25/30 - 15/30| - 0.5/30}{2.74/30} = \frac{|.83 - .50| - .0167}{.091}$$

$$= \frac{.3167}{.091} = 3.47$$

Step 5 We evaluate this result at $\alpha = .05$: $p_{\text{sample}} = .83$ is disturbingly far from the distribution's center. The probability is less than .05 that an outcome lies this far from center. Therefore, H_0 is rejected at $\alpha = .05$. Instead, we infer, p_{pop} does not equal .50.

EXAMPLE 8.14

A sample of 64 rats is to be tested in a maze. The maze has one choice point, where a rat can turn right or left. First, though, the investigator wants to know whether rats have a preference for turning right or left. He therefore tests each rat once, with this hypothesis: The proportion of right-turners in the population is $\frac{1}{2}$; $p_{pop} = .50$.

In the one sample, 48 rats turned right; they comprised $\frac{48}{64} = 0.75$ of the entire sample.

Adopt the 5 percent level of significance to test H_0.

Solution This problem can be solved in two different ways. Method 1 illustrates the procedure of Sec. 6.7, while Method 2 applies σ_p. The two methods, of course, give the very same conclusion.

Method 1 (sample result reported as a frequency)	Method 2 (sample result reported as a proportion)
1. *Hypothesis:* $p_{pop} = .50$ 2. *Alternative:* $p_{pop} \neq .50$ 3. *Sampling distribution:*	1. *Hypothesis:* $p_{pop} = .50$ 2. *Alternative:* $p_{pop} \neq .50$ 3. *Sampling distribution:*

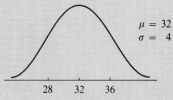

$$\mu = 32$$
$$\sigma = 4$$

28   32   36

Frequency of right-turners
for different samples

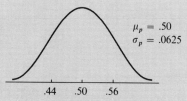

$$\mu_p = .50$$
$$\sigma_p = .0625$$

.44   .50   .56

Proportion of right-turners
for different samples

4. *Data:* 48 animals in the sample turned right.

$$z = \frac{|48 - 32| - 0.5}{4}$$

$$= \frac{15.5}{4} = 3.9$$

4. *Data:* 0.75 of the sample's animals turned right.

$$z = \frac{|0.75 - 0.50| - 0.5/N}{.0625}$$

$$= \frac{0.75 - 0.50 - 0.5/64}{.0625}$$

$$= \frac{0.24}{.0625} = 3.9$$

5. *Decision* ($\alpha = .05$): Hypothesis rejected. The probability is less than .05 that the sample outcome is a chance deviation from the hypothesized center.

5. *Decision* ($\alpha = .05$): Hypothesis rejected. The probability is less than .05 that the sample outcome is a chance deviation from the hypothesized center.

APPENDIX: *Proof*

Proof 8.1 *Proof that* $\dfrac{\sum (X - A)^2}{N}$ *is smallest when A equals* $\bar{X}$—*that* $\dfrac{\sum (X - \bar{X})^2}{N}$
is the smallest possible value.

Let A equal the hypothesized values of μ in Table 8.3. In Case 1, $A = 13$; in Case 2, $A = 14$; in Case 3, $A = 15$; in Case 4, $A = 16$. When A equals $\bar{X}$ (Case 3), $(X - A)^2$ is the same as $(X - \bar{X})^2$. In all the other cases, A differs from $\bar{X}$; A equals $\bar{X}$ plus something more: $A = \bar{X} + a$. In Case 1, $A = \bar{X} + (-2)$; in Case 2, $A = \bar{X} + (-1)$; in Case 4, $A = \bar{X} + (+1)$.

The data express each score as a squared deviation from A. These squared deviations then get summed: $\sum (X - A)^2$. Notice the different sums: For Case 1, $\sum (X - A)^2 = 400$. For Case 2, $\sum (X - A)^2 = 370$. For Case 3, $\sum (X - A)^2 = 360$. For Case 4, $\sum (X - A)^2 = 370$. The sum is smallest when A equals $\bar{X}$ (Case 3). When A differs from $\bar{X}$, the sum is larger.

Let us examine this result algebraically. First replace A by $(\bar{X} + a)$.

$$\sum (X - A)^2 = \sum [X - (\bar{X} + a)]^2$$

$$= \sum [X^2 - 2X(\bar{X} + a) + (\bar{X} + a)^2]$$

$$= \sum [X^2 - 2X\bar{X} - 2Xa + \bar{X}^2 + 2a\bar{X} + a^2]$$

$$= \sum X^2 - 2\bar{X} \sum X - 2a \sum X + N\bar{X}^2 + 2Na\bar{X} + Na^2$$

$$= \sum X^2 - 2\frac{\sum X}{N} \sum X - 2a \sum X + N\frac{(\sum X)^2}{N^2} + 2Na\frac{\sum X}{N} + Na^2$$

$$= \sum X^2 - \frac{(\sum X)^2}{N} + Na^2$$

$\sum X^2 - (\sum X)^2/N$ is the same as $\sum (X - \bar{X})^2$. Therefore:

$$\sum (X - A)^2 = \sum (X - \bar{X})^2 + Na^2$$

Now divide each part by N:

$$\frac{\sum (X - A)^2}{N} = \frac{\sum (X - \bar{X})^2}{N} + \frac{Na^2}{N}$$

$$= S^2 + a^2$$

Thus, $[\sum (X - A)^2]/N$ equals S^2 plus something more, a^2. If A equals $\bar{X}$ then $a = 0$; and $\sum (X - A)^2$ equals $\sum (X - \bar{X})^2$.

If A differs from $\bar{X}$, though, a does not equal 0. And $[\sum (X - A)^2]/N$ exceeds S^2: it equals $S^2 + a^2$. Squared deviations around $\bar{X}$ sum to S^2. Squared deviations around any other value give a larger sum, $S^2 + a^2$. Therefore, $[\sum (X - \mu)^2]/N$ exceeds S^2 whenever μ differs from $\bar{X}$.

EXERCISES

8.1 A population of scores contains these 6 scores and no others: 2, 3, 6, 6, 8, 11.
   (a) Compute the mean of the population.
       Answer: $\mu = 6$
   (b) Compute the standard deviation of the population.
       Answer: $\sigma = 3$

(c) Consider all the different samples of $N = 2$ scores that you could draw from this population. There are $6 \times 6 = 36$ different samples. One sample would be: {2,2}. Another would be: {2,3}. Another: {2,6}. And so on. List all of the 36 samples and their respective means.

(d) Compute the mean of this exhaustive sampling distribution of means.

Answer: $\mu = \dfrac{216}{36} = 6$

(e) Compute the standard deviation of this sampling distribution of means. (This value equals the standard error of the mean.)

Answer: σ *of means* $= \sqrt{4.5} = 2.12$

(f) Compute the theoretical value of the standard error of the mean. Make sure that it agrees with the value computed in (e).

Answer: $\sigma_{\bar{x}} = \dfrac{3}{\sqrt{2}} = 2.12$

(g) Make a frequency distribution which shows the sampling distribution of means.

8.2 Suppose the mean IQ for the general population is 100 and the standard deviation is 17. For a sample of 289 cases:

(a) What is the probability that the sample's mean is 101 or more?
Answer: Probability $= .1587$

(b) What is the probability that the sample's mean is 98 or less?
Answer: Probability $= .0228$

8.3 Suppose the standard deviation of a certain population of scores is known to be 20. How large a sample would you need in order for the standard error of the mean to be 2 points?
Answer: N = 100

8.4 A sample of 144 scores has a standard deviation of 12. If the sample mean is 153, what is the 95 percent confidence interval for the population mean? What is the 99 percent confidence interval?
Answer: 95 percent limits: 151.04 to 154.96; 99 percent limits: 150.42 to 155.58

8.5 An experimenter is planning to measure subjects' reaction times to a task. From pilot data, he has estimated σ to be 10. Now he wants to estimate the mean reaction time for the entire population. He therefore plans to draw one sample. In making the estimate, he wants to be sure, at the 90 percent level of confidence, that his observed $\bar{X}$ does not differ from μ by more than 3.3 sec. How large should his sample be?
Answer: 25 cases

8.6 A chewing gum manufacturer claims that its brand of chewing gum will hold its flavor significantly longer than other comparable brands. Measurements on a large number of different brands show that the average specimen holds its flavor 13 min with a standard deviation of 2 min (the population parameters). Sixteen specimens of the company's brand hold their flavor an average of 14.1 min. Is the company using false advertising?
Answer: z = 2.2. At the .05 level, H_0 *is rejected.*

8.7 For a test of verbal aptitude, $\mu = 90$ and $\sigma = 5$. A representative sample of 100 people is tested. What is the probability that the sample's mean differ from μ by one point or more?
Answer: .046

8.8 A personality test is composed of 3 subtests: A, B, and C. The value of r between any two subtests is 0. Here are the standard deviations of the three parts: $S_A = 2$; $S_B = 4$; $S_C = 4$. Suppose each subject is given a total score, $A + B + C$. What would the standard deviation of these total scores be?
Answer: 6

8.9 Suppose you draw a sample of $N = 3$ scores from a population, and the scores are 90, 99, and 102.
(a) What is your best estimate of the population *variance*?
Answer: Mean of the three $\overline{X}$'s $= 97$. $s^2 = 39$
(b) If you know that $\mu = 95$, what would be your best estimate of the population variance?
Answer: $(\sum X - \mu)^2 = 30$

8.10 From the following sample of scores, compute the best estimate of σ: 17, 19, 19, 19, 21.
Answer: $s = \sqrt{2} = 1.4$

8.11 Suppose 10,000 samples of 9 scores are drawn from a population whose $\sigma = 9$.
(a) If S is computed for every sample, the mean value of S throughout the samples would be (choose one): (i) less than 9; (ii) equal to 9; (iii) greater than 9.
Answer: (i)
(b) If $(\overline{X} - \mu)^2$ were computed for every sample, the mean over all samples would equal _____.
Answer: 9

8.12 For a sample of scores, $\overline{X} = 89$ and $S^2 = 9$. If $\mu = 91$, your best estimate of σ^2 would be _____.
Answer: 13

8.13 A sample of 9 scores has $s^2 = 9$. What is the mean of the sample's squared deviation scores?
Answer: 8

8.14 For a population of scores $\sigma = 20$. Samples of $N = 100$ are drawn. A new statistic, the half-mean, is defined as half the mean: $H = 1/2(\overline{X})$. The standard error of H for these data would equal _____.
Answer: $1/2(2) = 1.00$

8.15 For a population of scores, $\sigma = 10$ and $N = 100$; a new statistic "1/5 mean $+ 14$" is computed for a sample. The standard error of this statistic equals

_____.
Answer: 0.2

8.16 The "standard error of a median" is defined as the standard deviation of a sampling distribution of medians. This standard error is written σ_{Mdn} and it equals $1.25\sigma_{\bar{x}}$.

Imagine a sample of eight scores whose median is 135. In this sample $\sum (X - \bar{X})^2 = 56$.

(a) What is your best estimate of σ?

Answer: $\sqrt{8}$

(b) What is the 68 percent confidence interval for the population's median?

Answer: 135 ± 1.25

9

TESTING THE
DIFFERENCE BETWEEN
TWO MEANS

Chapter 8 described $\sigma_{\bar{X}}$, the standard error of the mean. $\sigma_{\bar{X}}$ was defined as the standard deviation of a sampling distribution of means. It was used to evaluate hypotheses about a population's μ: In testing that kind of hypothesis, an investigator examines one sample and compares his one sample's mean to the hypothesized μ.

In many experiments, though, the experimenter needs to study *two* samples, not one. Perhaps he wants to test one sample under Condition X and another sample under Condition Y. First he notes each sample's mean—$\bar{X}$ and $\bar{Y}$—and then considers the difference between them: Is $\bar{X} - \bar{Y}$ a *real* difference, he wonders, or is it just a chance affair—really no difference at all?

An educator, for example, might teach subjects by two different methods.

Some subjects might be taught by a lecture method, other subjects by a group-discussion method. After the training, each subject's performance would be measured. The experimenter would note each group's mean and compare the two means. Is the difference genuine, or just a fluke?

Or a physiologist might investigate diet and body weight. Two groups of animals might be fed different diets—Diet A and Diet B. Six months later each animal's weight would be noted. The mean of each group would be computed, and the means would be compared. Can the experimenter safely generalize beyond his data?

9.1   AN EXAMPLE WITH DATA

An experimenter was studying the properties of a tranquilizer. He wanted to examine the tranquilizer's effect on automobile driving: Does a tranquilized subject produce more errors? Is his reaction time slower? Does his attention waver more often? The experimenter wanted to compare performance under two conditions—(a) just after a subject took a tranquilizer, and (b) just after a subject took a placebo. (A placebo is an inert substance that resembles a drug but has no physiological effects: The subject would not notice a difference between drug and placebo, so psychologically, the two conditions would be comparable.) The experimenter decided to record the number of errors each subject made. The more errors, the worse the performance.

The study itself could be designed in several different ways. Consider two possible experimental designs. Let us call one the "Independent Groups" design, the other the "Paired Observations" design. In an "Independent Groups" design, the experimenter would test two separate, independent groups of people. Each subject would be selected at random and assigned to a condition at random. One group would receive the tranquilizer, the other group, the placebo. Then the experimenter would measure the number of errors each subject produced.

Illustrative data are shown below. In these data, ten people were tested—five in Group T and five in Group P. (In practice, of course, an experimenter

One experimental design: Independent groups

Condition T		Condition P	
Subject's name	*Score*	*Subject's name*	*Score*
Adams	32	Ferguson	26
Bergstrom	32	Goldsmith	28
Cohen	30	Hrenko	30
Delgado	29	Ikemoto	31
Espinosa	27	Johnson	25
Mean:	30	Mean:	28

would study many more subjects than that.) The mean of Group T is denoted $\bar{T}$; the mean of Group P, $\bar{P}$. In these data $\bar{T} = 30$, while $\bar{P} = 28$. The means show more errors for Group T. But statistically, we need to evaluate the two-point difference: Is it large enough to trust?

"Independent Groups" is a common experimental design. It does have one drawback, though: By chance, one group might have drawn subjects with more ability. The subjects in Group P, for example, might be more experienced as drivers, or more skillful. Hence, the difference between means would be ambiguous: It could be due to the different treatments (drug vs. placebo), or to the group's differing abilities, or to both factors.

To control a variable like ability, the experimenter might design the study differently. He might test every subject in *both* conditions. Subjects would be selected at random, but every subject would be tested twice (say a week apart) —once with the tranquilizer, once with the placebo. (Some subjects would receive the placebo first; other subjects would receive the tranquilizer first.) Then the groups would certainly be comparable in ability; they would contain the very same people. This kind of design is called either "Repeated Measurements" or "Paired Observations."

Data that illustrate Repeated Measurements are shown below. In these data, five subjects were tested, but each subject was tested twice. With this kind of data, an experimenter could compute a correlation coefficient relating a subject's performance in one condition to his performance in the other condition. (In these data, for example, $r = .92$.) Usually data like these do exhibit some correlation. For this reason the Repeated Measurements design is sometimes called "Correlated Observations."

Another experimental design: Repeated measurements

Subject's Name	Score in Condition T	Score in Condition P
Vandermeer	32	31
Wong	32	30
Xelowski	30	28
Yates	29	26
Zeigler	27	25
Means:	30	28

Now let us consider more realistic data. Suppose an experimenter adopted the Repeated Measurements design. Suppose he tested 40 subjects, and suppose every subject were tested twice. Perhaps the test simulated real highway conditions, and perhaps errors were recorded automatically. Say the testings were separated by a week: Some subjects received the tranquilizer first; other subjects, the placebo first. Ideally, an experiment like this would

TABLE 9.1 Data to illustrate Repeated Measurements

Subject	Errors in Driving Tranquilizer (T)	Placebo (P)	Difference Score (D) (Tranquilizer—Placebo)
1	26	22	4
2	24	19	5
3	22	20	2
4	33	32	1
5	27	30	−3
6	36	37	−1
7	30	24	6
8	38	39	−1
9	30	29	1
10	34	28	6
11	24	27	−3
12	22	21	1
13	34	30	4
14	36	37	−1
15	30	29	1
16	33	27	6
17	26	21	5
18	38	32	6
19	30	28	2
20	27	28	−1
21	30	25	5
22	26	29	−3
23	22	21	1
24	38	32	6
25	27	28	−1
26	33	31	2
27	30	26	4
28	34	35	−1
29	24	18	6
30	36	35	1
31	38	36	2
32	34	28	6
33	33	34	−1
34	24	23	1
35	30	26	4
36	27	28	1
37	26	29	−3
38	30	24	6
39	36	35	1
40	22	17	5
	$\bar{T} = 30$	$\bar{P} = 28$	$\bar{D} = 2$

$$s_\mathrm{D} = \sqrt{\frac{\Sigma(D - \bar{D})^2}{N - 1}}$$

$$= \sqrt{\frac{360}{39}} = 3.04$$

be performed "double blind": Neither the subject nor the examiner would know which drug the subject had received. In that way subtle biases could be avoided.

Hypothetical data are shown in Table 9.1. In these data $\bar{T} = 30$ and $\bar{P} = 28$. What conclusion can the experimenter draw? If another experimenter repeated the experiment, would $\bar{T}$ still be the higher? In theory, suppose *many* experimenters repeated the experiment: Would $\bar{T} - \bar{P}$ generally be positive, or might the average $\bar{T} - \bar{P}$ equal 0?

We can pose the question this way: Suppose every subject in the population were tested. Would the *population* show a difference between the two conditions? Let us label the population's two means μ_T and μ_P. Would $\mu_T - \mu_P$ equal 0? According to the data, $\bar{T} - \bar{P}$ equals 2; but the experimenter wants to generalize *beyond* the data—to $\mu_T - \mu_P$.

Let us therefore examine the data. The procedure we describe can be used whenever the samples are large. (A sample is considered large if it has more than 30 subjects. If it has less than 30 subjects, the procedure needs to be modified. These modifications are described in Chap. 10.)

9.2 TESTING THE DIFFERENCE BETWEEN MEANS: REPEATED MEASUREMENTS (PAIRED OBSERVATIONS)

Now consider the data in Table 9.1. Two scores were entered for every subject—a tranquilizer score and a placebo score. For example, Subject 1 earned 26 and 22; thus, the tranquilizer produced four more errors. A pair of scores appears for every subject.

To analyze the data, let us define a new kind of score. This new score is called a difference score. It is the difference between two values—the tranquilizer score minus the placebo score. If the two scores are denoted T and P, the new score is $T - P$. It is usually labeled D (for "difference score") so $D = T - P$. Each subject's D score also appears in Table 9.1.

Now consider the mean of the D scores; it is denoted $\bar{D}$. In Table 9.1, $\bar{D} = 2.0$. This mean difference score also equals "$\bar{T} - \bar{P}$": $30 - 28 = 2$. Let us prove that $\bar{D}$ equals $\bar{T} - \bar{P}$:

$$\bar{D} = \frac{\sum D}{N} = \frac{\sum (T - P)}{N} = \frac{\sum T}{N} - \frac{\sum P}{N}$$

$$\bar{D} = \bar{T} - \bar{P}$$

In general,

$$\bar{D} = \bar{X} - \bar{Y} \tag{9.1}$$

Thus, there are two ways to compute the mean difference score. You can average the D scores directly: $\bar{D} = \sum D/N = 80/40 = 2.0$. Or you can compute $\bar{T}$ and $\bar{P}$, and then compute their difference: $\bar{T} - \bar{P} = 30 - 28 = 2.0$. The two results are identical.

To test whether the means differ significantly, the following procedure is used. First, we examine each subject's difference score and treat that number as the subject's score. We ignore the original T and P scores and view the 40 difference scores as any sample of 40 scores. Table 9.1 shows this sample. Think of it as a sample from a population of difference scores. As usual, the mean of the population is denoted μ—in this case, μ_D to indicate that the scores are difference scores.

The investigator needs to test a hypothesis about μ_D. Usually he wants to test the hypothesis that $\mu_D = 0$. Perhaps the average person's difference score is 0. If so, the tranquilizer and placebo would have equal effects on the average. To test this hypothesis, we consider the sample of difference scores and note its mean. This mean is reported in Table 9.1: $\bar{D} = 2.0$. We also need to estimate σ of the population; to estimate σ, we compute the sample's s. Again, since the scores are difference scores, the population value is denoted σ_D, and the estimate is denoted s_D. For the sample's data:

$$s_{\bar{D}} = \sqrt{\frac{\sum (D - \bar{D})^2}{N - 1}} \tag{9.2}$$

$$= \sqrt{\frac{360}{39}} = 3.04$$

Let us now test the hypothesis that μ_D equals 0. First, we state $H_0 : \mu_D = 0$. (This particular hypothesis is sometimes called a *null* hypothesis—it claims that the population's mean, a mean difference score, is *zero*.) Let us adopt the 1 percent level of significance.

Next we state $H_1 : \mu_D \neq 0$. (If μ_D exceeds 0, more errors occur under a tranquilizer; if μ_D is less than 0, more errors occur under a placebo.)

Third, we consider the sampling distribution of $\bar{D}$'s. According to the null hypothesis, this distribution's mean is 0. We also need its standard error. In general, $\sigma_{\bar{X}}$ equals $\sigma/\sqrt{N}$. But the population's scores are difference scores, so every mean is $\bar{D}$ and the standard error is $\sigma_{\bar{D}}$. This standard error equals:

$$\sigma_{\bar{D}} = \frac{\sigma_D}{\sqrt{N}}$$

To estimate $\sigma_{\bar{D}}$, we need to estimate σ_D. σ_D is not usually known, so it is estimated from the sample's data as s_D. Then we use s_D in place of σ_D.

$$s_{\bar{D}} = \text{Estimate of } \sigma_{\bar{D}} = \frac{s_D}{\sqrt{N}} \tag{9.3}$$

$$= \frac{3.04}{\sqrt{40}} = 0.48$$

Thus, "0.48" estimates the theoretical variability among $\bar{D}$'s.

Now we can describe the sampling distribution of $\bar{D}$'s. If the original scores are normally distributed, the difference scores are also normal. Thus, we

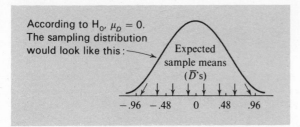

According to H_0, $\mu_D = 0$.
The sampling distribution
would look like this:——→

Expected
sample means
($\bar{D}$'s)

$-.96$ $-.48$ 0 $.48$ $.96$

FIG. 9.1

imagine a population of normally distributed difference scores. An experimenter draws one sample and notes its mean. In theory, many experimenters might perform the same experiment. All the different $\bar{D}$'s would form a normal distribution (Fig. 9.1). According to the null hypothesis, their mean would equal 0; their standard deviation, 0.48.

Next we locate $\bar{D} = 2.0$ in this distribution. Expressed as a z score, it becomes:

$$z = \frac{2.0 - 0}{0.48} = 4.2$$

This z score is sometimes called a critical ratio and written:

$$\text{C.R.} = z = \frac{\bar{D} - 0}{\text{estimate of } \sigma_{\bar{D}}} = \frac{\bar{D}}{s_{\bar{D}}} \tag{9.4}$$

Since $\bar{D}$ equals $\bar{T} - \bar{P}$, the formula can also be written:

$$\text{C.R.} = z = \frac{\bar{T} - \bar{P}}{s_{\bar{D}}}$$

Finally, the investigator makes his decision. According to H_0, the population's mean is 0. But the sample's $\bar{D}$ is far from 0—4.2 standard deviations away. Therefore, the sample's mean, $\bar{D} = 2.0$, *does* fall in the 1 percent rejection region. Hence, H_0 gets rejected, and the alternate hypothesis is accepted: $\mu_D \neq 0$. Apparently, μ_T *is* different from μ_P, so the tranquilizer *does* seem to cause more errors.

EXAMPLE 9.1

An experimenter studied 50 pairs of rats. He selected his rats from 50 different litters; the rats of each pair came from the same litter. Within each pair, one rat was handled (Rat X), the other was not (Rat Y). Rat X received 30 min of handling every day for six months. Rat Y, on the other hand, remained in

TABLE 9.2 Data showing each animal's activity level

Pair of littermates	(X) handled	(Y) nonhandled	(D = X − Y) difference score
1	50	34	16
2	46	42	4
3	42	46	−4
4	64	46	18
5	52	50	2
6	70	54	16
7	58	58	0
8	74	58	16
9	58	62	−4
10	66	70	−4
11	52	38	14
12	57	47	10
13	64	56	8
14	43	41	2
15	63	68	−5
16	49	51	−2
17	56	40	16
18	68	54	14
19	42	37	5
20	74	59	15
21	53	60	−7
22	46	50	−4
23	62	44	18
24	69	58	11
25	50	55	−5
26	65	65	0
27	66	44	22
28	54	45	9
29	73	69	4
30	44	34	10
31	61	61	0
32	60	49	11
33	66	64	2
34	45	48	−3
35	70	52	18
36	51	35	16
37	56	57	−1
38	71	70	1
39	47	52	−5
40	58	42	16
41	60	62	−2
42	57	63	−6
43	55	43	12
44	67	60	7

45	48	36	12
46	72	67	5
47	59	53	6
48	50	39	11
49	58	46	12
50	59	66	−7

$$\sum X = 2{,}900 \qquad \sum Y = 2{,}600 \qquad \sum D = 300$$

$$\sum X^2 = 172{,}330 \qquad \sum Y^2 = 140{,}546 \qquad \sum D^2 = 5{,}220$$

$$\bar{X} = 58.0 \qquad \bar{Y} = 52.0 \qquad \bar{D} = 6.0$$

$$\sum (D - \bar{D})^2 = \sum D^2 - \frac{(\sum D)^2}{N}$$

$$= 5{,}220 - \frac{(300)^2}{50}$$

$$= 3.420$$

$$s_D = \sqrt{\frac{\sum (D - \bar{D})^2}{N - 1}}$$

$$= \sqrt{\frac{3{,}420}{49}} = 8.35$$

the home cage for six months. Finally, every rat was tested. The "open field test" was administered: Each rat was placed in a strange and bare surrounding, and the experimenter scored the animal's activity. The resulting scores are shown in Table 9.2.

Nonhandled rats earned a mean of 52 points; handled rats, a mean of 58 points. A difference score was computed for every pair; the mean of all these difference scores ($\bar{D} = X - Y$) was 6.0. Does this mean differ significantly from 0? Assume that the scores are normally distributed, use a two-tailed test, and adopt the .01 level of significance.

Solution   The difference scores are shown in Table 9.2. Ignore the original X scores and Y scores; consider only the D scores. The mean of the 50 D scores ($\bar{D}$) equals 6.0.

Step 1   State H_0: $\mu_D = 0$. According to this null hypothesis, littermates in the population show a mean D score of 0.

Step 2 H_1: $\mu_D \neq 0$. (A two-tailed test is needed.)

Step 3   Describe the sampling distribution of means: According to H_0, $\mu_D = 0$. Therefore, the average sample's $\bar{D}$ should equal 0. $\sigma_{\bar{D}}$ describes the variability among these means; $\sigma_{\bar{D}}$ equals $\sigma_D/\sqrt{N}$. We use s_D to estimate σ_D.

$$s_{\bar{D}} = \text{Estimate of } \sigma_{\bar{D}} = \frac{s_D}{\sqrt{N}} = \frac{8.35}{\sqrt{50}} = \frac{8.35}{7.07} = 1.18$$

The sampling distribution would look like this:

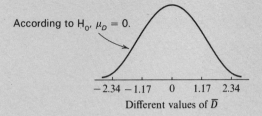

According to H_0, $\mu_D = 0$.

$-2.34 \quad -1.17 \quad 0 \quad 1.17 \quad 2.34$
Different values of $\bar{D}$

Step 4 Next we locate $\bar{D} = 6.0$ in the hypothesized sampling distribution. Expressed as a z score, it becomes:

$$\text{C.R.} = z = \frac{\bar{D} - 0}{s_{\bar{D}}} = \frac{6.0 - 0}{1.18} = 5.08$$

Step 5 z exceeds 2.58, so the sample's $\bar{D}$ does not fit comfortably in the hypothesized distribution. It falls in the .01 rejection region. H_0 is therefore rejected, and H_1 is accepted: $\mu_D \neq 0$.

μ_D also equals $\mu_X - \mu_Y$. If μ_D is not 0, then $\mu_X - \mu_Y$ is not 0. Therefore, μ_X differs from μ_Y. Apparently, handled rats *are* more active.

Let us summarize. Every subject's difference score was computed, and since they were normally distributed, they were treated like any sample of scores: The mean was noted ($\bar{D}$), an estimate of σ_D was computed (s_D), and $\sigma_{\bar{D}}$ was estimated. Then the critical ratio was formed: $\bar{D}/s_{\bar{D}}$. The ratio tells whether $\bar{D}$ differs significantly from 0. This procedure is simple and straightforward. Always use it when you analyze difference scores if they are normally distributed.

Many textbooks describe an alternate procedure, too. This other procedure is less efficient and in general should not be used. However, it is important theoretically and in Sec. 9.3 it will help us extend the theory. Let us therefore consider this other method. It mainly differs in the way s_D is computed.

Alternate method (less preferred)

When an investigator records difference scores $(X - Y)$, the variance of the difference scores is related to the variance of the X's and the variance of the Y's. This relationship holds whether we are thinking of S^2 or s^2. Here is the relationship in each form:

$$S^2{}_D = S^2{}_X + S^2{}_Y - 2r_{XY}S_X S_Y$$

$$s^2{}_D = s^2{}_X + s^2{}_Y - 2r_{XY}s_X s_Y$$

In other words, the variance of the difference scores could be computed from the variance of each part (and r_{XY}). The derivation[1] of these relationships is shown in the Appendix as Proofs 9.1 and 9.2. If we needed to estimate σ_D, we would write:

$$s_D = \sqrt{s^2{}_X + s^2{}_Y - 2r_{XY}s_X s_Y} \tag{9.5}$$

Thus, an investigator could compute s_D in either of two ways. He could list all the D scores and compute their s directly. Or he could consider the X scores and the Y scores separately, compute s_X and s_Y, and then use Eq. (9.5) to compute s_D. To use Eq. (9.5), though, he would need to compute r_{XY}, and r_{XY} is usually laborious to compute.

Now Eq. (9.5) can help us understand $s_{\bar{D}}$ better. $s_{\bar{D}}$, the standard error of the mean, equals $s_D/\sqrt{N}$; so we now replace s_D by $\sqrt{s^2{}_X + s^2{}_Y - 2r_{XY}s_X s_Y}$.

$$s_{\bar{D}} = \frac{s_D}{\sqrt{N}} = \frac{\sqrt{s^2{}_X + s^2{}_Y - 2r_{XY}s_X s_Y}}{\sqrt{N}}$$

$$= \sqrt{\frac{s^2{}_X}{N} + \frac{s^2{}_Y}{N} - 2r_{XY}\frac{s_X}{\sqrt{N}}\frac{s_Y}{\sqrt{N}}}$$

$$= \sqrt{s^2{}_{\bar{X}} + s^2{}_{\bar{Y}} - 2r_{XY}s_{\bar{X}}s_{\bar{Y}}} \tag{9.6}$$

Thus, $s_{\bar{D}}$ contains three ingredients: $s_{\bar{X}}$, $s_{\bar{Y}}$, and a subtracted term that involves r_{XY}. Let us apply this formula to the data of Table 9.2. (We have already computed $s_{\bar{D}}$ as 1.18, so the formula will let us check that answer.)

---

[1] A difference score has two parts—Part X and Part Y. The derivation shows that the variance of the difference scores is related to the variance of Part X and the variance of Part Y. The term *variance*, though, is a little ambiguous; it sometimes refers to a sample's variance (S^2), sometimes to a population's variance (σ^2), and sometimes to an estimate of the population's variance (s^2). However, the same relationship holds for all three forms:

$$S^2{}_D = S^2{}_X + S^2{}_Y - 2r_{XY}S_X S_Y$$
$$\sigma^2{}_D = \sigma^2{}_X + \sigma^2{}_Y - 2r_{\bar{X}\bar{Y}(\text{pop})}\sigma_X \sigma_Y$$
$$s^2{}_D = s^2{}_X + s^2{}_Y - 2r_{XY}s_X s_Y$$

The corresponding formulas for the standard deviation are:

$$S_D = \sqrt{S^2{}_X + S^2{}_Y - 2r_{XY}S_X S_Y} \qquad \text{(Standard deviation of a sample's difference scores)}$$

$$\sigma_D = \sqrt{\sigma^2{}_X + \sigma^2{}_Y - 2r_{XY(\text{pop})}\sigma_X \sigma_Y} \qquad \text{(Standard deviation of a population's difference scores)}$$

$$s_D = \sqrt{s^2{}_X + s^2{}_Y - 2r_{XY}s_X s_Y} \qquad \text{(Best estimate of a population's } \sigma_D\text{)}$$

First, we compile information for each condition. Then we estimate each standard error of the mean—the one for X scores and the one for Y scores.

	Handled (X)	Nonhandled (Y)
Estimate of population's standard deviation	$s_X = 9.18$	$s_Y = 10.45$
Number of cases (N)	$N_X = 50$	$N_Y = 50$
Correlation coefficient (r_{XY})	$r_{XY} = +0.64$	
Estimated standard error of the mean	$s_{\bar{X}} = \dfrac{s_X}{\sqrt{N_X}}$ $= \dfrac{9.18}{\sqrt{50}} = 1.30$	$s_{\bar{Y}} = \dfrac{s_Y}{\sqrt{N_Y}}$ $= \dfrac{10.45}{\sqrt{50}} = 1.47$

Then we compute $s_{\bar{D}}$.

$$s_{\bar{D}} = \sqrt{s_{\bar{X}}^2 + s_{\bar{Y}}^2 - 2r_{XY}s_{\bar{X}}s_{\bar{Y}}}$$
$$= \sqrt{(1.30)^2 + (1.47)^2 - 2(+0.64)(1.30)(1.47)}$$
$$= \sqrt{1.42} = 1.18$$

Thus, the two formulas for $s_{\bar{D}}$ agree.

Equation 9.6 relates $s_{\bar{D}}$ to $s_{\bar{X}}$ and $s_{\bar{Y}}$. We could also follow the very same steps to derive an analogous equation which relates the theoretical standard errors. That equation would be:

$$\sigma_{\bar{D}} = \sqrt{\sigma_{\bar{X}}^2 + \sigma_{\bar{Y}}^2 - 2r_{XY}\sigma_{\bar{X}}\sigma_{\bar{Y}}}$$

In this formula, $\sigma_{\bar{D}}$ is the theoretical standard error of the mean for difference scores; $\sigma_{\bar{X}}$ and $\sigma_{\bar{Y}}$ are the theoretical standard errors of the mean for X and Y scores. $r_{XY_{(\text{pop})}}$ is the population's correlation coefficient.

Again, $\sigma_{\bar{D}}$ describes a sampling distribution of means; the means, though, are *mean difference scores*. Now a mean difference score ($\bar{D}$) can also be viewed as a difference between two means ($\bar{X} - \bar{Y}$). Thus, we can imagine either a sampling distribution of $\bar{D}$'s or a sampling distribution of $\bar{X} - \bar{Y}$'s. Either way, the standard error is the same. For this reason $\sigma_{\bar{D}}$ has two different labels. It is sometimes called the standard error of *mean differences*, and it is sometimes called the standard error of the *difference between two means*. Furthermore, in some textbooks it is denoted $\sigma_{\bar{X} - \bar{Y}}$.

$\sigma_{\bar{D}}$ and $\sigma_{\bar{X} - \bar{Y}}$ are really identical, but they each emphasize a different view of the standard error. $\sigma_{\bar{D}}$ emphasizes the $\bar{D}$. This notation suggests a population of difference scores: A sample is drawn and the mean is noted; if the procedure were repeated by many experimenters, each experimenter would contribute one $\bar{D}$, and the distribution of $\bar{D}$'s would form a sampling distribution. $\sigma_{\bar{D}}$ is the standard deviation of this theoretical distribution.

The other notation, $\sigma_{\bar{X}-\bar{Y}}$, emphasizes the $\bar{X} - \bar{Y}$. To understand this notation, imagine two populations—Population X and Population Y. The mean of one population is μ_X; that of the other, μ_Y. The difference between μ's is: $\mu_X - \mu_Y$. Suppose the experimenter drew two samples—one from X and one from Y. He would note each sample's mean and compute $\bar{X} - \bar{Y}$. In theory, the procedure could be repeated by many experimenters. Each experimenter would contribute one $\bar{X} - \bar{Y}$. The distribution of all $\bar{X} - \bar{Y}$'s would form a sampling distribution. (This distribution is exactly the same as the distribution of $\bar{D}$'s.) Its standard deviation is the standard error—$\sigma_{\bar{X}-\bar{Y}}$ or $\sigma_{\bar{D}}$.

Either view can be adopted. Sometimes we think of a population of difference scores: Its mean is μ_D. Other times we think of two population means (μ_X and μ_Y); the difference between them is $\mu_X - \mu_Y$. Either way, the standard error is the same.

This section has described an experiment with paired observations. Designs of this kind always contain *pairs* of scores: Each score in one condition accompanies some score in the other condition. The scores of a pair may describe the same person, or they may describe different people who have been matched. Other examples of paired observations are shown below.

Subject	Experimental condition	Control condition	Family	Wife's score	Husband's score
Subject 1	27	23	Family 1	27	23
Subject 2	14	16	Family 2	14	16
Subject 3	21	19	Family 3	21	19
Subject 4	24	23	Family 4	24	23

Litter	Experimental animal	Control animal	IQ level	Experimental subject	Control subject
Litter 1	27	23	IQ 130–139	27	23
Litter 2	14	16	IQ 120–129	14	16
Litter 3	21	19	IQ 110–119	21	19
Litter 4	24	23	IQ 100–109	24	23

Other kinds of designs also exist. The experiment may involve two separate, unrelated groups of subjects. The groups are then said to be independent. Subjects in one group are not matched with subjects in the other group. One group might contain 50 boys, the other group, 47 girls; there is no basis for matching any boy with any one girl. That kind of design, called Independent Observations, is considered next.

9.3 TESTING THE DIFFERENCE BETWEEN MEANS: INDEPENDENT OBSERVATIONS

Suppose an experimenter studied two independent groups and computed their means—$\bar{\text{B}}$ for the boys, $\bar{\text{G}}$ for the girls. And suppose he wanted to evaluate the difference $\bar{\text{B}} - \bar{\text{G}}$. He might like to know whether the two *population* means differ: Does $\mu_B - \mu_G$ differ from 0?

To answer that question, the experimenter would have to consider the sampling distribution of $\bar{\text{B}} - \bar{\text{G}}$'s. He would need to estimate the distribution's standard error, $\sigma_{\bar{D}}$. What does $\sigma_{\bar{D}}$ equal? In Sec. 9.2 we expressed $\sigma_{\bar{D}}$ this way: $\sigma_{\bar{D}} = \sqrt{\sigma_X^2 + \sigma_Y^2 - 2r_{XY_{(\text{pop})}} \sigma_{\bar{X}} \sigma_{\bar{Y}}}$. (For the groups B and G, the formula becomes: $\sigma_{\bar{D}} = \sqrt{\sigma_{\bar{B}}^2 + \sigma_{\bar{G}}^2 - 2r_{BG_{(\text{pop})}} \sigma_{\bar{B}} \sigma_{\bar{G}}}$.) But what is the meaning of r_{XY} or r_{BG}? The scores are not paired, so boys' scores cannot be correlated with girls' scores. Suppose we paired the scores arbitrarily: If we selected pairs *at random*, r_{BG} would equal 0. And if $r_{BG} = 0$, the formula for $\sigma_{\bar{D}}$ becomes:

$$\sigma_{\bar{D}} = \sqrt{\sigma_X^2 + \sigma_Y^2} \qquad \text{or} \qquad \sqrt{\sigma_{\bar{B}}^2 + \sigma_{\bar{G}}^2} \tag{9.7}$$

For independent groups, then, the correlation term is zero. And $\sigma_{\bar{D}}$ only has two components: $\sigma_{\bar{X}}$ and $\sigma_{\bar{Y}}$. The experimenter has to estimate these two terms by computing $s_{\bar{X}}$ and $s_{\bar{Y}}$.

$$s_{\bar{D}} = \sqrt{s_{\bar{X}}^2 + s_{\bar{Y}}^2} \tag{9.8}$$

Example 9.2 illustrates the full procedure.

EXAMPLE 9.2

A test of extraversion was administered to two groups of subjects—49 adolescent boys and 64 adolescent girls. The mean score of each group is shown below. Assume that both populations are normally distributed, so the population of the difference scores would also be normal. Do the two groups' means differ significantly?

	Boys	*Girls*
N	$N_B = 49$	$N_G = 64$
Mean	$\bar{B} = 26.20$	$\bar{G} = 23.28$
s	$s_B = 4.0$	$s_G = 8.0$

Solution   First estimate the standard error of the mean for each group.

For the boys, $s_{\bar{B}} = \dfrac{s_B}{\sqrt{N_B}} = \dfrac{4.0}{\sqrt{49}} = 0.57$

For the girls, $s_{\bar{G}} = \dfrac{s_G}{\sqrt{N_G}} = \dfrac{8.0}{\sqrt{64}} = 1.00$

Then compute $s_{\bar{D}}$.

$$s_{\bar{D}} = \sqrt{s_{\bar{B}}^2 + s_{\bar{G}}^2} = \sqrt{(.57)^2 + (1.00)^2} = 1.15$$

This figure, 1.15, is an estimate of $\sigma_{\bar{D}}$. Now we can test the null hypothesis.

Step 1 State H_0: $\mu_B - \mu_G = 0$. Let us test this hypothesis at the 5 percent level of significance.

Step 2 State H_1: $\mu_B - \mu_G \neq 0$. (H_1 claims that the two μ's do differ. μ_B may exceed μ_G, or μ_G may exceed μ_B. A two-tailed test is needed.)

Step 3 Consider the sampling distribution which H_0 implies. In theory, suppose the experiment were repeated many times. Each experimenter would compute one value of $\bar{B} - \bar{G}$; the different $\bar{B} - \bar{G}$'s would be normally distributed. According to H_0, their mean would equal 0. Their standard deviation would approximately equal 1.15.

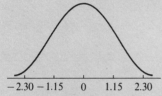

$$-2.30 \quad -1.15 \quad 0 \quad 1.15 \quad 2.30$$
Different values of $\bar{B} - \bar{G}$

Step 4 In the data, $\bar{B} - \bar{G} = 26.20 - 23.28 = 2.92$. Locate this result in the sampling distribution.

$$\text{C.R.} = \frac{(\bar{B} - \bar{G}) - 0}{s_{\bar{D}}} = \frac{(26.20 - 23.28) - 0}{1.15} = \frac{2.92}{1.15}$$
$$= 2.54$$

Step 5 z exceeds 1.96, so the sample's $\bar{B} - \bar{G}$ falls in the 5 percent rejection region. H_0 is therefore rejected at the .05 level. μ_B does seem to differ from μ_G, so the sexes do seem to differ in extraversion.

EXAMPLE 9.3

An investigator administered a test of musical ability to two groups—a group of tenth graders and a group of eighth graders. His results are shown below. Does musical ability really improve during that two-year period? Do the two groups differ significantly? Assume that the populations are normal, and use the 1 percent level of significance.

	Tenth graders (X)	Eighth graders (Y)
Mean	99.32	90.76
s	18.36	19.32
N	200	200

Solution First estimate the standard error for each group. For the tenth graders, $s_{\bar{X}} = 18.36/\sqrt{200} = 1.30$. For the eighth graders, $s_{\bar{Y}} = 19.32/\sqrt{200} = 1.37$. Next compute $s_{\bar{D}}$. ($s_{\bar{D}}$ estimates the theoretical population value, $\sigma_{\bar{D}}$.)

$$s_{\bar{D}} = \sqrt{s_{\bar{X}}^2 + s_{\bar{Y}}^2} = \sqrt{(1.30)^2 + (1.37)^2} = 1.89$$

Step 1 State H_0: $\mu_X - \mu_Y = 0$. The 1 percent level is adopted.

Step 2 State H_1: $\mu_X - \mu_Y > 0$. (According to this hypothesis, $\mu_X > \mu_Y$. A one-tailed test is therefore needed.)

Step 3 Consider the sampling distribution which H_0 implies. In theory, suppose the experiment were repeated many times. Each experimenter would compute one $\bar{X} - \bar{Y}$. The different $\bar{X} - \bar{Y}$'s would be normally distributed. According to H_0, their mean would equal 0. Their standard deviation would approximately equal 1.89.

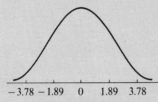

$-3.78 \ -1.89 \quad 0 \quad 1.89 \quad 3.78$
Different values $\bar{X} - \bar{Y}$

Step 4 In the data, $\bar{X} - \bar{Y} = 99.32 - 90.76 = 8.56$. Locate "8.56" in the hypothesized distribution.

$$\text{C.R.} = z = \frac{8.56 - 0}{1.89} = 4.53$$

Step 5 z exceeds 2.33, so the sample's $\bar{X} - \bar{Y}$ falls in the 1 percent rejection region. (A one-tailed test was adopted.) H_0 is therefore rejected at the .01 level of significance. μ_X does exceed μ_Y, so the experimenter concludes that tenth graders *are* superior.

Usually, H_0 is a *null* hypothesis—claiming that $\mu_X - \mu_Y$ equals 0. Sometimes, though, an experimenter has some other H_0 to test. He might want to test the hypothesis that $\mu_X - \mu_Y$ equals 10. H_0 would then claim that $\mu_X - \mu_Y = 10$. And H_1 would claim that $\mu_X - \mu_Y \neq 10$. Example 9.4 illustrates this kind of test.

EXAMPLE 9.4

When a puff of air strikes a subject's eye, the subject blinks. Now suppose an experimenter sounds a tone each time the puff occurs. Eventually, the *tone* would make the subject blink. An investigator compared schizophrenic subjects and normal subjects through this procedure. After the subject was thoroughly trained, the experimenter presented the tone alone. The subject was tested 200 times. The data show how often the subject blinked throughout these trials.

Schizophrenics (Y)	Normals (X)
$N = 100$	$N = 100$
$\bar{Y} = 150.0$	$\bar{X} = 159.0$
$s = \quad 8.0$	$s = \quad 6.0$
$s_{\bar{Y}} = \quad 0.8$	$s_{\bar{X}} = \quad 0.6$
$s_{\bar{D}} = 1.0$	

Test the hypothesis that schizophrenics and normals differ by 10.0 points— that $\mu_X - \mu_Y = 10.0$. Assume that the populations are normal, and adopt the 1 percent level.

Solution

Step 1   State H_0: $\mu_Y - \mu_X = 10.0$. (The .01 level is adopted.)

Step 2   State H_1: $\mu_Y - \mu_X \neq 10.0$. (A two-tailed test is needed.)

Step 3   In theory, suppose the experiment were repeated many times. Each experimenter would compute one $\bar{X} - \bar{Y}$. Different $\bar{X} - \bar{Y}$'s would be normally distributed. According to H_0, their mean would equal 10.0. Their standard deviation would approximately equal 1.0.

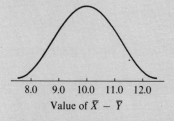

8.0	9.0	10.0	11.0	12.0

Value of $\bar{X} - \bar{Y}$

Step 4   In the data, $\bar{X} - \bar{Y} = 9.0$. How far is 9.0 from the hypothesized center, 10.0?

$$\text{C.R.} = z = \frac{(\bar{X} - \bar{Y}) - (\mu_X - \mu_Y)}{s_{\bar{D}}} = \frac{(159.0 - 150.0) - 10.0}{1.00}$$

$$= -1.00$$

Step 5   "9.0" fits comfortably into this distribution, so H_0 is accepted. We therefore accept the claim that $\mu_X - \mu_Y = 10.0$.

9.4 ESTABLISHING A CONFIDENCE INTERVAL FOR μ_D

In Example 9.1, the mean difference score, $\bar{D}$, was 6.00 and $s_{\bar{D}}$ was 1.18. In that problem $\bar{D}$ was the difference in activity level between handled and non-handled rats. The hypothesis was tested (and rejected) that $\mu_D = 0$. Thus, we concluded that μ_D is not 0; instead, μ_D seems to exceed 0. But what is μ_D? How much does an animal's activity increase on the average if the animal is handled? Some investigators like to establish a confidence interval at this point as a way of estimating μ_D.

Let us therefore establish the 95 percent confidence interval for μ_D. Following the procedure of Sec. 8.3, we consider the sample's $\bar{D}$ and compute $\bar{D} \pm 1.96 s_{\bar{D}}$:

$$95\% \text{ confidence interval:} \qquad \bar{D} \pm 1.96 s_{\bar{D}}$$
$$= 6.00 \pm 1.96(1.18)$$
$$= 6.00 \pm 2.31$$

Thus, the 95 percent confidence interval extends from 3.69 to 8.31; so μ_D probably lies between 3.69 and 8.31. (If the sample value, $\bar{D} = 6.00$, happens to be unusually high, μ_D is closer to 3.69; if the sample value happens to be unusually low, μ_D is closer to 8.31.)

Let us also compute the 99 percent confidence interval: $\bar{D} \pm 2.58 s_{\bar{D}}$. The 99 percent confidence interval would be $6.00 \pm 2.58(1.18)$. It would range from 2.96 to 9.04. Thus, at the 99 percent level of confidence, the population mean difference, μ_D, lies between 2.96 and 9.04.

Some investigators feel that it is more helpful to establish a confidence interval than simply test a null hypothesis. Hypothesis testing, they feel, only provides a yes or no answer: H_0 is accepted or H_0 is rejected. By establishing a confidence interval, though, one learns the range of likely values for μ_D, and this range may be more informative than a simple yes or no.

*9.5 TESTING THE DIFFERENCE BETWEEN PROPORTIONS: INDEPENDENT OBSERVATIONS

The Stanford-Binet Intelligence Test contains various kinds of problems and tasks. Psychologists who developed this test collected problems which differentiate children of one age from those of another age. Imagine one kind of problem that they tested—a word problem: The child was shown some scrambled words, and he was asked to arrange them into a meaningful sentence; he was allowed half a minute to solve the problem. Two groups of children were tested—12-year-olds and 13-year-olds. Each child either succeeded or not; his score was 1 or 0. Here are some hypothetical data:

* This section can be omitted in a shorter course.

	13-year-olds (X)	*12-year-olds* (Y)
Number of children (N)	$N_X = 100$	$N_Y = 100$
Frequency of 1s	80	60
Frequency of 0s	20	40
Proportion of 1s	$p_X = .80$	$p_Y = .60$

Does this item differentiate the two groups? Are 13-year-olds more apt to pass the item? Is p_X significantly greater than p_Y?

Consider p_X—the proportion of 13-year-olds who succeeded. Earlier we showed that a proportion is really a mean, a mean of 1s and 0s: Imagine a list of eighty 1s (the 80 "passes") and twenty 0s (the 20 "fails"). The mean of these 100 numbers is p_X: 80/100, or .80. Likewise, p_Y is the mean of sixty 1s and forty 0s: 60/100, or .60. And $p_X - p_Y$ is the difference between these means: .80 − .60, or .20.

Thus, the problem can be phrased this way: The mean of one group is .80; that of the other group, .60. Do these two means differ significantly? To answer this question, we need to determine $\sigma_{\bar{D}}$. In general, $\sigma_{\bar{D}}$ equals $\sqrt{\sigma_X{}^2 + \sigma_Y{}^2}$. But what is σ_X? Or σ_Y?

When scores are dichotomous, $\sigma_{\bar{X}}$ equals $\sqrt{(p_{pop}q_{pop})/N}$, as shown in Sec. 8.6. p_{pop} is the proportion of 1s in the population, q_{pop} the proportion of 0s. Thus, $\sigma_{\bar{X}}$ becomes $\sqrt{(p_{pop}q_{pop})/N}$ for the X population (13-year-olds). And $\sigma_{\bar{Y}}$ becomes $\sqrt{(p_{pop}q_{pop})/N}$ for the Y population (12-year-olds). We can denote these two standard errors this way:

$$\sigma_{\bar{X}} = \sqrt{\frac{p_{X(pop)}q_{X(pop)}}{N_X}} \quad \text{and} \quad \sigma_{\bar{Y}} = \sqrt{\frac{p_{Y(pop)}q_{Y(pop)}}{N_Y}}$$

Now we can determine $\sigma_{\bar{D}}$. Since the means are proportions, let us denote it $\sigma_{p_X - p_Y}$.

$$\sigma_{\bar{D}} \text{ or } \sigma_{p_X - p_Y} = \sqrt{\sigma_{\bar{X}}{}^2 + \sigma_{\bar{Y}}{}^2} = \sqrt{\frac{p_{X(pop)}q_{X(pop)}}{N_X} + \frac{p_{Y(pop)}q_{Y(pop)}}{N_Y}}$$

Usually in this type of problem, the experimenter wants to test a *null* hypothesis. He wants to test the claim that the two population proportions are equal—that $p_{X(pop)} = p_{Y(pop)}$. If these two proportions are *equal*, then either of them can be called p_{pop}. And when we test the null hypothesis, $\sigma_{p_X - p_Y}$ becomes:

$$\sigma_{p_X - p_Y} = \sqrt{\frac{p_{pop}q_{pop}}{N_X} + \frac{p_{pop}q_{pop}}{N_Y}}$$

But how shall we estimate p_{pop}? Let us consider all $N_X + N_Y = 200$ cases. Of all these children, $80 + 60 = 140$ passed the item, so the overall proportion of passes was $140/200 = .70$. The best estimate of p_{pop} is therefore .70. And the best estimate of $\sigma_{p_X - p_Y}$ becomes:

$$\text{Estimate of } \sigma_{p_X - p_Y} = \sqrt{\frac{pq}{N_X} + \frac{pq}{N_Y}}$$

$$= \sqrt{\frac{(.70)(.30)}{100} + \frac{(.70)(.30)}{100}} \tag{9.9}$$

$$= \sqrt{.0042} = .065$$

According to the null hypothesis, $p_{X(pop)}$ equals $p_{Y(pop)}$—both approximately .70. According to H_1, the two values differ: $p_{X(pop)}$ is higher. Now suppose the experiment were repeated many times. Each experimenter would compute one $p_X - p_Y$, and the sampling distribution would be normal. The mean would equal 0, and the standard deviation, .065.

Now consider the data of one sample: $p_X - p_Y$ equals $.80 - .60$, or .20. How far is this $p_X - p_Y$ from the hypothesized 0? The z score, or critical ratio, becomes:

$$\text{C.R.} = z = \frac{(p_X - p_Y) - 0}{\sigma_{p_X - p_Y}} \tag{9.10}$$

$$= \frac{(.80 - .60) - 0}{.065}$$

$$= 3.00$$

A one-tailed test is applied, and H_0 is rejected at the .01 level. Thus, the task *does* discriminate between the two groups.

EXAMPLE 9.5

Two groups were polled on a certain issue; one was a sample of Democrats, the other a sample of Republicans. The investigator recorded the proportion of people who voted each way. Let p denote each group's proportion of "yes" votes. Do the two groups differ significantly at the .05 level?

Here are the data:

	Republicans (R)	Democrats (D)
Sample size	$N_R = 200$	$N_D = 100$
Frequency of "yes" votes	90	55
Proportion of "yes" votes	$p_R = \dfrac{90}{200} = .45$	$p_D = \dfrac{55}{100} = .55$

$$\text{For all 300 cases: } p = \frac{90 + 55}{300} = .48$$

$$q = .52$$

$p_{R_{(pop)}}$ tells the proportion of "yes" votes in the Republican population; $p_{D_{(pop)}}$, in the Democrat population. We need to test the hypothesis that $p_{R_{(pop)}} - p_{D_{(pop)}} = 0$.

Solution

Step 1   State H_0: $p_{R_{(pop)}} - p_{D_{(pop)}} = 0$. The .05 level is adopted.

Step 2   State H_1: $p_{R_{(pop)}} - p_{D_{(pop)}} \neq 0$. A two-tailed test is needed.

Step 3   Estimate the standard error.

$$\text{Estimate of } \sigma_{p_R - p_D} = \sqrt{\frac{pq}{N_R} + \frac{pq}{N_D}}$$

$$= \sqrt{\frac{(.48)(.52)}{200} + \frac{(.48)(.52)}{100}}$$

$$= .06$$

According to the null hypothesis, the sampling distribution is normal; its mean is 0, and its standard error is about .06.

According to H_0, the mean of the sampling distribution is 0.

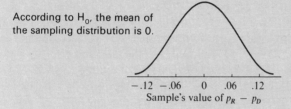

$$
\begin{array}{ccccc}
-.12 & -.06 & 0 & .06 & .12
\end{array}
$$
Sample's value of $p_R - p_D$

Step 4   The result of the one experiment showed that $p_R - p_D$ equals $.45 - .55 = -.10$. Let us locate $-.10$ in the sampling distribution.

$$z = \frac{(p_R - p_D) - 0}{\text{Estimate of } \sigma_{p_X - p_Y}} = \frac{(.45 - .55) - 0}{.06} = -1.6$$

Step 5   The observed difference fits comfortably into the sampling distribution. It *does* jibe with H_0. At the .05 level, then, H_0 is accepted; Republicans and Democrats do not seem to differ.

*9.6   TESTING THE DIFFERENCE BETWEEN TWO PROPORTIONS: CORRELATED OBSERVATIONS

Suppose a certain group of subjects is tested twice. Perhaps a film is shown, and the subjects are polled before the film, then again after the film. The investigator notes how many people say "yes" before and after. Then he

* This section can be omitted in a shorter course.

summarizes the data as two proportions—p_{Before} and p_{After}. He wants to know whether a significant change has occurred in p. Is p_{After} significantly greater than p_{Before}? Does their difference exceed 0?

Suppose p_{Before} equals .55, while p_{After} equals .65. Here are some hypothetical data. Let us call the data Case 1.

Case 1

		After Seeing the Film		
		"No"	"Yes"	
	"Yes"	0^A	55^B	$55 \to p_{Before}$
Before Seeing the Film	"No"	35^C	10^D	45
		35	65	100
			↓	
			p_{After}	

In these data 100 people were tested. The table shows how they responded on each occasion. Cell A describes people who said "yes" before and "no" afterward; not a single subject fell in that category. Cell B, on the other hand, describes people who said "yes" on both occasions; 55 subjects fell in that category. The entire top row—Cell A + Cell B—tells the number of yes votes before the film: $0 + 55 = 55$. From this figure we compute p_{Before}: $55/100 =$ .55. To compute p_{After} consider the subjects in Cell B and Cell D. These two frequencies—$55 + 10$—tell the number of yes votes after the film. p_{After} therefore equals $65/100 = .65$.

Cell B describes people who said "yes" on both occasions. These 55 subjects are therefore included both in p_{Before} and in p_{After}:

$$p_{Before} = \frac{\overset{\text{Cell A}}{\underset{\downarrow}{0}} + \overset{\text{Cell B}}{\underset{\downarrow}{55}}}{100} \quad \text{and} \quad p_{After} = \frac{\overset{\text{Cell B}}{\underset{\downarrow}{55}} + \overset{\text{Cell D}}{\underset{\downarrow}{10}}}{100}$$

Thus, Cell B is common to *both* proportions; therefore, it does not contribute to the difference between the p's. Instead, two other cells produce the difference—Cell A and Cell D. Cell A only appears in p_{Before}; it describes people who changed from yes to no. (Nobody did.) Cell D only appears in p_{After}; it describes people who changed from no to yes. (10 people fell in that cell.) Thus, 10 people changed one way, and no one changed the other way.

Should we attribute the $10:0$ difference to chance? Perhaps we could explain the difference this way: Certain subjects are fickle—they change their minds often and in unreliable ways. At one moment they change from no to yes; the next moment they change from yes to no. Perhaps the sample contained 10 fickle subjects of this kind, and perhaps by chance, all 10 of them shifted the same way—from no to yes.

Thus, the *consistent* subjects (Cell B and Cell C) can be ignored. Consistent subjects do not help us understand the attitude change. Instead, we examine the *inconsistent* subjects (Cell A and Cell D). Does the number of no to yes changes (Cell D) exceed the number of yes to no changes (Cell A)? Perhaps the two kinds of changes are equally probable; in the population perhaps they are equally common. If so, consider the probability that *all 10* subjects fell in Cell D. This probability is like the probability that 10 pennies all happen to fall heads.

Let us therefore consider a group of 10 such subjects. Let p denote the proportion who change from no to yes. (In the data, $p = 10/10 = 1.0$.) Test the hypothesis that p_{pop} equals .50. According to this hypothesis, as many subjects change one way as the other.

To test the hypothesis, we compute σ_p.

$$\sigma_p = \sqrt{\frac{pq}{N}} = \sqrt{\frac{(.50)(.50)}{10}} = .158$$

H_0 claims that p_{pop} is .50. H_1 claims that p_{pop} exceeds .50. (A one-tailed test is appropriate.) The sampling distribution would describe many 10-person samples. According to H_0, that distribution's mean would equal .50; its standard deviation, .158. In our sample, $p = 1.0$. Now how far is this value from the distribution's center?

$$z = \frac{|1.0 - .50| - \dfrac{.5}{N}}{.158} = \frac{.45}{.158} = 2.85$$

Therefore, H_0 gets rejected at the .01 level. Thus, p_{pop} *does* seem to differ from .50. Significantly more subjects changed from no to yes, so the attitude change *is* significant.

In this problem, then, p_{Before} (.55) really does differ from p_{After} (.65) since Cell A and Cell D differ significantly. Let us now consider three other cases. In these cases the attitude change is weaker, but the p's are still .55 and .65. Particularly notice the subjects in Cell A and Cell D. Those values have been darkened.

		Case 1					*Case 2*		
		After					After		
		No	Yes				No	Yes	
Before	Yes	**0**	55	55	Yes	**10**	45	55
	No	35	**10**	45	No	25	**20**	45
		35	65				35	65	

		Case 3					*Case 4*		
		After					After		
		No	Yes				No	Yes	
Before	Yes	**20**	35	55	Yes	**35**	20	55
	No	15	**30**	45	No	0	**45**	45
		35	65				35	65	

Case 4 is striking for its large number of changes: 35 people changed from yes to no, 45 from no to yes. Altogether 80 people changed their minds! If people change their minds *at random*, 40 should change each way. Does the 45 : 35 split really differ from a 40 : 40 split? The situation is like a toss of 80 pennies with 45 heads and 35 tails. Does this result differ significantly from an even split? If so, the attitude change is significant.

Let us consider the 80 changes in Case 4. The proportion in Cell D is $45/80 = .5625$. Does this p differ significantly from the hypothesized .50?

$$\sigma_p \text{ equals } \sqrt{\frac{pq}{N}} = \sqrt{\frac{(.50)(.50)}{80}} = .056$$

According to H_0, $p_{\text{pop}} = .50$; according to H_1, $p_{\text{pop}} \neq .50$. The sampling distribution would describe various 80-person samples. According to H_0, its mean would be .50, its standard deviation, .056. In our sample, $p = .5625$. How far is this p from the hypothesized center, .50?

$$z = \frac{|.5625 - .50| - \dfrac{.5}{80}}{.056} = \frac{.0565}{.056} = 1.0$$

The z is small, so the data jibe with H_0. In Case 4, then, the attitude change is *not* significant.

9.7   TYPE I AND TYPE II ERRORS

Suppose H_0 is valid. Only then can a Type I error occur: The null hypothesis is perfectly true, but the investigator gets misled; his sample is atypical and it fails to jibe with H_0. Then, misled by the sample, the investigator rejects H_0. α tells the probability of this error. Actually, α is a *conditional* probability: It tells the probability that an investigator rejects H_0—given that H_0 is valid.

On the other hand, suppose H_0 is *not* valid. Then a different kind of error can occur. H_0 ought to be rejected for it is false. But suppose the sample is atypical and happens to *jibe* with H_0. The investigator really should not accept H_0, but he does. The probability of this error is also a conditional probability. It tells the probability that the investigator accepts H_0—given that H_0 is false.

The two kinds of errors are described in the following table.

		The truth of the matter	
		H_0 *is valid* (*and should be accepted*)	H_0 *is not valid* (*and should be rejected*)
Investigator's conclusion	He accepts H_0		Type II Error
	He rejects H_0	Type I Error	

Some data

Let us consider some data and examine the two errors further. Suppose an experimenter tested two independent groups, an experimental group and a control group. Hypothetical data are shown in Table 9.3.

TABLE 9.3   Hypothetical data for two independent groups

Experimental Group (E)	*Control Group* (C)
$N_E = 100$ $\bar{E} = 129.0$ $s_E = 30.0$	$N_C = 100$ $\bar{C} = 125.0$ $s_C = 40.0$
$s_{\bar{E}} = \dfrac{30}{\sqrt{100}} = 3.0$	$s_{\bar{C}} = \dfrac{40}{\sqrt{100}} = 4.0$
$s_{\bar{D}} = \sqrt{s_{\bar{E}}^2 + s_{\bar{C}}^2} = \sqrt{3^2 + 4^2} = 5.0$	

Suppose the investigator now tests the null hypothesis. According to the null hypothesis $\mu_E - \mu_C$ equals 0. In the data $\bar{E} - \bar{C}$ equals 4.0. Furthermore, $s_{\bar{D}} = 5$, so the critical ratio becomes:

$$\text{C.R.} = \frac{(\bar{E} - \bar{C}) - 0}{s_{\bar{D}}} = \frac{(129.0 - 125.0) - 0}{5.0} = 0.80$$

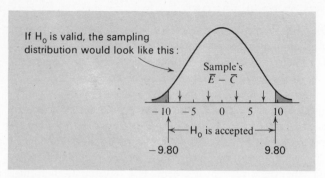

FIG. 9.2

The C.R. is small—less than 1.96—so H_0 is accepted. Thus, the sample's $\bar{E} - \bar{C}$ does not differ significantly from 0.

How large would $\bar{E} - \bar{C}$ have to be for the experimenter to reject H_0? The sampling distribution is shown in Fig. 9.2. α has been set at .05, and the rejection region falls beyond $z = 1.96$; $(1.96)(s_{\bar{D}}) = (1.96)(5.0) = 9.80$ points. Thus 95 percent of the distribution falls between -9.80 and $+9.80$; the rejection region falls outside these limits. If H_0 is true, most samples would fall within these limits: Generally speaking, $\bar{E} - \bar{C}$ would lie between -9.80 and $+9.80$, and the experimenter would accept H_0.

The procedure can be summarized this way: The experimenter *accepts* H_0 whenever $\bar{E} - \bar{C}$ lies between -9.80 and $+9.80$. If $\bar{E} - \bar{C}$ is 7.2, or -3.8, or 9.1, or -0.4, the experimenter accepts H_0. Let us record this fact; we will need it later.

For data like those of Table 9.3, the experimenter accepts the null hypothesis if the sample's $\bar{E} - \bar{C}$ falls between -9.80 and $+9.80$.

Of course, H_0 might not be true: $\mu_E - \mu_C$ might not equal 0. We never know for sure what it equals. But theoretically, we can imagine some Omniscient Being who views the whole population and knows The Truth. Perhaps this Omniscient Being finds that H_0 is perfectly true. On the other hand, perhaps He finds that H_0 is false and that μ_E exceeds μ_C by, say, 11 points. Only the Omniscient Being knows this truth. We humans can only theorize about it.

Table 9.4 lists two theoretical possibilities; they appear as the two columns: In one case, μ_E equals μ_C; in the other case, μ_E differs from μ_C. The rows of the table tell what conclusions the experimenter might draw. He might accept H_0, he might reject H_0. Thus, each cell of the table describes a different

TABLE 9.4 Meaning of two kinds of errors

		Truth about the population (seen by the omniscient being)	
		$\mu_E - \mu_C = 0$ (ideally, the experimenter should accept H_0)	$\mu_E - \mu_C \neq 0$ (ideally, the experimenter should reject H_0)
The experimenter's statistical inference	$\mu_E - \mu_C = 0$ (experimenter accepts H_0)	Cell M Probability $= 1 - \alpha$	Cell Q Type II error probability $= \beta$
	$\mu_E - \mu_c \neq 0$ (experimenter rejects H_0)	Cell N Type I error probability $= \alpha$	Cell R Probability $= 1 - \beta$

situation. In Cell M, for example, $\mu_E - \mu_C$ equals 0 and the experimenter *accepts* H_0. In contrast, Cell N describes the Type I error; $\mu_E - \mu_C$ equals 0 but the experimenter *rejects* H_0. The first column, then, considers cases where H_0 is valid. For those cases, the probability of Cell N is α; the probability of Cell M, $1 - \alpha$.

Type II error

Now consider the right-hand column. The Omniscient Being surveys the population and sees a real difference: μ_E differs from μ_C. For the sake of argument, suppose μ_E is actually 11 points bigger; $\mu_E - \mu_C$ equals 11. H_0 should be rejected since the difference is not zero. If the experimenter *accepts* H_0, he commits a Type II error. Now how often would this error occur?

Consider the sampling distribution (Fig. 9.3). $\mu_E - \mu_C$ equals 11.0, and the standard error is estimated to be 5.0. In general, $\bar{E} - \bar{C}$ would fall near 11.0.

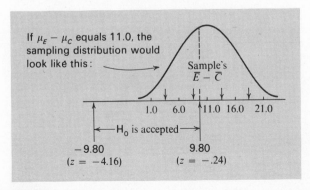

If $\mu_E - \mu_C$ equals 11.0, the sampling distribution would look like this:

Sample's $\bar{E} - \bar{C}$

1.0   6.0   11.0 16.0   21.0

← H_0 is accepted →

−9.80   9.80
($z = -4.16$)   ($z = -.24$)

FIG. 9.3

The experimenter tests the null hypothesis as usual: If $\bar{E} - \bar{C}$ falls between -9.80 and $+9.80$, he accepts H_0. How often would $\bar{E} - \bar{C}$ fall between -9.80 and $+9.80$? How much of the distribution lies between -9.80 and $+9.80$? When

$$\bar{E} - \bar{C} = +9.80 \qquad z = \frac{9.80 - 11}{5.0} = \frac{-1.20}{5.0} = -0.24$$

When

$$\bar{E} - \bar{C} = -9.80 \qquad z = \frac{-9.80 - 11}{5.0} = \frac{-20.80}{5.0} = -4.16$$

About 40 percent of the curve lies between these two z scores. So the probability of accepting H_0 is about .40.

Let us summarize the procedure: If $\mu_E - \mu_C$ is 11.0, sample outcomes would vary about 11.0. The sample's $\bar{E} - \bar{C}$ might equal 14.0 (and H_0 would get rejected); or the sample's $\bar{E} - \bar{C}$ might equal 7.1 (and H_0 would get accepted). Whenever $\bar{E} - \bar{C}$ fell between -9.80 and $+9.80$, the investigator would accept H_0—and commit a Type II error.

In this example, the Type II error would occur 40 percent of the time. The probability of a Type II error is denoted β. Thus, if $\mu_E - \mu_C$ is 11.0, $\beta = .40$.

Of course, $\mu_E - \mu_C$ need not be 11.0; it might equal 17.0. Then the sampling distribution would look as in Fig. 9.4. How often would $\bar{E} - \bar{C}$ fall between -9.80 and $+9.80$? Seven percent of the distribution falls in that region, so β would equal .07. The Type II error is not as likely when $\mu_E - \mu_C$ is large.

We can imagine many different cases. $\mu_E - \mu_C$ might be very small—say 6.0. Or it might be large—say, 13.0 or 104.0. (For each case, we still estimate $\sigma_{\bar{D}}$ to be 5.0.) And for each case β can be computed. Table 9.5 shows these probabilities.

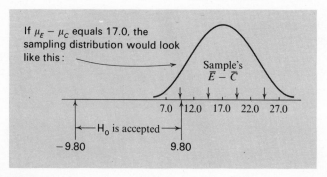

FIG. 9.4

TABLE 9.5 Probability of a Type II error for different values of $\mu_E - \mu_C$

The size of $\mu_E - \mu_C$	The probability of a Type II error, β	Power $1 - \beta$
1.0	.946	.054
2.0	.932	.068
3.0	.908	.092
4.0	.874	.126
5.0	.829	.171
6.0	.775	.225
7.0	.711	.289
8.0	.641	.359
9.0	.564	.436
10.0	.484	.516
11.0	.405	.595
12.0	.330	.670
13.0	.261	.739
14.0	.200	.800
15.0	.149	.851
16.0	.107	.893
17.0	.075	.925
18.0	.051	.949
19.0	.033	.967
20.0	.021	.979
$\vdots$	$\vdots$	$\vdots$
100.0	.000+	.999+

Check some of these probabilities for yourself. For example, suppose $\mu_E - \mu_C$ is 100. The sampling distribution becomes as shown in Fig. 9.5. Values between -9.80 and $+9.80$ are extremely rare; their probability is practically

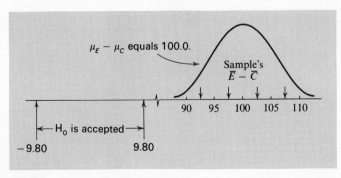

FIG. 9.5

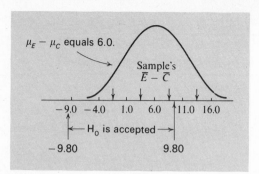

FIG. 9.6

zero. On the other hand, suppose $\mu_E - \mu_C$ is 6 (Fig. 9.6). The z score at 9.80 is: $(9.80 - 6.0)/5.0 = 0.76$. And the z score at -9.80 is: $(-9.80 - 6.0)/5.0 = -3.16$. These two values bound 77 percent of the distribution. Thus, the probability of a Type II error is high. If $\mu_E - \mu_C$ equals 6.0, $\beta = .77$. The smaller the difference, the larger the β.

EXAMPLE 9.6

Suppose an experimenter is about to analyze some data. In the data $\sigma_D = 1.0$. The data require a two-tailed test, and the experimenter adopts the .05 level of significance.

TABLE 9.6 Probability of accepting H_0 and rejecting H_0 for different sizes of $\mu_E - \mu_c$

$\mu_E - \mu_C$ (true mean difference)	Probability of accepting H_0	An error to accept H_0?	Probability of rejecting H_0	An error to reject H_0?
4.0	.021	Type II Error	.979	Not an error: $\mu_D \neq 0$
3.5	.062	,,	.938	,,
3.0	.149	,,	.851	,,
2.5	.295	,,	.705	,,
2.0	☐	,,	.516	,,
1.5	.677	,,	.323	,,
1.0	.830	,,	.170	,,
.5	.921	,,	.079	,,
.0	.950	Not an error: $\mu_D = 0$	.050	Type I Error
− .5	.921	Type II Error	.079	Not an error: $\mu_D \neq 0$
−1.0	.830	,,	.170	,,
−1.5	.677	,,	.323	,,
−2.0	.484	,,	.516	,,
−2.5	.295	,,	.705	,,
−3.0	.149	,,	.851	,,
−3.5	.062	,,	.938	,,
−4.0	.021	,,	.979	,,

Let us consider differences of various sizes: Let $\mu_E - \mu_C$ range from -4.0 to $+4.0$. Then for each value, we compute the probability of a Type II error. Table 9.6 reports all of the probabilities but one. Compute that missing value.

Solution H_0 would be accepted whenever $\bar{E} - \bar{C}$ fell between -1.96 (1.0) and $+1.96$ (1.0). Suppose $\mu_E - \mu_C$ equaled 2.0: How often would $\bar{E} - \bar{C}$ fall between -1.96 and $+1.96$?

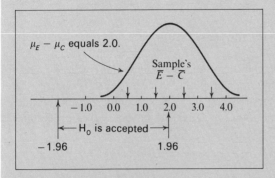

At 1.96, $z = (1.96 - 2.00)/1.0 = -.04$. At -1.96, $z = (-1.96 - 2.00)/1.0 = -3.96$. This region includes .48 of the distribution. So the probability of a Type II error is .48.

Power

According to Table 9.5, when $\mu_E - \mu_C$ is 14.0, β is .20. Therefore, the probability is .20 that H_0 get accepted. Now what is the probability that H_0 be rejected—as it should be? That probability is: $1 - .20 = .80$.

$1 - \beta$, or .80 in this case, is called the *power* of the test. It tells the probability that the experimenter reject H_0 when he should. Table 9.5 reports the power for each value of $\mu_E - \mu_C$. These values also appear in the graph of Fig. 9.7.

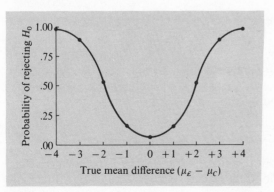

FIG. 9.7

Factors that affect the Type II error

A Type II error depends on several factors. First, a Type II error is more likely when $\mu_E - \mu_C$ is small. *Small* differences frequently get overlooked since the experimenter tends to call them "not significant."

Second, a Type II error is more common when α is strict—say, .01 or .001. Consider some data. Say $\sigma_{\bar{D}} = 10$ and the experimenter is about to test the null hypothesis. For what values of $\bar{E} - \bar{C}$ would H_0 be accepted? Let us consider three significance levels. First, suppose α is .05. The acceptance region would extend from $-1.96\,\sigma_{\bar{D}}$ to $+1.96\,\sigma_{\bar{D}}$: H_0 would get accepted whenever $\bar{E} - \bar{C}$ fell between $-1.96\,(10)$ and $+1.96\,(10)$—between -19.6 and $+19.6$. But when α is .01, the acceptance region is broader: It extends from -25.8 to $+25.8$. Thus, H_0 gets accepted more often, so the Type II error becomes more likely. Finally, when α is .001, the acceptance region is even broader: -32.9 to $+32.9$. Thus, as α grows more stringent: The acceptance region broadens, H_0 gets accepted more often, and Type II errors have a higher probability.

9.8   SUMMARY AND IMPLICATIONS FOR EXPERIMENTAL DESIGN

This chapter examined a common type of experiment: The experimenter studies two groups and compares their means, $\bar{X}$ and $\bar{Y}$ or $\bar{X}_1$ and $\bar{X}_2$. He then needs to evaluate the difference between these means. Do they differ significantly? Can we generalize to the whole population? Can we generalize to μ_1 and μ_2?

The statistical procedure usually begins with a null hypothesis. According to this null hypothesis, $\mu_1 - \mu_2$ is 0, or $p_{pop(1)} - p_{pop(2)}$ is 0. Then the experimenter considers the sampling distribution of differences—$\bar{X}_1 - \bar{X}_2$ or $p_1 - p_2$. He imagines the distribution's center, 0, and its standard deviation, $\sigma_{\bar{D}}$ or $\sigma_{p_1-p_2}$. Next he locates his sample's difference in this distribution by forming a z score (or critical ratio): He notes how far $\bar{X}_1 - \bar{X}_2$ is from 0 and divides by the size of the standard error. When the groups are independent, the formula is written:

$$\text{C.R.} = \frac{(\bar{X}_1 - \bar{X}_2) - 0}{\sigma_{\bar{D}}} = \frac{\bar{X}_1 - \bar{X}_2}{\sqrt{\sigma_{\bar{X}_1}^2 + \sigma_{\bar{X}_2}^2}} = \frac{\bar{X}_1 - \bar{X}_2}{\sqrt{\dfrac{\sigma_1^2}{N_1} + \dfrac{\sigma_2^2}{N_2}}}$$

In this formula σ_1 and σ_2 are population parameters; they need to be estimated from the data through s_1 and s_2. We therefore replace σ_1^2 and σ_2^2 by the two estimates, s_1^2 and s_2^2.

$$\text{C.R.} = \frac{\bar{X}_1 - \bar{X}_2}{\sqrt{(s_1^2/N_1) + (s_2^2/N_2)}}$$

Eventually, then, the critical ratio is formed. The experimenter's final decision depends on this ratio. If the ratio is small, he accepts H_0. If the ratio is large, he rejects H_0. Thus, the formula contains all the ingredients that affect the decision. It contains a difference, a measure of variability, and the sample size. Let us consider each of these ingredients separately.

Ingredients of a statistical test

First, the ratio's numerator contains a difference—$(\overline{X}_1 - \overline{X}_2)$ minus 0, or simply $\overline{X}_1$ minus $\overline{X}_2$. The larger the difference, the larger the C.R. Large differences make us reject H_0: If $\overline{X}_1$ is far from $\overline{X}_2$, then μ_1 probably differs from μ_2.

Second, the formula contains $s_1{}^2$ and $s_2{}^2$, measures of variability. These terms describe the variability within each group. They appear in the denominator, so large s^2 terms produce *smaller* C.R.'s. In general, the more variable the scores, the smaller the C.R. If the scores do not vary much, the C.R. is larger. Let $\overline{X}_1 - \overline{X}_2$ be an 8-point difference, and suppose the scores are extremely variable. Then the denominator would be large and the C.R. quite small. On the other hand, let $\overline{X}_1 - \overline{X}_2$ be an 8-point difference, and suppose the scores do *not* vary much. Then the denominator would be small, and the C.R. would be larger. The significance of the 8-point difference depends on the variabilities.

Finally, the formula contains N_1 and N_2, the number of cases in each group. These N's appear in the standard error's *denominator*. Thus, *large N's produce small* standard errors; and small standard errors produce *large* ratios. Therefore, with other things equal, large N's produce large C.R.'s.

Implications

Suppose μ_1 really differed from μ_2. The experimenter would want the critical ratio to be large, so ideally, the standard error should be small—the smaller the better. Now how could the experimenter minimize the standard error? What steps would help reduce its size?

For one thing, the experimenter could choose a large sample. A large N helps keep the standard error small. Second, the experimenter could take steps to reduce the variances. The less the scores vary, the smaller the standard error.

But how could an experimenter reduce the scores' variance? One way is to standardize the experiment's conditions. When all the subjects in a group are treated alike, the scores vary less. An experimenter should therefore aim for uniformity—identical instructions, identical testing conditions, identical incentives. This uniformity keeps the scores more alike and their variances smaller.

The size of the standard error also depends on the design of the experiment. An experiment can usually be designed in several different ways. Some designs produce smaller standard errors, others produce larger standard errors. In general, the smaller the standard error, the better the design. Let us therefore consider three ways to design an experiment.

Three experimental designs

Suppose an experimenter wants to see how marijuana affects memory. Perhaps he plans to administer marijuana in the experimental condition and a placebo in the control condition. Every subject is to be tested on a standard test of memory, and the two means will be compared—$\bar{E}$ for the experimental (marijuana) condition, $\bar{C}$ for the control (placebo) condition.

One possible design is the Independent Groups design. The experimenter selects a group of subjects at random. Then he randomly assigns half of them to one condition and half to the other condition. All the subjects are treated alike. The drug and placebo look alike, taste alike, and smell alike. Ideally, the testing is *double-blind*: Neither the subject nor the examiner knows who receives what drug. This design is schematized below:

Design 1: Independent Groups (100 subjects are tested. Each subject is tested once.)

Experimental condition (*marijuana is administered*)	*Control condition* (*placebo is administered*)
24	20
17	21
⋮	⋮
(50 scores)	(50 scores)

The standard error for this design is: $\sigma_{\bar{D}} = \sqrt{\sigma_{\bar{E}}^2 + \sigma_{\bar{C}}^2}$.

In this design subjects are assigned to a condition at random. By chance, though, the two groups might differ in some irrelevant way: One group might have higher IQs, more verbal aptitude, or more interest in the task. Irrelevant variables like these could affect the subject's memory: The group with the higher IQ, say, would have the better memory. A difference of this kind would obscure the drug's real effect. To avoid irrelevant influences, then, an experimenter should make sure his groups are comparable—alike in all important ways. If IQ is relevant, he should note each group's average IQ. If motivation is relevant, he should equalize the groups' motivations.

Sometimes two groups are deliberately matched in some way. The next design achieves this goal. Suppose IQ is relevant, and the experimenter wants to equalize his groups. He might select *pairs* of equally bright subjects: He would randomly draw a subject from the population and then find another subject with the same IQ. Many such pairs would be formed. Finally, one member of each pair would be randomly assigned to one condition, the other member to the other condition. This design is called a Groups with Matched Subjects design: it is schematically shown below. It can be viewed as a variation of the Repeated Measurements design.

Design 2: Groups with Matched Subjects (50 pairs of subjects are tested. The subjects within each pair are comparable in IQ.)

	Experimental condition	Control condition	Difference score
Pair 1 (The IQs equal 80)	9	7	2
$\vdots$	$\vdots$	$\vdots$	$\vdots$
Pair 50 (The IQs equal 120)	22	23	-1

Since this design contains paired observations, the experimenter would list the scores pair by pair, compute 50 difference scores, and then estimate $\sigma_{\bar{D}}$. Earlier we considered two ways of estimating $\sigma_{\bar{D}}$. One was to estimate σ_D and divide by $\sqrt{N}$. The other involved a formula containing the correlation coefficient:

$$\sigma_{\bar{D}} = \sqrt{\sigma_X^2 + \sigma_Y^2 - 2r_{XY}\sigma_X\sigma_Y}$$

This formula is generally not practical, but it does show the advantage of matching: For independent groups, $\sigma_{\bar{D}}$ equals $\sqrt{\sigma_X^2 + \sigma_Y^2}$. For groups with matched subjects, an additional term gets subtracted, so $\sigma_{\bar{D}}$ tends to be smaller. The subtracted term contains the correlation coefficient; hence, the higher the correlation, the smaller the $\sigma_{\bar{D}}$. When r_{XY} is high, then, the standard error is smaller. (When r_{XY} is zero, of course, the matching has no effect: $\sigma_{\bar{D}}$ equals $\sqrt{\sigma_X^2 + \sigma_Y^2}$, and the groups are independent.)

Ideally, matched subjects should be equal in every important respect. If an experimenter could arrange to test pairs of identical twins, the match would be very good. Or better still, perhaps he could test the same person twice, once in each condition. Then each score would be *perfectly* matched with a corresponding other score. The two subjects would have identical IQs, identical verbal abilities, identical physiological characteristics, identical motivations, and so on. That is the ultimate in matching: The same people serve in both conditions. Irrelevant group differences could not occur.

When a subject serves in both conditions, the design is a Repeated Measurements design. Like the Groups with Matched Subjects, it contains paired observations. It is schematized below. In this example 50 people are tested, and each one is tested twice.

Design 3: Repeated Measurements (50 subjects are tested. Each subject is tested twice, once in each condition.)

	Experimental condition	Control condition	Difference score
Subject 1	17	16	1
$\vdots$	$\vdots$	$\vdots$	$\vdots$
Subject 50	20	18	2

In this kind of design, the correlation between sets is generally high. The higher the correlation, the larger the subtracted term—and the smaller the standard error. In this design, then, the standard error tends to be smaller. And that is why the design is preferred.

In some experiments, of course, the Repeated Measurements design cannot be used. Perhaps an experimenter wants to train subjects in some skill and needs to compare two different methods of training. A subject trained by one method is no longer naive, so he could not participate in the other condition as well. Thus, some other design would have to be used. Each subject of one condition might be matched with a subject of comparable ability in the other condition. Matching of this kind could help reduce the standard error. On the other hand, if matching were not feasible, the experimenter would have to content himself with the Independent Groups design and a larger standard error.

APPENDIX: *Proofs*

Proof 9.1   *Proof that* $S^2_D = S^2_X + S^2_Y - 2r_{XY} S_X S_Y$.

To derive the formula for S^2_D, express each $X - Y$ as a deviation from their mean, $\bar{X} - \bar{Y}$. The deviation scores are then squared, summed, and divided by N.

$$S^2_D = \frac{\sum [(X - Y) - (\bar{X} - \bar{Y})]^2}{N}$$

$$= \frac{\sum [(X - \bar{X}) - (Y - \bar{Y})]^2}{N} = \frac{\sum [x - y]^2}{N}$$

Next perform the squaring and then sum.

$$S^2_D = \frac{\sum [x^2 + y^2 - 2xy]}{N} = \frac{\sum x^2}{N} + \frac{\sum y^2}{N} - 2\frac{\sum xy}{N}$$

$$= S^2_X + S^2_Y - 2r_{XY} S_X S_Y$$

If $r_{XY} = 0$, S^2_D equals $S^2_X + S^2_Y$. (When X and Y are uncorrelated, then, the variance of the *difference* scores, S^2_{X-Y}, equals the variance of the sums, S^2_{X+Y}.)

Proof 9.2   *Proof that* $s^2_D = s^2_X + s^2_Y - 2r_{XY} s_X s_Y$.

S^2_D is not the best estimate of the population variance, σ^2_D. To obtain the best estimate, multiply S^2_D by $N/N - 1$.

$$s^2_D = \frac{N}{N-1} S^2_D$$

From Proof 9.1, $S^2_D = S^2_X + S^2_Y - 2r_{XY} S_X S_Y$. Therefore:

$$s^2_D = \frac{N}{N-1} [S^2_X + S^2_Y - 2r_{XY} S_X S_Y]$$

$$= \frac{N}{N-1} S^2_X + \frac{N}{N-1} S^2_Y - 2r_{XY} \frac{N}{N-1} S_X S_Y$$

$$= s^2_X + s^2_Y - 2r_{XY} \sqrt{\frac{N}{N-1}} S_X \sqrt{\frac{N}{N-1}} S_Y$$

$$= s^2_X + s^2_Y - 2r_{XY} \cdot s_X \cdot s_Y$$

EXERCISES

9.1 The anxiety level of 100 subjects is measured before psychotherapy and after psychotherapy. A subject's change score is defined as his initial level minus his final level. The mean change score is 5, and the s of the change scores is 20. Estimate $\sigma_{\bar{D}}$, and establish the 95 percent confidence interval for the population mean, μ_D.

Answer: 95 percent confidence interval: $5 \pm 1.96(2)$: 1.08 to 8.92

9.2 A set of 81 difference scores $(X - Y)$ has a mean of 10. The data show that s for the difference scores is 36. Do the two sample means differ significantly at the 5 percent level of significance with a two-tailed test?

Answer: $z = \dfrac{10 - 0}{4} = 2.5$. *Null hypothesis rejected; the two means differ significantly.*

9.3 In an experiment on reading errors in dial readings, a large group of men and women were tested. The mean number of errors for men was 15.0 and the standard error of this mean was 1.5. The mean number of errors for the women was 17.5 and the standard error of this mean was 2.0. Is there a true difference between the number of errors made by men and by women?

Answer: $z = \dfrac{17.5 - 15.0}{2.5} = 1.0$. *Difference not significant at .05 level.*

9.4 An investigator wondered whether praise affects children's school work. He selected a large group of children and divided them randomly into two groups. From time to time the pupils of one group were praised for their work while those of the other group were ignored. Then, at the end of the year a test of academic achievement was given to each group. The praised group earned a mean score of 217 with a standard error of the mean of 6. The ignored group earned a score of 206 with a standard error of the mean of 8.

(a) Is the difference in mean performance statistically significant at the 5 percent level of significance?

Answer: $z = \dfrac{217 - 206}{10} = 1.10$. *Not statistically significant.*

(b) If the 5 percent level of significance is used, what is the probability of a Type II error when the true mean difference is, in fact, 9 points?
Answer:

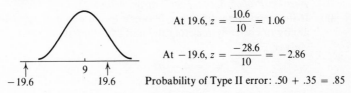

At 19.6, $z = \dfrac{10.6}{10} = 1.06$

At -19.6, $z = \dfrac{-28.6}{10} = -2.86$

Probability of Type II error: $.50 + .35 = .85$

9.5 Data have been reported in the literature for the mean length of boys and girls at birth. A sample of 900 boys showed the mean length to be 50.51 cm with $s = 3$. A sample of 900 girls showed the mean length to be 49.90 cm with $s = 3$. Is there a genuine sex difference in length at birth?

Answer: $z = \dfrac{.61}{\sqrt{.02}} = \dfrac{.61}{.14} = 4.4.$ *Difference statistically significant;* $p < .01.$

9.6 Suppose a two-tailed test is used to test the null hypothesis at the .05 level of significance. Suppose further that the standard error of the difference between means is 3 points.

(a) If the true difference in the population between μ_X and μ_Y is 6 points, the probability of correctly rejecting the null hypothesis is _____.

Answer:

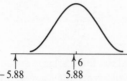

At 5.88, $z = \dfrac{-0.12}{3} = -0.04$

At -5.88, $z = \dfrac{-11.88}{3} = -3.96$

Probability of correctly rejecting $H_0 = .52$

(b) If the true difference is 12 points, the probability of correctly rejecting the null hypothesis is _____.

Answer: At 5.88, $z = \dfrac{5.88 - 12}{3} = 2.04.$ *Probability of correctly reject-*

ing $= .98.$

(c) If the true difference is 0 points, what is the probability of rejecting H_0? Of accepting H_0?

Answer: If true difference $= 0$, *probability of rejecting* H_0 *(erroneously) is* .05; *of accepting* H_0 *is* .95.

(d) If a one-tailed test had been used instead of a two-tailed test (still using the .05 level of significance), the probability of a Type I error would be

_____.

Answer: Probability of Type I error still .05.

9.7 Suppose a two-tailed test is used, the .05 level of significance is adopted, the difference between two sample means is 3, and the standard error of the difference between means is 2.

(a) Would the null hypothesis be rejected?

Answer: H_0 *would be accepted,* $z = \dfrac{3 - 0}{2} = 1.5.$

(b) What is the probability of a Type I error?

Answer: Probability of Type I error $= .05.$

(c) If the population difference between the means is 6, what is the probability of correctly rejecting the null hypothesis?

Answer:

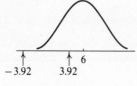

At 3.92, $z = \dfrac{3.92 - 6}{2} = -1.04$

Probability of correctly rejecting $H_0 = .85$

(d) If the population difference between the means is 0, what is the probability of making a Type II error?

Answer: If $\mu_x - \mu_y = 0$, it is not an error to accept H_0. Hence, probability of Type II error is 0.

9.8   In a class of 50 students, two tests are given. Test X has a mean of 80 and an s of 20. Test Y has a mean of 50 and an s of 10. The correlation coefficient, r_{XY}, between scores on the two tests is 0.50. Suppose difference scores were computed (Test $X -$ Test Y) for each student. What would the mean difference score be? What would the s of the difference scores be?

Answer: Mean $= 30$. $s = \sqrt{300} = 17.32$.

9.9   Suppose each individual in a population has two scores, X and Y. In this population, $\mu_x = 159$, $\mu_y = 150$, and $\sigma_D = 90$. Suppose a variety of 100-person samples were examined. What proportion of them would show $\overline{X} - \overline{Y} < 0$ (that is, $\overline{Y}$ greater than $\overline{X}$)?

Answer: .16

9.10 A two-tailed test of a mean difference is appropriate and the .046 level of significance is adopted (corresponding to a z cutoff point of 2). If $\sigma_{\overline{X} - \overline{Y}} = 4$, how big must the true difference be for the probability of a Type II error to equal .023?

Answer: 16

9.11 Psychotherapy was administered to 200 disturbed children. Each child was rated on various abnormal traits before the therapy and then again after the therapy. Before therapy 80 of these children were rated "restless" and 120 were rated "not restless." The detailed data are listed below. Has psychotherapy produced a change in restlessness? (Use the 1 percent level of significance.)

		After		
		Restless	Not restless	
Before	Restless	5	75	80
	Not restless	25	95	120
		30	170	200

Answer: $z = \dfrac{|.75 - .50| - \dfrac{.5}{100}}{.05}$

$= 4.9, p < .01$

9.12 Some authors write very "readably," while others do not. One investigator wondered whether such readability influences (in either direction) the amount a person can later remember. He asked two groups of subjects to read a passage and then recall as best they could. The passage read by Group 1 differed in only one important respect from the passage read by Group 2—it was more readable.

Each subject in Group 1 was matched with a subject in Group 2 on the basis of age, IQ, verbal ability, time of testing, and so on. The recall scores for these subjects are listed in the table below. The column of difference scores has only been completed for subjects 1 to 10.

Table of recall scores for two groups of subjects

Pair	Group 1	Group 2	Difference	Pair	Group 1	Group 2	Difference
1	18	18	0	26	16	13	
2	16	16	0	27	14	12	
3	14	12	2	28	13	20	
4	17	15	2	29	12	13	
5	12	14	−2	30	18	17	
6	11	13	−2	31	26	25	
7	12	13	−1	32	24	19	
8	18	14	4	33	16	12	
9	14	13	1	34	18	11	
10	17	19	−2	35	11	16	
11	16	18		36	22	17	
12	12	12		37	15	15	
13	15	12		38	18	14	
14	14	12		39	17	11	
15	11	13		40	20	16	
16	22	20		41	12	12	
17	24	21		42	15	13	
18	14	19		43	20	17	
19	15	19		44	18	15	
20	14	13		45	14	14	
21	11	16		46	12	11	
22	17	13		47	11	12	
23	18	20		48	16	12	
24	20	17		49	13	15	
25	22	13		50	15	13	
				Sum	800	750	50
				N	50	50	50
				$\bar{X}$	16.0	15.0	1.0
				s			3.22

(a) The mean difference score for all pairs of subjects is _____.
Answer: 1

(b) The difference between the mean recall of Group 1 and that of Group 2 is _____.
Answer: 1

(c) The s of the difference scores is _____. (Do not use the scores of Group 1 and Group 2; use the difference scores themselves.)
Answer: 3.22

(d) The estimate of $\sigma_{\bar{D}}$ for these difference scores is _____.

Answer: $\dfrac{3.22}{\sqrt{50}} = 0.455$

(e) The null hypothesis asserts that _____.

Answer: $\mu_D = 0$ or $\mu_1 - \mu_2 = 0$
     or $\mu_1 = \mu_2$

(f) Draw a normal curve to show the sampling distribution of mean differences that the null hypothesis implies. Label the hypothesized mean of the sampling distribution, and also label the outcome for this one sample.

(g) What is the standard deviation for the distribution you have drawn in (f)?
Answer: .455

(h) Compute the critical ratio (i.e., the z ratio).

Answer: $z = \dfrac{1.0 - 0}{.455} = 2.19$

(i) Is the obtained difference statistically significant at the .01 level?
Answer: No

(j) If you adopt the .01 level of significance, what is the probability of a Type I error?
Answer: .01

(k) What would you conclude about the effect of readability on recall?
Answer: Readability does affect the amount recalled; the difference is significant at the .05 level.

(l) Establish the 95 percent confidence interval for estimating μ_D, the mean difference score in the population.
Answer: $1.0 \pm 1.96(.455)$: 0.11 to 1.89

10

THE *t* TEST: HYPOTHESES ABOUT μ FOR A SMALL SAMPLE

In Chaps. 8 and 9 we tested hypotheses about μ, the population mean. Those examples dealt with fairly large samples—usually 50 or more cases. But sometimes an experimenter is limited to a small sample: Perhaps subjects are very scarce, or perhaps the testing is long and tedious. Then a large sample is not feasible. When a sample has less than 30 cases, it is considered small. Small samples pose a special problem which we shall examine in this chapter. We shall also consider the method for handling such problems.

10.1 A COMPLICATION IN THEORY AND METHOD

First let us review the procedure for testing a hypothesis about μ. Suppose an investigator has measured the IQs of 121 ghetto children, a relatively large sample. The sample is drawn at random, the mean is 92, and $s = 22$. The investigator wants to test the hypothesis that $\mu = 100$.

Since $N = 121$, $\sigma_{\overline{X}}$ is estimated this way:

$$s_{\overline{X}} = \text{est } \sigma_{\overline{X}} = \frac{\text{est } \sigma}{\sqrt{N}} = \frac{22}{\sqrt{121}} = 2$$

The critical ratio (or z) becomes: $z = (92 - 100)/2 = -4.00$. From this result, the investigator concludes that μ is not 100.

This procedure has one essential ingredient: We have to estimate $\sigma_{\overline{X}}$. To estimate $\sigma_{\overline{X}}$, we first estimate σ by computing $s = \sqrt{[\Sigma(X - \overline{X})^2]/(N - 1)}$; then we form $s_{\overline{X}} = s/\sqrt{N}$. And once $s_{\overline{X}}$ is computed, we treat it like $\sigma_{\overline{X}}$, placing it in the denominator of the z ratio: $(\overline{X} - \mu)/\sigma_{\overline{X}}$. Thus, we have assumed—and this is an important assumption—that $s_{\overline{X}}$ closely approximates $\sigma_{\overline{X}}$: that $s_{\overline{X}}$ can be treated like $\sigma_{\overline{X}}$.

For large samples, the assumption is safe; one sample's $s_{\overline{X}}$ is close to another's, so the $s_{\overline{X}}$ of any sample approximates $\sigma_{\overline{X}}$. But small samples vary more and two $s_{\overline{X}}$'s might be quite different. Therefore, a small sample's $s_{\overline{X}}$ cannot be treated as though it equaled $\sigma_{\overline{X}}$.

To examine the problem more closely, imagine many experimenters drawing samples. Let us first consider large samples. Table 10.1 shows the means of many large samples. The population's μ is 75, and the sample $\overline{X}$'s are normally distributed. The table also shows each $\overline{X}$ as a deviation from μ. These deviation values appear in the right-hand section of the table.

TABLE 10.1 Distribution of sample means (for each sample, $N = 100$)

Sample's mean ($\overline{X}$)	Category's midpoint	Frequency	Means expressed as $\overline{X} - \mu$	Frequency
77.25–77.74	77.5	1	2.25 to 2.74	1
76.75–77.24	77.0	4	1.75 to 2.24	4
76.25–76.74	76.5	6	1.25 to 1.74	6
75.75–76.24	76.0	8	0.75 to 1.24	8
75.25–75.74	75.5	17	0.25 to 0.74	17
74.75–75.24	75.0	24	-0.25 to 0.24	24
74.25–74.74	74.5	16	-0.75 to -0.24	16
73.75–74.24	74.0	9	-1.25 to -0.74	9
73.25–73.74	73.5	6	-1.75 to -1.24	6
72.75–73.24	73.0	3	-2.25 to -1.74	3
72.25–72.74	72.5	2	-2.75 to -2.24	2
		96 samples		

These means were drawn from a normal population whose $\mu = 75$ and whose $\sigma = 10$. For each sample, $N = 100$, so theoretically, $\sigma_{\overline{X}} = 1$. The mean of the 96 $\overline{X}$'s is 74.98, and the standard deviation is 1.01.

For this population, $\sigma_{\bar{X}} = 1$. Therefore, each $\bar{X} - \mu$ can be divided by $\sigma_{\bar{X}}$ to form z scores. The different z's would be normally distributed too. Whenever scores in the population are normally distributed, z's of this kind are normally distributed too: Since the scores are normally distributed, the $\bar{X}$'s are normally distributed. Then, since the $\bar{X}$'s are normally distributed, the different values of $\bar{X} - \mu$ are normally distributed. Finally, every $\bar{X} - \mu$ is divided by the constant $\sigma_{\bar{X}}$, so the resulting z's are normally distributed.

The complication with small samples

Now suppose each sample is very small. Perhaps each experimenter draws a 10-score sample; he computes $\bar{X}$, s, and eventually $s_{\bar{X}}$. Some typical results are shown in Table 10.2. Perhaps 96 samples are examined altogether.

TABLE 10.2   Data from 96 small samples (for each sample, $N = 10$)

	$\bar{X}$	s^2	s	$s_{\bar{X}} = \dfrac{s}{\sqrt{N}}$
Sample 1	71.2	138.0	11.75	$11.75/\sqrt{10} = 3.71$
Sample 2	82.4	92.4	9.61	$9.61/\sqrt{10} = 3.04$
Sample 3	73.0	87.6	9.36	$9.36/\sqrt{10} = 2.96$
Sample 4	74.7	151.2	12.30	$12.30/\sqrt{10} = 3.89$
Sample 5	76.1	118.7	10.89	$10.89/\sqrt{10} = 3.45$
Sample 6	72.8	76.1	8.72	$8.72/\sqrt{10} = 2.76$
Sample 7	70.9	103.5	10.17	$10.17/\sqrt{10} = 3.22$
Sample 8	76.8	225.9	15.03	$15.03/\sqrt{10} = 4.75$
Sample 9	78.3	109.3	10.45	$10.45/\sqrt{10} = 3.31$
Sample 10	75.1	64.8	8.05	$8.05/\sqrt{10} = 2.55$
Sample 11	67.5	84.4	9.19	$9.19/\sqrt{10} = 2.91$
$\vdots$	$\vdots$	$\vdots$	$\vdots$	$\vdots$
Sample 96	80.6	78.4	8.85	$8.85/\sqrt{10} = 2.80$

Let us examine these results in detail. First, consider the means; their distribution is shown in Table 10.3. The distribution is normal, like the one in Table 10.1. The $\bar{X} - \mu$ values are also normally distributed.

Table 10.4 shows the s^2 values from the various samples. The average s^2 equals 97.3, so for the average sample, s equals $\sqrt{97.3} = 9.9$, a close approximation to the population value $\sigma = 10$. However, the distribution is far from normal. The median is 92.8, and 91 percent of the cases lie between 10 and 170; all the rest lie beyond 170, extending to values around 300. The general form of the distribution is related to the chi-square distribution, a theoretical distribution which we shall examine in Chap. 13.

TABLE 10.3   Means of 96 small samples (for each sample, $N = 10$)

Mean ($\overline{X}$)	Midpoint	Frequency	Means expressed as $\overline{X} - \mu$	Frequency
81.50–82.49	82.0	1	6.50 to 7.49	1
80.50–81.49	81.0	2	5.50 to 6.49	2
79.50–80.49	80.0	4	4.50 to 5.49	4
78.50–79.49	79.0	5	3.50 to 4.49	5
77.50–78.49	78.0	7	2.50 to 3.49	7
76.50–77.49	77.0	8	1.50 to 2.49	8
75.50–76.49	76.0	11	0.50 to 1.49	11
74.50–75.49	75.0	16	−0.50 to 0.49	16
73.50–74.49	74.0	11	−1.50 to −0.49	11
72.50–73.49	73.0	9	−2.50 to −1.49	9
71.50–72.49	72.0	7	−3.50 to −2.49	7
70.50–71.49	71.0	7	−4.50 to −3.49	7
69.50–70.49	70.0	4	−5.50 to −4.49	4
68.50–69.49	69.0	2	−6.50 to −5.49	2
67.50–68.49	68.0	1	−7.50 to −6.49	1
66.50–67.49	67.0	1	−8.50 to −7.49	1
		96 samples		

These means were drawn from a population whose $\mu = 75$ and whose $\sigma = 10$. For each sample, $N = 10$, so theoretically, $\sigma_{\overline{X}} = 3.16$. The mean of the 96 $\overline{X}$'s is 74.8, and the standard deviation is 3.08.

TABLE 10.4 s^2 values of 96 small samples (for each sample, $N = 10$)

s^2	Category's midpoint	Frequency
290.0–309.9	300.0	1
270.0–289.9	280.0	0
250.0–269.9	260.0	1
230.0–249.9	240.0	0
210.0–229.9	220.0	1
190.0–209.9	200.0	2
170.0–189.9	180.0	4
150.0–169.9	160.0	7
130.0–149.9	140.0	9
110.0–129.9	120.0	11
90.0–109.9	100.0	14
70.0–89.9	80.0	21
50.0–69.9	60.0	13
30.0–49.9	40.0	8
10.0–29.9	20.0	4
		96 samples

These s^2 values were drawn from a population whose $\sigma^2 = 100$ ($\sigma = 10$). For each sample, $N = 10$. The mean of all the s^2 values is 97.3. (This mean corresponds to an s of 9.9.) Notice how skewed the distribution is.

Be sure to notice two features of the distribution: The s^2 values are highly variable, and their distribution is very skewed. If we were to compute each sample's s or $s_{\bar{X}}$, that distribution would also be skewed.

Now suppose each experimenter forms the ratio $(\bar{X} - \mu)/s_{\bar{X}}$. He divides each sample's $\bar{X} - \mu$ by its $s_{\bar{X}}$. Table 10.5 shows these values for representative samples. A ratio of this kind is called a t ratio. The numerator of the t ratio is normally distributed; the denominator is not. Therefore, t ratios are not normally distributed.

TABLE 10.5 t values for representative samples

	$\bar{X}$	$s_{\bar{X}}$	$t = \dfrac{\bar{X} - \mu}{s_{\bar{X}}}$
Sample 1	71.2	3.71	−1.02
Sample 2	82.4	3.04	2.43
Sample 3	73.0	2.96	−0.68
Sample 4	74.7	3.89	−0.08
Sample 5	76.1	3.45	0.32
Sample 6	72.8	2.76	−0.80
Sample 7	70.9	3.22	−1.27
Sample 8	76.8	4.75	0.38
Sample 9	78.3	3.31	1.00
Sample 10	75.1	2.55	0.04
Sample 11	67.5	2.91	−2.58
⋮	⋮	⋮	⋮
Sample 96	80.6	2.80	2.00

Be sure to differentiate between t and z. z equals $(\bar{X} - \mu)/\sigma_{\bar{X}}$; the denominator is a constant quantity. t equals $(\bar{X} - \mu)/s_{\bar{X}}$; the denominator is a variable quantity. t signifies that $s_{\bar{X}}$ has been used as an estimate of $\sigma_{\bar{X}}$: For small samples $s_{\bar{X}}$ varies in a non-normal way. z, on the other hand, suggests that the experimenter knows $\sigma_{\bar{X}}$ exactly, or has approximated $\sigma_{\bar{X}}$ from a large sample. z's of different samples are normally distributed; t's are not.

10.2   THE DISTRIBUTION OF t'S

Table 10.6 shows the t ratio for each sample. Superficially, the distribution looks normal: The values are symmetrical, their mean is 0. But actually, the distribution is *leptokurtic*; that is, it is tall and thin in the center, and its tails contain more area than a normal curve's tails. Therefore, the distribution seems to have a greater spread, and extreme values are more common. Notice how many t's in Table 10.6 exceed 1.96. In a normal distribution z's of this size occur $2\frac{1}{2}$ percent of the time. In a distribution of t's, they occur more often—in Table 10.6, about 7 percent of the time.

TABLE 10.6   Resulting distribution of *t*'s

t value	*Frequency*
2.685 to 3.250	1
2.262 to 2.685	1
1.833 to 2.262	3
1.383 to 1.833	4
1.100 to 1.383	6
0.703 to 1.100	9
0.000 to 0.703	24
−0.703 to −0.000	24
−1.100 to −0.703	10
−1.383 to −1.100	5
−1.833 to −1.383	4
−2.262 to −1.833	2
−2.685 to −2.262	2
−3.250 to −2.685	1
	96 samples

The theoretical *t* distribution

A theoretical *t* distribution is shown in Fig. 10.1 next to a normal distribution. Like the normal distribution, the *t* distribution is bell-shaped and symmetrical. It is highest at the center. Its mean, median, and mode are all equal. The distribution is also asymptotic to the X axis. It mainly differs from the normal curve in the way its area is distributed. More area lies in the tails, less in the center.

The normal curve has .025 of its area above $z = 1.96$. The *t* distribution, though, has more area in that region: In the figure $P(t > 1.96)$ is greater—approximately .06.

Actually, there are many different *t* distributions, depending on the sample's size. The smaller the sample, the more leptokurtic the distribution.

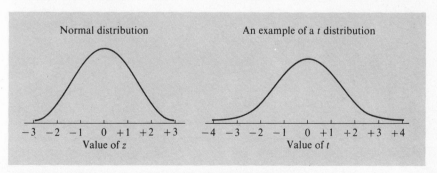

FIG. 10.1 A normal distribution and a theoretical distribution.

If the samples are really small, the tails contain even more of the area. Therefore, extreme t's are more common in small samples.

A sample's t is characterized by the term *degrees of freedom*. The degrees of freedom associated with a t equal $N - 1$. The larger the N, the greater the degrees of freedom. For a sample of 5 scores, the t is said to have $5 - 1 = 4$ degrees of freedom. For a sample of 24 scores, the t has 23 degrees of freedom.

We first encountered $N - 1$ in the denominator of the formula for s: $s = \sqrt{[\Sigma(X - \overline{X})^2]/(N - 1)}$. Mathematical statisticians have shown that the sampling distribution of s depends partly on this $N - 1$. Once $N - 1$ is stated, the distribution of s can be described mathematically. Therefore, the distribution of $s_{\overline{x}}$ also depends on $N - 1$.

The t distribution is mathematically derived by combining a normal distribution in the numerator with the distribution of $s_{\overline{x}}$ in the denominator. Therefore, the t distribution also depends on $N - 1$. Once $N - 1$ is stated, the shape of the t distribution can also be described mathematically. Therefore, the distribution of t's from 5-score samples is called "a t distribution with 4 degrees of freedom."

The number of degrees of freedom is denoted df. If we considered samples of 9 scores, the t would have 8 df. The t distribution would be a t distribution with 8 df. A t distribution with 8 degrees of freedom is not as leptokurtic as one with 4 degrees of freedom.

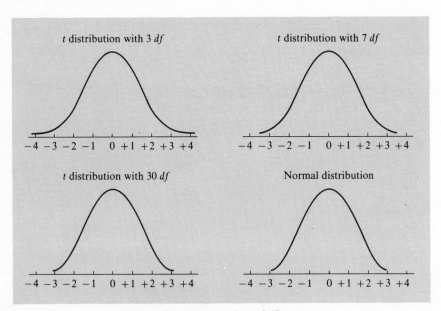

FIG. 10.2 Various t distributions for different values of df.

Different *t* distributions are shown in Fig. 10.2. As the sample size increases, the *t* distribution gradually comes to resemble the normal distribution. With 30 or more degrees of freedom, the *t* distribution looks very much like the normal distribution.

A table of the *t* distribution appears in the appendix. It tells the probability that a sample's *t* exceeds specified values. Table 10.7 shows part of that table.

TABLE 10.7 Partial table of the *t* distribution
(A more complete table appears as Table A.2 in the appendix.)

Number of degrees of freedom (df)	Critical t when $\alpha = .10$	Critical t when $\alpha = .05$	Critical t when $\alpha = .01$
1	6.314	12.706	63.657
5	2.015	2.571	4.032
7	1.895	2.365	3.499
10	1.812	2.228	3.169
12	1.782	2.179	3.055
18	1.734	2.101	2.878
30	1.697	2.046	2.750
60	1.671	2.000	2.660
∞ (Normal distribution)	1.645	1.960	2.576

First consider the *t* distribution with 5 df. *t* values above 2.015 occur 5 percent of the time, so the two values, −2.015 and +2.015, bound the middle 90 percent of the distribution. The table also tells what values bound the middle 95 percent of the distribution. Those values are −2.571 and +2.571. The values −4.032 and +4.032 bound the middle 99 percent.

The table also describes the *t* distribution with 10 degrees of freedom. The *t* values that are critical for $\alpha = .10$, $\alpha = .05$, and $\alpha = .01$ are 1.812, 2.228, and 3.169. When df = 30, the corresponding three values are 1.697, 2.046, and 2.750. Notice the progression: As the number of degrees of freedom increases, the critical *t* values approach the corresponding values of a normal distribution. In a normal distribution the corresponding *z*'s are: 1.645, 1.960, and 2.576.

The equation for the *t* distribution was first derived by W. S. Gosset in 1908. Gosset published under the pen name of "Student," so the distribution is sometimes called "the Student distribution" or "Student's distribution." It is only used to make inferences about means.

In the next two sections we shall apply the *t* distribution to problems. Always remember the basic assumption behind the *t* distribution. Scores in the population are assumed to be normally distributed. That way sample $\overline{X}$'s are normally distributed, $(\overline{X} - \mu)$'s are normally distributed, and ratios of the form $(\overline{X} - \mu)/s_{\overline{X}}$ follow the *t* distribution.

10.3　APPLICATIONS: TESTING A HYPOTHESIS ABOUT μ

EXAMPLE 10.1

Ten subjects were randomly drawn from a population. Scores in the population were normally distributed, and the sample's mean was 103.8. For the data $\Sigma X = 1{,}038$, and $\Sigma X^2 = 107{,}888$. Test the hypothesis that $\mu = 100$. Adopt the .05 level of significance.

Solution　First we need to compute s:

$$\Sigma(X - \bar{X})^2 = \Sigma X^2 - \frac{(\Sigma X)^2}{N} = 107{,}888 - \frac{(1{,}038)^2}{10}$$

$$= 143.6$$

$$s = \sqrt{\frac{\Sigma(X - \bar{X})^2}{N - 1}} = \sqrt{\frac{143.6}{9}} = 3.99$$

Then $s_{\bar{X}}$ can be computed:

$$s_{\bar{X}} = \frac{s}{\sqrt{N}} = \frac{3.99}{\sqrt{10}} = 1.26$$

"1.26" is the sample's estimate of $\sigma_{\bar{X}}$. (The sample is small, so other samples would give quite different estimates.)

To test the hypothesis that $\mu = 100$, we form the t ratio:

$$t = \frac{\bar{X} - \mu}{s_{\bar{X}}} = \frac{103.8 - 100}{1.26} = 3.02$$

How likely are t values of 3.02 or more? The sample has 9 df, so we consider a t distribution with 9 df. A table of the t distribution shows that t values beyond 2.262 occur 5 percent of the time: $t_{.05}(9 \text{ df}) = 2.262$. The observed t, 3.02, is even greater than the tabled value. We therefore reject H_0, and infer that $\mu \neq 100$.

EXAMPLE 10.2

A 10-score sample has a mean of 103.8. $s_{\bar{X}}$ equals 1.26. Establish the 95 percent confidence interval for μ.

Solution　If we knew $\sigma_{\bar{X}}$, we would compute $\bar{X} + 1.96\,\sigma_{\bar{X}}$ and $\bar{X} - 1.96\,\sigma_{\bar{X}}$. But the figure "1.96" comes from the normal curve which is not appropriate. Instead, we need the corresponding value from the t distribution with 9 df.

In that t distribution, what values bound the middle 95 percent? The critical values are -2.262 and $+2.262$. Therefore, the 95 percent confidence limits are:

Upper limit: $103.8 + 2.262(1.26) = 106.65$

Lower limit: $103.8 - 2.262(1.26) = 100.95$

Thus, μ probably lies between 100.95 and 106.65.

In this way, confidence limits can be established by using $s_{\bar{X}}$ and the appropriate value of t. When a sample contains n degrees of freedom, its t is sometimes denoted $t(n \text{ df})$.

Let us, therefore, use $t_{.05}(n \text{ df})$ to denote the value of t that bounds the middle 95 percent of the distribution. Then the 95 percent confidence limits would be: $\bar{X} \pm [t_{.05}(n \text{ df})]s_{\bar{X}}$.

10.4 APPLICATIONS: TESTING A HYPOTHESIS ABOUT A DIFFERENCE BETWEEN TWO μ'S

The t distribution can also be used to test a difference between two means. Let us examine a type of problem we considered before (Example 9.1). This time, though, the sample is considerably smaller—10 pairs of littermates instead of 50.

EXAMPLE 10.3

Ten pairs of littermates were studied from birth. One animal of each pair was raised under stress conditions, the other under nonstress conditions. The two means differed by 6 points. Here are the data:

Pair of littermates	(X) Nonstress	(Y) Stress	$D = (X - Y)$ Difference
A	50	34	16
B	46	42	4
C	42	46	-4
D	64	46	18
E	52	50	2
F	70	54	16
G	58	58	0
H	74	58	16
I	58	62	-4
J	66	70	-4
	$\bar{X} = 58.0$	$\bar{Y} = 52.0$	$\bar{D} = 6$

Do the two means differ significantly? Test the hypothesis that $\mu_D = 0$. Use the .05 level of significance.

Solution　First we record the various difference scores. We view them as a 10-score sample from a population of difference scores. For these 10 difference scores: $\Sigma D = 60$ and $\Sigma D^2 = 1,160$. Then we compute s_D:

$$\Sigma(D - \bar{D})^2 = \Sigma D^2 - \frac{(\Sigma D)^2}{N}$$

$$= 1,160 - \frac{(60)^2}{10} = 800$$

$$s_D = \sqrt{\frac{\Sigma(D - \bar{D})^2}{N - 1}} \tag{10.1}$$

$$= \sqrt{\frac{800}{9}} = 9.43$$

The best estimate of σ_D, then, is

$$s_{\bar{D}} = \frac{s_D}{\sqrt{N}} \tag{10.2}$$

$$= \frac{9.43}{\sqrt{10}} = 2.98$$

Does the observed $\bar{D}$ deviate significantly from the hypothesized $\mu_D = 0$? A t ratio is formed:

$$t = \frac{\bar{D} - \mu_D}{s_{\bar{D}}} \tag{10.3}$$

$$= \frac{6 - 0}{2.98} = 2.01$$

We now consider a t distribution with 9 degrees of freedom. From a table of the t distribution, $t_{.05}(9 \text{ df}) = 2.262$. The t values -2.262 and $+2.262$ bound the middle 95 percent of the distribution. The observed t does fit comfortably within these limits, so the null hypothesis is tenable: $\mu_D = 0$.

A comment on "degrees of freedom"

The form of a t distribution depends on the sample's degrees of freedom. If a sample contains seven scores, then the s is said to have $N - 1 = 6$ df, and the corresponding t distribution has 6 df.

Let us consider the concept further. Suppose a sample contains seven scores: 15, 17, 18, 18, 20, 22, 23. For this sample, $\bar{X} = 19$. If we wanted to estimate the population's variance, we would need to consider each $X - \bar{X}$.

A variance, after all, is a mean of squared deviation scores. To estimate the population variance, then, we need a *random sample of deviation scores*: We square that sample's deviation scores and average them.

Let us therefore consider the seven deviation scores—$(15 - 19)$, $(17 - 19)$, $(18 - 19)$, $(18 - 19)$, $(20 - 19)$, $(22 - 19)$, and $(23 - 19)$: Are they a random sample of the population's deviation scores? To be *random*, they would have to be *independent* of each other. But they really are not independent: If you list any six of them, you can automatically figure out the seventh one. (Altogether the deviation scores have to sum to 0: $\Sigma(X - \overline{X}) = 0$.) If six deviation scores are -4, -2, 1, 0, 0, and 3, the seventh one has to be 2. We therefore say that the seventh deviation score *depends on* the other six. *Six* deviation scores are independent; there is no way of determining one from the others. But the seventh one depends on the other six. This fact is summarized by the phrase "6 degrees of freedom"—six are independent, the seventh is not.

This interpretation will help explain the next example. In that example the *t* test is used to tell whether two unrelated sample means differ significantly.

EXAMPLE 10.4

Two separate groups of subjects were tested. The experimental group (Group E) had 10 subjects; the control group (Group C), 9 subjects. Group E's scores are called X scores, Group C's are called Y scores. Here are the data. Assume that the data are normal.

Group E	Group C
12	10
13	13
16	14
14	12
15	15
12	16
15	12
14	14
13	11
16	

$\Sigma X = 140$	$\Sigma Y = 117$
$\Sigma X^2 = 1,980$	$\Sigma Y^2 = 1,551$
$N_X = 10$	$N_Y = 9$
$\overline{X} = 14.0$	$\overline{Y} = 13.0$

Do the two means differ significantly? Adopt the .05 level of significance.

Solution The null hypothesis states that $\mu_X - \mu_Y = 0$. According to this hypothesis, the two groups are from a common population. As a first step we estimate this population's σ. To estimate σ, consider each group's squared deviation scores:

<table>
<tr><td align="center">*For Group E*</td><td align="center">*For Group C*</td></tr>
<tr><td>$\Sigma x^2 = \Sigma(X - \bar{X})^2$</td><td>$\Sigma y^2 = \Sigma(Y - \bar{Y})^2$</td></tr>
<tr><td>$= \Sigma X^2 - \dfrac{(\Sigma X)^2}{N}$ (10.4)</td><td>$= \Sigma Y^2 - \dfrac{(\Sigma Y)^2}{N}$ (10.5)</td></tr>
<tr><td>$= 1{,}980 - \dfrac{(140)^2}{10}$</td><td>$= 1{,}551 - \dfrac{(117)^2}{9}$</td></tr>
<tr><td>$= 20$</td><td>$= 30$</td></tr>
</table>

Altogether the data provide 19 squared deviation scores; they sum to 50: $\Sigma x^2 + \Sigma y^2 = 20 + 30 = 50$. The degrees of freedom from each set sum to 17: $(N_X - 1)$ from Group E and $(N_Y - 1)$ from Group C. For small samples, statisticians recommend pooling the squared deviation scores and pooling the degrees of freedom. The best estimate of σ^2 becomes:

$$\text{est } \sigma^2 = s^2 = \frac{\Sigma x^2 + \Sigma y^2}{(N_X - 1) + (N_Y - 1)}$$

$$= \frac{20 + 30}{9 + 8}$$

$$= 2.94 \tag{10.6}$$

s equals $\sqrt{2.94} = 1.71$. Therefore, "1.71" is the best single estimate of the population's σ. This estimate is said to have $[(N_X - 1) + (N_Y - 1)] = 17$ degrees of freedom.

We now need to estimate $\sigma_{\bar{D}}$. Theoretically:

$$\sigma_{\bar{D}} = \sqrt{\sigma_{\bar{X}}^2 + \sigma_{\bar{Y}}^2} = \sqrt{\left(\frac{\sigma}{\sqrt{N_X}}\right)^2 + \left(\frac{\sigma}{\sqrt{N_Y}}\right)^2}$$

$$= \sqrt{\frac{\sigma^2}{N_X} + \frac{\sigma^2}{N_Y}} \tag{10.7}$$

The *estimate* of $\sigma_{\bar{D}}$ becomes $\sqrt{(1.71)^2/10 + (1.71)^2/9} = .79$. This estimate of $\sigma_{\bar{D}}$ is denoted $s_{\bar{D}}$.

Finally, the t ratio becomes:

$$t = \frac{(\bar{X} - \bar{Y}) - 0}{s_{\bar{D}}}$$

$$= \frac{(14.0 - 13.0)}{.79} \tag{10.8}$$

$$= 1.27$$

The sample has 17 degrees of freedom, so we need to consider the t distribution with 17 df. From a table of the t distribution, $t_{.05}(17 \text{ df}) = 2.101$. The observed t equals 1.27 and lies comfortably within the theoretical chance distribution. We therefore accept the null hypothesis: $\mu_D = 0$.

On using small samples

If an experimenter *has* to use a small sample, the t distribution is appropriate. In general, though, an investigator should try to avoid small samples. For one thing, a small sample does not allow the investigator to tell whether the population's scores are normal. With a larger sample, he can check the assumptions more readily.

Furthermore, as a rule of thumb, small samples should be avoided for another reason. When the sample is small, the chances of a Type II error are greater. $s_{\bar{D}}$ is larger, so the investigator is more apt to overlook a real difference, calling it nonsignificant. In general, the best way to minimize a Type II error is to use a larger N. Thus, if an experimenter is concerned about Type II errors, he should try to use larger samples.

EXERCISES

10.1   A small sample of 13 scores is drawn from a population whose $\sigma = 15$. If you were testing a hypothesis about the population mean, which would be appropriate—a table of the normal curve or a table of the t distribution? *Answer: Table of normal curve appropriate, since σ is known.*

10.2   A set of data contains 25 scores, and $S^2 = 96$. (This is not the best estimate of σ^2.) The mean of the sample is 16. Test the hypothesis that the population mean is 20. *Answer: $s^2 = 100$; $s_{\bar{x}} = 2$; $t(24) = -2$; H_0 accepted at .05 level.*

10.3   Scores on a test of spatial ability are normally distributed in the population. A random sample of 16 subjects was drawn, and the sample's mean was 108. Furthermore, $\Sigma X = 1,728$, and $\Sigma X^2 = 187,005$. Test the hypothesis at $\alpha = .05$ that $\mu = 105$. *Answer: $s_{\bar{x}} = 1.26$, $t(15) = 2.38$. H_0 is rejected; $\mu \neq 105$.*

10.4 A sample of 16 scores has a mean of 108; $s_{\bar{x}} = 1.26$.
   (a) Establish the 95 percent confidence interval for μ.
        Answer: 105.32 to 110.68
   (b) Establish the 99 percent confidence interval for μ.
        Answer: 104.28 to 111.72

10.5 An investigator wanted to determine whether the administration of benze-drine would affect the performance of students in a repetitive monotonous task. He tested 10 students with and without the drug in a carefully con-trolled experiment and obtained the results below. Is the difference between the mean scores statistically significant at the 1 percent level of significance?

Student	With Benzedrine	Without Benzedrine	Difference Score
A	95	87	8
B	76	77	−1
C	81	70	11
D	93	91	2
E	86	86	0
F	72	69	3
G	86	80	6
H	94	87	7
I	86	77	9
J	94	89	5

$$\Sigma D = 50$$
$$\Sigma(D - \bar{D})^2 = 140$$

Answer: $s_D{}^2 = 15.56$; $s_{\bar{D}} = 1.25$; $t(9) = 4$; H_0 rejected at .01 level.

10.6 An experimenter tested 12 pairs of rabbits; each pair came from a common litter. Animal D was injected with a drug and Animal P with a placebo. Test the hypothesis that $\mu_D - \mu_P = 0$. Adopt the .05 level of significance.

Pair	Animal D	Animal P	Difference
1	67	75	8
2	58	70	12
3	63	62	−1
4	59	71	12
5	60	68	8
6	68	68	0
7	71	69	−2
8	62	69	7
9	61	70	9
10	59	72	13
11	65	71	6
12	66	72	6

Answer: $\bar{D} = 6.5$; $s_{\bar{D}} = 1.47$; $t(11) = 4.42$; H_0 *is rejected; the groups differ significantly.*

10.7 In a study with guinea pigs, littermates were separated from birth. One was placed in a stimulus-rich environment, the other in a stimulus-impoverished environment. Later each animal was tested to determine its activity level; the higher the score, the more active the animal. Do the two conditions differ significantly? Adopt the .05 level of significance.

Litter	Enriched	Impoverished	Difference Score
1	46	34	12
2	42	42	0
3	41	31	10
4	42	35	7
5	34	39	−5
6	37	40	−3
7	44	37	7

Answer: $\bar{D} = 4.0$; $s_{\bar{D}} = 2.50$; $t(6) = 1.60$. H_0 *is accepted; the groups do not differ significantly.*

10.8 A study was performed to determine whether the nature of the instructions affects performance on a particular task. Ten men from a large college population earned the following scores under the two instruction conditions.

Subject	Instruction A	Instruction B
1	120	128
2	130	131
3	118	127
4	140	132
5	140	141
6	135	137
7	126	118
8	130	132
9	125	130
10	127	135

Establish the 95 percent confidence interval for the population mean difference.
Answer: 2.0 ± 4.34

10.9 The performances of a control and an experimental group are to be compared. These groups contain different people who have not been systematically matched. Performance scores of the subjects are given below. Is the difference between the mean scores statistically significant at the 10 percent level of significance?

Control (X)	Experimental (Y)
10	7
5	3
6	5
7	7
10	8
6	4
7	5
8	6
6	3
5	2
$\Sigma X = 70$	$\Sigma Y = 50$
$\Sigma X^2 = 520$	$\Sigma Y^2 = 286$

Answer: $s^2 = 3.67$; $s_{\bar{D}} = 0.86$; $t(18) = 2.33$. H_0 rejected at 10 percent level.

10.10   Two-year-olds were studied for attachment behavior. The children in one group had working mothers, those in the other group had nonworking mothers. The following scores report how much time each child spent with his mother during a session in a playroom. Do the means differ significantly at the .05 level?

Working mothers	Nonworking mothers
8	9
6	12
9	8
4	7
8	10
8	9
9	8
8	8
11	10
8	
9	

Answer: $\bar{D} = 1.0$; $s_{\bar{D}} = 0.75$; $t(18) = 2.10$. H_0 is accepted; the groups do not differ significantly.

10.11   Two groups of adolescent boys were tested for political liberalism. Group R contained sons of Republicans, Group D, sons of Democrats. The scores on a test of liberalism are shown below. Do the two means differ significantly at the .05 level?

Group R	Group D
10	12
7	16
17	10
11	9
10	14
12	19
13	11
9	13
10	

Answer: $\bar{D} = 2.0$; $s_{\bar{D}} = 1.49$; $t(15) = 1.34$. H_0 *is accepted; the groups do not differ significantly.*

11

ANALYSIS OF VARIANCE

This chapter describes a technique called the *analysis of variance*. It was first devised by Sir Ronald Fisher, an English statistician. It is used to compare *several* means to tell whether they differ significantly. By studying variations of the technique, an experimenter comes to appreciate the different options he has when he designs an experiment. In this chapter, we shall consider the more basic forms.

To begin with, consider a simple experiment. Suppose an investigator wants to compare three styles of print for making highway signs. Perhaps he wants to determine which style is most legible. As one way of designing

This chapter can be omitted in a shorter course.

the experiment, he could select three separate groups of subjects; call them Groups 1, 2, and 3. Each group would be tested on a different style of print. The investigator would note how many errors each subject made, and he would compute the mean number of errors in each condition. Let us call the means $\overline{X}_1$, $\overline{X}_2$, and $\overline{X}_3$. The experimenter would want to know whether the three means differed significantly. This experimental arrangement resembles the "Independent Groups" design which involved two separate groups. Now, through the analysis of variance, we can extend the design to three or more conditions. We would diagram it this way:

Style of Print		
Style 1	Style 2	Style 3
24	30	27
19	41	33
.	.	.
.	.	.

The "Repeated Measurements" design can also be extended to three or more conditions: Each experimental treatment would be administered to every subject. The data would be recorded this way:

	Style of Print		
	Style 1	Style 2	Style 3
Subject 1	24	27	26
Subject 2	19	25	22
.	.	.	.
.	.	.	.
Subject n	22	30	29

Again, the investigator would compute the three means; then he would want to see if they differed significantly. This analysis would differ slightly from the one for Independent Groups.

Each of these designs could be elaborated further. Suppose the investigator wanted to study *two* variables simultaneously. He might want to study each style of print (*a*) when the subject was intoxicated and (*b*) when the subject was sober. The extended design would be diagramed this way:

		Style of Print		
		Style 1	Style 2	Style 3
Level of Alcohol	Intoxicated	31 29 . .	25 22 . .	29 30 . .
	Sober	15 21 . .	17 21 . .	9 15 . .

Six different groups of subjects would have to be studied. Three groups would be intoxicated—one would be tested on Style 1, another on Style 2, a third on Style 3; and three other groups would be sober. If four subjects were tested in each group, the complete experiment would require $6 \times 4 = 24$ different subjects. With this design, the investigator could determine whether the three styles of print differed (*a*) for intoxicated subjects and (*b*) for sober subjects.

Similarly, the Repeated Measurements design could be expanded. Each subject would be tested under all six conditions. In some testings the subject would be intoxicated; in others, he would be sober. Sometimes Style 1 would be tested, other times, Style 2 or Style 3 would be tested. The design would be diagramed this way:

	Style of Print					
	Style 1		Style 2		Style 3	
	Intoxicated	Sober	Intoxicated	Sober	Intoxicated	Sober
Subject 1	21	18	24	19	22	17
Subject 2	30	21	31	21	29	19
. .	.	.	.	.	.	.
Subject *n*	19	14	19	15	19	15

Notice that every subject has 6 scores. If 4 subjects were tested, the data would contain 24 scores.

The next two sections will lay the groundwork for the analysis of variance. Then we shall examine the technique for the simplest design, the one-variable Independent Groups design. Later we shall extend it to the Repeated Measurements design.

11.1   PRELIMINARY CONSIDERATIONS: THE F DISTRIBUTION AND THE F TEST

To perform an analysis of variance, the investigator needs to understand a simple but important test, the F test. In this section we shall consider that test and later we shall apply it to the analysis of variance.

The F test is used to tell whether two samples' variances differ significantly. For each sample, we estimate σ^2. Suppose one sample's s^2 is 147.62, and the other's is 50.21. To perform the test, we form a ratio of the two variance estimates, placing the larger one in the numerator: $147.62/50.21 = 2.94$. Then we use a table to interpret this ratio. The test is simple to apply. To understand its meaning, though, we need to consider the theory behind it. Let us therefore examine the theory.

Suppose an investigator randomly selects five scores from a normal population and computes s^2; perhaps s^2 equals 14. Other investigators might also draw a five-score sample, and perhaps each of them computes s^2. Then we could imagine an entire distribution of s^2 values. That distribution would be very skewed.

Now suppose the investigator selects, not one, but *two* samples from the population, and suppose he computes each sample's s^2. Perhaps one sample contains 9 scores, the other, 16 scores. Here are the results:

One sample	*The other sample*
$s_1{}^2 = 14$	$s_2{}^2 = 12$
$N_1 = 9$	$N_2 = 16$
Degrees of freedom $= N_1 - 1 = 8$	Degrees of freedom $= N_2 - 1 = 15$

Then the investigator forms a ratio of the variance estimates: $s_1{}^2/s_2{}^2 = 14/12 = 1.17$. This ratio is called an F ratio. F is used in honor of Sir Ronald Fisher.

Other investigators could examine similar pairs of samples—in each case, a 9-score and a 16-score sample. We could imagine each investigator computing $s_1{}^2$, $s_2{}^2$, and the F ratio. Then we could imagine a sampling distribution of these F's. The shape of this theoretical distribution has been studied mathematically. It is a skewed distribution like the one shown in Fig. 11.1.

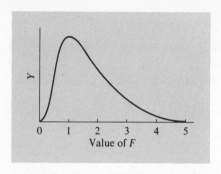

Value of F

FIG. 11.1 An example of a theoretical F distribution.

Thus, an F ratio is a ratio of two s^2 values. Theoretically, each s^2 is an estimate of σ^2. Therefore, the numerator and the denominator are both estimates of σ^2, and their ratio is generally somewhere near 1. By chance, some F's would be less than 1, others would exceed 1.

Let us consider this F distribution further. How much of its area lies above an F of 2.0? How often do F's above 2.0 occur by chance? How much of the area lies above 3.2? Tables are available to answer these questions. Table 11.1 gives information of this kind. It shows that 10 percent of the

TABLE 11.1 Characteristics of the F distribution shown in Fig. 11.1

Value of F	Percent of the distribution that exceeds this F
1.62	20.0
2.12	10.0
2.64	5.0
3.20	2.5
4.00	1.0
4.67	0.5
6.47	0.1

distribution lies above the F value 2.12: The probability is therefore .10 that an F exceed 2.12. The table also tells the 5 percent and the 1 percent cutoff points: 5 percent of the time the F would exceed 2.64; 1 percent of the time it would exceed 4.00. These F's are also shown graphically in Fig. 11.2. This distribution is valid if the original population was normal.

The equation for this F distribution is complicated, but it depends mainly on two numbers—(a) the degrees of freedom associated with the *numerator's* s^2, and (b) the degrees of freedom associated with the *denominator's* s^2. Let us call these two numbers df_N ("N" for "numerator") and df_D ("D" for "denominator"): In the example, $df_N = 8$ and $df_D = 15$.

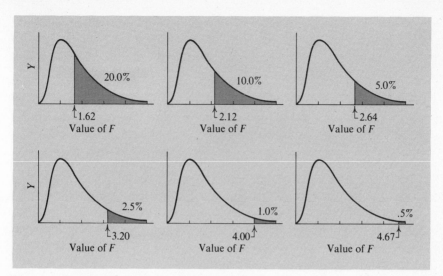

FIG. 11.2   Graphs showing the cutoff points described in Table 11.1.

The equation of the F distribution in Fig. 11.1 therefore depends on the two numbers 8 and 15. The two df's are usually expressed this way: We write $F(8, 15)$ to show that the theoretical distribution has 8 and 15 degrees of freedom. df_N is written first, df_D second. For the 9- and 16-score samples, then, the F would be: $F(8, 15) = 14/12 = 1.17$.

The theoretical distribution of $F(8, 15)$ is not the only F distribution. A different distribution could be drawn for each combination of df_N and df_D. These different distributions are described in an F table. Part of an F table appears in Table 11.2.

TABLE 11.2   Values of F which are critical at the .05 level. (A more complete table appears as Table A.3 in the appendix.)

| | | df_N (*Corresponding to the numerator's s^2*) | | |
		2	5	8
df_D	5	5.79	5.05	4.82
	7	4.74	3.97	3.73
	10	4.10	3.33	3.07
(Corresponding	15	3.68	2.90	2.64
to the	20	3.49	2.71	2.45
denominator's	30	3.32	2.53	2.27
s^2)	40	3.23	2.45	2.18
	120	3.07	2.29	2.02

Each entry in Table 11.2 refers to some particular F distribution. The entry tells which F value bounds the distribution's highest 5 percent. To use this table, read *across* the table to the column containing df_N. Then read *down* to the row containing df_D. The table's entry in that row and that column tells the critical F—the value that bounds the most extreme 5 percent. For the distribution with $df_N = 8$ and $df_D = 15$, the critical F is 2.64; "2.64" separates the top 5 percent from everything below. We express the critical value this way: $F_{.05}(8, 15) = 2.64$. Check a few other F's in the table: $F_{.05}(2, 10) = 4.10$; $F_{.05}(8, 120) = 2.02$. A more complete version of this table appears in the appendix.

Table 11.3 tells which F's are critical at the .01 level. Again, each entry describes some particular F distribution; it tells which F separates the top 1 percent from everything below. For example, $F_{.01}(8, 5) = 10.29$; $F_{.01}(8, 10) = 5.06$. A more complete version of this table also appears in the appendix.

TABLE 11.3   Values of F which are critical at the .01 level. (A more complete table appears as Table A.3 in the appendix.)

		df_N (*Corresponding to the numerator's* s^2)		
		2	5	8
df_D	5	13.27	10.97	10.29
	7	9.55	7.46	6.84
(Corresponding	10	7.56	5.64	5.06
to the	15	6.36	4.56	4.00
denominator's	20	5.85	4.10	3.56
s^2)	30	5.39	3.70	3.17
	40	5.18	3.51	2.99
	120	4.79	3.17	2.66

Familiarize yourself with these tables. Suppose $df_N = 2$. Check various entries in the column where $df_N = 2$: $F_{.01}(2, 10) = 7.56$; $F_{.01}(2, 40) = 5.18$; and $F_{.01}(2, 120) = 4.79$. For any column, the critical F gets smaller as df_D gets larger. Likewise, for any row. Therefore, large F's are more common when the sample is small. Large samples rarely yield large F's.

A table of the F distribution only reports F's above 1.00. Very small F's (like .08 and .15) are unusual too, but that side of the distribution is not tabled. In practice, therefore, we form an F ratio by placing the larger s^2 in the numerator and the smaller one in the denominator. That way the F ratio is always 1.0 or more.

The following example illustrates how the F test is used to test hypotheses.

EXAMPLE 11.1

An investigator examined two samples, a sample of boys and a sample of girls. He wanted to know whether girls are significantly more variable than boys. He obtained the following information:

Boys	Girls
8 cases	9 cases
$s^2 = 50.21$	$s^2 = 147.62$
$df = 7$	$df = 8$

Assume that the scores are normal, and adopt the .05 level of significance.

Solution A null hypothesis can be stated this way: $H_0: \sigma^2_G = \sigma^2_B$. According to this hypothesis, the population variances are identical, so the ratio s^2_G/s^2_B should be close to 1. The alternate hypothesis, H_1, claims that σ^2_G is greater. $H_1: \sigma^2_G > \sigma^2_B$.

Next, the F ratio is formed; the larger s^2 is placed in the numerator. And the ratio has 8 and 7 df:

$$F(8, 7) = s^2_G/s^2_B = 147.62/50.21 = 2.94$$

Finally a table of the F distribution is needed to determine whether "2.94" should be considered unusual. The .05 level has been adopted, and $F_{.05}(8, 7) = 3.73$. Any F above 3.73 would lead us to reject H_0. The observed F, however, is only 2.94. It does fit comfortably in the hypothesized chance distribution. Therefore, H_0 is accepted: Boys and girls do not seem to differ in variability.

Notice that the F test is really a one-tailed test: In the example H_1 claims that σ^2_G *exceeds* σ^2_B. "The most extreme part of the distribution" refers to F's above 3.73; it does not include unusually small F's. In other problems, though, H_1 might claim that $\sigma^2_G \neq \sigma^2_B$. Then a two-tailed test would be needed: "The most extreme 5 percent of the distribution" would refer to both ends of the distribution—F values that are unusually large and ones that are unusually small. If we had a detailed F table, we would find that 5 percent of the distribution lies above 3.73 and 5 percent lies below 0.268.[1] In that case $F(8, 7) = 3.73$ would be the 10 percent cutoff value: 5 percent of the distribution exceeds 3.73, and 5 percent lies below 0.268.

---

[1] $F = 3.73$ cuts off the highest 5 percent of the distribution. It happens mathematically that the F which cuts off the *lowest* 5 percent of the distribution can be computed this way: $1/3.73 = 0.268$. Therefore, 5 percent of the distribution lies below 0.268, and 5 percent lies above 3.73.

EXAMPLE 11.2

An experimenter produced two kinds of lesions in monkeys—Lesion 1 in one group, Lesion 2 in another group. Then he observed each animal for a month after surgery and rated the amount of aggression each animal displayed. He theorized that the two groups would differ primarily in variability. Here are the data:

Lesion 1	Lesion 2
$\bar{X} = 95.3$	$\bar{X} = 94.8$
$s^2 = 27.4$	$s^2 = 6.13$
$N = 31$	$N = 31$

Do the groups differ in variability? Assume that the scores are normal, and use the .02 level of significance.

Solution First state H_0: $\sigma_1^2 = \sigma_2^2$. Then state H_1: $\sigma_1^2 \neq \sigma_2^2$. H_1 does not specify which variance is greater, so a two-tailed test is needed. Now consider the implications of H_0: A chance distribution of F's is expected, and the distribution has 30 and 30 degrees of freedom. From an F table: $F_{.01}(30, 30) = 2.38$. The F which cuts off the *lowest* 1 percent is $1/2.38 = 0.418$. For a two-tailed test, then, F's of 0.418 and 2.38 bound the middle 98 percent.

Now, consider the experiment's result: $F(30, 30) = 27.4/6.13 = 4.47$. This F does not fit comfortably in the hypothesized distribution; it lies in the most unusual 2 percent of the distribution. Therefore, we reject H_0 and conclude that the groups do differ in variability.

11.2 PRELIMINARY CONSIDERATIONS: A REVIEW OF TWO IMPORTANT POINTS

We shall need two principles from earlier chapters. One concerns $\sigma_{\bar{X}}$, the standard error of the mean. The other concerns s, the estimate of σ. This section therefore reviews those principles.

The standard error of the mean

The standard error of the mean ($\sigma_{\bar{X}}$) tells how variable sample means are. This term is related to the standard deviation of scores in the population (σ). Two important ingredients appear in the formula—σ and N.

$$\sigma_{\bar{X}} = \frac{\sigma}{\sqrt{N}}$$

In a certain population, suppose $\mu = 74$ and $\sigma = 20$. An investigator draws a sample of 100 scores from this population. The standard error equals $20/\sqrt{100} = 2.0$. We can therefore visualize two different distributions: We can visualize *scores* in the population ($\mu = 74$, $\sigma = 20$), or we can visualize *means* of different samples (the average mean is 74, $\sigma_{\bar{X}} = 2.0$).

EXAMPLE 11.3
Samples of seven cases are drawn. $\sigma_{\bar{X}} = 3$. Determine σ.

Solution $\sigma_{\bar{X}} = \sigma/\sqrt{N}$. Squaring both sides, $\sigma_{\bar{X}}^2 = \sigma^2/N$. Therefore, $\sigma^2 = N\sigma_{\bar{X}}^2$. For these data, $N = 7$, so:

$$\sigma^2 = N\sigma_{\bar{X}}^2 = 7(3^2) = 63$$

The population's standard deviation is $\sqrt{63} = 7.9$.

EXAMPLE 11.4
An investigator collected 50 different samples; each sample contained 17 scores. He studied the 50 means and estimated $\sigma_{\bar{X}}^2$ to be 2.9. Estimate σ^2 of the original population.

Solution $\sigma^2 = N\sigma_{\bar{X}}^2$. Since $\sigma_{\bar{X}}^2$ is estimated to be 2.9, σ^2 is estimated to equal 17 (2.9) = 49.3.

Best estimate of σ
We will also need to use s, the best estimate of σ. To estimate σ^2, we usually compute $[\sum(X - \bar{X})^2]/(N - 1)$. The denominator, $N - 1$, is called the degrees of freedom associated with this estimate. If S^2 has already been computed, we correct it by the formula:

$$s^2 = \text{est of } \sigma^2 = \frac{N}{N-1} S^2$$

EXAMPLE 11.5
Here is a small sample of data. Compute S^2 and s^2.

X

5    $\sum X = 16$
8
2    $\sum X^2 = 94$
1

Solution

$$\sum(X - \bar{X})^2 = \sum X^2 - \frac{(\sum X)^2}{N} = 94 - \frac{(16)^2}{4} = 30$$

Then: $S^2 = [\sum(X - \bar{X})^2]/N = 30/4 = 7.5$. On the other hand,

$$s^2 = \frac{\sum(X - \bar{X})^2}{N - 1} = \frac{30}{3} = 10.0$$

As usual, S^2—7.5—*under*estimates the population's variance; the best estimate—10.0—is larger.

EXAMPLE 11.6

For a certain sample, $S = 4$ and $S^2 = 16$. The sample contains 9 cases. Estimate σ.

Solution

$$s^2 = \frac{N}{N - 1} S^2 = \frac{9}{8}(16) = 18$$

Therefore $s = \sqrt{18} = 4.24$.

The next two examples combine these principles. They are rarely used this way in practice, but they will help clarify the theory we develop.

EXAMPLE 11.7

An investigator drew three samples from a population. Each sample contained 16 scores. The means were $\bar{X}_1 = 152$, $\bar{X}_2 = 156$, and $\bar{X}_3 = 157$. (*a*) Use the three means to compute their variance. (*b*) Then compute the best estimate of $\sigma_{\bar{X}}$.

Solution   (*a*) The three sample means are three numbers—152, 156, and 157 —and their mean is 155. We can compute the variance and denote it $S^2_{\bar{X}}$:

$$S^2_{\bar{X}} = \frac{[(152 - 155)^2 + (156 - 155)^2 + (157 - 155)^2]}{3}$$

$$= 14\tfrac{2}{3}$$

(*b*) Now "$14\tfrac{2}{3}$" is not the best estimate of $\sigma^2_{\bar{X}}$. As usual, it needs to be corrected:

$$\text{est } \sigma_{\bar{X}}^2 = \tfrac{3}{2}S^2_{\bar{X}} = \tfrac{3}{2}(14\tfrac{2}{3}) = 7.0$$

Therefore, the best estimate of $\sigma_{\bar{X}}$ is $\sqrt{7.0} = 2.6$.

EXAMPLE 11.8

The same investigator now wants to estimate σ from his estimate of $\sigma_{\bar{X}}$. Each sample contained 16 scores; use this fact to estimate σ.

Solution   In Example 11.7, $\sigma_{\bar{X}}$ was estimated as 2.6. Each sample's N was 16, so we can use the formula that relates $\sigma_{\bar{X}}$ to σ: $\sigma_{\bar{X}} = \sigma/\sqrt{N}$:

$$\sigma = \sigma_{\bar{X}} \cdot \sqrt{N}$$

$$\text{est } \sigma = 2.6(\sqrt{16}) = 10.4$$

In this way σ can be estimated from the means of several random samples.

11.3   AN OVERVIEW OF THE METHOD

The next three sections describe the simplest analysis of variance. Let us begin with the data of Table 11.4. These data represent an Independent Groups design. Three groups of subjects were tested, each group on a different style of print. There were four subjects in each group, and the table reports each group's mean. We assume that the scores are drawn from a normal population.

TABLE 11.4   Data for a simple analysis of variance

Style 1	Style 2	Style 3
5	4	8
8	9	12
2	10	14
1	5	6
$\bar{X}_1 = 4.0$	$\bar{X}_2 = 7.0$	$\bar{X}_3 = 10.0$

Do these means differ significantly? The investigator could perform several *t* tests—a *t* test comparing Style 1 and Style 2, one comparing Style 1 and Style 3, and third comparing Style 2 and Style 3. But that procedure is objectionable since it allows the investigator *several* chances of finding a significant difference. An experiment with four conditions would require six *t* tests; one with five conditions would require 10 *t* tests. With that many *t* tests, one of them would probably be significant by chance. Therefore, some statistical test is needed that considers *all* the means simultaneously.

Here is the general plan. The analysis of variance is designed to yield two different estimates of σ^2. The two estimates are obtained in quite different ways. One comes from *actual scores*: The investigator examines the subjects' scores and estimates σ^2. The other comes from the different *means*: The investigator notes how the means vary, and from that information he derives an estimate of σ^2. If the means only differ from each other by chance, the two estimates of σ^2 should be very close.

The first estimate comes directly from the scores; let us consider that estimate first. We examine the scores in each condition and note their variance. The scores in Condition 1 are 5, 8, 2, 1; their variance is 7.5. We write: $S^2_{\text{Within Condition 1}} = 7.5$. For Condition 2 the scores are 4, 9, 10, 5; their variance is 6.5: $S^2_{\text{Within Condition 2}} = 6.5$. For Condition 3 the scores are 8, 12, 14, 6; their variance is 10: $S^2_{\text{Within Condition 3}} = 10$. Then these three values are averaged. That average is called "Average $S^2_{\text{Within conditions}}$." Roughly speaking, it approximates σ^2. (Later, we shall refine it further.)

One estimate of σ^2:	Average $S^2_{\text{Within conditions}} \rightarrow$ An estimate of σ^2

The other estimate comes from the means. The three means are 4.0, 7.0, and 10.0. Suppose these means only differ by chance. We can measure this variance; it equals 6.0. We write: $S^2_{\text{Between means}} = 6.0$. From $S^2_{\text{Between means}}$ we can then estimate the theoretical quantity, $\sigma_{\bar{X}}^2$. And $\sigma_{\bar{X}}^2$ is related to σ^2. ($\sigma_{\bar{X}} = \sigma/\sqrt{N}$, so $\sigma_{\bar{X}}^2 = \sigma^2/N$.) Therefore, we can estimate σ^2 from $S^2_{\text{Between means}}$. Thus, the second estimate of σ^2 comes from the means.

The other estimate of σ^2:	$S^2_{\text{Between means}} \rightarrow \sigma_{\bar{X}}^2 \rightarrow$ Another estimate of σ^2

(Later we shall refine this estimate too.)

Once the two estimates are determined, they get compared through an F test. *If the means only differ by chance*, one estimate should roughly equal the other; the F should be about 1. We therefore examine the F ratio. If it is close to 1.0, the two estimates are similar; the means only vary the way you would expect them to vary by chance.

Thus, the two estimates are compared through an F test. In fact, that is the goal of the analysis of variance. All our computations lead up to this F. These computations are summarized in a summary table. An example of a summary table is shown in Table 11.5.

Particularly notice the column marked "Variance Estimate." This column gives the two estimates of σ^2. The entry "36.0" is called the "between conditions" estimate. "Between conditions" refers to the variation between the means of the conditions; it is the estimate of σ^2 that is obtained from $S^2_{\text{Between means}}$.

TABLE 11.5 A typical summary table

Sources of variance	Sum of squares	df	Variance esimate or Mean square	F
Total	168	11		
Between conditions	72	2	36.0	3.37
Within conditions	96	9	10.7	

The entry "10.7" is called the "within conditions" estimate. "Within conditions" refers to variation among the scores within each condition. It is the estimate that is obtained from the term "Average $S^2_{\text{Within conditions}}$."

In the last column an F ratio is formed. That ratio equals $36.0/10.7 = 3.37$. It is said to have "2 and 9 degrees of freedom." (The reason for "2 and 9 df" will emerge in Sec. 11.4.) We therefore write: $F(2,9) = 3.37$. To evaluate it, consult an F table. From the table, $F_{.05}(2,9) = 4.26$. Thus, "3.37" is small enough to fit comfortably into the chance distribution, so the two estimates *do* seem comparable. Therefore, the means do not differ significantly.

Section 11.4 will show how to compute these two estimates in a cookbook manner. Then Sec. 11.5 will examine their meaning more fully.

11.4 THE COMPUTATIONAL PROCEDURE

To compute each estimate of σ^2, first compute the "sum of squares" terms, then compute the "degrees of freedom" terms. Then divide each sum of squares by the corresponding df to obtain an estimate of σ^2.

Computing the sum of squares terms

Three "sum of squares" terms need to be computed—a "total" sum of squares (ss_T), a "between" sum of squares (ss_B) and a "within" sum of squares (ss_W). The total sum of squares, ss_T, is the sum of the 12 squared deviation scores in Table 11.4: $(X - \overline{X})^2$. In the summary table it equals 168. This term can be divided into two component parts—ss_B and ss_W. Normally we compute ss_T and ss_B directly; then we compute ss_W by subtraction: $ss_W = ss_T - ss_B$.

Let us begin with the total sum of squares. The simplest formula is:

$$ss_T = \sum_k \sum_n X^2 - \frac{\left(\sum_k \sum_n X\right)^2}{N} \tag{11.1}$$

This formula requires some comment. The small letter n is the number of scores in each group; k is the number of groups. If all the groups are the same size, $kn = N$. The expression "$\sum_k \sum_n X$" is a double summation; it is an instruction, first, to sum the n scores of each condition $\left(\sum_n X\right)$ and then to sum these sums. The complete term could be written $\sum_k \left(\sum_n X\right)$, but we usually omit the parentheses. If there is no ambiguity, we simply write: $\sum \sum X$.

Likewise, $\sum_k \sum_n X^2$ is an instruction to square each X and then to sum all the squared scores. It can be simplified to $\sum \sum X^2$.

For the data of Table 11.4, $\sum \sum X^2 = 756$, and $\sum \sum X = 84$. Therefore,

$$ss_T = \sum \sum X^2 - \frac{(\sum \sum X)^2}{N}$$

$$= 756 - \frac{(84)^2}{12} = 168$$

Next we need to compute ss_B. First sum each column: $\sum_n X$. For simplicity, let us call each column's total T. The three T's are: 16, 28, and 40. Each total is based on $n = 4$ scores. The formula for ss_B is:

$$ss_B = \sum_n \frac{T^2}{n} - \frac{(\sum \sum X)^2}{N} \tag{11.2}$$

In this formula ss_B is the difference between two terms. One term, $(\sum \sum X)^2/N$, has already appeared in the formula for ss_T: $(\sum \sum X)^2/N = (84)^2/12 = 588$. To compute the other term, $\sum_k T^2/n$, square each T and divide it by $n = 4$. Do this for each column's total and sum the k terms. ss_B equals:

$$ss_B = \left[\frac{16^2}{4} + \frac{28^2}{4} + \frac{40^2}{4}\right] - \frac{(84)^2}{12}$$

$$= 72$$

Finally, compute ss_W:

$$ss_W = ss_T - ss_B \tag{11.3}$$
$$= 168 - 72 = 96$$

Then enter ss_T, ss_B, and ss_W in the summary table.

Computing the degrees of freedom

Now consider each entry in the "degrees of freedom" column. Let us designate the three entries df_T, df_B, and df_W. First we compute df_T.

$$df_T = N - 1 \tag{11.4}$$
$$= 12 - 1 = 11$$

For 12 numbers, there are 11 degrees of freedom.

The "between" term is based on 3 numbers (the three means, 4.0, 7.0, and 10.0). Its df equals:

$$df_B = k - 1 \qquad\qquad (11.5)$$
$$= 3 - 1 = 2$$

When a variance estimate is derived from three numbers, it has 2 degrees of freedom.

Finally, df_W is computed by subtraction:

$$df_W = df_T - df_B \qquad\qquad (11.6)$$
$$= 11 - 2 = 9$$

This term can also be computed directly: Compute $n - 1$ for each group and sum these terms—$3 + 3 + 3 = 9$. If each group's n is the same, df_W equals $k(n - 1)$—in this example, $3(4 - 1) = 9$. The variance estimate within each condition has 3 df; for k conditions, there are $k(4 - 1) = 9$ df altogether.

Computing the other terms

Finally, we compute the two estimates of σ^2. These estimates are also called "mean square" terms. One is the "between" mean square; it is denoted ms_B. The other is the "within" mean square denoted ms_W.

To compute ms_B, divide ss_B by df_B. We write:

$$ms_B = \frac{ss_B}{df_B} = \frac{72}{2} = 36.0$$

To compute ms_W, divide ss_W by df_W.

$$ms_W = \frac{ss_W}{df_W} = \frac{96}{9} = 10.7$$

The two variance estimates, then, are 36.0 and 10.7.

Finally, the F ratio gets formed: $F = ms_B/ms_W$. The numerator has 2 df, the denominator, 9 df. Thus, F $(2,9) = 36.0/10.7 = 3.37$. This F is then compared with $F_{.05}$ $(2,9) = 4.26$. "3.37" is relatively small, so the null hypothesis is accepted. The means do not differ significantly.

EXAMPLE 11.9

An investigator was studying the effect of certain drugs on people's moods. He selected five comparable groups of subjects. A different drug was administered to each group. After a month on the drug, each subject's mood was rated.

Here are the data. Let n_i denote the number of subjects in each group; n_i varies from group to group. Each group's mean is also reported. Do the means differ significantly? Assume normality, and adopt the .01 level of significance.

	Drug A	Drug B	Drug C	Drug D	Drug E
	13	17	16	13	19
	15	17	17	14	14
	12	16	18	16	14
	14	21	16	15	13
	18	22	19	14	18
	14	17	20	17	16
	19	15		12	14
		18		13	
T_i	105	143	106	114	108
n_i	7	8	6	8	7
Mean	15.0	17.9	17.7	14.2	15.4

$$\sum\sum X = 576$$
$$\sum\sum X^2 = 9{,}440$$
$$N = 36$$

Solution Altogether there are $N = 36$ scores. The sum of all 36 scores is $\sum\sum X = 576$. The sum of the squared scores is $\sum\sum X^2 = 9{,}440$.

Step 1 According to H_0, the five means only differ by chance. Imagine a population tested under Drug A; its mean would be μ_A. Also imagine a population tested under Drug B; its mean would be μ_B. According to the null hypothesis, $\mu_A = \mu_B = \mu_C = \mu_D = \mu_E$.

Step 2 The alternate hypothesis H_1 claims that these μ's are not all equal; at least one of them differs from the others.

Step 3 Consider the implications of H_0. If the μ's are all equal, the five sample means—15.0, 17.9, 17.7, 14.2, 15.4—only differ by chance. The analysis of variance uses the variance among the $\bar{X}$'s to estimate σ^2. It also considers a more direct estimate of σ^2.

First compute the sum of squares terms:

$$\text{SS}_T = \sum\sum X^2 - \frac{(\sum\sum X)^2}{N} = 9{,}400 - \frac{(576)^2}{36} = 224.00$$

$$\text{SS}_B = \sum\frac{T^2}{n} - \frac{(\sum\sum X)^2}{N} = \left[\frac{105^2}{7} + \frac{143^2}{8} + \frac{106^2}{6} + \frac{114^2}{8} + \frac{108^2}{7}\right] - \frac{(576)^2}{36}$$

$$= 78.58$$

$$\text{SS}_W = \text{SS}_T - \text{SS}_B = 224.00 - 78.58 = 145.42$$

Then begin a summary table:

Source	Sum of squares	df	Mean square	F
Total	224.00			
Between	78.58			
Within	145.42			

Fill in the degrees of freedom.

$$df_T = N - 1 = 36 - 1 = 35$$
$$df_B = k - 1 = 5 - 1 = 4$$
$$df_W = df_T - df_B = 35 - 4 = 31$$

Then compute the mean square terms and enter them in the table. They are the estimates of σ^2.

$$ms_B = \frac{ss_B}{df_B} = \frac{78.58}{4} = 19.64$$

$$ms_W = \frac{ss_W}{df_W} = \frac{145.42}{31} = 4.69$$

Finally, form the F ratio:

$$F = \frac{ms_B}{ms_W} = \frac{19.64}{4.69} = 4.19$$

Here is the complete summary table:

Source	Sum of squares	df	Mean square	F
Total	224.00	35		
Between	78.58	4	19.64	4.19
Within	145.42	31	4.69	

Now consult a table of the F distribution. $F_{.01}$ (4,31) is not tabled, but $F_{.01}$ (4,30) *is*; $F_{.01}$ (4,30) = 4.02. The F in the summary table exceeds 4.02, so ms_B is significantly greater than ms_W. Therefore, H_0 is rejected: The means *do* differ significantly at the .01 level.

Procedures exist to tell which means are the deviant ones. For example, Mean B and Mean C seem to be unusually high. Tests of this kind are described in more advanced texts.

The analysis of variance can also be used when $k = 2$. If there are two experimental conditions, the analysis of variance is equivalent to a t test. And the value of t is related to the value of F: $F = t^2$. The following example illustrates both methods and shows their equivalence.

EXAMPLE 11.10

An experimenter compared two groups, an experimental group and a control group. Each group contained 10 subjects. Do the two means differ significantly? Assume normality, and adopt the .05 level of significance.

	Control	Experimental
	10	7
	5	3
	6	5
	7	7
	10	8
	6	4
	7	5
	8	6
	6	3
	5	2
$\sum X^2$	520	286
T	70	50
n	10	10

Solution using the analysis of variance   First compute each sum of squares.

$$\text{ss}_T = \sum \sum X^2 - \frac{(\sum \sum X)^2}{N} = 806 - \frac{(120)^2}{20} = 86$$

$$\text{ss}_B = \sum \frac{T^2}{n} - \frac{(\sum \sum X)^2}{N} = \left[\frac{70^2}{10} + \frac{50^2}{10} \right] - \frac{(120)^2}{20} = 20$$

$$\text{ss}_W = \text{ss}_T - \text{ss}_B = 86 - 20 = 66$$

Then form the summary table:

Source of Variation	ss	df	ms	F
Total	86.0	19		
Between Conditions	20.0	1	20.0	5.40
Within Conditions	66.0	18	3.67	

The F is significant at the .05 level: $F_{.05}(1,18) = 4.41$, and "5.40" exceeds this critical value.

Solution using the t *test*   (The following procedure was described more fully in Example 10.4.) First compute $\sum x^2$ for each group. [$\sum x^2$ is the same as $\sum(X - \bar{X})^2$].

For the control group:

$$\sum x^2 = \sum X^2 - \frac{(\sum X)^2}{N} = 520 - \frac{(70)^2}{10} = 30$$

For the experimental group:

$$\sum x^2 = \sum X^2 - \frac{(\sum X)^2}{N} = 286 - \frac{(50)^2}{10} = 36$$

Then estimate σ:

$$\text{est } \sigma = s = \sqrt{\frac{\sum x_E^2 + \sum x_C^2}{N_E + N_C - 2}} = \sqrt{\frac{30 + 36}{18}} = \sqrt{3.67} = 1.92$$

Then estimate $\sigma_{\bar{D}}$:

$$s_{\bar{D}} = \sqrt{\frac{s^2}{N_E} + \frac{s^2}{N_C}} = \sqrt{\frac{3.67}{10} + \frac{3.67}{10}} = 0.86$$

Finally, form a t ratio. The two means are: $\bar{E} = 7.0$ and $\bar{C} = 5.0$. Therefore:

$$t = \frac{\bar{E} - \bar{C}}{s_{\bar{D}}} = \frac{7.0 - 5.0}{0.86} = 2.33$$

The critical $t_{.05}$ (with 18 df) is 2.10. Therefore, 2.33 is significant at the .05 level.

Notice that $F = t^2$. In the example F equals 5.40 and t equals 2.33. 5.40 = $(2.33)^2$. The two theoretical distributions are also related. For example, $F_{.05}(1,18) = 4.41$, and $t_{.05}(18$ df$) = 2.10$: $4.41 = (2.10)^2$. The proof that $F = t^2$ is shown in the chapter appendix as Proof 11.1.

11.5   THE MEANING OF THE MEAN SQUARE TERMS

This section examines the meaning of ms_B and ms_W more fully. In the data of Table 11.4, $k = 3$ (3 conditions) and $n = 4$ (4 scores per condition). The table contains $N = nk = 12$ scores altogether.

We began the analysis with a null hypothesis. According to the null hypothesis, the population's μ is the same for all three styles of print. Each group can therefore be viewed as a random sample from the population; the three sample means only differ by chance.

The "between" estimate of σ^2

The three sample means were 4.0, 7.0, and 10.0. From these means, we can estimate $\sigma_{\bar{X}}$. Then, since $\sigma_{\bar{X}}$ is related to σ, we can estimate σ^2.

On page 290 we computed the variance among the three means: $S^2_{\text{Between means}}$ = 6.0. But "6.0" is not a good estimate of $\sigma_{\bar{X}}^2$. To improve it, we convert S^2 to s^2. $S^2_{\text{Between means}}$ contained $k = 3$ numbers. Therefore, we correct it this way: $\dfrac{k}{k-1} S^2_{\text{Between means}} = \tfrac{3}{2} S^2_{\text{Between means}} = \tfrac{3}{2}(6.0) = 9.0$.

"9.0" is now a good estimate of $\sigma_{\bar{X}}^2$. And from it we can estimate σ^2: Each mean was based on n scores, so $\sigma_{\bar{X}} = \sigma/\sqrt{n}$. Therefore, $\sigma^2 = n\sigma_{\bar{X}}^2$. Thus, our estimate of σ^2 equals $4(9.0) = 36.0$. "36.0" appeared in the summary table as ms_{B}; it is one estimate of σ^2.

Thus, $S^2_{\text{Between means}}$ has been corrected in two ways. The first correction made it a good estimate of $\sigma_{\bar{X}}^2$. The second correction produced an estimate of σ^2.

Correction 1 (to make $S^2_{\text{Between means}}$ an unbiased estimate of $\sigma_{\bar{X}}^2$)		Correction 2 (to convert "est $\sigma_{\bar{X}}^2$" to "est σ^2")		Original uncorrected variance		Estimate of σ^2
$\left(\dfrac{k}{k-1}\right)$	$\times$	(n)	$\times$	$S^2_{\text{Between means}}$	$=$	ms_{B}
$\left(\dfrac{3}{2}\right)$	$\times$	(4)	$\times$	6.0	$=$	36.0

Be sure to notice one point. We always expect sample means to vary. Just as *scores* are expected to vary, means are also expected to vary. For a given amount of *score* variability (σ), we expect a certain amount of *mean* variability ($\sigma_{\bar{X}}$). The statistical test tells whether the means vary *more* than that.

The "within" estimate of σ^2

To get a "within" estimate of σ^2, we consider k terms: $S^2_{\text{Within Condition 1}} = 7.5$; $S^2_{\text{Within Condition 2}} = 6.5$; and $S^2_{\text{Within Condition 3}} = 10.0$. The mean of these terms is: $(7.5 + 6.5 + 10.0)/3 = 8.0$. This mean is called the "Average $S^2_{\text{Within conditions}}$."

Let us now improve this measure to yield another estimate of σ^2. Consider any condition's variance—say, $S^2_{\text{Within Condition 1}}$. This variance was based on n scores: $\sum (X - \bar{X})^2/n$. To make it a best estimate, we should multiply by $n/(n-1)$. In the same way, each condition's variance should be corrected. Therefore, the estimate of σ^2 becomes: $n/(n-1)$ Average $S^2_{\text{Within conditions}}$ = $\tfrac{4}{3}(8.0) = 10.7$. "10.7" appeared in the summary table as ms_{W}.

Thus, the "Average $S^2_{\text{Within conditions}}$" only needs one correction.

Correction (*to make each condition's* S^2 *an unbiased estimate of* σ^2)		Uncorrected variance	=	Estimate of σ^2
$\left(\dfrac{n}{n-1}\right)$	$\times$	Average S^2 Within conditions	=	ms$_W$
$\left(\dfrac{4}{3}\right)$	$\times$	8.0	=	10.7

The relationship between the two uncorrected variances

The two uncorrected terms, S^2 Between means and Average S^2 Within conditions, have an interesting relationship which will be useful in the next section. To see this relationship, first consider the variance among all 12 scores; call it S^2 Total. (To compute S^2 Total, we would consider all 12 scores and compute their mean, 7.0. Then we would compute all the squared deviation scores, sum them, and divide by N: S^2 Total $= 14$.)

Now S^2 Between means and Average S^2 Within conditions equal S^2 Total:

$$S^2_{\text{Total}} = S^2_{\text{Between means}} + \text{Average } S^2_{\text{Within conditions}}$$
$$14.0 = 6.0 + 8.0$$

This equation appears as Proof 11.2 in the appendix to this chapter. Let us briefly consider the nature of the proof. First, each score gets expressed as a deviation from the overall mean: $X - \overline{X}$. This deviation score can be divided into two parts:

$$X - \overline{X} = X - \overline{X}_c + \overline{X}_c - \overline{X}$$

Total deviation score	=	Part 1 (Within variation)	+	Part 2 (Between variation)

Part 1 tells how far the score is from the mean of its condition ($X - \overline{X}_c$). Part 2 tells how far its mean is from the overall mean ($\overline{X}_c - \overline{X}$). The score 14, for example, appeared in Condition 3. Condition 3's mean is 10, so the "within" component is $14 - 10 = 4$; and the "between" component is $10 - 7 = 3$.

$$X - \overline{X} \ = \ X - \overline{X}_c \ + \ \overline{X}_c - \overline{X}$$
$$14 - 7 \ = \ 14 - 10 \ + \ 10 - 7$$

Now consider the variance of all 12 scores. To compute S^2_{Total}, we need to square the deviation scores. As $(X - \overline{X})$ gets squared, the two right-hand terms also get squared. As Proof 11.2 shows, one part eventually becomes $S^2_{\text{Within conditions}}$; the other part becomes $S^2_{\text{Between means}}$.

11.6 THE MEANING OF "SUM OF SQUARES" AND "DEGREES OF FREEDOM"

Section 11.5 showed that ms_B is related to $S^2_{\text{Between means}}$:

$$\text{ms}_B = n \frac{k}{k-1} S^2_{\text{Between means}}$$

Since $N = nk$:

$$\text{ms}_B = \frac{NS^2_{\text{Between means}}}{k-1}$$

$$= \frac{72}{2}$$

$$= 36.0$$

The numerator is: $NS^2_{\text{Between means}}$. This numerator is the "between" sum of squares. In the summary table, ss_B equals 72. Notice that $NS^2_{\text{Between means}} = 12\,(6.0) = 72$.

The denominator is $k - 1 = 3 - 1 = 2$. This denominator is the "between" degrees of freedom. (k numbers were used to compute $S^2_{\text{Between means}}$ so df_B is $k - 1$.)

To summarize: ms_B equals $\text{ss}_B / \text{df}_B$. The numerator, ss_B, equals: $NS^2_{\text{Between means}}$; the denominator, df_B, equals $k - 1$.

There is an easier way to compute ss_B. Since ss_B equals $NS^2_{\text{Between means}}$:

$$\text{ss}_B = NS^2_{\text{Between means}} = nkS^2_{\text{Between means}}$$

$$= nk \frac{\sum_k (\overline{X}_c - \overline{X})^2}{k}$$

$$= n \sum_k (\overline{X}_c - \overline{X})^2$$

If this term is expanded, the formula becomes:

$$\text{ss}_B = \sum_k \frac{T^2}{n} - \frac{(\sum \sum X)^2}{N}$$

The complete derivation is shown in the chapter's appendix as Proof 11.4.
Now consider ms_W.

$$\text{ms}_W = \frac{n}{n-1} (\text{Average } S^2_{\text{Within conditions}})$$

Let us multiply this term by k/k. Its value does not change; it still equals 10.7: $\frac{3}{3} \frac{4}{3}(8.0) = 10.7$.

$$\text{ms}_W = \frac{k}{k} \frac{n}{n-1} (\text{Average } S^2_{\text{Within conditions}})$$

$$= \frac{N(\text{Average } S^2_{\text{Within conditions}})}{k(n-1)}$$

$$= \frac{12}{9}(8.0) = 10.7$$

The numerator is: $N(\text{Average } S^2_{\text{Within conditions}})$. This numerator is the "within" sum of squares. In the summary table, ss_W equals 96.0. Notice that $N(\text{Average } S^2_{\text{Within conditions}}) = 12\,(8.0) = 96.0$.

The denominator is $k(n-1)$. This denominator is the "within" degrees of freedom: $k(n-1) = 3(4-1) = 9$. It tells how many degrees of freedom were used in making the "within" estimate of σ^2. There were $k = 3$ conditions, and each condition contained $n - 1 = 3$ df. Altogether, there were $k(n-1) = 9$ df.

Again, there is an easier way to compute ss_W. Since ss_W equals $N(\text{Average } S^2_{\text{Within conditions}})$:

$$\text{ss}_W = N \, (\text{Average } S^2_{\text{Within conditions}})$$

$$= nk \quad \frac{1}{k} \sum_{c=1}^{k} \frac{\sum_{i=1}^{n} (X - \overline{X}_c)^2}{n}$$

For any one group
Averaged across all k groups

$$= nk \frac{1}{k} \frac{\sum_k \sum_n (X - \overline{X}_c)^2}{n}$$

$$= \sum_k \sum_n (X - \overline{X}_c)^2$$

If this term is expanded, the formula becomes:

$$ss_W = \sum \sum_k X^2 - \sum \frac{T^2}{n}$$

$$= ss_T - ss_B$$

The complete derivation is shown in the chapter appendix as Proof 11.5.

Additivity of ss and df

The sum of squares terms and the df terms have an important additive property. To see this additivity, first consider S^2_{Total} and its two component parts:

$$S^2_{Total} = S^2_{Between\ means} + Average\ S^2_{Within\ conditions}$$

$$14 = 6 + 8$$

Now let us multiply each term by N.

$$NS^2_{Total} = NS^2_{Between\ means} + N(Average\ S^2_{Within\ conditions})$$
$$12(14) = 12(6) + 12(8)$$

Each term now equals the corresponding sum of squares.

$$ss_T = ss_B + ss_W$$
$$168 = 72 + 96$$

Thus, the sum of squares terms are additive.

The df terms are also additive. Altogether the scores contain $N - 1$ degrees of freedom. The "between" estimate was based on k means, so $df_B = k - 1$. The "within" estimate was based on $n - 1$ degrees of freedom for each condition—altogether, $k(n - 1)$ df. These three df's have the following relationship.

$$df_T = df_B + df_W$$
$$N - 1 = k - 1 + k(n - 1)$$
$$= k - 1 + kn - k$$

For the data,

$$11 = 3 - 1 + 3(4 - 1)$$
$$= 2 + 9$$

Therefore, df_W is usually computed by subtraction: $df_W = df_T - df_B$.

To compute the ms terms, we then divide each ss by the corresponding df. Only two ms terms are really of interest: $ms_B = ss_B/df_B$ and $ms_W = ss_W/df_W$. Finally, the F ratio is formed: $F = ms_B/ms_W$. The larger the F, the more the two mean squares differ.

The various relationships are summarized in Table 11.6.

TABLE 11.6 Summary of the relationships among various terms

Source of variance	Sum of squares	Degrees of freedom	Estimates of σ^2 (mean square)
Total	$ss_T = NS^2_{Total}$ **equals**	$df_T = N - 1$ **equals**	
1. Between conditions (i.e., variations between the means of the different conditions)	$ss_B = NS^2_{Between\ means}$ $+$	$df_B = k - 1$ $+$	$ms_B = \dfrac{ss_B}{df_B}$
2. Within conditions (i.e., variation among the scores within a condition, averaged across all conditions)	$ss_W =$ $N(\text{Average }S^2_{Within\ conditions})$	$df_W = k(n - 1)$	$ms_W = \dfrac{ss_W}{df_W}$

* 11.7 THE FORMAL MODEL

We have now examined the basic ideas of the analysis of variance; but we still need to consider the theory in more detail. This section will state the assumptions and explain the theory. Readers who are not interested in the formal theory might skip this section and proceed to Sec. 11.8.

First consider the fictitious data in Table 11.7. There are three conditions

TABLE 11.7 Some fictitious data

	Condition 1	Condition 2	Condition 3	
	49	51	52	
	44	57	50	
	47	64	45	
	$\bar{X}_1 = 46.7$	$\bar{X}_2 = 57.3$	$\bar{X}_3 = 49.0$	$\bar{X}_T = 51.0$
(And suppose:	$\mu_1 = 46.0$	$\mu_2 = 56.0$	$\mu_3 = 48.0$	$\mu_T = 50.0$)
	$\alpha_1 = 46 - 50 = -4$	$\alpha_2 = 56 - 50 = 6$	$\alpha_3 = 48 - 50 = -2$	

* This section can be omitted in a shorter course.

with three scores in each condition. The means are: $\overline{X}_1 = 46.7$; $\overline{X}_2 = 57.3$, and $\overline{X}_3 = 49.0$. The overall mean, $\overline{X}_T$, equals 51.0. Naturally, we never know the population means (μ_1, μ_2, and μ_3). But for the sake of argument, suppose $\mu_1 = 46.0$, $\mu_2 = 56.0$; and $\mu_3 = 48.0$. μ_T, the overall mean, is 50.0.

The meaning of an "effect"

To begin with, the theory considers each condition's "effect" on the scores. For example, consider Condition 2's effect. μ_2 is 56.0—higher than the other μ's—so Condition 2's effect is positive: It *raises* the subjects' scores. The *effect* itself is expressed as $\mu_2 - \mu_T$. An effect is denoted α—for Condition 2, α_2. Thus, $\alpha_2 = \mu_2 - \mu_T = 56 - 50 = 6$. The effect of the *j*th experimental condition is written: $\alpha_j = \mu_j - \mu_T$.

In Table 11.7, $\alpha_1 = -4$; $\alpha_2 = 6$; and $\alpha_3 = -2$. Normally we do not know the different α's; we can only form hypotheses about them. When we state a *null* hypothesis, we assume that each α equals 0; thus every μ_j equals μ_T.

The theory

Each score is denoted X_{ij}—"the *i*th score in the *j*th condition." The theory proposes that every score be divided into three parts. One part equals the overall mean μ_T. The second part equals α_j—the effect of Condition *j*. The third part is any remaining part. This third part is due to many extraneous factors—subject characteristics, situational factors, and so on. It is denoted e_{ij}. We therefore write:

$$X_{ij} \quad = \quad \mu_T \quad + \quad \alpha_j \quad + \quad e_{ij}$$

$$\text{Part 1} \qquad \text{Part 2} \qquad \text{Part 3}$$

In Table 11.7, for example, the first entry is 49. "49" is analyzed into: $\mu_T = 50$, $\alpha_1 = -4$, and $e_{ij} = 3$. In the same way, every score can be analyzed into three components. This analysis is shown in Table 11.8.

TABLE 11.8 Analysis of scores into theoretical components

Condition 1	Condition 2	Condition 3
$X_{ij} = \mu_T + \alpha_1 + e_{ij}$	$X_{ij} = \mu_T + \alpha_2 + e_{ij}$	$X_{ij} = \mu_T + \alpha_3 + e_{ij}$
$49 = 50 + (-4) + 3$	$51 = 50 + (6) + -5$	$52 = 50 + (-2) + 4$
$44 = 50 + (-4) + -2$	$57 = 50 + (6) + 1$	$50 = 50 + (-2) + 2$
$47 = 50 + (-4) + 1$	$64 = 50 + (6) + 8$	$45 = 50 + (-2) + -3$

Two scores in *different* conditions have different α's and different e_{ij}'s. But two scores in the *same* conditions have identical α's; only their e_{ij}'s differ. For example, the scores in Condition 2 are: 51, 57, and 64. In each case $\alpha = 6$; the corresponding e_{ij}'s are: -5, $+1$, and $+8$.

Assumptions

At this point the theory makes three assumptions. First, we consider the scores in any one condition and assume that they have been drawn at random. The scores only differ if the e_{ij}'s differ, so the e_{ij}'s can also be viewed as a random sample.

Second, we consider the variance of the scores in each condition. The variance of the *scores* is the same as the variance of the e_{ij}'s. In the population, too, the variance of one equals the variance of the other: σ^2 (the variance of the *scores*) equals σ_e^2 (the variance of the e_{ij}'s). The theory assumes that this variance, σ^2, is the same within each experimental condition.

Finally, we assume that the scores in each condition are normally distributed. If the *scores* are normally distributed, the e_{ij}'s are normally distributed. Thus, the e_{ij}'s are assumed to be normal. This assumption allows us to use the F test.

The expectation of ms_B and ms_W

Next we consider the two mean squares, ms_B and ms_W. Imagine computing ms_B and ms_W for many different samples, and consider their expectations— $E(ms_B)$ and $E(ms_W)$. In the appendix a derivation is performed to show that $E(ms_W) = \sigma^2$. A second derivation examines $E(ms_B)$; $E(ms_B)$ equals σ^2 plus another term which depends on the size of the different effects. This derivation shows that $E(ms_B) = \sigma^2 + n \sum \alpha_j^2/(k - 1)$. If all the effects are 0, $\sum \alpha_j^2$ equals 0, and $E(ms_B)$, like $E(ms_W)$, equals σ^2. These two derivations appear as Proofs 11.6 and 11.7 in the appendix to this chapter.

When the null hypothesis is true, $\sum \alpha_j^2 = 0$, the effects are all 0. In that case, $E(ms_B) = E(ms_W)$; and the F ratio should be close to 1.

*11.8   REPEATED MEASUREMENTS DESIGN

In this section we apply the analysis of variance to a Repeated Measurements design. Again, suppose three styles of print are compared; but this time let every subject be tested under all styles of print. Data are shown in Table 11.9. Each *condition* total is reported, and so is each *subject* total. Let us denote each condition's total as T_c and each subject's total as T_s. The table also reports the number of scores in each column and the number of scores in each row.

---

* This section can be omitted in a shorter course.

TABLE 11.9 Data for a Repeated Measurements design

| | | Condition | | Each subject's | |
	Style 1	Style 2	Style 3	total (T_s)	n_s
Subject 1	5	4	8	17	3
Subject 2	8	9	12	29	3
Subject 3	2	10	14	26	3
Subject 4	1	5	6	12	3
Each condition's total (T_c)	16	28	40	84	
n_c	4	4	4		

The variance of all 12 numbers, S^2_{Total}, is 14. This variance can be divided into three parts—Part 1, Part 2, and Part 3. Part 1 is the variance of the column means, $S^2_{Between\ column\ means}$; it equals 6. Part 2 is the variance of the row means, $S^2_{Between\ row\ means}$; it equals 5.17. Part 3 is any other variance that remains in S^2_{Total}. This remaining variance is called the residual variance, $S^2_{Residual}$.

$S^2_{Residual}$ equals: $14.00 - 6.00 - 5.17 = 2.83$. It represents unexplained variation in the original 12 numbers. We ascribe it to a variety of unknown factors; it is sometimes called *error variance*.

$S^2_{Between\ row\ means}$ describes the variation among the means of different subjects. Subject 4, for example, is systematically low, while Subject 2 is systematically high. These subject differences cause some of the variance in the data. Through the analysis of variance we can remove that part of the variance. And once it is removed, we can examine the remaining two parts.

Then we obtain one estimate of σ^2 from $S^2_{Between\ column\ means}$ and another estimate from $S^2_{Residual}$. Finally, we perform an F test to compare the two estimates.

Let us now perform the analysis itself. The complete summary table is shown in Table 11.10. First compute the total sum of squares. The computa-

TABLE 11.10 Summary table for the analysis of variance. (The original data are shown in Table 11.7.)

Source of variance	Sum of squares	df	Mean square	F
Total	168.0	11		
Between conditions	72.0	2	36.0	6.3
Between subjects	62.0	3		
Residual	34.0	6	5.7	

tion is exactly like the one for Independent Groups.

$$ss_T = \sum \sum X^2 - \frac{(\sum \sum X)^2}{N} \tag{11.7}$$

$$= 756 - \frac{(84)^2}{12} = 168$$

Then compute the "between conditions" (or "between columns") sum of squares. This computation is also like the one for Independent Groups:

$$ss_{\text{Between conditions}} = \sum \frac{T_c^2}{n_c} - \frac{(\sum \sum X)^2}{N} \tag{11.8}$$

$$= \left[\frac{16^2}{4} + \frac{28^2}{4} + \frac{40^2}{4}\right] - \frac{(84)^2}{12} = 72.0$$

Then compute the "between subjects" (or "between rows") sum of squares. To compute this term, we need T_s, each subject's total, and n_s, the number of scores in each total.

$$ss_{\text{Between subjects}} = \sum \frac{T_s^2}{n_s} - \frac{(\sum \sum X)^2}{N} \tag{11.9}$$

$$= \left[\frac{17^2}{3} + \frac{29^2}{3} + \frac{26^2}{3} + \frac{12^2}{3}\right] - \frac{(84)^2}{12}$$

$$= 62.0$$

Finally, we compute the residual sum of squares by subtraction.

$$ss_{\text{Residual}} = ss_T - ss_{\text{Between conditions}} - ss_{\text{Between subjects}} \tag{11.10}$$

$$= 168.0 - 72.0 - 62.0 = 34.0$$

Enter the sum of squares terms in the summary table. Then compute the degrees of freedom: $df_T = N - 1 = 11$. $df_{\text{Between conditions}} = k - 1 = 2$. To compute $df_{\text{Between subjects}}$, consider the number of subjects (n) minus 1: $n - 1 = 4 - 1 = 3$. Finally, df_{Residual} is computed by subtraction:

$$df_{\text{Residual}} = df_T - df_{\text{Between conditions}} - df_{\text{Between subjects}} \tag{11.11}$$

$$= 11 - 2 - 3 = 6$$

Finally, compute the mean square terms and the F ratio.

$$ms_{\text{Between conditions}} = \frac{ss_{\text{Between conditions}}}{df_{\text{Between conditions}}} = \frac{72}{2} = 36.0$$

$$ms_{\text{Residual}} = \frac{ss_{\text{Residual}}}{df_{\text{Residual}}} = \frac{34}{6} = 5.7$$

The F ratio is:

$$F = \frac{ms_{\text{Between conditions}}}{ms_{\text{Residual}}} \tag{11.12}$$

$$= \frac{36.0}{5.7} = 6.3$$

This F has 2 and 6 df. To evaluate it, we consult a table of the F distribution: $F_{.05}(2, 6) = 5.14$. "6.3" exceeds the table value, so the two variance estimates *do* differ significantly. Therefore, the column means are significantly different.

More advanced textbooks of psychological statistics discuss the assumptions behind this test. The same assumptions are made as are made for the simpler analysis of Independent Groups. In addition, a further assumption is needed about the correlation between scores in one condition and those in another condition: We need to assume that all such correlations are basically equal, differing from one another only by chance.

This kind of design is frequently used in psychology: The subject is the unit of analysis, and every subject gets tested repeatedly. Other kinds of units are also possible. A small *group* might be the unit: Suppose an investigator studied many groups. Each group might be tested under various conditions, and the investigator might measure the group's efficiency or work output under each condition.

The unit could also be a group of matched subjects. Suppose an experimenter formed three-person groups, making the subjects in each group comparable in some way—comparable in socioeconomic level, say, or in IQ, or in some ability. Then one subject of each group would be assigned to Condition A, another to Condition B, a third to Condition C. In this case a *group of matched subjects* would be the unit of analysis. Example 11.11 illustrates this variation of the design.

EXAMPLE 11.11

An investigator performed an experiment with four experimental conditions. He wanted to learn whether distracting lights, odors, and touches affect a person's ability to understand tape-recorded messages. The experimenter selected four-member groups. The four subjects within each group were matched for their auditory acuity. One subject was then assigned at random to each condition. Here are the results:

| | Condition | | | | | |
	Distracting lights	Distracting odors	Distracting touches	Control	T_s	n_s
Group 1 (excellent auditory ability)	25	30	25	25	105	4
Group 2 (good auditory ability)	23	22	23	21	89	4
Group 3 (medium auditory ability)	19	23	20	24	86	4
Group 4 (fair auditory ability)	15	17	16	21	69	4
Group 5 (poor auditory ability)	15	15	15	24	69	4
T_c	97	107	99	115	418	
n_c	5	5	5	5		20

Do the conditions differ significantly? Make all the necessary assumptions.

Solution   First compute the sum of squares terms:

$$\text{SS}_T = \sum \sum X^2 - \frac{(\sum \sum X)^2}{N} = 9{,}086 - \frac{(418)^2}{20} = 349.8$$

$$\text{SS}_{\text{Between conditions}} = \sum \frac{T_c{}^2}{n_c} - \frac{(\sum \sum X)^2}{N}$$

$$= \left[\frac{97^2}{5} + \frac{107^2}{5} + \frac{108^2}{5} + \frac{106^2}{5} \right] - \frac{(418)^2}{20}$$

$$= 40.6$$

$$\text{SS}_{\text{Between groups}} = \sum \frac{T_s{}^2}{n_s} - \frac{(\sum \sum X)^2}{N}$$

$$= \left[\frac{105^2}{4} + \frac{89^2}{4} + \frac{86^2}{4} + \frac{69^2}{4} + \frac{69^2}{4} \right] - \frac{(418)^2}{20}$$

$$= 229.8$$

$$\text{SS}_{\text{Residual}} = \text{SS}_T - \text{SS}_{\text{Between conditions}} - \text{SS}_{\text{Between groups}}$$

$$= 349.8 - 40.6 - 229.8 = 79.4$$

Then compute the df's:

$$\text{df}_T = N - 1 = 20 - 1 = 19$$

$$\text{df}_{\text{Between conditions}} = k - 1 = 4 - 1 = 3$$

$$\text{df}_{\text{Between groups}} = n - 1 = 5 - 1 = 4$$

$$\text{df}_{\text{Residual}} = \text{df}_T - \text{df}_{\text{Between conditions}} - \text{df}_{\text{Between groups}} = 19 - 3 - 4 = 12$$

The summary table is shown below. It reports the mean square terms and the final F. For these data, $F(3, 12) = 2.0$. From a table of the F distribution, $F_{.05}(3, 12) = 3.49$. Therefore, the means do not differ significantly.

Source of variation	ss	df	ms	F
Total	349.8	19		
Between conditions	40.6	3	13.5	2.0
Between groups	229.8	4		
Residual	79.4	12	6.6	

APPENDIX: *Proofs*

Proof 11.1 *Proof that $F = t^2$ when $k = 2$.*

Suppose an experiment contains two conditions ($k = 2$), and suppose there are n scores in each condition. Then $N = 2n$. In this case, the term $S^2_{\text{Between means}}$ can be simplified:

$$S^2_{\text{Between means}} = \frac{(\bar{X}_1 - \bar{X})^2 + (\bar{X}_2 - \bar{X})^2}{2}$$

$$= \frac{\left(\bar{X}_1 - \frac{(\bar{X}_1 + \bar{X}_2)}{2}\right)^2 + \left(\bar{X}_2 - \frac{(\bar{X} + \bar{X}_2)}{2}\right)^2}{2}$$

$$= \frac{\left(\frac{2\bar{X}_1 - \bar{X}_1 - \bar{X}_2}{2}\right)^2 + \left(\frac{2\bar{X}_2 - \bar{X}_1 - \bar{X}_2}{2}\right)^2}{2}$$

$$= \frac{(\bar{X}_1 - \bar{X}_2)^2 + (\bar{X}_2 - \bar{X}_1)^2}{8}$$

$$= \frac{2(\bar{X}_1 - \bar{X}_2)^2}{8}$$

$$= \frac{1}{4}(\bar{X}_1 - \bar{X}_2)^2$$

Now consider the F ratio.

$$F = \frac{ms_B}{ms_W} = \frac{ss_B/1}{ss_W/2(n-1)}$$

$$= \frac{NS^2_{\text{Between means}}}{\frac{ss_W}{2(n-1)}} = \frac{(2n)S^2_{\text{Between means}}}{\frac{ss_W}{2(n-1)}}$$

$$= \frac{(2n)\frac{1}{4}(\bar{X}_1 - \bar{X}_2)^2}{\frac{\sum x_1^2 + \sum x_2^2}{2(n-1)}}$$

$$= \frac{\frac{1}{2}n(\bar{X}_1 - \bar{X}_2)^2}{\dfrac{\sum x_1{}^2 + \sum x_2{}^2}{n + n - 2}}$$

$$= \frac{\dfrac{n}{2}(\bar{X}_1 - \bar{X}_2)^2}{s^2} = \frac{(\bar{X}_1 - \bar{X}_2)^2}{\dfrac{2}{n}s^2}$$

$$= \frac{(\bar{X}_1 - \bar{X}_2)^2}{\dfrac{s^2}{n} + \dfrac{s^2}{n}} = \frac{(\bar{X}_1 - \bar{X}_2)^2}{s_{\bar{D}}{}^2} = t^2$$

Proof 11.2   *Proof that* $S^2{}_{\text{Total}} = S^2{}_{\text{Between means}} + Average\ S^2{}_{\text{Within conditions}}$.
Section 11.5 considered each score as a deviation from the overall mean $\bar{X}$. Each deviation score was divided into two parts:

$$(X - \bar{X}) \qquad = \qquad (X - \bar{X}_c) \qquad + \qquad (\bar{X}_c - \bar{X})$$

Total deviation score	=	Part 1 (Within variation)	+	Part 2 (Between variation)

Consider the scores within one condition. First square each deviation score:

$$(X - \bar{X})^2 = (X - \bar{X}_c)^2 + (\bar{X}_c - \bar{X})^2 + 2(\bar{X}_c - \bar{X})(X - \bar{X}_c)$$

Then, to compute $S^2{}_{\text{Total}}$, sum these squared deviation scores:

(Within one condition)
$$\sum_n (X - \bar{X})^2 = \sum_n (X - \bar{X}_c)^2 + n(\bar{X}_c - \bar{X})^2 + 2(\bar{X}_c - \bar{X}) \sum_n (X - \bar{X}_c)$$
$$= \sum_n (X - \bar{X}_c)^2 + n(\bar{X}_c - \bar{X})^2$$

Do the same for each condition and sum for all k conditions.

(Across all conditions)
$$\sum_k \sum_n (X - \bar{X})^2 = \sum_k \sum_n (X - \bar{X}_c)^2 + n \sum_k (\bar{X}_c - \bar{X})^2$$

Divide by N.

$$\frac{\sum_k \sum_n (X - \bar{X})^2}{N} = \frac{\sum_k \sum_n (X - \bar{X}_c)^2}{N} + \frac{n \sum_k (\bar{X}_c - \bar{X})^2}{N}$$

Since $N = nk$:

$$\frac{\sum_k \sum_n (X - \bar{X})^2}{N} = \frac{1}{k} \sum_k \frac{\sum_n (X - \bar{X}_c)^2}{n} + \frac{\sum_k (\bar{X}_c - \bar{X})^2}{k}$$

$$S^2{}_{\text{Total}} = \frac{1}{k} \sum_k S^2{}_{\text{Within one condition}} + S^2{}_{\text{Between means}}$$

$$S^2{}_{\text{Total}} = Average\ S^2{}_{\text{Within conditions}} + S^2{}_{\text{Between means}}$$

Proof 11.3   *Computational formula for* SS_T.

$$SS_T = NS^2_{Total}$$

$$= \sum_k \sum_n (X - \bar{X})^2$$

$$= \sum_k \sum_n (X^2 - 2\bar{X}X + \bar{X}^2)$$

$$= \sum_k \sum_n X^2 - 2\bar{X} \sum_k \sum_n X + N\bar{X}^2$$

$$= \sum_k \sum_n X^2 - 2\frac{(\sum_n \sum_n X)^2}{N} + \frac{N(\sum_k \sum_n X)^2}{N^2}$$

$$= \sum_k \sum_n X^2 - \frac{(\sum_k \sum_n X)^2}{N}$$

Proof 11.4   *Computational formula for* SS_B.

$$SS_B = NS^2_{Between\ means}$$

$$= nkS^2_{Between\ means}$$

$$= nk\frac{\sum_k (\bar{X}_c - \bar{X})^2}{k}$$

$$= n\sum_k (\bar{X}_c - \bar{X})^2$$

$$= n\sum_k (\bar{X}_c^2 - 2\bar{X}_c\bar{X} + \bar{X}^2)$$

$\bar{X}_c$, the mean of the condition, equals $\dfrac{\sum_n X}{n}$. If we denote the total T, then $\bar{X}_c = \dfrac{T}{n}$.

Then:

$$SS_B = n\sum_k \left[\left(\frac{T^2}{n^2}\right) - 2\bar{X}\left(\frac{T}{n}\right) + \bar{X}^2 \right]$$

$$= \sum_k \left[n\frac{T^2}{n^2} - 2n\bar{X}\frac{T}{n} + n\bar{X}^2 \right]$$

$$= \sum_k \left[\frac{T^2}{n} - 2\bar{X}T + n\bar{X}^2 \right]$$

$$= \sum_k \frac{T^2}{n} - 2\bar{X}\left(\sum_k \sum_n X \right) + kn\bar{X}^2$$

$$= \sum_k \frac{T^2}{n} - \frac{\left(\sum_k \sum_n X \right)^2}{N}$$

Proof 11.5 *Computational formula for* ss_W

Section 11.6 showed that $ss_W = N(\text{Average } S^2{}_{\text{Within conditions}}) = \sum_k \sum_n (X - \bar{X}_c)^2$. Therefore:

$$ss_W = \sum_k \sum_n [X^2 - 2\bar{X}_c X + \bar{X}_c{}^2]$$

$$= \sum_k \sum_n \left[X^2 - 2\frac{T}{n} X + \left(\frac{T}{n}\right)^2 \right]$$

$$= \sum_k \left[\sum_n X^2 - 2\frac{T}{n} \sum_n X + n\frac{T^2}{n^2} \right]$$

$$= \sum_k \left[\sum_n X^2 - 2\frac{T^2}{n} + \frac{T^2}{n} \right]$$

$$= \sum_k \left[\sum_n X^2 - \frac{T^2}{n} \right]$$

$$= \sum_k \sum_n X^2 - \sum_k \frac{T^2}{n}$$

$$= ss_T - ss_B$$

Proof 11.6 *Proof that* $E(ms_W) = \sigma^2$.

ms_W equals ss_W/df_W. Earlier we showed that ss_W equals N (Average $S^2{}_{\text{Within conditions}}$), which in turn is $\sum \sum (X_{ij} - \bar{X}_j)^2$. To compute ss_W, we need to consider each score's deviation from the condition's mean. If we consider any one group—say, Group j—these squared deviations are written: $\sum_n (X_{ij} - \bar{X}_j)^2$. Now Condition j has n scores; to estimate σ^2, we divide the sum by $n - 1$.

$$E\left[\frac{\sum\limits_n (X_{ij} - \bar{X}_j)^2}{n - 1} \right] = \sigma^2$$

For any one condition, then: $E\left[\sum\limits_n (X_{ij} - \bar{X}_j)^2 \right] = (n - 1)\sigma^2$

This expectation is the same in each condition; in each case it equals $(n - 1)\sigma^2$. Now let us consider the squared deviation scores over *all* conditions; that expectation is k times "$(n - 1)\sigma^2$."

$$E\left[\sum_k \sum_n (X_{ij} - \bar{X}_j)^2 \right] = k(n - 1)\sigma^2$$

$\sum_k \sum_n (X_{ij} - \bar{X}_j)^2$ is the "within" sum of squares. To compute ms_W, we divide by the degrees of freedom, $k(n - 1)$. Therefore, the expectation for ms_W becomes:

$$E(ms_W) = \frac{k(n - 1)\sigma^2}{k(n - 1)} = \sigma^2$$

Proof 11.7 *Proof that* $E(ms_B) = \sigma^2 + n \sum \alpha_j^2/(k-1)$.

ms_B equals ss_B/df_B. Earlier we showed that ss_B equals $NS^2_{\text{Between means}}$, which in turn is $n \sum_k (\bar{X}_j - \bar{X}_T)^2$. The mean of each condition $(\bar{X}_j)$ is $\dfrac{\sum X_{ij}}{n}$. But $X_{ij} = \mu_T + \alpha_j + e_{ij} = \mu_T + (\mu_j - \mu_T) + e_{ij} = \mu_j + e_{ij}$. Thus, each score in Condition j can be viewed as "$\mu_j + e_{ij}$." And the mean of these values equals μ_j plus the mean e_{ij}. Let us denote the mean e_{ij} as $\bar{e}$:

$$\bar{X}_j = \text{mean of "} \mu_j + e_{ij}\text{"} = \mu_j + \bar{e}$$

Similarly, the overall mean, $\bar{X}_T$, equals μ_T plus the overall mean of the e_{ij}'s:

$$\bar{X}_T = \mu_T + \bar{e}_T$$

Therefore,

$$\bar{X}_j - \bar{X}_T = (\mu_j + \bar{e}] - (\mu_T + \bar{e}_T)$$
$$\qquad\qquad\quad \uparrow \qquad\qquad \uparrow$$
$$\qquad\qquad\quad \bar{X}_j \qquad\qquad \bar{X}_T$$

Rearranging the terms:

$$\bar{X}_j - \bar{X}_T = (\mu_j - \mu_T) + (\bar{e} - \bar{e}_T)$$

Since $(\mu_j - \mu_T)$ is α_j:

$$\bar{X}_j - \bar{X}_T = \alpha_j + (\bar{e} - \bar{e}_T)$$

Thus, each $\bar{X}_j - \bar{X}_T$ equals α_j plus another term. This other term is the condition's mean e_{ij} expressed as a deviation from the overall mean e_{ij}.

Let us now examine ss_B:

$$ss_B = n \sum_k (\bar{X}_j - \bar{X}_T)^2$$

$$= n \sum_k [\alpha_j + (\bar{e} - \bar{e}_T)]^2$$

$$= n[\sum \alpha_j^2 + \sum (\bar{e} - \bar{e}_T)^2 + 2 \sum \alpha_j (\bar{e} - \bar{e}_T)]$$

$$= n \sum \alpha_j^2 + n \sum (\bar{e} - \bar{e}_T)^2 + 2n \sum_k \alpha_j (\bar{e} - \bar{e}_T)$$

Since the e_{ij}'s have been drawn at random, $\bar{e} - \bar{e}_T$ is not correlated with α_j. Therefore, the last term becomes 0 when it is averaged over many samples.

$$E(ss_B) = [E(n \sum \alpha_j^2) + E(n \sum (\bar{e} - \bar{e}_T)^2]$$

$$= nE(\sum \alpha_j^2) + nE[\sum (\bar{e} - \bar{e}_T)^2]$$

$\sum \alpha_j^2$ is an exact theoretical quantity; its expectation is $\sum \alpha_j^2$. But $\sum (\bar{e} - \bar{e}_T)^2$ varies from sample to sample; let us now consider *its* expectation. $\sum (\bar{e} - \bar{e}_T)^2$ is the sum of k squared numbers. Each number tells how far the condition's mean e_{ij} deviates from the overall mean, $\bar{e}_T$. Let us divide this quantity by $k-1$: $[\sum (\bar{e} - \bar{e}_T)^2]/(k-1)$. This term estimates $\sigma_{\bar{e}}^2$, the variance of the different $\bar{e}$'s. ($\sigma_{\bar{e}}$ is a standard error of the mean—in this case, a standard error of the mean e_{ij}.)

Therefore:

$$\mathrm{E}\,\frac{\left[\sum_{k} (\bar{e} - \bar{e}_\mathrm{T})^2\right]}{k-1} = \sigma_{\bar{e}}^2$$

$$\mathrm{E}\left[\sum_{k} (\bar{e} - \bar{e}_\mathrm{T})^2\right] = (k-1)\sigma_{\bar{e}}^2$$

The expectation of ss_B therefore becomes:

$$\mathrm{E}(ss_\mathrm{B}) = n \sum \alpha_j^2 + n(k-1)\sigma_{\bar{e}}^2$$

But $\sigma_{\bar{e}}$, like any σ_X, is related to the corresponding σ; in this case it is related to σ_e, the standard deviation of the e_{ij}'s: $\sigma_{\bar{e}}^2 = \sigma_e^2/n$. And σ_e^2, according to the theory, is the same as σ^2. Therefore:

$$\mathrm{E}(ss_\mathrm{B}) = n \sum \alpha_j^2 + n(k-1)\frac{\sigma^2}{n}$$

$$= n \sum \alpha_j^2 + (k-1)\sigma^2$$

To compute ms_B, then, we divide ss_B by $k-1$. The expectation becomes:

$$\mathrm{E}(ms_\mathrm{B}) = \frac{\mathrm{E}(ss_\mathrm{B})}{k-1}$$

$$= \frac{n \sum \alpha_j^2}{k-1} + \frac{(k-1)\sigma^2}{k-1}$$

$$= \frac{n \sum \alpha_j^2}{k-1} + \sigma^2$$

EXERCISES

11.1   Use the F table to find the values of the following F's.

(a) $F_{.05}\,(5,24)$
       Answer: 2.62

(b) $F_{.01}\,(5,24)$
       Answer: 3.90

(c) $F_{.05}\,(24,5)$
       Answer: 4.53

(d) $F_{.01}\,(24,5)$
       Answer: 9.47

(e) $F_{.05}\,(2,10)$
       Answer: 4.10

(f) $F_{.05}\,(2,25)$
       Answer: 3.38

(g) $F_{.05}\,(2,125)$
       Answer: 3.07

(h) $F_{.05}\,(5,125)$
       Answer: 2.29

11.2   An experimenter wanted to determine whether a certain drug makes subjects' scores more variable. For 11 subjects tested under the drug, $\sum (X - \bar{X})^2 = 180$. For 11 other subjects tested under a placebo $\sum (X - \bar{X})^2 = 60$. Do the two groups differ significantly in variability? Use the .05 level of significance. *Answer: $F(10,10) = 3.0$. The difference is significant at the .05 level.*

11.3   Imagine 25 samples from a population. Suppose each sample contains 30 scores. The experimenter studies the $\bar{X}$'s and estimates $\sigma_{\bar{X}}$ to be 3. Estimate σ^2. *Answer: 270*

11.4   An experimenter compares two groups. For Group X, $\bar{X} = 41$, $s = 4$, and $N = 17$. For Group Y, $\bar{Y} = 41$, $s = 2$, and $N = 13$. The experimenter plans to pool the variances of the two groups to derive one estimate of σ. Why should he not do this? *Answer: The two s's differ significantly; $F(16,12) = 4.0$.*

11.5   Here are the means of two experimental groups: $\bar{X}_1 = 5.0$, $\bar{X}_2 = 7.0$. Each group contained eight subjects. The two groups do not differ significantly in any respect (e.g., in mean, median, variance). Use the two means' variability to estimate the population's σ. *Answer: $s_{\bar{X}}^2 = 2.0$. σ^2 is estimated to equal $2(8) = 16$; $s = 4$.*

11.6   An experimenter compared two groups of pigeons in discrimination learning. One group was rewarded with desirable food, the other group with less desirable food. Do the two groups differ significantly in variability?

Group 1 (desirable food)	Group 2 (less desirable food)
$\bar{X} = 78.4$	$\bar{Y} = 76.1$
$s = 3$	$s = 4$
$N = 31$	$N = 25$

Answer: $F(24,30) = 1.78$; the difference is not significant at the .05 level.

11.7   Five different treatments were administered to separate groups of subjects. Here are the resulting data. Do the five treatment means differ significantly at the .01 level of significance?

	I	II	III	IV	V	
	4	5	15	35	17	
	7	6	18	27	26	
	9	12	21	29	17	
	9	12	26	30	20	
	14	7	20	25	12	
T or $\sum X$	43	42	100	146	92	$\sum\sum X = 423$
$\sum X^2$	423	398	2,066	4,320	1,798	$\sum\sum X^2 = 9,005$

Answer:

	ss	df	ms	F
Total	1847.8	24		
Between	1521.4	4	380.4	23.3*
Within	326.4	20	16.32	

$$*p < .01$$

11.8 Rats were tested under four conditions, and their error scores in a maze were tabulated. Do the means of the four groups differ significantly at the .01 level of significance?

	I	II	III	IV	
	16	24	16	25	
	7	6	15	19	
	19	15	18	16	
	24	25	19	17	
	31	32	6	42	
		24	13	45	
		29	18		
T or $\sum X$	97	155	105	164	$\sum\sum X = 521$
$\sum X^2$	2,203	3,903	1,695	5,320	$\sum\sum X^2 = 13,121$

Answer:

	ss	df	ms	F
Total	2263.4	24		
Between	513.3	3	171.1	2.05*
Within	1750.1	21	83.3	

$$*p > .01$$

11.9 Here are some data obtained from an experiment with three conditions. The data meet the requirements for an analysis of variance.

	I	II	III	
# scores/condition	10	10	10	
$\bar{X}$	7.4	8.3	11.3	
$\sum X^2$	649	755	1,263	$\sum\sum X^2 = 2,667$

Do the treatment means differ significantly?
Answer:

Group I: $\sum X = 74$
Group II: $\sum X = 83$
Group III: $\sum X = 113$

	ss	df	ms	F
Total	237	29		
Between	83.4	2	41.7	7.3*
Within	153.6	27	5.7	

$*p < .01$

12

CORRELATION AND
PREDICTION

In Chap. 4 we considered r, the coefficient of correlation, as a descriptive statistic. At that time r was defined but not examined in detail. We also suggested that correlations can be used to make predictions: Given a person's height, we can predict his weight; given his IQ, we can predict his performance in school. Thus, the concept would seem to have special significance to the psychologist. Let us now examine r in detail.

Definition

We have defined r_{XY} by several formulas. The basic formula described r as a mean of z score products:

$$r_{XY} = \frac{\sum z_X z_Y}{N} \qquad (12.1)$$

$$= \frac{\sum xy}{N S_X S_Y}$$

This formula is convenient as a definition. When an investigator wants to *compute* r, though, the following formula is more convenient:

$$r_{XY} = \frac{N \sum XY - (\sum X)(\sum Y)}{\sqrt{N \sum X^2 - (\sum X)^2} \sqrt{N \sum Y^2 - (\sum Y)^2}} \qquad (12.2)$$

The value of r can range from -1 through 0 to $+1$. When r equals $+1$ or -1, the datum points on a graph fall along a perfectly straight line. When r lies between 0 and $+1$ or between 0 and -1, the datum points fall *around* a straight line, not necessarily on it. As r moves closer to 0, the datum points become more and more scattered on the graph.

This measure of correlation is very much related to the geometry of a straight line. In this chapter, we shall first consider how a straight line can be used to describe a set of data. Then we shall examine its relationship to r. If you would like to review the geometry of a straight line, you might refer to Chapter Appendix 1 on page 351.

12.1   REGRESSION LINE

Consider the 10 pairs of observations in Table 12.1. Let us say that 10 subjects have been tested, and that every subject has been assigned two scores, an X score and a Y score. The value of r is $+0.60$, so the two variables are positively related.

The data are shown in the graph of Fig. 12.1. Each subject's pair of scores appears as a dot in the figure. The dots do not fall along a perfectly straight line, but they do seem to fall *around* a line. What line would best describe the trend of the data? What is the equation of that line? If you look ahead for a moment, you will see the ultimate answer: $Y = 1.2X + 14$. Eventually this equation will be used to describe the trend.

We need an equation of this kind for two reasons. For one thing; it describes the relationship between X and Y. It says that the Y score can be viewed as 1.2 times the X score, with the constant 14 added. More important, though, the equation can also be used to make predictions about other individuals. If we trust the sample of 10 subjects, we can generalize beyond the data: Say an individual has only been tested on X; perhaps $X = 20$. Then we can use

TABLE 12.1 Data for 10 subjects on test X and test Y

Subject	X score (personality test)	Y score (improvement in psychotherapy)	z_X	z_Y
A	26	32	−0.80	−1.80
B	24	40	−1.20	−1.00
C	22	44	−1.60	−0.60
D	33	44	+0.60	−0.60
E	27	48	−0.60	−0.20
F	36	52	+1.20	+0.20
G	30	56	+0.00	+0.60
H	38	56	+1.60	+0.60
I	30	60	+0.00	+1.00
J	34	68	+0.80	+1.80

$$\sum X = 300 \qquad \sum Y = 500$$
$$\sum X^2 = 9{,}250 \qquad \sum Y^2 = 26{,}000$$
$$\sum XY = 15{,}300$$
$$N = 10$$
$$\bar{X} = 30 \qquad \bar{Y} = 50$$
$$S_X = 5 \qquad S_Y = 10$$

the equation to predict his Y score: $Y = 1.2X + 14 = 1.2(20) + 14 = 38$. From the X score, then, we can predict the Y score.

But how shall we select values for b and a in the equation $Y = bX + a$? Occasionally an investigator fits a line to his data "by eye." That is, he draws an arbitrary line on the graph, making half the datum points fall above the line and half fall below the line. Then he determines the equation of the line and reports that equation. The resulting line would be arbitrary, of course,

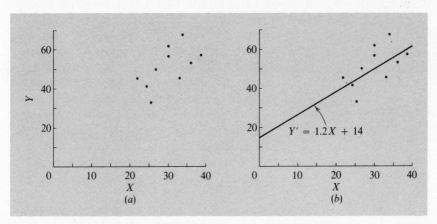

FIG. 12.1 (a) Graph of data. (b) Same graph, regression equation.

and two investigators might describe the same data quite differently. There-fore, a more objective, precise method is needed. The preferred procedure is called the *least-squares solution*. It is described next.

Least-squares solution

A straight line is needed so that we can ultimately predict a subject's Y score from his X score. To avoid confusion, let us make an important distinction. We need to distinguish between (*a*) a *prediction* that we might make about a subject's Y score, and (*b*) the Y score itself. A *predicted* Y score is usually denoted Y'. The predicted Y score equals "$bX + a$," so from now on, let us write: $Y' = bX + a$. On the other hand, Y denotes the Y score itself. The only way to determine Y is to administer Test Y. For Subject A in Table 12.1, $Y = 32$.

Our major goal, though, is prediction. Ultimately we hope to measure a person's X score, predict his Y', and not need to measure the Y score at all. After all, Variable Y might be quite difficult to measure: Perhaps X denotes a person's score on a college admission test, and perhaps Y denotes his success in four years of college. If we are to measure Y, the person would have to spend four years of effort, time, and money in college. But if we could *predict* Y in advance, the person might be spared ultimate frustration, expense, and heartache.

As a first step we need actual measures of both variables. The subjects in Table 12.1, for example, have been tested directly on X and Y. For these 10 subjects, then, we have values of X and of Y; and once we have determined the equation, we shall also have values of Y'.

A prediction is rarely perfect, so Y' is bound to differ from Y at least a little. Ideally the two should be close, and the difference, $Y - Y'$, should be small—as small as possible. Ideally the average value of $Y - Y'$ should equal 0. The mean $Y - Y'$ *is* 0 when $\sum (Y - Y')$ is 0. That is, for some of our subjects Y might be higher than the prediction, and for others, Y might be lower. If the sum is 0, then the positive discrepancies offset the negative ones. One criterion for our line, then, is this: b and a should be chosen in such a way that the resulting Y' values make $\sum (Y - Y') = 0$.

It is also desirable to have the sum of the *squared* difference as small as possible. That is, $\sum (Y - Y')^2$ should be a minimum. The reason for this goal will become clear later. It happens that when $\sum (Y - Y')^2$ is as small as pos-sible, $\sum (Y - Y')$ equals 0, so both criteria can be satisfied at the same time. This second goal is called the *least-squares criterion*.

To summarize, we want to find an equation that relates X scores and Y scores. We ultimately hope to predict Y scores, so the equation is written: $Y' = bX + a$. Our goal is to find the best b and a for this equation. The values of b and a should be chosen so as to satisfy the least-squares criterion— $\sum (Y - Y')^2$ should be a minimum, and $\sum (Y - Y')$ should be 0.

Methods of calculus show how to achieve this goal. The mathematical procedure appears at the end of this chapter as Proof 12.1. For now, let us just examine the answer.

To satisfy the least-squares criterion, compute b as follows:

$$b = \frac{N \sum XY - (\sum X)(\sum Y)}{N \sum X^2 - (\sum X)^2} \tag{12.3}$$

Then use the value of b to compute a:

$$a = \overline{Y} - b\overline{X} \tag{12.4}$$

For the data of Table 12.1, the values are:

$$b = \frac{10(15,300) - (300)(500)}{10(9,250) - (300)^2} = 1.2$$

$$a = 50 - (1.2)(30) = 14$$

The equation becomes: $Y' = 1.2X + 14$.

If the investigator is willing to generalize beyond his data to other individuals in the same population, he only needs this equation and the individual's X score to make a prediction. If for some new subject, $X = 30$, then $Y' = 1.2(30) + 14 = 50$.

Consider the 10 subjects of Table 12.2 and note their Y' scores; compare these values with their actual Y scores. Two subjects of the group, Subject G and Subject I, had X scores of 30; for both of them, $Y' = 50$. In both cases the prediction happens to be too low. For Subject G, the Y' value is off by 6 points; for Subject I, by 10 points. We summarize these results this way: For Subject G, $Y - Y' = 6$; for Subject I, $Y - Y' = 10$. On the other hand, the prediction for Subject H was too high: $Y' = 1.2(38) + 14 = 59.6$. For Subject H, therefore, $Y - Y' = 56 - 59.6 = -3.6$.

Errors of prediction

$Y - Y'$ is called an error of prediction; it is the difference between a subject's actual Y score and his predicted Y score. These errors can be positive or negative, as shown in the last column of Table 12.2. Notice that their sum is 0, so the mean error is also 0.

Figure 12.2 shows the same data on a graph. Especially notice Subject J's datum point. For him, $X = 34$ (and $Y = 68$). The line at $X = 34$ makes the prediction for Subject J: $Y' = 54.8$. The datum point, on the other hand, tells his actual Y score: $Y = 68$. The vertical distance between the dot and the line tells how large the error is. The farther the dot is from the line, the greater the $Y - Y'$. Since $\sum (Y - Y') = 0$, the distance of dots above the line equals the distance of dots below the line.

You might also notice that the least-squares criterion is met in these data. If you squared each error to obtain $\sum (Y - Y')^2$, your total would be 640.0.

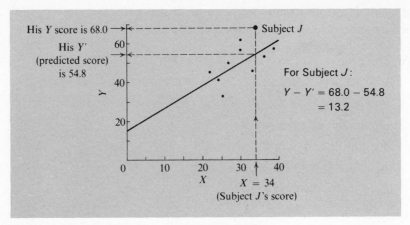

FIG. 12.2   The meaning of $Y - Y'$ shown graphically.

Any other value of a and b would yield Y' values which made $\sum (Y - Y')^2$ larger than 640.0. The squared error scores will reappear later.

Relationship between b and r
The formula for b happens to resemble the formula for r. A simple relationship exists between them.

$$b = r_{XY} \frac{S_Y}{S_X} \tag{12.5}$$

TABLE 12.2   Each subject's error of prediction, $Y - Y'$

Subject	X score	Y score	Y' score (i.e., $1.2X + 14$)	$Y - Y'$
A	26	32	45.2	−13.2
B	24	40	42.8	−2.8
C	22	44	40.4	3.6
D	33	44	53.6	−9.6
E	27	48	46.4	1.6
F	36	52	57.2	−5.2
G	30	56	50.0	6.0
H	38	56	59.6	−3.6
I	30	60	50.0	10.0
J	34	68	54.8	13.2

$$\sum (Y - Y') = 0$$
$$\text{Mean } (Y - Y') = 0$$

(To prove this relationship, you might write the formulas for r, S_Y, and S_X:

$$r\frac{S_Y}{S_X} = \frac{N\sum XY - (\sum X)(\sum Y)}{\sqrt{N\sum X^2 - (\sum X)^2}\sqrt{N\sum Y^2 - (\sum Y)^2}} \cdot \frac{\frac{1}{N}\sqrt{N\sum Y^2 - (\sum Y)^2}}{\frac{1}{N}\sqrt{N\sum X^2 - (\sum X)^2}}$$

Various terms cancel, and the result is:

$$\frac{N\sum XY - (\sum X)(\sum Y)}{N\sum X^2 - (\sum X)^2}$$

And this term equals b.)

If you know the values of r and the two standard deviations, then you can compute b very easily.

EXAMPLE 12.1

An investigator has data on 1,000 individuals who have been in psychotherapy for five years. Variable X tells the score the individual received on a personality test. Variable Y tells his improvement in psychotherapy over the five years. Here are the data: $\sum XY = 30,000$. $\sum X = 3,000$. $\sum X^2 = 14,000$. $\sum Y = 5,000$.

(*a*) Compute the value of b in the regression equation.

Solution

$$b = \frac{N\sum XY - (\sum X)(\sum Y)}{N\sum X^2 - (\sum X)^2}$$

$$= \frac{1,000(30,000) - (3,000)(5,000)}{1,000(14,000) - (3,000)^2} = 3.0$$

(*b*) What is the regression equation?

Solution From the above data, $\bar{X} = 3$ and $\bar{Y} = 5$.

$$a = \bar{Y} - b\bar{X} = 5 - (3)(3) = -4$$

Therefore the equation is: $Y' = 3X - 4$.

(*c*) Predict the improvement score of a subject with $X = 4$.

Solution $Y' = 3(4) - 4 = 8$.

(*d*) If $S_Y = 10$, compute r.

Solution   From the above data,

$$S_x = \frac{1}{N} \sqrt{N \sum X^2 - (\sum X)^2}$$

$$= \frac{1}{1,000} \sqrt{1,000(14,000) - (3,000)^2}$$

$$= 2.24$$

Furthermore,

$$b = r \cdot \frac{S_Y}{S_X}$$

$$3 = r \frac{10}{2.24}$$

Therefore

$$r = \frac{3(2.24)}{10} = +0.67$$

The equation for predicting Y' from a given X score is called a *regression equation*, and b is called the *regression coefficient*. The regression coefficient is sometimes written $b_{Y \cdot X}$ as a reminder that Y is being predicted from X. Then the regression equation itself would be written: $Y' = b_{Y \cdot X} X + a_{Y \cdot X}$. The subscripts stress that Y is being predicted, not X. Usually "$Y \cdot X$" is read "Y dot X," "Y from X," "Y on X," or "Y given X." Anytime there is ambiguity about the variable being predicted, this notation should be used.

EXAMPLE 12.2

A firm tested 500 new employees on an aptitude test (X). Three years later they collected supervisors' ratings of each employee's success on the job (Y). The data yielded the following statistics: $\bar{X} = 100$, $S_x = 10$, $\bar{Y} = 130$, $S_Y = 20$, $r_{XY} = .70$. (*a*) Compute the best-fitting regression equation for predicting Y. (*b*) Compute Y' for $X = 90$. (*c*) Compute Y' for $X = 125$.

Solution   (*a*) The regression coefficient is: $b_{Y \cdot X} = r_{XY} \cdot S_Y / S_X$.

$$b_{Y \cdot X} = (.70) \frac{20}{10} = 1.4$$

$$a_{Y \cdot X} = \bar{Y} - b_{Y \cdot X} \bar{X} = 130 - (1.4)(100) = -10$$

Therefore, the regression equation is: $Y' = 1.4X - 10$.

(*b*) If $X = 90$, $Y' = 1.4(90) - 10 = 116$.
(*c*) If $X = 125$, $Y' = 1.4(125) - 10 = 165$.

Notice how reasonable these two answers are. When $X = 90$, the X score is low—one standard deviation below $\bar{X}$. Since the correlation is positive we expect Y' to be low, too. On the other hand, if $X = 125$, the X score is high, so Y' should also be high.

EXAMPLE 12.3

Here are some data that exhibit a strong negative correlation. Compute the regression equation and predict the Y score for someone with $X = 164$.

$$\bar{X} = 200 \qquad \bar{Y} = 90 \qquad r_{XY} = -0.90$$
$$S_X = 9 \qquad S_Y = 5$$

Solution

$$b_{Y \cdot X} = r \cdot \frac{S_Y}{S_X} = (-0.90)\frac{5}{9} = -0.5$$

$$a_{Y \cdot X} = \bar{Y} - b\bar{X} = 90 - (-0.5)(200) = 190$$

Regression equation: $Y' = -0.5X + 190$.

Notice that the regression coefficient is negative. When X is large, Y' is relatively small. When X is small, Y' is relatively large. These figures make sense since the correlation is negative.

If $X = 164$, then $Y' = (-0.5)(164) + 190 = 108$. In this case the value of X is *below* average, and the resulting Y' is *above* average.

Predicting X from Y

Usually an investigator lets Y designate the variable he intends to predict. But occasionally, he needs to predict the X score from the subject's Y score. The regression equation is then written: $X' = b_{X \cdot Y} Y + a_{X \cdot Y}$. Values of $b_{X \cdot Y}$ and $a_{X \cdot Y}$ are needed which make $\sum (X - X') = 0$ and which minimize

$$\sum (X - X')^2$$

Again the least-squares method can be applied, and the resulting values of b and a are:

$$b_{X \cdot Y} = \frac{N \sum XY - (\sum X)(\sum Y)}{N \sum Y^2 - (\sum Y)^2} = r_{XY} \cdot \frac{S_X}{S_Y}$$

$$a_{X \cdot Y} = \bar{X} - b_{X \cdot Y} \bar{Y}$$

The formula for $b_{X \cdot Y}$ is very similar to the formula for $b_{Y \cdot X}$. The only change is that every X in one formula changes to Y in the other and vice versa. In the same way, the formulas for $a_{Y \cdot X}$ and $a_{X \cdot Y}$ are very similar.

If the two regression coefficients $b_{Y \cdot X}$ and $b_{X \cdot Y}$ are multiplied together, their product equals r_{XY}^2 :

$$(b_{Y \cdot X})(b_{X \cdot Y}) = \left(r_{XY} \cdot \frac{S_Y}{S_X}\right)\left(r_{XY} \cdot \frac{S_X}{S_Y}\right) = r_{XY}^2$$

Therefore, whenever you multiply the two b's, the product must be positive; r^2 cannot be negative. Hence, the two b's must have the same sign; both must be positive or both must be negative.

EXAMPLE 12.4

What is wrong with these values of b reported for a set of data:

(a) $b_Y._X = -1$ and $b_X._Y = 0.50$?

Solution According to these values, $r^2 = (-1)(0.50) = -0.50$. But this value of r^2 is impossible, so the two b's are inconsistent.

(b) $b_Y._X = -1$ and $b_X._Y = -3$?

Solution According to these values, $r^2 = (-1)(-3) = +3$. Since r cannot exceed 1, r^2 cannot exceed 1. Hence, the b's are inconsistent.

Also notice the value of b when the standard deviations are equal. In that case, $b_{Y \cdot X} = b_{X \cdot Y} = r_{XY}$. Suppose $S_X = 10$, $S_Y = 10$, and $r_{XY} = .60$. Then

$$b_{Y \cdot X} = r_{XY}\frac{S_Y}{S_X} = (.60)\frac{10}{10} = .60$$

Likewise, if both variables were changed to z scores, both standard deviations would equal 1; so for z scores, $b_{Y \cdot X} = b_{X \cdot Y} = r$.

This result is of historical interest. An early measure of correlation was Sir Francis Galton's measure, which Karl Pearson later elaborated into r. Galton's procedure first equated the variability of the two sets of scores and then determined a best-fitting straight line. The *slope* of this line was Galton's measure of correlation.

12.2 ANALYZING THE Y SCORE INTO COMPONENTS

So far we have examined the predicted Y' values, but we have not yet examined their accuracies. Let us next consider how good the Y' values are and how severe the errors are.

It is convenient to think of a Y score as having two parts: (a) To some extent the score is predictable from X, and (b) to some extent, it is not. That is, Y' makes up one part of the Y score, and $Y - Y'$ the other.

$$Y = Y' + (Y - Y')$$

(Actual score) = (Predicted part) + (Error of prediction)

If Y' happens to equal Y, the error is 0. More usually, though, Y is not predicted perfectly, so there is some error.

Table 12.3 shows each Y score analyzed into its two components. As you know, the mean error equals 0. Also notice the mean Y' value. In Table 12.3 this mean is 50; it equals the mean of the original Y scores. That is,

$$\overline{Y}' = \overline{Y}$$

On the *average*, then, the Y' values are perfect; their mean equals $\overline{Y}$ and the average error is 0.

$$\text{Mean of } (Y - \overline{Y}) = 0$$

The proofs of these points are given at the end of the chapter in Proofs 12.2 and 12.3.

TABLE 12.3 Each subject's Y score analyzed into its two parts

Subject	X	Y score Y	=	Predicted part Y' (i.e., $1.2X + 14$)	+	Error of prediction $Y - Y'$
A	26	32		45.2		−13.2
B	24	40		42.8		−2.8
C	22	44		40.4		3.6
D	33	44		53.6		−9.6
E	27	48		46.4		1.6
F	36	52		57.2		−5.2
G	30	56		50.0		6.0
H	38	56		59.6		−3.6
I	30	60		50.0		10.0
J	34	68		54.8		13.2
$r_{XY} = 0.60$		$\sum Y = 500$ Mean of $Y = 50.0$		$\sum Y' = 500$ Mean of $Y' = 50.0$		$\sum (Y - Y') = 0$ Mean of $(Y - Y') = 0.0$
		$S_Y^2 = 100$		$S_{Y'}^2 = 36$		$S_{Y-Y'}^2 = 64$

Analyzing the variance

Now consider the variability of each set of scores in Table 12.3. The variances are labeled S_Y^2, $S_{Y'}^2$, and $S_{Y-Y'}^2$. Each variance is reported at the bottom of its column. To compute $S_{Y-Y'}^2$, for example, you would subtract the mean of $Y - Y'$ (which equals 0) from each error score, square the deviations, sum them, and divide by N (which equals 10).

As Table 12.3 shows, $S_Y^2 = 100$ and the variances of the parts are: $S_{Y'}^2 = 36$ and $S_{Y-Y'}^2 = 64$. Notice that the variances of the parts together equal the variance of the Y scores.

This relationship is always true. Just as we analyzed the Y score earlier into two parts, we now analyze the Y score *variance* into two corresponding parts:

$$S_Y^2 = S_{Y'}^2 + S_{Y-Y'}^2$$

If $S_Y^2 = 276$ and $S_{Y'}^2 = 176$, then $S_{Y-Y'}^2$ equals 100.

Figure 12.3 shows two graphs. One of them reports each subject's Y score, while the other reports the Y' scores. In the graph on the left, notice the variability among the Y scores. The Y scores range from 32 to 68, and their variance is 100.

Why do the subjects vary so much in their Y scores? Why do they differ from one another? There are many reasons, of course; one important reason is this: Subjects differ in Y *because they differ in X*. Variables X and Y are correlated, so a person who is low on X is probably also low on Y. The correlation between X and Y really *requires* that subjects must differ on one variable if they differ on the other.

The graph on the right shows how much Y score variability is required by variable X: The equation $Y' = 1.2X + 14$ describes the idealized relationship between X and Y, and the X scores range from 22 to 38. Therefore,

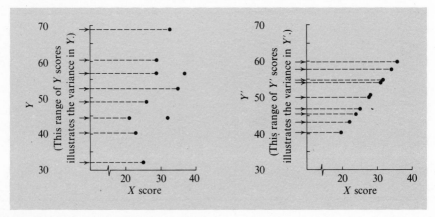

FIG. 12.3 Interpretation of SY^2 and S^2Y'.

given the X-Y relationship, the Y scores must vary, too, from a low of 40.4 (for a subject whose $X = 22$) to a high of 59.6 (for a subject whose $X = 38$). The term $S_{Y'}{}^2$ tells how much Y score variance is expected because of the relationship: 36 points of variance in Y is expected by the variation in X. In this sense, the relationship "explains" some, but not all, of the 100 points of Y score variance. $S_{Y'}{}^2$ is sometimes called "explained" or "predicted" variance.

However, the relationship between X and Y does not fully explain the Y score variance. We still do not understand, for example, why the Y scores can be as low as 32, or as high as 68. Variable X has only explained one part of the Y score variance; the remaining variance is unexplained. This unexplained variance is reflected by the term $S^2{}_{Y-Y'}$. It is sometimes called the "unexplained" or "unpredicted" variance. It tells what part of the Y score variance the regression equation fails to explain. That, by the way, is why we wanted $\sum (Y - Y')^2$ to be small in the first place. The least-squares criterion was designed to minimize $S^2_{Y-Y'}$ so as to *maximize* the explained variance, $S_{Y'}{}^2$.

To summarize, the Y score variance can be analyzed into two parts, $S_{Y'}{}^2$ and $S^2_{Y-Y'}$. The former is called "predicted" or "explained" variance; it tells how much variance in Y can be explained by Y's correlation with X. The latter is called "unpredicted" or "unexplained" variance and tells how much variance in Y cannot be explained.

Variance, uncertainty, and reduction in uncertainty

The more the scores in a set vary, the harder it is to guess any one person's score. If S_Y equaled 0, the Y scores would all be alike. Every subject's score would equal the mean score, and there would be no uncertainty about anybody's score. But as S_Y increases, the range of scores broadens, and our uncertainty about any one person also increases. The larger the variance, the more the uncertainty.

Now suppose I want to anticipate the weight of a man who is about to arrive for testing. Men vary in weight, and I expect these weights to range from, say, 100 lb to 300 lb. Since the scores vary so much, I am uncertain about the weight of the one particular newcomer.

But suppose some variable is correlated with weight—say, height—and suppose I know the newcomer's *height*. My uncertainty about his weight would certainly be reduced to some extent: If he is 6 ft 4 in. tall, I would expect him to be heavy. If he is 4 ft 8 in. tall, I would expect him to be light. As soon as I know his height, my uncertainty is reduced about his weight. Information about X helps to reduce my uncertainty about Y. (Some uncertainty would still exist, of course, since some short people are heavy and some tall people are light: The correlation is not perfect, so $S^2_{Y-Y'}$ is not 0. But if the correlation *were* perfect, no uncertainty would remain at all; I could predict Y without error.)

The term $S_Y{}^2$ describes our uncertainty about a subject's Y score when we have no other information about him. But if X is correlated with Y and we know his X score, then we have less uncertainty about Y. The term $S^2_{Y-Y'}$ tells how much uncertainty continues to exist after X has been used as a predictor.

Relationship to r

So far we have analyzed the Y score variance $(S_Y{}^2)$ into the two parts $S_{Y'}{}^2$ and $S^2_{Y-Y'}$.

$$S_Y{}^2 = S_{Y'}{}^2 + S^2_{Y-Y'}$$
$$100 = \quad 36 + 64$$

What proportion of $S_Y{}^2$ has gone into each part? Clearly, $36/100 = .36$ of it has become explained variance, and $64/100 = .64$ of it has become unexplained variance. These two proportions are related to r.

The term $S_{Y'}{}^2$ is always equal to r^2 of $S_Y{}^2$. (See Proof 12.5 at the end of the chapter.) In the data of Table 12.3, $r^2 = (.60)^2 = .36$; and $.36$ of $S_Y{}^2$ equals $S_{Y'}{}^2$.

$$S_{Y'}{}^2 = r^2 \times S_Y{}^2 \tag{12.6}$$

Or:

$$\frac{S_{Y'}{}^2}{S_Y{}^2} = r^2$$

The term $S^2_{Y-Y'}$ always equals the remaining part of $S_Y{}^2$. It equals $(1 - r^2)$ of $S_Y{}^2$. In the data of Table 12.3, $(1 - r^2) = (1 - .60^2) = .64$; and $.64$ of $S_Y{}^2$ equals $S^2_{Y-Y'}$.

$$S^2_{Y-Y'} = (1 - r^2) \times S_Y{}^2 \tag{12.7}$$

Or:

$$\frac{S^2_{Y-Y'}}{S_Y{}^2} = (1 - r^2)$$

These relationships are summarized below:

$$S_Y{}^2 = S_{Y'}{}^2 + S^2_{Y-Y'}$$

Dividing every term by $S_Y{}^2$:
$$\frac{S_Y{}^2}{S_Y{}^2} = \frac{S_{Y'}{}^2}{S_Y{}^2} + \frac{S^2_{Y-Y'}}{S_Y{}^2}$$

$$1 = r^2 + (1 - r^2)$$

The two proportions, of course, must sum to 1. If $r = .90$, then $.81$ of the Y score variance becomes $S_{Y'}{}^2$, and the remaining $.19$ of the Y score variance becomes $S_{Y-Y'}^2$. If $r = 1.00$, then all of the Y score variance becomes $S_{Y'}{}^2$. In that case, the Y score variance is fully explained, and the error score variance equals 0. When $r = 1.00$, predictions are perfect.

How about the case when $r = 0$? If $r = 0$, $S_{Y'}{}^2 = 0$ and all of the Y score variance becomes error variance. Consider some concrete data. Suppose in a set of data $\overline{X} = 30$, $S_X = 10$, $\overline{Y} = 50$, $S_Y = 10$, and $r_{XY} = 0.00$. Let us write the regression equation for predicting Y':

$$b = r \cdot \frac{S_Y}{S_X} = 0 \cdot \frac{10}{10} = 0$$

$$a = \overline{Y} - b\overline{X} = 50 - 0(30) = 50$$

The regression equation, then, is $Y' = 50$. For every subject, Y' is the same, namely 50; and this Y' happens to equal $\overline{Y}$. (In the absence of a correlated variable, the best single prediction is the mean.) Since all Y' values are the same, $S_{Y'}{}^2 = 0$. A subject's error of prediction, $Y - Y'$, then equals $Y - \overline{Y}$. And the variance of these errors is the same as the variance of the Y scores themselves. When $r = 0$, then, all of the Y score variance becomes $S_{Y-Y'}^2$.

EXAMPLE 12.5

In a set of scores, $S_Y = 15$ and $r_{XY} = .20$. Suppose the regression equation were determined and Y' were computed for each subject. (a) What would the standard deviation of the Y' values be? (b) What would the standard deviation of the errors of prediction be?

Solution (a) $S_{Y'}{}^2 = r^2 \times S_Y{}^2 = (.20)^2 \times (15)^2 = .04(225) = 9.0$. Therefore $S_{Y'} = 3.0$.

(b) $S_{Y-Y'}^2$ can be computed in either of two ways:

(i) $S_{Y-Y'}^2 = S_Y{}^2 - S_{Y'}{}^2 = 225 - 9 = 216$
(ii) $S_{Y-Y'}^2 = (1 - r^2) \times (S_Y{}^2)$
$= (1 - .20^2) \times 15^2 = .96(225) = 216$

Therefore, $S_{Y-Y'} = \sqrt{216} = 14.7$.

12.3 STANDARD ERROR OF ESTIMATE

The variance of the $Y - Y'$ values has a special significance in statistical work. Expressed as a standard deviation, it is written $S_{Y-Y'}$ and is called the *standard error of estimate*. To examine this term more fully, consider the following fictitious situation.

Suppose an investigator were performing research on hypnosis. Whenever he studied an experimental subject, he would have to determine whether or not the individual was susceptible to hypnosis. Therefore, he would first administer a scale of hypnotic susceptibility. That scale, though, might require two hours of the experimenter's time; and if the subject were not susceptible, the two hours would have been wasted. If there were some way to predict in advance who is susceptible, the experimenter could select subjects more efficiently. Therefore, he might first look for some predictor of hypnotic susceptibility.

Perhaps he notes that IQ data exist for most people, and he feels that IQ scores might correlate with hypnotic susceptibility. To test this hunch, he administers a scale of hypnotic susceptibility to a large group of subjects and also obtains their IQs. The data are reported in Table 12.4. The value of r between the two measures is .48, and the best-fitting regression equation is: $Y' = .19X - 9.58$.

TABLE 12.4 Scattergram: IQ data and hypnotic susceptibility scores

Y scores (hypnotic susceptibility)		*X scores IQ* 75–79	80–84	85–89	90–94	95–99	100–104	105–109	110–114	115–119	120–124	*Frequency of Y scores* ↓
		77	82	87	92	97	102	107	112	117	122	
18–19	18.5					1	1	1	2	1	1	7
16–17	16.5				1	3	5	8	7	4	1	29
14–15	14.5		1	1	4	10	19	21	15	7	2	80
12–13	12.5		1	4	13	30	43	38	21	7	2	159
10–11	10.5	1	2	10	30	54	60	43	19	5	1	225
8–9	8.5	1	6	19	43	60	54	30	10	3	1	227
6–7	6.5	2	7	21	38	43	30	13	4	1		159
4–5	4.5	2	6	15	21	19	10	4	1			78
2–3	2.5	2	4	7	7	5	3	1				29
0–1	0.5	0	1	2	2	1	1					7
Frequency of → *X scores*		8	28	79	159	226	226	159	79	28	8	1,000

For these data, $S_Y^2 = 11.30$ (so the standard deviation is 3.36). This variance, of course, can be analyzed into two parts, as usual: $S_{Y'}^2$ and $S_{Y-Y'}^2$.

$$S_{Y'}^2 = r^2 \times S_Y^2 = (.48)^2 \times 11.30 = 2.82$$
$$S_{Y-Y'}^2 = (1 - r^2) \times S_Y^2 = (1 - .48^2) \times 11.30 = 8.48$$

The errors of prediction clearly account for most of the Y score variance—about three-fourths of it.

The standard error of estimate equals $\sqrt{8.48} = 2.91$. This is the figure that we need to consider more fully.

$$S_{Y-Y'} = \sqrt{(1 r - ^2)(S_Y^2)} = S_Y\sqrt{1 - r^2} \qquad (12.8)$$
$$= 2.91$$

Interpretation of $S_{Y-Y'}$

Consider a prediction about one individual—say a subject whose $X = 87$. For him, Y' would equal 7:

$$Y' = .20X - 10.4 = .20(87) - 10.4 = 7.0$$

Now consider *all* the subjects whose X score is 87. Their data appear in one strip of the scattergram, the column for $X = 87$. That strip is shaded in Table 12.4, and it reappears in Table 12.5 as a separate frequency distribution. This distribution is sometimes called a *conditional distribution*—the distribution

TABLE 12.5 Frequency distribution of Y scores for subjects whose $X = 87$

Interval	Y score (midpoint of interval)	Frequency
14–15	14.5	1
12–13	12.5	4
10–11	10.5	10
8–9	8.5	19
6–7	6.5	21
4–5	4.5	15
2–3	2.5	7
0–1	0.5	2
		—
		79

$$\text{Mean} = \text{Lowest midpoint} + i \cdot \frac{\sum(f \times d)}{N}$$

$$= .5 + 2\left(\frac{257}{79}\right) \approx 7.0$$

$$S = \frac{i}{N}\sqrt{N\sum fd^2 - (\sum fd)^2} = \frac{2}{79}\sqrt{79(1,003) - (257)^2} \approx 2.91$$

of Y scores when $X = 87$. It contains 79 cases (79 people had $X = 87$) and its mean and standard deviation are also reported: $\overline{X} = 7.0$ and $S = 2.91$.

Notice in particular that the mean of the distribution equals Y' and the standard deviation equals $S_{Y-Y'}$. Thus, Y' tells the average Y score for all subjects who earned that X score. If $Y' = 7$ when $X = 87$, then the *average* subject with $X = 87$ earned a Y score of 7.0. Furthermore, the value of $S_{Y-Y'}$ tells how much the Y scores vary around Y' (their mean). The larger $S_{Y-Y'}$, the more these subjects vary in their Y scores.

As another illustration, consider a subject in Table 12.4 with $X = 112$. For him, $Y' = 0.20(112) - 10.4 = 12.0$. Notice the distribution of Y scores when $X = 112$; this distribution appears in Table 12.6. The mean and standard deviation are also reported: The mean equals 12.0 and S equals 2.91. Again, Y' tells the average Y score for subjects with $X = 112$. And $S_{Y-Y'}$ tells the distribution's standard deviation.

To summarize: For any given X, there is an entire distribution of Y scores. When the regression equation supplies Y', it tells us the mean of these Y scores. And the standard error of estimate tells us the distribution's standard deviation. A separate distribution of Y scores occurs for each particular X. If these distributions are normal, they can be described as in Fig. 12.4.

The data of Table 12.4 illustrate the theoretically ideal case: N is very large, the regression equation $Y' = bX + a$ passes through the mean Y score

TABLE 12.6 Frequency distribution of Y scores for subjects whose $X = 112$

Interval	Y score (midpoint of interval)	Frequency
18–19	18.5	2
16–17	16.5	7
14–15	14.5	15
12–13	12.5	21
10–11	10.5	19
8–9	8.5	10
6–7	6.5	4
4–5	4.5	1
		—
		79

$$\text{Mean} = \text{Lowest midpoint} + i \cdot \frac{\sum (f \times d)}{N}$$

$$= 4.5 + 2\left(\frac{296}{79}\right) \approx 12.0$$

$$S = \frac{i}{N} \sqrt{N \sum fd^2 - (\sum fd)^2} = \frac{2}{79} \sqrt{79(1,276) - (296)^2} \approx 2.91$$

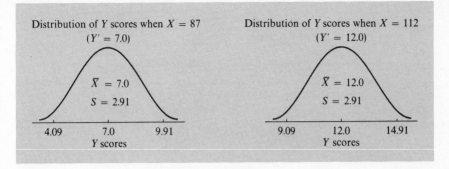

Distribution of Y scores when X = 87 (Y' = 7.0)

$\bar{X} = 7.0$
S = 2.91

4.09   7.0   9.91
Y scores

Distribution of Y scores when X = 112 (Y' = 12.0)

$\bar{X} = 12.0$
S = 2.91

9.09   12.0   14.91
Y scores

FIG. 12.4

of each column, and each distribution has the same standard deviation. In practice, data do not quite achieve this ideal. Instead Y' *approximately* equals the mean of that column's Y scores, and the standard deviation usually varies a little from one column to the next. In fact, $S_{Y-Y'}$ can be viewed as an average of the different column standard deviations. If you assume that these standard deviations differ from one another only by chance, $S_{Y-Y'}$ is an estimate of any one of them.

Two other features of the data of Table 12.4 deserve some comment. First, notice that $S_{Y-Y'}$ is smaller than S_Y. In any given column, the Y scores do not vary as much as the entire set of 1,000 Y scores. With no information about a person's X score, your uncertainty about his Y score is reflected by $S_Y = 3.36$: The person probably falls within 3.36 points of the overall mean. But if you know that $X = 87$, or if you know that $X = 112$, then your uncertainty is reduced. In that case, your uncertainty is reflected by $S_{Y-Y'} = 2.91$: The person probably falls within 2.91 points of Y'.

Secondly, notice the relationship between $S_{Y-Y'}$ and r. When $r = 0$, $S_{Y-Y'} = S_Y$; in that case, $S_{x-Y'}$ is large. However, as r gets closer to 1.00 (or to -1.00), $S_{Y-Y'}$ gets smaller. When r is very large, the X score helps greatly in reducing uncertainty about the Y score. In fact, when $r = 1.00$ (or when $r = -1.00$), no uncertainty remains at all; $S_{Y-Y'} = 0$. In that case, everyone with a given X achieves the same Y score and all of these Y scores are equal to Y'. Perfect predictions occur.

EXAMPLE 12.6
Here are some data: $r_{XY} = .80$, $\bar{X} = 200$, $S_X = 20$, $\bar{Y} = 150$, $S_Y = 15$. (a) Compute the regression equation. (b) If $X = 180$, compute Y'. (c) Suppose the Y scores are normally distributed. Describe the distribution of Y scores for subjects with $X = 180$. (d) If a subject's X score is 180, what is the probability that his Y score is 150 or more?

Solution

(a) $b_{Y \cdot X} = r_{XY} \dfrac{S_Y}{S_X} = (.80)\dfrac{15}{20} = 0.60$

$a_{Y \cdot X} = \bar{Y} - b_{Y \cdot X}\bar{X} = 150 - (.60)(200) = 30$

$Y' = 0.60X + 30$

(b) If $X = 180$, $Y' = 0.60(180) + 30 = 138$

(c) The mean Y score would equal 138. To compute the standard deviation:

$S_{Y-Y'}^2 = (1 - r^2)(S_Y^2) = (1 - .80^2)(15^2) = (.36)(225) = 81$

$S_{Y-Y'} = \sqrt{81} = 9$

The distribution would have this form:

For $X = 180$

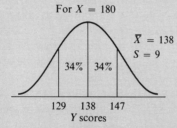

$\bar{X} = 138$
$S = 9$

34% 34%

129   138   147
Y scores

(d) If $X = 180$, the z score for $Y = 150$ in this distribution is:

$z_Y = \dfrac{150 - 138}{9} = \dfrac{12}{9} = 1.33$

Hence, .09 of this distribution falls above 150. If $X = 180$, the probability is .09 that Y exceeds 150—i.e., that Y exceeds $\bar{Y}$. This answer, of course, could be stated as a conditional probability:

$P(Y > 150 \,|\, X = 180) = .09$

Assumptions

Whenever we use the procedures of this chapter, we make certain assumptions, and these assumptions need to be made explicit. They are called the assumptions of *linearity*, *homoscedasticity*, and *normality*.

First, we assume that the relationship between the two variables is *linear*, that is, we assume that a straight line is the best way to describe the relationship. To tell whether data really are linear, you should examine them on a graph. Figure 12.5 shows two examples of *non*linear relationships. *r* would not be appropriate in these cases since *r* tells how well a *straight line* describes the trend, and in these cases a straight line is not the best description. Other techniques exist for fitting a *curve* to data and for measuring the curvilinear correlation.

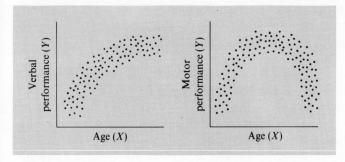

FIG. 12.5

The second assumption is called *homoscedasticity*: Whenever we use the standard error of estimate, $S_{Y-Y'}$, we assume that the Y scores in any single column have essentially the same standard deviation—namely, $S_{Y-Y'}$. "Homoscedasticity" can be translated as "similar variability" in each column of Y scores.

Figure 12.6 is an example of data that are not homoscedastic. If you consider some *low* X score, the Y scores show relatively little variability. But if you consider a high X score, the Y scores show somewhat more variability. For low X scores, the datum points are close to the regression line; for high X scores, they show more scatter about the line. In this kind of case, you would not want to use $S_{Y-Y'}$ as your estimate of every column's standard deviation; it would be too large an estimate for some columns and too small an estimate for others.[1]

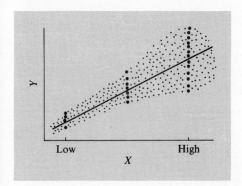

FIG. 12.6

[1] Sometimes, when the data are not homoscedastic, it is possible to transform the scores in some way to make them homoscedastic. For example, each Y could be converted to a logarithm, calling it "log Y." Even though the Y scores do not have equal variabilities, the log Y scores might. Then, if X were plotted against log Y, the homoscedasticity assumption would now be met. The investigator could then proceed to compute the correlation between X and log Y, and the standard error of estimate would now be meaningful.

For data of this kind, the investigator might report results separately for high and low X scores. For low X scorers, the datum points are close to the regression line, so r is high. For high X scorers, the correlation would not be nearly as large. (This feature of the data, by the way, is certainly more interesting than a single value of r. For reasons of this kind, an investigator should always plot his data on a graph before computing r.)

Finally, we sometimes assume that the Y scores within any one column are normally distributed. An investigator usually makes this assumption when he uses the standard error of estimate. If he concludes, for example, that "68 percent of a distribution lies within 2.91 points of 7.0," the figure "68 percent" comes from a table of the normal curve. If the Y scores are not normally distributed to begin with, the inference, of course, is not valid.

Confidence intervals

In Chap. 8 we distinguished between a "point estimate" and an "interval estimate" of μ. The point estimate reports a *single number* as the estimate, while the interval estimate reports a *range* of possible values. The range (or interval) is constructed in such a way that it probably contains μ; the probability that it actually does is called the *level of confidence*. Likewise, when we predict Y from a regression equation, we can state our prediction as a single number Y' (a point estimate), or we can report it as a confidence interval.

Let us illustrate the procedure for establishing a confidence interval with the earlier data that related IQ scores (X) to hypnotic susceptibility scores (Y). In those data, $r = 0.48$ and $S_{Y-Y'} = 2.91$. For $X = 87$, the Y scores formed a normal distribution with a mean of 7.0 (the value of Y') and $S = 2.91$ (the value of $S_{Y-Y'}$) (Fig. 12.7).

If $X = 87$, the best *point* estimate of Y, of course, is $Y' = 7.00$. The following statement, though, might be more informative: The probability is .68 that an individual with $X = 87$ falls within one standard error (i.e., 2.91 points) of 7.00; the probability is .68 that he falls between 4.09 and 9.91. The 68 percent confidence interval, then, is 4.09–9.91.

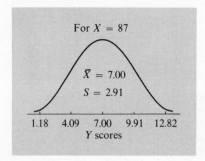

For $X = 87$

$\bar{X} = 7.00$
$S = 2.91$

| 1.18 | 4.09 | 7.00 | 9.91 | 12.82 |

Y scores

FIG. 12.7

The 95 percent confidence interval reports the Y scores that lie within 1.96 standard errors of center. The 95 percent confidence interval extends $(1.96)(2.91) = 5.70$ points on either side of 7.00. The probability, then, is .95 that the individual falls between 1.30 and 12.70. If the person's IQ is 87, he is not at all apt to have a hypnotic susceptibility score of 0, 1, 13, 14, 15, 16, 17, 18, or 19.

In this way the regression equation and the standard error of estimate enable us to establish a confidence interval for predicting a subject's Y score. The procedure can be summarized this way:

68 % confidence interval: $Y' \pm 1\ S_{Y-Y'}$ (12.9)

95 % confidence interval: $Y' \pm 1.96\ S_{Y-Y'}$ (12.10)

99 % confidence interval: $Y' \pm 2.58\ S_{Y-Y'}$ (12.11)

EXAMPLE 12.7

For a set of data, $r = .90$, $S_Y = 10$, and the best-fitting regression equation is $Y' = 1.2X + 17$. A subject has an X score of 80. Establish the 99 percent confidence interval for his Y score.

Solution $Y' = 1.2(80) + 17 = 113$. The standard error of estimate is:

$$S_{Y-Y'} = S_Y\sqrt{1 - r^2} = 10\sqrt{1 - .90^2} = 10\sqrt{.19} = 4.35$$

The 99 percent confidence interval is therefore:

$$Y' \pm 2.58\ S_{Y-Y'} = 113 \pm 2.58(4.35) = 113 \pm 11.22$$

It extends from 101.78 to 124.22.

Procedure with small samples

In Chap. 8 we showed that the standard deviation, $S = \sqrt{\sum (X - \overline{X})^2/N}$, is not a perfect estimate of the population value σ; S systematically underestimates σ. When the sample is large, the bias is minor and can be ignored. But when the sample is small, the bias is severe enough to worry about. A better, unbiased, estimate of σ is $s = \sqrt{\sum (X - \overline{X})^2/(N - 1)}$.

In the same way, $S_{Y-Y'}$ is a biased estimate of the population value. Let us call the population value $\sigma_{Y-Y'}$. If an investigator knew the population value, he would gladly use it whenever he wanted to establish a confidence interval of Y'. But normally he has to estimate the population value from his sample. When the sample is large, he can use $S_{Y-Y'}$ as his estimate. But when the sample contains less than 50 pairs of observations, $S_{Y-Y'}$, seriously underestimates $\sigma_{Y-Y'}$. In that case, a better estimate is:

$$s_{Y-Y'} = \sqrt{\frac{NS_Y^2(1-r^2)}{N-2}} \tag{12.12}$$

This formula is derived from the analysis of variance in more advanced texts.

12.4 REGRESSION TOWARD THE MEAN

An interesting statistical phenomenon, called *regression toward the mean*, is related to the problem of correlation. This phenomenon had historical significance in the development of r, and originally the letter r stood for the word "regression." The phenomenon can be described this way: Let us say that two variables are correlated, but not perfectly. Now suppose we examine people with some given X score. Perhaps the X score is one standard deviation above $\bar{X}$, and perhaps 93 people have this X score. Then suppose we note the Y score of each person in this group and compute their mean. Now the mean of these Y scores would be closer to $\bar{Y}$ than the X score was to $\bar{X}$. If the X score were one standard deviation above $\bar{X}$, the average Y score might be .8 standard deviation above $\bar{Y}$. If the X score were 1.4 standard deviations below $\bar{X}$, the average Y score might be 1.1 standard deviations below $\bar{Y}$. We say that the average Y score for a given X "regresses toward $\bar{Y}$."

To be more concrete, let us consider some fictitious data. Suppose an investigator correlates the IQs of fathers (X) with the IQs of their sons (Y). Imagine data from a very large sample; say $r_{XY} = .80$. For simplicity, let the mean IQ of each generation be 100 and let the S be 15. Then: $\bar{X} = 100$, $S =_X 15$, $\bar{Y} = 100$, $S_Y = 15$, and $r_{XY} = .80$.

Now consider the regression equation for predicting Y (the son's IQ) from X (the father's IQ).

$$b_{Y \cdot X} = r\frac{S_Y}{S_X} = .80\frac{(15)}{(15)} = .80$$

$$a_{Y \cdot X} = \bar{Y} - b_{Y \cdot X}\bar{X} = 100 - (.80)(100) = 20$$

The regression equation is: $Y' = .80X + 20$. Now consider the fathers with IQs of 120; let us predict their sons' IQs: $Y' = .80(120) + 20 = 116$. Therefore, men with IQs of 120, on the average, have sons with IQs of 116. The son's IQ, on the average, is closer to his generation's overall mean, 100, than the father's was. Statistically, we say that the average son's IQ has regressed toward the mean.

On the other hand, consider fathers with IQs of 70. For their sons, $Y' = .80(70) + 20 = 76$. Here, too, the average son has regressed toward the mean; the son's IQ is closer to 100 than the father's was. No matter which X value you select, Y' is closer to 100.

It may seem that the generation of sons is growing more mediocre than the generation of fathers. Generation after generation, you might argue, the scores all seem to be approaching $\overline{Y}$. But this is an illusion. Consider, for example, the geniuses in the two generations. Genius-fathers, in general, produce sons who are not as outstanding as they themselves. However, the younger generation still has its share of geniuses; they do not come exclusively from genius-fathers though: Some are produced by superior fathers, others by lesser fathers, and others occasionally by average, or even below-average, fathers. If you only consider the sons of genius-fathers, you will not spot all the geniuses in the younger generation.

[Regression also occurs in the other direction. Suppose the regression equation were written to predict X (the son's IQ) from Y (the father's IQ). For any given Y, we could then determine the X'. For example, we could consider all the genius-sons and predict their fathers' IQ. Again, the regression phenomenon would be seen: X' would be closer to $\overline{X}$ than Y was to $\overline{Y}$.]

To further clarify this phenomenon, let us transform the raw scores of the regression equation into z score form: The equation itself is $Y' = bX + a$. If X equals $\overline{X}$, the resulting Y' equals $\overline{Y}$. (See Proof 12.4 at the end of this chapter.) Therefore, we can write two equations:

(1) $Y' = bX + a$ (Regression equation, raw score form)   (12.13)

(2) $\overline{Y} = b\overline{X} + a$ (See Proof 12.4)

Subtracting each part of one equation from the corresponding part of the other,

$$(1) - (2) \quad Y' - \overline{Y} = bX - b\overline{X} + a - a$$
$$= b(X - \overline{X})$$

Now let y' represent $(Y' - \overline{Y})$ and let x represent $(X - \overline{X})$. The equation becomes:

$$y' = bx \qquad\qquad (12.14)$$

$$y' = r\frac{S_Y}{S_X}x$$

Rearranging the terms:

$$\frac{y'}{S_Y} = r\frac{x}{S_X}$$

The left term of this equation tells the location of Y' in the distribution of Y scores. This term really reports Y' as a z score: Its deviation from $\overline{Y}$

is divided by S_Y. Let us call this term the "predicted z_Y" and denote it z_Y'. Furthermore, x/S_X equals z_X, so the regression equation can be written:

$$\frac{Y' - \overline{Y}}{S_Y} = r \frac{X - \overline{X}}{S_X}$$

$$z_Y' = rz_X \qquad\qquad (12.15)$$

Therefore, when all scores are in z score form, the regression equation is very much simplified: The slope becomes r, and no other terms are needed.

The regression equation for the father-son IQ data could be written: $z_Y' = .80z_X$. With all scores expressed as z scores, the best prediction of a son's IQ is .80 of his father's IQ. If the father's score is one standard deviation above average ($z_X = 1.00$), the son's score is predicted to be: $z_Y' = .80(1.00) = .80$. Thus, the son is not expected to be as outstanding as the father. In general, sons of such fathers fall less than one standard deviation above average.

What if z_X were negative—say, $z_Y = -2.00$? Then $z_Y' = .80(-2.00) = -1.60$. The predicted value is also negative, but not as extreme as z_X. Again, z_Y' regresses toward the mean value 0.

Regression also occurs when r is negative. In that case z_Y differs in sign from z_X, but its absolute value is closer to 0. For example, if $r = -0.60$ and $z_X = 2.00$, then $z_Y' = rz_X = (-.60)(2.00) = -1.20$.

The amount of regression depends on the size of r. If $r = 1.00$, $z_Y' = z_X$ so the Y score does not regress at all. It remains just as outstanding as X. When $r = 1.00$, the z scores of each pair are identical. On the other hand, if $r = 0$, $z_Y' = 0$ no matter what z_X equals: For any z_X, we expect the Y score to equal $\overline{Y}$. Thus, when $r = 0.00$, regression is complete; for any X, the average Y score is $\overline{Y}$.

The graphs of Fig. 12.8 illustrate the regression phenomenon for different values of r. All scores are plotted as z scores. For $r = 1.00$, the best-fitting line is steepest; its slope equals 1.00. As r gets smaller, the slope becomes flatter; and when $r = 0.00$, the slope becomes 0.

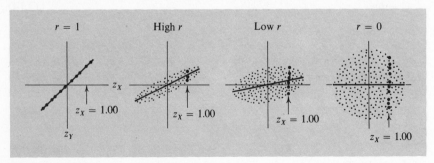

FIG. 12.8

The practical significance of regression

An investigator should always consider the regression phenomenon when he designs a study. Suppose he wants to determine whether a film affects people's attitudes. He might administer a five-point attitude scale to 1,000 subjects and select the 50 highest-scoring subjects. Say their average score is 4.7. These subjects would then see the film, and a week later they would be retested. This time perhaps their mean is 3.9. "3.9" is certainly lower than "4.7." But the drop need not be due to the film. For consider the 1,000 subjects who were tested initially. Suppose all these subjects were tested twice without ever seeing the film. For them, r might equal .80. Perhaps the data would look as in Fig. 12.9.

Notice the subjects who were actually tested on both occasions. Their mean on Occasion 1 is 4.7. And because of regression, their mean on Occasion 2 is lower. Thus, lower ratings are expected on purely statistical grounds. A careful investigator therefore needs a control group for comparison. This control group would be tested on both occasions without ever seeing the film. That way the experimental group's change would be compared to the control group's change.

Subtler examples of regression also occur. Suppose two groups of children are to be tested—one, a brain-damaged group; the other, a normal group. Suppose the groups are to come from two different populations: The brain-damaged population has, say, a mean IQ of 85, and the normal population, a mean IQ of 100. The two populations can be diagramed as two sets (Fig. 12.10).

Now suppose the investigator adopts this strategy: First he draws subjects from the brain-damaged population. Perhaps the scores are 87, 83, 91, and so on; say the mean is 84. Then he locates *normal* subjects to match the brain-damaged subjects. That group's mean would also be 84. (For normal subjects, of course, 84 is 16 points below the population's μ.)

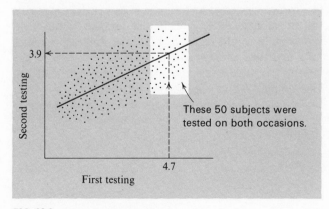

FIG. 12.9

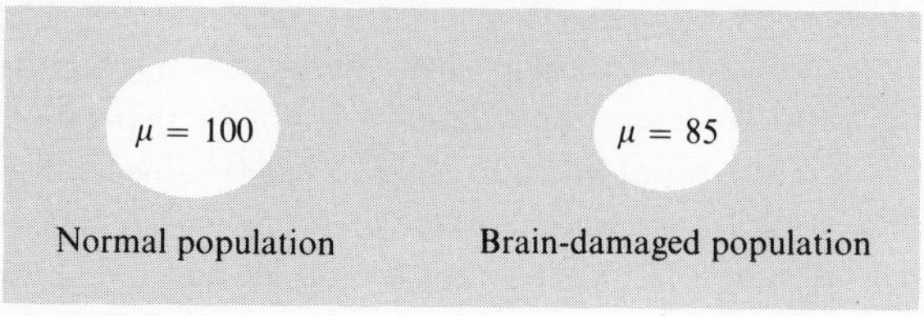

$\mu = 100$ $\mu = 85$

Normal population   Brain-damaged population

FIG. 12.10

Then the two groups might be trained by the same method, and a year later, their IQs would be reassessed. Suppose the training had no effect on IQ. On the second testing the normal subjects would still regress. Their scores had been far below μ on Occasion 1; so on Occasion 2, their mean would rise to, say, 91. The mean of the brain-damaged group, on the other hand, still hovers around its population μ, 85. Thus, the normal subjects, by regressing, would gain 6 points, while the brain-damaged subjects would remain unchanged. In this way the groups could differ on Occasion 2 for purely statistical reasons.

12.5   THE POPULATION PARAMETERS

Throughout this chapter we have discussed the data of *samples*. Ideally, though, an investigator would like to know about the *population*. In theory, we can imagine a regression equation for the entire population: In place of $b_{Y \cdot X}$ we would write $\beta_{Y \cdot X}$, the population parameter. In place of $a_{Y \cdot X}$, we would write $\alpha_{Y \cdot X}$. And the regression equation would become:

$$Y' = \beta_{Y \cdot X} X + \alpha_{Y \cdot X} \quad \text{(Theoretical regression equation for the population)}$$

Thus, a sample's $b_{Y \cdot X}$ can be viewed as an estimate of $\beta_{Y \cdot X}$. And a sample's $a_{Y \cdot X}$ can be viewed as an estimate of $\alpha_{Y \cdot X}$. Different samples would yield different b's, and their average would equal β. Likewise, different samples would yield different a's, and their average would equal α.

Finally, the population's r is usually denoted ρ (rho). Just as b is related to r, β is related to ρ. The sample's b and r are related this way:

$$b_{Y \cdot X} = r_{XY} \frac{S_Y}{S_X}$$

Therefore, in the population:

$$\beta_{Y \cdot X} = \rho_{XY} \frac{\sigma_Y}{\sigma_X}$$

Each sample value, then, is an estimate of some corresponding population value: r is an estimate of ρ; S_Y/S_X is an estimate[1] of σ_Y/σ_X; and $b_{Y \cdot X}$ is an estimate of $\beta_{Y \cdot X}$.

12.6 TESTING THE SIGNIFICANCE OF r

Like any descriptive statistic, r varies from sample to sample. Suppose an investigator examines a sample of 18 cases and computes these data: $r = .60$, $S_X = 2$, $S_Y = 10$, and $b_{Y \cdot X} = 3.0$. Other samples from the same population would yield slightly different values of r, and you can imagine an entire sampling distribution of different sample r's. Furthermore, the mean of this sampling distribution equals ρ, the population value. Usually the value of ρ is not known, so we can only state hypotheses about it. Therefore, we need some procedure to test such hypotheses.

One of the most important questions is this: When $r = .60$, could $\rho = 0$? Could the sample value $r = .60$ be a chance deviation from the population value 0? If so, we would not want to trust the sample's regression equation for making predictions.

Thus, we need to test the null hypothesis that $\rho = 0$. To evaluate this hypothesis, a t test is usually performed. The t test requires that different sample r's be normally distributed; they *are* normally distributed when $\rho = 0$. The t has $N - 2$ degrees of freedom, and it is computed this way:

$$t = \frac{r}{\sqrt{(1 - r^2)/(N - 2)}}$$

$$= \frac{r\sqrt{N - 2}}{\sqrt{1 - r^2}} \tag{12.16}$$

N refers to the number of pairs of observations.

For the data reported above, $r = .60$ and $N = 18$. Let us adopt the .01 level of significance. t (with 16 degrees of freedom) equals:

$$t = \frac{.60\sqrt{16}}{\sqrt{1 - .60^2}} = \frac{.60(4)}{.80} = 3.00$$

---

[1] S_Y is not a good estimate of σ_Y, but S_Y/S_X *is* a good estimate of σ_Y/σ_X. After all, the two S's have identical denominators:

$$S_X = \sqrt{\frac{\sum x^2}{N}} \quad \text{and} \quad S_Y = \sqrt{\frac{\sum y^2}{N}}$$

Therefore, in the ratio S_Y/S_X, these denominators cancel one another. Thus S_Y/S_X is the same as s_Y/s_X. And either ratio estimates σ_Y/σ_X.

A large t would imply that the data and the hypothesis are not compatible. According to a table of the t distribution, $t_{.01} = 2.92$. The sample's $t = 3.00$ exceeds this value, so we reject the null hypothesis at the .01 level; $\rho \neq 0$. Thus, the sample r differs significantly* from 0.

Another way to ask about the significance of r is to ask whether the *slope of the regression line* differs significantly from a population value of 0. Different samples would yield slightly different regression equations, and each one would have its own particular regression coefficient. Again, you can imagine a sampling distribution of sample b's. The mean of the sampling distribution would equal $\beta_{Y \cdot X}$, the population value of b.

Let us therefore ask this question: Could $\beta_{Y \cdot X} = 0$? Might the sample $b_{Y \cdot X} = 3.0$ be a chance deviation from the hypothesized $\beta_{Y \cdot X} = 0$?

The test of this hypothesis happens to be exactly the same as the t test for evaluating hypotheses about ρ. To test the significance of b, first compute the standard error of $b_{Y \cdot X}$:

$$s_{b_Y \cdot x} = \frac{S_Y \sqrt{1 - r^2}}{S_X \sqrt{N - 2}}$$

For the data above:

$$s_{b_Y \cdot x} = \frac{10 \sqrt{1 - .60^2}}{2 \sqrt{16}} = \frac{10(.80)}{2(4)} = 1.00$$

Then perform the following t test with $N - 2$ degrees of freedom:

$$t = \frac{b_{Y \cdot X} - 0}{s_{b_Y \cdot x}}$$

$$= \frac{3.00 - 0}{1.00} = 3.00$$

As before, of course, this t is significant at the .01 level. Hence, the sample $b_{Y \cdot X}$ differs significantly from the hypothesized $\beta_{Y \cdot X} = 0$.

The r-to-z[1] transformation

If ρ is not 0, sample r's are not normally distributed. Therefore, a t test cannot be used to test hypotheses. For example, if $\rho = .80$, the sampling distribution is highly skewed: While sample r's could fall very much *below* .80, they could not fall much *above* .80. In other words, the sampling distribution is negatively skewed. And the farther ρ is from 0, the more skewed it is.

R. A. Fisher, an English statistician, has devised a way to transform different values of r so as to normalize the sampling distribution. He called his

---

[1] Tables exist to tell how large an r is needed for significance at different levels of significance. One such table appears in the appendix as Table A.5.

transformation an "r-to-z transformation," but his z bears no relation to the z score. To avoid confusion, let us call Fisher's value z^* and speak of an "r-to-z^* transformation."

The r-to-z^* transformation can be used for samples of any size and for r's of any value. First the investigator converts his r to a z^*. Then the sampling distribution is normal, so the investigator can perform statistical tests on z^*. The formula for computing z^* is:

$$z^* = \tfrac{1}{2}[\log_e(1 + r) - \log_e(1 - r)]$$

If $r = .40$,

$$z^* = \tfrac{1}{2}[\log_e(1.40) - \log_e(.60)] = 0.424$$

Tables exist for making the conversion automatically; one of these tables appears in the appendix as Table A.6.

Suppose a population has $\rho = .40$; for this population, $z^* = 0.424$. If different samples were drawn from this population, the values of r would not be normally distributed, but the sample values of z^* would be. Sample values of z^* would form a normal distribution around the distribution's mean, 0.424.

The standard error of this sampling distribution is:

$$\sigma_{z^*} = \frac{1}{\sqrt{N - 3}} \tag{12.17}$$

Notice that this standard error only depends on one thing, the sample size. If $N = 28$, $\sigma_{z^*} = 1/\sqrt{N-3} = 1/\sqrt{28-3} = 0.20$. Thus, the standard deviation of the sampling distribution equals 0.20 (Fig. 12.11). Again suppose $\rho = .40$ (so the population $z^* = 0.424$) and suppose a sample of 28 cases is drawn. What value of z^* would you expect for this sample? Since $\sigma_{z^*} = .20$, 95 percent of all random samples would have z^* values in the region: $.424 \pm (1.96)(0.20) = .424 \pm .392$. The probability is therefore .95 that a sample z^* fall between .032 and .816. These values would be more meaningful if they were expressed as r's. With Table A.6 you can convert them back to r's: For $z^* = .032$, $r = .03$; for $z^* = .816$, $r = .67$. Therefore, the probability is .95 that a sample r falls between .03 and .67.

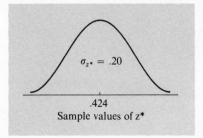

$\sigma_{z^*} = .20$

.424
Sample values of z^*

FIG. 12.11

EXAMPLE 12.8

From a sample of 103 cases, $r = .80$. (a) Establish the 95 percent confidence interval for the correlation coefficient. (b) Test the hypothesis that $\rho = .90$.

Solution   (a) The standard error of z^* is:

$$\sigma_{z^*} = \frac{1}{\sqrt{N-3}} = \frac{1}{\sqrt{103-3}} = .10$$

If $r = .80$, $z^* = 1.099$. The probability is .95 that this z^* is within 1.96 standard errors of the population value. Therefore, the 95 percent confidence interval equals: $1.099 \pm (1.96)(0.10)$. The confidence interval extends from 0.903 to 1.295. Expressed as correlation coefficients, the confidence interval extends from .72 to .86. Therefore, ρ probably lies between .72 and .86.

(b) If $\rho = .90$, the population value of z^* equals 1.472. According to this hypothesis, a sample value of z^* should fall near 1.472. Furthermore, when $N = 103$, $\sigma_{z^*} = 0.10$. Let us now evaluate the hypothesis that $\rho = .90$: Should we consider the sample value $z^* = 1.099$ a chance deviation from the hypothesized $z^* = 1.472$?

$$z = \frac{1.099 - 1.472}{0.10} = \frac{-0.373}{0.10} = -3.73$$

From a table of the normal curve, this z is extreme. Therefore, the two values differ significantly and the hypothesis that $\rho = .90$ can be rejected at the .01 level of significance. The r of .80 does not seem to be a chance deviation from the hypothesized $\rho = .90$.

Testing the difference between two sample r's

The r-to-z^* transformation is also used to tell whether two independent sample r's differ significantly from each other. Suppose an investigator collects two sets of data: The data for 48 girls show $r_{XY} = .72$, and the data for 53 boys show $r_{XY} = .61$. Let us call the former value r_G (for "girls") and the latter value r_B (for "boys"). Do the two r's differ significantly? Does the population of girls show a significantly stronger correlation than the population of boys? Test the hypothesis that $\rho_G = \rho_B$.

Values of z^* are normally distributed, so sample differences $z_1^* - z_2^*$ are also normally distributed. Following the usual pattern, the standard error of the $z_1^* - z_2^*$ difference equals:

$$\sigma_{z_1^* - z_2^*} = \sqrt{\sigma_{z_1^*}^2 + \sigma_{z_2^*}^2}$$

$$= \sqrt{\frac{1}{N_1 - 3} + \frac{1}{N_2 - 3}} \tag{12.18}$$

For these data:

$$\sigma_{z_1{}^*-z_2{}^*} = \sqrt{\frac{1}{45} + \frac{1}{50}} = 0.202$$

Now $r_G = .72$ and $r_B = .61$; as z^* values, they become: $z_G{}^* = .908$ and $z_B{}^* = .709$; and their difference equals 0.199. The standard error of this difference is 0.202.

According to the null hypothesis, the value of $z_1{}^* - z_2{}^*$ in the population equals 0. Does the observed difference, 0.199, differ significantly from 0?

$$\text{C.R.} = \frac{(z_1{}^* - z_2{}^*) - 0}{\sigma_{z_1{}^*-z_2{}^*}} \tag{12.19}$$

$$= \frac{0.199}{0.202} = 0.99$$

This value is then referred to the normal curve. Since the C.R. is small, the null hypothesis is tenable, and the two r's do not differ significantly.

APPENDIX 1: *The Geometry of a Straight Line*

Consider a graph whose X axis and Y axis are ruled off in equal units. Any point on the graph is identified by a pair of numbers: The first number locates the point on the X axis, the second number locates it on the Y axis. A point denoted (3,2) falls at $+3$ on the X axis and $+2$ on the Y axis. A point denoted $(0,-4)$ falls at 0 on the X axis and at -4 on the Y axis. Let us identify the point $(0,-4)$ as P_1 and the point (3,2) as P_2. These two points are shown in the figure below.

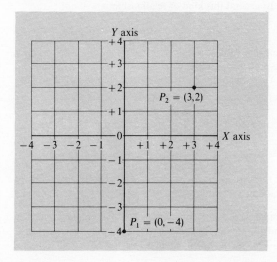

Consider the distance that separates P_1 and P_2—the distance along the X dimension as well as the distance along the Y dimension. Along the X axis there is a 3-point separation. It is customary to call this separation ΔX (delta X):

$$\Delta X = X_2 - X_1 = 3 - 0 = 3$$

Likewise, you can specify the distance between the two points on the Y axis. This distance is called ΔY and equals 6:

$$\Delta Y = Y_2 - Y_1 = 2 - (-4) = 6$$

The slope of the line connecting the two points. Suppose you draw a line connecting P_1 and P_2. The slope of this line is defined as $\Delta Y / \Delta X$. The slope thus equals the change in the Y dimension divided by the corresponding change in the X dimension. For the line connecting P_1 with P_2, the slope is 2. The slope of a line is usually designated b.

$$b = \frac{\Delta Y}{\Delta X} = \frac{6}{3} = 2$$

The following lines exhibit a variety of different slopes.

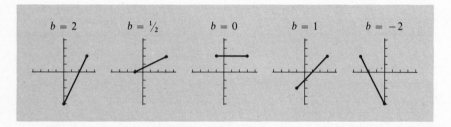

Equation of a straight line. Next consider an equation that tells how X and Y are related. Say the equation is $Y = 3X - 1$. In this relationship Y is a multiple of X with a constant added: Y equals the tripled value of X plus the constant -1. If X is 2, $Y = 3(2) - 1 = 5$. If X is 4, $Y = 3(4) - 1 = 11$. In general this kind of relationship is written:

$$Y = bX + a$$

In the equation b and a refer to constant values.

For the equation $Y = 3X - 1$, consider some different possible values of X and compute the corresponding values of Y. If $X = 2$, then $Y = 5$. If $X = 0$, then $Y = -1$. The following table shows five such pairs:

	If X is:	Then Y is:
Pair 1	-1	-4
Pair 2	0	-1
Pair 3	1	2
Pair 4	2	5
Pair 5	3	8

Each pair in the table can be plotted as a point on a graph. The five points would be: $(-1,-4)$, $(0,-1)$, $(1,2)$, $(2,5)$, and $(3,8)$; they are shown on the graph below. Notice that they fall along a straight line. The equation of this line is said to be $Y = 3X - 1$.

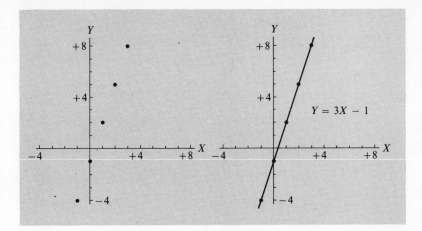

What is the slope of this line? The slope of the line is always the value of b—in this case, 3. To illustrate the slope of 3, choose *any* two points on the line—say, the point (2,5) and the point (3,8). The slope between these two points is $\Delta Y/\Delta X = (8 - 5)/(3 - 2) = 3$. For *any* two points on the line, the slope would be the same. For the points $(0,-1)$ and (2,5), the slope is still 3: $b = (5 - (-1))/(2 - 0) = 3$. Therefore, we say that the line " $Y = 3X - 1$ " has a slope of 3. To report the slope of a straight line, just read the value of b in its equation.

(The term a in the equation tells the value of Y when $X = 0$. In the equation $Y = 3X + 4$, $a = 4$: When X equals 0, then $Y = 4$. The point (0,4) is sometimes called the Y intercept.)

Fractional, zero, and negative slopes. The equation $Y = \frac{1}{3}X - 4$ has a fractional slope, $\frac{1}{3}$. As this line moves from one point to the next, the change in Y is only $\frac{1}{3}$ of the change in X: As X changes 3 points, Y only changes 1 point.

The equation $Y = 0X + 12$, which is usually written $Y = 12$, has a slope of 0. As X changes from one value to the next, Y exhibits no change at all; it always equals 12. Hence ΔY is always 0, so the slope is 0.

Finally, consider an equation with a negative slope: $Y = -4X + 13$. One point on this line is (1,9); another point is (2,5). As X increases one point, Y *decreases* four points. The slope is: $\Delta Y/\Delta X = (5 - 9)/(2 - 1) = -4/1 = -4$. A negative slope reveals a negative relationship; as one variable increases, the other decreases.

APPENDIX 2: *Proofs*

Proof 12.1 *Least-squares solution for determining a and b of regression equation.*

Given: $Y' = bX + a$
Goal: $\sum (Y - Y')^2$ should be a minimum.

First expand $\sum (Y - Y')^2$.

$$\sum (Y - Y')^2 = \sum [Y - (bX + a)]^2 = \sum [Y - bX - a]^2$$
$$= \sum [Y^2 + b^2 X^2 + a^2 - 2bXY - 2aY + 2abX]$$
$$= \sum Y^2 + b^2 \sum X^2 + Na^2 - 2b \sum XY - 2a \sum Y + 2ab \sum X$$

Then differentiate this function with respect to a and with respect to b.

(1) $\dfrac{\partial[\sum (Y - Y')^2]}{\partial a} = 2aN - 2\sum Y + 2b\sum X$

(2) $\dfrac{\partial[\sum (Y - Y')^2]}{\partial b} = 2b\sum X^2 - 2\sum XY + 2a\sum X$

(The symbol ∂ is used in calculus. It is an instruction to take a partial derivative with respect to some variable.) Now set each partial derivative equal to 0.

(1) $2aN - 2\sum Y + 2b\sum X = 0$

$\therefore \ \sum Y = b\sum X + Na$

(2) $2b\sum X^2 - 2\sum XY + 2a\sum X = 0$

$\therefore \ \sum XY = b\sum X^2 + a\sum X$

From these two simultaneous equations, solve for a and b.
First solve for b:

(1) $\sum Y = b\sum X + Na$

(2) $\sum XY = b\sum X^2 + a\sum X$

(1') $\sum X[\sum Y = b\sum X + Na]$

(2') $N[\sum XY = b\sum X^2 + a\sum X]$

(1') $(\sum X)(\sum Y) = b(\sum X)^2 + Na\sum X$

(2') $N\sum XY = Nb\sum X^2 + Na\sum X$

(2' − 1') $N\sum XY - (\sum X)(\sum Y) = Nb\sum X^2 - b(\sum X)^2$

$\qquad\qquad N\sum XY - (\sum X)(\sum Y) = b[N\sum X^2 - (\sum X)^2]$

$$b = \frac{N\sum XY - (\sum X)(\sum Y)}{N\sum X^2 - (\sum X)^2}$$

Now use the value of b to solve for a:

$\sum Y = b\sum X + Na$

$\dfrac{\sum Y}{N} = \dfrac{b\sum X}{N} + \dfrac{Na}{N}$

$\bar{Y} = b\bar{X} + a$

$$a = \bar{Y} - b\bar{X}$$

Proof 12.2   *Proof that* $\overline{Y}' = \overline{Y}$.

Given: $Y' = bX + a$ for every subject.

First sum Y' for all subjects.

$$\sum Y' = \sum (bX + a)$$
$$\sum Y' = b \sum X + Na$$

But, from Proof 12.1, $\sum Y = b \sum X + Na$. Therefore:

$$\sum Y' = \sum Y$$
$$\frac{\sum Y'}{N} = \frac{\sum Y}{N}$$

$$\overline{Y}' = \overline{Y}$$

Proof 12.3   *Proof that the mean* $Y - Y' = 0$.
To compute the mean error score, first sum the error scores:

$$\sum (Y - Y') = \sum Y - \sum Y'$$

As shown in Proof 12.2, though, $\sum Y = \sum Y'$. Therefore:

$$\sum Y - \sum Y' = 0$$

Hence: $\sum (Y - Y') = 0$

$$\text{Mean } (Y - Y') = 0$$

Proof 12.4   *Proof that* $Y' = \overline{Y}$ *when* $X = \overline{X}$.
In general, $Y' = bX + a$.
If $X = \overline{X}$, then:

$$Y' = b\overline{X} + a$$

$$= b\frac{\sum X}{N} + a$$

$$= \frac{b \sum X + Na}{N}$$

$$= \frac{\sum Y}{N}$$

$$Y' = \bar{Y}$$

Proof 12.5 *Proof that r^2 equals the ratio $S_{Y'}^2/S_Y^2$.*
First write Y' and X as deviation scores, as shown in Eq. (12.14). The regression equation becomes:

$$y' = bx$$

Using the deviation score, y', write the variance of the Y' values:

$$S_{Y'}^2 = \frac{\sum y'^2}{N}$$

$$= \frac{\sum (bx)^2}{N} = \frac{b^2 \sum x^2}{N}$$

$$= b^2 S_X^2$$

The ratio then becomes:

$$\frac{S_{Y'}^2}{S_Y^2} = \frac{b^2 S_X^2}{S_Y^2} = \left(b \frac{S_X}{S_Y} \right)^2$$

But $b = r(S_Y/S_X)$. That is, $r = b(S_X/S_Y)$.
Therefore:

$$\frac{S_{Y'}^2}{S_Y^2} = r^2$$

EXERCISES

12.1 Sketch a graph to fulfill the required conditions. Example: r_{XY} is positive and a single regression line best describes the data:

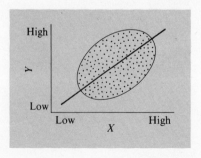

(a)   When X is below $\bar{X}$, $r = .90$; when $X \geq \bar{X}$, $r = .40$.
Answer:

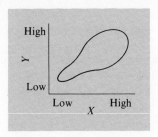

(b)   When X is below $\bar{X}$, r is positive; when $X \geq \bar{X}$, r is negative.
Answer:

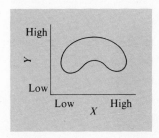

(c)   When X is below $\bar{X}$, r is positive; when $X \geq \bar{X}$, r is zero.
Answer:

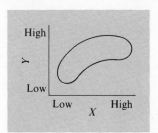

12.2   (a)   The following datum points fall along a line parallel to the X axis ($Y = 4$). Therefore, r equals: (choose one)

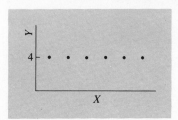

　　(i)　1
　　(ii)　½
　　(iii)　−1
　　(iv)　0
　　(v)　cannot be determined from the information given.
　　Answer: iv

(b)　Datum points all fall along the line $Y' = 0.4X + 9$. Therefore r is: (choose one)
　　(i)　1.0
　　(ii)　1.4
　　(iii)　high and positive
　　(iv)　none of these
　　Answer: i

12.3　(a)　For the following data, r would be:

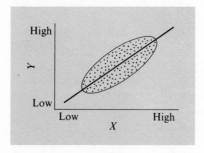

　　(i)　positive and high
　　(ii)　negative and high
　　(iii)　positive and low
　　(iv)　negative and low
　　Answer: i

(b)　For the following data, r would be:

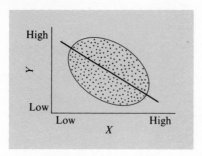

　　(i)　positive and high
　　(ii)　positive and low
　　(iii)　negative and high
　　(iv)　negative and low
　　Answer: iv

12.4 Compute the regression equation for the following sets of data:

(a) X	Y	(b) X	Y	(c) X	Y	(d) X	Y
0	1	−1	2	−2	0	0	0
1	3	0	1	0	2	1	2
2	2	3	−1	2	3	2	3
3	4						
4	5						

Answer: (a) $Y' = .9X + 1.2$

(b) $Y' = \dfrac{-19}{26} X + \dfrac{15}{13}$ or $26Y' + 19X = 30$

(c) $Y' = \frac{3}{4}X + \frac{5}{3}$ or $12Y' = 9X + 20$
(d) $Y' = \frac{3}{2}X + \frac{1}{6}$ or $6Y' = 9X + 1$

12.5 Think of the z score formula for r: In what ways can all of the X scores be manipulated without changing the correlation between X and Y?
Answer: Every score can be increased, decreased, multiplied by, or divided by a constant, and r does not change.

12.6 In a certain set of data, $S_Y = 10$ and $S_{Y'} = 8$.
(a) Compute the standard error of estimate.
Answer: $S_{Y-Y'} = 6$
(b) Compute the value of r_{XY}.
Answer: $r_{XY} = +.80$ or $r_{XY} = -.80$

12.7 Here are three sets of data:

Set A		Set B		Set C	
X	Y	X	Y	X	Y
0	25	3	69	16	0
12	25	9	57	20	52
14	17	12	51	22	84
20	5	15	45	22	18
20	31	19	37	24	74
20	33	21	33	26	40
20	45	25	25	28	96
26	25	28	19	28	48
28	19	31	13	30	116
40	25	37	1	34	132

$\sum X = 200$ $\sum Y = 250$		$\sum X = 200$ $\sum Y = 350$		$\sum X = 250$ $\sum Y = 660$	
$\sum X^2 = 5{,}000$ $\sum Y^2 = 7{,}250$		$\sum X^2 = 5{,}000$ $\sum Y^2 = 16{,}250$		$\sum X^2 = 6{,}500$ $\sum Y^2 = 59{,}560$	
$\sum XY = 5{,}000$		$\sum XY = 5{,}000$		$\sum XY = 18{,}100$	

$\bar{X}$	20		20		25
S_X	10		10		5.0
$\bar{Y}$	25		35		66
S_Y	10		20		40
r_{XY}					

(a) Compute the value of r for each set.
Answer: 0, -1, .80

(b) Plot each set of data on a separate sheet of graph paper. Do not connect the datum points.

(c) Calculate the regression equation for predicting Y from X by the least-squares solution. Draw this line on the graph.
Answer: $Y' = 25$; $Y' = -2X + 75$; $Y' = 6.4X - 94$

(d) What is the slope of this best-fitting line?
Answer: 0, -2, 6.4

(e) Using the regression equation, list a column of Y' scores (i.e., Y score that would be predicted by the equation for each subject).
Answer: Every Y' equals 25; every Y' equals the Y score; 8.4, 34.0, 46.8, 46.8, 59.6, 72.4, 85.2, 85.2, 98.0, 123.6.

(f) Also list a column of $(Y - Y')$ scores—i.e., the errors of prediction.
Answer: Every $Y - Y'$ equals $Y - 25$; every $Y - Y'$ equals 0; -8.4, 18.0, 37.2, -28.8, 14.4, -32.4, 10.8, -37.2, 18.0, 8.4

(g) What is the mean of the Y' column? of the $(Y - Y')$ column?
Answer: 25, 0; 35, 0; 66, 0

(h) What is the total variance of the Y scores?
Answer: 100; 400; 1,600

(i) What is the variance of the "predicted Y-scores"?
Answer: 0; 400; 1,024

(j) What is the variance of the "errors of prediction"?
Answer: 100; 0; 576

(k) Of the total Y variance, what proportion is predictable from the regression equation?
Answer: 0; 1.00; .64

(l) What proportion of the total Y variance is not predictable from the regression equation?
Answer: 1.00; 0; .36

12.8 In a psychological study of stress, 100 subjects were tested on a motor skill task. The same subjects were tested both in a stress condition and in a relaxed condition. The study yielded the following data:

Relaxed Condition (X)   Stress Condition (Y)
$\sum X = 1,000$ $\sum Y = 920$
$\sum X^2 = 10,900$ $\sum Y^2 = 10,064$
$$\sum XY = 9,650$$
$$N = 100$$

(a) Is there a significant correlation between the scores obtained under the two conditions?
Answer: $r = .375$; $t = 4.01$, $p < .01$

(b) What is the regression equation for predicting "stress" scores from "relaxed" scores?
Answer: $Y' = .5X + 4.2$

(c) A new subject comes into the laboratory and under the relaxed condition earns a score of 13. Predict what his score would be under the stress condition.
Answer: Y' = 10.7

(d) Express your answer to (c) as a confidence interval. Report (i) the 68 percent level of confidence, and (ii) the 95 percent level of confidence.
Answer: (i) 10.7 ± 3.7; (ii) 10.7 ± 7.25

12.9 $S_X{}^2 = 4$; $S_Y{}^2 = 4$; $\bar{X} = 0$; $\bar{Y} = 0$; $r = .60$. If $X = 5$, the best prediction of Y is _____.
Answer: 3

12.10 For these data: $\bar{X} = 55$, $\bar{Y} = 100$, $S_X = 5$, $S_Y = 10$, $r_{XY} = 0.50$:

(a) What is the slope of the regression equation for predicting Y from X?
Answer: b = 1.0; Y' = 130

(b) If a person has an X score of 85, what is your best prediction of his Y score?
Answer: 130

12.11 Suppose you computed two regression lines—one for predicting Y from X and one for predicting X from Y. For each pair of numbers below, indicate whether the pair could be the slopes of the two regression lines.

(a) 0.5, 1.5
Answer: Yes

(b) 1.5, 1.0
Answer: No

(c) 0.5, −0.5
Answer: No

(d) −0.5, −0.5
Answer: Yes

12.12 If $r = .5$ and $z_X = 2.0$, $z_{Y'}$ equals _____.
Answer: 1

12.13 Here are some data for two variables:

$$\bar{X} = 50 \qquad \bar{Y} = 100$$
$$S_X = 5 \qquad S_Y = 10$$
$$r_{XY} = .90$$

Consider a person who is exactly one standard deviation above the mean on X. What is the probability that his Y score is below $\bar{Y}$?
Answer: P(Y < 100 | X = 55) = .019

12.14 Test X correlates with both Test A and Test B. $r_{XA} = .90$ and $r_{XB} = .80$. The standard deviation of Test A scores is 10, while the standard deviation of Test B scores is 6. Would Test X give more reliable (trustworthy) predictions of A scores or of B scores? Why?
Answer: A is better; smaller standard error.

12.15   For a set of data, the regression equation is $Y' = .4X + 5$. $r = .8$ and $S_Y = 16$.

(a)   Consider people whose $X = 120$. Describe the distribution of their Y scores.
Answer: Mean = 53, S = 9.6

(b)   If a subject's X score is 120, what is the probability that his Y score is 40 or less?
Answer: $z_{40} = -1.35$; probability = .09

(c)   Establish the 95 percent confidence interval for the Y scores of a person whose X is 120.
Answer: 34.2 to 71.8

12.16   Say IQ scores for a given generation of subjects have $\bar{X} = 100$ and $S = 15$. Furthermore, say the value of r between IQs of fathers and IQs of their sons is .70.

(a)   Consider all fathers whose $z = 2.00$. What is the mean IQ of their sons?
Answer: 121

(b)   Consider all sons with IQs of 130. What is the mean IQ of their fathers?
Answer: 121

12.17   Here are some data: $\bar{X} = 40$, $\bar{Y} = 50$, $S_X = 8$, $S_Y = 6$, and $r_{XY} = 0.0$.

(a)   Compute the mean and standard deviation of the "$X + Y$" scores.
Answer: Mean = 90; $S_{Y+X} = 10$

(b)   Compute the mean and standard deviation of the "$Y - X$" scores (the difference scores).
Answer: Mean = 10; $S_{Y-X} = 10$

12.18   In a certain set of data, the standard deviation of difference scores computed from the z scores ($z_X - z_Y$) is .40. What is the value of r between X and Y?
Answer: $S_{X-Y}^2 = S_X{}^2 + S_Y{}^2 - 2r_{XY}S_XS_Y$, but for z scores, $S_X = S_Y = 1$. Thus, $r_{XY} = .92$.

12.19   A sample of $N = 27$ cases shows that $r = .40$. Test the hypothesis that $\rho = 0$. Use the .05 level of significance.
Answer: $t(25) = 2.2$, H_0 is rejected, $p < .05$

12.20   For a sample of 67 cases, $r = .4$.

(a)   Establish the 99 percent confidence interval for ρ.
Answer: .10 to .63

(b)   Test the hypothesis that $\rho = .3$. Let $\alpha = .05$.
Answer: At $z^* = .310$, C.R. $= 0.92$, so H_0 is accepted.

12.21   Parents' attitudes were correlated with their children's behavior. For 53 mothers, $r = .49$; for 73 fathers, $r = .59$. Do the two r's differ significantly at the .05 level?
Answer: $\sigma_{z_1{}^* - z_2{}^*} = .185$; $z = .76$; $p > .05$; H_0 is accepted.

12.22 Consider the two regression lines for a given set of data:

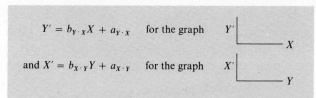

$Y' = b_{Y \cdot X}X + a_{Y \cdot X}$ for the graph Y' [graph: axis X]

and $X' = b_{X \cdot Y}Y + a_{X \cdot Y}$ for the graph X' [graph: axis Y]

(a) Under what condition would $b_{Y \cdot X}$ equal $b_{X \cdot Y}$?
Answer: $S_X = S_Y$

(b) Under what condition would $b_{Y \cdot X}$ and $b_{X \cdot Y}$ both be negative?
Answer: r_{XY} is negative.

(c) Is it possible for one slope to equal 0 and the other to differ from 0?
Answer: No

(d) If $b_{Y \cdot X} = 3$, what are the possible values of $b_{X \cdot Y}$?
Answer: $0 < b_{X \cdot Y} \leq \frac{1}{3}$

12.23 Suppose you read the following statement in an article: "The relationship between X and Y seems to be higher for people with low X scores than it is for people with high X scores." What does this statement imply?
Answer: Nonhomoscedasticity—e.g.,

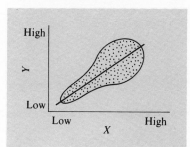

12.24 Suppose the correlation between X and Y is .60 for males, and suppose the correlation between X and Y is also .60 for females. (Think of the data on a graph.) Let both sets of data fall along the same straight line, and let the standard error of estimate be the same for both sets. Try to think of some situation that would cause r to be higher (e.g., .80) when the data of males and females are presented together as one set.
Answer:

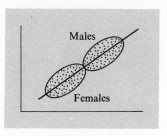

12.25 Algebraically prove that the value of r between the Y' scores and the $(Y - Y')$ scores is 0.

$$Answer: r_{Y'(Y-Y')} = \frac{\sum y'(y-y')}{NS_{Y'}S_{Y-Y'}} = \frac{\sum bx(y-bx)}{NS_{Y'}S_{Y-Y'}} = \frac{\sum bxy - \sum(bx)^2}{NS_{Y'}S_{Y-Y'}}$$

$$= \frac{r_{XY}bS_X S_Y - b^2 S_X^2}{S_{Y'}S_{Y-Y'}} = \frac{r_{XY}bS_X S_Y - b\left(r\dfrac{S_Y}{S_X}\right)S_X^2}{S_{Y'}S_{Y-Y'}} = 0$$

12.26 Algebraically prove that the value of r between the Y' scores and the Y scores is r_{XY}.

$$Answer: r_{Y(Y')} = \frac{\sum yy'}{NS_Y S_{Y'}} = \frac{\sum bxy}{NS_Y S_{Y'}} = \frac{b\sum xy}{NS_Y(bS_X)}$$

$$= \frac{\sum xy}{NS_X S_Y} = r_{XY}$$

13

THE CHI-SQUARE TEST

Statistical methods are based on theoretical distributions. The two most basic distributions are the binomial distribution and the normal distribution. In this chapter we consider one more theoretical distribution—the chi-square distribution. This distribution is derived from the normal distribution. Other distributions—like the t distribution and the F distribution—can then be derived from the chi-square distribution.

The chi-square distribution is mainly used to analyze *categorized* data. The data might report the number of schizophrenics, manic-depressives, and paranoids in a sample; or the number of animals that turned right in a maze and the number that turned left; or the number of Caucasian, Oriental, Chicano, Black, and American Indian children in a school. If an experimenter has a hypothesis about the relative frequency of each category in the population, he could use the chi-square test to compare these hypothesized frequencies with the frequencies he observed in his data.

The chi-square test is also used to study a *relationship* between two variables. Sometimes a variable is not numerical; instead, its "values" are categories. Consider the variable "ethnic origin" and the variable "psychiatric disorder." An investigator might want to see if these two variables are correlated: Perhaps people of Mediterranean descent are more prone to one disorder, while those of Nordic descent are more prone to another disorder. The chi-square test can be used to examine this kind of relationship.

Let us begin by considering the simplest application of the chi-square test. The problem we consider can also be treated by the binomial distribution, using the method of Chap. 7. After we have treated the problem by both methods, we shall examine the relationship between them.

13.1   DATA TREATED BY TWO METHODS

Let us test a hypothesis about a population's p. First we shall use the binomial distribution, then we shall use the chi-square distribution.

EXAMPLE 13.1

An investigator studied 64 rats. Each rat was placed in a two-choice maze. The animal could turn right or left. A different odor occurred in each arm of the maze, so the experimenter could determine the animal's preference. Forty-four rats turned right. Use the .01 level, and test the hypothesis that the population's p equals .50.

Solution H_0 claims that $p_{pop} = .50$. H_1 claims that $p_{pop} \neq .50$. According to H_0, the sampling distribution of 64 rat samples would be described by the binomial expansion $(.50 + .50)^{64}$:

$$(p + q)^{64} = (\tfrac{1}{2} + \tfrac{1}{2})^{64} = (\tfrac{1}{2})^{64} + 64(\tfrac{1}{2})^{63}(\tfrac{1}{2}) + \cdots$$

The distribution's mean is $\mu = np = 32$; its standard deviation is $\sigma = \sqrt{npq} = 4$. This binomial distribution can be approximated by the normal curve:

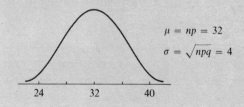

$$\mu = np = 32$$
$$\sigma = \sqrt{npq} = 4$$

In the one sample, 44 animals turned right. To evaluate this result, we form a z score:

$$z = \frac{|44 - 32| - \frac{1}{2}}{4} = 2.875$$

(Without the correction for continuity, the z score would be: $z = (44 - 32)/4 = 3.00$. This value is not quite as accurate, but the error is small when n is large.) Finally, we make a decision. z is large, so H_0 is rejected at $p < .01$.

Now let us treat the data by the chi-square test. First we need to prepare a table that tells how many animals turned right and how many turned left. These frequencies are called "observed frequencies"; they are denoted as f_i. Then we compute the theoretical frequencies: H_0 claims that $p_{pop} = .50$. According to this hypothesis, .50 (64) = 32 rats should turn right, and 32 rats should turn left. These hypothesized frequencies are called "expected frequencies"; they are denoted as F_i. The two sets of frequencies are shown in Table 13.1.

TABLE 13.1   Observed and expected frequencies in Example 13.1

	Number of right turns	Number of left turns	Total
Observed frequencies (f_i)	44	20	64
Expected frequencies (F_i)	32	32	64

To perform a chi-square test, note each column's f_i and F_i. Column 1's frequencies are denoted f_1 and F_1; they equal 44 and 32. Column 2's frequencies are denoted f_2 and F_2; they equal 20 and 32. If H_0 is valid, each f_i should be close to the corresponding F_i. Now consider each difference and square it: $(f_i - F_i)^2$. Then divide this squared quantity by F_i. Do the same for each column and sum. If there are k columns, we write the sum as:

$$\sum_k \frac{(f_i - F_i)^2}{F_i}$$

The resulting quantity is called a *chi-square*; we denote it χ^2, using the Greek letter χ (pronounced *kye*). This quantity is sometimes called the Pearson χ^2 in honor of the statistician Karl Pearson who devised it. For the data:

$$\chi^2 = \sum_k \frac{(f_i - F_i)^2}{F_i} \tag{13.1}$$

$$= \frac{(44 - 32)^2}{32} + \frac{(20 - 32)^2}{32}$$

$$= \frac{(12)^2}{32} + \frac{(-12)^2}{32} = 9.0$$

A correction for continuity can also be incorporated into this χ^2. This correction makes the computation a little more precise. To use it, subtract .5 from the absolute difference $|f_i - F_i|$ and square the result. Then divide by F_i and sum:

$$\chi^2_{\text{With correction for continuity}} = \frac{(|44 - 32| - \frac{1}{2})^2}{32} + \frac{(|20 - 32| - \frac{1}{2})^2}{32}$$

$$= \frac{(11.5)^2}{32} + \frac{(11.5)^2}{32} = 8.265625$$

The χ^2 obtained in this way is related to the z in the example. When the z is squared, it equals χ^2.

With the correction for continuity: $z = 2.875$
$$\chi^2 = 8.265625 = (2.875)^2 = z^2$$

Without the correction for continuity: $z = 3.00$
$$\chi^2 = 9.00 = (3.00)^2 = z^2$$

Thus χ^2 can be viewed as z^2 in examples of this kind. Table 13.2 summarizes the computations. And Proof 13.1 in the chapter appendix proves that they are equivalent.

How shall we interpret the χ^2 statistic? Suppose the observed and expected frequencies agreed perfectly. Then every $f_i - F_i$ would be 0. The resulting χ^2 would equal 0. When $\chi^2 = 0$, the observed frequencies perfectly match the hypothesized frequencies. When f_i and F_i disagree, the χ^2 is larger. In general the larger the difference, the larger the χ^2. A large χ^2 shows that observed frequencies do not jibe with hypothesized frequencies.

Usually, of course, f_i and F_i differ a little by chance. We need to know how large a χ^2 is usual. What values are expected by chance? A table exists to answer such questions; it is called a table of the chi-square distribution. Table 13.3 shows part of that table.

According to the table, the probability is .25 that χ^2 is 1.323 or higher. The probability is only .05 that χ^2 is 3.841 or higher. A χ^2 beyond 6.635 is very rare; such values only occur .01 of the time.

In Example 13.1, $\chi^2 = 9.0$ (with the correction for continuity, 8.3). How often do χ^2 values this large or larger occur by chance? According to the table, such values rarely happen by chance—$p < .01$. Therefore, H_0 is rejected at the .01 level of significance.

The following examples further illustrate the chi-square test. Example 13.2 repeats the problem that was described in Example 7.2 and solves it by the chi-square method.

TABLE 13.2 Two ways to test the hypothesis that $p_{pop} = .50$

Using the binomial distribution	Using the chi-square distribution
DATA: 44 animals out of 64 turned right	DATA: 44 animals out of 64 turned right

ACCORDING TO H_0:

$\mu = np = 32$

$\sigma = \sqrt{npq} = 4$

TABLE:

	Right	Left
f_i (observed)	44	20
F_i (expected)	32	32

TEST: $z = \dfrac{X - \mu}{\sigma}$

$= \dfrac{44 - 32}{4} = 3.0$

$= 3.0$

TEST: $\chi^2 = \sum_k \dfrac{(f_i - F_i)^2}{F_i}$

$= \dfrac{(44 - 32)^2}{32} + \dfrac{(20 - 32)^2}{32}$

$= 9.0 = (3.0)^2$

WITH CORRECTION FOR CONTINUITY:

$z = \dfrac{|X - \mu| - \frac{1}{2}}{4}$

$= \dfrac{|44 - 32| - \frac{1}{2}}{4}$

$= 2.875$

WITH CORRECTION FOR CONTINUITY:

$\chi^2 = \sum_k \dfrac{(|f_i - F_i| - \frac{1}{2})^2}{32}$

$= \dfrac{(|44 - 32| - \frac{1}{2})^2}{32} + \dfrac{(|20 - 32| - \frac{1}{2})^2}{32}$

$= 8.265625 = (2.875)^2$

TABLE 13.3 Part of a table of the chi-square distribution

Value of χ^2	.004	.016	.102	.455	1.323	2.706	3.841	6.635	10.828
Chance probability of this χ^2 or any larger value	.98	.90	.75	.50	.25	.10	.05	.01	.001

EXAMPLE 13.2

An investigator conducted a political poll. One hundred people were polled; 60 of them favored the issue and voted "yes." Test the hypothesis that $p_{pop} = .50$. Adopt the .05 level of significance.

Solution First state $H_0: p_{pop} = .50$. Then state $H_1: p_{pop} \neq .50$. According to H_0, half the people should vote "yes," and half should vote "no." The following table shows the expected frequencies. It also shows the observed frequencies.

	Yes votes	No votes
Observed frequencies	60	40
Expected frequencies	50	50

Next we compute χ^2:

$$\chi^2_{\text{With correction for continuity}} = \sum \frac{(|f_i - F_i| - \frac{1}{2})^2}{F_i}$$

$$= \frac{(|60 - 50| - \frac{1}{2})^2}{50} + \frac{(|40 - 50| - \frac{1}{2})^2}{50}$$

$$= 3.61$$

According to the tabled values, this χ^2 is not unusual; values this size or larger occur more than .05 of the time. Therefore, we accept the hypothesis that $p_{\text{pop}} = .50$. The observed frequencies are compatible with the expected frequencies.

Again notice the relationship between χ^2 and the z score reported in Example 7.2. In that example $z = 1.90$. In the present example, $\chi^2 = (1.90)^2 = 3.61$.

EXAMPLE 13.3

One hundred voters were polled on an issue. Sixty voted "yes" and 40 voted "no." Test the hypothesis that $p_{\text{pop}} = .70$.

Solution First state H_0: $p_{\text{pop}} = .70$. Then state H_1: $p_{\text{pop}} \neq .70$. According to H_0, $.70(100) = 70$ people should vote "yes." The following table shows the observed and expected frequencies.

	Yes votes	No votes
Observed frequencies	60	40
Expected frequencies	70	30

Then we compute χ^2.

$$\chi^2_{\text{With correction for continuity}} = \frac{(|60 - 70| - \frac{1}{2})^2}{70} + \frac{(|40 - 30| - \frac{1}{2})^2}{30}$$

$$= \frac{(9.5)^2}{70} + \frac{(9.5)^2}{30} = 4.30$$

The critical χ^2 at the .05 level is 3.841. Thus, 4.30 is extreme. Values this size or larger have a low chance probability: $p < .05$. Therefore, H_0 is rejected; we infer that $p_{\text{pop}} \neq .70$.

13.2 GENERATING A CHI-SQUARE DISTRIBUTION

What is the chi-square distribution, and how is it generated? In theory, it is derived from the normal curve. Imagine a normal distribution of X scores. Suppose each score is converted to a z score; then the z scores are normally distributed, too. Then suppose every z score is squared. This distribution of squared z scores is a chi-square distribution.

To be more concrete, let us approximate a normal distribution. Consider the binomial expansion $(p + q)^n = (\frac{1}{2} + \frac{1}{2})^9$. This distribution is shown in Table 13.4. Its scores range from 0 to 9. Its mean is 4.5, and its standard deviation is 1.5. Distributions of this kind were described in Chap. 6.

TABLE 13.4 An approximation of the normal distribution through $(p + q)^n = (\frac{1}{2} + \frac{1}{2})^9$

X score	Probability	z score	Probability
9	.001953125	3.0000	.001953125
8	.017578125	2.3333	.017578125
7	.070312500	1.6667	.070312500
6	.164062500	1.0000	.164062500
5	.246093750	0.3333	.246093750
4	.246093750	-0.3333	.246093750
3	.164062500	-1.0000	.164062500
2	.070312500	-1.6667	.070312500
1	.017578125	-2.3333	.017578125
0	.001953125	-3.0000	.001953125

The binomial expansion lets us record each score's probability. The probability of m successes is $[n!/m! \, (n - m)!] \, (\frac{1}{2})^m (\frac{1}{2})^{n-m}$. The probability of the score 6, for example, equals $[9!/6! 3!] \, (\frac{1}{2})^6 \, (\frac{1}{2})^3 = .164$. To approximate the normal curve, we view each score as a category. The score "6" extends from 5.5 to 6.5. Theoretically, then, the probability is .164 that a score lies between 5.5 and 6.5.

We can also convert each score to a z score. The score "7" becomes: $(7 - 4.5)/1.5 = 1.67$. "7" is therefore 1.67 standard deviations from the center. Table 13.4 shows the various z scores too. From now on, let us think in terms of z scores, rather than X scores: The z scores are normally distributed, their mean is 0, and their standard deviation is 1.0. We can also consider the *probability* of each z score. These probabilities are shown in Table 13.4. The probability that $z = 3.00$ is .002—the same as the probability that $X = 9$.

Figure 13.1 shows the probabilities graphically. We could describe these probabilities by a histogram or by a polygon. The smooth curve in Fig. 13.1 approximates the normal curve.

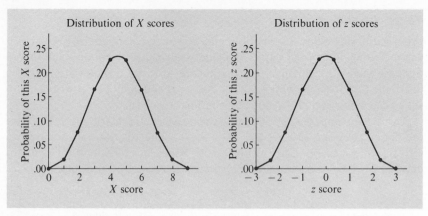

FIG. 13.1   An approximation of the normal curve through $(p + q)^n = (\frac{1}{2} + \frac{1}{2})^9$.

The distribution can also be drawn in ogive form. Suppose we wanted to know the probability that z equals 2.33 or more. Table 13.5 reports probabilities of this kind. To compute these probabilities, select any X score—say, 6. What is the probability that X equals 6 or more? "6" really denotes a category from 5.5 to 6.5. The category as a whole has a probability of .164. Therefore, we divide the probability in half to describe just the scores between 6.0 and 6.5: $\frac{1}{2}$ (.164) = .082. The probability of "6" or more is therefore taken to be: .082 plus the probability of each higher category: .082 + .070 + .018 + .002 = .172. Probabilities of this kind are shown in Fig. 13.2. Again, the graph can be plotted in terms of X scores or z scores.

Now let us consider *squared* z scores. For example, what is the probability that $z^2 = 9$? z^2 equals 9 when $z = 3.00$ and when $z = -3.00$. How often

TABLE 13.5   The probability of each score or any higher value

X score	Probability of this score or any higher value	z score	Probability of this score or any higher value
9	.0009765625	3.0000	.0009765625
8	.0107421875	2.3333	.0107421875
7	.0546875000	1.6667	.0546875000
6	.1718750000	1.0000	.1718750000
5	.3769531250	0.3333	.3769531250
4	.6230468750	−0.3333	.6230468750
3	.8281250000	−1.0000	.8281250000
2	.9453125000	−1.6667	.9453125000
1	.9892578125	−2.3333	.9892578125
0	.9990234375	−3.0000	.9990234375

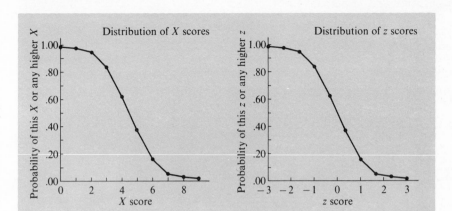

FIG. 13.2 An approximation of the normal curve (in ogive form).

does that happen? From Table 13.6, each probability is .002. Therefore, the probability that z is "$+3.00$ or -3.00" equals $.002 + .002 = .004$. The probability is therefore .004 that $z^2 = 9.00$. This result is shown in Table 13.6.

How about the probability that $z^2 = 1.00$? $z = 1.00$ when $z = +1.00$ and when $z = -1.00$. The probability that $z^2 = 1.00$ therefore equals: $.164 + .164 = .328$. The probability of each z^2 value is computed the same way.

TABLE 13.6 An approximation of the chi-square distribution

z score	z^2 (or χ^2)	Probability of this z^2
$+3.0000$ or -3.0000	9.0000	2 (.001953125) = .003906250
$+2.3333$ or -2.3333	5.4444	2 (.017578125) = .035156250
$+1.6667$ or -1.6667	2.7778	2 (.070312500) = .140625000
$+1.0000$ or -1.0000	1.0000	2 (.164062500) = .328125000
$+0.3333$ or -0.3333	0.1111	2 (.246093750) = .492187500

The z^2 value is called a χ^2. Figure 13.3 shows each χ^2 and its probability. The graph as a whole is called a chi-square distribution. Notice how skewed it is. All values are positive (since they are *squared* numbers). And the larger the value, the less probable it is.

The distribution can also be drawn as an ogive. Table 13.7 reports the probabilities in ogive form. For example, it tells the probability that χ^2 equals 0.11 or more; that probability is .754. These *ogive probabilities* are shown in Fig. 13.4.

A table of the chi-square distribution describes that kind of distribution. Suppose we needed the probability that χ^2 is 8.3 or more. We could consult

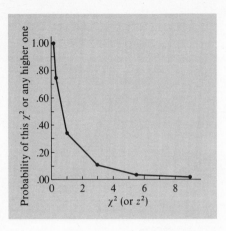

FIG. 13.3   An approximation of the chi-square distribution.

TABLE 13.7   An approximation of the chi-square distribution with probabilities reported as ogive probabilities

z^2 (or χ^2)	Probability of this z^2 or any higher value
9.0000	.0019531250
5.4444	.0214843750
2.7778	.1093750000
1.0000	.3437500000
0.1111	.7539062500

Fig. 13.4 or Table 13.3: Values above 8.3 are rare; they occur less than .01 of the time.

Thus, the binomial distribution can be used to approximate a chi-square distribution. To derive the theoretical chi-square distribution, though, we

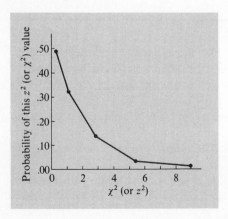

FIG. 13.4   An approximation of the chi-square distribution (in ogive form).

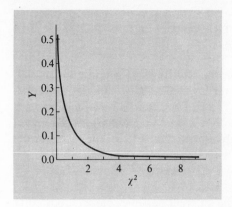

FIG. 13.5 A theoretical chi-square distribution.

would begin with the normal curve itself. Using the methods of calculus, we would square each z score and examine the resulting curve. The theoretical distribution is shown in Fig. 13.5.

Let us summarize. To derive the chi-square distribution, we consider a variable that is normally distributed. This variable gets converted to z score form; its mean is 0 and its standard deviation is 1. Its scores can be positive or negative, and 68 percent of them lie between $z = -1$ and $z = +1$.

Then we square each z score. The distribution of z^2 values is the chi-square distribution. Unlike the normal distribution, it is very skewed. Its values are only positive. In a *normal* distribution, 68 percent of the cases fall between $z = -1$ and $z = +1$; as *squared* values, they fall between 0 and 1. Therefore, 68 percent of the chi-square distribution falls between $z^2 = 0$ and $z^2 = 1$.

This chi-square distribution is said to have 1 degree of freedom; we usually denote the chi-square value $\chi^2_{(1)}$. The meaning of the term *1 degree of freedom* will become clear in the next section.

EXAMPLE 13.4

A distribution of scores is normally distributed. Its mean is 100, and its standard deviation is 10. What is the probability that a score lies more than 19.6 points away from the mean (in either direction)? First use the normal curve to answer the question; then use the chi-square distribution.

Solution The scores that are 19.6 points from the mean are 80.4 and 119.6. The corresponding z scores are -1.96 and $+1.96$. Therefore, .025 of the normal curve's area falls in each tail, so the probability is .05.

To use the chi-square distribution, let us square the z score: $\chi^2_{(1)} = z^2 = (1.96)^2 = 3.84$. How often do χ^2 values exceed 3.84? According to the information in Table 13.3, that probability is .05.

13.3   THE CHI-SQUARE DISTRIBUTION WITH 2 OR MORE DEGREES OF FREEDOM

Imagine a normal distribution of z scores. But this time suppose the investigator draws *two* z scores. He selects them independently, squares each one, and adds them together: $z_1^2 + z_2^2$. We call this quantity a *chi-square with 2 degrees of freedom*: $\chi^2_{(2)} = z_1^2 + z_2^2$. Now suppose the procedure is repeated many times. We can imagine a distribution of these $\chi^2_{(2)}$ values. This distribution is the chi-square distribution with 2 degrees of freedom.

To approximate this distribution, we consider the z^2 values in Table 13.7. The z^2 values are: 0.11, 1.00, 2.78, 5.40, and 9.00. Suppose we select two values at random and sum them; what are the different possible combinations? 0.11 might combine with 0.11; or with 1.00; or with 2.78; and so on. For each combination, we could record the value of $z_1^2 + z_2^2$. We could also compute its probability: suppose $z_1^2 = 2.78$ and $z_2^2 = 5.40$; their sum is 8.18. The probability of this combination is $(.141)(.035) = .005$. Or suppose $z_1^2 = 5.40$ and $z_2^2 = 1.00$; their sum is 6.40. The probability of this combination is $(.035)(.328) = .011$.

In this way we record each sum and its probability. Table 13.8 shows all the combinations, and Table 13.9 presents them as a frequency distribution. Table 13.9, then, describes the different $\chi^2_{(2)}$ values and their probabilities. Figure 13.6 shows the distribution graphically.

The distribution in Fig. 13.6 is based on the binomial distribution so it only *approximates* the theoretical distribution. Theoretically the distribution is derived from the normal curve; the theoretical distribution is shown in Fig. 13.7.

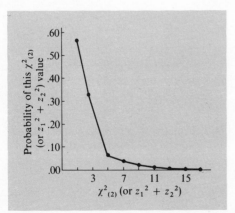

FIG. 13.6   An approximation of the chi-square distribution (based on Table 13.9).

TABLE 13.8 Different values of $z_1^2 + z_2^2$ (the probability of each value is also reported)

		Value of z_2^2			
		0.11	1.00	2.78	5.40	9.00
Value of z_1^2	0.11	0.22 $P = (.492)(.492)$ $= .242$	1.11 $P = (.492)(.328)$ $= .161$	2.89 $P = (.492)(.141)$ $= .069$	5.51 $P = (.492)(.035)$ $= .017$	9.11 $P = (.492)(.004)$ $= .002$
	1.00	1.11 $P = (.328)(.492)$ $= .161$	2.00 $P = (.328)(.328)$ $= .108$	3.78 $P = (.328)(.141)$ $= .046$	6.40 $P = (.328)(.035)$ $= .011$	10.00 $P = (.328)(.004)$ $= .001$
	2.78	2.89 $P = (.141)(.492)$ $= .069$	3.78 $P = (.141)(.328)$ $= .046$	5.56 $P = (.141)(.141)$ $= .020$	8.18 $P = (.141)(.035)$ $= .005$	11.78 $P = (.141)(.004)$ $= .001$
	5.40	5.51 $P = (.035)(.492)$ $= .017$	6.40 $P = (.035)(.328)$ $= .011$	8.18 $P = (.035)(.141)$ $= .005$	10.80 $P = (.035)(.035)$ $= .001$	14.40 $P = (.035)(.004)$ $= .000$
	9.00	9.11 $P = (.004)(.492)$ $= .002$	10.00 $P = (.004)(.328)$ $= .001$	11.78 $P = (.004)(.141)$ $= .001$	14.40 $P = (.004)(.035)$ $= .000$	18.00 $P = (.004)(.004)$ $= .000$

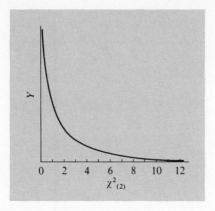

FIG. 13.7 Theoretical chi-square distribution when df = 2.

In general, the values of $\chi^2_{(2)}$ are larger than those of $\chi^2_{(1)}$: What is the mean value of $\chi^2_{(2)}$? To answer this question, we compute the expectation[1] of $z_1^2 + z_2^2$.

$$
\begin{aligned}
\mathrm{E}[z_1^2 + z_2^2] &= \mathrm{E}[z_1^2] + \mathrm{E}[z_2^2] \\
&= \quad 1 \quad + \quad 1 \\
&= \quad 2
\end{aligned}
$$

Thus, the average value of $\chi^2_{(2)}$ is 2.

Tables exist for describing the theoretical distribution of $\chi^2_{(2)}$. One of these tables appears as Table A.4 in the appendix. To use this table, consult the line labeled "2 df." According to the table, "5.991" cuts off the highest 5 percent of the distribution, and "9.210" cuts off the highest 1 percent.

We can also define $\chi^2_{(3)}$ as the sum of *three* independent z^2 values. $\chi^2_{(3)} = z_1^2 + z_2^2 + z_3^2$. Suppose an experimenter independently draws three z^2 values and sums them. If the procedure is repeated many times, an entire distribution could be formed. This distribution is the chi-square distribution with 3 df. Its mean is 3.

In general, we can imagine any number of squared z scores summed together. Suppose there are v of them. (v is the Greek letter nu.) The resulting sum is denoted $\chi^2_{(v)}$. The distribution of these sums is called a chi-square

---

[1] The concept of "expectation" was discussed in Sec. 5.2. A term's expectation is the value we expect on the average. The expectation of X is μ—the value we expect in the long run. Section 8.5 considered another expectation, the expectation of s^2: Over many samples, the average value of s^2 is σ^2. Therefore, the expectation of s^2 is σ^2; $\mathrm{E}(s^2) = \sigma^2$.

To do this derivation, we need to consider the expectation of z^2. $\mathrm{E}(z^2)$ is the value of z^2 expected in the long run—the mean value. Suppose we average z^2 over many, many cases: $\Sigma z^2/N$. This average is the same as the *variance* of many z scores. And, the variance of a set of z scores is 1 (see Sec. 4.6). Therefore, we expect z^2 to equal 1 on the average, so the expectation of z^2 is 1: $\mathrm{E}(z^2) = 1$.

TABLE 13.9 Frequency distribution to show different values of $z_1{}^2 + z_2{}^2$

Value of $z_1{}^2 + z_2{}^2$	Probability
18.00–19.99	.000
16.00–17.99	.000
14.00–15.99	.000
12.00–13.99	.000
10.00–11.99	.005
8.00–9.99	.014
6.00–7.99	.022
4.00–5.99	.054
2.00–3.99	.338
0.00–1.99	.564

distribution with v df. Thus, v is the number of degrees of freedom;[1] it tells how many z^2 values have been summed. The distribution's mean always equals v.

Some representative distributions are shown in Fig. 13.8. For low values of v, the distribution is skewed. As v increases, the distribution becomes less skewed. And as v gets very large, the distribution comes to resemble a normal distribution.

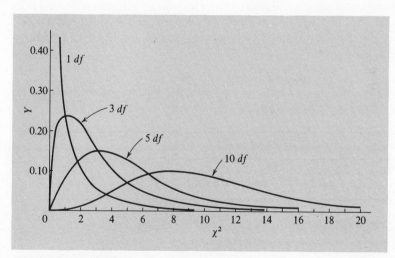

FIG. 13.8 Various theoretical chi-square distributions.

[1] The number of degrees of freedom is denoted in either of two ways—v or df.

Table A.4 in the appendix describes various chi-square distributions. For each value of v, it tells the critical values of χ^2. For example, consider the chi-square distribution with 7 degrees of freedom: 14.067 bounds the highest 5 percent of the distribution; 18.475 bounds the highest 1 percent. As another example, consider the distribution with 13 degrees of freedom: 22.362 bounds the highest 5 percent of that distribution; 27.688 bounds the highest 1 percent.

13.4   APPLICATIONS: GOODNESS OF FIT TESTS

Now let us examine some applications. In each problem the data are categorized. The investigator wants to test a hypothesis about each category's relative frequency in the population. The chi-square test is used to compare the observed and expected frequencies.

We have already examined data in two categories. In the 2-category case, the χ^2 amounts to a z^2. When the data contain three categories, the χ^2 amounts to a $z_1^2 + z_2^2$. That is, the χ^2 has 2 degrees of freedom. Thus, a 3-category χ^2 has 2 degrees of freedom. In general, for data in k categories, the χ^2 has $k - 1$ degrees of freedom.

EXAMPLE 13.5

An experimenter wanted to compare 3 brands of dog pellets; call them Brands A, B, and C. He observed 90 dogs. Each dog was given a choice of the brands, and the experimenter noted which brand the animal preferred. The results showed that 41 dogs preferred A, 20 preferred B, and 29 preferred C. Test the hypothesis that the foods are equally attractive. Use the 5 percent level of significance.

Solution   The observed frequencies are shown below. According to H_0, one third of the animals prefer each brand. The following table shows the observed and expected frequencies.

	Brand A	Brand B	Brand C	Total
Observed frequencies	41	20	29	90
Expected frequencies	30	30	30	90

The resulting χ^2 has $k - 1 = 3 - 1 = 2$ degrees of freedom. It equals:

$$\chi^2_{(2)} = \frac{(41 - 30)^2}{30} + \frac{(20 - 30)^2}{30} + \frac{(29 - 30)^2}{30}$$

$$= 7.4$$

(A correction for continuity is not used when the χ^2 has more than 1 df.)

From a table of the chi-square values, 7.4 is large. Values this large occur less than .05 of the time. Therefore, the hypothesis is rejected: The three brands are not equally attractive. The animals seem to prefer Brand A.

EXAMPLE 13.6

An anthropologist studied 99 people from a certain ethnic group. He classified them into 5 physical types; call the types A, B, C, D, and E. According to his theory, C and D should be more common. He expected their frequencies to have the ratio: $1 : 2 : 3 : 3 : 2$. (Since these numbers sum to 11, $\frac{1}{11}$ of the cases should be of Type A; $\frac{2}{11}$ of Type B; $\frac{3}{11}$ of Type C; $\frac{3}{11}$ of Type D; and $\frac{2}{11}$ of Type E.) The data showed the following frequencies:

	Type A	B	C	D	E	Total
Observed frequencies	8	17	23	35	16	99

Do these frequencies agree with the hypothesis?

Solution First compute the expected frequencies. $\frac{1}{11}$ of the cases means: $\frac{1}{11}(99) = 9$ cases. $\frac{2}{11}$ means: $\frac{2}{11}(99) = 18$ cases. And so on. The following table shows the observed and expected frequencies:

	Type A	B	C	D	E	Total
Observed frequencies (f_i)	8	17	23	35	16	99
Expected frequencies (F_i)	9	18	27	27	18	99

The resulting value of χ^2 is:

$$\chi^2_{(4)} = \frac{(8-9)^2}{9} + \frac{(17-18)^2}{18} + \frac{(23-27)^2}{27} + \frac{(35-27)^2}{27} + \frac{(16-18)^2}{18}$$

$$= 3.35$$

This χ^2 has 4 df. From a chi-square table, 3.35 is quite small; the probability that χ^2 exceeds 3.35 is more than .50. Thus, the data agree with the hypothesis. The investigator's theory is supported.

EXAMPLE 13.7

A geneticist classified tomato plants along two dimensions. Each plant was tall or short, and its leaf showed a cut-leaf pattern or a potato-leaf pattern.

Thus, there were four types of plants—tall cut-leaf, short cut-leaf, tall potato-leaf, and short potato-leaf. In a certain generation of plants, the plants' frequencies were expected to show the ratio $9:3:3:1$. The following table shows the observed and expected frequencies.

	Tall cut-leaf	Short cut-leaf	Tall potato-leaf	Short potato-leaf	Total
Observed (f_i)	93	28	29	10	160
Expected (F_i)	90	30	30	10	160

Test the hypothesis that the observed and expected frequencies agree. Use the 5 percent level of significance.

Solution

$$\chi^2_{(3)} = \frac{(93-90)^2}{90} + \frac{(28-30)^2}{30} + \frac{(29-30)^2}{30} + \frac{(10-10)^2}{10}$$

$$= 0.26$$

The probability is very high that $\chi^2_{(3)}$ will exceed 0.26 by chance: $p > .95$. Therefore, the observed and expected frequencies do agree.

Another interpretation of the df concept

Theoretically, a chi-square's degrees of freedom tell how many independent z^2 terms have been added together to produce the χ^2. This section describes another interpretation of the concept.

Imagine a problem with 1 df. Perhaps we toss a coin 60 times, expecting 30 heads and 30 tails. And suppose the data show 36 heads and 24 tails:

	Number of heads	Number of tails	Total number of tosses
Observed (f_i)	36	24	60
Expected (F_i)	30	30	60

Notice each $f_i - F_i$. For one category $f_i - F_i$ equals $36 - 30 = +6$. For the other category it equals $24 - 30 = -6$. The two discrepancies, then, are $+6$ and -6; they sum to 0. Once one discrepancy is known, the other is also known.

The two discrepancies are not independent of one another. We say that *one* of them is free to vary; it determines a particular z score. The other is related to the first and adds nothing new. Its z score is the negative of the first. That is why we speak of 1 degree of freedom. The χ^2 amounts to a single computation, the z score.

Now imagine a three-category problem. Subjects might be classified as left-eye dominant, right-eye dominant, or ambiocular (neither eye is dominant). Perhaps the investigator hypothesizes that ambiocular subjects are twice as common as left- or right-dominant subjects. Suppose the data show these results:

	Left-eye dominant	Right-eye dominant	Ambiocular	Total
Observed (f_i)	57	49	94	200
Expected (F_i)	50	50	100	200

Again, notice each $f_i - F_i$. For the first category, $f_i - F_i = 57 - 50 = +7$; for the second category, it equals $49 - 50 = -1$; for the third category, $94 - 100 = -6$. Again, the three discrepancies sum to 0. If you know any two of them, you can reconstruct the third. The third discrepancy " depends on " the other two. The χ^2 here amounts to a sum of two squared z scores, and we speak of 2 degrees of freedom.

In general, when there are k categories, the k discrepancies sum to 0. Therefore, $k - 1$ of them are independent. The last one depends on the other $k - 1$. Therefore, the χ^2 has $k - 1$ degrees of freedom.

Testing the normality of a distribution

The chi-square test can also be used to tell whether a frequency distribution is normal. Suppose a normal distribution is divided into tenths; each section would contain 10 percent of the cases. What z scores would bound each tenth? From a table of the normal curve, one-tenth would lie between $z = .00$ and $z = .25$; another tenth, between $z = .25$ and $z = .52$. And so on. In a normal distribution, 200 scores would be distributed this way:

Category (in z scores)	Expected frequency
1.28 to ∞	20
.84 to 1.28	20
.52 to .84	20
.25 to .52	20
.00 to .25	20
$-$ .25 to .00	20
$-$ .52 to $-$ .25	20
$-$ .84 to $-$ .52	20
-1.28 to $-$ .84	20
$-\infty$ to -1.28	20
	200 cases altogether

Now suppose an investigator has collected 200 scores and wants to test their normality. He could convert each score to a z score and tally the z scores. Then, to assess the normality, he would compare the observed with the expected. Example 13.8 illustrates the procedure.

EXAMPLE 13.8

An experimenter collected 200 scores. He estimated the population's μ to be 59.3 and the population's σ to be 8.2. (μ was estimated from $\bar{X}$; σ was estimated from s.) Then he expressed each score as a z score. μ was taken to be 59.3; σ, 8.2. A typical score—say, 68—became: $z = (68 - 59.3)/8.2 = 1.06$.

Finally, the z scores were tallied. The results are shown in the following table. Test the hypothesis that the data are normally distributed. Use the 1 percent level of significance.

Category (in z scores)	Observed frequency (f_i)	Expected frequency (F_i)
1.28 to ∞	3	20
.84 to 1.28	11	20
.52 to .84	13	20
.25 to .52	40	20
.00 to .25	39	20
−.25 to .00	34	20
−.52 to −.25	30	20
−.84 to −.52	15	20
−1.28 to −.84	10	20
−∞ to −1.28	5	20

Solution   From the table we compute the χ^2:

$$\chi^2 = \frac{(3-20)^2}{20} + \frac{(11-20)^2}{20} + \frac{(13-20)^2}{20} + \frac{(40-20)^2}{20} + \frac{(39-20)^2}{20}$$

$$+ \frac{(34-20)^2}{20} + \frac{(30-20)^2}{20} + \frac{(15-20)^2}{20} + \frac{(10-20)^2}{20} + \frac{(5-20)^2}{20}$$

$$= 91.30$$

This chi-square is very large so f_i and F_i do not agree. Thus, the data do not seem to be normally distributed.

This kind of problem differs from the earlier problems in a way which affects the degrees of freedom. To solve this problem, we had to estimate two population parameters, μ and σ. More advanced textbooks show that these estimates cost 2 more degrees of freedom. That is, they constrain the $f_i - F_i$

values in two more ways. The degrees of freedom are reduced to $k - 3 = 10 - 3 = 7$. Only 7 "$f_i - F_i$" values are independent.

Therefore, $\chi^2_{(7)} = 91.30$; $p < .01$. The hypothesis is rejected that the data are normal.

*13.5 THE MULTINOMIAL DISTRIBUTION FOR COMPUTING EXACT PROBABILITIES

A two-category χ^2 is related to the binomial distribution. The binomial distribution $(A + B)^n$ describes the different outcomes of a two-category experiment; each event is an A or a B. But suppose an experiment has more than two categories—perhaps the three categories A, B, and C. Then we could extend the binomial to include all three categories: $(A + B + C)^n$. The extended distribution is called the multinomial distribution.

To use the multinomial distribution, imagine n independent events, and suppose each event has three possible outcomes A, B, or C. The expansion $(A + B + C)^n$ describes all the different outcomes. For example, suppose 7 animals are tested in a maze. And suppose each animal can turn right (A), turn left (B), or continue straight (C). The expansion $(A + B + C)^7$ describes the different outcomes. One term, for example, contains $A^3 B^2 C^2$; that term describes the outcomes with 3 A's, 2 B's, and 2 C's. Its coefficient would be: $7!/3! 2! 2! = 210$; the whole term would be: $(7!/3! 2! 2!) A^3 B^2 C^2$. Let f_A denote the fequency of A's; f_B, the frequency of B's; and f_C, the frequency of C's. The coefficient would be: $n!/f_A! f_B! f_C!$. And the whole term would be: $(n!/f_A! f_B! f_C!) A^{f_A} B^{f_B} C^{f_C}$.

To compute the *probability* of this outcome, replace A, B, and C by the corresponding probabilities. Suppose the three events are equally probable: $p_A = p_B = p_C = \frac{1}{3}$. Then the probability of the $A^3 B^2 C^2$ outcome equals:

$$\frac{7!}{3! \, 2! \, 2!} (\tfrac{1}{3})^3 (\tfrac{1}{3})^2 (\tfrac{1}{3})^2 = .096$$

In this way we can determine exact probabilities.

When we use the chi-square test, we are really approximating multinomial probabilities. But when n is small, it is more exact to compute the probability directly. Example 13.9 illustrates this procedure.

EXAMPLE 13.9

An experimenter wanted to compare three brands of dog pellets—Brands A, B, and C. He studied seven dogs and noted each dog's preference. His results showed that five dogs preferred Brand A, one preferred Brand B, and one

* This section can be omitted in a shorter course.

preferred Brand C. Suppose the brands are really equally attractive: $p_A = p_B = p_C = \frac{1}{3}$. What is the chance probability of a result as extreme as 5 A's, 1 B, and 1 C?

Solution This result can be described by the notation $A^5 B^1 C^1$. Let us consider all the cases with 5 or more A's: $A^5 B^1 C^1$; $A^5 B^2 C^0$; $A^5 B^0 C^2$; $A^6 B^1 C^0$; $A^6 B^0 C^1$; and $A^7 B^0 C^0$. From the multinomial distribution, we can compute the probability of each outcome:

$$A^5 B^1 C^1: \quad \frac{7!}{5!\,1!\,1!} \quad (\tfrac{1}{3})^5 (\tfrac{1}{3})^1 (\tfrac{1}{3})^1 = \tfrac{42}{2187} = .0192$$

$$A^5 B^2 C^0: \quad \frac{7!}{5!\,2!\,0!} \quad (\tfrac{1}{3})^5 (\tfrac{1}{3})^2 (\tfrac{1}{3})^0 = \tfrac{21}{2187} = .0096$$

$$A^5 B^0 C^2: \quad \frac{7!}{5!\,0!\,2!} \quad (\tfrac{1}{3})^5 (\tfrac{1}{3})^0 (\tfrac{1}{3})^2 = \tfrac{21}{2187} = .0096$$

$$A^6 B^1 C^0: \quad \frac{7!}{6!\,1!\,0!} \quad (\tfrac{1}{3})^6 (\tfrac{1}{3})^1 (\tfrac{1}{3})^0 = \tfrac{7}{2187} = .0032$$

$$A^6 B^0 C^1: \quad \frac{7!}{6!\,0!\,1!} \quad (\tfrac{1}{3})^6 (\tfrac{1}{3})^0 (\tfrac{1}{3})^1 = \tfrac{7}{2187} = .0032$$

$$A^7 B^0 C^0: \quad \frac{7!}{7!\,0!\,0!} \quad (\tfrac{1}{3})^7 (\tfrac{1}{3})^0 (\tfrac{1}{3})^0 = \tfrac{1}{2187} = .0005$$

Therefore, the probability of an outcome that contains 5 or more A's is: $.0192 + .0096 + .0096 + .0032 + .0032 + .0005 = .0453$.

In the same way, we could consider events with 5 or more B's. Their probabilities also sum to .0453. Then we could consider events with 5 or more C's. Their probabilities also sum to .0453. The probability of an outcome with 5 or more of a kind therefore equals $3(.0453) = .1359$.

If we solved this problem by a chi-square test, the result would not be quite as precise. The $\chi^2_{(2)}$ would equal 4.0. From a chi-square table, the chance probability of "4.0 or more" lies between .10 and .20. This conclusion agrees with ".1359."

13.6 ASSUMPTIONS AND COMMON ERRORS

Now let us review three assumptions behind the chi-square test. First, we assume that the sampling distribution of each $f_i - F_i$ is normal. Second, we assume that the categories are mutually exclusive. Third, we assume that the observations are randomly drawn. Let us examine each of these assumptions.

Normality of $f_i - F_i$
First of all, the chi-square distribution is derived from a normal distribution. Recall the data that appeared in Example 13.1:

	Number of animals that turned right	Number of animals that turned left
Observed frequencies	44	20
Expected frequencies	32	32

The χ^2 was 9.0; it equalled the squared z score, $(3.0)^2$. To obtain the z score, we computed:

$$z = \frac{X - \mu}{\sigma} = \frac{X - np}{\sqrt{npq}} = \frac{44 - 32}{\sqrt{64(1/2)(1/2)}} = \frac{44 - 32}{4}$$

In theory, we imagine a sampling distribution of z's like this one. We assume that the sampling distribution is normal. Now the z's are normally distributed if their numerators are normally distributed. The numerator in the example is $44 - 32$—or $f_i - F_i$. Thus, we assume that the sampling distribution of $f_i - F_i$ is normal.

$f_i - F_i$ is not normally distributed when F_i is very small. For suppose F_i is 2. And consider some possible values of f_i. f_i might be less than F_i: 0 or 1. It might *equal* F_i: 2. Or it might *exceed* F_i: 3, 4, 5, 6, 7, ... Therefore, $f_i - F_i$ could be -2, -1, 0, 1, 2, 3, 4, 5, 6, and so on. Now on the average, the difference would be 0, so the sampling distribution would be very skewed—two differences below 0 (which occur often) and many differences above 0 (which occur less often). When F_i is small, then, the sampling distribution is skewed.

For this reason, statisticians generally recommend that each F_i be 5 or more. If any F_i is less than 5, some other procedure should be used. Exact probabilities, for example, could be computed through the binomial or the multinomial distribution.

Mutually exclusive categories
The second assumption is that the categories are mutually exclusive. A subject tallied in one category should not fall in any other category. Suppose we were classifying neurotic behaviors; we might form the categories: "Irrational fears," "Depression," "Somatic complaints," and so on. But a subject might exhibit multiple symptoms; he might fall into two or three categories. Then the chi-square test could not be used.

Independent sampling
Finally, we assume that the subjects have been selected at random. According to this assumption, every subject is selected independently. Any one subject cannot be tested twice to increase the n. His responses on the two occasions would be correlated.

Three common errors

Investigators seem to make three common errors in using the chi-square test. First, they sometimes perform too many chi-square tests on the same data. Suppose an investigator computes a four-category chi-square and finds that the χ^2 is not significant. Thus, Categories A, B, C, and D would not differ significantly. Then, eager to find a difference, suppose the investigator examines each three-category subset—Categories A, B, and C; Categories A, C, and D; and every other three-category comparison. And suppose he computes a chi-square for each three-category comparison. In the same way, he could also perform many *two*-category comparisons. Thus, the investigator might perform 4 three-category tests and 6 two-category tests—a total of 10 chi-square tests. One of these tests would probably be significant by chance alone.

Another error occurs when an investigator performs a chi-square test on percentages instead of frequencies. Suppose 60 percent of the voters in a poll favor A, while 40 percent favor B. To compute χ^2, we need the original frequencies: If 10 votes were polled, the chi-square would *not* be significant; if 400 were polled, it *would* be significant.

A final error is to combine correlated observations. Suppose an investigator interviews 25 subjects and asks each subject four questions. He could not treat the data as though n equals $25 \times 4 = 100$. The 100 responses would not be independent. To illustrate this point, suppose 20 subjects participate in a memory test, and each subject's errors are sorted into two types, Type A and Type B. Perhaps the experimenter wants to determine whether Type A occurs more often. Suppose Subject 1 makes 4 A-errors and 2 B-errors; Subject 2 makes 6 A-errors and 5 B-errors; and so on. Various scores are shown below. The A-errors sum to 83, while the B-errors sum to 59.

	Number of A-errors	Number of B-errors
Subject 1	4	2
Subject 2	6	5
Subject 3	6	4
Subject 4	0	1
Subject 5	5	3
⋮	⋮	⋮
Subject 20	⋮	⋮
	83	59

A chi-square test is not appropriate for data of this type since the 142 responses are not independent. Therefore, it is not valid to compare the observed " 83 versus 59 " with an expected " 71 versus 71." Instead, a *t* test or an analysis of variance should be used.

The chi-square test *would* be appropriate if the experimenter rearranged the data. He might note how many subjects made more A-errors, and how many made more B-errors. Suppose 16 subjects made more A-errors, and 4 made more B-errors. The chi-square test could then be used to tell whether the two categories differ in their frequencies:

	More A-errors	More B-errors	Total
Observed frequencies	16	4	20
Expected frequencies	10	10	20

In this case $n = 20$. Now the observations are independent: They reflect 20 independent subjects. Tests of this kind will be discussed further in Chap. 14.

13.7 APPLICATIONS: ASSESSING A CORRELATION BETWEEN TWO VARIABLES

The chi-square test is also used to tell whether two variables are correlated. Imagine two non-numerical variables—say, "type of highway accident" and "season of the year." These two variables may be correlated: Perhaps one kind of accident tends to occur in the winter, while another kind tends to occur in the summer. The chi-square test can be used to evaluate a correlation of this type.

Sometimes a variable's categories can be ordered. Levels of IQ, for example, can be ordered. Perhaps three categories are formed: low IQ, medium IQ, and high IQ. The statistical procedure ·is the same whether or not the categories are ordered.

Let us begin with an example. Suppose an investigator has studied 100 patients. And suppose the patients have been classified in two ways: "Diagnostic category" is one variable—schizophrenic, manic-depressive, or paranoid. And "level of IQ" is the other variable—low IQ or high IQ. The data are shown in Table 13.10.

TABLE 13.10 Data relating two categorized variables: Observed frequencies (f_i)

Diagnostic category	Level of IQ		Total
	High (*Above* 100)	Low (*Below* 100)	
Schizophrenic	20	30	50
Manic-depressive	10	10	20
Paranoid	30	0	30
	60	40	100

Each cell of the table describes one diagnostic category at one IQ level. The table shows the number of subjects in each cell: 20 patients are high-IQ schizophrenics; 30 are low-IQ schizophrenics. The data suggest that schizophrenics are more often low in IQ. On the other hand, the paranoids are all high in IQ. Thus, the variables seem to be correlated: One kind of patient tends to be higher in IQ, another kind tends to be lower in IQ.

Consider each row's total; the row totals show 50 schizophrenics, 20 manic-depressives, and 30 paranoids. Then consider each column's total. The column totals show 60 high-IQ patients and 40 low-IQ patients. We can summarize these overall totals in a table:

Diagnostic Category	High IQ	Low IQ	
Schizophrenic			50
Manic-depressive			20
Paranoid			30
	60	40	

Now let us consider whether the variables are correlated. If they *are* correlated, we expect many low-IQ schizophrenics and many high-IQ paranoids. As before, let us begin with a *null* hypothesis: Suppose the variables are *not* correlated. There are 50 schizophrenics and 60 high-IQ patients. If the variables are not correlated (independent), how many high-IQ schizophrenics are expected?

Altogether, there are 60 high-IQ patients. Therefore, 60 percent of the patients are high in IQ. If the variables are independent, 60 percent of each diagnostic group should be high in IQ: 60 percent of the schizophrenics, 60 percent of the manic-depressives, and 60 percent of the paranoids. "Sixty percent of the schizophrenics" refers to .60(50) = 30 people. Thus, the first cell's expected frequency is 30.

And how many manic-depressives should be high in IQ? .60(20) = 12 people. In this way, we can determine each cell's expected frequency. These expected frequencies are shown in Table 13.11. They are implied by the null hypothesis.

TABLE 13.11   Each cell's expected frequency (F_i)

	IQ above 100	IQ below 100	Total
Schizophrenic	30	20	50
Manic-depressive	12	8	20
Paranoid	18	12	30
	60	40	100

Now let us compare the two tables. One shows observed frequencies; the other shows expected frequencies. To examine their difference, we compute a χ^2. If the χ^2 is small, the two sets agree.

$$\chi^2 = \frac{(20-30)^2}{30} + \frac{(30-20)^2}{20} + \frac{(10-12)^2}{12} + \frac{(10-8)^2}{8} + \frac{(30-18)^2}{18}$$

$$+ \frac{(0-12)^2}{12}$$

$$= 29.16$$

This χ^2 is very large. Thus, the two frequencies do not agree, so the null hypothesis is rejected. Therefore, the variables *do* seem to be correlated. Apparently, paranoids tend to be brighter, and schizophrenics tend to be duller.

Degrees of freedom

Now let us consider the degrees of freedom. Let k denote the number of columns, and r, the number of rows. To compute the degrees of freedom, multiply $(k-1)$ by $(r-1)$. In the example, df $= (k-1)(r-1) = (2-1)(3-1) = 2$.

If df $= 2$, then 2 "$f_i - F_i$" values are independent. The others are not independent. Consider the schizophrenic categories first. For the high-IQ schizophrenics, $f_i - F_i$ equals $20 - 30 = -10$. But the number of schizophrenics is fixed at 50, so for low-IQ schizophrenics, $f_i - F_i$ has to equal $30 - 20 = +10$.

Now consider the high-IQ categories: For high-IQ schizophrenics, $f_i - F_i$ is -10. For high-IQ manic-depressives, it equals $10 - 12 = -2$. How about the high-IQ paranoids? The number of high-IQ patients is fixed at 60. $f_i - F_i$ equals -10 for schizophrenics and -2 for manic-depressives; therefore, it has to equal $+12$ for paranoids.

In this way we can show that the data have 2 degrees of freedom: $\chi^2_{(2)} = 29.16$, $p < .001$. This chi-square is extremely large, so the f's and F's do not agree. There are fewer high-IQ schizophrenics than expected, and more high-IQ paranoids.

How to compute the expected frequencies

There is an easy way to compute expected frequencies. First, we need to develop a notation. Let n_{R_i} denote the number of cases in Row i. Let n_{C_j} denote the number of cases in Column j. And let N denote the total number of cases. To compute the expected frequencies for the cell in Row i, Column j, multiply n_{R_i} by n_{C_j}, and divide the product by N. Let us call this expected frequency F_{ij}.

$$F_{ij} = \frac{(n_{R_i})(n_{C_j})}{N} \tag{13.2}$$

For example, consider the high-IQ schizophrenics. n_{R_i} (the number of schizo-phrenics) is 50. n_{C_j} (the number of high-IQ patients) is 60. And N is 100. Therefore, that cell's F_{ij} is $(50)(60)/100 = 30$.

Table 13.10 is called a contingency table. It has r rows and k columns, so we call it an "r by k contingency table." Each expected frequency is denoted F_{ij}. "i" refers to the ith row, and "j" refers to the jth column. Thus, F_{31} is the expected frequency of Row 3, Column 1. f_{31} is the observed frequency of Row 3, Column 1. In Table 13.10, $f_{31} = 30$. And in Table 13.11, $F_{31} = 18$. Now we can write the formula for chi-square more precisely:

$$\chi^2_{(r-1)(k-1)} = \sum \frac{(f_{ij} - F_{ij})^2}{F_{ij}} \tag{13.3}$$

Let us prove that F_{ij} equals $\dfrac{(n_{R_i})(n_{C_j})}{N}$. Consider any cell—say, Row 1, Column 1—the high-IQ schizophrenics. What is the probability of a high-IQ schizophrenic? If the two variables are independent:

$$P(\text{High-IQ} \cap \text{Schizophrenic}) = P(\text{High-IQ}) \times P(\text{Schizophrenic})$$

Therefore, we need two simple probabilities: $P(\text{High-IQ})$ and $P(\text{Schizophrenic})$. From the data:

$$P(\text{Schizophrenic}) = \frac{n_{R_1}}{N} = \frac{50}{100} = .50$$

$$P(\text{High-IQ}) \quad = \frac{n_{C_1}}{N} = \frac{60}{100} = .60$$

Therefore, the joint probability is:

$$
\begin{aligned}
P(\text{High-IQ} \cap \text{Schizophrenic}) &= P(R_1 \cap C_1) \\
&= P(\text{Schizophrenic}) \times P(\text{High-IQ}) \\
&= P(R_1) \times P(C_1) \\
&= \frac{n_{R_1}}{N} \times \frac{n_{C_1}}{N} \\
&= \frac{50}{100} \times \frac{60}{100} \\
&= .30
\end{aligned}
$$

If the two variables are independent, then .30 tells the cell's probability. In general, for two independent variables:

$$P(R_i \cap C_j) = \left(\frac{n_{R_i}}{N}\right)\left(\frac{n_{C_j}}{N}\right)$$

From this probability we can then compute the expected frequency. With 100 individuals altogether, we expect $(.30)(N) = .30 \ (100) = 30$ high-IQ schizophrenics. And in general:

$$F_{ij} = [P(R_i \cap C_j)] \cdot N = \left(\frac{n_{R_i}}{N}\right)\left(\frac{n_{C_j}}{N}\right) \cdot N$$

$$= \frac{(n_{R_i})(n_{C_j})}{N}$$

The following examples illustrate the complete procedure.

EXAMPLE 13.10

An experimenter asked 180 subjects to perform a difficult task. Half the subjects were told they succeeded; half were told they failed. Later the subject was asked to contribute to a charity. Some subjects were willing to contribute, others were not. The results are shown in the following table:

| | Subject's performance was labeled: | | |
	Success	Failure	
Subject contributed to charity	80	40	120
Subject refused	10	50	60
	90	90	180

Is the subject's altruism related to his prior "success"?

Solution First we state a null hypothesis: The two variables are independent. Suppose the variables are independent; what frequencies are expected? For the first cell, the expected frequency is:

$$F_{11} = \frac{(n_{R_1})(n_{C_1})}{N} = \frac{(120)(90)}{180} = 60$$

The various F_{ij}'s appear in the following table:

| | Subject's performance was labeled: | | |
	Success	Failure	
Subject contributed to charity	60	60	120
Subject refused	30	30	60
	90	90	180

To compare the two sets of frequencies, we compute a chi-square.

$$\chi^2 = \frac{(80-60)^2}{60} + \frac{(10-30)^2}{30} + \frac{(40-60)^2}{60} + \frac{(50-30)^2}{30}$$
$$= 40.0$$

This chi-square has $(k-1)(r-1) = (2-1)(2-1) = 1$ df. The probability is very small that $\chi^2_{(1)}$ exceed 40.0 by chance. Therefore, H_0 is rejected. Apparently, the variables *are* related.

EXAMPLE 13.11

Children of five different ages were asked to solve a problem. Twenty children were tested at each age level. The results show the number of children who solved the problem.

			Age			
	5	7	9	11	13	Total
Succeeded	8	10	10	13	12	52
Failed	12	10	10	7	8	48
	20	20	20	20	20	100

Do older children solve the problem more readily? Use the 5 percent level of significance.

Solution According to the null hypothesis, the two variables are independent. If so, the following frequencies are expected:

			Age			
	5	7	9	11	13	Total
Succeeded	10.4	10.4	10.4	10.4	10.4	52
Failed	9.6	9.6	9.6	9.6	9.6	48
	20.0	20.0	20.0	20.0	20.0	100

Then the χ^2 is computed. This χ^2 has $(k-1)(r-1) = (5-1)(2-1) = 4$ df. Therefore:

$$\chi^2 = \frac{(8-10.4)^2}{10.4} + \frac{(10-10.4)^2}{10.4} + \frac{(10-10.4)^2}{10.4} + \frac{(13-10.4)^2}{10.4}$$
$$+ \frac{(12-10.4)^2}{10.4} + \frac{(12-9.6)^2}{9.6} + \frac{(10-9.6)^2}{9.6} + \frac{(10-9.6)^2}{9.6}$$
$$+ \frac{(7-9.6)^2}{9.6} + \frac{(8-9.6)^2}{9.6}$$
$$= 3.08$$

A chi-square this large occurs readily by chance; $p > .05$. Therefore, the observed and expected frequencies do not differ significantly. The null hypothesis is accepted, and the variables seem to be independent. Success is not related to age.

APPENDIX: *Proof*

Proof 13.1 *Proof that $\chi^2 = z^2$ in a two-category problem.*
Consider two categories, Category 1 and Category 2. Let the observed frequencies be f_1 and f_2. The hypothesized frequencies are F_1 and F_2. Then:

$$\chi^2 = \sum_k \frac{(f_i - F_i)^2}{F_i}$$

$$= \frac{(f_1 - F_1)^2}{F_1} + \frac{(f_2 - F_2)^2}{F_2}$$

According to H_0, p is the probability of Category 1 in the population; and q is the probability of Category 2. n is the number of observations. Therefore $F_1 = np$. And $F_2 = nq = n(1 - p)$. Therefore:

$$\chi^2 = \frac{(f_1 - np)^2}{np} + \frac{(f_2 - nq)^2}{nq}$$

Now put both terms over a common denominator:

$$\chi^2 = \frac{q(f_1 - np)^2 + p(f_2 - nq)^2}{npq}$$

Consider the term in the numerator: $f_2 - nq$. It equals:

$$f_2 - nq = f_2 - n(1 - p) = f_2 - n + np$$

Now $n = f_1 + f_2$. Therefore $f_2 - n = -f_1$. And:

$$(f_2 - nq) = f_2 - n(1 - p) = f_2 - n + np = -f_1 + np$$

$$(f_2 - nq)^2 = (-f_1 + np)^2 = (f_1 - np)^2$$

Therefore:

$$\chi^2 = \frac{q(f_1 - np)^2 + p(f_1 - np)^2}{npq} = \frac{(f_1 - np)^2[p + q]}{npq}$$

Since $p + q = 1$:

$$\chi^2 = \frac{(f_1 - np)^2}{npq} = \frac{(f_1 - \mu)^2}{npq} = \frac{(X - \mu)^2}{\sigma^2} = \left(\frac{X - \mu}{\sigma}\right)^2 = z^2$$

EXERCISES

13.1 What percent of the χ^2 distribution with 1 df lies between $\chi^2 = 0$ and $\chi^2 = 6.66$? (Use both the normal distribution and the χ^2 distribution to answer this question.) Notice that $(2.58)^2 = 6.66$.
Answer: .99

13.2 (a) When we perform a χ^2 test for frequencies in k categories, the χ^2 has _____ degrees of freedom.
Answer: k — 1

(b) When we perform a "goodness of fit" test to see if frequencies follow those expected from a normal distribution, the test has _____ degrees of freedom.
Answer: k — 3

(c) When we use a χ^2 test to assess a correlation between two categorized variables, the number of degrees of freedom equals _____.
Answer: (r — 1)(k — 1)

13.3 Four hundred people changed their attitudes after viewing a film—176 people changed in the negative direction; 224 changed in the positive direction. Do these figures differ from a 50/50 split? Adopt the .05 level of significance. Perform the test in two ways: (a) using the normal curve's approximation to the binomial distribution; (b) using the chi-square test.
Answer: z = 2.4; χ^2 = 5.76. Significantly more change in positive direction.

13.4 Ninety people performed two tasks and then stated which one seemed easier. Fifty-five thought Task 1 was easier; 35 thought Task 2 was easier. Do the tasks differ significantly in their perceived difficulty? Let $\alpha = .05$.
Answer: χ^2 = 4.0; p < .05; the tasks do differ significantly.

13.5 Suppose a penny is tossed 100 times. How many heads would lead you to conclude, at the .01 level of significance, that the coin was biased?
Answer: Fewer than 38 or more than 62.

13.6 A geneticist crossed two species of flowers and examined the offspring. Theoretically, the four kinds of offspring should exhibit frequencies in a ratio of 9 : 3 : 3 : 1. The data showed the following frequencies: 120, 48, 36, 13. Do the observed frequencies significantly depart from the theory?
Answer: χ^2 = 1.91; accept H_0.

13.7 Two hundred children were shown an array of six toys. Each child was allowed to choose one toy. The frequencies below show the number of children who selected each toy. Did the toys differ significantly in their appeal?

Toy:	A	B	C	D	E	F
Frequency of selection:	30	27	29	31	40	43

Answer: χ^2 = 6.40; accept H_0.

13.8 In a certain population the μ and σ are known. An experimenter collected 100 scores which he converted to z scores. The distribution of scores is shown below. Test the hypothesis that the data are normally distributed. Let $\alpha = .05$.

Category (in z scores)	Observed frequencies	Expected frequencies
Above 1.28	7	10
.84 to 1.28	8	10
.52 to .84	12	10
.25 to .52	14	10
.00 to .25	15	10
−.25 to .00	11	10
−.52 to −.25	10	10
−.84 to −.52	9	10
−1.28 to −.84	8	10
Below −1.28	6	10
	100	100

Answer: $\chi^2_{(7)} = 8.0$. *The distribution can be considered normal.*

13.9 In a certain population $\mu = 100$ and $\sigma = 10$. Samples of $N = 25$ are to be drawn. (Compute $\sigma_{\bar{x}}$.) Now suppose someone randomly draws 100 different samples of $N = 25$ scores and records the means. He finds the following distribution of means:

Mean	Below 98	Between 98 and 102	Above 102
Frequency	10	65	25

Is there reason to believe that the population is non-normal?
Answer: $\chi^2 = 7.44$; *reject* H_0. *Distribution is significantly non-normal.*

13.10 Subjects were asked to perform a certain task, and the nature of the instructions varied. In one condition, the subject was led to feel coerced; in the other condition, he was not. The experimenter noted how many subjects complied with the request and how many refused. The resulting data are shown below. Do the two conditions differ significantly?

Subject's behavior	Experimental condition Coerced	Not coerced	
Refused	20	20	40
Complied	40	70	110
	60	90	150

Answer: $\chi^2_{(1)} = 2.3$; *the relationship is not statistically significant.*

13.11 An experimenter examined the relationship between the amount of training given to production line workers and their supervisors' later ratings. The following results were obtained:

	Ratings		
	Excellent	Good	Poor
1 day	6	12	0
3 days	12	25	6
1 week	14	31	12
2 weeks	2	23	7

Amount of training

Is there significant association (at the .01 level) between the two variables?
Answer: $\chi^2_{(6)} = 10.86$; $p > .05$; *the association is not significant.*

14

NONPARAMETRIC TESTS
OF SIGNIFICANCE

We have now examined the classical statistical tests—tests which are sometimes called *parametric* tests. Each of these tests is based on certain assumptions. When we use the normal curve, for example, or the t distribution, or the F distribution, we assume that scores in the population are normally distributed. When we perform an analysis of variance, we assume that the scores in each condition are normal and that they have equal variances. Strictly speaking, the classical statistical tests are only valid if these assumptions are valid.

At times, though, an investigator cannot make assumptions of normality or of equal variances. Perhaps the data are very skewed; or perhaps the experimental groups have grossly different variances. Then we need statistical

This chapter can be omitted in a shorter course.

tests that do not make assumptions of this kind. Such tests are called *non-parametric* tests or *distribution-free* tests. When they are used, the investigator need not worry about violating distributional assumptions.

Nonparametric tests do have one drawback, though. In general, they are less powerful. If the assumptions behind a parametric test can be met, then the parametric test is better able to spot a real difference. The nonparametric test tends to overlook small differences and produce a Type II error.

Before we examine the nonparametric tests, let us review the way we compare two statistical tests. Suppose an investigator is considering an experiment with two experimental conditions, Condition E and Condition C; he wants to test a hypothesis about $\mu_E - \mu_C$. Perhaps each experimental group contains 30 subjects (so $N = 60$), and α is set at .05. The investigator could then consider different values of $\mu_E - \mu_C$ and compute the power $(1 - \beta)$ for each possible difference. He could then plot a power function for each statistical test and compare the two tests.

When $\mu_E - \mu_C$ is a 5-point difference, for example, the power of Test A might be .83, and that of Test B, .71. We could express the result this way:

> When $N = 60$: Test A's power is .83; Test B's power is .71.

Now how large would N have to be to make the power of Test B equal to .83? We could compute that N: Say it equals 90. Then we could write:

> Test A's power for $N = 60$ equals Test B's power for $N = 90$.

A 60-score sample with Test A gives the same power as a 90-score sample with Test B. Test A is clearly more efficient. Statisticians sometimes form a ratio of these two N's: $60/90 \times 100 = 67$ percent. This percentage is called the *power efficiency* of Test B relative to Test A.

This kind of information is used to evaluate a nonparametric statistical test. From such information, we conclude that nonparametric tests are less powerful. That is why the parametric tests are preferred. If the parametric assumptions cannot be met, though, the nonparametric test is preferred.

This chapter describes six major nonparametric tests. Two of them, the simplest ones, are called *sign tests*—one for matched groups and one for independent groups. Although they are easy to apply, they have low power efficiency. Other tests, the *rank tests*, are generally more powerful and often very useful.

14.1 A SIGN TEST FOR MATCHED GROUPS (THE "SIGN TEST")

Suppose every subject in an experiment has been tested twice. Data of this type appeared in Chap. 9, Table 9.1. The subject was tested under two conditions of automobile driving—one under a drug, the other under a placebo. A parametric test was performed, and the mean difference was significantly greater than 0. Let us now test the same data another way.

First, consider every subject's difference score and note the *sign* of the difference. Is it positive or negative? When the difference score is positive, record $+$; when it is negative, record $-$. (Difference scores of 0 are just ignored.) The data of Table 9.1 contain 40 difference scores; 28 are positive and 12 are negative.

If the drug and the placebo have similar effects, $+$'s and $-$'s should occur equally often in the population. The null hypothesis would claim that half the population's difference scores are positive and half are negative. According to H_0, then, the probability of a $+$ is .50.

To test this hypothesis, we consider a sampling distribution for samples of 40 observations:

$$\mu_{\text{binomial}} = np = 40(.50) = 20; \quad \sigma_{\text{binomial}} = \sqrt{npq} = \sqrt{(40)(.50)(.50)} = 3.16$$

Then we evaluate the outcome "28 $+$'s":

$$z = \frac{|28 - 20| - \frac{1}{2}}{3.16} = 2.37$$

This z is large, so H_0 gets rejected at $\alpha = .05$. The probability of a $+$ in the population is apparently not .50: The $+$'s seem to outnumber the $-$'s, so the drug *does* seem to affect a subject's performance.

This procedure is called a *sign test*. It is very easy to apply, but notoriously low in power. One way to see its inefficiency is to compare "$z = 2.37$" with the z of Chap. 9, which was based on a parametric test. In Chap. 9, the z equaled 4.20—considerably larger than 2.37. The sign test ignores information about the actual magnitude of difference scores, and the price we pay is a lower z value. In general, if a parametric test is appropriate, it more readily detects a real difference.

EXAMPLE 14.1

Two types of dials were compared. A subject was asked to read each dial many times, and the experimenter recorded his errors. Altogether 12 subjects were tested. The data show how many errors each subject produced. Do the two conditions differ significantly? Use the .05 level of significance.

| | Number of errors | | Sign of difference |
	Type A	Type B	
Subject A	3	1	+
Subject B	4	2	+
Subject C	0	0	tie
Subject D	1	1	tie
Subject E	1	0	+
Subject F	2	3	−
Subject G	1	0	+
Subject H	1	0	+
Subject I	2	0	+
Subject J	1	1	tie
Subject K	3	2	+
Subject L	1	0	+

Solution Subjects C, D, and J showed no difference, so their data are ignored. The remaining data show 8 positive differences and 1 negative difference. What is the chance probability of a result as extreme as this?
The appropriate binomial distribution is:

$$(A + B)^9 = A^9 + 9 A^8 B + \frac{(9)(8)}{2} A^7 B^2 + \cdots$$

The chance probability of 8 or more pluses is: $(\frac{1}{2})^9 + 9(\frac{1}{2})^8(\frac{1}{2}) = {}^{10}\!/_{512} = .02$. The probability of 8 or more pluses *or* 8 or more negatives is .04. Thus, the chance probability is .04 that data show a result as extreme as the one observed. The null hypothesis is therefore rejected. The two types of dial do differ significantly at the .05 level; Style A seems to produce more errors.

14.2   A SIGN TEST FOR INDEPENDENT GROUPS (THE MEDIAN TEST)

Next we consider a similar test for two independent groups. Again, perhaps the data are skewed, so the investigator does not want to use a parametric test.

Suppose an investigator compared two groups of subjects. The subjects in one group were selected to be intellectually rigid, while those in the other group were not. Then each subject was tested on a perceptual task. The subject's perceptual distortions were scored to determine whether intellectual rigidity affects perceptual accuracy. The resulting scores are shown in Table 14.1.

TABLE 14.1   Degree of rigidity on a perceptual task.

Intellectually rigid	Control
9	8
9	7
9	9
9	9
9	8
7	8
9	7
9	7
9	6
8	8
	8
	9
10 scores	12 scores

Median of all 22 scores = 8.5

To apply the median test, first determine the median of all 14 scores. In Table 14.1, the median is 8.5. Then note how many subjects in each group fell above the median and how many fell below the median. The data of Table 14.1 can be summarized this way:

	Intellectually rigid	Control	Total
Above median	8	3	11
Below median	2	9	11
Total	10	12	22

If the two types of people do not really differ, half of each group should fall above the median, and half should fall below the median. There should be no relationship between the rows and the columns. A χ^2 test can be used to evaluate the relationship. The expected value for the cells in the left-hand column is 5.0; for the cells in the right-hand column, 6.0.

$$\chi^2 = \frac{(8-5)^2}{5} + \frac{(2-5)^2}{5} + \frac{(3-6)^2}{6} + \frac{(9-6)^2}{6}$$
$$= 6.60$$

This χ^2 has 1 degree of freedom; it is significant at the .05 level. Thus, the relationship is stronger than expected by chance. Intellectually rigid subjects do seem to have higher scores.

The median test can also be used for data in three or more conditions. The investigator determines the median of all N scores and notes how many scores fall above the median in each condition. The results get summarized in a table, and a chi-square is computed. Example 14.2 illustrates the procedure.

EXAMPLE 14.2

Reaction times were measured with four kinds of stimuli. Some subjects were tested with visual stimuli, others with auditory stimuli, others with tactile stimuli, and others with olfactory stimuli. Fourteen subjects were tested in each group. Each subject's reaction time is shown in Table 14.2. Do the four groups differ significantly at the .05 level of significance?

TABLE 14.2   Reaction times to different kinds of stimuli

Visual	Auditory	Tactile	Olfactory
0.4	0.4	0.4	1.1
0.5	0.4	0.5	0.6
0.5	0.5	0.5	0.4
0.6	0.4	0.6	0.7
0.5	0.4	0.6	0.6
0.6	0.4	0.5	0.5
0.4	0.4	0.7	0.6
0.5	0.5	0.9	0.7
0.5	0.5	0.8	0.8
0.4	0.4	0.5	0.8
0.4	0.4	0.5	0.6
0.5	0.4	1.0	0.7
0.4	0.5	0.9	0.8
0.5	0.7	0.6	0.5

Solution   First consider the median of all 56 scores. "0.4" occurred 16 times; "0.5" occurred 18 times; the other scores occurred 22 times. If we computed the median, it would equal 0.52. We cannot divide the scores into two equal halves. Instead, we arbitrarily divide them into two convenient groups—those above the median (0.6 and above) and those below the median (0.5 and below):

	Visual	Auditory	Tactile	Olfactory	Total
Above the median (0.6 and above)	2	1	8	11	22
Below the median (0.5 and below)	12	13	6	3	34
	14	14	14	14	56

Then we compute χ^2. The expected value for each cell in the top row is 5.5; for each cell in the bottom row, 8.5:

$$\chi^2 = \frac{(2 - 5.5)^2}{5.5} + \frac{(1 - 5.5)^2}{5.5} + \frac{(8 - 5.5)^2}{5.5} + \frac{(11 - 5.5)^2}{5.5}$$
$$+ \frac{(12 - 8.5)^2}{8.5} + \frac{(13 - 8.5)^2}{8.5} + \frac{(6 - 8.5)^2}{8.5} + \frac{(3 - 8.5)^2}{8.5}$$
$$= 20.66$$

Thus χ^2 (with 3 df) = 20.66. This result is significant at the .05 level. The visual and auditory stimuli seem to produce faster reaction times.

14.3 A RANK TEST FOR MATCHED GROUPS (THE WILCOXON MATCHED-PAIRS SIGNED-RANKS TEST)

As we noted, sign tests are easy to apply, but they are not very powerful. They tend to overlook small differences, calling them nonsignificant. Other nonparametric tests, like the ones we consider next, are more powerful. Even when the assumptions of the parametric tests are met, these tests are almost as efficient as the parametric ones.

The tests we shall consider are based on ranks. Before we examine them, we should consider some facts about ranks.

Converting scores to ranks

Consider the scores 95, 96, 97, 115, 148. Perhaps they are reaction times, which are known to be skewed. Then the investigator could replace each score by its rank. We usually let " 1 " be the rank of the lowest score; " 2," the rank of the next higher score; and so on. Thus, the scores 95, 96, 97, 115, 148 would be assigned the ranks 1, 2, 3, 4, 5.

Sometimes two scores are tied for a given rank. If the scores were 95, 97, 97, 115, 148, then two scores would be tied for ranks 2 and 3. In that case, the tied scores are assigned the mean of the two ranks—2.5. The ranks would be: 1, 2.5, 2.5, 4, 5.

If the scores were 95, 97, 97, 97, 148, three scores would be tied. The mean of the ranks 2, 3, and 4 would be assigned to them. The ranks would be: 1, 3, 3, 3, 5.

Mean and variance of ranks

Now consider the set of N ranks 1, 2, 3, ..., N. The sum of N ranks equals: $N(N + 1)/2$. For the ranks 1, 2, 3, 4, 5, the sum equals $5(6)/2 = 15$. The *mean* of the ranks would be this sum divided by N:

$$\text{Mean of } N \text{ ranks} = \frac{\sum X}{N} = \frac{N(N + 1)}{2} \div N = \frac{(N + 1)}{2} \tag{14.1}$$

For the ranks 1, 2, 3, 4, 5, the mean equals $(N + 1)/2 = (5 + 1)/2 = 3$.

Now consider the variance of N ranks. To compute the variance, we would first need ΣX^2: We would square each rank (1^2, 2^2, 3^2, ...) and sum the squared ranks. The sum of N squared ranks always equals $N(N + 1)(2N + 1)/6$. When $N = 5$, the sum $1^2 + 2^2 + 3^2 + 4^2 + 5^2$ equals $(5)(6)(11)/6 = 55$.

This term could be used to derive a formula for the variance of N ranks. The derivation would begin:

$$\text{Variance} = \frac{1}{N}\left[\sum X^2 - \frac{(\sum X)^2}{N}\right]$$

For N ranks:

$$\text{Variance} = \frac{1}{N}\left[\frac{N(N + 1)(2N + 1)}{6} - \frac{\left(\frac{N(N + 1)}{2}\right)^2}{N}\right]$$

When the algebra is completed, the formula becomes:

$$\text{Variance} = \frac{N^2 - 1}{12} \tag{14.2}$$

Thus, for the ranks $1, 2, 3, 4, 5$, the variance is: $(N^2 - 1)/12 = (5^2 - 1)/12 = 2$. And the standard deviation of the five ranks is $\sqrt{2} = 1.4$.

A rank test

A rank test has been developed for paired observations. Let us begin with a set of paired observations. Perhaps matched subjects have been tested on two different drugs, and each subject's performance has been measured.

	Drug A	Drug B	Difference (d)
Pair A	22	25	−3
Pair B	22	21	1
Pair C	22	15	7
Pair D	19	15	4
Pair E	30	21	9

First, we compute the difference score (d) for each pair. Then we ignore the sign of each difference score—$|d|$—and rank-order these $|d|$ values; the smallest is assigned the rank 1. Then we consider the sign of the original d value and attach this sign to the rank. Some ranks become positive and others become negative:

	Difference (d)	$\lvert d \rvert$	Rank of $\lvert d \rvert$	Signed rank Negative	Signed rank Positive
Pair A	-3	3	2	-2	
Pair B	1	1	1		$+1$
Pair C	7	7	4		$+4$
Pair D	4	4	3		$+3$
Pair E	9	9	5		$+5$
					$T = 13$

Then we compute the sum of the positive ranks and denote it T. For the data, $T = 13$.

To evaluate this result, we need to consider the sampling distribution of T. Suppose the null hypothesis is valid, and the two groups only differ by chance. Half the difference scores should be positive, and half should be negative. The sum "$1 + 2 + 3 + 4 + 5 = 15$" should therefore be divided about equally between the positives and the negatives. Thus, T should be about $15/2 = 7.5$.

How far is the observed "$T = 13$" from the expected value 7.5? Tables exist to evaluate an observed T; we shall examine one of those tables shortly. Before we do, though, let us generate the sampling distribution ourselves. We need to consider all possible values of T. Five difference scores, which are rank-ordered, could be positive or negative.

According to the null hypothesis, the probability is 1/2 that a difference score is positive. By chance, some ranks are positive and others are negative. As one outcome, for example, all five difference scores might be positive; in that case, T would be 15. As another outcome, the smallest difference score (rank 1) might be negative, and the other four positive; in that case T would equal $2 + 3 + 4 + 5 = 14$. There are 32 possible outcomes; they are shown in Table 14.3 along with the values of T.

A frequency distribution of the T values appears in Table 14.4. This distribution is the theoretical distribution of T for 5-pair samples. The mean is 7.5, and the standard deviation is 3.71. From this distribution we can compute the probability that T is 13 or more; that probability is $3/32 = .094$. Table 14.4 yields probabilities of this kind for different values of T. The information could also be presented this way:

If T equals:	The probability of this T or a more extreme one is:
0 or 15	.031
1 or 14	.062
2 or 13	.094
3 or 12	.156

Thus, when $T = 13$, the corresponding probability is .094. The difference is not significant when $T = 13$. To be significant at $\alpha = .05$, T would have to be as small as 0 or as large as 15.

Table A.7 in the appendix was compiled from probabilities like these. In Table A.7, N is the number of pairs of observations. The table tells the value of T that is needed to reach significance at different α's.

TABLE 14.3   Different possible sample outcomes for five pairs of observations

Different possible outcomes	The rank order of the sample's $|d|$ values					T
	1	2	3	4	5	
1	+	+	+	+	+	15
2	−	+	+	+	+	14
3	+	−	+	+	+	13
4	+	+	−	+	+	12
5	+	+	+	−	+	11
6	+	+	+	+	−	10
7	−	−	+	+	+	12
8	−	+	−	+	+	11
9	−	+	+	−	+	10
10	−	+	+	+	−	9
11	+	−	−	+	+	10
12	+	−	+	−	+	9
13	+	−	+	+	−	8
14	+	+	−	−	+	8
15	+	+	−	+	−	7
16	+	+	+	−	−	6
17	−	−	−	+	+	9
18	−	−	+	−	+	8
19	−	−	+	+	−	7
20	−	+	−	−	+	7
21	−	+	−	+	−	6
22	−	+	+	−	−	5
23	+	−	−	−	+	6
24	+	−	−	+	−	5
25	+	−	+	−	−	4
26	+	+	−	−	−	3
27	−	−	−	−	+	5
28	−	−	−	+	−	4
29	−	−	+	−	−	3
30	−	+	−	−	−	2
31	+	−	−	−	−	1
32	−	−	−	−	−	0

TABLE 14.4 The sampling distribution of T for samples with five pairs of observations

T	f
15	1
14	1
13	1
12	2
11	2
10	3
9	3
8	3
7	3
6	3
5	3
4	2
3	2
2	1
1	1
0	1
	32

$$\mu = 7.5$$
$$\sigma = 3.71$$

EXAMPLE 14.3

An investigator studied the amount of dependency that children showed in comparable activities at home and at nursery school. Eight children were tested. Raters rated each child on a 10-point scale. The mean ratings are shown below. Was rated dependency significantly higher at school? Use the .05 level of significance.

Child	Rated dependency In school	Rated dependency At home	d	Signed rank Negative	Signed rank Positive
A	9.1	4.6	4.5		+6
B	8.8	7.6	1.2		+1
C	1.7	4.5	−2.8	−4	
D	3.2	3.2	tie		
E	3.3	5.0	−1.7	−2.5	
F	9.1	2.4	6.7		+7
G	1.0	2.7	−1.7	−2.5	
H	5.4	1.9	3.5		+5
				$T = 19$	

Solution Subject D's ratings were the same in both conditions, so we eliminate that pair of scores from the analysis; thus $N = 7$. Then the absolute differences are rank-ordered, the signs are replaced, and the positive ranks are summed: $T = 19$.

According to the null hypothesis, the positive ranks should equal the negative ranks; both should be about 14. We need to determine whether the observed 19 is significantly greater than 14. According to Table A.7 in the appendix (with $N = 7$), T must be 26 or more to be significant at the .05 level by a two-tailed test. Therefore, 19 is not unusual; such values occur quite often by chance. The null hypothesis is therefore accepted at $\alpha = .05$.

Normal curve approximation

As N increases, the sampling distribution of T becomes normal. For large samples, the normal curve can be used to approximate the sampling distribution.

Suppose an experimenter examined 42 pairs of matched animals. Say he studied the animals' performance and found that $T = 532$. The sum of all the ranks from 1 to 42 is $42(43)/2 = 903$. If the null hypothesis is valid, half the ranks should be positive, so T should be approximately $\frac{1}{2}(903) = 451.5$. The distribution's mean and standard deviation can be computed by the following formulas:

$$\mu_T = \frac{N(N + 1)}{4} \tag{14.3}$$

$$= \frac{42(43)}{4} = 451.5$$

$$\sigma_T = \sqrt{\frac{N(N + 1)(2N + 1)}{24}} \tag{14.4}$$

$$= \sqrt{\frac{(42)(43)(85)}{24}} = 79.98$$

Thus we imagine a normal distribution whose $\mu = 451.5$ and whose $\sigma = 79.98$. To evaluate the observed T, we then compute a z score. A correction for continuity can also be included to increase the accuracy:

$$z = \frac{|534 - 451.5| - 1/2}{79.98} = \frac{82}{79.98} = 1.03$$

The z is small, so T fits comfortably into the hypothesized sampling distribution. Therefore, the null hypothesis is accepted. The two conditions do not differ significantly.

EXAMPLE 14.4

In a psycholinguistic experiment subjects read a series of statements and decided whether each statement was true or false. The experimenter measured the subject's reaction time to each statement. He computed the median reaction time to the true statements and to the false statements. The difference was noted for each subject. Altogether 32 subjects were tested. The data are shown in Table 14.5. Do false statements have longer reaction times? Use the .01 level of significance and a one-tailed test.

TABLE 14.5   Data for the psycholinguistic experiment

Subject	d	Signed rank Negative	Signed rank Positive
1	1.5		+12
2	1.2		+10
3	1.6		+15
4	−0.5	−3	
5	0		—
6	0		—
7	3.5		+27.5
8	2.4		+21
9	2.5		+23
10	2.5		+23
11	1.6		+15
12	−0.5	−3	
13	1.9		+19.5
14	0.7		+ 6
15	0.9		+ 7
16	2.5		+23
17	1.6		+15
18	1.9		+19.5
19	1.6		+15
20	0		—
21	−0.6	−5	
22	0.5		+ 3
23	2.9		+26
24	−1.1	−8.5	
25	1.1		+ 8.5
26	3.5		+27.5
27	−1.6	−15	
28	1.4		+11
29	−0.4	−1	
30	0		—
31	1.8		+18
32	2.8		+25
			$T = 370.5$

Solution First the difference scores of 0 are eliminated. That leaves 28 non-zero difference scores, so $N = 28$. Then the absolute difference scores are rank-ordered, the signs are replaced, and the positive ranks are summed: $T = 370.5$.

Then the sampling distribution is described. Its mean is: $N(N + 1)/4 = 28(29)/4 = 203$. Its standard deviation is

$$\sqrt{N(N + 1)(2N + 1)/24} = \sqrt{(28)(29)(57)/24} = 43.91$$

Finally, the z score is computed:

$$z = \frac{|370.5 - 203| - 1/2}{43.91} = 3.80$$

This z is significant at $\alpha = .01$, so the null hypothesis is rejected. Apparently, true statements are comprehended faster.

14.4 A RANK TEST FOR INDEPENDENT GROUPS (THE RANK SUM TEST)

Next we consider the rank sum test, a test which compares two independent groups. Suppose some experimental animals were reinforced to imitate a leader. Does "learning to imitate" generalize to other situations? If an animal learned to imitate a leader in one situation, would it imitate the leader in other situations? Experimental animals were studied over a period of time. Each animal's behavior was scored to report the number of times it imitated the leader. Here are the data:

Experimental Group (Reinforced for imitating)	Control Group (Not reinforced for imitating)
87	118
52	54
55	51
49	50
	98

The data are skewed so the investigator does not use a t test or an analysis of variance.

The experimental group has four scores, and the control group has five scores: $n_E = 4$ and $n_C = 5$. Altogether there are $N = 9$ scores. To use the test, we first rank-order all N scores. The ranks become:

Experimental Group	Control Group
7	9
4	5
6	3
1	2
	8
$n_E = 4$	$n_C = 5$
Sum $= 18$	Sum $= 27$

Then we consider the *smaller* sample (the experimental group) and sum its ranks. Let us denote this sum W: $W = 18$. The rank sum test is designed to evaluate the sum 18. A table is available for evaluating W; but before we examine that table, let us generate the sampling distribution without a table. We need to consider the different possible values of W.

If the four lowest scores were in Group E, the ranks would be 1, 2, 3, and 4; their sum would be 10. If the four highest scores were in Group E, the ranks would be 6, 7, 8, and 9; their sum would be 30. Therefore, W lies somewhere between 10 and 30.

If the two groups do not differ significantly, Group E's ranks should resemble Group C's ranks. The mean for all 9 ranks is $(N + 1)/2 = (9 + 1)/2 = 5$. If a group has n scores, its total should be n(mean rank). Group E has four scores, so its total should be roughly $4(5) = 20$. Thus W lies between 10 and 30—and probably near 20.

We could systematically list each value of W. Perhaps the experimental group has the ranks "1, 2, 3, 4" or "1, 2, 4, 7" or "2, 4, 5, 9." For each possibility, we could compute W and then determine the complete sampling distribution. That distribution is shown in Table 14.6. The sampling distribution is symmetrical, and its mean is 20. From this distribution we can determine the probability of "18 or less." That probability is .365.

Tables have been compiled to summarize these probabilities. For each W the table would tell the probability of that W or a more extreme one. To use the table, we would need to specify the size of each sample. Table 14.7 shows part of such a table. It describes the probabilities when the smaller group has four cases and the larger group has five cases.

Locate "$W = 18$" in the table. As the table shows, the probability is .365 that W is 18 or less. Thus, the chances are high that the rank sum is 18 or less.

This probability is one-tailed—18 or *less*. But suppose a two-tailed probability were needed—the probability that W is 18 or less *or* 22 or more. Then we would double .365. The two-tailed probability would equal $2(.365) = .720$. This probability tells the likelihood that W is as far from the center as 18. The null hypothesis would obviously be accepted.

Table A.8 in the appendix tells the value of W that is needed to reach significance at different α's.

TABLE 14.6 Sampling distribution of W when $n_{smaller} = 4$ and $n_{larger} = 5$

Possible value of W	Its chance probability
30	.008
29	.008
28	.016
27	.024
26	.039
25	.048
24	.063
23	.072
22	.087
21	.087
20	.096
19	.087
18	.087
17	.072
16	.063
15	.048
14	.039
13	.024
12	.016
11	.008
10	.008

(The probability is .365 that W is 18 or lower)

TABLE 14.7 Sampling distribution of W when $n_{smaller} = 4$ and $n_{larger} = 5$

W	The probability of this W or a more extreme one
10 or 30	.008
11 or 29	.016
12 or 28	.032
13 or 27	.056
14 or 26	.095
15 or 25	.143
16 or 24	.206
17 or 23	.278
18 or 22	.365
19 or 21	.452
20 or 20	.548

EXAMPLE 14.5

Psychiatric patients rated their daily moods on a scale from 0 to 100. Two different drugs were administered to the patients—Drug A to Group A, Drug B to Group B. Each patient's rating after a week on the drug was recorded. The data are shown below. Do the two groups differ significantly? Adopt the .05 level of significance, and use a two-tailed test.

Mood ratings: Original data		Ranks	
Group A	Group B	Group A	Group B
40	62	4	8
40	80	4	11
40	63	4	9
36	72	1	10
54	37	6	2
61	83	7	12

Solution First rank-order the 12 scores. Then sum the smaller group's ranks. Since both groups are the same size, let us arbitrarily consider Group A: For Group A, $W = 26$.

Then consult Table A.8 in the appendix. $n_{smaller} = 6$ and $n_{larger} = 6$. To be significant at the .05 level by a two-tailed test, W must be "26 or smaller" or "52 or larger." Therefore the observed difference is significant, and we reject the null hypothesis. The two groups do differ significantly at the .05 level.

Normal curve approximation

As N increases, the sampling distribution of W comes to resemble a normal distribution. The distribution's mean (μ_W) and standard deviation (σ_W) can be computed by the following formulas:

$$\mu_W = \frac{n_{smaller}(N + 1)}{2} \tag{14.5}$$

$$\sigma_W = \sqrt{\frac{n_{smaller}\, n_{larger}(N + 1)}{12}} \tag{14.6}$$

The observed W can then be expressed as a z score. A correction for continuity can also be included to increase the accuracy.

$$z = \frac{|W - \mu_W| - \frac{1}{2}}{\sigma_W} \tag{14.7}$$

The procedure is shown in Example 14.6.

EXAMPLE 14.6

Are authoritarian people more conforming? An investigator studied two groups of subjects with 15 subjects in each group. The subjects in one group were judged to be authoritarian, those in the other group were not. Each subject was interviewed, and the interview was scored to tell how many conforming remarks the subject emitted. The data were very skewed, so the investigator converted each conformity score to a rank. For the authoritarian group, the sum of the ranks (W) was 284.

Were the authoritarian subjects more conforming? Test the hypothesis at the 5 percent level of significance with a one-tailed test.

Solution With 15 subjects per group, $N = 15 + 15 = 30$. First compute the mean and standard deviation of the sampling distribution of W:

$$\mu_W = \frac{n_{smaller}(N + 1)}{2} = \frac{15(31)}{2} = 232.5$$

$$\sigma_W = \sqrt{\frac{n_{smaller}\,n_{larger}(N + 1)}{12}} = \sqrt{\frac{(15)(15)(31)}{12}} = 24.11$$

Then approximate the sampling distribution of W by a normal curve whose $\mu = 232.5$ and whose $\sigma = 24.11$. Finally, locate the observed W in this distribution:

$$z = \frac{|W - \mu_W| - \frac{1}{2}}{\sigma_W}$$

$$= \frac{|284 - 232.5| - \frac{1}{2}}{24.11} = 2.12$$

This z exceeds 1.65, so the observed W lies in the highest 5 percent of the sampling distribution. Therefore, we reject the null hypothesis. The groups do differ significantly. Apparently, authoritarian subjects are more conforming.

14.5 A RANK TEST FOR k INDEPENDENT GROUPS (THE KRUSKAL-WALLIS TEST)

Imagine an experiment with several experimental conditions. An analysis of variance would be used if the data were normal; otherwise, a nonparametric test is needed. Kruskal and Wallis have developed a powerful test to handle such data. As an example, consider an experiment with three conditions; $k = 3$. There are 16 scores altogether, so $N = 16$.

	Condition	
I	*II*	*III*
96	82	115
128	124	132
83	149	171
61	135	147
101	109	155
		193

To apply the Kruskal-Wallis test, first rank-order all N scores; the ranks extend from 1 to 14. Then sum the ranks in each condition; each sum is denoted R_i.

		Condition	
	I	*II*	*III*
	4	2	7
	9	8	10
	3	13	15
	1	11	12
	5	6	14
			16
Sum of ranks (R_i)	22	40	74
n_i	5	5	6

According to the null hypothesis, the three conditions do not really differ; the mean rank should be about the same in each group. Kruskal and Wallis developed a measure, H, which describes the means' variability. The larger H is, the more the conditions differ.

To compute H, consider each condition's sum (R_i) and the number of scores in that sum (n_i). For each group, compute R_i^2/n_i. Then sum all these terms. H is defined as follows:

$$H = \left[\frac{12}{N(N+1)}\right]\left[\sum \frac{R_i^2}{n_i}\right] - 3(N+1) \tag{14.8}$$

For the data:

$$H = \left[\frac{12}{16(17)}\right]\left[\frac{22^2}{5} + \frac{40^2}{5} + \frac{74^2}{6}\right] - 3(17)$$

$$= \left[\frac{12}{272}\right][1329.5] - 51$$

$$= 7.65$$

If each n_i is 5 or more, the distribution of H follows the chi-square distribution with $k - 1$ degrees of freedom. In the example, $H = 7.65$. To evaluate this result, we consider a chi-square distribution with 2 df. Let $\alpha = .05$; then the critical value of χ^2 is 5.99. In the example, H exceeds this value, so the groups do differ significantly.

When two or more scores are tied, the value of H has to be corrected slightly. The corrected value is denoted $H_{corrected}$.

$$H_{corrected} = \frac{H}{\text{Correction factor}} \tag{14.9}$$

To compute the correction factor, consider each case of tied scores. Note how many scores are tied, and denote that number t. (If three scores are tied, $t = 3$.) For each case, compute $t^3 - t$. Then sum all of these values. The correction factor equals:

$$\text{Correction factor} = 1 - \frac{\Sigma(t^3 - t)}{N^3 - N}$$

The complete procedure is shown in Example 14.7.

EXAMPLE 14.7

Lesions were produced in four different hypothalamic locations in experimental rats. The experimenter then measured the amount of water each animal drank during a subsequent period. A control group was also tested. Do the five groups differ significantly? Use the .05 level of significance.

Lesion A	Lesion B	Lesion C	Lesion D	Control
35	6	9	41	22
14	29	5	7	8
6	4	4	4	11
6	64	80	14	5
13	13	14	21	14
14	64	51		42
64		84		71
				97

Solution   First convert the data to ranks:

	Lesion A	Lesion B	Lesion C	Lesion D	Control
	23	7	11	24	21
	17	22	4.5	9	10
	7	2	2	2	12
	7	28	31	17	4.5
	13.5	13.5	17	20	17
	17	28	26		25
	28		32		30
					33
R_i	112.5	100.5	123.5	72	152.5
n_i	7	6	7	5	8
$\sum \dfrac{R_i^2}{n_i}$	1,808.04	1,683.38	2,178.89	1,036.80	2,906.03

Then sum the ranks in each condition and compute H:

$$H = \left[\frac{12}{N(N+1)}\right]\left(\sum \frac{R_i^2}{n_i}\right) - 3(N+1)$$

$$= \left[\frac{12}{33(34)}\right][1,808.04 + 1,683.38 + 2,178.89 + 1,036.80$$

$$+ 2,906.03] - 3(34)$$

$$= 0.83$$

Then correct for tied scores. Let us prepare a table which shows the ties:

Scores	t (Number of tied scores)	$t^3 - t$
4, 4, 4	3	$3^3 - 3 = 24$
5, 5	2	$2^3 - 2 = 6$
6, 6, 6	3	$3^3 - 3 = 24$
13, 13	2	$2^3 - 2 = 6$
14, 14, 14, 14, 14	5	$5^3 - 5 = 120$
64, 64, 64	3	$3^3 - 3 = 24$
		$\sum(t^3 - t) = 204$

For each case of tied scores, compute $t^3 - t$. Then sum all of these terms: $\sum(t^3 - t) = 204$. The correction factor becomes:

$$\text{Correction factor} = 1 - \frac{\sum(t^3 - t)}{N^3 - N}$$

$$= 1 - \frac{204}{33^3 - 33} = 1 - .01 = .99$$

Finally, compute $H_{\text{corrected}}$:

$$H_{\text{corrected}} = \frac{H}{\text{Correction factor}}$$

$$= \frac{0.83}{0.99} = 0.84$$

This value of H is viewed as a χ^2 with $k - 1 = 5 - 1 = 4$ degrees of freedom. "0.84" is so small that the null hypothesis is accepted at $\alpha = .05$. The five conditions do not differ significantly.

14.6 FRIEDMAN TWO-WAY ANALYSIS OF VARIANCE BY RANKS

Finally, we need to consider one other nonparametric test. This test analyzes the data of a Repeated Measurements design when the data do not meet the assumptions of an analysis of variance. In Sec. 11.8 we examined the Repeated Measurements design. In that design, every subject was tested in each experimental condition. For example, consider the data in Table 14.8; every subject was tested in three experimental conditions.

TABLE 14.8 Data for a Repeated Measurements design: $k = 3, n = 5$

	Condition A	Condition B	Condition C
Subject 1	27	21	22
Subject 2	39	30	21
Subject 3	24	21	49
Subject 4	91	47	34
Subject 5	56	21	39

To use Friedman's test, we convert each subject's scores to ranks. In Table 14.8, for example, each subject's scores are converted to ranks from 1 to 3. We do this for every subject. The results are shown in Table 14.9. Then we sum each row and column.

TABLE 14.9 Data of Table 14.8 converted to ranks

	Condition A	Condition B	Condition C	Sum
Subject 1	3	1	2	6
Subject 2	3	2	1	6
Subject 3	2	1	3	6
Subject 4	3	2	1	6
Subject 5	3	1	2	6
Sum (R_i)	14	7	9	30

The row sums are all equal—$1 + 2 + 3 = 6$—but the column sums differ. The test is designed to tell whether they differ significantly. In Table 14.9, Condition B seems to have lower ranks, while Condition A seems to have higher ranks. According to the null hypothesis, the differences are due to chance.

Friedman's test concerns the variance among the column means. Friedman[1] has shown how to compare the variance among the means with the variance expected by chance. First of all, we know how a set of ranks should vary *theoretically*. For n ranks, the theoretical variance is: $(n^2 - 1)/12$. Therefore, we can express the theoretical variance within each condition. Second, from the analysis of variance, we can compute $ms_{\text{Between conditions}}$. If the null hypothesis is valid, the means only differ by chance; and $ms_{\text{Between conditions}}$ estimates σ^2. The ratio of these terms—$ms_{\text{Between conditions}}/\sigma^2$—follows the chi-square distribution.

Friedman has derived a convenient formula to express this ratio. In the formula, k is the number of columns, and n is the number of subjects. To use the formula, sum each column, denoting the sum R_i. Then square each R_i and sum the squared totals. The formula is denoted χ_r^2:

$$\chi_r^2 = \left[\frac{12}{nk(k+1)}\right] \left(\sum R_i^2\right) - 3n(k+1) \tag{14.10}$$

From the data of Table 14.8, $\sum R_i^2$ equals $14^2 + 7^2 + 9^2 = 326$. χ_r^2 becomes:

$$\chi_r^2 = \left[\frac{12}{(5)(3)(4)}\right] (14^2 + 7^2 + 9^2) - (3)(5)(4)$$
$$= 5.20$$

When k and n are small, a special table is needed to evaluate χ_r^2. This table appears in textbooks of nonparametric statistics.[2] When we consult this table

[1] Friedman, M. The use of ranks to avoid the assumption of normality implicit in the analysis of variance. *Journal of the American Statistical Association*, 1937, **32**, 675–701.
[2] One standard text is Siegel, S. *Nonparametric Statistics*, McGraw-Hill Book Co., New York, 1956.

for $k = 3$ and $n = 5$, we obtain the following information:

χ_r^2	Probability of this χ_r^2 or a larger one
0.0	1.000
1.2	.691
2.8	.367
5.2	.093
6.4	.039
7.6	.024
8.4	.0085
10.0	.00077

Thus, "5.2" is not statistically significant at the .05 level. The groups do not differ significantly.

When the sample is large enough, the sampling distribution of χ_r^2 follows the chi-square distribution. When k is greater than 3 and n is greater than 4, consult the chi-square distribution with $k - 1$ degrees of freedom. Example 14.8 illustrates a problem of this type. That example reanalyzes the data of Example 11.11.

EXAMPLE 14.8

An investigator performed an experiment with four experimental conditions. He wanted to learn whether distracting lights, odors, and touches affect a person's comprehension of tape-recorded messages. Five-person groups were tested. The subjects within each group were matched for their auditory acuity.

	Condition			
	Distracting lights	Distracting odors	Distracting touches	Control
Group 1 (excellent auditory acuity)	25	30	25	25
Group 2 (good auditory acuity)	23	22	23	21
Group 3 (medium auditory acuity)	19	23	20	24
Group 4 (fair auditory acuity)	15	17	16	21
Group 5 (poor auditory acuity)	15	15	15	24

Do the groups differ significantly?

Solution   First change each row's scores to ranks. Tied scores are assigned the mean of the ranks they would otherwise receive.

	Distracting lights	Distracting odors	Distracting touches	Control	Sum
Group 1 (excellent auditory acuity)	2	4	2	2	10
Group 2 (good auditory acuity)	3.5	2	3.5	1	10
Group 3 (medium auditory acuity)	1	3	2	4	10
Group 4 (fair auditory acuity)	1	3	2	4	10
Group 5 (poor auditory acuity)	2	2	2	4	10
Sum (R_i)	9.5	14	11.5	15	50

Sum each column's ranks, square each total, and sum the squared totals: $\sum R_i^2 = 9.5^2 + 14^2 + 11.5^2 + 15^2 = 643.5$. Finally compute χ_r^2:

$$\chi_r^2 = \left[\frac{12}{nk(k+1)} \right] (\sum R_i^2) - 3n(k+1)$$

$$= \frac{12}{5(4)(5)} (9.5^2 + 14^2 + 11.5^2 + 15^2) - 3(5)(5)$$

$$= 2.22$$

To evaluate "2.22," consult a chi-square distribution with $k - 1 = 3$ df. According to the table, χ_r^2 must equal 7.82 to be significant at the .05 level. Since "2.22" is so small, the four conditions do not differ significantly.

EXERCISES

14.1 Subjects were tested under two viewing conditions—a monocular condition and a binocular condition. Each score reported how often the subject perceived correctly (as a percentage of a maximum score). Use the sign test to determine whether the two conditions differ significantly. Adopt the 5 percent level of significance.

	Binocular Condition	Monocular Condition
Subject A	76	62
Subject B	21	20
Subject C	35	39
Subject D	48	39
Subject E	94	80
Subject F	19	14
Subject G	67	53

Answer: Probability of 5 or more pluses or 5 or more minuses is $14/64$; H_0 accepted

14.2   Members of a speed-reading class were tested for their reading speed before and after the course. The data are shown below. Use the sign test to determine whether the overall change was significant.

Subject	Before	After
A	73	50
B	80	45
C	65	60
D	61	62
E	90	59
F	69	54
G	70	49
H	60	30

Answer: Probability of 7 or more pluses = .035; H_0 is rejected at the .05 level

14.3   Fifty subjects were tested on a visual task with each eye. Performance was better with the dominant eye in 32 cases, and better with the other eye in 17 cases. (There was one case of a tie.) Is the eye difference significant?
Answer: $\mu_{binomial} = 24.5$; $\sigma_{binomial} = 3.5$; $z = 2.0$; H_0 is rejected.

14.4   An investigator compared subjects' memory for words under two conditions. In one condition the subjects were asked to visualize the object; in the other condition, they were not. The data report the number of words each subject remembered. Use the median test to tell whether the groups differed significantly.

Instructed to Visualize	Not Instructed
10	4
9	6
5	5
8	6
9	6
4	7
8	5
8	6
4	7
7	7

Answer: $\chi^2_{(1)} = 3.20$; $p > .05$; H_0 is accepted.

14.5   The median reaction time for a population of subjects is 117.9. A sample of seven hospitalized subjects was tested. The subjects gave the following reaction times: 90, 90, 90, 92, 111, 116, 158. Make up a statistical test—the simplest one you can think of—to test the hypothesis that the seven subjects comprise a random sample from the general population. Adopt the 5 percent level of significance.

Answer: Probability of 5 or more pluses or 5 or more minuses is $14/64$*;* H_0 *accepted.*

14.6 Convert the following scores to ranks: 5, 3, 7, 3, 4, 5, 9, 5, 7. What is the mean of these ranks? What is the variance of these ranks?
Answer: 5, 1.5, 7.5, 1.5, 3, 5, 9, 5, 7.5; mean = 5; variance = 6.67

14.7 An investigator studied the activity level of subjects before and after lunch. Use the rank test for matched groups to tell whether the two activity levels differ significantly.

Subject	Before	After
1	52	50
2	45	49
3	55	55
4	50	48
5	47	43
6	50	49
7	46	47
8	50	45
9	56	55
10	55	53

Answer: $T = 35.5, p > .05$*,* H_0 *is accepted.*

14.8 Two groups of children were rated for their aggressive behavior. The children in Group 1 each had an older sibling; those in Group 2 each had a younger sibling. Use the rank-sum test to tell whether the groups differ significantly in their rated degree of aggressiveness.

Group 1	Group 2
20	60
25	35
19	45
28	25
22	29
25	34
30	30
26	

Answer: $W = 78.5, p < .01$*;* H_0 *is rejected.*

14.9 Do children adopt their parents' prejudices? An investigator tested two groups of adolescents—20 children from highly prejudiced parents and 25 children from less prejudiced parents. He interviewed each child and scored the child's degree of prejudice. The data were ranked, and the sum of the ranks for the prejudiced group was 570. Use the rank sum test to tell whether the groups differ significantly.
Answer: $\mu_W = 460, \sigma_W = 43.78, z = 2.50, p < .05$*;* H_0 *is rejected.*

14.10 Three samples of animals were tested in a maze. One group was reinforced with a sugar solution, another with a saccharine solution, and a third with plain water. Use the Kruskal-Wallis test to tell whether the three groups differ significantly.

Mean Number of Errors

Sugar	Saccharine	Control
10	6	16
15	10	48
8	12	19
11	10	21
30	9	22
58	35	
	60	

Answer: $H_{corrected} = 2.20$, with 2 df, $p > .05$; H_0 is accepted.

14.11 Four methods were compared for teaching slow learners to read. Each subject was matched with subjects of the other groups for initial reading ability. The subject's final reading score is reported below. Use the Friedman two-way analysis of variance by ranks to tell whether the different methods produced significant differences.

	Method 1	Method 2	Method 3	Method 4
Best readers	30	17	40	20
Next best	13	38	23	12
Next best	10	20	25	9
Poorest readers	15	18	20	7

Answer: $\chi^2_r = 7.8$; $p = .036$; H_0 rejected.

GLOSSARY

α	(alpha) Probability of a Type I error.
β	(beta) Probability of a Type II error.
μ	(mu) Mean of a population.
ν	(nu) Number of degrees of freedom.
π	(pi) 3.1416.
ρ	(rho) Correlation coefficient of a population.
σ	(sigma: small letter) Standard deviation of a population.
$\sum, \sum_{k}, \sum_{i=1}^{N}$	(sigma: capital letter) Instruction to sum.
χ^2	(chi-square) The value of the statistic computed in the chi-square test. The distribution of such values follows the χ^2 distribution.

$\lvert a \rvert$	Absolute value of a: $\lvert -5 \rvert = 5$; $\lvert +5 \rvert = 5$.
$A \cup B$	Union of sets A and B.
$A \cap B$	Intersection of sets A and B.
$P(A \mid B)$	Conditional probability; probability of A given that B has occurred.
$n!$	n factorial: $4! = 4 \cdot 3 \cdot 2 \cdot 1 = 24$.
$\sqrt{a}$	Square root of a.
∞	Infinity.
$a > b$	a is greater than b.
$a \geq b$	a is greater than or equal to b.
$a < b$	a is less than b.
$a \leq b$	a is less than or equal to b.
$a = b$	a equals b.
$a \neq b$	a does not equal b.
$a, a_{Y \cdot X}$	Constant in the regression equation for predicting Y from X. It tells the value of Y that is predicted when X equals 0.
A.D.	Average deviation.
$b, b_{Y \cdot X}$	Regression coefficient. It tells the slope of the regression equation for predicting Y from X.
cf	Cumulative frequency. It tells the number of cases that fall at or below a given value.
$_nC_r$	Number of combinations that can be formed from n objects when r of them are drawn at a time.
C.R.	Critical ratio. It tells the value formed when a sample value is expressed as a z score within a hypothesized sampling distribution.
d	(1) Coded deviation values. In a frequency distribution it tells the category's distance from the lowest category. (2) In the Wilcoxon matched-pairs signed-ranks test, the difference between the two scores of a pair.
D	A difference score. It tells the difference between two paired measurements: $Y - X$.
$_nD_n$	Number of permutations of n objects that are distinguishably different.
$\bar{D}$	Mean of a set of difference scores.
df	Number of degrees of freedom.
e	Base of Naperian logarithms, 2.7183.
e_{ij}	Amount of error in a score X_{ij}. It primarily appears in the theory behind the analysis of variance.
E_1	A simple event like the toss of a coin.
$E(X)$	Expected value of X. It equals the mean of the X scores.
$E(X - \mu)^2$	Expected value of the squared deviation scores. It equals σ^2.
f	Frequency of scores in some category of a frequency distribution.

f_i, f_{ij}	Observed frequency in some category when a chi-square test is performed.
F_i, F_{ij}	Expected frequency in some category when a chi-square test is performed.
F	Ratio of two variance estimates. The distribution of such values follows the theoretical F distribution.
H	Value of the statistic computed in the Kruskal-Wallis Test.
H_0	Hypothesis that is tested by a statistical test, often a null hypothesis.
H_1	Alternate hypothesis to the one being tested.
i	Width of each category in a frequency distribution.
ms	Mean square term in the analysis of variance. It is an estimate of the population variance.
N	Number of observations in a sample.
n_{R_i}, n_{C_i}	Number of observations in a given row or column of an r by k table. It is used in the chi-square test.
n	Number of simple events that enter into a binomial experiment.
P_i	ith percentile score. P_{75} is the 75th percentile score; 75 percent of the cases lie below it.
$P, P(A)$	Probability of some outcome (A).
$_nP_n$	Number of permutations of n objects.
$_nP_r$	Number of permutations of r objects from a supply of n objects.
p	Probability in a binomial situation that one of the two alternatives occurs.
q	Probability in a binomial situation that the other alternative occurs: $q = 1 - p$.
Q	Quartile deviation.
Q_1	First quartile score. It equals P_{25}.
Q_3	Third quartile score. It equals P_{75}.
r, r_{XY}	Correlation coefficient of a sample.
S, S_X, S_Y	Standard deviation of a sample.
s, s_X, s_Y	Best estimate of the standard deviation of a population based on the scores of a sample.
$S^2, S_X{}^2, S_Y{}^2$	Variance of a sample.
$s^2, s_X{}^2, s_Y{}^2$	Best estimate of the variance of the population based on the scores of a sample.
$S_{\bar{X}}$	An estimate of the standard error of the mean in which S has been used to estimate σ.
$s_{\bar{X}}$	An estimate of the standard error of the mean in which s has been used to estimate σ.
$S_{\bar{X}-\bar{Y}}$	An estimate of the standard error of the difference between two means in which S_{X-Y} has been used to estimate σ_{X-Y}.

$s_{\bar{X}-\bar{Y}}$	An estimate of the standard error of the difference between two means in which $s_{\bar{X}-\bar{Y}}$ has been used to estimate $\sigma_{\bar{X}-\bar{Y}}$.
$S_{Y-Y'}$	Standard error of estimate when Y is predicted from X.
ss	Sum of squares term in the analysis of variance. It equals the sum of squared deviation scores.
T	(1) A score normalized in such a way that the mean of the entire set is 50 and the standard deviation is 10.
	(2) In the analysis of variance, the total of a set of scores. T_c is the total for a given column; T_s is the total for a given subject.
	(3) Value of the statistic computed in the Wilcoxon matched-pairs signed-ranks test.
t	(1) A ratio that follows the t distribution. The numerator is normally distributed and the denominator follows the chi-square distribution.
	(2) Number of tied observations in a set of ranks.
W	Value of the statistic computed in the rank sum test.
X, X_i, Y, Y_i	A variable.
x, y	A variable with every observation expressed as a deviation from the mean—e.g., $x = X - \bar{X}$.
$\bar{X}, \bar{Y}$	Mean of a sample. A bar over a symbol always denotes the mean value.
Y'	Value of Y predicted from the best-fitting regression equation. $Y' = b_{Y \cdot X} X + a_{Y \cdot X}$.
z	Standard score, $\dfrac{X - \bar{X}}{S_X}$. It tells how many standard deviations X is from $\bar{X}$.
z^*	A transformed value of r which normalizes the sampling distribution of r.

APPENDIXES

A: MAJOR STATISTICAL TABLES

TABLE A.1 Area under the normal curve between the center and a given z score

z score	Area between mean and that z score	z score	Area between mean and that z score	z score	Area between mean and that z score
0.00	.0000	0.30	.1179	0.60	.2257
0.01	.0040	0.31	.1217	0.61	.2291
0.02	.0080	0.32	.1255	0.62	.2324
0.03	.0120	0.33	.1293	0.63	.2357
0.04	.0160	0.34	.1331	0.64	.2389
0.05	.0199	0.35	.1368	0.65	.2422
0.06	.0239	0.36	.1406	0.66	.2454
0.07	.0279	0.37	.1443	0.67	.2486
0.08	.0319	0.38	.1480	0.68	.2517
0.09	.0359	0.39	.1517	0.69	.2549
0.10	.0398	0.40	.1554	0.70	.2580
0.11	.0438	0.41	.1591	0.71	.2611
0.12	.0478	0.42	.1628	0.72	.2642
0.13	.0517	0.43	.1664	0.73	.2673
0.14	.0557	0.44	.1700	0.74	.2704
0.15	.0596	0.45	.1736	0.75	.2734
0.16	.0636	0.46	.1772	0.76	.2764
0.17	.0675	0.47	.1808	0.77	.2794
0.18	.0714	0.48	.1844	0.78	.2823
0.19	.0753	0.49	.1879	0.79	.2852
0.20	.0793	0.50	.1915	0.80	.2881
0.21	.0832	0.51	.1950	0.81	.2910
0.22	.0871	0.52	.1985	0.82	.2939
0.23	.0910	0.53	.2019	0.83	.2967
0.24	.0948	0.54	.2054	0.84	.2995
0.25	.0987	0.55	.2088	0.85	.3023
0.26	.1026	0.56	.2123	0.86	.3051
0.27	.1064	0.57	.2157	0.87	.3078
0.28	.1103	0.58	.2190	0.88	.3106
0.29	.1141	0.59	.2224	0.89	.3133

Continued

TABLE A.1 *Continued*

z score	Area between mean and that z score	z score	Area between mean and that z score	z score	Area between mean and that z score
0.90	.3159	1.30	.4032	1.70	.4554
0.91	.3186	1.31	.4049	1.71	.4564
0.92	.3212	1.32	.4066	1.72	.4573
0.93	.3238	1.33	.4082	1.73	.4582
0.94	.3264	1.34	.4099	1.74	.4591
0.95	.3289	1.35	.4115	1.75	.4599
0.96	.3315	1.36	.4131	1.76	.4608
0.97	.3340	1.37	.4147	1.77	.4616
0.98	.3365	1.38	.4162	1.78	.4625
0.99	.3389	1.39	.4177	1.79	.4633
1.00	.3413	1.40	.4192	1.80	.4641
1.01	.3438	1.41	.4207	1.81	.4649
1.02	.3461	1.42	.4222	1.82	.4656
1.03	.3485	1.43	.4236	1.83	.4664
1.04	.3508	1.44	.4251	1.84	.4671
1.05	.3531	1.45	.4265	1.85	.4678
1.06	.3554	1.46	.4279	1.86	.4686
1.07	.3577	1.47	.4292	1.87	.4693
1.08	.3599	1.48	.4306	1.88	.4699
1.09	.3621	1.49	.4319	1.89	.4706
1.10	.3643	1.50	.4332	1.90	.4713
1.11	.3665	1.51	.4345	1.91	.4719
1.12	.3686	1.52	.4357	1.92	.4726
1.13	.3708	1.53	.4370	1.93	.4732
1.14	.3729	1.54	.4382	1.94	.4738
1.15	.3749	1.55	.4394	1.95	.4744
1.16	.3770	1.56	.4406	1.96	.4750
1.17	.3790	1.57	.4418	1.97	.4756
1.18	.3810	1.58	.4429	1.98	.4761
1.19	.3830	1.59	.4441	1.99	.4767
1.20	.3849	1.60	.4452	2.00	.4772
1.21	.3869	1.61	.4463	2.01	.4778
1.22	.3888	1.62	.4474	2.02	.4783
1.23	.3907	1.63	.4484	2.03	.4788
1.24	.3925	1.64	.4495	2.04	.4793
1.25	.3944	1.65	.4505	2.05	.4798
1.26	.3962	1.66	.4515	2.06	.4803
1.27	.3980	1.67	.4525	2.07	.4808
1.28	.3997	1.68	.4535	2.08	.4812
1.29	.4015	1.69	.4545	2.09	.4817

TABLE A.1 *Continued*

z score	Area between mean and that z score	z score	Area between mean and that z score	z score	Area between mean and that z score
2.10	.4821	2.50	.4938	2.90	.4981
2.11	.4826	2.51	.4940	2.91	.4982
2.12	.4830	2.52	.4941	2.92	.4982
2.13	.4834	2.53	.4943	2.93	.4983
2.14	.4838	2.54	.4945	2.94	.4984
2.15	.4842	2.55	.4946	2.95	.4984
2.16	.4846	2.56	.4948	2.96	.4985
2.17	.4850	2.57	.4949	2.97	.4985
2.18	.4854	2.58	.4951	2.98	.4986
2.19	.4857	2.59	.4952	2.99	.4986
2.20	.4861	2.60	.4953	3.00	.4987
2.21	.4864	2.61	.4955	3.01	.4987
2.22	.4868	2.62	.4956	3.02	.4987
2.23	.4871	2.63	.4957	3.03	.4988
2.24	.4875	2.64	.4959	3.04	.4988
2.25	.4878	2.65	.4960	3.05	.4989
2.26	.4881	2.66	.4961	3.06	.4989
2.27	.4884	2.67	.4962	3.07	.4989
2.28	.4887	2.68	.4963	3.08	.4990
2.29	.4890	2.69	.4964	3.09	.4990
2.30	.4893	2.70	.4965	3.10	.4990
2.31	.4896	2.71	.4966	3.11	.4991
2.32	.4898	2.72	.4967	3.12	.4991
2.33	.4901	2.73	.4968	3.13	.4991
2.34	.4904	2.74	.4969	3.14	.4992
2.35	.4906	2.75	.4970	3.15	.4992
2.36	.4909	2.76	.4971	3.16	.4992
2.37	.4911	2.77	.4972	3.17	.4992
2.38	.4913	2.78	.4973	3.18	.4993
2.39	.4916	2.79	.4974	3.19	.4993
2.40	.4918	2.80	.4974	3.20	.4993
2.41	.4920	2.81	.4975	3.21	.4993
2.42	.4922	2.82	.4976	3.22	.4994
2.43	.4925	2.83	.4977	3.23	.4994
2.44	.4927	2.84	.4977	3.24	.4994
2.45	.4929	2.85	.4978	3.30	.4995
2.46	.4931	2.86	.4979	3.40	.4997
2.47	.4932	2.87	.4979	3.50	.4998
2.48	.4934	2.88	.4980	3.60	.4998
2.49	.4936	2.89	.4981	3.70	.4999

TABLE A.2   Critical values of the *t* distribution

	Proportion of *t* distribution in shaded region:									
	.005	.01	.025	.05	.10	.20	.25	.30	.40	.45
	Level of significance for a two-tailed test									
df	.01	.02	.05	.10	.20	.40	.50	.60	.80	.90
1	63.66	31.82	12.71	6.31	3.08	1.376	1.000	.727	.325	.158
2	9.92	6.96	4.30	2.92	1.89	1.061	.816	.617	.289	.142
3	5.84	4.54	3.18	2.35	1.64	.978	.765	.584	.277	.137
4	4.60	3.75	2.78	2.13	1.53	.941	.741	.569	.271	.134
5	4.03	3.36	2.57	2.02	1.48	.920	.727	.559	.267	.132
6	3.71	3.14	2.45	1.94	1.44	.906	.718	.553	.265	.131
7	3.50	3.00	2.36	1.90	1.42	.896	.711	.549	.263	.130
8	3.36	2.90	2.31	1.86	1.40	.889	.706	.546	.262	.130
9	3.25	2.82	2.26	1.83	1.38	.883	.703	.543	.261	.129
10	3.17	2.76	2.23	1.81	1.37	.879	.700	.542	.260	.129
11	3.11	2.72	2.20	1.80	1.36	.876	.697	.540	.260	.129
12	3.06	2.68	2.18	1.78	1.36	.873	.695	.539	.259	.128
13	3.01	2.65	2.16	1.77	1.35	.870	.694	.538	.259	.128
14	2.98	2.62	2.14	1.76	1.34	.868	.692	.537	.258	.128

15	2.95	2.60	2.13	1.75	1.34	.866	.691	.536	.258	.128
16	2.92	2.58	2.12	1.75	1.34	.865	.690	.535	.258	.128
17	2.90	2.57	2.11	1.74	1.33	.863	.689	.534	.257	.128
18	2.88	2.55	2.10	1.73	1.33	.862	.688	.534	.257	.127
19	2.86	2.54	2.09	1.73	1.33	.861	.688	.533	.257	.127
20	2.84	2.53	2.09	1.72	1.32	.860	.687	.533	.257	.127
21	2.83	2.52	2.08	1.72	1.32	.859	.686	.532	.257	.127
22	2.82	2.51	2.07	1.72	1.32	.858	.686	.532	.256	.127
23	2.81	2.50	2.07	1.71	1.32	.858	.685	.532	.256	.127
24	2.80	2.49	2.06	1.71	1.32	.857	.685	.531	.256	.127
25	2.79	2.48	2.06	1.71	1.32	.856	.684	.531	.256	.127
26	2.78	2.48	2.06	1.71	1.32	.856	.684	.531	.256	.127
27	2.77	2.47	2.05	1.70	1.31	.855	.684	.531	.256	.127
28	2.76	2.47	2.05	1.70	1.31	.855	.683	.530	.256	.127
29	2.76	2.46	2.04	1.70	1.31	.854	.683	.530	.256	.127
30	2.75	2.46	2.04	1.70	1.31	.854	.683	.530	.256	.127
40	2.70	2.42	2.02	1.68	1.30	.851	.681	.529	.255	.126
60	2.66	2.39	2.00	1.67	1.30	.848	.679	.527	.254	.126
120	2.62	2.36	1.98	1.66	1.29	.845	.677	.526	.254	.126
∞	2.58	2.33	1.96	1.645	1.28	.842	.674	.524	.253	.126

Source: Table A.2 is taken from Table III of Fisher and Yates: *Statistical Tables for Biological, Agricultural and Medical Research*, published by Oliver & Boyd, Edinburgh, and by permission of the authors and publishers.

TABLE A.3 Critical values of F distribution, .05 level and .01 level

.05 level

n_1 / n_2	1	2	3	4	5	6	8	12	24	∞
1	161.4	199.5	215.7	224.6	230.2	234.0	238.9	243.9	249.0	254.3
2	18.51	19.00	19.16	19.25	19.30	19.33	19.37	19.41	19.45	19.50
3	10.13	9.55	9.28	9.12	9.01	8.94	8.84	8.74	8.64	8.53
4	7.71	6.94	6.59	6.39	6.26	6.16	6.04	5.91	5.77	5.63
5	6.61	5.79	5.41	5.19	5.05	4.95	4.82	4.68	4.53	4.36
6	5.99	5.14	4.76	4.53	4.39	4.28	4.15	4.00	3.84	3.67
7	5.59	4.74	4.35	4.12	3.97	3.87	3.73	3.57	3.41	3.23
8	5.32	4.46	4.07	3.84	3.69	3.58	3.44	3.28	3.12	2.93
9	5.12	4.26	3.86	3.63	3.48	3.37	3.23	3.07	2.90	2.71
10	4.96	4.10	3.71	3.48	3.33	3.22	3.07	2.91	2.74	2.54
11	4.84	3.98	3.59	3.36	3.20	3.09	2.95	2.79	2.61	2.40
12	4.75	3.88	3.49	3.26	3.11	3.00	2.85	2.69	2.50	2.30
13	4.67	3.80	3.41	3.18	3.02	2.92	2.77	2.60	2.42	2.21
14	4.60	3.74	3.34	3.11	2.96	2.85	2.70	2.53	2.35	2.13
15	4.54	3.68	3.29	3.06	2.90	2.79	2.64	2.48	2.29	2.07
16	4.49	3.63	3.24	3.01	2.85	2.74	2.59	2.42	2.24	2.01
17	4.45	3.59	3.20	2.96	2.81	2.70	2.55	2.38	2.19	1.96
18	4.41	3.55	3.16	2.93	2.77	2.66	2.51	2.34	2.15	1.92
19	4.38	3.52	3.13	2.90	2.74	2.63	2.48	2.31	2.11	1.88
20	4.35	3.49	3.10	2.87	2.71	2.60	2.45	2.28	2.08	1.84
21	4.32	3.47	3.07	2.84	2.68	2.57	2.42	2.25	2.05	1.81
22	4.30	3.44	3.05	2.82	2.66	2.55	2.40	2.23	2.03	1.78
23	4.28	3.42	3.03	2.80	2.64	2.53	2.38	2.20	2.00	1.76
24	4.26	3.40	3.01	2.78	2.62	2.51	2.36	2.18	1.98	1.73
25	4.24	3.38	2.99	2.76	2.60	2.49	2.34	2.16	1.96	1.71
26	4.22	3.37	2.98	2.74	2.59	2.47	2.32	2.15	1.95	1.69
27	4.21	3.35	2.96	2.73	2.57	2.46	2.30	2.13	1.93	1.67
28	4.20	3.34	2.95	2.71	2.56	2.44	2.29	2.12	1.91	1.65
29	4.18	3.33	2.93	2.70	2.54	2.43	2.28	2.10	1.90	1.64
30	4.17	3.32	2.92	2.69	2.53	2.42	2.27	2.09	1.89	1.62
40	4.08	3.23	2.84	2.61	2.45	2.34	2.18	2.00	1.79	1.51
60	4.00	3.15	2.76	2.52	2.37	2.25	2.10	1.92	1.70	1.39
120	3.92	3.07	2.68	2.45	2.29	2.17	2.02	1.83	1.61	1.25
∞	3.84	2.99	2.60	2.37	2.21	2.10	1.94	1.75	1.52	1.00

Source: Table A.3 is taken from Table V of Fisher and Yates: *Statistical Tables for Biological, Agricultural and Medical Research*, published by Oliver & Boyd, Edinburgh, and is used by permission of the authors and publishers.

TABLE A.3 *Continued*

.01 level

n_2 \ n_1	1	2	3	4	5	6	8	12	24	∞
1	4052	4999	5403	5625	5764	5859	5982	6106	6234	6366
2	98·50	99·00	99·17	99·25	99·30	99·33	99·37	99·42	99·46	99·50
3	34·12	30·82	29·46	28·71	28·24	27·91	27·49	27·05	26·60	26·12
4	21·20	18·00	16·69	15·98	15·52	15·21	14·80	14·37	13·93	13·46
5	16·26	13·27	12·06	11·39	10·97	10·67	10·29	9·89	9·47	9·02
6	13·74	10·92	9·78	9·15	8·75	8·47	8·10	7·72	7·31	6·88
7	12·25	9·55	8·45	7·85	7·46	7·19	6·84	6·47	6·07	5·65
8	11·26	8·65	7·59	7·01	6·63	6·37	6·03	5·67	5·28	4·86
9	10·56	8·02	6·99	6·42	6·06	5·80	5·47	5·11	4·73	4·31
10	10·04	7·56	6·55	5·99	5·64	5·39	5·06	4·71	4·33	3·91
11	9·65	7·20	6·22	5·67	5·32	5·07	4·74	4·40	4·02	3·60
12	9·33	6·93	5·95	5·41	5·06	4·82	4·50	4·16	3·78	3·36
13	9·07	6·70	5·74	5·20	4·86	4·62	4·30	3·96	3·59	3·16
14	8·86	6·51	5·56	5·03	4·69	4·46	4·14	3·80	3·43	3·00
15	8·68	6·36	5·42	4·89	4·56	4·32	4·00	3·67	3·29	2·87
16	8·53	6·23	5·29	4·77	4·44	4·20	3·89	3·55	3·18	2·75
17	8·40	6·11	5·18	4·67	4·34	4·10	3·79	3·45	3·08	2·65
18	8·28	6·01	5·09	4·58	4·25	4·01	3·71	3·37	3·00	2·57
19	8·18	5·93	5·01	4·50	4·17	3·94	3·63	3·30	2·92	2·49
20	8·10	5·85	4·94	4·43	4·10	3·87	3·56	3·23	2·86	2·42
21	8·02	5·78	4·87	4·37	4·04	3·81	3·51	3·17	2·80	2·36
22	7·94	5·72	4·82	4·31	3·99	3·76	3·45	3·12	2·75	2·31
23	7·88	5·66	4·76	4·26	3·94	3·71	3·41	3·07	2·70	2·26
24	7·82	5·61	4·72	4·22	3·90	3·67	3·36	3·03	2·66	2·21
25	7·77	5·57	4·68	4·18	3·86	3·63	3·32	2·99	2·62	2·17
26	7·72	5·53	4·64	4·14	3·82	3·59	3·29	2·96	2·58	2·13
27	7·68	5·49	4·60	4·11	3·78	3·56	3·26	2·93	2·55	2·10
28	7·64	5·45	4·57	4·07	3·75	3·53	3·23	2·90	2·52	2·06
29	7·60	5·42	4·54	4·04	3·73	3·50	3·20	2·87	2·49	2·03
30	7·56	5·39	4·51	4·02	3·70	3·47	3·17	2·84	2·47	2·01
40	7·31	5·18	4·31	3·83	3·51	3·29	2·99	2·66	2·29	1·80
60	7·08	4·98	4·13	3·65	3·34	3·12	2·82	2·50	2·12	1·60
120	6·85	4·79	3·95	3·48	3·17	2·96	2·66	2·34	1·95	1·38
∞	6·64	4·60	3·78	3·32	3·02	2·80	2·51	2·18	1·79	1·00

TABLE A.4 Critical values of the χ^2 distribution

Proportion of χ^2 distribution in shaded region (*level of significance*)

df	.995	.99	.975	.95	.90	.75	.50	.25	.10	.05	.025	.01	.005
1	.0000	.0002	.0010	.0039	.0158	.102	.455	1.32	2.71	3.84	5.02	6.63	7.88
2	.0100	.0201	.0506	.103	.211	.575	1.39	2.77	4.61	5.99	7.38	9.21	10.6
3	.072	.115	.216	.352	.584	1.21	2.37	4.11	6.25	7.81	9.35	11.3	12.8
4	.207	.297	.484	.711	1.06	1.92	3.36	5.39	7.78	9.49	11.1	13.3	14.9
5	.412	.554	.831	1.15	1.61	2.67	4.35	6.63	9.24	11.1	12.8	15.1	16.7
6	.676	.872	1.24	1.64	2.20	3.45	5.35	7.84	10.6	12.6	14.4	16.8	18.5
7	.989	1.24	1.69	2.17	2.83	4.25	6.35	9.04	12.0	14.1	16.0	18.5	20.3
8	1.34	1.65	2.18	2.73	3.49	5.07	7.34	10.2	13.4	15.5	17.5	20.1	22.0
9	1.73	2.09	2.70	3.33	4.17	5.90	8.34	11.4	14.7	16.9	19.0	21.7	23.6
10	2.16	2.56	3.25	3.94	4.87	6.74	9.34	12.5	16.0	18.3	20.5	23.2	25.2
11	2.60	3.05	3.82	4.57	5.58	7.58	10.3	13.7	17.3	19.7	21.9	24.7	26.8
12	3.07	3.57	4.40	5.23	6.30	8.44	11.3	14.8	18.5	21.0	23.3	26.2	28.3
13	3.57	4.11	5.01	5.89	7.04	9.30	12.3	16.0	19.8	22.4	24.7	27.7	29.8
14	4.07	4.66	5.63	6.57	7.79	10.2	13.3	17.1	21.1	23.7	26.1	29.1	31.3

15	32.8	30.6	27.5	25.0	22.3	18.2	14.3	11.0	8.55	7.26	6.26	5.23	4.60
16	34.3	32.0	28.8	26.3	23.5	19.4	15.3	11.9	9.31	7.96	6.91	5.81	5.14
17	35.7	33.4	30.2	27.6	24.8	20.5	16.3	12.8	10.1	8.67	7.56	6.41	5.70
18	37.2	34.8	31.5	28.9	26.0	21.6	17.3	13.7	10.9	9.39	8.23	7.01	6.26
19	38.6	36.2	32.9	30.1	27.2	22.7	18.3	14.6	11.7	10.1	8.91	7.63	6.84
20	40.0	37.6	34.2	31.4	28.4	23.8	19.3	15.5	12.4	10.9	9.59	8.26	7.43
21	41.4	38.9	35.5	32.7	29.6	24.9	20.3	16.3	13.2	11.6	10.3	8.90	8.03
22	42.8	40.3	36.8	33.9	30.8	26.0	21.3	17.2	14.0	12.3	11.0	9.54	8.64
23	44.2	41.6	38.1	35.2	32.0	27.1	22.3	18.1	14.8	13.1	11.7	10.2	9.26
24	45.6	43.0	39.4	36.4	33.2	28.2	23.3	19.0	15.7	13.8	12.4	10.9	9.89
25	46.9	44.3	40.6	37.7	34.4	29.3	24.3	19.9	16.5	14.6	13.1	11.5	10.5
26	48.3	45.6	41.9	38.9	35.6	30.4	25.3	20.8	17.3	15.4	13.8	12.2	11.2
27	49.6	47.0	43.2	40.1	36.7	31.5	26.3	21.7	18.1	16.2	14.6	12.9	11.8
28	51.0	48.3	44.5	41.3	37.9	32.6	27.3	22.7	18.9	16.9	15.3	13.6	12.5
29	52.3	49.6	45.7	42.6	39.1	33.7	28.3	23.6	19.8	17.7	16.0	14.3	13.1
30	53.7	50.9	47.0	43.8	40.3	34.8	29.3	24.5	20.6	18.5	16.8	15.0	13.8
40	66.8	63.7	59.3	55.8	51.8	45.6	39.3	33.7	29.1	26.5	24.4	22.2	20.7
50	79.5	76.2	71.4	67.5	63.2	56.3	49.3	42.9	37.7	34.8	32.4	29.7	28.0
60	92.0	88.4	83.3	79.1	74.4	67.0	59.3	52.3	46.5	43.2	40.5	37.5	35.5
70	104.2	100.4	95.0	90.5	85.5	77.6	69.3	61.7	55.3	51.7	48.8	45.4	43.3
80	116.3	112.3	106.6	101.9	96.6	88.1	79.3	71.1	64.3	60.4	57.2	53.5	51.2
90	128.3	124.1	118.1	113.1	107.6	98.6	89.3	80.6	73.3	69.1	65.6	61.8	59.2
100	140.2	135.8	129.6	124.3	118.5	109.1	99.3	90.1	82.4	77.9	74.2	70.1	67.3

Source: Table A.4 is taken from Table IV of Fisher and Yates: *Statistical Tables for Biological, Agricultural and Medical Research*, published by Oliver & Boyd, Edinburgh, and is used by permission of the authors and publishers. The version reproduced here is from Murray R. Spiegel: *Problems of Statistics*, Schaum Publishing Company.

TABLE A.5 Critical values of r

(Each entry tells how large r needs to be to differ significantly from 0 at that level of significance)

Degrees of freedom (N − 2)	.05	.025	.01	.005	.0005
1	.98769	.99692	.999507	.999877	.9999988
2	.90000	.95000	.98000	.990000	.99900
3	.8054	.8783	.93433	.95873	.99116
4	.7293	.8114	.8822	.91720	.97406
5	.6694	.7545	.8329	.8745	.95074
6	.6215	.7067	.7887	.8343	.92493
7	.5822	.6664	.7498	.7977	.8982
8	.5494	.6319	.7155	.7646	.8721
9	.5214	.6021	.6851	.7348	.8471
10	.4973	.5760	.6581	.7079	.8233
11	.4762	.5529	.6339	.6835	.8010
12	.4575	.5324	.6120	.6614	.7800
13	.4409	.5139	.5923	.6411	.7603
14	.4259	.4973	.5742	.6226	.7420
15	.4124	.4821	.5577	.6055	.7246

Degrees of freedom (N − 2)	.05	.025	.01	.005	.0005
16	.4000	.4683	.5425	.5897	.7084
17	.3887	.4555	.5285	.5751	.6932
18	.3783	.4438	.5155	.5614	.6787
19	.3687	.4329	.5034	.5487	.6652
20	.3598	.4227	.4921	.5368	.6524
25	.3233	.3809	.4451	.4869	.5974
30	.2960	.3494	.4093	.4487	.5541
35	.2746	.3246	.3810	.4182	.5189
40	.2573	.3044	.3578	.3932	.4896
45	.2428	.2875	.3384	.3721	.4648
50	.2306	.2732	.3218	.3541	.4433
60	.2108	.2500	.2948	.3248	.4078
70	.1954	.2319	.2737	.3017	.3799
80	.1829	.2172	.2565	.2830	.3568
90	.1726	.2050	.2422	.2673	.3375
100	.1638	.1946	.2301	.2540	.3211

Source: Table A.5 is taken from Table VI of Fisher and Yates: Statistical Tables for Biological, Agricultural and Medical Research, published by Oliver & Boyd, Edinburgh, and reproduced here by permission of the authors and publishers.

TABLE A.6 Transformation of r to z^*

$$\left(\text{In this transformation } z^* = \frac{1}{2} \log_e \frac{(1 + r)}{(1 - r)} \right)$$

r	z^*	r	z^*	r	z^*
.00	.0000	.35	.3654	.70	.8673
.01	.0100	.36	.3769	.71	.8872
.02	.0200	.37	.3884	.72	.9076
.03	.0300	.38	.4001	.73	.9287
.04	.0400	.39	.4118	.74	.9505
.05	.0500	.40	.4236	.75	0.973
.06	.0601	.41	.4356	.76	0.996
.07	.0701	.42	.4477	.77	1.020
.08	.0802	.43	.4599	.78	1.045
.09	.0902	.44	.4722	.79	1.071
.10	.1003	.45	.4847	.80	1.099
.11	.1104	.46	.4973	.81	1.127
.12	.1206	.47	.5101	.82	1.157
.13	.1307	.48	.5230	.83	1.188
.14	.1409	.49	.5361	.84	1.221
.15	.1511	.50	.5493	.85	1.256
.16	.1614	.51	.5627	.86	1.293
.17	.1717	.52	.5763	.87	1.333
.18	.1820	.53	.5901	.88	1.376
.19	.1923	.54	.6042	.89	1.422
.20	.2027	.55	.6184	.90	1.472
.21	.2132	.56	.6328	.91	1.528
.22	.2237	.57	.6475	.92	1.589
.23	.2342	.58	.6625	.93	1.658
.24	.2448	.59	.6777	.94	1.738
.25	.2554	.60	.6931	.95	1.832
.26	.2661	.61	.7089	.96	1.946
.27	.2769	.62	.7250	.97	2.092
.28	.2877	.63	.7414	.98	2.298
.29	.2986	.64	.7582	.99	2.647
.30	.3095	.65	.7753		
.31	.3205	.66	.7928		
.32	.3316	.67	.8107		
.33	.3428	.68	.8291		
.34	.3541	.69	.8480		

Source: The original data appeared as Table 14 of the *Biometrika Tables for Statisticians*, 3d ed., 1966, edited by E. S. Pearson and H. O. Hartley. These data are used here with the kind permission of Prof. E. S. Pearson and the Biometrika Trustees.

TABLE A.7 Critical values of T in Wilcoxon's matched-pairs signed-ranks test

	Level of significance for one-tailed test			
	.05	.025	.01	.005
	Level of significance for two-tailed test			
N	.10	.05	.02	.01
5	0 or smaller, 15 or larger			
6	2, 19	0 or smaller, 21 or larger		
7	3, 25	2, 26	0 or smaller, 28 or larger	
8	5, 31	3, 33	1, 35	0 or smaller, 36 or larger
9	8, 37	5, 40	3, 42	1, 44
10	10, 45	8, 47	5, 50	3, 52
11	13, 53	10, 56	7, 59	5, 61
12	17, 61	13, 65	10, 68	7, 71
13	21, 70	17, 74	12, 79	10, 81
14	25, 80	21, 84	16, 89	13, 92
15	30, 90	25, 95	19, 101	16, 104
16	35, 101	30, 106	23, 113	20, 116
17	41, 112	35, 118	28, 125	24, 129
18	47, 124	40, 131	33, 138	28, 143
19	53, 137	46, 144	38, 152	33, 157
20	60, 150	52, 158	43, 167	38, 172

Source: The original data for Table A.7 appeared in F. Wilcoxon, S. K. Katti, and Roberta Wilcox, Critical values and probability levels for the Wilcoxon rank sum test and the Wilcoxon signed rank test, 1968; published by Lederle Laboratories Division, American Cyanamid Company, in cooperation with the Department of Statistics, The Florida State University. The material is used here by permission of Lederle Laboratories Division, American Cyanamid Company.

TABLE A.8 Critical values of W in Wilcoxon's rank sum test for independent groups

		Level of significance for one-tailed test			
		.05	.025	.01	.005
		Level of significance for two-tailed test			
$n_{smaller}$	n_{larger}	.10	.05	.02	.01
2	5	3 or smaller, 13 or larger			
	6	3 / 15			
	7	3 / 17			
	8	4 / 18	3 or smaller, 19 or larger		
	9	4 / 20	3 / 21		
	10	4 / 22	3 / 23		
3	3	6 / 15			
	4	6 / 18			
	5	7 / 20	6 / 21		
	6	8 / 22	7 / 23		
	7	8 / 25	7 / 26	6 or smaller, 27 or larger	
	8	9 / 27	8 / 28	6 / 30	
	9	10 / 29	8 / 31	7 / 32	6 or smaller, 33 or larger
	10	10 / 32	9 / 33	7 / 35	6 / 36
4	4	11 / 25	10 / 26		
	5	12 / 28	11 / 29	10 / 30	
	6	13 / 31	12 / 32	11 / 33	10 / 34
	7	14 / 34	13 / 35	11 / 37	10 / 38
	8	15 / 37	14 / 38	12 / 40	11 / 41
	9	16 / 40	15 / 41	13 / 43	11 / 45
	10	17 / 43	15 / 45	13 / 47	12 / 48

Continued

Source: The original data for Table A.8 appeared in F. Wilcoxon, S. K. Katti, and Roberta Wilcox, Critical values and probability levels for the Wilcoxon rank sum test and the Wilcoxon signed rank test, 1968; published by Lederle Laboratories Division, American Cyanamid Company, in cooperation with the Department of Statistics, The Florida State University. The material is used here by permission of Lederle Laboratories Division, American Cyanamid Company.

TABLE A.8 Continued

		Level of significance for one-tailed test							
		.05		.025		.01		.005	
		Level of significance for two-tailed test							
$n_{smaller}$	n_{larger}	.10		.05		.02		.01	
5	5	19	36	17	38	16	39	15	40
	6	20	40	18	42	17	43	16	44
	7	21	44	20	45	18	47	17	48
	8	23	47	21	49	19	51	18	52
	9	24	51	22	53	20	55	18	57
	10	26	54	23	57	21	59	19	61
6	6	28	50	26	52	24	54	23	55
	7	29	55	27	57	25	59	24	60
	8	31	59	29	61	27	63	25	65
	9	33	63	31	65	28	68	26	70
	10	35	67	32	70	29	73	28	74
7	7	39	66	36	69	34	71	32	73
	8	41	71	38	74	36	76	34	78
	9	43	76	40	79	37	82	35	84
	10	45	81	42	84	39	87	37	89
8	8	51	85	49	87	46	90	44	92
	9	54	90	51	93	48	96	45	99
	10	56	96	53	99	50	102	47	105
9	9	66	105	63	108	59	112	57	114
	10	69	111	65	115	61	119	59	121
10	10	82	128	78	132	74	136	71	139

B: OTHER METHODOLOGICAL AND COMPUTATIONAL AIDS

TABLE B.1   Random numbers

09188	20097	32825	39527	83389	87374	86304	04220	64278	58044
90045	85497	51981	50654	91870	76150	81997	94938	68476	64659
73189	50207	47677	26269	27124	67018	64464	62290	41361	82760
75768	76490	20971	87749	95375	05871	12272	90429	93823	43178
54016	44056	66281	31003	20714	53295	27398	00682	07706	17813
08358	69910	78542	42785	04618	97553	58873	13661	31223	08420
28306	03264	81333	10591	32604	60475	07893	40510	94119	01840
53840	86233	81594	13628	28466	68795	90290	51215	77762	20791
91757	53741	61613	62269	55781	76514	90212	50263	83483	47055
89415	92694	00397	58391	48949	72306	17646	12607	94541	37408
77513	03820	86864	29901	51908	13980	82774	68414	72893	55507
19502	37174	69979	20288	74287	75251	29773	55210	65344	67415
21818	59313	93278	81757	07082	85046	73156	05686	31853	38452
51474	66499	68107	23621	42836	09191	91345	94049	08007	45449
99559	68331	62535	24170	74819	78142	12830	69777	43860	72834
33713	48007	93584	72869	58303	29822	64721	51926	93174	93972
85274	86893	11303	22970	73515	90400	34137	28834	71148	43643
84133	89640	44035	52166	61222	60561	70091	73852	62327	18423
56732	16234	17395	96131	85496	57560	91622	10123	81604	18880
65138	56806	87648	85261	45875	21069	65861	34313	85644	47277
38001	02176	81719	11711	74219	64049	92937	71602	65584	49698
37402	96397	01304	77586	47324	62605	10086	56271	40030	37438
97125	40348	87083	31417	75237	62047	39250	21815	15501	29578
21826	41134	47143	34072	49139	06441	85902	64638	03856	54552
73135	42742	95719	09035	08789	88156	74296	85794	64691	19202

Continued

Source: This table is reproduced from *A Million Random Digits with 100,000 Normal Deviates.* Rand Corporation, 1955. Free Press, Glencoe, Illinois, with the kind permission of the Rand Corporation.

TABLE B.1 *Continued*

07638	77929	03061	18072	96207	44156	23821	99538	04713	66994
60528	83441	07954	19814	59175	20695	05533	52139	61212	06455
83596	35655	06958	92983	05128	09719	77433	53783	92301	50498
10850	62746	99599	10507	13499	06319	53075	71839	06410	19362
39820	98952	43622	63147	64421	80814	43800	09351	31024	73167
59580	06478	75569	78800	88835	54486	23768	06156	04111	08408
38508	07341	23793	48763	90822	97022	17719	04207	95954	49953
30692	70668	94688	16127	56196	80091	82067	63400	05462	69200
65443	95659	18288	27437	49632	24041	08337	65676	96299	90836
27267	50264	13192	72294	07477	44606	17985	48911	97341	30358
91307	06991	19072	24210	36699	53728	28825	35793	28976	66252
68434	94688	84473	13622	62126	98408	12843	82590	09815	93146
48908	15877	54745	24591	35700	04754	83824	52692	54130	55160
06913	45197	42672	78601	11883	09528	63011	98901	14974	40344
10455	16019	14210	33712	91342	37821	88325	80851	43667	70883
12883	97343	65027	61184	04285	01392	17974	15077	90712	26769
21778	30976	38807	36961	31649	42096	63281	02023	08816	47449
19523	59515	65122	59659	86283	68258	69572	13798	16435	91529
67245	52670	35583	16563	79246	86686	76463	34222	26655	90802
60584	47377	07500	37992	45134	26529	26760	83637	41326	44344
53853	41377	36066	94850	58838	73859	49364	73331	96240	43642
24637	38736	74384	89342	52623	07992	12369	18601	03742	83873
83080	12451	38992	22815	07759	51777	97377	27585	51972	37867
16444	24334	36151	99073	27493	70939	85130	32552	54846	54759
60790	18157	57178	65762	11161	78576	45819	52979	65130	04860

TABLE B.1 *Continued*

10097	32533	76520	13586	34673	54876	80959	09117	39292	74945
37542	04805	64894	74296	24805	24037	20636	10402	00822	91665
08422	68953	19645	09303	23209	02560	15953	34764	35080	33606
99019	02529	09376	70715	38311	31165	88676	74397	04436	27659
12807	99970	80157	36147	64032	36653	98951	16877	12171	76833
66065	74717	34072	76850	36697	36170	65813	39885	11199	29170
31060	10805	45571	82406	35303	42614	86799	07439	23403	09732
85269	77602	02051	65692	68665	74818	73053	85247	18623	88579
63573	32135	05325	47048	90553	57548	28468	28709	83491	25624
73796	45753	03529	64778	35808	34282	60935	20344	35273	88435
98520	17767	14905	68607	22109	40558	60970	93433	50500	73998
11805	05431	39808	27732	50725	68248	29405	24201	52775	67851
83452	99634	06288	98083	13746	70078	18475	40610	68711	77817
88685	40200	86507	58401	36766	67951	90364	76493	29609	11062
99594	67348	87517	64969	91826	08928	93785	61368	23478	34113
65481	17674	17468	50950	58047	76974	73039	57186	40218	16544
80124	35635	17727	08015	45318	22374	21115	78253	14385	53763
74350	99817	77402	77214	43236	00210	45521	64237	96286	02655
69916	26803	66252	29148	36936	87203	76621	13990	94400	56418
09893	20505	14225	68514	46427	56788	96297	78822	54382	14598
91499	14523	68479	27686	46162	83554	94750	89923	37089	20048
80336	94598	26940	36858	70297	34135	53140	33340	42050	82341
44104	81949	85157	47954	32979	26575	57600	40881	22222	06413
12550	73742	11100	02040	12860	74697	96644	89439	28707	25815
63606	49329	16505	34484	40219	52563	43651	77082	07207	31790

Continued

TABLE B.1 *Continued*

61196	90446	26457	47774	51924	33729	65394	59593	42582	60527
15474	45266	95270	79953	59367	83848	82396	10118	33211	59466
94557	28573	67897	54387	54622	44431	91190	42592	92927	45973
42481	16213	97344	08721	16868	48767	03071	12059	25701	46670
23523	78317	73208	89837	68935	91416	26252	29663	05522	82562
04493	52494	75246	33824	45862	51025	61962	79335	65337	12472
00549	97654	64051	88159	96119	63896	54692	82391	23287	29529
35963	15307	26898	09354	33351	35462	77974	50024	90103	39333
59808	08391	45427	26842	83609	49700	13021	24892	78565	20106
46058	85236	01390	92286	77281	44077	93910	83647	70617	42941
32179	00597	87379	25241	05567	07007	86743	17157	85394	11838
69234	61406	20117	45204	15956	60000	18743	92423	97118	96338
19565	41430	01758	75379	40419	21585	66674	36806	84962	85207
45155	14938	19476	07246	43667	94543	59047	90033	20826	69541
94864	31994	36168	10851	34888	81553	01540	35456	05014	51176
98086	24826	45240	28404	44999	08896	39094	73407	35441	31880
33185	16232	41941	50949	89435	48581	88695	41994	37548	73043
80951	00406	96382	70774	20151	23387	25016	25298	94624	61171
79752	49140	71961	28296	69861	02591	74852	20539	00387	59579
18633	32537	98145	06571	31010	24674	05455	61427	77938	91936
74029	43902	77557	32270	97790	17119	52527	58021	80814	51748
54178	45611	80993	37143	05335	12969	56127	19255	36040	90324
11664	49883	52079	84827	59381	71539	09973	33440	88461	23356
48324	77928	31249	64710	02295	36870	32307	57546	15020	09994
69074	94138	87637	91976	35584	04401	10518	21615	01848	76938

TABLE B.2 The value of $n!$ for the numbers 1 through 50

n	$n!$	n	$n!$
1	1	26	4.03291×10^{26}
2	2	27	1.08889×10^{28}
3	6	28	3.04888×10^{29}
4	24	29	8.84175×10^{30}
5	120	30	2.65253×10^{32}
6	720	31	8.22283×10^{33}
7	5040	32	2.63131×10^{35}
8	40320	33	8.68331×10^{36}
9	362880	34	2.95232×10^{38}
10	3.62880×10^{6}	35	1.03331×10^{40}
11	3.99168×10^{7}	36	3.71993×10^{41}
12	4.79002×10^{8}	37	1.37637×10^{43}
13	6.22702×10^{9}	38	5.23022×10^{44}
14	8.71783×10^{10}	39	2.03979×10^{46}
15	1.30767×10^{12}	40	8.15914×10^{47}
16	2.09227×10^{13}	41	3.34525×10^{49}
17	3.55686×10^{14}	42	1.40500×10^{51}
18	6.40235×10^{15}	43	6.04152×10^{52}
19	1.21645×10^{17}	44	2.65827×10^{54}
20	2.43290×10^{18}	45	1.19622×10^{56}
21	5.10909×10^{19}	46	5.50262×10^{57}
22	1.12400×10^{21}	47	2.58623×10^{59}
23	2.58520×10^{22}	48	1.24139×10^{61}
24	6.20488×10^{23}	49	6.08218×10^{62}
25	1.55112×10^{25}	50	3.04141×10^{64}

TABLE B.3 Binomial coefficients

$$\left(\text{This table tells the value of } _nC_r = \frac{n!}{r!(n-r)!} \text{ for different values of } n \text{ and } r \right)$$

		Value of r										
		0	1	2	3	4	5	6	7	8	9	10
	1	1	1									
	2	1	2	1								
	3	1	3	3	1							
	4	1	4	6	4	1						
Value	5	1	5	10	10	5	1					
	6	1	6	15	20	15	6	1				
of	7	1	7	21	35	35	21	7	1			
	8	1	8	28	56	70	56	28	8	1		
n	9	1	9	36	84	126	126	84	36	9	1	
	10	1	10	45	120	210	252	210	120	45	10	1
	11	1	11	55	165	330	462	462	330	165	55	11
	12	1	12	66	220	495	792	924	792	495	220	66
	13	1	13	78	286	715	1287	1716	1716	1287	715	286
	14	1	14	91	364	1001	2002	3003	3432	3003	2002	1001
	15	1	15	105	455	1365	3003	5005	6435	6435	5005	3003
	16	1	16	120	560	1820	4368	8008	11440	12870	11440	8008
	17	1	17	136	680	2380	6188	12376	19448	24310	24310	19448
	18	1	18	153	816	3060	8568	18564	31824	43758	48620	43758
	19	1	19	171	969	3876	11628	27132	50388	75582	92378	92378
	20	1	20	190	1140	4845	15504	38760	77520	125970	167960	184756

TABLE B.4 The square, square root, and reciprocal of the numbers 1 to 1,000

N	N^2	$\sqrt{N}$	$1/N$	N	N^2	$\sqrt{N}$	N^2
1	1	1.0000	1.000000	51	2601	7.1414	.019608
2	4	1.4142	.500000	52	2704	7.2111	.019231
3	9	1.7321	.333333	53	2809	7.2801	.018868
4	16	2.0000	.250000	54	2916	7.3485	.018519
5	25	2.2361	.200000	55	3025	7.4162	.018182
6	36	2.4495	.166667	56	3136	7.4833	.017857
7	49	2.6458	.142857	57	3249	7.5498	.017544
8	64	2.8284	.125000	58	3364	7.6158	.017241
9	81	3.0000	.111111	59	3481	7.6811	.016949
10	100	3.1623	.100000	60	3600	7.7460	.016667
11	121	3.3166	.090909	61	3721	7.8102	.016393
12	144	3.4641	.083333	62	3844	7.8740	.016129
13	169	3.6056	.076923	63	3969	7.9373	.015873
14	196	3.7417	.071429	64	4096	8.0000	.015625
15	225	3.8730	.066667	65	4225	8.0623	.015385
16	256	4.0000	.062500	66	4356	8.1240	.015152
17	289	4.1231	.058824	67	4489	8.1854	.014925
18	324	4.2426	.055556	68	4624	8.2462	.014706
19	361	4.3589	.052632	69	4761	8.3066	.014493
20	400	4.4721	.050000	70	4900	8.3666	.014286
21	441	4.5826	.047619	71	5041	8.4261	.014085
22	484	4.6904	.045455	72	5184	8.4853	.013889
23	529	4.7958	.043478	73	5329	8.5440	.013699
24	576	4.8990	.041667	74	5476	8.6023	.013514
25	625	5.0000	.040000	75	5625	8.6603	.013333
26	676	5.0990	.038462	76	5776	8.7178	.013158
27	729	5.1962	.037037	77	5929	8.7750	.012987
28	784	5.2915	.035714	78	6084	8.8318	.012821
29	841	5.3852	.034483	79	6241	8.8882	.012658
30	900	5.4772	.033333	80	6400	8.9443	.012500
31	961	5.5678	.032258	81	6561	9.0000	.012346
32	1024	5.6569	.031250	82	6724	9.0554	.012195
33	1089	5.7446	.030303	83	6889	9.1104	.012048
34	1156	5.8310	.029412	84	7056	9.1652	.011905
35	1225	5.9161	.028571	85	7225	9.2195	.011765
36	1296	6.0000	.027778	86	7396	9.2736	.011628
37	1369	6.0828	.027027	87	7569	9.3274	.011494
38	1444	6.1644	.026316	88	7744	9.3808	.011364
39	1521	6.2450	.025641	89	7921	9.4340	.011236
40	1600	6.3246	.025000	90	8100	9.4868	.011111
41	1681	6.4031	.024390	91	8281	9.5394	.010989
42	1764	6.4807	.023810	92	8464	9.5917	.010870
43	1849	6.5574	.023256	93	8649	9.6437	.010753
44	1936	6.6332	.022727	94	8836	9.6954	.010638
45	2025	6.7082	.022222	95	9025	9.7468	.010526
46	2116	6.7823	.021739	96	9216	9.7980	.010417
47	2209	6.8557	.021277	97	9409	9.8489	.010309
48	2304	6.9282	.020833	98	9604	9.8995	.010204
49	2401	7.0000	.020408	99	9801	9.9499	.010101
50	2500	7.0711	.020000	100	10000	10.0000	.010000

Continued

Source: The original data for Table B.4 appeared in *Handbook of Statistical Nomographs, Tables, and Formulas* by J. W. Dunlap and A. K. Kurtz, 1932, World Book Company, New York. The data are used here with the kind permission of Dr. Jack W. Dunlap.

TABLE B.4 *Continued*

N	N^2	$\sqrt{N}$	$1/N$	N	N^2	$\sqrt{N}$	$1/N$
101	10201	10.0499	.00990099	151	22801	12.2882	.00662252
102	10404	10.0995	.00980392	152	23104	12.3288	.00657895
103	10609	10.1489	.00970874	153	23409	12.3693	.00653595
104	10816	10.1980	.00961538	154	23716	12.4097	.00649351
105	11025	10.2470	.00952381	155	24025	12.4499	.00645161
106	11236	10.2956	.00943396	156	24336	12.4900	.00641026
107	11449	10.3441	.00934579	157	24649	12.5300	.00636943
108	11664	10.3923	.00925926	158	24964	12.5698	.00632911
109	11881	10.4403	.00917431	159	25281	12.6095	.00628931
110	12100	10.4881	.00909091	160	25600	12.6491	.00625000
111	12321	10.5357	.00900901	161	25921	12.6886	.00621118
112	12544	10.5830	.00892857	162	26244	12.7279	.00617284
113	12769	10.6301	.00884956	163	26569	12.7671	.00613497
114	12996	10.6771	.00877193	164	26896	12.8062	.00609756
115	13225	10.7238	.00869565	165	27225	12.8452	.00606061
116	13456	10.7703	.00862069	166	27556	12.8841	.00602410
117	13689	10.8167	.00854701	167	27889	12.9228	.00598802
118	13924	10.8628	.00847458	168	28224	12.9615	.00595238
119	14161	10.9087	.00840336	169	28561	13.0000	.00591716
120	14400	10.9545	.00833333	170	28900	13.0384	.00588235
121	14641	11.0000	.00826446	171	29241	13.0767	.00584795
122	14884	11.0454	.00819672	172	29584	13.1149	.00581395
123	15129	11.0905	.00813008	173	29929	13.1529	.00578035
124	15376	11.1355	.00806452	174	30276	13.1909	.00574713
125	15625	11.1803	.00800000	175	30625	13.2288	.00571429
126	15876	11.2250	.00793651	176	30976	13.2665	.00568182
127	16129	11.2694	.00787402	177	31329	13.3041	.00564972
128	16384	11.3137	.00781250	178	31684	13.3417	.00561798
129	16641	11.3578	.00775194	179	32041	13.3791	.00558659
130	16900	11.4018	.00769231	180	32400	13.4164	.00555556
131	17161	11.4455	.00763359	181	32761	13.4536	.00552486
132	17424	11.4891	.00757576	182	33124	13.4907	.00549451
133	17689	11.5326	.00751880	183	33489	13.5277	.00546448
134	17956	11.5758	.00746269	184	33856	13.5647	.00543478
135	18225	11.6190	.00740741	185	34225	13.6015	.00540541
136	18496	11.6619	.00735294	186	34596	13.6382	.00537634
137	18769	11.7047	.00729927	187	34969	13.6748	.00534759
138	19044	11.7473	.00724638	188	35344	13.7113	.00531915
139	19321	11.7898	.00719424	189	35721	13.7477	.00529101
140	19600	11.8322	.00714286	190	36100	13.7840	.00526316
141	19881	11.8743	.00709220	191	36481	13.8203	.00523560
142	20164	11.9164	.00704225	192	36864	13.8564	.00520833
143	20449	11.9583	.00699301	193	37249	13.8924	.00518135
144	20736	12.0000	.00694444	194	37636	13.9284	.00515464
145	21025	12.0416	.00689655	195	38025	13.9642	.00512821
146	21316	12.0830	.00684932	196	38416	14.0000	.00510204
147	21609	12.1244	.00680272	197	38809	14.0357	.00507614
148	21904	12.1655	.00675676	198	39204	14.0712	.00505051
149	22201	12.2066	.00671141	199	39601	14.1067	.00502513
150	22500	12.2474	.00666667	200	40000	14.1421	.00500000

TABLE B.4 *Continued*

N	N^2	$\sqrt{N}$	$1/N$	N	N^2	$\sqrt{N}$	$1/N$
201	40401	14.1774	.00497512	251	63001	15.8430	.00398406
202	40804	14.2127	.00495050	252	63504	15.8745	.00396825
203	41209	14.2478	.00492611	253	64009	15.9060	.00395257
204	41616	14.2829	.00490196	254	64516	15.9374	.00393701
205	42025	14.3178	.00487805	255	65025	15.9687	.00392157
206	42436	14.3527	.00485437	256	65536	16.0000	.00390625
207	42849	14.3875	.00483092	257	66049	16.0312	.00389105
208	43264	14.4222	.00480769	258	66564	16.0624	.00387597
209	43681	14.4568	.00478469	259	67081	16.0935	.00386100
210	44100	14.4914	.00476190	260	67600	16.1245	.00384615
211	44521	14.5258	.00473934	261	68121	16.1555	.00383142
212	44944	14.5602	.00471698	262	68644	16.1864	.00381679
213	45369	14.5945	.00469484	263	69169	16.2173	.00380228
214	45796	14.6287	.00467290	264	69696	16.2481	.00378788
215	46225	14.6629	.00465116	265	70225	16.2788	.00377358
216	46656	14.6969	.00462963	266	70756	16.3095	.00375940
217	47089	14.7309	.00460829	267	71289	16.3401	.00374532
218	47524	14.7648	.00458716	268	71824	16.3707	.00373134
219	47961	14.7986	.00456621	269	72361	16.4012	.00371747
220	48400	14.8324	.00454545	270	72900	16.4317	.00370370
221	48841	14.8661	.00452489	271	73441	16.4621	.00369004
222	49284	14.8997	.00450450	272	73984	16.4924	.00367647
223	49729	14.9332	.00448430	273	74529	16.5227	.00366300
224	50176	14.9666	.00446429	274	75076	16.5529	.00364964
225	50625	15.0000	.00444444	275	75625	16.5831	.00363636
226	51076	15.0333	.00442478	276	76176	16.6132	.00362319
227	51529	15.0665	.00440529	277	76729	16.6433	.00361011
228	51984	15.0997	.00438596	278	77284	16.6733	.00359712
229	52441	15.1327	.00436681	279	77841	16.7033	.00358423
230	52900	15.1658	.00434783	280	78400	16.7332	.00357143
231	53361	15.1987	.00432900	281	78961	16.7631	.00355872
232	53824	15.2315	.00431034	282	79524	16.7929	.00354610
233	54289	15.2643	.00429185	283	80089	16.8226	.00353357
234	54756	15.2971	.00427350	284	80656	16.8523	.00352113
235	55225	15.3297	.00425532	285	81225	16.8819	.00350877
236	55696	15.3623	.00423729	286	81796	16.9115	.00349650
237	56169	15.3948	.00421941	287	82369	16.9411	.00348432
238	56644	15.4272	.00420168	288	82944	16.9706	.00347222
239	57121	15.4596	.00418410	289	83521	17.0000	.00346021
240	57600	15.4919	.00416667	290	84100	17.0294	.00344828
241	58081	15.5242	.00414938	291	84681	17.0587	.00343643
242	58564	15.5563	.00413223	292	85264	17.0880	.00342466
243	59049	15.5885	.00411523	293	85849	17.1172	.00341297
244	59536	15.6205	.00409836	294	86436	17.1464	.00340136
245	60025	15.6525	.00408163	295	87025	17.1756	.00338983
246	60516	15.6844	.00406504	296	87616	17.2047	.00337838
247	61009	15.7162	.00404858	297	88209	17.2337	.00336700
248	61504	15.7480	.00403226	298	88804	17.2627	.00335570
249	62001	15.7797	.00401606	299	89401	17.2916	.00334448
250	62500	15.8114	.00400000	300	90000	17.3205	.00333333

Continued

TABLE B.4 *Continued*

N	N^2	$\sqrt{N}$	$1/N$	N	N^2	$\sqrt{N}$	$1/N$
301	90601	17.3494	.00332226	351	123201	18.7350	.00284900
302	91204	17.3781	.00331126	352	123904	18.7617	.00284091
303	91809	17.4069	.00330033	353	124609	18.7883	.00283286
304	92416	17.4356	.00328947	354	125316	18.8149	.00282486
305	93025	17.4642	.00327869	355	126025	18.8414	.00281690
306	93636	17.4929	.00326797	356	126736	18.8680	.00280899
307	94249	17.5214	.00325733	357	127449	18.8944	.00280112
308	94864	17.5499	.00324675	358	128164	18.9209	.00279330
309	95481	17.5784	.00323625	359	128881	18.9473	.00278552
310	96100	17.6068	.00322581	360	129600	18.9737	.00277778
311	96721	17.6352	.00321543	361	130321	19.0000	.00277008
312	97344	17.6635	.00320513	362	131044	19.0263	.00276243
313	97969	17.6918	.00319489	363	131769	19.0526	.00275482
314	98596	17.7200	.00318471	364	132496	19.0788	.00274725
315	99225	17.7482	.00317460	365	133225	19.1050	.00273973
316	99856	17.7764	.00316456	366	133956	19.1311	.00273224
317	100489	17.8045	.00315457	367	134689	19.1572	.00272480
318	101124	17.8326	.00314465	368	135424	19.1833	.00271739
319	101761	17.8606	.00313480	369	136161	19.2094	.00271003
320	102400	17.8885	.00312500	370	136900	19.2354	.00270270
321	103041	17.9165	.00311526	371	137641	19.2614	.00269542
322	103684	17.9444	.00310559	372	138384	19.2873	.00268817
323	104329	17.9722	.00309598	373	139129	19.3132	.00268097
324	104976	18.0000	.00308642	374	139876	19.3391	.00267380
325	105625	18.0278	.00307692	375	140625	19.3649	.00266667
326	106276	18.0555	.00306748	376	141376	19.3907	.00265957
327	106929	18.0831	.00305810	377	142129	19.4165	.00265252
328	107584	18.1108	.00304878	378	142884	19.4422	.00264550
329	108241	18.1384	.00303951	379	143641	19.4679	.00263852
330	108900	18.1659	.00303030	380	144400	19.4936	.00263158
331	109561	18.1934	.00302115	381	145161	19.5192	.00262467
332	110224	18.2209	.00301205	382	145924	19.5448	.00261780
333	110889	18.2483	.00300300	383	146689	19.5704	.00261097
334	111556	18.2757	.00299401	384	147456	19.5959	.00260417
335	112225	18.3030	.00298507	385	148225	19.6214	.00259740
336	112896	18.3303	.00297619	386	148996	19.6469	.00259067
337	113569	18.3576	.00296736	387	149769	19.6723	.00258398
338	114244	18.3848	.00295858	388	150544	19.6977	.00257732
339	114921	18.4120	.00294985	389	151321	19.7231	.00257069
340	115600	18.4391	.00294118	390	152100	19.7484	.00256410
341	116281	18.4662	.00293255	391	152881	19.7737	.00255754
342	116964	18.4932	.00292398	392	153664	19.7990	.00255102
343	117649	18.5203	.00291545	393	154449	19.8242	.00254453
344	118336	18.5472	.00290698	394	155236	19.8494	.00253807
345	119025	18.5742	.00289855	395	156025	19.8746	.00253165
346	119716	18.6011	.00289017	396	156816	19.8997	.00252525
347	120409	18.6279	.00288184	397	157609	19.9249	.00251889
348	121104	18.6548	.00287356	398	158404	19.9499	.00251256
349	121801	18.6815	.00286533	399	159201	19.9750	.00250627
350	122500	18.7083	.00285714	400	160000	20.0000	.00250000

TABLE B.4 *Continued*

N	N^2	$\sqrt{N}$	$1/N$	N	N^2	$\sqrt{N}$	$1/N$
401	160801	20.0250	.00249377	451	203401	21.2368	.00221729
402	161604	20.0499	.00248756	452	204304	21.2603	.00221239
403	162409	20.0749	.00248139	453	205209	21.2838	.00220751
404	163216	20.0998	.00247525	454	206116	21.3073	.00220264
405	164025	20.1246	.00246914	455	207025	21.3307	.00219780
406	164836	20.1494	.00246305	456	207936	21.3542	.00219298
407	165649	20.1742	.00245700	457	208849	21.3776	.00218818
408	166464	20.1990	.00245098	458	209764	21.4009	.00218341
409	167281	20.2237	.00244499	459	210681	21.4243	.00217865
410	168100	20.2485	.00243902	460	211600	21.4476	.00217391
411	168921	20.2731	.00243309	461	212521	21.4709	.00216920
412	169744	20.2978	.00242718	462	213444	21.4942	.00216450
413	170569	20.3224	.00242131	463	214369	21.5174	.00215983
414	171396	20.3470	.00241546	464	215296	21.5407	.00215517
415	172225	20.3715	.00240964	465	216225	21.5639	.00215054
416	173056	20.3961	.00240385	466	217156	21.5870	.00214592
417	173889	20.4206	.00239808	467	218089	21.6102	.00214133
418	174724	20.4450	.00239234	468	219024	21.6333	.00213675
419	175561	20.4695	.00238663	469	219961	21.6564	.00213220
420	176400	20.4939	.00238095	470	220900	21.6795	.00212766
421	177241	20.5183	.00237530	471	221841	21.7025	.00212314
422	178084	20.5426	.00236967	472	222784	21.7256	.00211864
423	178929	20.5670	.00236407	473	223729	21.7486	.00211416
424	179776	20.5913	.00235849	474	224676	21.7715	.00210970
425	180625	20.6155	.00235294	475	225625	21.7945	.00210526
426	181476	20.6398	.00234742	476	226576	21.8174	.00210084
427	182329	20.6640	.00234192	477	227529	21.8403	.00209644
428	183184	20.6882	.00233645	478	228484	21.8632	.00209205
429	184041	20.7123	.00233100	479	229441	21.8861	.00208768
430	184900	20.7364	.00232558	480	230400	21.9089	.00208333
431	185761	20.7605	.00232019	481	231361	21.9317	.00207900
432	186624	20.7846	.00231481	482	232324	21.9545	.00207469
433	187489	20.8087	.00230947	483	233289	21.9773	.00207039
434	188356	20.8327	.00230415	484	234256	22.0000	.00206612
435	189225	20.8567	.00229885	485	235225	22.0227	.00206186
436	190096	20.8806	.00229358	486	236196	22.0454	.00205761
437	190969	20.9045	.00228833	487	237169	22.0681	.00205339
438	191844	20.9284	.00228311	488	238144	22.0907	.00204918
439	192721	20.9523	.00227790	489	239121	22.1133	.00204499
440	193600	20.9762	.00227273	490	240100	22.1359	.00204082
441	194481	21.0000	.00226757	491	241081	22.1585	.00203666
442	195364	21.0238	.00226244	492	242064	22.1811	.00203252
443	196249	21.0476	.00225734	493	243049	22.2036	.00202840
444	197136	21.0713	.00225225	494	244036	22.2261	.00202429
445	198025	21.0950	.00224719	495	245025	22.2486	.00202020
446	198916	21.1187	.00224215	496	246016	22.2711	.00201613
447	199809	21.1424	.00223714	497	247009	22.2935	.00201207
448	200704	21.1660	.00223214	498	248004	22.3159	.00200803
449	201601	21.1896	.00222717	499	249001	22.3383	.00200401
450	202500	21.2132	.00222222	500	250000	22.3607	.00200000

Continued

TABLE B.4 *Continued*

N	N^2	$\sqrt{N}$	$1/N$	N	N^2	$\sqrt{N}$	$1/N$
501	251001	22.3830	.00199601	551	303601	23.4734	.00181488
502	252004	22.4054	.00199203	552	304704	23.4947	.00181159
503	253009	22.4277	.00198807	553	305809	23.5160	.00180832
504	254016	22.4499	.00198413	554	306916	23.5372	.00180505
505	255025	22.4722	.00198020	555	308025	23.5584	.00180180
506	256036	22.4944	.00197628	556	309136	23.5797	.00179856
507	257049	22.5167	.00197239	557	310249	23.6008	.00179533
508	258064	22.5389	.00196850	558	311364	23.6220	.00179211
509	259081	22.5610	.00196464	559	312481	23.6432	.00178891
510	260100	22.5832	.00196078	560	313600	23.6643	.00178571
511	261121	22.6053	.00195695	561	314721	23.6854	.00178253
512	262144	22.6274	.00195312	562	315844	23.7065	.00177936
513	263169	22.6495	.00194932	563	316969	23.7276	.00177620
514	264196	22.6716	.00194553	564	318096	23.7487	.00177305
515	265225	22.6936	.00194175	565	319225	23.7697	.00176991
516	266256	22.7156	.00193798	566	320356	23.7908	.00176678
517	267289	22.7376	.00193424	567	321489	23.8118	.00176367
518	268324	22.7596	.00193050	568	322624	23.8328	.00176056
519	269361	22.7816	.00192678	569	323761	23.8537	.00175747
520	270400	22.8035	.00192308	570	324900	23.8747	.00175439
521	271441	22.8254	.00191939	571	326041	23.8956	.00175131
522	272484	22.8473	.00191571	572	327184	23.9165	.00174825
523	273529	22.8692	.00191205	573	328329	23.9374	.00174520
524	274576	22.8910	.00190840	574	329476	23.9583	.00174216
525	275625	22.9129	.00190476	575	330625	23.9792	.00173913
526	276676	22.9347	.00190114	576	331776	24.0000	.00173611
527	277729	22.9565	.00189753	577	332929	24.0208	.00173310
528	278784	22.9783	.00189394	578	334084	24.0416	.00173010
529	279841	23.0000	.00189036	579	335241	24.0624	.00172712
530	280900	23.0217	.00188679	580	336400	24.0832	.00172414
531	281961	23.0434	.00188324	581	337561	24.1039	.00172117
532	283024	23.0651	.00187970	582	338724	24.1247	.00171821
533	284089	23.0868	.00187617	583	339889	24.1454	.00171527
534	285156	23.1084	.00187266	584	341056	24.1661	.00171233
535	286225	23.1301	.00186916	585	342225	24.1868	.00170940
536	287296	23.1517	.00186567	586	343396	24.2074	.00170648
537	288369	23.1733	.00186220	587	344569	24.2281	.00170358
538	289444	23.1948	.00185874	588	345744	24.2487	.00170068
539	290521	23.2164	.00185529	589	346921	24.2693	.00169779
540	291600	23.2379	.00185185	590	348100	24.2899	.00169492
541	292681	23.2594	.00184843	591	349281	24.3105	.00169205
542	293764	23.2809	.00184502	592	350464	24.3311	.00168919
543	294849	23.3024	.00184162	593	351649	24.3516	.00168634
544	295936	23.3238	.00183824	594	352836	24.3721	.00168350
545	297025	23.3452	.00183486	595	354025	24.3926	.00168067
546	298116	23.3666	.00183150	596	355216	24.4131	.00167785
547	299209	23.3880	.00182815	597	356409	24.4336	.00167504
548	300304	23.4094	.00182482	598	357604	24.4540	.00167224
549	301401	23.4307	.00182149	599	358801	24.4745	.00166945
550	302500	23.4521	.00181818	600	360000	24.4949	.00166667

TABLE B.4 *Continued*

N	N^2	$\sqrt{N}$	$1/N$	N	N^2	$\sqrt{N}$	$1/N$
601	361201	24.5153	.00166389	651	423801	25.5147	.00153610
602	362404	24.5357	.00166113	652	425104	25.5343	.00153374
603	363609	24.5561	.00165837	653	426409	25.5539	.00153139
604	364816	24.5764	.00165563	654	427716	25.5734	.00152905
605	366025	24.5967	.00165289	655	429025	25.5930	.00152672
606	367236	24.6171	.00165017	656	430336	25.6125	.00152439
607	368449	24.6374	.00164745	657	431649	25.6320	.00152207
608	369664	24.6577	.00164474	658	432964	25.6515	.00151976
609	370881	24.6779	.00164204	659	434281	25.6710	.00151745
610	372100	24.6982	.00163934	660	435600	25.6905	.00151515
611	373321	24.7184	.00163666	661	436921	25.7099	.00151286
612	374544	24.7386	.00163399	662	438244	25.7294	.00151057
613	375769	24.7588	.00163132	663	439569	25.7488	.00150830
614	376996	24.7790	.00162866	664	440896	25.7682	.00150602
615	378225	24.7992	.00162602	665	442225	25.7876	.00150376
616	379456	24.8193	.00162338	666	443556	25.8070	.00150150
617	380689	24.8395	.00162075	667	444889	25.8263	.00149925
618	381924	24.8596	.00161812	668	446224	25.8457	.00149701
619	383161	24.8797	.00161551	669	447561	25.8650	.00149477
620	384400	24.8998	.00161290	670	448900	25.8844	.00149254
621	385641	24.9199	.00161031	671	450241	25.9037	.00149031
622	386884	24.9399	.00160772	672	451584	25.9230	.00148810
623	388129	24.9600	.00160514	673	452929	25.9422	.00148588
624	389376	24.9800	.00160256	674	454276	25.9615	.00148368
625	390625	25.0000	.00160000	675	455625	25.9808	.00148148
626	391876	25.0200	.00159744	676	456976	26.0000	.00147929
627	393129	25.0400	.00159490	677	458329	26.0192	.00147710
628	394384	25.0599	.00159236	678	459684	26.0384	.00147493
629	395641	25.0799	.00158983	679	461041	26.0576	.00147275
630	396900	25.0998	.00158730	680	462400	26.0768	.00147059
631	398161	25.1197	.00158479	681	463761	26.0960	.00146843
632	399424	25.1396	.00158228	682	465124	26.1151	.00146628
633	400689	25.1595	.00157978	683	466489	26.1343	.00146413
634	401956	25.1794	.00157729	684	467856	26.1534	.00146199
635	403225	25.1992	.00157480	685	469225	26.1725	.00145985
636	404496	25.2190	.00157233	686	470596	26.1916	.00145773
637	405769	25.2389	.00156986	687	471969	26.2107	.00145560
638	407044	25.2587	.00156740	688	473344	26.2298	.00145349
639	408321	25.2784	.00156495	689	474721	26.2488	.00145138
640	409600	25.2982	.00156250	690	476100	26.2679	.00144928
641	410881	25.3180	.00156006	691	477481	26.2869	.00144718
642	412164	25.3377	.00155763	692	478864	26.3059	.00144509
643	413449	25.3574	.00155521	693	480249	26.3249	.00144300
644	414736	25.3772	.00155280	694	481636	26.3439	.00144092
645	416025	25.3969	.00155039	695	483025	26.3629	.00143885
646	417316	25.4165	.00154799	696	484416	26.3818	.00143678
647	418609	25.4362	.00154560	697	485809	26.4008	.00143472
648	419904	25.4558	.00154321	698	487204	26.4197	.00143266
649	421201	25.4755	.00154083	699	488601	26.4386	.00143062
650	422500	25.4951	.00153846	700	490000	26.4575	.00142857

Continued

TABLE B.4 *Continued*

N	N^2	$\sqrt{N}$	$1/N$	N	N^2	$\sqrt{N}$	$1/N$
701	491401	26.4764	.00142653	751	564001	27.4044	.00133156
702	492804	26.4953	.00142450	752	565504	27.4226	.00132979
703	494209	26.5141	.00142248	753	567009	27.4408	.00132802
704	495616	26.5330	.00142045	754	568516	27.4591	.00132626
705	497025	26.5518	.00141844	755	570025	27.4773	.00132450
706	498436	26.5707	.00141643	756	571536	27.4955	.00132275
707	499849	26.5895	.00141443	757	573049	27.5136	.00132100
708	501264	26.6083	.00141243	758	574564	27.5318	.00131926
709	502681	26.6271	.00141044	759	576081	27.5500	.00131752
710	504100	26.6458	.00140845	760	577600	27.5681	.00131579
711	505521	26.6646	.00140647	761	579121	27.5862	.00131406
712	506944	26.6833	.00140449	762	580644	27.6043	.00131234
713	508369	26.7021	.00140252	763	582169	27.6225	.00131062
714	509796	26.7208	.00140056	764	583696	27.6405	.00130890
715	511225	26.7395	.00139860	765	585225	27.6586	.00130719
716	512656	26.7582	.00139665	766	586756	27.6767	.00130548
717	514089	26.7769	.00139470	767	588289	27.6948	.00130378
718	515524	26.7955	.00139276	768	589824	27.7128	.00130208
719	516961	26.8142	.00139082	769	591361	27.7308	.00130039
720	518400	26.8328	.00138889	770	592900	27.7489	.00129870
721	519841	26.8514	.00138696	771	594441	27.7669	.00129702
722	521284	26.8701	.00138504	772	595984	27.7849	.00129534
723	522729	26.8887	.00138313	773	597529	27.8029	.00129366
724	524176	26.9072	.00138122	774	599076	27.8209	.00129199
725	525625	26.9258	.00137931	775	600625	27.8388	.00129032
726	527076	26.9444	.00137741	776	602176	27.8568	.00128866
727	528529	26.9629	.00137552	777	603729	27.8747	.00128700
728	529984	26.9815	.00137363	778	605284	27.8927	.00128535
729	531441	27.0000	.00137174	779	606841	27.9106	.00128370
730	532900	27.0185	.00136986	780	608400	27.9285	.00128205
731	534361	27.0370	.00136799	781	609961	27.9464	.00128041
732	535824	27.0555	.00136612	782	611524	27.9643	.00127877
733	537289	27.0740	.00136426	783	613089	27.9821	.00127714
734	538756	27.0924	.00136240	784	614656	28.0000	.00127551
735	540225	27.1109	.00136054	785	616225	28.0179	.00127389
736	541696	27.1293	.00135870	786	617796	28.0357	.00127226
737	543169	27.1477	.00135685	787	619369	28.0535	.00127065
738	544644	27.1662	.00135501	788	620944	28.0713	.00126904
739	546121	27.1846	.00135318	789	622521	28.0891	.00126743
740	547600	27.2029	.00135135	790	624100	28.1069	.00126582
741	549081	27.2213	.00134953	791	625681	28.1247	.00126422
742	550564	27.2397	.00134771	792	627264	28.1425	.00126263
743	552049	27.2580	.00134590	793	628849	28.1603	.00126103
744	553536	27.2764	.00134409	794	630436	28.1780	.00125945
745	555025	27.2947	.00134228	795	632025	28.1957	.00125786
746	556516	27.3130	.00134048	796	633616	28.2135	.00125628
747	558009	27.3313	.00133869	797	635209	28.2312	.00125471
748	559504	27.3496	.00133690	798	636804	28.2489	.00125313
749	561001	27.3679	.00133511	799	638401	28.2666	.00125156
750	562500	27.3861	.00133333	800	640000	28.2843	.00125000

TABLE B.4 *Continued*

N	N^2	$\sqrt{N}$	$1/N$	N	N^2	$\sqrt{N}$	$1/N$
801	641601	28.3019	.00124844	851	724201	29.1719	.00117509
802	643204	28.3196	.00124688	852	725904	29.1890	.00117371
803	644809	28.3373	.00124533	853	727609	29.2062	.00117233
804	646416	28.3549	.00124378	854	729316	29.2233	.00117096
805	648025	28.3725	.00124224	855	731025	29.2404	.00116959
806	649636	28.3901	.00124069	856	732736	29.2575	.00116822
807	651249	28.4077	.00123916	857	734449	29.2746	.00116686
808	652864	28.4253	.00123762	858	736164	29.2916	.00116550
809	654481	28.4429	.00123609	859	737881	29.3087	.00116414
810	656100	28.4605	.00123457	860	739600	29.3258	.00116279
811	657721	28.4781	.00123305	861	741321	29.3428	.00116144
812	659344	28.4956	.00123153	862	743044	29.3598	.00116009
813	660969	28.5132	.00123001	863	744769	29.3769	.00115875
814	662596	28.5307	.00122850	864	746496	29.3939	.00115741
815	664225	28.5482	.00122699	865	748225	29.4109	.00115607
816	665856	28.5657	.00122549	866	749956	29.4279	.00115473
817	667489	28.5832	.00122399	867	751689	29.4449	.00115340
818	669124	28.6007	.00122249	868	753424	29.4618	.00115207
819	670761	28.6182	.00122100	869	755161	29.4788	.00115075
820	672400	28.6356	.00121951	870	756900	29.4958	.00114943
821	674041	28.6531	.00121803	871	758641	29.5127	.00114811
822	675684	28.6705	.00121655	872	760384	29.5296	.00114679
823	677329	28.6880	.00121507	873	762129	29.5466	.00114548
824	678976	28.7054	.00121359	874	763876	29.5635	.00114416
825	680625	28.7228	.00121212	875	765625	29.5804	.00114286
826	682276	28.7402	.00121065	876	767376	29.5973	.00114155
827	683929	28.7576	.00120919	877	769129	29.6142	.00114025
828	685584	28.7750	.00120773	878	770884	29.6311	.00113895
829	687241	28.7924	.00120627	879	772641	29.6479	.00113766
830	688900	28.8097	.00120482	880	774400	29.6648	.00113636
831	690561	28.8271	.00120337	881	776161	29.6816	.00113507
832	692224	28.8444	.00120192	882	777924	29.6985	.00113379
833	693889	28.8617	.00120048	883	779689	29.7153	.00113250
834	695556	28.8791	.00119904	884	781456	29.7321	.00113122
835	697225	28.8964	.00119760	885	783225	29.7489	.00112994
836	698896	28.9137	.00119617	886	784996	29.7658	.00112867
837	700569	28.9310	.00119474	887	786769	29.7825	.00112740
838	702244	28.9482	.00119332	888	788544	29.7993	.00112613
839	703921	28.9655	.00119190	889	790321	29.8161	.00112486
840	705600	28.9828	.00119048	890	792100	29.8329	.00112360
841	707281	29.0000	.00118906	891	793881	29.8496	.00112233
842	708964	29.0172	.00118765	892	795664	29.8664	.00112108
843	710649	29.0345	.00118624	893	797449	29.8831	.00111982
844	712336	29.0517	.00118483	894	799236	29.8998	.00111857
845	714025	29.0689	.00118343	895	801025	29.9166	.00111732
846	715716	29.0861	.00118203	896	802816	29.9333	.00111607
847	717409	29.1033	.00118064	897	804609	29.9500	.00111483
848	719104	29.1204	.00117925	898	806404	29.9666	.00111359
849	720801	29.1376	.00117786	899	808201	29.9833	.00111235
850	722500	29.1548	.00117647	900	810000	30.0000	.00111111

Continued

TABLE B.4 *Continued*

N	N^2	$\sqrt{N}$	$1/N$	N	N^2	$\sqrt{N}$	$1/N$
901	811801	30.0167	.00110988	951	904401	30.8383	.00105152
902	813604	30.0333	.00110865	952	906304	30.8545	.00105042
903	815409	30.0500	.00110742	953	908209	30.8707	.00104932
904	817216	30.0666	.00110619	954	910116	30.8869	.00104822
905	819025	30.0832	.00110497	955	912025	30.9031	.00104712
906	820836	30.0998	.00110375	956	913936	30.9192	.00104603
907	822649	30.1164	.00110254	957	915849	30.9354	.00104493
908	824464	30.1330	.00110132	958	917764	30.9516	.00104384
909	826281	30.1496	.00110011	959	919681	30.9677	.00104275
910	828100	30.1662	.00109890	960	921600	30.9839	.00104167
911	829921	30.1828	.00109769	961	923521	31.0000	.00104058
912	831744	30.1993	.00109649	962	925444	31.0161	.00103950
913	833569	30.2159	.00109529	963	927369	31.0322	.00103842
914	835396	30.2324	.00109409	964	929296	31.0483	.00103734
915	837225	30.2490	.00109290	965	931225	31.0644	.00103627
916	839056	30.2655	.00109170	966	933156	31.0805	.00103520
917	840889	30.2820	.00109051	967	935089	31.0966	.00103413
918	842724	30.2985	.00108932	968	937024	31.1127	.00103306
919	844561	30.3150	.00108814	969	938961	31.1288	.00103199
920	846400	30.3315	.00108696	970	940900	31.1448	.00103093
921	848241	30.3480	.00108578	971	942841	31.1609	.00102987
922	850084	30.3645	.00108460	972	944784	31.1769	.00102881
923	851929	30.3809	.00108342	973	946729	31.1929	.00102775
924	853776	30.3974	.00108225	974	948676	31.2090	.00102669
925	855625	30.4138	.00108108	975	950625	31.2250	.00102564
926	857476	30.4302	.00107991	976	952576	31.2410	.00102459
927	859329	30.4467	.00107875	977	954529	31.2570	.00102354
928	861184	30.4631	.00107759	978	956484	31.2730	.00102249
929	863041	30.4795	.00107643	979	958441	31.2890	.00102145
930	864900	30.4959	.00107527	980	960400	31.3050	.00102041
931	866761	30.5123	.00107411	981	962361	31.3209	.00101937
932	868624	30.5287	.00107296	982	964324	31.3369	.00101833
933	870489	30.5450	.00107181	983	966289	31.3528	.00101729
934	872356	30.5614	.00107066	984	968256	31.3688	.00101626
935	874225	30.5778	.00106952	985	970225	31.3847	.00101523
936	876096	30.5941	.00106838	986	972196	31.4006	.00101420
937	877969	30.6105	.00106724	987	974169	31.4166	.00101317
938	879844	30.6268	.00106610	988	976144	31.4325	.00101215
939	881721	30.6431	.00106496	989	978121	31.4484	.00101112
940	883600	30.6594	.00106383	990	980100	31.4643	.00101010
941	885481	30.6757	.00106270	991	982081	31.4802	.00100908
942	887364	30.6920	.00106157	992	984064	31.4960	.00100806
943	889249	30.7083	.00106045	993	986049	31.5119	.00100705
944	891136	30.7246	.00105932	994	988036	31.5278	.00100604
945	893025	30.7409	.00105820	995	990025	31.5436	.00100503
946	894916	30.7571	.00105708	996	992016	31.5595	.00100402
947	896809	30.7734	.00105597	997	994009	31.5753	.00100301
948	898704	30.7896	.00105485	998	996004	31.5911	.00100200
949	900601	30.8058	.00105374	999	998001	31.6070	.00100100
950	902500	30.8221	.00105263	1000	1000000	31.6228	.00100000

INDEX

Topic	Formula	Equation Number
Inference from a single mean	95% confidence interval: $\bar{X} \pm t_{.05} s_{\bar{X}}$	See Example 10.2
	99% confidence interval: $\bar{X} \pm t_{.05} s_{\bar{X}}$	See Example 10.2
Inference from a difference between means (pair observations)	$t = \dfrac{\bar{D} - \mu_D}{s_{\bar{D}}} = \dfrac{\bar{D} - \mu_D}{\dfrac{s_D}{\sqrt{N}}}$	10.3
Inference from a difference between means (independent observations)	$\Sigma x^2 = \Sigma X^2 - \dfrac{(\Sigma X)^2}{N}$	10.4
	$\Sigma y^2 = \Sigma Y^2 - \dfrac{(\Sigma Y)^2}{N}$	10.5
	$s^2 = \dfrac{\Sigma x^2 + \Sigma y^2}{(N_X - 1) + (N_Y - 1)}$	10.6
	$s_{\bar{D}} = \sqrt{\dfrac{s^2}{N_X} + \dfrac{s^2}{N_Y}}$	10.7
	$t = \dfrac{\bar{D} - \mu_D}{s_{\bar{D}}}$	10.8
Analysis of variance		
One-way design	$ss_T = \Sigma\,\Sigma\,X^2 - \dfrac{(\Sigma\,\Sigma\,X)^2}{N}$	11.1
	$ss_B = \Sigma\,\dfrac{T^2}{n} - \dfrac{(\Sigma\,\Sigma\,X)^2}{N}$	11.2
	$ss_W = SS_T - SS_B$	11.3
	$df_T = N - 1$	11.4
	$df_B = k - 1$	11.5
	$df_W = df_T - df_B$	11.6
	$ms_B = SS_B / df_B$	See Sec. 11.4
	$ms_W = SS_W / df_B$	See Sec. 11.4
	$F = \dfrac{\text{one estimate of } \sigma^2}{\text{other estimate of } \sigma^2} = \dfrac{ms_B}{ms_W}$	See Sec. 11.1 and Sec. 11.4
Repeated measurements:	$ss_T = \Sigma\,\Sigma\,X^2 - \dfrac{(\Sigma\,\Sigma\,X)^2}{N}$	11.7
	$ss_{\text{Between conditions}} = \Sigma\,\dfrac{T_c^{\,2}}{n_c} - \dfrac{(\Sigma\,\Sigma\,X)^2}{N}$	11.8
	$ss_{\text{Between subjects}} = \Sigma\,\dfrac{T_s^{\,2}}{n_s} - \dfrac{(\Sigma\,\Sigma\,X)^2}{N}$	11.9
	$ss_{\text{Residual}} = ss_T - ss_{\text{Between conditions}} - ss_{\text{Between subjects}}$	11.10
	$df_T = N - 1$	See Sec. 11.8
	$df_{\text{Between conditions}} = k - 1$	See Sec. 11.8
	$df_{\text{Between subjects}} = n - 1$	See Sec. 11.8
	$df_{\text{Residual}} = df_T - df_{\text{Between conditions}} - df_{\text{Between subjects}}$	11.11
	$F = \dfrac{ms_{\text{Between conditions}}}{ms_{\text{Residual}}}$	11.12
For both designs:	$F = t^2$	See Example 11.10 and Proof 11.1
Correlation	$r_{XY} = \dfrac{\Sigma\,z_X z_Y}{N}$	12.1
	$= \dfrac{N\,\Sigma\,XY - (\Sigma\,X)(\Sigma\,Y)}{\sqrt{N\,\Sigma\,X^2 - (\Sigma\,X)^2}\;\sqrt{N\,\Sigma\,Y^2 - (\Sigma\,Y)^2}}$	12.2
	$b = \dfrac{N\,\Sigma\,XY - (\Sigma\,X)(\Sigma\,Y)}{N\,\Sigma\,X^2 - (\Sigma\,X)^2}$ (for predicting Y from X)	12.3